INTRODUCTION TO
HOUSING

INTRODUCTION TO HOUSING

SECOND EDITION

EDITED BY
KATRIN B. ANACKER
ANDREW T. CARSWELL
SARAH D. KIRBY
KENNETH R. TREMBLAY

THE UNIVERSITY OF GEORGIA PRESS
ATHENS

© 2018 by the University of Georgia Press
Athens, Georgia 30602
www.ugapress.org
All rights reserved
Designed by Kaelin Chappell Broaddus
Set in 10/12 Minion Pro Regular by Kaelin Chappell Broaddus
Printed and bound by Thomson-Shore, Inc.
The paper in this book meets the guidelines for
permanence and durability of the Committee on
Production Guidelines for Book Longevity of the
Council on Library Resources.

Most University of Georgia Press titles are
available from popular e-book vendors.

Printed in the United States of America
22 21 20 19 18 C 5 4 3 2 1

Library of Congress Cataloging-in-Publication Data

Names: Anacker, Katrin B., editor.
Title: Introduction to housing / edited by Katrin B. Anacker
    [and three others].
Description: Second edition. | Athens : University of Georgia Press, [2017] |
    Includes bibliographical references and index.
Identifiers: LCCN 2017047635| ISBN 9780820349688 (hardcover : alk. paper) |
    ISBN 9780820349695 (ebook)
Subjects: LCSH: Housing.
Classification: LCC HD7287 .I74 2017 | DDC 363.5—dc23
    LC record available at https://lccn.loc.gov/2017047635

Dedicated to the memory of
Kenneth R. Tremblay

Contents

Editors' Introduction to *Introduction to Housing*, second edition
KATRIN B. ANACKER, ANDREW T. CARSWELL, AND SARAH D. KIRBY   ix

SECTION I   **INTRODUCTION**

Chapter 1. Current Trends in the U.S. Housing Market
RACHEL BOGARDUS DREW   3

Chapter 2. Influences on Housing Choice
JULIA O. BEAMISH AND ROSEMARY CARUCCI GOSS   21

SECTION II   **HOUSING DESIGN**

Chapter 3. Kitchen and Bathroom Design
KATHLEEN R. PARROTT AND JULIA O. BEAMISH   43

Chapter 4. Single-Family Residential Design
SUK-KYUNG KIM AND MIRA AHN   64

Chapter 5. Multifamily Residential Design
BECKY L. YUST   80

Chapter 6. Universal Design in Housing
SANDRA C. HARTJE, HEIDI H. EWEN, AND KENNETH R. TREMBLAY   98

SECTION III   **HOMEOWNERSHIP**

Chapter 7. Home Buying and Homeownership
MARILYN J. BRUIN AND DEBORAH MITCHELL   121

Chapter 8. The Housing Finance Industry
KATRIN B. ANACKER   139

Chapter 9. Renting
CHERIE STUEVE, MARTIN C. SEAY, AND ANDREW T. CARSWELL   156

Chapter 10. Housing Affordability
CHRISTINE C. COOK, MARILYN J. BRUIN, AND BECKY L. YUST   167

Chapter 11. Homelessness
DANIEL TREGLIA, ANN ELIZABETH MONTGOMERY, AND DENNIS PATRICK CULHANE **183**

SECTION IV HOUSING POLICY

Chapter 12. Housing and Community
KATHRYN HOWELL **199**

Chapter 13. Neighborhood Amenities
ELIZABETH MUELLER **218**

Chapter 14. Federal Housing Policy
KIRK MCCLURE **235**

Chapter 15. The Great Recession
KATRIN B. ANACKER **255**

SECTION V SPECIAL TOPICS IN HOUSING

Chapter 16. Housing and Racial and Ethnic Diversity
KATRIN B. ANACKER **275**

Chapter 17. Housing and Aging
DEIRDRE PFEIFFER **294**

Chapter 18. Home Environments and Health
KATHLEEN R. PARROTT AND JORGE H. ATILES **316**

Chapter 19. Sustainable Housing
JOSEPH LAQUATRA **341**

Chapter 20. Housing and Disasters
SARAH D. KIRBY AND ANNIE HARDISON-MOODY **356**

SECTION VI HOUSING IN A GLOBAL CONTEXT

Chapter 21. Housing in Asia
SUK-KYUNG KIM **377**

Chapter 22. Housing in Europe
JEAN MEMKEN AND SHIRLEY NIEMEYER **396**

Chapter 23. Housing in Latin America and the Caribbean
ROSA E. DONOSO AND MARJA ELSINGA **409**

Chapter 24. Housing in Africa
AKIN S. AKINYEMI, PETRA L. DOAN, AND LINDSAY SLAUTTERBACK **425**

Chapter 25. Global Housing Challenges in the Twenty-First Century
CORIANNE PAYTON SCALLY **441**

Glossary **453**

Contributors **467**

Index **471**

Editors' Introduction to *Introduction to Housing*, second edition

Housing can be understood in a number of different ways. For an individual, it may be a place to lay down roots or the center of household life—or it may be a place characterized by household challenges (Edin & Shaefer, 2015). For a homeowner, it may be a solid foundation for building long-term wealth—or it may have resulted in foreclosure and difficulties reestablishing one's credit history (Barofsky, 2012; Bernanke, 2015; Blinder, 2014; Dayen, 2016; Engel & McCoy, 2011; Graham, 2017; Immergluck, 2015; Martin & Niedt, 2015; Mian & Sufi, 2014; Paulson, 2010). For a neighborhood, it may be the location of a well-maintained housing stock, enabling thriving community life—or it may be the location of vacancies, vandalism, and squatting (Hollander, 2011; Jacobs, 1992; Mallach, 2009, 2010; Satter, 2009). For a city, it may be a source of high revenue streams through property taxes—or there may be the case of overwhelming liability, resulting in the need to condemn an entire building, board up windows, mow the front lawn, or remove snow (Brash, 2011; Hartman & Squires, 2013). For a society, it may result in people being well-housed in a safe, affordable, and attractive housing stock, or in people struggling to find affordable, high-quality housing (Abramsky, 2013; Desmond, 2016; Woldoff, Morrison, & Glass, 2016). For housing scholars, housing can be understood as a commodity—or as a right (Bratt, Stone, & Hartman, 2006; Brenner, Marcuse, and Mayer, 2012; Pattillo, 2013). In summary, there are many ways to understand housing.

Over the past few decades or so, the housing landscape in the United States has changed rapidly. For example, the United States experienced a national house price bubble that ended in the spring of 2006 and then triggered the national subprime and foreclosure crises. These developments in turn resulted in the Great Recession, which started in December 2007 and technically ended in June 2009, although many impacts are still visible, especially in multiple local housing and labor markets. In the meantime, the national homeownership rate has declined, returning to the level of the mid-1990s due to foreclosures, decreased household formation rates, increased debt burdens, including student debt, and extremely tight lending requirements. Policy makers in Washington, D.C., have responded to these developments in multiple ways. For example, they nationalized Fannie Mae and Freddie Mac during the financial crisis of 2008 and the subsequent Wall Street bailout. In addition, the U.S. Congress helped to establish several programs to assist homeowners who were on the brink of foreclosure.

The demographic and socioeconomic environment of the United States has changed rapidly as well. While baby boomers (i.e., those born between 1946 and 1964) have been much studied over the past several decades, millennials (i.e., those born between 1985 and 2000) have only recently been discussed as they have surpassed baby boomers in terms of numbers and become large drivers of the future housing market. Perhaps surprisingly, each group is different in terms of its characteristics and housing and lifestyle choices. For example, some baby boomers move to retirement communities, possibly in the Sunbelt, while others choose to age in the communities in which they have resided for a long time. Some baby boomers sell their single-family homes in the suburbs to move to condominiums or apartments downtown while others age in place. Some baby boomers live comfortable lives while others struggle financially, thus possibly taking on one or several part-time jobs. With regard to housing, there may be issues related to affordability, maintenance, and the use, lack, or abundance of space.

Millennials can be divided into three broad groups. First, there are those who have a four-year or higher college degree, have secured well-paying jobs with benefits, and have an upward career trajectory yet also have student debt. Second, there are those who have some college experience, possibly an associate's degree, and medium or low skills, and who might struggle with job security and stability. Third, there are those who do not have any college experience, do not have skills appreciated by the labor market, and have been struggling to be successful. Many millennials have postponed forming households and having children, although very recent developments have pointed out a slight increase in household formation rates. The question remains, what proportion will keep postponing forming households and families, and what proportion will forego these activities?

All millennial groups are likely to struggle in the housing market: the first group with access to credit for homeownership, the second group with rental affordability and/or credit for homeownership, and the third group with rental housing affordability. Also, unlike many baby boomers, millennials have greater interest in mixed-income housing communities. Furthermore, many millennials have entered and continued in a job market that does not have the stability that baby boomers have experienced, which has made them a different kind of consumer in the housing market.

The field of housing design and construction has been evolving rapidly. Current approaches include a focus on resilience in terms of disaster fortification, sustainability, and green design. Housing design approaches have focused on aging in place, universal design, and visitability. Also, housing affordability approaches that incorporate innovative solutions such as transit-oriented development (TOD) and Accessory Dwelling Units (ADUs) have been emerging.

Over the past few decades, U.S. housing policy has continued to be fragmented, and there is a trend toward attempting to accomplish more with fewer resources. This development has been especially challenging given the lingering impacts of the housing crisis and the Great Recession, discussed above, and the gridlock in Congress and its focus on reining in spending, especially on social issues like housing.

The second edition of *Introduction to Housing* discusses many current and future challenges of the housing market. This book has six sections. The first five focus on the United States and the sixth focuses on international housing.

Section I ("Introduction") lays the groundwork for the twenty-five chapters in this book. Rachel Bogardus Drew provides an overview of current trends in the U.S. housing market and discusses trends in construction, transactions, housing characteristics, and household composition as well as emerging trends in homeownership, housing affordability, and future housing demand. In the following chapter, Julia O. Beamish and Rosemary Carucci Goss discuss influences on housing choice. Based on a conceptual framework, they argue that housing choice is influenced by a household's desire to fulfill normative behavior related to housing while still reflecting its demographic, socioeconomic, and psychographic characteristics.

Design matters. Good design may facilitate the development process, may result in a longer lifecycle for the building, and may positively influence a resident's quality of life. Section II ("Housing Design") focuses on interior, single-family and multifamily housing, and universal design. Kathleen R. Parrott and Julia O. Beamish introduce the history of and trends in kitchen and bath design as well as the design process for kitchen and bath planning. In the following chapter, authored by Suk-Kyung Kim and Mira Ahn, single-family residential design, including a brief history of and influences on design, the design process, and exterior and interior space design, are discussed. Then, Becky L. Yust analyzes aspects of multifamily residential design, including the importance and the definition of good design, precedents of multifamily residential design, types of multifamily housing communities, and design considerations and design trends in multifamily housing. In the following chapter, Sandra C. Hartje, Heidi H. Ewen, and Kenneth R. Tremblay focus on universal design in housing. They discuss the conceptualization, the evolution, the foundations, the integration, and the benefit of universal design in housing. They also cover the design principles of a universally designed house and policies and programs to implement universal design in housing.

Although the subprime lending and foreclosure crises and the following Great Recession have caused the national homeownership rate, especially the homeownership rates of blacks/African Americans and Hispanics/Latinos, to decrease, homeownership has nevertheless remained a good strategy to build long-term wealth due to lack of other attainable investment strategies for most low- and middle-income households. Section III ("Homeownership") focuses on the home-buying process, the housing finance industry, the main alternative to homeownership (renting), housing affordability, and homelessness. The first chapter in this section, authored by Marilyn J. Bruin and Deborah Mitchell, is about the process of home buying and select aspects of the responsibilities of homeownership. The next chapter, by Katrin B. Anacker, focuses on the evolution of the housing finance industry, exemplified by building and loan societies, mortgage banks, the Federal Housing Administration (FHA), the Federal National Mortgage Association (Fannie Mae), and the Federal Home Loan Mortgage Corporation (Freddie Mac). Next, Cherie Stueve, Martin C. Seay, and Andrew T. Carswell discuss advantages and disadvantages of renting, the historical social status of renters, and demand, supply, characteristics, and demographic and socioeconomic drivers of rental housing. The following chapter, authored by Christine C. Cook, Marilyn J. Bruin, and Becky L. Yust, is about select housing affordability challenges and solutions. The authors discuss land use, building cost, and finance cost strategies, followed by public policies and approaches pursued by nonprofit housing organizations to address housing affordability challenges. Finally, Daniel Treglia, Ann Elizabeth Montgomery, and Dennis Patrick Culhane conceptualize homelessness and then discuss counts and characteristics of the homeless population, analyze reasons for homelessness, and discuss strategies and policies for ending homelessness.

Public policy has played an important role in housing and may be seen as a status leveler or a status enhancer. In the case of the former, many affordable housing programs, for example HOPE VI or the Housing Choice Voucher Program, benefit those who are less well off; in the case of the latter, the Mortgage Interest Deduction disproportionately benefits those who are better off. While the earlier part of Section IV ("Housing Policy") focuses on neighborhoods, the later part focuses on housing. Kathryn Howell writes about housing in the context of community and the ways neighborhoods have been defined and represented by residents, policy makers, and advocates. Howell also examines the effects of these definitions and representations on housing and planning policies. Finally, she examines historical changes in the discourse of community and how they have affected the way that residents interact within those communities. Next, Elizabeth Mueller traces the evolution of thinking about the benefits of residence in a particular place by discussing neighborhood context and home values. She elaborates on the uneven landscape of neighborhood amenities, in particular focusing on income and racial segregation and the effects of living in a poor neighborhood. She then discusses how neighborhood amenities can be recast as opportunities and how these features can be linked to a broader definition of well-being. In the following chapter, Kirk McClure discusses federal housing policy, in particular direct project-based, tenant-based, and place-based subsidies and indirect subsidies in the forms of loan insurance and tax breaks. McClure then focuses on the evolution of select federal legislation and housing programs, the scale of federal programs, and the future of federal housing policy. In the final chapter of this section, Katrin B. Anacker discusses the effects of the Great Recession on homeownership and housing policy, followed by a consideration of the long-term and short-term aspects of the national foreclosure crisis and the national policy response to both the Great Recession and the foreclosure crisis.

Section V ("Special Topics in Housing") focuses on population groups that will become an increasing focus in housing in the near and distant future, for example, people of color, who will surpass non-Hispanic whites as a proportion of the U.S. population in 2044 (Frey, 2014), or people over age sixty-five, who made up 13 percent of the U.S. population in 2010 and are projected to increase to more than 20 percent in 2050 (Vincent & Velkoff, 2010). This section also focuses on topics that have witnessed an increase in attention over the past few years and that will continue to do so, for example, home environments and health, sustainable housing, and housing and disasters, partly triggered by the increase in select population groups and by anticipated climate change. The first chapter, authored by Katrin B. Anacker, is about the racial and ethnic diversity of renters and homeowners and individual, macroeconomic, and policy factors that influence homeownership by race and ethnicity. In the following chapter, Deirdre Pfeiffer discusses housing and aging. She reviews the demographics of aging in America and addresses the ways that seniors are reshaping their homes and communities.

She then explores diverse strategies to help seniors age in places that are affordable, nurturing, and well matched to their capacities. Then, Kathleen R. Parrott and Jorge H. Atiles present an overview of the impact of the home on the health of the people who live within it based on a systems approach. They provide information on individual home hazards and building science principles associated with home environments and health. In the following chapter, Joseph Laquatra focuses on sustainable housing, including waste management at the construction site, energy efficiency, the use of renewable energy, green building, and sustainable communities. Finally, Sarah D. Kirby and Annie Hardison-Moody discuss the effects of disasters on communities and their housing stock, especially the complicated reactions of individuals and families to the physical and emotional loss of home and community. The authors then discuss disaster response, housing and community disaster resilience, mitigation, and rebuilding.

Over the next years and decades many communities in the United States as well as across the world will face increasing housing challenges, for example, the right to adequate housing, tenure security, ensuring the quality of housing and basic services, housing affordability, residential segregation and discrimination, and environmental sustainability. The chapters in section VI ("Housing in a Global Context") focus on select challenges. Suk-Kyung Kim discusses housing in Asia, Jean Memken and Shirley Niemeyer discuss housing in Europe, Rosa E. Donoso and Marja Elsinga discuss housing in Latin America and the Caribbean, and Akin S. Akinyemi, Petra L. Doan, and Lindsay Slautterback discuss housing in Africa. Finally, Corianne Payton Scally introduces housing challenges in the global context in the twenty-first century.

Books, including edited volumes, are ultimately the outcome of collaborative efforts over many years. The first edition of *Introduction to Housing* was published in 2006. The need for a second edition was deliberated at the Housing Education and Research Association (HERA) conference in Roanoke, Virginia, in 2012 and then formally discussed at the HERA conference in Tulsa, Oklahoma, in 2013. The editors presented status updates at the HERA conferences in Kansas City, Missouri, in 2014 and in Springfield, Illinois, in 2015 and also solicited feedback from the HERA board during quarterly telephone conferences in 2014 and 2015. We thank HERA presidents Sarah D. Kirby, Martha Keel, Andrew T. Carswell, Michael Goldschmidt, Pamela Turner, and Leslie Green-Pimentel for helpful guidance; the HERA board and HERA conference participants and members for constructive suggestions; and HERA's former executive director Michael Vogel and executive director Barbara Allen for assistance. We thank the Center for Real Estate Entrepreneurship at George Mason University for support. We also thank Helen McManus, public policy and management studies liaison librarian at George Mason University's Arlington campus, for assistance with references. Claudia Holland, former head of the Scholarly Communication and Copyright Office at University Libraries at George Mason University's Fairfax campus, competently and promptly answered many questions about copyright agreements. Matthew Ogborn and Joy Margheim provided superb copy editing services. Finally, we thank James Patrick Allen, our commissioning editor at the University of Georgia Press, and his incredible team.

The journey from the idea to publish a second edition to submitting the final manuscript has been an enjoyable one, with one exception. On February 12, 2015, we lost our fourth editor, Kenneth R. Tremblay. He had served as an influential coeditor of the first edition of *Introduction to Housing* and provided much appreciated institutional memory for this second edition. Ken was one of the brightest minds in housing, authoring over 270 publications for scholarly and lay audiences and giving countless paper and poster presentations at conferences while remaining unassuming and approachable. Over his several-decades-long HERA membership he served as president in 2010, editor of *Housing and Society*, an at-large representative on the board of directors for three terms, and a member of several committees. All these and other accomplishments earned him the Distinguished Service Award at the 2014 HERA conference. We miss him dearly and dedicate *Introduction to Housing*, second edition, to him.

REFERENCES

Abramsky, S. (2013). *The American way of poverty: How the other half still lives*. New York: Nation Books.

Barofsky, N. (2012). *Bailout: An inside account of how Washington abandoned Main Street while rescuing Wall Street*. New York: Free Press.

Bernanke, B. S. (2015). *The courage to act: A memoir of a crisis and its aftermath*. New York: W. W. Norton.

Blinder, A. S. (2014). *After the music stopped: The financial crisis, the response, and the work ahead*. New York: Penguin Books.

Brash, J. (2011). *Bloomberg's New York: Class and governance in the luxury city*. Athens: University of Georgia Press.

Bratt, R. G., Stone, M. E., & Hartman, C. (2006). *A right to housing: Foundation for a new social agenda*. Philadelphia: Temple University Press.

Brenner, N., Marcuse, P., & Mayer, M. (Eds.). (2012). *Cities for people, not for profit: Critical urban theory and the right to the city*. New York: Routledge.

Dayen, D. (2016). *Chain of title: How three ordinary Americans uncovered Wall Street's great foreclosure fraud*. New York: The New Press.

Desmond, M. (2016). *Evicted: Poverty and profit in the American city*. New York: Crown.

Edin, K. J., & Shaefer, L. (2015). *$2.00 a day: Living on almost nothing in America*. Boston: Houghton Mifflin Harcourt.

Engel, K. C., & McCoy, P. A. (2011). *The subprime virus: Reckless credit, regulatory failure, and next steps*. Oxford: Oxford University Press.

Frey, W. H. (2014). *New projections point to a majority minority nation in 2044*. Washington, D.C.: Brookings Institution.

Graham, C. (2017). *Happiness for all? Unequal hopes and lives in pursuit of the American Dream*. Princeton, N.J.: Princeton University Press.

Hartman, C., & Squires, G. D. (2013). *From foreclosure to fair lending: Advocacy, organizing, occupy, and the pursuit of equitable access to credit*. New York: New Village Press.

Hollander, J. B. (2011). *Sunburnt cities: The Great Recession, depopulation, and urban planning in the American sunbelt*. New York: Routledge.

Immergluck, D. (2015). *Preventing the next mortgage crisis: The meltdown, the federal response, and the future of housing in America*. Lanham, Md.: Rowman & Littlefield.

Jacobs, J. (1992). *The death and life of great American cities*. New York: Vintage Books.

Mallach, A. (2009). *A decent home: Planning, building, and preserving affordable housing*. Chicago: American Planning Association Press.

Mallach, A. (2010). *Bringing buildings back: From abandoned properties to community assets*. Montclair, N.J.: National Housing Institute.

Martin, I. W., & Niedt, C. (2015). *Foreclosed America*. Stanford, Calif.: Stanford University Press.

Mian, A., & Sufi, A. (2014). *House of debt: How they (and you) caused the Great Recession, and how we can prevent it from happening again*. Chicago: University of Chicago Press.

Pattillo, M. (2013). Housing: Commodity versus right. *Annual Review of Sociology, 39*, 509–531.

Paulson, H. M. (2010). *On the brink: Inside the race to stop the collapse of the global financial system*. New York: Business Plus.

Satter, B. (2009). *Family properties: How the struggle over race and real estate transformed Chicago and urban America*. New York: Picador.

Vincent, G., & Velkoff, V. (2010). *The next four decades: The older population in the United States: 2010 to 2050: Population estimates and projections*. Washington, D.C.: U.S. Bureau of the Census.

Woldoff, R. A., Morrison, L. M., & Glass, M. R. (2016). *Priced out: Stuyvesant Town and the loss of middle-class neighborhoods*. New York: New York University Press.

INTRODUCTION TO
HOUSING

SECTION I
INTRODUCTION

Chapter 1

Current Trends in the U.S. Housing Market

RACHEL BOGARDUS DREW

In the United States, the market for housing is large, varied, and complex. It represents over 133 million dwellings, with a value of over $20 trillion in 2014 and spending activity that contributes over 15 percent to the GDP (Federal Reserve Board, 2015; U.S. Bureau of the Census, n.d.d). The market consists of single-unit structures and multiunit apartments, primary residences and vacation homes, all in a wide range of styles, locations, and conditions. There are also many types of housing market activities, including building, buying, renting, furnishing, renovating, and financing homes (Green & Malpezzi, 2003) (see chapters 3, 5, 6, 7, 8, and 9). Most of these activities are locally oriented, though they are often discussed and analyzed at a national level and have important ramifications for the national economy. The housing market is also strongly influenced by external forces, such as changes in economic conditions, public policy, and social preferences (Green & Malpezzi, 2003; Schwartz, 2015) (see chapter 15).

Housing markets are also important to study because of the commodity on which they are based. Housing provides shelter and sanctuary from the outside world and a place of convening for families and friends, as well as serving as the site of many daily activities (see chapter 2). With the exception of houseboats and mobile homes, most housing is located in fixed places that shape where and how people interact with their communities, whether through work, education, public and private services, or leisure time (see chapters 12 and 13). For people who own their homes, housing also represents a major financial investment with the potential to both appreciate and depreciate in value (see chapters 2, 7, 10, 15, and 16). Of course, for those without safe and sound shelter, the lack of housing presents a major obstacle to living a healthy, satisfying, and productive life (Ronald, 2008) (see chapter 11). Housing markets are therefore about much more than just physical buildings (see chapter 8).

This chapter provides short summaries that act as an overview of the basic concepts and metrics used to discuss current and emerging trends in the U.S. housing market and sets the stage for more detailed descriptions of specific aspects of housing in subsequent chapters in *Introduction to Housing*. These concepts and metrics are necessary for understanding the role that housing markets play in the physical, economic, and social contexts that are discussed in this book. Readers interested in learning more about specific elements of the housing market are therefore referred to the many references cited throughout and listed at the end of the chapter.

The trends discussed below also offer a glimpse of the status of the housing market in the wake of the economic downturn, also called the Great Recession, which officially lasted from December 2007 to June 2009. This recession followed a period of unprecedented growth in the U.S. economy, and especially in the housing market (see chapter 15). Starting in the mid-1990s, demand for housing grew as a series of policy and industry innovations made it easier and less expensive to buy homes (Drew, 2013; Shlay, 2006). Buoyed by lower interest rates for mortgage borrowing, millions of households were able to purchase their own homes for the first time, while existing homeowners benefited from rising house values and the opportunity to refinance their mortgages and extract equity or lower their housing costs (Schwartz, 2015). Home sales, prices, and construction all rose in response, which further bolstered the housing market and the national economy (Schwartz, 2015). Meanwhile, the mortgage industry sought to reach an even larger pool of potential home buyers by introducing still more novel and exotic means of financing home purchases and refinances. The risks inherent in lending to lower-income and less-qualified borrowers were offset by packaging loans into tradable securities, which were sold to a wide range of investors on Wall Street who were looking to benefit from the boom in the housing market (Cannato, 2010; Schwartz, 2015) (see chapter 8).

The cycle of lending to ever-riskier borrowers seeking to buy homes in an environment with rapidly rising prices, and obscuring those risks within complex investment securities, eventually reached its end in the mid-2000s, when the torrid pace of the housing market began to slow. A small group of homeowners with so-called subprime mortgages, which have variable costs and higher interest rates than conventional loans, began to have trouble keeping up with their rising mortgage payments (Schwartz, 2015). Unable to find buyers for their homes, they went into default on their mortgages, which in turn lowered the value of securities backed by those loans. Demand for these investments evaporated, and with them demand for more mortgage originations and home purchases. Thus a new cycle was started, characterized by decreasing house prices, a higher number of defaults and foreclosures, a lower number of home sales, and decreased mortgage borrowing, which all but collapsed the housing finance industry (Schwartz, 2015). The effects of the housing market breakdown on the mortgage-backed investment market, meanwhile, rippled through the entire economy and brought on the worst economic downturn since the Great Depression (Couch, 2013; Schwartz, 2015) (see chapter 15).

The dramatic rise and fall of the housing market leading up to the Great Recession is evident in many of the trends covered in this chapter. The chapter begins with a description of what constitutes the housing market and the distinctions between different types of dwellings and households. It then covers four different types of trends within the housing market: construction, transactions, housing characteristics, and household composition. It concludes by looking at three additional aspects of housing that merit closer inspection and consideration: homeownership, housing affordability, and housing demand. These three trends are not only important to the current state of the housing market but are poised to play important roles in shaping the future course of housing in the United States (see chapters 2, 7, and 10).

KEY TERMS AND CONCEPTS

Before delving into different trends and metrics on housing, it is useful to first clarify the basic terminology used in the housing field. A housing *unit* refers to a specific completed dwelling, distinguished from all other dwellings by its unique address (i.e., unit number, house number, street name, and postal or zip code). The majority (70 percent as of 2013) of housing units in the United States are *single-family units*, which can be either stand-alone structures or attached structures separated by ground-to-roof walls, such as townhouses (U.S. Bureau of the Census, n.d.a, n.d.f). Even when attached, single-family units typically do not share any common spaces or utilities. Another 24 percent of housing units are *multifamily units*, which do share some common exterior features, such as hallways, garages, and shared entryways. A single apartment building, therefore, may be home to several multifamily units, which may or may not share utilities. The remaining 6 percent of housing units are *manufactured homes*, also called mobile homes, which are self-contained units that lack a foundation or other permanent attachment to the property on which they are located (U.S. Bureau of the Census, n.d.f).

At any given time, a housing unit can be either occupied or vacant. An *occupied* unit is characterized by the residence of a *household*, which is defined as an individual or a group of individuals who coreside in the unit (U.S. Bureau of the Census, n.d.f). The unit is considered occupied even if the household is temporarily living elsewhere, such as in a seasonal or second home, as long as the occupied unit is still considered the household's primary residence for legal purposes. A *vacant* unit is any dwelling that is not currently occupied as a primary residence, regardless of how long it has been in that state (U.S. Bureau of the Census, 2013). Vacant units thus include units that are intended for primary use but do not have a current occupant, either because they are in the process of a transfer between households or because of lack of demand for that unit. Vacant units can also be units held for occasional use (e.g., seasonal and second homes) and units that have been abandoned (U.S. Bureau of the Census, 2013).

Occupied units can be further identified by the relationship between their owners and residents. Units that are the primary residence of their owner are called *owner-occupied* units, and a resident owner is referred to as a *homeowner* (see chapter 7). Owners who do not live in their units typically opt to lease them to other households, called *renters*, thus designating the unit as a *rental unit* and the owner as the *landlord* (see chapter 9). Both arrangements are generally codified in legal contracts that specify the terms and conditions of residency, allowable uses of the property, rights and responsibilities of the owner and residents, and how the residents pay for their use of the unit (Belsky & Drew, 2008). Many homeowners, for example, finance their homes with a combination of a down payment and money borrowed from a mortgage lender, which they typically pay back with interest over a period of decades (see chapter 8). Renters, meanwhile, generally pay landlords a monthly fee in exchange for use of the unit, for a lease period of a few months to a few years, and sometimes with one to three months of rent paid in advance as a deposit against damage to the unit or early termination of the lease (Belsky & Drew, 2008) (see chapter 9). The owner/renter status of a housing unit, as well as that of the household in the unit, is referred to as *housing tenure* (U.S. Bureau of the Census, n.d.d).

TRENDS IN CONSTRUCTION

There is a constant need for new housing in the United States, both to house the ever-growing population and to replace dwellings deemed unsuitable due to age, condition, location, or style. Almost all housing in the United States is professionally planned, designed, and built in accordance with local, state, and federal government standards and regulations. The construction process typically involves three steps: the permitting of a new building, the start of construction, and the completion of the dwelling. The length of time between these steps is generally zero to two months between permitting and starting construction and three to nine months between the start and completion of construction (U.S. Bureau of the Census, n.d.f) (see chapters 3, 6, 18, and 19). The U.S. Bureau of the Census collects data from local governments and permitting authorities on the number of units that go through these stages annually, making it fairly straightforward to track these trends over time.

The amount of new housing construction that occurs varies greatly over time. Construction activity generally coincides with cycles in the broader economy, declining in the lead-up to recessions and expanding during periods of economic growth (see figure 1.1). During the housing market boom of the early 2000s, for example, all three indicators of housing construction showed significant gains, with permits and starts both increasing by over 30 percent between 2001 and 2005 alone. Housing completions, meanwhile, did not increase quite as dramatically, as some units permitted or started were abandoned before completion when concerns about the housing market emerged mid-decade. Subsequently, housing construction declined sharply, with permits and starts falling by over 70 percent from their 2005 peak to new record-low levels by 2009. All three measures of housing construction remained low until 2011, when they once again began to increase, though the number of new units added to the housing stock remained well below prior highs (U.S. Bureau of the Census, n.d.f).

Construction data can also be used to track how much new housing is built as single-family units, multifamily units, and manufactured housing. As with the total amount of new housing, the mix of single-family and multifamily units generally fluctuates with changes in the broader economy, though changes in housing policy and consumer taste can also influence how much housing of each type is added in a given year. The rise in new construction during the 2000s housing market boom, driven largely by increases in demand for owner-occupied housing, was fueled entirely by single-family units, starts of which grew from 1.2 million in 2000 to 1.7 million in 2005, a 39 percent increase in just five years. Meanwhile, multifamily and manufactured housing starts actually declined by 15 percent over the same period (U.S. Bureau of the Census, n.d.e, n.d.f). When housing starts subsequently dropped, single-family homes also accounted for most of the decline, falling by 74 percent to just 445,000 in 2009, though multifamily

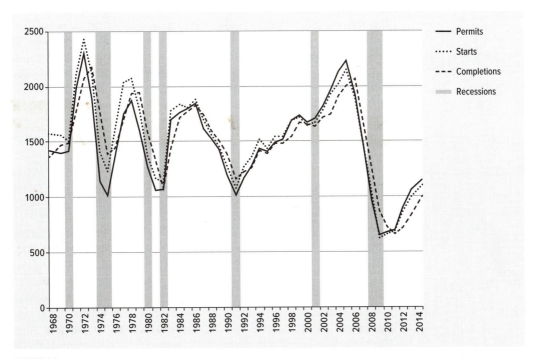

FIGURE 1.1
U.S. Housing Permits, Starts, and Completions, 1968–2014
Source: U.S. Bureau of the Census, n.d.f.
Note: Areas shaded in gray indicate national recessions as defined by the National Bureau of Economic Research, U.S. Business Cycle Expansions and Contractions.

and manufactured housing starts also decreased by 67 percent over the same period (U.S. Bureau of the Census, n.d.e, n.d.f) (see chapter 15).

Housing construction trends are not only an indicator of strength and activity in the housing market but also a signal of housing's contribution to local and regional economies. That contribution comes from employment and spending on materials in the construction process, as well as consumption spending of the households that occupy new dwellings. Value put-in-place is one measure of this financial impact, reflecting the dollar value of the construction work done to erect new homes, including spending on labor and materials, architectural and engineering work, taxes paid during construction, and contractor profits (U.S. Bureau of the Census, n.d.b). Separate figures are collected for single-family and multifamily residential structures, as well as for improvements made to the existing housing stock.

The total value put-in-place reflects both how much new construction occurs and how much the per-unit cost of that construction changes over time. When the amount of construction declines greatly, then the total value put-in-place will also decrease, even if per-unit spending remains steady, as was the case from 2005 to 2007, when per-unit spending rose from $306,000 to $333,000, while total value put-in-place declined from $525 billion to $348 billion (U.S. Bureau of the Census, n.d.b). When both starts and per-unit costs fall simultaneously, however, value put-in-place declines even more precipitously; in 2011, total value put-in-place bottomed out at $114 billion as per-unit costs dropped to $264,000. It takes strength in both trends, therefore, for construction value to increase, as it did after 2011 (U.S. Bureau of the Census, n.d.b).

Another way that the housing stock stays current with needs and contributes to local economies is through the remodeling of homes (i.e., improvements made to existing housing to update or change features of the dwelling) (Joint Center for Housing Studies of Harvard University, 2015a).

This process can include anything from minor design upgrades, such as replacing fixtures or adding custom-built components to a single room, to major renovations or rehabilitation of entire structures (see chapters 3, 5, 6, and 18). While remodeling activity and spending typically follow economic conditions, they also reflect how much households are willing to invest in their current dwellings versus building or buying a new one. During the late 2000s, for example, the fall in the value of improvements to existing owner-occupied homes was less than the decline of new construction, with the former experiencing a peak-to-trough decline of 27 percent (from 2007 to 2011) versus a 78 percent decline in the value of new construction (from 2005 to 2009) as many homeowners opted to renovate their existing homes rather than buy and sell in a volatile economy (Joint Center for Housing Studies of Harvard University, 2015a) (see chapter 15).

The annual volume and value of housing construction and remodeling activity in the United States, while impressive in its scale, still represents only a fraction of all housing market activity that occurs annually. The 437,000 newly constructed single-family homes sold in 2014, for example, accounted for only 9 percent of all single-family home sales, while the value of those new home sales (i.e., the number of sales times average sale price), at $123 billion, was just 12 percent of the total value of all homes sold that year (Joint Center for Housing Studies of Harvard University, 2015b). We should therefore look beyond new construction to fully understand how the housing market operates.

TRENDS IN TRANSACTIONS

Existing housing that is not newly constructed plays a considerable role in the national economy, primarily through transactions between buyers and sellers or landlords and tenants. Such transactions occur when a household moves from one dwelling to another, incurring costs along the way. These include fees paid to brokers for assisting in the marketing and processing of the transactions, payments for hiring movers or trucks to transport household goods, costs of repairs or modifications prior to occupancy, and purchases of new furnishings and equipment suitable to the new dwelling (Belsky & Drew, 2008). In addition, the process of transferring properties is not seamless; it requires considerable time and effort to search for a new residence, negotiate terms and financing, and plan and carry out a move (see chapter 7). For these reasons, households tend to move infrequently, and only in response to a change in their needs or taste (Belsky & Drew, 2008). Tracking trends in housing transactions can thus both explicitly reveal much about changing demand for different housing types and implicitly reveal the changing composition of households themselves.

Housing transactions differ by the tenure status of the unit. Renters tend to move more often, in part because the costs to move from a rented residence are much less than those associated with owned homes (Belsky & Drew, 2008) (see chapter 9). Home sales are also more legally complex, which adds additional costs and time to the home-buying process (see chapter 7). These tenure-related differences are observed in the vacancy rates for for-rent and for-sale housing, with the latter consistently much lower than the former (see figure 1.2).

Both trends are highly sensitive to conditions in the home-buying mar-

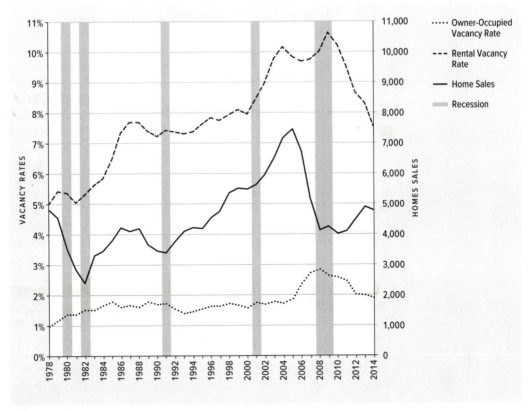

FIGURE 1.2
U.S. Housing Vacancy Rates by Tenure and U.S. Home Sales, 1978–2014

Source: U.S. Bureau of the Census, n.d.c, n.d.d; U.S. Department of Housing and Urban Development, 2015a.

Note: Areas shaded in gray indicate national recessions as defined by the National Bureau of Economic Research, U.S. Business Cycle Expansions and Contractions. Vacancy rates are for primary residences only and do not include vacation/seasonally occupied dwellings. Sales are expressed in thousands of units and include both existing and newly constructed homes.

ket, with rental vacancy rates generally rising with home purchases and owner vacancy rates tending to increase during periods of declining home sales. This is clearly observed in the vacancy rate and home-sales trends from the late 1970s through the mid-2010s. During the dual recessions of the early 1980s, for example, sales of new and existing single-family homes experienced a sharp drop when high interest rates and a poor economy made home purchases expensive and difficult (U.S. Department of Housing and Urban Development, 2015a). The owner vacancy rate increased by 50 percent in response, from 1.0 percent to 1.5 percent, between 1978 and 1982, resulting in over three hundred thousand more vacant for-sale units (U.S. Bureau of the Census, n.d.d). The subsequent increase in home sales, however, caused rental vacancy rates to increase sharply, from 5.1 percent in 1981 to 7.7 percent by 1987, or 1.2 million units.

This pattern repeated itself during the homeownership boom of the 1990s and early 2000s as well, when home sales and rental vacancy rates rose in tandem. Vacancy rates for for-sale homes, meanwhile, remained steady throughout most of this period. When the faltering housing market brought about a sharp drop in home sales, from 7.5 million in 2005 to 4.1 million just three years later, however, owner vacancy rates rose by over a third, reaching a record high of 2.9 percent, or 2.2 million vacant for-sale units by 2008. With fewer home sales and millions of foreclosed owners in need of new housing, demand for rentals resurged, lowering the rental vacancy rate back to early 1990s levels by 2014 (U.S. Bureau of the Census, n.d.d).

Another indicator of transactions in the housing market is the median sales price of existing homes. Similar to sales, house prices increased steeply during the homeownership boom of the 1990s through the mid-2000s, rising from an average of $180,000 for an existing single-family home in 1995 to an average of $264,000 for an existing single-family home by 2005, when measured in 2014 dollars adjusted for inflation (Joint Center for Housing Studies of Harvard University, 2015b). Unlike other indicators of the sudden downturn in housing markets after 2005, however, house prices did not immediately drop after reaching their peak, instead plateauing for two years. This reflects the delayed reaction to changes in the market of home buyers and sellers, who were initially unsure whether declining sales, rising defaults, and the falloff in new construction were short-term corrections rather than signs of a systemic collapse (Couch, 2013). Once the effects of the downturn began to manifest in investment markets and the broader economy, bringing with them tightening mortgage standards and reduced ability of households to purchase homes, house prices began to fall more dramatically, finally bottoming out in 2011 at an average sales price of $173,000 (in 2014 dollars) for an existing single-family home (Joint Center for Housing Studies of Harvard University, 2015b) (see chapter 15).

In the five years following the end of the Great Recession, most measures of housing transactions showed steady, if slow, improvement. Sales of new and existing single-family homes, which held fast at around four million units a year between 2008 and 2011, rose back to just under five million in 2013 (U.S. Bureau of the Census, n.d.f; U.S. Department of Housing and Urban Development, 2015a). House prices likewise increased after 2011, surpassing $200,000 on average for an existing single-family home in 2014 (Joint Center for Housing Studies of Harvard University, 2015b). Meanwhile, vacancy rates for owner and renter units both declined to pre-boom levels by 2014, as activity in both the for-sale and for-rent markets continued to increase (U.S. Bureau of the Census, n.d.d). The path of these trends, however, is an open question. Higher sales volumes and house prices may encourage more homeowners to place their homes on the market, sustaining the recovery further. Yet as of 2015, mortgage lending still remained constrained, limiting home-buying opportunities for many would-be homeowners (Carr & Anacker, 2015). The future course of the housing market, therefore, will depend greatly on the interplay of both transactions and residential finance availability.

TRENDS IN HOUSING CHARACTERISTICS

Single-family 1500 to 2500 sf

Just as housing construction and housing transactions have varied over time, so too have the characteristics of housing units themselves. Changes in taste, technology, the economy, household demographics, and socioeconomics all influence the features residents desire in their housing, including size, location, quality, and structure type. A newly available feature may become standard over time (e.g., central air conditioning), while older technologies are phased out of the stock (e.g., wood-burning stoves). Again, observing these trends reveals how both housing and households have changed over the years and decades (see chapters 2, 3, 5, 6, and 18).

1 One big change in housing over time has been its size. The median number of square feet in a newly constructed single-family home has increased from around fifteen hundred in the early 1980s to nearly twenty-five hundred by 2014 (U.S. Bureau of the Census, n.d.f). This growth has not oc-

FIGURE 1.3
Indicators of Housing Quality, 1985–2013
Source: U.S. Bureau of the Census, n.d.a.

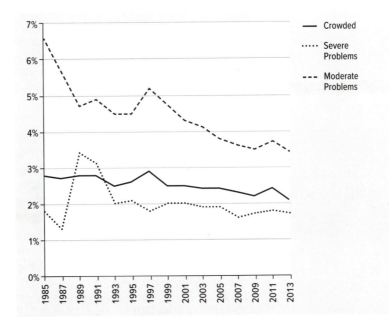

[Margin note: Square footage increased per single-family but the size of the family decreased.]

curred, however, as a result of an increase in the average household size, which has actually declined from 2.75 to 2.54 persons per household over this period (U.S. Bureau of the Census, n.d.c). Instead, this trend is a reflection of people's preferences for more space in their homes. Similarly, the proportion of newly constructed single-family homes with at least four bedrooms has increased from under 20 percent in the mid-1980s to 46 percent in 2014, as households increasingly desire additional rooms to serve as guest rooms, home offices, or playrooms (U.S. Bureau of the Census, n.d.f) (see chapter 2).

[Margin: 2] The locations of new housing have also been changing over time, as the population has been gradually shifting away from the older centers in the Northeast and Midwest and toward newer communities in the South and West. The share of all housing located in the South, for example, increased from 32 percent in the 1970s to 38 percent by 2009 (U.S. Bureau of the Census, n.d.c). The share in the Northeast, meanwhile, declined from 23 to 18 percent over the same period. At the same time, more housing has been located in the suburbs in recent years, accounting for fully half of all units as of 2014 (U.S. Bureau of the Census, n.d.c).

With larger, newer construction constantly improving the quality of the housing stock, incidences of poor-quality housing are rare. The shares of occupied housing with either moderate or severe quality problems are low and gradually declining with each year (see figure 1.3). Moderate problems include nonfunctioning toilets, unvented heating, lack of kitchen facilities, and potentially hazardous fixtures. Severe problems include the lack of running water, complete lack of heating or electricity, persistent leaks or holes exposed to the outside, and rodent infestations. Incidences of crowding, defined as more than one person per room residing in the unit, are also low and falling (U.S. Bureau of the Census, n.d.a) (see chapter 12).

Better-quality housing over time, however, does not mean that all housing is suitable and affordable to all households. Discrepancies remain between the location, size, features, and cost of housing and the needs and

CURRENT TRENDS IN THE U.S. HOUSING MARKET 11

TRENDS IN HOUSEHOLD COMPOSITION

Since the 1970s, there have been noticeable changes in the racial and ethnic composition of households, as immigration and higher rates of natural increase (i.e., births) among people of color have more than doubled the share of households headed by a person of color nationally, from 15 percent in 1976 to 34 percent as of 2014 (see figure 1.4). Nearly all of this growth is accounted for by Hispanic and Asian/other (including multirace) household heads, while the share of black household heads increased only slightly over this period. This trend is expected to continue in the near future, with the share of households headed by non-Hispanic whites decreasing to under 60 percent by the year 2035 (McCue, 2014) (see chapter 16).

A less consistent trend in household characteristics is the age distribution of household heads, which fluctuates not only with swings in generational rates of births and immigration but also with trends in household formation and dissolution. This is evident over time in the share of households headed by young adults (i.e., those under thirty-five years old). In the 1970s, for instance, this age group mostly consisted of baby boomers (i.e., those born between 1946 and 1964), who not only were the largest generation at the time but also were forming more households in their twenties and thirties relative to prior generations (Goodman, Pendall, & Zhu, 2015). The result was an increase in the share of households headed by someone under thirty-five years old, from 25 percent in 1970 to 31 percent in 1980 (U.S. Bureau of the Census, n.d.c). In the 1990s, however, the baby boomers aged out of young adulthood and were replaced in this age segment by the Generation X population (i.e., those born between 1965 and 1984). Generation X was not only smaller in numbers relative to the baby boomers, but its members were also

FIGURE 1.4
Share of U.S. Households Headed by a Person of Color, 1976–2014

Source: U.S. Bureau of the Census, n.d.c.

Note: Blacks and Asian/others are non-Hispanic. Hispanics may be of any race. Balance of distribution represents households headed by non-Hispanic whites.

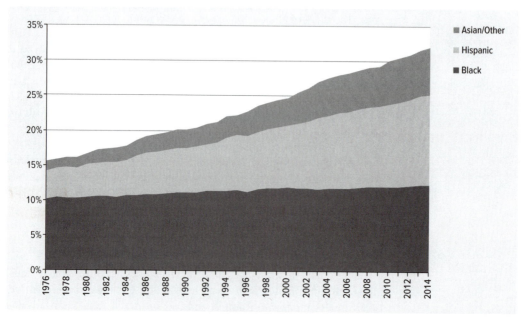

less likely to form households in their twenties and early thirties, as many of this generation remained in their parental homes longer, sought higher education, and delayed marriage and parenthood. Thus the share of young adult households fell to 23 percent by 2000, when Generation X accounted for all householders under thirty-five years old (U.S. Bureau of the Census, n.d.c) (see chapter 2).

Over the next two decades, further shifts in the age composition are expected as the baby boomers enter their retirement years and increase the share of households headed by someone at least sixty-five years old, from 24 percent in 2015 to 32 percent in 2035 (McCue, 2014). The next generation to enter young adulthood, meanwhile, are the millennials (i.e., those born between 1985 and 2004). While numerically larger than Generation X and even the baby boomers (McCue, 2014), millennials are expected to continue the trend of deferring household formation in favor of more time spent living at home, pursuing education, or living with roommates. The young adult share of all households, therefore, is expected to remain at around 20 percent through 2035 (McCue, 2014).

An additional aspect of household composition relevant to housing is the family type, which often influences the size and location of housing preferred by households. Over the past two decades, the most notable change in family type has been the declining share of married couples with children (see figure 1.5). This shift is directly related to the aging of the baby boomers into their retirement years (and thus no longer living with children), as well as declines in the fertility rates of younger women (Vespa, Lewis, & Kreider, 2013). Replacing these families have been increasing shares of single persons, other families (i.e., single parents and unmarried couples with children), and nonfamily households (i.e., unrelated roommates).

These shifts in the distributions of households have important implications for housing demand. Higher shares of older and childless households in particular will require housing that matches their needs and lifestyles (i.e., units offering accessibility and amenities suitable for an aging population)

FIGURE 1.5
U.S. Household Distribution by Family Type, 1995–2014
Source: U.S. Bureau of the Census, n.d.c.

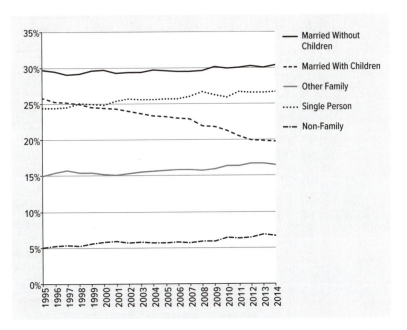

CURRENT TRENDS IN THE U.S. HOUSING MARKET

(Joint Center for Housing Studies of Harvard University, 2014). The increasing number and proportion of single-person households, meanwhile, may increase demand for smaller, more affordable units, particularly in denser urban locations (Been, Gross, & Infranca, 2014). How the nation's housing stock can be adjusted to meet these needs has ramifications not just for housing markets but for the economic and social well-being of the population as well (see chapters 2 and 17).

EMERGING TRENDS

As the preceding discussions show, the first decade of the 2000s was a period of substantial change in housing construction, transactions, characteristics, and household composition (see chapter 2). The effects of the early 2000s housing boom and subsequent recession on these trends are likely to be enduring, affecting not just the building and buying of structures but also people's preferences for particular housing types and locations (see chapters 15 and 16). Three trends in particular bear watching, as each will be an important component in determining the direction of housing markets going forward: homeownership, housing affordability, and future housing demand (see chapters 7, 10, and 25).

Homeownership

The nation's homeownership rate, or the share of households who live in owner-occupied homes, is often regarded as not just an indicator of housing market activity but also of national prosperity. Homeownership is associated with a wide range of benefits for both families and communities (Drew, 2013). Living in an owned home, for example, correlates with better social and educational outcomes for children, more knowledge of and involvement in community affairs, and an increased feeling of achievement and independence (Dietz & Haurin, 2003) (see chapter 12). Owning a home is also an investment vehicle through which owners can build wealth through the appreciation of house values over time; indeed, homeownership has been the primary means of wealth creation for middle-class households since at least the 1960s (Wolff, 2012) (see chapter 7).

The myriad benefits associated with homeownership have made this tenure form popular not only among individual households but also among policy makers as a means of improving social and economic conditions, especially for low-income households (Drew, 2013; Shlay, 2006) (see chapter 12). Indeed, higher homeownership rates and wealth building were among the objectives that motivated many of the policy and market initiatives introduced in the 1980s and 1990s to liberalize and expand mortgage lending to populations with traditionally low homeownership rates, including households of color (Drew, 2013; Shlay, 2006). New mortgage products with low initial payments and low down payment requirements, less stringent qualifying criteria, and the proliferation of mortgage brokers operating outside the regulatory constraints imposed on banks all served to increase the availability and affordability of mortgage credit and thus the opportunity to buy a home (Drew, 2013). The result of these efforts was a dramatic rise in the national homeownership rate, from 64 percent in 1994 to 69 percent by 2004 (see figure 1.6; see chapter 8).

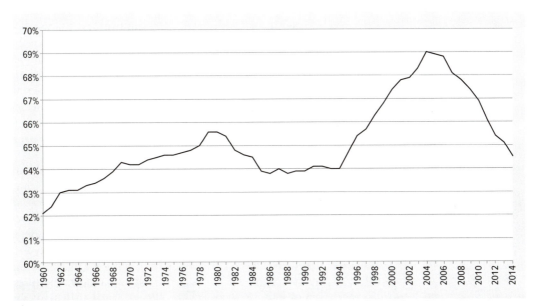

FIGURE 1.6
National Homeownership Rate, 1960–2014
Source: U.S. Bureau of the Census, n.d.d.

The onset of the housing market downturn in the mid-2000s, however, put an end to the homeownership boom, as concerns over the riskiness of nontraditional mortgage products caused mortgage credit to contract sharply (Drew, 2013). Despite falling house prices improving the affordability of homeownership, the lack of mortgage options prevented many would-be home buyers from making purchases. At the same time, an estimated six million existing homeowners who could no longer afford their mortgage payments ended up losing their homes to foreclosure between 2007 and 2014 (CoreLogic, 2015). Federal policy efforts to encourage and reinforce homeownership, such as first-time homebuyer tax credits and mortgage remediation programs for distressed homeowners, helped some households acquire or retain their owned homes but could not completely turn the tide of declining homeownership (Couch, 2013). The national homeownership rate fell almost as quickly as it had risen, and by 2014 it was back to its mid-1990s level of under 64 percent (U.S. Bureau of the Census, n.d.d) (see chapter 15).

In the wake of this dramatic rise and fall in the national homeownership rate, concerns have arisen over the future of homeownership in the United States. Given its historical associations with positive outcomes, the federal government still promotes homeownership as a policy priority through favorable tax treatment of interest paid on mortgage loans and proceeds from home sales (Drew, 2013; Shlay, 2006) (see chapter 7). The government has also long supported the mortgage market itself, initially by creating a pair of government-sponsored enterprises (GSEs), known as Fannie Mae and Freddie Mac, to provide liquidity to lenders so that they could make more loans than their own reserves allowed. While the GSEs operated as private companies with an implicit federal guarantee for most of their history, their transfer into federal conservatorship during the housing crisis in 2008 was a clear signal of the policy importance of preserving homeownership opportunities. Finally, the Federal Housing Administration (FHA) provides guarantees on loans, as well as low-down-payment programs for qualified low-income borrowers, all for the purpose of encouraging more home buying (Carr & Anacker, 2014; Drew, 2013). Persistent tightness in mortgage markets, along with new regulations imposed on mortgage lenders after the downturn, however, have continued to limit home-buying opportunities (Couch, 2013). With the experience of millions of households losing their homes to foreclosure and the evaporation of nearly $7 trillion in housing wealth during the downturn, policy makers are uncertain about whether and how to continue using policy measures to expand homeownership opportunities lest the mistakes of the past be repeated (Federal Reserve Board, 2015) (see chapter 8).

At the same time that mortgage market conditions are inhibiting home buying, demographic and social conditions in the United States are having their own effects on the share of households owning their own home. The baby boom generation, which entered its peak home-buying years just as the housing boom took off in the 1990s, is expected to decrease its homeownership rate starting in 2020 as its members retire and gradually exit the owner-occupied housing market (Goodman, Pendall, & Zhu, 2015). The smaller Generation X cohort will not be able to fully offset these departures, while the incoming millennial generation, though larger than the baby boomers, is expected to include higher shares of nonfamily households and households of color, who have lower homeownership rates than family and non-Hispanic white households (McCue, 2014). Only a concerted effort to increase homeownership rates among these younger households in a safe and sustainable way that does not introduce undue risks to homeowners or the housing market will increase homeownership rates once again (see chapter 2).

Housing Affordability

As the quality and accessibility of homes have increased over time, so too have their costs. Even with the decline in housing prices and rents during the 2000s recession, housing expenses for many owners and renters remained high and a significant draw on their resources. The share of households that exceeds the federal standard for affordable housing (i.e., paying more than 30 percent of their income on shelter) was 34 percent in 2013 (U.S. Bureau of the Census, n.d.a) (see chapter 10). The share among renters (49 percent) is higher than among owners (26 percent), and it is higher among households with incomes below $75,000 (48 percent) than those with higher incomes (7 percent) (Joint Center for Housing Studies of Harvard University, 2015b) (see chapter 9).

The ramifications of millions of households facing such housing cost burdens are significant. With such high proportions of their income spent on housing, many households have difficulty affording other basic needs, such as food, transportation to work, health care, and clothing (Joint Center for Housing Studies of Harvard University, 2015b). Governmental resources available to alleviate housing affordability burdens, meanwhile, generally fall far short of the growing need for assistance. The Department of Housing and Urban Development (HUD) estimated that in 2013 only one in four low-income renters eligible for federal housing assistance actually received a subsidy to offset their housing costs (U.S. Department of Housing and Urban Development, 2015b) (see chapter 14).

The prospects for improving housing affordability are, unfortunately, dim. Housing costs are expected to continue increasing as demand from an ever-growing population places pressure on the existing supply of dwellings while new construction is hampered by the high cost of land (Joint Center for Housing Studies of Harvard University, 2015b). Stagnant or declining real wages for many workers will further exacerbate these burdens, especially in housing markets with high rents and low vacancies, where housing costs have been rising faster than inflation (Joint Center for Housing Studies of Harvard University, 2015b). The long-term effects of expensive housing, meanwhile, will continue to wreak havoc on households struggling to afford their dwellings, leaving them resource depleted and unable to save for the future. The trend of high housing costs and burdens is thus an important one to monitor going forward (see chapter 10).

Future Housing Demand

A third important trend in the housing market is the level and pace of household growth. The net number of households added each year determines how many new housing units will be needed, which in turn impacts construction levels, transactions, and housing conditions across the country. The demographic composition of those households, meanwhile, shapes preferences for the types, locations, and tenure of housing. Understanding the drivers of household formation, therefore, is essential for predicting future housing demand and supply trends (see chapter 25).

The largest driver of household growth is population increase. Between 2000 and 2010, the U.S. population grew by 27.3 million people, or 9.7 percent, which translated into 11.2 million new households, or a 10.7 percent increase (Lofquist, Lugaila, O'Connell, & Feliz, 2012). This rate of population growth represents a slowdown relative to earlier decades, however, due to changes in key demographic and social trends. For one, long-running declines in fertility rates among women, from later ages of first births to fewer children born per female, have reduced the rate of natural increase of the U.S. population (Goodman, Pendall, & Zhu, 2015). For another, annual immigration numbers in the 2000s were well below the high levels observed in the 1980s and 1990s due to worsening economic conditions and political uncertainties in the United States (McCue, 2014). The effects of these demographic shifts have been especially noticeable among adults in their late twenties to midforties, which is traditionally the cohort responsible for most new household formations.

Population alone, however, does not determine household growth. The other component to consider is the headship rate, or the share of the population age fifteen or older that head their own households. The national headship rate, which was 50 percent in the mid-1970s, actually rose to 52 percent as of 2003 (U.S. Bureau of the Census, n.d.c). While only a small change in percentage terms, this increase represents around eight million additional households formed than there would have been if 1970s headship rates had persisted. This increase is largely a result of higher numbers of single-person households among all age segments of the population. With marriage rates on the decline since the 1960s, more young adults are delaying or deferring matrimony and thus living longer as individuals. Seniors and middle-age adults, meanwhile, are living longer postmarriage lives (i.e., after being widowed or divorced), thus further adding to the number of single-person households (McCue, 2014) (see chapters 2 and 17).

There are also nondemographic forces that influence how many households are formed. In periods of weak economic growth or recessions, household growth generally declines because fewer people have the income and resources to live on their own, thus staying with family or roommates longer. Indeed, headship rates declined slightly during the Great Recession, to 51.5 percent in 2012 (U.S. Bureau of the Census, n.d.c). The effect of poor economic conditions on headship rates is generally short lived, however, as people who deferred forming their own households eventually do so once the economy improves (McCue, 2014) (see chapters 2 and 15).

Using information about expected population growth and demographic trends, researchers project that the pace of household formation will gradually slow down, from an average growth of around 1.33 million households per year between 2013 and 2015 to an estimated average growth of 1.29 million households per year between 2015 and 2020, and then further to an estimated average growth of 1.19 million households per year between 2020 and 2025 (McCue, 2014). These projections, however, are based on an assumption that headship rates will remain constant among the population, segmented by age and race and ethnicity, at their average growth rate as observed between 2010 and 2012, a period directly following a recession. If economic conditions continue to improve in the latter half of the 2010s and beyond, actual headship rates may rise again and temper the decline in household formations somewhat.

CONCLUSION

The trends in housing discussed in this chapter offer some perspective on how housing has changed over the past few decades, including the effects of the Great Recession and the downturn in the home-buying market. These trends focus on the general status of housing markets and households and provide context for many of the detailed discussions about housing in the chapters of this book. They do not, however, portend what the future of housing will look like. Caution should therefore be used in extrapolating recent trends into predictions going forward. Indeed, the Great Recession was such an unusual occurrence in regional and local housing markets that its effects are likely to linger on for several years, and possibly decades (see chapter 15).

Housing will continue to play an important role in the social and economic life of Americans. Beyond providing the basic necessity of shelter and protection from the elements, housing serves many other purposes. It determines where and how people live, with whom they associate, and what opportunities are available to them, and it can be a source of economic gains or distress. Yet even beyond these direct effects, housing also represents part of people's identity and is often seen as a measure of prosperity, both for individuals and the nation. The marking of trends in housing markets, while important, thus describes only part of the story (see chapters 2, 12, and 13). The subsequent chapters of *Introduction to Housing* help fill in more of this story and complete the picture of how housing shapes the economy and society at large.

REFERENCES

Been, V., Gross, B., & Infranca, J. (2014). *Responding to changing households: Regulatory challenges for micro-units and accessory dwellings.* New York: NYU Furman Center.

Chapter 2: Influences on Housing Choice

JULIA O. BEAMISH AND
ROSEMARY CARUCCI GOSS

Choosing a place to live may seem like a fairly simple decision. Yet many factors influence the actual choice of dwelling for an individual or a family. For example, an apartment, a townhouse, or a single-family home in an urban, suburban, or rural location could be appropriate for a certain individual, but each one may not be feasible or appropriate for the same person at every point in life. Income and household size might make an apartment feasible for a young couple just getting started, while a large home in the country might be too expensive and too much work for this same couple.

Several concepts have been used to explain the relationship between individuals and their housing. One of these, Maslow's hierarchy of human needs, discussed below, has been used to explain the important role that shelter plays in people's lives and how it can fulfill some of their basic physical and psychological needs. Other research has examined demographic and socioeconomic characteristics of housing preferences. Housing values, consumer lifestyles, and housing norms have also been considered in explaining the housing choices and housing satisfaction of consumers.

The conceptual framework for influences on housing choice developed by Beamish, Goss, and Emmel (2001) identifies and explains factors influencing housing choice and is the focus of this chapter. Briefly, it suggests that housing choice is influenced by demographic, socioeconomic, and psychographic characteristics of the household and by housing norms.

In 1942 Abraham Maslow presented a theoretical structure of human needs to a psychoanalytic society in his hierarchy of human needs (Maslow, 1970). This theory explains human motivation and has been adapted by many fields, including housing. According to this framework, there are five levels of needs that humans try to satisfy (see figure 2.1). Lower-level needs must be satisfied before higher-level needs can be addressed. Physiological needs are the lowest level. These are needs that must be met for human survival: food, protection from the elements, and maintenance of body temperature. Basic shelter is essential for humans in most climates and areas. The second level is security and safety, which reflect a need to protect oneself and control one's life. Housing can help meet these needs by offering a space that is healthful and free of hazards. The third level is social need or a sense

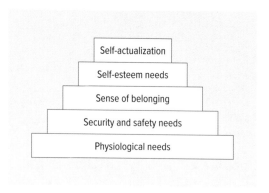

FIGURE 2.1
Maslow's Hierarchy of Human Needs
Source: Authors, based on Maslow, 1970.

of belonging. Family socialization in the home environment is an important focus of this level of needs. The fourth level is self-esteem or ego needs. In the United States, housing is often an expression of one's image of self. The final level is self-actualization, occurring when a person is able to meet his or her fullest potential; here the home can provide a setting that allows for creative expression. Authors of books on housing have used Maslow's framework to describe the role of housing in supporting human life (Beamish et al., 2001; Lindamood & Hanna, 1979; Newmark & Thompson, 1977).

Many housing choices are available to consumers in the United States. A variety of locations, structure types, sizes, styles, materials, and construction types provide opportunities for many unique living environments. Most of these housing choices could fulfill the human housing needs discussed above. How do households choose among the array of available housing choices? What influences their preferences and final choice of housing? How and why does a match between a household and a home occur? The next section will explore the answers to these questions in three major sections: demographic and socioeconomic characteristics, psychographic characteristics, and housing norms.

CONCEPTUAL FRAMEWORK FOR INFLUENCES ON HOUSING CHOICE

Beamish, Goss, and Emmel developed the conceptual framework for influences on housing choice in 2001. The framework, revised and presented here, identifies demographic and socioeconomic characteristics as key concepts that influence a variety of psychographic characteristics, which in turn influence housing norms. Ultimately housing choice is influenced by the household's desire to fulfill normative behavior related to housing while still reflecting its demographic, socioeconomic, and psychographic characteristics (see figure 2.2).

Demographic and socioeconomic characteristics are concepts used to explain the population in terms such as age, income, and occupation (see chapters 7, 8, 9, 10, and 17). As presented in this framework, psychographic characteristics include housing values, lifestyle, cultural orientation, and generational differences (see chapters 12, 13, 16, and 17). Housing values are internalized standards that materially affect the way a person will react when confronted with a situation permitting more than one option. These values have been identified as a guide for making decisions (J. Montgomery, 1966;

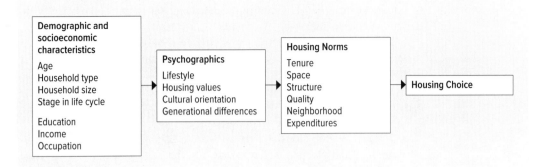

FIGURE 2.2
Conceptual Framework for Influences on Housing Choice
Source: Authors.

Roske, 1983). Lifestyle is an individual's whole way of living. It refers to a style of living that has a significant impact on one's housing norms, not to the style of one's furnishings or look. Cultural orientation and generational differences reflect concepts that have been developed by researchers and marketers to help explain attitudes and housing preferences of different segments of the population.

Housing norms have been discussed extensively by Morris and Winter (1978), who identify six housing norms present in the United States. Three of these norms (tenure type, space, and structure type) have determined the type of housing that most Americans live in today: the single-family detached home that is owner occupied and has a sufficient number of bedrooms for the occupants. The three other housing norms (housing quality, housing expenditures, and neighborhood) have more varied outcomes depending on the demographic, socioeconomic, and psychographic factors influencing the household (see chapters 12 and 13).

In the next several sections each of the concepts presented in the framework will be explained in more detail.

Demographic and Socioeconomic Characteristics

Demographers and other social scientists often categorize information about individuals and households to explain in broad terms how a population lives. We can study household decisions about housing by looking at data such as the homeownership rate by age, race, or ethnicity. In the United States several sources are frequently used to provide demographic and socioeconomic information about housing. The U.S. Census was started in 1790 and is conducted by the U.S. Bureau of the Census every 10 years during years ending in 0. The census is used as a means for reapportioning the U.S. House of Representatives and serves as an important source of information for government agencies to use in planning and allocating resources. A detailed housing section was added to the census survey in 1940 to provide an assessment of the current housing stock and, over time, to allow a comparison of the housing stock across decades. However, by 2010 very little housing information was gathered in the decennial count, which used a short form of ten questions that collected data on household size, race, ethnicity (i.e., Hispanic status), gender, and age of members of each household, as well as housing tenure (see chapters 1, 7, 9, 10, 16, and 17).

Other sources for explaining demographic and socioeconomic characteristics and providing housing information are available, with each providing different types of useful housing-related data. For example, the U.S. Bureau of the Census started conducting the American Community Survey (ACS) to provide more detailed information about households in communities throughout the country. It relies on a statistical sample of households that is collected annually. Data from the Current Population Survey (CPS) are also used to provide information about households and labor force trends. This survey is sponsored by the U.S. Bureau of the Census and the U.S. Department of Labor and is gathered monthly.

The American Housing Survey (AHS) is used frequently by housing researchers and planners. It is sponsored by the U.S. Department of Housing and Urban Development (HUD) and is collected on a biannual basis by the U.S. Bureau of the Census. The AHS uses the housing unit as a basis for its sample, thus providing information about the housing stock of the nation. The survey returns to the same housing unit each time it is collected, and housing units are added or subtracted to reflect recent additions to and recent deductions from the housing stock (see chapters 1, 12, and 13).

DEMOGRAPHIC CHARACTERISTICS OF HOUSEHOLDS

The U.S. Bureau of the Census defines a household as a group of individuals who are living together in a housing unit. A family household is defined as a specific type of household in which the members are related by blood, marriage, or adoption. Nonfamily households include single persons and persons sharing housing who are not related. In 2012 the majority of American households (66 percent) were still classified as families, although the proportion of households in this category has steadily declined since 1970, when it was 81 percent (Vespa, Lewis, & Kreider, 2013). As the proportion of nonfamily households increases, housing norms may also be changing because traditional cultural norms related to housing, such as space preferences, are often based on families rather than on households (Klinenberg, 2012).

In recent years the rate of growth in household formation has slowed (Timiraos, 2014). Primarily, this slowdown is due to young adults being unable to form separate households. Relatively high unemployment rates among young adults with relatively low incomes have resulted in an increased number of young adults living with their parents or with roommates. Also, people in this age group are marrying later than previous generations. The decrease in the number of immigrants coming into the United States due to the impact of the Great Recession and stricter enforcement of immigration policies has also contributed to the decrease in the number of households formed. In sum, the decrease in the number of new households formed has a significant impact on the number of existing housing units available and the need to develop new housing units (see also chapters 1 and 15).

Householder Age. Age is an important way to categorize the population. Current population statistics show that in the United States there is a very large age group called the baby boomers, whose members were born between 1946 and 1964. The demographic echo of the baby boomer generation is the millennial generation, born between 1981 and 1996 (Pew Research Center, 2010). The size of this cohort surpassed the baby boomer cohort in 2015, 75.3 million versus 74.6 million, due to the increased number of immigrants among the millennials and the increasing mortality rate of the baby boomers (Fry, 2015; see also chapter 17).

Household Type. The various types of families and households in the United States are recognized by official sources. The family household data in the CPS has been grouped into multiple categories: married couples without children, married couples with children, unmarried couples with children, mother only with children, and father only with children. Other family households have also been identified: grandparents with grandchildren (multigenerational families), parents with adult children, and householders with parents. Further, the U.S. Bureau of the Census has been able to classify households as same-sex and opposite-sex partners (Vespa et al., 2013).

Household Size. In 2010 the average household size in the United States was 2.58 members and the average family size was 3.14 members (Lofquist, Lugaila, O'Connel, & Feliz, 2012). This average varied among race and ethnic origin, with Hispanic-origin families being the largest (3.69 members). Non-Hispanic white families were smaller (3.08) than Asian (3.38) and black (3.28) families. The size of the family or household has a great influence on the number of bedrooms and bathrooms that may be needed in a housing unit (see chapter 1).

Stage in the Life Cycle. The concept of life cycle can be applied to the transformation (maturation, generation, and decline) of any living organism or organization (O'Rand & Krecker, 1990). Life cycle is not a demographic variable, but in the housing literature it has often been viewed in the context of the family and referred to as family life cycle. The term offers a way to group the influences of age of householders and the presence and age of children in an effort to identify patterns that help explain resource allocation. Since the middle of the twentieth century, numerous researchers have identified stages that families go through during their lifetime. The earlier models focused on nuclear families, with marriages that remained intact throughout a couple's lives. The stages usually gave minimal consideration to the period before marriage and after retirement or widowhood. These models are perhaps less reflective of today's households, which are made up of people who stay single or childless, may divorce one or more times during their lifetime, and remain in the aging family stage longer because of longevity. Table 2.1 discusses examples of stages in the family life cycle.

TABLE 2.1
Examples of Stages in the Family Life Cycle

Duvall, 1957	Carter and McGoldrick, 1989
Single: under 35, no children	Leaving home: single young adults
Couple: married, no children	Joining of families through marriage: the new couple
Childbearing family: married, birth of first child	
Preschool family: married, young children	Families with young children
School-age family: married, older children	Families with adolescents
Launching family: married, oldest child has left home	Launching children and moving on
Middle-age family: head over age forty-five, no children at home, empty nest	
Aging family: retirement to death	Families in later life

Source: Duvall, 1957; Carter & McGoldrick, 1989.

The complexity of current family and household living arrangements indicates that a simple linear-stage approach to family development is not an accurate depiction of today's society. Patterns that exist today include delayed marriages, cohabitation, divorces, remarriages, blended families, multigenerational families, same-sex marriages, and singleness.

However, the life-cycle stage approach does have some implications for consumer behavior, including housing choices. Since the stages in the family life cycle present normative expectations for family life, housing norms often parallel this cycle. For example, a young single person will probably expect to rent an apartment, but a married couple with a child will have hopes to buy a home. A move to a larger home might coincide with the arrival of more children and the space needs of older children. Some retired couples will move into smaller housing units once their children have left home (see chapter 17).

SOCIOECONOMIC CHARACTERISTICS OF HOUSEHOLDS

Another set of factors affecting psychographic attitudes, housing norms, and ultimately housing choice are socioeconomic characteristics. *Socioeconomic status* or *social class* are terms that have been used by social scientists to describe the hierarchical clustering of demographic characteristics including education, income, and occupation. People in different socioeconomic classes may have different expectations for personal and family behavior and different housing preferences and choices. Although most class systems identify only three classes (upper, middle, and lower), Michelson (1976: 112) identified five levels of social class in relation to housing:

1. **Lower class:** low income; often no steady job or one subject to the whims of the employer; little education;
2. **Working class:** regular blue-collar employment;
3. **Lower middle class:** regular white-collar employment, usually for others; moderate salary at most;
4. **Upper middle class:** high amount of education; comfortable salary or fees; sometimes self-employed but skills are transferable regardless; and
5. **Upper class:** great personal wealth either at present or within the family at some past date; at least moderate education; occupation, if any, is respectable.

These levels represent a generalization. Many variations and distinctions could be made within each level. These categories also reflect a stereotype of social structure that is suitable for the industrial age, with laborers, management, and owners composing the top four levels, as listed above. As society moves more deeply into the technology age, these class distinctions may not hold true. While some nontraditional occupations may only require modest levels of education yet lead to large incomes, other occupations may require extensive education but not lead to the highest-paying jobs. Discussions of socioeconomic characteristics allow identification of the current status of households. These characteristics within society may vary over the life cycle and over time, reflecting the changing status of occupations and education and their impact on income.

Householder Education. In the United States education is viewed as a way to increase one's income and social status. Education can prepare individuals for specialized jobs as well as provide for a well-rounded and knowledgeable public. In the highest-paying occupations, advanced and professional degrees are typically required. In 2013 the annual median household salary for someone with a doctorate was $121,284; a professional degree, $130,643; a master's degree, $95,948; a bachelor's degree, $79,522; an associate's degree, $56,185; some college but no degree, $49,683; a high school diploma (includes equivalent), $40,701; ninth–twelfth grade, no diploma, $25,672; and less than ninth grade, $24,194 (Statista, 2015). Lack of education, leading to lower-paying jobs, is a factor that can constrain groups within society from affording adequate housing (see chapters 1, 7, 9, and 10).

Household Income. The real median household income in the United States in 2012 was 8.3 percent lower than it was in December 2007, just before the Great Recession started (DeNavas-Walt, Proctor, & Smith, 2013) (see chapter 15). Income can vary greatly among household groups. The average income level of married-couple families was significantly higher than the income of single-parent families, and among these single-parent families, female-headed families had an average income significantly lower than male-headed families. Households with heads in the forty-five to fifty-four age range had the highest median income, while the lowest median income was among households with heads over age sixty-five and those between fifteen and twenty-four. Differences in income also exist among racial and ethnic groups. Asians and Pacific Islanders had the highest median income, followed by non-Hispanic whites, while blacks/African Americans had the lowest median income (see chapters 1, 16, and 17).

The association between income and housing is evident because income is a key indication of what a household is able to pay for housing. By the fourth quarter of 2014 households with incomes above the median had homeownership rates of approximately 79 percent, while those with incomes below the median had ownership rates of 49 percent (Callis & Kresin, 2015).

Householder Occupation. There are many classifications of occupation, and certain occupations tend to be associated with the social class categories identified above. For example, workers in factories or trades may be considered working class, while professors and doctors would be considered upper middle class. The U. S. Bureau of Labor Statistics has identified twenty-two standard occupational categories (SOCs). In 2012 (U.S. Bureau of Labor Statistics, 2014b) the highest annual incomes were for physicians and surgeons (including specialists within those fields), chief executives, dentists (including specialists in that field), nursing anesthetists, petroleum engineers, architectural and engineering managers, air traffic controllers, computer and information systems managers, and marketing managers. The U.S. Bureau of Labor Statistics (2014a) indicated that the lowest-paying occupations were in food preparation and service; farming, fishing, and forestry; personal care and service; building and grounds cleaning and maintenance; and healthcare support occupations. With its direct relationship to income, occupation can be a very important factor in determining the type of housing a household can afford.

Psychographic Characteristics

While demographic and socioeconomic data may characterize general housing choices and allow for exploration of relationships between characteristics, it does not always answer questions about why people choose different housing situations. Psychographic research has long been used by marketers to describe the factors that impact consumer choices relating to values, lifestyle, attitudes, opinions, and interests. Historically, housing researchers often focused on the impact of housing values and norms on the selection of a dwelling. Today, lifestyle, cultural orientation, and generational differences have all been shown to influence one's housing behavior. This section will examine these factors and explore how they affect housing norms and ultimately housing choice.

HOUSING VALUES

In the early stages of housing research, housing values were considered important concepts to explain people's preferences and choices in selecting housing and therefore determining what type of housing should be built. The major frameworks for housing values were developed by Cutler (1947) and Beyer, Mackesey, and Montgomery (1955). Cutler identified ten housing values: beauty, comfort, convenience, location, health, personal interests, privacy, safety, friendship activities, and economy. A household with a strong economy value might select a home that is inexpensive and efficient to operate, while a household with privacy values might want to select a home with private bedrooms for each family member.

Beyer et al. (1955) developed a list of nine housing values: economy, family centrism, physical health, aesthetics, leisure, equality, freedom, mental health, and social prestige. Their research suggests a hierarchy clustered around four main values: economy, family (including physical and mental health and family centrism), personal (aesthetics, leisure, and equality), and social prestige.

In the 1980s and 1990s, housing values were again explored in relation to households in the southern region. Beamish, McCray, Weber, and Brewer (1989) confirmed the value clusters that Beyer et al. (1955) identified and determined two patterns of value hierarchy: family-economy-personal-social (FEPS) and family-personal-economy-social. Ha and Weber (1992) compared the two value patterns and found that people in rural areas with low incomes and education were more likely to put the economy value above the personal value. When the top three values were used in a regional housing study, family and economy values were found to influence measures of housing affordability (Goss, 1994), and the economy value was found to influence measures of housing quality (Beamish, 1994).

LIFESTYLE

The early housing values research has been superseded by the marketing concept of lifestyle to help explain housing preferences and choice. Lifestyle, as a concept to predict behavior, was first introduced in marketing by Lazer in 1963 (Plummer, 1974). Over the years there have been many efforts to develop and refine lifestyle measurements. A popular demographic and lifestyle descriptor, PRIZM, developed in the 1970s by the Claritas Corporation, clustered the United States into forty neighborhood types that describe consumers' lifestyles and purchase behaviors (Weiss, 1988). This target-marketing system has evolved over time, and today it divides U.S. households into sixty-six demographic and behavior types.

One of the most popular lifestyle measures has been the activity, interest, and opinion (AIO) rating statements developed by Wells and Tigert (1971).

As a basis for examining lifestyle influences on preferences of multifamily housing residents, Lee, Goss, and Beamish (2007) developed fifty-nine AIO and values statements. Their research identifies four lifestyles factors: well-being, social, space, and envirotech. In a second study (Lee, Beamish, & Goss, 2008), the authors found that residents with a social lifestyle preferred to live in a downtown/urban area, while those more focused on well-being, space, the environment, and technology preferred to live in rural and suburban areas. Kwon, Lee, and Beamish (2016) examined baby boomer households between the ages of fifty and sixty-five to determine their lifestyle and housing preferences. Four boomers' lifestyles (the beautiful home, the economical, the engaged, and the family centric) and four housing preferences for later life (supportive housing, the apartment rental, the city townhouse, and the country house) were identified, and significant relationships between lifestyles and housing preferences were found.

Examining lifestyle information helps housing developers determine which type of housing features will appeal to various market segments. Consumers aware of their interests and activities can also seek a housing solution that matches their lifestyle.

CULTURAL ORIENTATION

Another way of viewing influences on housing preferences is by looking at the cultural orientation of people in society. Ray (1997) suggests that Americans live in three emerging subcultures of meaning and value. Most of U.S. society is either traditionalist (29 percent) or modernist (47 percent). Traditionalists believe in a nostalgic image of small towns and strong churches that defines the "Good Old American Way." Modernists place high value on personal success, consumerism, materialism, and technological rationality. However, a new movement called cultural creatives (24 percent) blossomed in the 1960s with the civil rights, women's rights, social justice, and ecology movements (Ray, 1997). Cultural creatives tend to be affluent, well-educated, and on the cutting edge of social change. About 60 percent are women. As housing consumers they tend to buy existing homes and remodel to suit their needs. They prefer established neighborhoods and like lots of privacy both inside (e.g., home offices away from children) and outside (e.g., hidden behind fences or lush landscaping) (Ray & Anderson, 2000). To them, a general architectural style, such as colonial or contemporary, is not important as long as it is authentic and fits into its proper place on the land (e.g., the California ranch style in California). They like eclectic interior design with original art and handmade crafts, walls of books, and nooks.

The concepts behind cultural creatives can be found in the later work of Brooks (2000), who coined the term "Bobos," or bourgeois bohemians, to describe hippies who grew up to become part of the mainstream business world. Florida (2002) takes this concept a step further, suggesting a new "creative class," which represents about 30 percent of the U.S. workforce and has become a major influence on the remainder of the population by setting consumer trends in such areas as housing. The creative class values creativity, individuality, diversity, and merit but does not flaunt its wealth.

GENERATIONAL DIFFERENCES

Certainly no lifestyle discussion would be complete without reflecting on the impact of the generations or age cohorts that strongly influence current lifestyles. An age cohort is a group of individuals who were born around the same time and experienced many of the same historic events at a similar age. Although some authors vary in what they call the generations, there seem to be more discrepancies as to the time spans for each generation than what they are called (Dent, 1998; Mitchell, 1995; Strauss & Howe, 1997; Zemke, Raines, & Filipczak, 2000). For example, social scientists usually define the baby boom generation as those born between 1946 and 1964 (Green, 2003; Smith & Clurman, 2007), although some have used birth dates that range from 1943 to 1964 (Lancaster & Stillman, 2002; Strauss & Howe, 1997; Zemke et al., 2000). For the purposes of this chapter, we define generational groups as millennials (sometimes also called Generation Y; born between 1981 and 1996), Generation X (born between 1965 and 1980), baby boomers (born between 1946 and 1964), and traditionalists, composed of the Silent Generation (born between 1928 and 1945) and the GI Generation (born before 1928). We will not discuss the youngest generation (Generation Z), those born after 1996, as their characteristics and their influences on housing are still evolving (see chapter 17).

Millennials are the most culturally diverse of all generational groups, as well as being the group most comfortable with diversity (Pew Research Center, 2010). They surpassed the size of the baby boomer generation in 2015 (R. Montgomery, 2015). Their doting parents, often described as helicopter parents, and their exposure to technology, especially the Internet, from the time they were born has had a significant impact on who they are and how they consume products (Johnson & Johnson, 2010). They are confident, computer savvy, and get along well with boomers and traditionalists (Quigley, 2016). They are much more likely to live at home with their parents than boomers or Generation Xers (Pew Research Center, 2010), not only because they seem to get along much better with them, but in many cases because starting salaries and student loan debt have made it difficult for them to form their own households (Joint Center for Housing Studies of Harvard University, 2014). When they do move out they are more likely to live in downtown lofts, or possibly apartments in mature suburbs that are connected to the city via public transportation, and they often share housing with roommates. They have shunned owning cars and instead ride bikes, share cars, or take public transportation (Badger, 2014; see also chapter 1).

Generation Xers reject the workaholic values of baby boomers and seek jobs that also allow enjoying life (Zemke et al., 2000). They prefer working on their own, rely on themselves for personal and professional development, and place their loyalties within themselves (Johnson & Johnson, 2010). This group was hit hardest by the national house price crash that preceded the Great Recession, in part because they purchased housing at peak prices in the early to mid-2000s, just before the house price bubble burst. Many in this group saw the value of their primary residences drop by over 20 percent (Bloomberg News, 2014). Some lost their jobs, had to relocate, and sold their homes at a loss.

Until the millennials surpassed them in 2015, baby boomers were the largest of the generations—almost eighty million strong. Boomers have often been described as optimistic, rule-breaking, option-driven idealists who are workaholics and who look for personal gratification in the goods and services they consume (Smith & Clurman, 2007; Zemke et al., 2000). As they are comfortable with debt and enjoy their relative affluence, they have continued to buy newer, bigger, and more elegant housing with more features and amenities (Smith & Clurman, 2007). Some baby boomers, due to their desire for self-expression, have chosen to move to New Urbanist communities and, more recently, have chosen renting apartments or buying condominiums in downtowns across the United States as they look to retirement and downsizing. Ruppies (retired urban people) like the youthful influence and mix of people who compose the downtown community (Ezell, 2006). Although some boomers will choose age-qualified communities at retirement, many will look for maintenance-free living in downtowns or in naturally occurring retirement communities (NORCs), resort areas, or college towns because they do not want to be associated with age-segregated housing that makes them feel old (Smith & Clurman, 2007).

The traditionalists are often divided into two groups—the Silent Generation, born between 1928 and 1945, and the GI Generation, born before 1928. Although these groups had different generational markers, they have similar values. They are conservative, conforming, patriotic, and believe in teamwork, hard work, authority, and sacrifice (Lancaster & Stillman, 2002; Zemke et al., 2000). The Silent Generation, labeled by *Time* magazine in 1952 because of their nonconfrontational nature (Howe, 2014; Johnson & Johnson, 2010), often find active adult communities desirable for their social lifestyle. Although many of the GI Generation remain in the homes they purchased after they returned from World War II and began raising the baby boomer generation, some started moving to retirement communities that were established in the mid-1960s, such as Sun City, Arizona, which was developed by Del Webb, the retirement community pioneer (Urban Land Institute, 2001). Today many members of this generation—often women—find that they need assistance with their housing and move to assisted living or nursing homes (see chapter 17).

Choices surrounding housing alternatives, such as apartments, townhomes, or single-family homes, will vary as the generations move through various stages in the life cycle, but each generation puts its own stamp on how that housing structure fits with its lifestyle. Marketers continue to study generations to determine what consumers want and how those wants differ by generation. For example, John Burns Real Estate Consulting recently reported on a study of twenty thousand new home shoppers and what was important to baby boomers, Generation Xers, and millennials as they looked for new homes (Carmichael, 2014). The top four desires were similar for all three groups. They all wanted a grocery store and restaurants close by and a fitness center and walking trails in the neighborhood or even in their building. Wi-Fi Internet access and a community intranet with events, clubs, and other amenities were more important to boomers than to the other two generations (see chapter 1).

Housing Norms

As individuals and families evaluate and make decisions about their housing, they are guided by norms. Housing norms, like other norms, are culturally defined standards for behavior. Each society establishes what it considers desirable behavior related to housing people. Most members of that society strive to meet or conform to this behavior.

Norms are transmitted from one generation to another through families, friends, mass media, and public interaction. Most people live their lives aspiring to certain housing norms, and the inability to achieve these norms is usually the result of constraints rather than different desires or attitudes

(Lindamood & Hanna, 1979). In their theoretical framework, Morris and Winter (1978) identify six housing norms—tenure, space, structure type, quality, neighborhood, and expenditures—for the United States. Most Americans aspire to fulfill the first three housing norms in the form of a single-family, owner-occupied home that contains a sufficient number of bedrooms or sleeping areas for all household members. There are sanctions, such as federal tax deductions for homeownership, local zoning restrictions, and occupancy standards, that encourage and reinforce these norms (see chapters 7, 10, 14, and 16). The latter three housing norms are much more dependent upon the demographic, socioeconomic, and psychographic characteristics of the household and will vary widely among U.S. households. Over the past years and decades these housing norms have evolved (see chapter 1).

TENURE TYPE

Tenure norms relate to owning or renting housing. The American Dream includes the desire to own one's own dwelling. While the portion of U.S. households who rent has increased substantially in recent years, the Board of Governors of the Federal Reserve System (2015) report that 81 percent of renters in 2014 preferred to own a home, but many could not because they could not afford the down payment or qualify for a mortgage. Historically, the U.S. government has provided tax incentives and financing programs that support and sanction homeownership (see chapters 1, 7, 8, 10, and 14).

Homeownership in the United States had reached a record high of 69 percent in 2004, but by 2015, after the end of the Great Recession and a slow economic recovery, the percentage of homeowners in the United States had dropped to 63.7 percent (Joint Center for Housing Studies of Harvard University, 2016). The decline in the homeownership rate was the result of the national foreclosure crisis that started in the first quarter of 2007 and the collapse of the mortgage market shortly thereafter, which resulted in tighter requirements for obtaining a mortgage (Parrott & Zandi, 2013; see chapters 7, 8, 10, and 15). The homeownership rate by age, race, and ethnicity has declined but is disproportionately lower among young, Hispanic/Latino, and black/African American households (Joint Center for Housing Studies of Harvard University, 2014; see chapter 16). While demographic and economic shifts have reduced the ownership rate among millennials and among those who are married and have two incomes to support a down payment, the rate is higher than in previous generations and will likely continue to increase as more of this generation find higher-paying employment and marry (Terrazas, 2014). For the general population, the homeownership rate for married couples with families (73.3 percent) far exceeds the ownership rate of single-parent families, with 37.9 percent for female-headed households and 56.5 percent for male-headed households (Vespa et al., 2013; see chapter 1).

As homeownership rates have declined over the past few years, renter rates have increased. The National Multifamily Housing Council (National Multifamily Housing Council, 2013) estimates that 35 percent of all U.S. households are renters, a reflection of the fact that not all households share or are able to attain the norm of homeownership. Many low-income households rent because they cannot afford to buy. The increase in the renter rate can be attributed to the increase in demand for rental housing due to the increase in millennials and the increase in housing affordability issues among low-income households and households that were foreclosed on. In addition to these groups, an increasing number of people with high incomes view renting as an attractive alternative to owning because of the focus on providing lifestyle amenities (Joint Center for Housing Studies of Harvard University, 1999). Renting also allows households to sign a lease for a specific period of time, often a year, thus allowing residents the ability to relocate to another city or part of town if required by their employment or household needs (Florida, 2010; see chapters 9, 10, and 14).

While 43 percent of renters occupy apartments in buildings of five or more units, 35 percent rent single-family homes, and 18 percent rent apartments in buildings with two (duplex) to four (quadraplex) units (National Multifamily Housing Council, 2013). During the Great Recession, institutional investors' interest in buying single-family housing in distressed markets helped stabilize the single-family housing market and increased the supply of single-family rentals (Joint Center for Housing Studies of Harvard University, 2014; see chapter 15).

SPACE

The amount and type of space that families desire and need are influenced by cultural space norms and are important aspects of selecting a residence. The amount of space needed is directly influenced by a household's size, composition, and stage in the life cycle and indirectly influenced by a household's lifestyle. Most households expect to have a kitchen, a bathroom, and a social space, such as a living room or great room, but they may have varied expectations about the adequate number of bedrooms. Different cultures have different norms about the gender and age of individuals who may share a sleeping room. When Americans evaluate space in a home, they consider the number of bedrooms and how they are distributed among household members. For most U.S. households, norms about sleeping spaces are fairly well defined, including a parental bedroom, single or shared bedrooms for children depending on age and gender, and individual bedrooms for other adult household members.

The types of spaces desired by homebuyers and included in new homes have changed over time. Many homebuyers are looking for larger kitchens, open multipurpose areas, additional bedrooms and bathrooms, and more space overall. Some homebuyers are willing to give up lot size to acquire more housing space, but this willingness varies with age and stage in the life cycle. By contrast, smaller homes are also being promoted as a more affordable and sustainable option. Smaller homes require fewer materials, are easier to heat and maintain, and can have a reduced carbon footprint. This may be especially true for older and smaller households.

STRUCTURE TYPE

The type of dwelling people choose to live in is influenced by norms for housing structure. The predominant physical housing structure in the United States has been the single-family detached home for most households. The desire to live in this type of structure is still very strong, despite the somewhat recent house price and foreclosure crises. In a 2013 national survey, 76 percent of respondents indicated that they preferred to live in a single-family detached home (National Association of Realtors, 2013).

Recently, alternative housing types have increased in popularity. Townhomes and other multifamily housing structures with community amenities (e.g., a pool, a community center, etc.), security, low maintenance, and ease of occupancy have been developed and appeal to retirees, young professionals, and the more mobile segments of the population. The 2012 *Statistical Abstract* (U.S. Bureau of the Census, 2012) indicates that 18.9 percent of all housing units in the United States in 2009 were multifamily housing of five or more units.

Manufactured housing, alternatively called mobile homes, is seldom included in the category of single-family detached homes, although it actually meets that definition. Manufactured housing must meet a national building code and can be built in one state and transported to another. Even though they meet a national building code, communities often restrict the placement of manufactured homes in traditional neighborhoods. As an alternative housing type, manufactured housing accounted for 6.5 percent of all housing units in 2009 (U.S. Bureau of the Census, 2012; see chapter 10).

QUALITY

Quality norms take into account acceptable structural quality, as well as amenities associated with the home. As individuals evaluate housing for quality, each may have a different idea of what is considered good or poor quality. The National Housing Act of 1949 (Government Printing Office, 1949: 1) set the goal of "a decent home in a suitable environment for every American family." In the 1940s the primary focus was on three attributes: plumbing facilities, general state of repair, and the relationship between the size of the home and the number of people living in it. The U.S. Bureau of the Census evaluated quality based upon such features as an equipped kitchen, central heating, complete indoor plumbing, and soundness of structure. In 1940, 45.2 percent of U.S. homes lacked some or all plumbing (Weicher, 1977). Since the 1950s problems related to physical qualities such as plumbing, heating/cooling, and overcrowding have decreased substantially in the United States (Baker, 2013). In 1995 only 5.1 percent of owner-occupied housing was considered moderately or severely inadequate, according to American Housing Survey data. By 2007 the proportion had dropped to 3.0 percent (2.27 million), but in 2011 the number of inadequate units had increased slightly (2.4 million). This increase reversed a trend in improved housing that had been occurring for decades, reflecting the decline in investments in existing housing by owners and the rise of foreclosed and abandoned properties during the Great Recession (Baker, 2013; see chapter 15).

Households of all income levels need to be aware of environmental issues that impact their health and the safety of their home. Some common concerns include the presence of lead paint and asbestos in older housing, radon, and problems with indoor air and water quality. Home inspections and/or testing may be performed to identify such problems (Parrott, 1997; see chapter 18).

Along with an increase in structural quality, the level of amenities desired and expected by households has also increased. Many U.S. households are now able to attain a standard for levels of interior and exterior amenities unrealized in earlier years. As one example, homes with 2.5 or more bathrooms increased from 20 percent to 55 percent of the U.S. housing stock during the years 1975 to 2002 (Joint Center for Housing Studies of Harvard University, 2002). The average number of bathrooms in new construction in 2012 was 2.56 (Emrath, 2013). Other amenities once considered extras that are now standard in new homes are dishwashers, microwave ovens, and garages.

NEIGHBORHOOD

Neighborhood norms prescribe that homebuyers not only prefer a safe and attractive area in which to live but also a neighborhood that is appropriate to a household's social and economic status. Neighborhoods can be defined by many characteristics or factors, including street design, lot sizes, landscaping, age, and nearby schools, recreation, shopping, and employment opportunities. Common neighborhood distinctions are by income, wealth, or social class, with lifestyle as a possible factor in neighborhood development and selection. For example, avid golfers may wish to live in a country club setting. Retirees may desire retirement communities that provide activities suited to their lifestyle. Downtown neighborhoods are growing in popularity, with multifamily living and public transportation supporting urban living for young professionals (see chapters 12 and 13).

EXPENDITURES

The proportion of money a household spends on housing is typically related to income, but housing norms also predict that individuals spend according to that income and lifestyle. For example, society would not look favorably upon a family neglecting the necessities of life to live in a home beyond its means, nor would it be expected to see a person with a high income living in a substandard dwelling (Morris & Winter, 1978).

Housing affordability has continued to be a problem for an increasing proportion of Americans, both in terms of the initial cost of purchasing or renting a dwelling and the long-term cost of energy, utilities, and maintenance. The rising cost of housing has increased the housing expense burden for many households, and the number of affordable housing units has continued to dwindle (see chapter 10).

CONCLUSION

The conceptual framework for influences on housing choice (Beamish et al., 2001) discussed in this chapter has divided the influences on housing choice into segments of demographic, socioeconomic, and psychographic characteristics, as well as housing norms that allow readers to explore a variety of concepts that influence the type of housing in which people choose to live. The final decision about one's housing is a mix and layering of these influences with the intent that a suitable and satisfactory housing environment will be selected and enjoyed. While housing choice is an individual decision, the housing industry is concerned about the culmination of these choices, and housing researchers study these characteristics to better understand what the housing options of the future will be.

Many of the demographic, socioeconomic, and psychographic characteristics discussed in this chapter indicate that changes are occurring within society. Some observable trends highlighted are a growing older population, more varied types of households and families, a decline in homeownership, especially among younger households, and an increased interest in living in urbanized areas (see chapters 7, 10, and 17).

Currently, many people still strive for a quality-built, single-family, owner-occupied detached home in a good neighborhood that costs less than 30 percent of their income. Over the life cycle of some households, some of these ideals may become stronger or weaker, depending on the composition and circumstances of these households (see chapter 10).

There are many housing choices available that address the norms for housing, but these options also make it possible for households to seek housing that matches their lifestyles, values, incomes, and personal interests. Community amenities might encourage physical activities, such as walking trails, swimming pools, golf courses, or marinas. Often, services such as childcare, dry cleaners, and business centers are being located in developments to support working lifestyles. The homes themselves may have features that reflect personal interests, such as office areas, media rooms, large bedrooms and bathrooms, and kitchens equipped with commercial-type cooking appliances. Builders and developers try to differentiate their homes to attract buyers and residents using the psychographic characteristics discussed in this chapter.

Basic factors such as demographic and socioeconomic characteristics shape lifestyles, values, and interests. The very nature of psychographic characteristics suggests that they are subject to change over time. Interests, life-cycle stages, incomes, and occupations will vary throughout our lives. Housing choices also will vary and change. People may start their adult lives in small apartments that give them freedom from parents and autonomy. After they marry and have children, a home in a suburban neighborhood may be the perfect place to raise children. Once their family grows, they may purchase a larger home and then, when the children have left home, they may return to a smaller home with amenities that support security, recreation, and personal interests. Psychographic characteristics explain how people refine their choices and select housing with the features that express who they are and what makes shelter home.

Families and households choose housing that meets their needs within the timeframe and society in which they live. Somewhat recent events, such as the Great Recession, as well as immigration and cultural diversity, more diverse family and household types, and an aging society, impact the demographic and psychographic characteristics of households and the nation and may impact the housing options that meet housing norms (see chapters 1, 15, 16, and 17).

REFERENCES

Badger, E. (2014, October 14). The many reasons millennials are shunning cars. *Washington Post*. Retrieved March 26, 2017, from http://www.washingtonpost.com/blogs/wonkblog/wp/2014/10/14/the-many-reasons-millennials-are-shunning-cars/.

Baker, K. (2013, February). The return of substandard housing. *Housing Perspectives*. Retrieved March 26, 2017, from http://housingperspectives.blogspot.com/2013/02/the-return-of-substandard-housing.html.

Beamish, J. (1994). A causal model of barriers and incentives to affordable housing in southern rural communities: Housing quality. *Housing and Society, 21*(1), 25–36.

Beamish, J., Goss, R. C., & Emmel, J. (2001). Lifestyle influences on housing preferences. *Housing and Society, 28*(1&2), 1–28.

Beamish, J., McCray, J., Weber, M., & Brewer, G. (1989). *Housing values of southern rural households*. (Monograph of S-194 Southern Regional Technical Committee, Serial Number 01-89). Auburn, Ala.: Auburn University.

Beyer, G. H., Mackesey, T. W., & Montgomery, J. E. (1955). *Houses are for people*. (Research Publication No. 3). Ithaca, N.Y.: Housing Research Center, Cornell University.

Kwon, H. J., Lee, H. J., & Bea... (2014a). *Economics new release: Occupational employment preferences for later life*. Retrieved March 26, 2017, from http://www.bls.gov/news 255–262.

Lancaster, L. C., & Stillman, ... (2014b). *Occupational outlook handbook: Highest paying Business*. ...March 26, 2017, from http://www.bls.gov/ooh/highest-paying

Lee, H. J., Beamish, J., & Gos... residents. *Housing and S...* (2012). *2012 statistical abstract: Construction and housing:*

Lee, H. J., Goss, R. C., & Bea...*teristics*. Retrieved March 26, 2017, from http://www.census ences of multifamily hou...ats/construction_housing/housing_units_and_characteristics

Lindamood, S., & Hanna, S. ...
St. Paul, Minn.: West. ...ider, R. M. (2013). *America's families and living arrangements:*

Lofquist, D., Lugaila, T., O'C...l Reports, P20-570). Washington, D.C.: U.S. Bureau of the (Current Census Briefs C...

Maslow, A. (1970). *Motivatio*...policy: Past, present and future. In D. Phares (Ed.), *A decent*

Michelson, W. (1976). *Man a*...*Housing urban America*. Cambridge, Mass.: Ballinger.

Mitchell, S. (1995). *The offici*...*ering of America*. New York: Harper and Row.

Montgomery, J. (1966). *Fami*...1971). Activities, interests, and opinions. *Journal of Advertis-* manuscript, Florida State

Montgomery, R. (2015), April...pczak, B. (2000). *Generations at work*. New York: (reprinted from the *Kans*

Morris, E. W., & Winter, M. ...
& Sons.

National Association of Real ...
Retrieved March 26, 2017
/2013/2013-community-p

National Multifamily Housin...
Retrieved March 26, 2017

Newmark, N. L., & Thomps...
Press.

O'Rand, A. M., & Krecker, M...
ings, and uses in the soci...

Parrott, J., & Zandi, M. (2013...

Parrott, K. (1997). Environm...
47–68.

Pew Research Center (2010, ...
Retrieved March 26, 2017
nials-confident-connecte...

Plummer, T. J. (1974). The co...
Marketing, 38(1), 33–37.

Quigley, M. W. (2016, March ...
als. *AARP*. Retrieved Ma...
/friends-family/blogs/inf...

Ray, P. H. (1997). The emergi...

Ray, P. H., & Anderson, S. R. ...
changing the world. New ...

Roske, M. D. (1983). *Housing*

Smith, J. W., & Clurman, A. ...

Statista. (2015). *Median hous...*
March 26, 2017, from http...
-income-in-the-united-s...

Strauss, W., & Howe, N. (199...

Terrazas, A. (2014). Stop sayi...
Research. Retrieved Marc...
-homeownership-2-7895...

Timiraos, N. (2014). Rate of ...
Time Economics. Retriev...
/2014/09/22/rate-of-amer...

Urban Land Institute. (2001)...
ton, D.C.: Urban Land In...

SECTION 11
HOUSING DESIGN

Chapter 3

Kitchen and Bathroom Design

KATHLEEN R. PARROTT AND
JULIA O. BEAMISH

A kitchen is more than a place to cook. It is a gathering and social space. Many household activities take place in the kitchen, including management, recreation, and entertainment. By contrast, the bathroom is a personal and private space. People will have different ideas about function, mood, and ambience in a bathroom. These people-centered, complex, and technical spaces are a particular challenge for the designer. However, kitchens and bathrooms remain two of the most important rooms that housing consumers consider when purchasing or remodeling a home (see chapter 7).

This chapter presents a brief historical review of the development of design standards for kitchens and bathrooms, followed by a discussion of current various trends and influences on kitchens and bathrooms in the United States and Canada. A short discussion on the design process follows, with specific information on designing kitchens and then bathrooms after that. Throughout the chapter, reference is made to planning guidelines, building codes, and other standards used in kitchen and bathroom design.

HISTORY OF KITCHEN AND BATHROOM DESIGN

The evolution of the American home is a history of social change, as well as a history of technology, science, and design. Kitchens and bathrooms were not present in early American homes, but the functional aspects of those spaces were evident. Food preparation in the colonial period was accomplished over an open fire in a cooking hearth, usually in the main room of the family home. As colonists became more prosperous, their homes increased in size and cooking was conducted in a second area, or "keeping room" (Plante, 1995). In the southern colonies, these rooms eventually began to be built in a separate building to remove heat and reduce fire hazards. In some homes the cooking area was placed in a lower level or basement and food was brought to dining areas in the main social space of the home. Women prepared the food, and they often worked in isolation in these spaces. More established homesteads would include small outbuildings for wells, smokehouses, food storage, and dairies (Olmert, 2009).

43

Bathrooms were not typically found in these early North American homes. Outhouses, or privies, with pit toilets were built some distance away from the home, joining the other outbuildings surrounding the main home. Within the home, chamber pots were placed in bedrooms for use at night. Grooming and dressing occurred in the bedrooms by washing hands, faces, and arms with water kept in a pitcher and a bowl placed on a piece of furniture. Bathing was not a common occurrence in most homes due to the belief that it could lead to sickness and because of the resources required to heat water and fill a tub large enough for a person to sit in (Parrott, Beamish, Emmel, & Peterson, 2013).

The Industrial Revolution

These labor-intensive and time-consuming processes and arrangements for daily living existed for most people in the United States and Canada for many years, especially in rural areas and small towns. By the middle of the 1800s, the Industrial Revolution had started to take hold in many areas, and cities were developing and expanding in various locations across the country. Increased density of housing and the change from an agrarian to a more urban society presented challenges. New technologies were invented to save time and improve the quality of life, especially for women (Beecher & Stowe, 1869).

In many cities, manufacturing facilities required new workers, and the housing available was of poor quality. New immigrants crowded into housing units in cities that did not have safe ways to remove waste. Disease and malnutrition led to outbreaks of yellow fever and cholera in urban areas that were fatal for some. Because of the more crowded and unpleasant aspects of cities, many wealthier people started moving out of cities, and suburban developments began to appear along streetcar lines (Clark, 1986; Wright, 1981). By the late 1800s, medical doctors and scientists had concluded that many diseases were due to unsanitary water and the inability to remove wastewater from the drinking supply. By the turn of the nineteenth century, sanitation systems were beginning to be installed in several larger cities. These systems provided clean water that could be used for drinking, food preparation, and cleaning, and they removed dirty water to a central location where bacteria and other harmful ingredients could be treated. This change, and the introduction of gas and electricity to the home, established the infrastructure that would encourage the development of modern kitchens and bathrooms (Beamish, Parrott, Emmel, & Peterson, 2013).

Modern Kitchen Design

The rise of industrial workers impacted the North American family and the role of women. In the eighteenth century, wealthier households frequently used domestic servants or slaves to manage the daily activities in the home. However, by the second half of the nineteenth century, slavery had ended and the need for factory workers, including women and children, gave servants other job opportunities. Many middle-class women had to manage their homes without assistance (Clark, 1986; Wright, 1981). The role of the homemaker evolved, and advice for managing the family and decorating and planning the home was prevalent in books and women's publications that promoted the ideology of domesticity (Wright, 1981).

Modern kitchens have their basis in ideas of work simplification and human factors that were promoted to enhance efficiency in manufacturing and the workplace. In 1869 Catherine Beecher and her sister Harriet Beecher Stowe, the famed writer and abolitionist, wrote a book for women, *American Woman's Home*, to provide advice on how to manage their homes. One chapter was devoted to the layout of the kitchen and included the concept of work centers for various tasks that incorporated storage and work surfaces. The sisters suggested bringing water into the kitchen and recommended painted walls that would be easier to clean. They also designed a more efficient cookstove (Beecher & Stowe, 1869).

By 1913 Christine Frederick had written several articles in the *Ladies Home Journal* on home management and had them published in a book titled *The New Housekeeping: Efficiency Studies in Home Management* (Frederick, 1913). She had undertaken work efficiency studies at her Applecroft Home Experiment Station in Greenlawn, New York, that led to the standardization of counter heights. Frederick was a proponent of the methodology of scientific management developed by Frederick Taylor to study the time-use and work patterns of food preparation in the kitchen (Wright, 1981).

In 1926 Austrian architect Margarete Schütte-Lihotzky designed a kitchen for worker housing in Germany, now known as the Frankfurt Kitchen and as the first "fitted" kitchen (figure 3.1). It used many of the principles Frederick had proposed to make a small, efficient work space. The Frankfurt Kitchen also included built-in cabinets and appliances that fit together to make continuous work surfaces and convenient and accessible storage (Museum of Modern Art, 2010).

The desire to make housework easier for women led to several other effi-

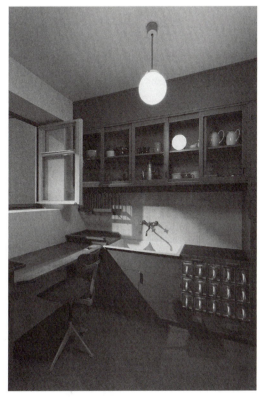

FIGURE 3.1
Frankfurt Kitchen, 1926–27
Source: Kinchin & O'Connor, n.d. Reprinted with permission.

ciency studies. These studies were typically conducted by home economists in the 1930s and 1940s at state and national agricultural experiment stations, and they aided in the development of recommendations for work aisles, wall cabinet heights, and the amount and placement of storage (Heiner & McCullough, 1948; Wilson, 1938). The Small Homes Council at the University of Illinois at Urbana-Champaign developed a series of publications that outlined recommendations for functional kitchen storage (Kapple, 1964; McCullough, 1949; Wanslow, 1965). At the same time, manufacturers of appliances, cabinets, and other household items developed products that would fit in standardized kitchens and promoted model kitchens and plans that could help interpret the ideas of an efficient kitchen (Beamish et al., 2013).

By the 1950s, many of these standardized space recommendations had been incorporated into the minimum property standards (MPS) used by the Federal Housing Administration (FHA) to guide the design of housing financed by this agency. This step had wide implications for the standardization of the modern American kitchen throughout the rest of the twentieth century, since many homes were built and financed using the FHA program (Beamish et al., 2013; see chapters 7, 8, and 10).

In the 1960s the National Kitchen and Bath Association (NKBA) began as a professional industry organization to promote the interests of the manufacturers, distributors, and designers associated with the kitchen and bathroom design industry. NKBA joined with the Small Homes Council in 1975 (Jones & Kapple, 1975) to issue *Kitchen Industry Technical Manuals* and identified twenty-one guidelines that designers should know and follow in order to become a Certified Kitchen Designer®. These guidelines have been reviewed and revised several times since their original publication by the NKBA to reflect changes in building codes and industry standards. The recommendations for designing kitchens made later in this chapter are based on current NKBA guidelines.

Modern Bathroom Design

The North American bathroom typically has three fixtures: toilet, bathtub, and lavatory (the common industry term for a bathroom sink), but it has not always been that way. The modern bathroom depended on the establishment of water and sewer systems that brought clean water to the home and removed wastewater. It took decades for clean water systems to reach cities and towns, so the bathroom evolved as the basic water and sewer infrastructure was developed and installed.

In some homes, cisterns that gathered rainwater and stored it in tanks in the attic provided water supplies that could support some bathroom activities on the second floor of Victorian homes before city water under pressure was available. The flush toilet was the first fixture to be plumbed, relying on gravity to feed the water from the cistern and remove it from the fixture. A bathtub also used the cistern system of running water and was included in the private bathroom. The lavatory was probably the last fixture to be added, and it was designed as a bowl on a pedestal (Parrott et al., 2013).

Once sanitation systems became available to homes, water was plumbed into the house and wastewater was removed through pipes. The three fixtures requiring running water were often placed close together in one room. Water pressure and mechanized ways to heat water also encouraged the development of the shower, which needed warm water to be dispensed through an overhead spray. The first home showers were considered therapeutic because of the strong spray of water and were not considered appropriate for women (Parrott et al., 2013).

The development of bathrooms in hotels spurred the idea that bathrooms should be part of the bedroom (Giedion, 1969). However, incorporating a bathroom into an older house often meant that the bathroom was placed in an awkward location. The bathroom could be added to the back of the house and tied into the kitchen plumbing, which was efficient, or it could go into an upstairs bedroom that was converted for this use. Bathroom expenses were high for the average family, so often only one bathroom was provided (Parrott et al., 2013).

By the 1920s, plumbing manufacturers had developed the three fixtures out of enameled ware, porcelain, or cast iron, and bathrooms became more affordable. They began to be incorporated into new homes, and a mechanical core that distributed the plumbing and sewer throughout the house was commonly incorporated into the construction. The space to hold the bathroom fixtures became smaller, eventually resulting in the standard 5-by-7-ft. bathroom that lines all the fixtures beside each other on one wall for efficient plumbing distribution. By the 1950s, plumbing codes had been developed that encouraged the further expansion of the standardized bathroom.

Research conducted by Kira (1966) at the Center for Housing and Environmental Studies at Cornell University during the 1950s and 1960s examined the human factors that applied to personal hygiene and began to promote the ergonomic design of bathroom fixtures. Further research from the Small Homes Council provided guidance on the space requirements needed to use the various fixtures in the bathroom. Many of these recommendations have been incorporated into the minimum requirements of the International Residential Code. The NKBA developed its first guidelines for bathrooms in 1992, and these have been used in the examinations required for their Certified Bathroom Designer® program (Parrott et al., 2013).

TRENDS AND INFLUENCES IN TODAY'S KITCHENS AND BATHROOMS

A thorough understanding of the client—or users of the space—is critical to a successful kitchen or bathroom design, but there are other considerations as well. The designer must also understand the milieu or environment in which the client lives and in which the home is located. There are important trends that influence the design process in kitchens and bathrooms, and these must be considered as part of a successful design. We will review five design influences: population characteristics, universal design, sustainability, technology, and material choices.

Population Characteristics

Both the United States and Canada collect data on the population to track key trends of particular interest to kitchen and bathroom designers, including household composition, types of food prepared and served, entertainment and social activities, and standards of privacy and modesty (see chapter 2). First, the United States and Canada are increasingly racially, ethnically, and culturally diverse, and there is diversity in terms of the types of households.

For example, it is estimated that by 2025, 36 percent of U.S. households will be minority households (Joint Center for Housing Studies of Harvard University, 2014; see chapter 16). Second, the proportion of older adults in the population continues to increase in both the United States and Canada. In the United States, the number of households aged over sixty-five years is expected to increase by 10.7 million households by 2025, while households aged over seventy years will account for two-thirds of the household growth in the same time period (Joint Center for Housing Studies of Harvard University, 2014). In Canada, people aged sixty-five years and older are expected to increase 24 to 28 percent as a proportion of the population between 2013 and 2063 (Statistics Canada, 2014). Third, a growing percentage of the population lives in multigenerational households (Lofquist, 2012; see chapter 17).

Universal Design

Universal design is generally defined as the design of products and spaces to provide access and be usable for as many people as possible, regardless of their size, age, and abilities (Beamish et al., 2013). The ability of people to perform tasks varies greatly depending on their cognitive and physical functioning, including sensory acuity, handedness, and mobility. Anthropometry is the study of human measurements. Anthropometric data are typically presented for population groups, such as by age, gender, race, or ethnicity. Structural, or static, anthropometric data pertain to a stationary body. Examples of structural anthropometric data are eye height, shoulder width, and hip breadth. Functional anthropometric data pertain to a body in motion. Examples of functional anthropometric data include sitting vertical reach height and forward grip reach. If a person uses a mobility aid, such as a cane or a walker, this information is generally included in his or her anthropometric information (Panero & Zelnik, 1979).

In the development of a universally designed kitchen or bathroom, anthropometric information is used to make the space accessible to and usable by the majority of people. Consideration is given to various factors, including how people fit the space, what they need to reach, and what is visible.

The Center for Universal Design at North Carolina State University developed the well-known seven principles of universal design (Story, Mueller,

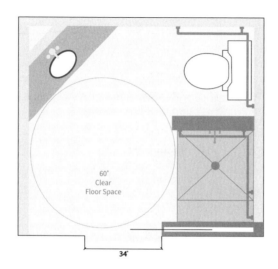

FIGURE 3.2
Accessible Bathroom Design
This accessible design provides access to bathroom fixtures, turning space for mobility aids, and grab bars for support.
Source: Caitlin Creative Works, LLC.

& Mace, 1998). Briefly, they are equitable use, flexibility in use, simple and intuitive use, perceptible information, tolerance for error, low physical effort, and size and space for approach and use (see chapter 18).

Applications of these principles in kitchen and bath design can lead to good design for everyone. For example, good-quality lighting on kitchen counters and at the bathroom mirror are helpful to everyone but may be especially useful and enhance safety when cutting vegetables or reading small type on medicine bottles (perceptible information and tolerance for error). Using rocker switches or motion-sensor controls for that lighting is useful for everyone (equitable use). Having work counters at multiple heights can accommodate tall and short users and could be designed to promote sitting to work if needed (flexibility in use). Lever-handled faucets are easy to understand and require little effort to control (simple and intuitive use and low physical effort). Placing stored items on shelves and cabinets that are within the universal reach range of most users is assuring, and providing clear floor space to stand at the storage provides people with access to the things they regularly use (size and space for approach and use) (figure 3.2; see chapter 6).

Sustainability

A well-designed kitchen or bathroom is environmentally friendly and healthy for the user and reflects sustainable use of resources. To design a sustainable space is to consider the idea of balance and minimize the impact on the future. Sustainability is a philosophical approach that guides design practices (Davis & Fisher, 2015).

In today's kitchen and bathroom industry, the concept of sustainability is represented by the term *green building*. Green building or sustainable practices include

- promoting healthy places to live;
- enhancing and protecting natural ecosystems and biodiversity;
- improving air and water quality;
- reducing solid waste; and
- conserving natural resources (Parrott et al., 2013).

These are lofty ideals; however, there are very practical and useful ways to implement these ideals that also result in good design in kitchens and bathrooms. In recent publications targeted to both professional and student designers, the National Kitchen and Bath Association recommends the following green and sustainable practices (Beamish et al., 2013; Davis & Fisher, 2015; Parrott et al., 2013):

- **Design small spaces.** Smaller, more compact spaces use fewer materials in construction and require less energy to heat, cool, and light.
- **Specify environmentally healthy building and interior finish materials.** This includes
    - selection of nontoxic, sustainably harvested, recycled, salvaged, repurposed, or renewable resource materials;
    - avoidance of materials manufactured with volatile organic compounds (VOCs); and
    - use of materials that are certified environmentally safe through independent, third-party testing programs.

- **Specify materials and products from local sources.** Selecting locally sourced materials potentially minimizes the energy use and pollution of transportation.
- **Specify products and appliances that are energy efficient and specify plumbing fixtures and appliances that conserve and use water efficiently.** In particular, use items that are identified as energy or water efficient through independent, third-party testing or certifications, such as EnerGuide, Energy Star®, or WaterSense®.
- **Design the kitchen with a convenient, easy-to-use recycling center.** This practice includes designing a system that facilitates household recycling and considers local community waste management and recycling practices. Flexibility is important, as community practices often change over time.
- **Maximize the use of daylight.** This reduces the need for artificial light sources.
- **Use energy-efficient light sources.** Lighting efficiency is measured in lumens per watt. Other factors will affect efficiency, including placement of light fixtures, fixture choice, and the surface to be lit. Designing lighting is complex, and planning is essential to provide both effective and efficient lighting.
- **Design kitchens or bathrooms with adequate exhaust ventilation.** Proper ventilation will remove excess moisture and control for potential problems with condensation and mold. A kitchen also needs ventilation to control grease and combustion by-products if there are gas cooking appliances. Kitchens must have an adequate source of replacement or make-up air to balance exhaust ventilation. A heat recovery ventilation system or energy recovery ventilation system is recommended for continuous whole-house ventilation with energy conservation. Local building codes specify ventilation requirements for kitchens or bathrooms.
- **Plan for energy efficiency and durability in construction.** For a kitchen or bathroom space, this includes properly insulated exterior walls with appropriately placed vapor retarders. Windows should be certified as energy efficient and appropriate to the climate zone by independent testing, such as the National Fenestration Rating Council or Energy Star®. The model 2012 *International Energy Conservation Code* can provide further information on energy-efficient construction and is incorporated into many local building codes.
    - If the kitchen or bathroom design project is part of a whole-house project, it may be appropriate to seek certification from a national, regional, or local green building program. These programs typically set detailed criteria for sustainable products, materials, and practices throughout the design and construction process. Examples of national green building programs include the ICC 700 National Green Building Standards™, LEED (Leadership for Energy and Environmental Design) for Homes, and R-2000, while EarthCraft House and Earth Advantage Institute are regional programs.

- **Plan the layout of the kitchen or bathroom to maximize the use of standard-size building materials and products.** This minimizes construction waste.
- **Recycle construction and demolition waste.** Serviceable cabinets, appliances, and fixtures removed in remodeling may be donated (see chapter 19).

Technology

The key words in evaluating the influence of technology are *choice* and *change*. Growth and development of technological options for kitchens and bathrooms give designers and their clients many options to meet their needs and wants. At the same time, technology is changing at a rapid pace, so the design of these important spaces must be flexible to adapt and accept new technology.

Laptop computers, cell phones, electronic games, and a variety of portable electronic devices are common in homes today. Multiple pieces of equipment, with multiple users, travel around the home. The kitchen is a common place to use these devices. Landing spaces for electronic devices, charging and docking stations, electrical connections, and accessories or peripherals need consideration. The interfaces between users and computers need to be designed from an *ergonomic* perspective, applying anthropometric knowledge (see chapter 2).

There are myriad choices of appliances for today's kitchens that offer a wide variety of cooking methods, often within the same appliance. Operating systems provide a variety of options to control and monitor the appliance but may or may not be easy to learn to use. Sizes and installation requirements will vary by manufacturer and model. Most consumers choose appliances that offer the benefit of current technology but are appropriate to their needs and abilities.

Despite today's emphasis on water conservation, many people want a luxury, spa-like experience in the bathroom. New developments in plumbing fittings and fixtures, such as low-flow showerheads and high-efficiency toilets, can conserve water but provide good performance. Third-party, independent testing programs, such as WaterSense®, certify fixtures and fittings and identify high-performance products. In addition, improved finishes on bathroom fixtures and fittings can be low maintenance and durable (see chapter 19).

Entertainment in the bathroom is also a result of technological development and is a relatively new phenomenon. Televisions and sound systems embedded in mirrors, whirlpool tubs, and toilets are available. Miniaturization and sealing of electronic components have helped make this possible in the warm, moist environment of the bathroom.

Much of the technological growth in kitchens and bathrooms depends on electricity. Even if a piece of equipment and or a product works on a battery, it typically has a base unit for recharging. Therefore, from a design and planning perspective, consideration must be given to the electrical system in the home. Where are the electrical receptacles? How many are there? What is the electrical capacity of the individual receptacles and the total system? If the design project is a remodel, does the electrical system need an upgrade to meet current and future needs, as well as the current code?

Materials

Selecting and specifying materials for kitchens and bathrooms is a complex process. There are a wide variety of choices, with many factors influencing the choices and many different material decisions to make. For example, a kitchen designer and client might consider ten different countertop materials in fifty different color and pattern combinations before making a selection. Then the same process needs to occur with other materials, including flooring, wall coverings, and cabinet finishes (see chapters 2 and 7).

However, there are general and useful criteria to consider in evaluating materials for kitchens and bathrooms related to the design and use of these spaces (Beamish et al., 2013; Parrott et al., 2013; Parrott, Beamish, Emmel, & Lee, 2008).

- **Function:** Function is related to the intended purpose or use of the material. For example, in a kitchen that is used frequently, is the flooring material comfortable for standing (resilient)? In a bathroom, will the wall coverings dry quickly in the moist atmosphere?
- **Maintenance:** Maintenance is partly related to frequency and type of use. Some materials are "high maintenance" but might be acceptable to a user if he or she is willing to perform the maintenance in exchange for the material of choice. For example, some types of stone and tile require regular sealing, and glass needs to be wiped down to remove water spots. Low maintenance may be a priority for some users, who select materials accordingly.
- **Durability:** Durability is related to the frequency of use, the type of use, and the maintenance provided by the user. High-quality materials may be more durable, but not always. As an example, stainless steel, currently a popular material in kitchens, is a durable material but takes regular maintenance and care to keep it free from scratches and discolorations. Over time, stainless steel may still be functional but will no longer appear pristine.
- **Safety:** People interested in safety might look for floor materials that are less likely to be slippery when wet. Countertop materials that reflect maximum light without glare are safe, functional, and efficient. Material installations with rounded edges are less likely to cause injury.

    Today there is interest in biological safety, and many materials are available with antimicrobial finishes. These finishes are incorporated to provide safety to the product itself. However, if dirt, skin cells, food waste, and other debris were to accumulate on the material due to poor maintenance, the antimicrobial finish may not protect the material from mold or bacterial growth.
- **Fashion and style:** Most people who are remodeling, building, or buying a home look at fashion trends in kitchens and bathrooms and want spaces that reflect contemporary trends and personal style. Material choices are important in achieving style and fashion. However, kitchens and bathrooms are very expensive and complex spaces in the home, and it can be disruptive to change these frequently used rooms. Designers often recommend the selection of simple, classic, or basic choices for colors, styles, or patterns of materials that "anchor" the space or are used in large quantity. Then, other materials, which

can be more easily changed in the future, can be used to offer fashion, style, accents, color contrast, and visual interest to the design.

In a kitchen, cabinetry and countertops typically account for half or more of the cost of the space and are major design elements. However, the walls, backsplash, floors, furnishings, and other accessories can be used to enhance and complement the cabinetry and countertops.

In the typically smaller space of a bathroom, wall coverings, flooring, lighting fixtures, and perhaps plumbing fittings, such as the lavatory faucet, are possibilities for fashion statements. Choice of color, material, and style offer many options for design. The bathroom is a private and personal space, which can influence the design choices.

THE DESIGN PROCESS

The *design process* is a multistage process that begins with an idea and moves to a completed product. As part of the design process, the kitchen or bathroom designer will gather information about the client for whom the space is being designed and the space to be designed. A *design program* is prepared to document and guide the design process and project development from start to finish.

The *needs assessment* is critical, as it is the basis for understanding how the kitchen or bathroom will be designed and constructed and for knowing what is possible. The needs assessment is used to gather detailed information about who will use the kitchen or bathroom space (client), how they will use the space (activities), what will be in the space (storage needs, appliances, furnishings, and equipment), and how the existing or to-be-constructed home influences the design of the space (size, style, materials, and covenants). Additionally, the needs assessment gathers other information that might influence the construction and project completion (job site). The designer might complete a needs assessment through a client interview. Also, checklists used by the client can help organize the process and ensure more detailed and complete information (Beamish et al., 2013; Parrott et al., 2013; see chapter 2).

KITCHEN PLANNING

Location and Types of Kitchens

Kitchens can be located in various parts of the home, depending on the design of the home or the lifestyle needs of the family or household. In past designs, kitchens would usually be placed at the back of the home and would be close to the backyard. This location was suited to families in which the woman was the primary cook and spent a great deal of time in the kitchen, as it allowed for a closed work area and supervision of children playing in the backyard.

Today the kitchen is more likely to be considered a central hub of the home, with a variety of users and with activities occurring in the kitchen and in nearby interior and exterior social areas. Wherever it is placed, it is important to consider which rooms or spaces are adjacent to the kitchen and how the household will be using all of these spaces. Locating the kitchen

FIGURE 3.3
Open Arrangements of Kitchens
The island and L-shaped kitchen arrangements are examples of designs that are open to other adjoining spaces so that people can circulate between spaces and socialize.
Source: Caitlin Creative Works, LLC.

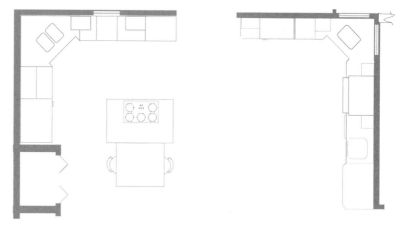

Island kitchen   L-shaped kitchen

near a service entry close to the garage or parking area, where groceries and other household items can be brought into the home, aids convenience. Locating kitchens close to dining areas, either within the kitchen area or in a separate room with circulation to the kitchen, is also recommended. Additionally, informal indoor and outdoor living areas can be supported by having a kitchen close by (see chapter 2).

Kitchens come in a variety of configurations, and these can be grouped into open arrangements that encourage interaction with nearby social spaces or closed arrangements that support a more enclosed work space (Beamish et al., 2013).

OPEN ARRANGEMENTS

- **L-shaped kitchen:** Appliances, sink(s), and cabinets with counters are arranged along two adjoining walls (figure 3.3).
- **One-wall kitchen:** Appliances, sink, and cabinets with counters are arranged on one wall in a room.
- **Corridor kitchen:** Appliances, sink(s), and cabinets with counters are arranged on two opposing walls with circulation openings at each end of the created corridor.
- **Island kitchen:** A work area with appliances, sink, and/or cabinets with counters is placed in a separate island. Seating for dining or snacking may be placed on the outside portion of the island (figure 3.3).

CLOSED ARRANGEMENTS:

- **U-shaped kitchen:** Appliances, sink(s), and cabinets with counters are placed along three adjoining walls with the circulation space at the end of the counters, outside the work area (figure 3.4).
- **Parallel or galley kitchen:** Appliances, sink(s), and cabinets with counters are placed on two opposing walls with one end closed off with a wall.
- **G-shaped kitchen:** Appliances, sink(s), and cabinets with counters are arranged along four sides with access to the kitchen work area through a break in the arrangement (figure 3.4).

FIGURE 3.4
Closed Arrangements of Kitchens

The U-shaped and G-shaped kitchens are examples of closed designs where the kitchen is more visually and spatially separate from other living areas of the home.

Source: Caitlin Creative Works, LLC.

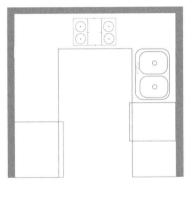

U-shaped kitchen

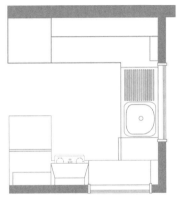

G-shaped kitchen

An *unfitted kitchen* may also be used in some arrangements. This type of kitchen has appliances, sink(s), and cabinets with counters and/or furniture pieces arranged as individual units on two, three, or four walls, with circulation at various corners in the room. Often this type of kitchen has a central work island or dining area that supports the work flow.

DESIGNING A KITCHEN BY CENTERS

A center in kitchen and bath design is an area where a particular task or function occurs, considering the user, space, fixtures, and other components. The center concept is a helpful approach to designing a kitchen because it arranges the appliances, sink, storage, and work areas by the tasks that are to be accomplished in the kitchen. It allows the designer to consider activities and the needed tools and space to accomplish those activities efficiently. In the kitchen there are three major centers: sink and preparation center, refrigerator center, and cooking center. Occasionally other centers are included, depending on the range of tasks performed in the kitchen by various households. In the kitchen, centers are composed of storage, work surface, one or more appliances or sinks, and floor space (Beamish et al., 2013).

- Storage is usually accommodated in base, wall, and pantry cabinets, although shelves, pot racks, and furniture pieces could provide this function.
    - Standardized base cabinets are 24 inches deep and 34½ inches tall with a 1½-inch-high countertop, making the work surface 36 inches high.
    - Wall cabinets are typically 12–15 inches deep and vary in height from thirty to forty-two inches. They are mounted on the wall or hung from the ceiling or a soffit, a framed construction element between the ceiling and the top of the wall cabinet. Wall cabinets are fifteen to eighteen inches above the base cabinets with countertop.
    - Pantry cabinets are tall cabinets that come in a variety of depths ranging from twelve to twenty-four inches.
    - Standard or stock cabinets in the United States are specified in three-inch increments. For instance, a base cabinet could be nine, twelve, fifteen, eighteen, twenty-one, twenty-four, twenty-

seven, thirty, thirty-three, thirty-six, thirty-nine, forty-two, forty-five, or forty-eight inches wide. In countries using the metric system, the cabinets are specified in millimeters or centimeters.[1]

- Countertops in the kitchen are considered the work surfaces. One type of work surface is the landing area, which is the counter area beside or across from an appliance or fixture in a center. The landing area provides a minimum amount of surface area that can be used for dishes, pots, pans, and other tools used in food preparation.
- Floor spaces in front of the appliances, sink, and work surfaces are called work aisles. In the kitchen, work aisles should be a minimum of thirty-six inches for one cook and forty-two inches when two or more people will be working in the kitchen (NKBA, 2012).

SINK AND PREPARATION CENTER

The sink is a central element in a kitchen design. Many activities occur at this center, including food preparation and cleanup during and after meal preparation and dining. Sinks are made of a variety of materials and of different sizes and configurations. To work efficiently in the kitchen, it is ideal to place the sink in between other centers.

When planning the sink center, eighteen inches of landing area is recommended on one side of the sink and twenty-four inches on the other (NKBA, 2012). The twenty-four-inch space will also accommodate a standard-sized dishwasher, which is typically a needed appliance for the cleanup activities that occur at the sink. Ideally, trash receptacles should be planned near the sink and food-preparation areas for cleanup.

A preparation area is needed for combining and mixing ingredients that will be cooked or served during the meal. It is recommended that this area be adjacent or close to the sink since a water source is typically needed in many food-preparation activities. The primary requirement is a work surface thirty-six inches wide and twenty-four inches deep (NKBA, 2012). Access to stored food and cooking equipment is also needed. Thus the preparation area is often planned between the sink and the cooking appliance or between the sink and the refrigerator. Specialized preparation areas may be devised for baking or to provide a seated preparation area. These areas will usually require a lower work height, such as thirty or thirty-two inches. No cabinets should be placed under a seated counter area (NKBA, 2012).

REFRIGERATION CENTER

The refrigerator is a cold-food storage appliance. During food preparation, the cook will go to the refrigerator to gather the needed food. It may also be used by others in the household to retrieve cold beverages and snacks. The refrigerator is often placed at one end of the kitchen arrangement because it is tall and an obstacle to efficient work flow during food preparation. A fifteen-inch landing area is recommended beside or across from the refrigerator (NKBA, 2012). Under-counter refrigerators, both cabinet and drawer

---

1. In the Canadian kitchen and bath industry, standard measurements are given in millimeters. Therefore, for example, a basic base cabinet would be 610 mm (24 inches) deep and 914 mm (36 inches) high with a countertop. In Beamish et al. (2013) and Parrott et al. (2013), all dimensions referenced are given in both imperial (inches) and metric (millimeters) measures.

models, are available and can be placed within the work areas of the kitchen or in a separate area, such as a bar or beverage center.

COOKING CENTER

Several different types of cooking appliances can be found in today's kitchens, and each has specialized requirements within the cooking center. Occasionally, these appliances are separated and moved to a secondary cooking center (Beamish et al., 2013).

- Surface cooking is accomplished by range or cooktop appliances. Food is prepared by such methods as frying and boiling, and the cook interacts frequently with the appliance. Landing areas are recommended on both sides on the cooking surface—fifteen inches on one side and twelve inches on the other. If the cooking surface is in an island or peninsula, then nine inches of counter space behind the cooking surface is recommended (NKBA, 2012).

    Ventilation is required for surface cooking, and several different types of fans and ventilation systems are available. If a range hood is used above the cooking surface, it should extend three inches beyond the cooking surface on each side and be placed at least twenty-four inches above the cooking surface (NKBA, 2012). Proximity ventilation is placed within the cooking appliance or adjacent to (usually behind) the cooking surface in the counter. Deeper counters are often planned to accommodate this extra appliance.

- Oven cooking is a more passive cooking activity, since prepared food is usually placed in the oven for a time determined by the recipe. Although frequently found in the range appliance, separate ovens can also be found in a location away from the main cooking center. A fifteen-inch landing area beside the appliance or on a counter across from the appliance is recommended (NKBA, 2012).

- Microwave cooking is available in almost all homes today. It can be used for a variety of activities. The microwave oven can be placed in several locations, depending on how it is used. It may be placed within the cooking center, close to the cooking surface or oven, if it is being actively used in cooking foods, or it may be placed next to the refrigerator if it is primarily used to reheat or defrost food coming out of the refrigerator. It could also be placed below the counter in a snack center, especially if children will be using the appliance. Recommendations for the height of the bottom of the microwave are three inches below the shoulder height of the primary user, or a maximum of fifty-four inches. A fifteen-inch landing area below, beside, or on a counter across from the microwave is recommended (NKBA, 2012).

Putting the Kitchen Centers Together

To enhance the workflow of the kitchen, the centers are usually arranged in a configuration that results in a work triangle. In this arrangement, the sink is in the middle and the range or cooktop is on one side with the refrigerator on the other. Appropriate landing areas and preparation areas are placed within this triangular arrangement, which also provides adequate storage. The recommendation for the size of the work triangle is no more than twenty-

TABLE 3.1
Recommendations for Shelf and Drawer Frontage in Small, Medium, and Large Kitchens (in inches)

	Small	Medium	Large
Wall	300	360	360
Base	520	615	660
Drawer	360	400	525
Pantry	180	230	310
Misc.	40	95	145
TOTAL	1,400	1,700	2,000

Source: Beamish et al., 2013. Reprinted with permission.

six feet. Each leg of the triangle should be no less than four feet and no more than nine feet. Ideally, there should not be a circulation path that interrupts the work triangle, and the work surfaces should not be interrupted by a tall cabinet or appliance.

Research conducted by Parrott, Beamish, and Emmel (2003) was the basis of recommendations for the overall amount of counter area and storage needed in kitchens. The recommendations were based on the analysis of items stored in recently designed small, medium, and large kitchens. A small kitchen is less than 150 square feet, a medium kitchen is 151–350 square feet, and a large kitchen is 351 square feet or more. The recommendations are for shelf/drawer frontage of cabinetry or other storage pieces (see table 3.1).

BATHROOM PLANNING

Types and Locations of Bathrooms

Different types of bathrooms are found in today's housing. The most common are described below (Parrott et al., 2013).

- **Half bathroom/powder room:** This bathroom includes only a lavatory and toilet and is usually located near social or family activity areas in the home.
- **Full bathroom:** This bathroom includes a lavatory, toilet, and tub and/or shower and is typically located near the private areas of the home.
- **Compartmentalized bathroom:** This is a full bathroom with one or more fixtures in its own compartment, allowing multiple users. It may be located near social or private areas to facilitate sharing.
- **Bathroom suite:** This bathroom, usually adjacent to a bedroom, may include multiple lavatories, toilets, showers or tubs, and other fixtures and features such as a bidet, vanity, or dressing area.
- **Bathroom spa:** This bathroom includes fixtures similar to a bathroom suite as well as one or more spa fixtures, such as a whirlpool or jetted tub, soaking tub, sauna, or steam shower.

Designing a Bathroom by Centers

Similar to the design of kitchens, an effective approach to the design of bathrooms is the center concept. A basic bathroom has three centers: grooming, bathing/showering, and toileting.

FIGURE 3.5
Bathroom Space Clearances
Recommended clearances shown in this drawing will give a person adequate space to safely and comfortably move around in the bathroom to complete normal activities.
Source: Caitlin Creative Works, LLC.

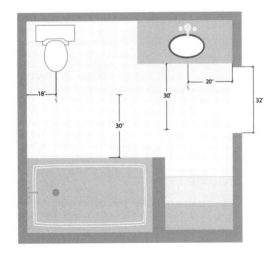

GROOMING CENTER

Multiple activities may take place in the grooming center, including washing hands and face, brushing teeth, applying facial care and makeup, shaving, brushing and styling hair, taking medicines, and providing first aid. The grooming center requires a lavatory, water source, and one or more mirrors at eye level for all users. Adequate storage is needed in the cabinetry and on countertops for frequently used items. Childproof storage may be needed for items such as medicines. Lighting should be placed to come from the side to minimize shadows and should be of a color that flatters skin tones, such as warm white.

Space requirements in the grooming center must consider the size and number of people using the center and whether seated use is required. Minimum clearances are based on the model 2012 *International Residential Code* (International Code Council, 2011). However, more generous clearances are typically recommended by the NKBA bathroom planning guidelines (NKBA, 2012; Parrott et al., 2013). Additionally, a bathroom designed for accessibility will need additional space for accommodating mobility aids, as reported in the NKBA planning guidelines with access standards (NKBA 2012; Parrott et al., 2013) (see figure 3.2).

Several important dimensions need to be considered in planning the grooming center. There should be twenty-one to thirty inches in front of the lavatory. There should be fifteen to twenty inches on center from the lavatory to a vertical obstruction such as a wall (figure 3.5). The height of the lavatory should ideally be about three inches below the users' elbow, but the actual height will vary with the user and with standing or seated use (NKBA, 2012).

BATHING/SHOWERING CENTER

The bathing/showering center is for cleansing the body and may include a bathtub, shower, or tub/shower combination. Body cleansing can be a utilitarian experience or it can be relaxing and sensual. A variety of cleansing products such as soaps, shampoo, conditioner, and bath oils, as well as accessories such as loofahs, sponges, razors, and sprayers, will need to be accommodated. Storage for towels is recommended, and hanging space for damp towels is necessary.

Ventilation is important for moisture control in the bathing/showering center. A ventilation fan that exhausts 50 cfm (cubic feet per minute) is recommended (NKBA, 2012). A humidistat control may be desirable. Variable levels of light will allow mood changes for more relaxing bathing or showering. However, electrical switches and fixtures must not be directly accessible from the bathtub or shower.

Safety is very important in the bathing/showering center, and appropriately placed grab bars are necessary to prevent falls. Water temperature controls should prevent scalding. All flooring should be nonslip and steps, especially for entering a tub, should be avoided. Tempered glass is required for any glazing.

Adequate space is needed in front of a bathtub: twenty-one to thirty inches for a user to sit on the edge of the tub, swing his or her legs over one at a time, and then safely ease into the tub (figure 3.5). The height of the tub should not exceed eighteen inches. The faucet controls for the tub should be placed so they are usable before entering the tub (NKBA, 2012).

The minimum size for a shower is thirty by thirty inches, with thirty-six by thirty-six inches preferred. As with the bathtub, twenty-one to thirty inches is needed in front of the shower, and the controls should be accessible before entering the shower spray (NKBA, 2012). A seat in the shower is a desirable feature. In households where showering is the preference, a walk-in shower is a recommended choice over a tub/shower combination. The walk-in shower can be safer, as there is no stepping over the side of the tub, and there are a variety of design possibilities (Parrott et al., 2013).

TOILETING CENTER

Toileting activities may be culturally influenced and can determine the choice of fixtures. In North America, women traditionally sit on the toilet while men stand to urinate and sit to defecate. While the height of a toilet for sitting is not ideal for men to stand to urinate, residential urinals are not common. Women also use the toilet for feminine hygiene during the menstrual cycle. Bidets, whether a separate fixture or combined with the toilet, are used for perineal cleansing after toileting activities and are becoming somewhat more available in North American homes.

Toilets are a major water-using fixture, and therefore environmental considerations and codes have mandated a change in toilet design in recent years. Low-flow toilets that use less water may be noisier, as water flows at a higher rate to achieve efficiency. Other water-efficient fixtures may require electrical connections for a pump assist.

Toilets vary in size, style, and design. Typical sizes run from a twenty-two-inch wall-hung toilet, to a twenty-five-inch standard bowl toilet, to a thirty-inch-deep elongated bowl. Generally, the height of the toilet seat is important for access, with older people or people with limited mobility preferring a higher seat, such as seventeen to nineteen inches (Parrott et al., 2013). Different toilet designs are increasingly available to specialized market groups, such as toilets sized for children or obese adults, or culturally or internationally specific styles, such as toilets used by squatting instead of sitting.

Adequate space of fifteen to eighteen inches measured from the center of the toilet to a vertical obstruction such as a wall or cabinet is needed on either side of a toilet. As with other fixtures in the bathroom, clear space of twenty-one to thirty inches is needed in front of the toilet (figure 3.5). The clearances for a bidet, which is typically installed next to a toilet, are the same as for a toilet (NKBA, 2012).

General Bathroom Design Considerations

In addition to the design of the bathroom centers, there are several general considerations in putting together the centers. First is the entry to the bathroom. The bathroom should have a door that gives a clear opening of thirty-two inches, which requires a minimum of a two-foot, ten-inch door (figure 3.5). If possible, the door should swing out so that if anyone falls in the bathroom, he or she would not block the door. Also, the placement of the door should not interfere with any of the activities in the three primary centers in the bathroom (NKBA, 2012).

A minimum ceiling height of eighty inches is required over each fixture in the bathroom as well as the clear area in front of each fixture (NKBA, 2012). In homes with very high ceilings, dropped ceilings may be desirable to create better proportion and sense of space in small bathrooms.

Circulation in a bathroom is typically limited. Consider carefully how and when people will be using the different fixtures and how to arrange the centers to prevent congestion. Make sure there is adequate space for access to each fixture, passage through the space, and, if needed, mobility aids.

CONCLUSION

Kitchens and bathrooms are the most complex, technical, frequently used, and expensive spaces in a typical home. They are also fascinating, challenging, and rewarding to design. This chapter has presented an overview of the many issues involved in designing a kitchen or bathroom that meets the needs of the user. We began with a brief historic review of the key influences on the evolution of today's kitchens and bathrooms, including new ideas about sanitation, technology, work simplification, human factors, and the role of women. We also reviewed the early and influential housing research that was critical in establishing the importance of functional and ergonomic design in kitchens and bathrooms. Five important design trends were identified and discussed as influences on kitchen and bath design today: population characteristics, universal design, sustainability, technology, and material choices.

Sections on kitchen design and bathroom design were presented, both organized around the concept of designing by centers. In the design information detailed, we emphasized an approach that was functional and ergonomic; recommended building to code and research-based standards; considered safety, accessibility, and independent living; promoted sustainability; and encouraged creativity.

In most North American homes, the kitchen is an emotional as well as a functional center of the home. The preparation, eating, and sharing of food is a central part of life for the household. The bathroom is a private space—a retreat, perhaps. However, the ability to function independently in the bathroom is critical for dignity and independent living. Thus the kitchen and bath designer has a critical role—and responsibility—to design these spaces to support and enhance people's lives successfully.

REFERENCES

Beamish, J. O., Parrott, K. R., Emmel, J., & Peterson, M. J. (2013). *Kitchen planning: Guidelines, codes, standards.* (2nd ed.). Hoboken, N.J.: John Wiley & Sons; Hackettstown, N.J.: National Kitchen and Bath Association.

Beecher, C., & Stowe, H. B. (1869). *The American woman's home.* New York: J. B. Ford.

Clark, C. E. (1986). *The American family home: 1800–1960.* Chapel Hill: University of North Carolina Press.

Davis, A., & Fisher, R. R. (2015). *Sustainable design: Conservation, materials, practices.* Hoboken, N.J.: John Wiley & Sons; Hackettstown, N.J.: National Kitchen and Bath Association.

Frederick, C. (1913). *The new housekeeping: Efficiency studies in home management.* Garden City, N.Y.: Doubleday, Page, and Co.

Giedion, S. (1969). *Mechanization takes command.* New York: W. W. Norton.

Heiner, M. K., & McCullough, H. E. (1948). *Functional kitchen storage.* (Cornell University Agricultural Experiment Station, Bulletin 846). Ithaca, N.Y.: Cornell University.

International Code Council (2011). *International residential code for one and two family dwellings.* Country Club Hills, Ill.: International Code Council.

Joint Center for Housing Studies of Harvard University. (2014). *State of the nation's housing 2014.* Retrieved January 26, 2017, from http://www.jchs.harvard.edu/research/state_nations_housing.

Jones, R. A., & Kapple, W. H. (1975). *Kitchen industry technical manual* (Vol. 5). National Kitchen and Bath Association and Small Homes Council. Urbana-Champaign: University of Illinois.

Kapple, W. H. (1964). *Kitchen planning standards.* (Small Homes Council—Building Research Council Circular Series C5.32). Urbana: University of Illinois Press.

Kinchin, J., & O'Connor, A. (n.d.). *Counterspace: Design and the Modern Kitchen.* New York: Museum of Modern Art.

Kira, A. (1966). *The bathroom.* Ithaca, N.Y.: Center for Housing and Environmental Studies, Cornell University.

Lofquist, D. A. (2012). *Multigenerational households: 2009–2011* (American Community Survey brief ACSRBR/11-03). Retrieved January 26, 2017, from http://www.census.gov/prod/2012pubs/acsbr11-03.pdf.

McCullough, H. E. (1949). *Cabinet space for the kitchen.* (Small Homes Council—Building Research Council Circular Series C5.31). Urbana: University of Illinois Press.

Museum of Modern Art. (2010). *Counter space design and the modern kitchen: The Frankfurt kitchen.* Retrieved January 26, 2017, from http://www.moma.org/interactives/exhibitions/2010/counter_space/the_frankfurt_kitchen.

NKBA (National Kitchen and Bath Association). (2012). *Kitchen & bathroom: Planning guidelines with access standards.* Hoboken, N.J.: John Wiley & Sons; Hackettstown, N.J.: National Kitchen and Bath Association.

Olmert, M. (2009). *Kitchens, smokehouses and privies.* Ithaca, N.Y.: Cornell University Press.

Panero, J., & Zelnik, M. (1979). *Human dimension and interior space: A source book of design reference standards.* New York: Whitney Library of Design.

Parrott, K., Beamish, J., & Emmel, J. (2003). *Kitchen storage research project.* Blacksburg: Virginia Tech.

Parrott, K. R., Beamish, J. O., Emmel, J. M., & Lee, S. J. (2008). Kitchen remodeling: Exploring the dream kitchen projects. *Housing and Society, 35*(2), 25–42.

Parrott, K. R., Beamish, J. O., Emmel, J., & Peterson, M. J. (2013). *Bath planning: Guidelines, codes, standards.* Hoboken, N.J.: John Wiley & Sons; Hackettstown, N.J.: National Kitchen and Bath Association.

Plante, E. M. (1995). *The American kitchen: 1700 to present.* New York: Facts on File.

Statistics Canada. (2014). *Population projections for Canada (2013 to 2063), Provinces and Territories (2013 to 2038): Highlights.* Retrieved January 26, 2017, from http://www.statcan.gc.ca/pub/91-520-x/2014001/hi-fs-eng.htm.

Story, M. F., Mueller, J. L., & Mace, R. L. (1998). *The universal design file: Designing for people of all ages and abilities.* Raleigh: Center for Universal Design, North Carolina State University.

Wanslow, R. (1965). *Kitchen planning guide*. Urbana: Small Homes Council—Building Research Council and University of Illinois.

Wilson, M. (1938). *The Willamette Valley farm kitchen*. Corvallis: Oregon State University Agricultural Experiment Station.

Wright, G. (1981). *Building the dream: A social history of housing in America*. Cambridge, Mass.: MIT Press.

Chapter 4   Single-Family Residential Design

SUK-KYUNG KIM AND MIRA AHN

Single-family housing, defined as an individual, freestanding, and unattached dwelling unit, has been a dominant housing type in the United States (U.S. Bureau of the Census, n.d.a). Although American homes have continuously changed in architectural style, size, and number of rooms, the overall single-family housing design has remained consistent in regard to design principles and strategies (Pile, 2007). To offer residents comfortable living environments, single-family home designers consider diverse factors that affect both design characteristics and final design solutions, including social trends and housing-related norms, residents' demographic characteristics and socioeconomic status, popular architectural as well as historic styles, and current construction technologies (McAlester & McAlester, 1984).

This chapter introduces the design features of selected historic styles that continue to be used in many single-family homes and then considers the diverse factors that influence current single-family home design. For readers interested in the details of design and space planning for a single-family home, this chapter explains the entire design and construction process and presents examples of interior space planning, while expounding on the functions of interior spaces in a single-family home.

SINGLE-FAMILY HOMES AS A DOMINANT HOUSING TYPE

The single-family home has been a dominant housing type for a long time in the United States. The share of single-family detached homes has remained fairly consistent, at 60 percent, over the past five decades or so (U.S. Bureau of the Census, n.d.b). While the distribution of the average number of stories of new single-family homes has remained the same, almost equally divided between one and a half and two stories, the average square footage has increased from 1,740 square feet in 1980 to 2,598 square feet in 2013 (U.S. Bureau of the Census, n.d.b). The number of bedrooms and bathrooms has also increased. In 1980, 63 percent of new single-family homes had three bedrooms and 20 percent had four or more bedrooms, while in 2013, 46 percent of new single-family homes had three bedrooms and 44 percent had four bedrooms. In 1980, almost no new single-family homes had three or more bathrooms, while in 2013, 33 percent of new single-family homes had three or more bathrooms. These percentages show that the size of single-family homes and the number of bedrooms and bathrooms have increased over time.

BRIEF HISTORY OF U.S. SINGLE-FAMILY RESIDENTIAL DESIGN

For *A Field Guide to American Houses*, McAlester and McAlester (1984) conducted intensive field research on American residential designs. In contrast to vernacular homes, "styled houses" are defined as those designed by architectural designers (McAlester & McAlester, 1984). Styled houses are categorized into several periods based on interior and exterior design features. Considering significant changes in housing forms, texture, and ornamentation, five periods for styled homes are commonly accepted (Kim et al., 2014): 1600–1820, colonial homes; 1820–80, romantic homes; 1860–1900, Victorian homes; 1880–1940, eclectic homes; and 1940–present, modern homes.

While each period has notable architects, Frank Lloyd Wright's designs have been continuously popular among many connoisseurs of residential design for a long time. Wright introduced the Prairie-style home between 1900 and 1920, with its massive square and rectangular piers of masonry to support porch roofs and its porches with widely overhanging eaves. Most of his homes have two stories with one-story wings or porches. Eaves, cornices, and façades emphasize horizontal lines (Kim et al., 2014; see figure 4.1).

While the common Prairie-style home with its elaborate and possibly luxurious details might be geared toward upper-income households, the common Craftsman-style home, with a somewhat plain design, might be more directed toward middle-income households. The characteristics of the Craftsman design include a low-pitched gable roof, occasionally hipped, with wide, unenclosed overhanging eaves and exposed roof rafters. Decorative beams or braces are often located under its gables. The home porches, either full or partial width, include a roof supported by tapered square columns or pedestals that extend to the ground level (Heinz, 2002; Kim et

FIGURE 4.1
Prairie-Style Home, Chicago, Illinois
Image credit: S.-K. Kim.

FIGURE 4.2
Typical U.S. Ranch-Style Home
Image credit: S.-K. Kim.

al., 2014). A variation of the Craftsman-style home is the American Four-Square home, also known as the "Prairie Box" or "Transitional Pyramid" design (McAlester & McAlester, 1984: 444). These types of homes, which borrow design elements from the Craftsman styles, appeared in the early 1900s in many neighborhoods and remained popular among families of diverse socioeconomic backgrounds until the 1930s (Kim et al., 2014).

Modern homes, for example, ranch homes, were among the most popular single-family housing styles between 1935 and the 1970s (McAlester & McAlester, 1984). These one-story homes commonly feature low-pitched roofs and broad and rambling façades, as shown in figure 4.2 (McAlester & McAlester, 1984). Several variations of ranch-style homes, such as split-level and raised-ranch styles, have wings and sunken garages. Common features of this style are a wide-open façade that is not blocked by columns, leading to the open floor plan. These main features of modern homes are still present in newly developed neighborhoods, but current versions show narrower façades than original modern-style homes.

In addition to ranch homes, different styles have been popular since the 1940s, often including *neo*, which means "new," in front of the style name. For example, there are neocolonial, neo-French, neo-Tudor, and neo-Mediterranean homes (McAlester & McAlester, 1984). Neocolonial homes are still common in many neighborhoods today. They have symmetrical façades that lack the regularly spaced pattern of windows and show lower or steeper roof pitches compared to traditional colonial homes, which have higher and wider roofs and symmetrical façades with detailed patterns of windows and dormers. Many architectural designers have interpreted this style in slightly different ways and have added some unique colonial details, such as door surrounds, colonnaded entry porches, and dentil cornices (Kim et al., 2014).

Rather than being based on a dominant home style, current single-family residential designs present various forms, structures, colors, and textures for both interiors and exteriors (Mayberry Homes, n.d.). They are also designed to accommodate diverse occupants' needs, such as the desire to achieve high energy efficiency and to incorporate smart home technologies that facilitate convenient living and positively influence well-being and aging in place.

INFLUENCES ON SINGLE-FAMILY RESIDENTIAL DESIGN

Residential design has been influenced by many different factors. Because living experiences vary by culture and time, many different prototypes of homes have emerged (Rapoport, 1969). Although the basic function of a home is to offer shelter, individual meanings of home and design preferences have been transformed in response to diverse influences.

Codes and Regulations

When designing a home, architects refer to housing codes and regulations prior to making any other design decisions in order to ensure the safety, health, and welfare of occupants (Kilmer & Kilmer, 1992). The International Residential Code (IRC), published in 2000 by the International Code Council (ICC), is the main code used for homes that have three stories or less. This code is a comprehensive, stand-alone residential code that defines the minimum requirements for construction, in particular plumbing, mechanical, fuel gas, energy, and electrical provisions for one- and two-family residences (Harmon & Kennon, 2014).

In providing for accessible single-family housing design, architects and interior designers refer to guidelines and standards provided by the Americans with Disabilities Act (ADA) (U.S. Department of Justice, 2010). Currently these standards are not required for all single-family homes, but they do have to be met for single- or multifamily housing units directly funded by the federal government. Common requirements for residential buildings are summarized in table 4.1.

In regard to energy efficiency, designers adhere to the International Energy Conservation Code (IECC), created by the ICC in 2000, which established the minimum energy performance for both residential and commercial buildings, similar to energy requirements in the IRC. Most states have adopted the IECC for individual dwellings (Harmon & Kennon, 2014).

Housing Norms

American single-family residential design is also influenced by norms and culture, lifestyle, and aesthetic preferences and tastes. Morris and Winter's (1978) housing adjustment theory encompasses U.S. households' unique housing norms in regard to tenure, structure type, and space quality. One of the strongest housing norms in the United States is the preference for an owner-occupied single-family detached home. This type of home typically has a private or semiprivate outdoor space, such as a backyard, patio, or porch, which influences the overall housing design (see chapter 2).

Space Quality, Privacy, and Special Needs

Other important influences for single-family housing design are space quality, privacy, and residents' special needs. Overcrowding and privacy were critical housing concerns at the beginning of the twentieth century, especially for needy families (Evans, 2006; Riis, 1890). Such issues are no longer critical for most homes in the United States, since the IRC recommends seventy square feet as the minimum for an inhabitable room. However,

TABLE 4.1
Common Requirements for Residential Buildings

Components	Requirements by the International Residential Code (IRC)
Construction types and building size	The IRC specifies many aspects of habitable residential spaces, including minimum room sizes and proper lighting, ventilation, and heating requirements. Although the total area of a residence is generally not regulated, the structure typically cannot be more than three stories high. If it has more than three stories, building codes will apply. However, the IRC does place minimum square footage and ceiling height requirements on each habitable room within the residence. For example, the minimum area of a habitable room, except for a kitchen, is 70 sq. ft. (6.5 m^2) and the ceiling height in a habitable room must typically be a minimum of 7 ft. (2,134 mm) above the finished floor (IRC 554).
Means of egress	Most homes rely on exterior windows as a means of egress during an emergency. The IRC sets minimum requirements for the size, height, and operation of these windows. It requires a minimum of one regulated exterior exit door in each residence (at least 3 ft. [914 mm] wide by 80 in. [2,032 mm] high). Other doors to the exterior are allowed to have smaller widths. Minimum corridor width is typically 3 ft. (914 mm). For all sleeping areas, the IRC requires an emergency means of egress. The code typically allows this exit to be an operable window. The bottom of the window cannot be more than 44 in. (1,118 mm) above the floor, and the window must have a clear opening of certain dimensions that allow a person to exit through the window in case of a fire or other emergency (IRC 554–555).
Fire resistance	The main separation requirement pertains to an attached garage. A one-hour assembly must separate any part of the garage that connects to the house, including walls and ceiling. Any door between the garage and the living area must be fire rated. The 2006 edition of the IRC requires that the door be self-closing and self-latching as well. Other fire code requirements are specified for items such as fireplaces and wood-burning stoves (IRC 555–556).
Fire protection	Fire and smoke detection consists mainly of smoke detectors. The IRC requires that all new homes have smoke detectors that are interconnected and tied into the electrical system with battery backup. Typically they must be installed in each sleeping room, outside each sleeping area, on all inhabitable floors, and in basements and garages (IRC 556–557).
Plumbing	The minimum requirements for plumbing fixtures typically include one kitchen sink, one water closet (toilet), one bathtub or shower unit, and one washing machine hookup. In addition, each water closet and bathtub or shower must also be installed in a room with privacy. The IRC specifies the size, clearances, installation requirements, and finishes for most fixture types. For example, a shower must have a minimum area of 900 sq. in. (0.581 m^2) (IRC 557).
Mechanical	Ventilation at home is directly related to the size and number of exterior windows and how much natural ventilation they supply. For example, the IRC specifies that a bathroom should have an operable window of a certain size. If it does not have a window, an exhaust fan with a duct leading directly to the exterior of the building is required. Dryer exhaust must be ducted to the outside, yet the code sets maximum length limitations that may restrict the location of a laundry room within the house. All HVAC (heating, ventilation, and air conditioning) must be located where they are easy to access and maintain (IRC 558).
Electrical	All electrical outlets must be a certain distance apart, and GFCI (ground fault circuit interrupter) outlets must be used in wet areas. All inhabitable rooms require a wall switch to control lighting, and all stairways must include at least one light fixture with a wall switch at each floor level (IRC 559).

Source: Harmon & Kennon, 2014. Reprinted with permission.

many designers are still making efforts to solve overcrowding issues with design-oriented approaches, such as utilizing efficient interior space design that considers proper layout, furniture arrangement, and color schemes (Kilmer & Kilmer, 1992).

Homes often reflect the demographic and socioeconomic status of their occupants through their overall design, which includes housing quality, home size, and amenities. For example, a home with a three-car garage or a luxurious foyer with double entry doors symbolizes a higher economic status than does a home with a carport or a narrow entry hall. However, such high-end features are now found in many middle-income-family homes (Centex Homes, n.d.). A significant number of developers offer various floor plans for different socioeconomic groups, based on personal preferences and ability to pay. Many customized homes for middle- or upper-income households show common design features, such as bigger garage spaces, high-quality interior finishes, and special-purpose rooms. Residential design for families with lower incomes shows simple exterior lines and shapes and utilizes cost-effective and durable interior and exterior materials and finishes to reduce construction costs (KB Homes, n.d.; Centex Homes, n.d.; Mayberry Homes, 2016).

Homes also accommodate residents' special needs. One example, to meet universal design guidelines and green home considerations, is the Life Wise Home developed by the National Association of Home Builders (NAHB) Research Center. Originally built as an experimental home, it demonstrates how residential design can reflect the needs of elderly or disabled residents (National Association of Home Builders Research Center, 2002; see chapters 6 and 17). It follows universal design guidelines and provides accessibility for wheelchair users and residents with limited mobility. The Life Wise Home design also considers indoor air quality, waste management, energy efficiency, and water conservation and incorporates green products, such as low-emissivity (or low-e) glass for windows and reclaimed flooring materials, to improve durability and cost-effective maintenance of the home. Many builders and designers have adopted the design features in this home when rehabilitating homes for elderly residents (National Association of Home Builders Research Center, 2002).

Single-family residential design is influenced by new construction technology, new exterior and interior materials, various residential technological systems and equipment, and environmental concerns (Kim & Lee, 2014). Examples of residential technological systems include home automation systems and energy-efficient HVAC systems (Kim & Ahn, 2010). An environmentally conscious design considers energy efficiency, green materials, site placement and design, and healthy home principles (see chapter 19). Technological and environmental aspects are reflected in recent green home designs. Examples of green homes are Energy Star® certified homes, the U.S. Green Building Council's LEED-certified homes, and homes certified by the National Association of Home Builders' (NAHB) National Green Building Programs (Kim & Lee, 2014; National Association of Home Builders, 2016; U.S. Green Building Council, 2013). These environmentally conscious homes utilize various technologies and building materials to reduce energy use and increase durability, comfort, and indoor environmental quality in the home. In addition, homes certified by LEED or NAHB consider how the home's location is aligned with transportation, sustainable site features such as redeveloped sites, and connectivity with communities. These homes pursue a holistic approach, from building design through postoccupancy evaluation, to achieve the green home rating systems' main goal of making homes sustainable (U.S. Green Building Council, 2016).

Some experimental homes, such as LaHouse at Louisiana State University (Reichel, n.d.) and the Gator Tech Smart House at the University of Florida, have also applied this green and technology-oriented home design concept. These homes were designed for elderly residents and tested various residential technologies (i.e., home automation, energy consumption management system, and motion detectors) to improve the functions of the entire home. The diverse functions can also support occupants with disabilities (Helal, 2015). These experimental homes, therefore, envision many possibilities of technology-implemented home designs for aging or disabled residents.

The popularity of prefabricated buildings also demonstrates the influence of technological development and environmental concerns on residential design. Prefabrication, which reduces construction and maintenance costs, has been a part of the construction process in the United States since the seventeenth century (Marquit, 2013). A famous example of a historic prefabricated home is Le Corbusier's Dom-Ino House, designed in 1914, which had a simple reinforced concrete structure supported by slim beams (McGuirk, 2014). Although it was never built, this project introduced a new concept in home construction for the masses. It included inexpensive and easily reproducible building modules that would decrease the construction period. Another famous example of prefabrication is the mail-order home by Sears, Roebuck & Company, which offered the popular mail-order American Four-Square home (Craven, n.d.). Prefabrication was also a popular method for building shelters for temporary workers and soldiers during World War II (Halberstam, 1993).

The popularity of the prefabricated home did not continue after the end of World War II due to a number of important factors. One of the main reasons was associated with a complicated decision-making process for prefabricated home residents to obtain the final design. Although homeowners were able to go through a simple process to purchase and build a prefabricated home without professional architectural services, they still had to review zoning and regulations and take care of many documents in order to build their own homes. Accordingly, they had to make many design decisions, which were not commonly understood and were difficult for them. Prefabricated homes thus became less popular among U.S. homeowners.

Recently, however, prefabrication has regained popularity in the United States as an option that can reduce construction costs. Considering the cost-effectiveness, easy delivery, and the construction process, prefabricated homes should remain popular for households looking for affordable housing.

DESIGN PROCESS AND INTERIOR SPACE DESIGN

Many designers plan residential spaces with the purpose of satisfying the functional, physical, and psychological needs of the home's residents (Kilmer & Kilmer, 1992). Designing a high-quality single-family residential environment is a difficult task because this environment serves a variety of personal and familial daily activities. Much of the literature indicates that numerous environmental factors affect residential satisfaction and residents' intention to remain in a particular home (Bruin & Cook, 1997; Weidemann & Anderson, 1985). An unsatisfactory or inappropriate residential environment may hinder or limit residential functions or harm residents' physical and psychological health (Lee & Kim, 2012). Therefore, designers of residential environments follow an evidence-based design process that includes various activities such as information gathering for research, design concept development, interior and exterior space planning, rough and detailed design idea development, and construction (Duerk, 1993) to create healthy, comfortable, and functional spaces for future occupants.

SINGLE-FAMILY HOUSING DESIGN PROCESS

The initial step toward a well-designed single-family home is to understand the existing constraints, such as regulations and code requirements, location, lot size, lot orientation, proximity to adjacent homes, setback, and number of stories. As discussed above, codes and regulations affect single-family home design in many ways. The location of a home may determine the home type (e.g., a one-story single-family home with a spacious patio and porch in a warm region compared to a two-story single-family home with less exterior exposure in a cold region). Design options may be limited by the size and orientation of the building lot and the proximity to adjacent homes.

In addition to codes and regulations and physical constraints, residential designers need to satisfy the needs of the occupants. Thus designers gather information about exterior and interior spaces and analyze their clients' residential needs by communicating with them several times. This information-gathering and analysis process helps designers develop well-defined space plans (Duerk, 1993).

Design concepts are the motivations or inspiration for the design. They can be conceptual, realistic, or imaginary. For instance, a concept for a single-family design can be happiness (conceptual), energy efficiency (realistic), or a spaceship (imaginary). Various design concepts inspire designers to create different residential design solutions (Duerk, 1993). The finalized design solution is initially presented in a schematic design and is cultivated in construction document details. The schematic design comprises various diagrams and sketches to present design ideas. The final step of the schematic design usually involves presenting technical and pictorial drawings, such as floor plans, elevations, or perspectives (Pile, 2007). Successful information gathering and analysis for a project allows designers to develop a schematic design that meets residential needs properly and accommodates any restrictions from the physical conditions surrounding the home.

Once the schematic design is developed, designers present to the client their final design that includes floor plans, elevations, perspectives, sketches, or rendered images of the home. Designers then develop construction drawings for the construction company. Once the client, the designer, and the construction company agree on all design details, the construction process begins, although a few minor modifications may happen along the way.

The construction period typically takes about 6.2 months, although this may vary depending on the site location, the construction materials, the structure of the home, the exterior and interior materials, the skills and experience of the construction workers, and the weather conditions during the construction (U.S. Bureau of the Census, 2014). Once the construction process is complete, an official from the city or township inspects the home to evaluate whether it is ready for occupancy. Once the home is approved, the client and a representative from the construction company walk through the home. Finally, the client moves into the home (Duerk, 1993).

After the resident moves into the home, the designer may conduct a voluntary postoccupancy evaluation (POE), assessing whether the home functions appropriately and as intended, whether it satisfies the resident's needs, and whether the design can be improved (Preiser, White, & Rabinowitz, 1988). Figure 4.3 explains the entire single-family housing design process. Although the process looks linear in this figure, several steps in the process

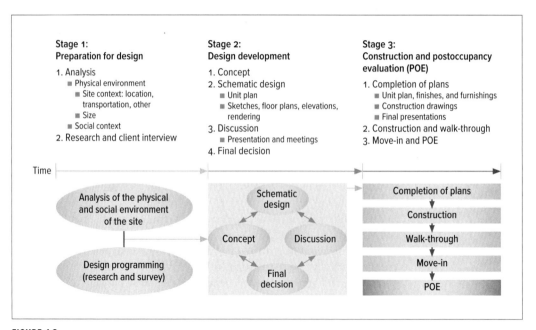

FIGURE 4.3
Single-Family Housing Design Process
Image credit: S.-K. Kim.

are repeated in many practices to find better design outcomes or to accommodate a client's needs for revising plans (Zeisel, 1984). All activities listed in figure 4.3 are thus interrelated in order to achieve the best design outcome.

Resident-Oriented Approach

A designer plans residential spaces to satisfy an occupant's needs. Understanding and synthesizing information regarding the future residents' needs is fundamental for creating an effective residential space plan (Kilmer & Kilmer, 1992). Figure 4.4 shows two interior space plans for single-family residential design that differ according to individual household characteristics. These space design ideas apply to two lots of the same size in suburban Michigan. The first single-family residential design is for a sixty-eight-year-old female householder (household #1) and the second is for a four-person household consisting of a couple and two children (household #2). Each household decided to build a two-story, 1,700-square-foot home with an additional 350 square feet of basement space. Figure 4.4 shows how the spaces were designed to meet the specific residential needs of each household within the same square footage.

The final space plan for household #1 has an open floor plan on both floors, with a living room, a kitchen, and a dining room on the first floor and a large master suite and a bedroom for the owner's grandchildren on the second floor. The final space plan for household #2 has the family's common spaces such as a living room, a kitchen, and a dining space on the first floor, three smaller bedrooms on the second floor, and a guest bedroom as well as a playroom for the children and their friends in the basement. These two examples represent how residential spaces can be organized differently depending on residents' needs.

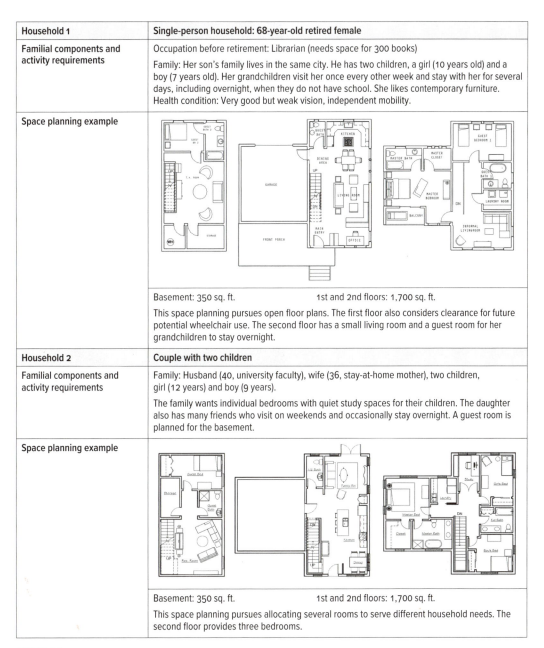

Household 1	Single-person household: 68-year-old retired female
Familial components and activity requirements	Occupation before retirement: Librarian (needs space for 300 books) Family: Her son's family lives in the same city. He has two children, a girl (10 years old) and a boy (7 years old). Her grandchildren visit her once every other week and stay with her for several days, including overnight, when they do not have school. She likes contemporary furniture. Health condition: Very good but weak vision, independent mobility.
Space planning example	Basement: 350 sq. ft. 1st and 2nd floors: 1,700 sq. ft. This space planning pursues open floor plans. The first floor also considers clearance for future potential wheelchair use. The second floor has a small living room and a guest room for her grandchildren to stay overnight.
Household 2	Couple with two children
Familial components and activity requirements	Family: Husband (40, university faculty), wife (36, stay-at-home mother), two children, girl (12 years) and boy (9 years). The family wants individual bedrooms with quiet study spaces for their children. The daughter also has many friends who visit on weekends and occasionally stay overnight. A guest room is planned for the basement.
Space planning example	Basement: 350 sq. ft. 1st and 2nd floors: 1,700 sq. ft. This space planning pursues allocating several rooms to serve different household needs. The second floor provides three bedrooms.

FIGURE 4.4
Interior Space Planning Examples for Different Household Needs
Image credit: S.-K. Kim.

Spatial Organization and Functions of Interior Spaces

The interior space of a typical single-family home consists of three types of zones: private, social, and service (Kilmer & Kilmer, 1992). As each interior zone fulfills different functions, the spatial organization of interior space should be viewed holistically. Figure 4.5 presents an overview of interior space planning in single-family homes with one or two stories. These plans present details for different types of spaces, based on needs for privacy and spatial functions.

Home type	Single-family home
Single-story home	The first floor includes all three zones. Spaces are horizontally separated, depending on the level of privacy. The social zone is located in the middle and service and personal zones are separated. 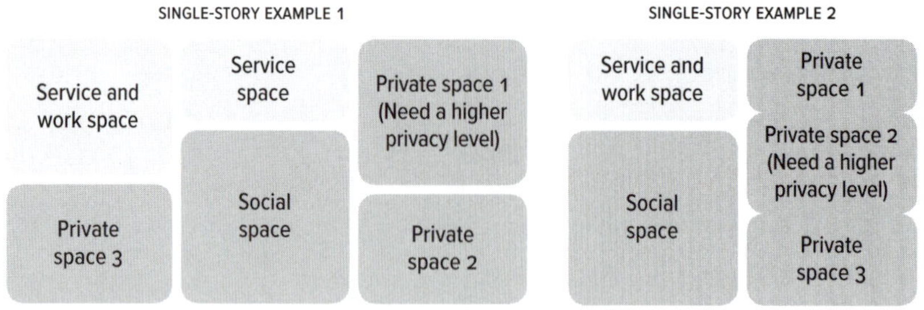 **SINGLE-STORY EXAMPLE 1** Service and work space / Service space / Private space 1 (Need a higher privacy level) / Private space 3 / Social space / Private space 2 **SINGLE-STORY EXAMPLE 2** Service and work space / Private space 1 / Social space / Private space 2 (Need a higher privacy level) / Private space 3
Two-story home	Spaces are vertically separated, depending on the level of privacy. Social and service spaces are located on the first floor. Additional social spaces are on the second floor, along with private spaces. An example of space planning is presented below. 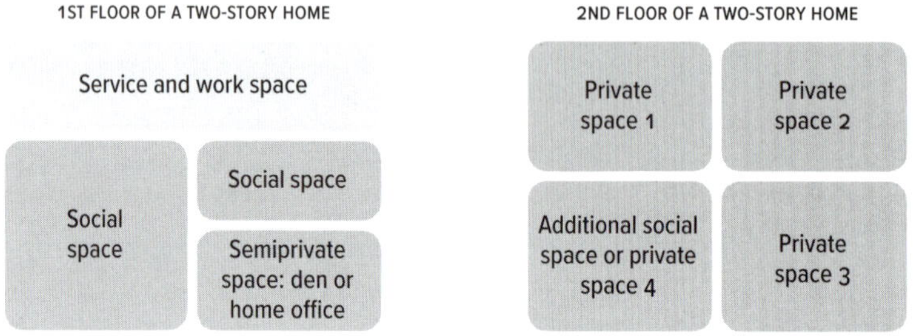 **1ST FLOOR OF A TWO-STORY HOME** Service and work space / Social space / Social space / Semiprivate space: den or home office **2ND FLOOR OF A TWO-STORY HOME** Private space 1 / Private space 2 / Additional social space or private space 4 / Private space 3

FIGURE 4.5
Interior Space Planning Guidelines
Image credit: S.-K. Kim

Private Zone

The private zone includes bedrooms and bathrooms. Such spaces are usually located on the second floor in a two-story single-family home, while the first floor is open to visitors, providing a lower level of privacy. In a single-story home bedrooms and bathrooms are not vertically separated from other spaces, although they are typically located at a corner rather than in the center of the home. The front and central portions of a single-story home are designated for social spaces such as living or recreational rooms (see figure 4.5).

Private spaces support diverse daily activities, just as social spaces do. When designing private spaces such as bedrooms and bathrooms, designers thus pay attention to their multiple functions: size; spatial layout; personal characteristics of users such as their age, preferences for colors and furniture, or their gender; and various functions the space will serve (Kilmer & Kilmer, 1992). Various activities, including sleeping, reading or studying, watching TV, conversation, stretching, or lifting weights are accommodated through different spatial layouts and within smaller spaces. A bedroom layout should provide for resting, casual social, and entertainment functions. Another private space is a bathroom adjacent to bedrooms. Bathrooms located on the second floor of a two-story home are more private than those on the first floor. In bathroom planning, designers consider reducing traffic within the interior space and enhancing the efficiency of spatial use (see chapter 3).

Social Zone

Major functions of social spaces in a single-family home are socializing, dining, and entertaining with family members or visitors (Pile, 2007). A contemporary single-family home typically has two or three social spaces—for example, the living room on the first floor of a home, another social space on the second floor, and yet another if the basement is habitable (Mayberry Homes, 2016). Well-designed social spaces can offer better opportunities for social interaction among family members. Social spaces in a home can be labeled as living rooms, recreational rooms, family rooms, or multipurpose rooms (Kilmer & Kilmer, 1992), depending on their functions and homeowners' preferences.

The living room is usually located on the first floor in the center of the home, determining the ambience of the entire residential design. The level of openness and the color scheme for the walls, the ceiling, and the floor, as well as the furniture in this space, can also affect the design of other spaces. Many contemporary single-family homes have open floor plans, allowing residents to modify the layout easily according to their needs.

Social spaces usually accommodate diverse activities, ranging from personal activities such as reading or studying to social activities such as conversing, playing games, or watching TV (Pile, 2007). The major element of the social space is the seating area, which mainly defines the furniture layout of the space and provides a spot for household members and visitors to gather. Major design features in social spaces are determined by the life cycle of the household and its demographic and socioeconomic characteristics. One example for a new development in the Grand Rapids area in Michigan is presented in figure 4.6. Its design focuses on creating a multifunctional living room. It shows an open floor plan, which facilitates different activities in the living room, such as cooking, dining, and allowing for family and social gatherings. In a corner of the living room is a small study area, because the client wanted to keep an eye on his children while working in the living room. To accommodate the residents' concerns about energy use and their interest in home automation systems, a system control board, or smart board, was installed on the living room wall to control and monitor heating, air conditioning, water, and electricity.

Dining space was once regarded as a part of the kitchen space in a home (Pile, 2007). However, dining spaces now frequently function as social spaces for family gatherings and socialization with visitors (Kim, Ahn, &

FIGURE 4.6
Open Floor Plan Multipurpose Room
Image credit: J. Son and S.-K. Kim.

FIGURE 4.7
Layout of a Dining Space for Family Gatherings
Image credit: S. Yoo and S.-K. Kim.

FIGURE 4.8
Furniture Layout in the Dining Space for Individual Dining
Image credit: S. Yoo and S.-K. Kim.

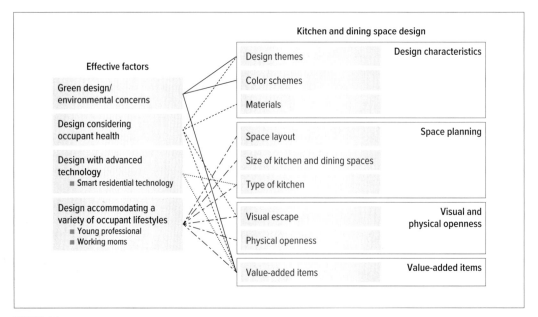

FIGURE 4.9
Effective Factors for Kitchen and Dining Space Designs
Source: Kim, Ahn, & Tremblay, 2008. Copyright © Housing Education and Research Association, reprinted by permission of Taylor and Francis Ltd., http://www.tandfonline.com, on behalf of Housing Education and Research Association.

Tremblay, 2008). Figure 4.7 shows a design idea for a dining space that connects the kitchen with the living room and also functions as a social space, providing a small gathering area for family members, supported by a flexible furniture layout. The dining table in Figure 4.7 may be clustered to serve the family-gathering function or may be moved and linearly arranged for family members' individual dining.

Service and Work Space

Service and work spaces in a single-family home include a kitchen, a laundry room, storage areas, and a garage (Pile, 2007). The kitchen has also evolved from an isolated area to one for social food preparation and social gathering (Kim et al., 2008). Many contemporary kitchens function as social, service, and work areas.

Contemporary kitchen designs address green design and environmental concerns, occupant health, advanced technology, and accommodation of various occupants' lifestyles, among other features. Figure 4.9 presents four features to be considered in kitchen design in single-family homes and specific items related to each feature (Kim et al., 2008; see chapter 3).

CONCLUSION

Since different housing styles were introduced in the 1600s, single-family home design has evolved in the United States. This chapter discussed the history and trends in single-family residential design, highlighted major single-family home styles—such as Prairie, American Four-Square, and ranch—including their interior and exterior design elements.

The main elements that affect single-family residential design were also discussed in this chapter. Codes and regulations, housing norms, households' demographic and socioeconomic characteristics, and technological development and environmental concerns were highlighted. Many elements of housing design and construction are determined by households' demographic and socioeconomic characteristics. This chapter thus showed examples of how interior space planning relates to households' characteristics and needs. The effects of green and sustainable design, high-tech integrated design, and aging in place were discussed with exemplary cases.

Residential designers go through a well-planned design process and collect information about clients' needs for their homes. Throughout the entire design process, designers should address their clients' needs and characteristics, which need to be reflected in the home design, including interior space planning, color coordination, material selections, and other issues. This chapter thus explained the single-family home design process in general and interior space planning strategies in detail. Interior spaces can be categorized into three zones depending on their major functions—private, public, and service—and the chapter presented actual design solutions in terms of specific functions and uses of different spaces.

Throughout the single-family housing design process, it is also important for designers to rely on a user-participatory design method that focuses on working with the client to arrive at the best design solution. Additionally, a postoccupancy evaluation may analyze the strengths and weaknesses of final design outcomes to improve them for future single-family residential design.

REFERENCES

Bruin, M. J., & Cook, C. C. (1997). Understanding constraints and residential satisfaction among low-income single-parent families. *Environment and Behavior, 29*(4), 532–553.

Centex Homes. (n.d.). Emerald Springs neighborhood in Indiana. Retrieved October 1, 2015, from http://www.centex.com/.

Craven, J. (n.d.). American foursquare. Retrieved February 1, 2016, from http://architecture.about.com/od/periodsstyles/ig/House-Styles/Foursquare.htm.

Duerk, D. P. (1993). *Architectural programming: Information management for design.* New York: John Wiley & Sons.

Evans, G. W. (2006). Child development and the physical environment. *Annual Review of Psychology, 57,* 423–451.

Halberstam, D. (1993). *The fifties.* New York: Villard Books.

Harmon, S. K., & Kennon, K. E. (2014). *The codes guidebook for interiors.* New York: John Wiley & Sons, Inc.

Heinz, T. (2002). *Frank Lloyd Wright's houses.* New York: Gramercy Book.

Helal, S. (2015). *The Gator Tech Smart House.* Retrieved March 3, 2015, from http://www.icta.ufl.edu/gt.htm.

KB Homes. (n.d.). Home design in this community: The Calderwood. Retrieved October 1, 2015, from http://www.kbhome.com/new-homes-raleigh-durham/the-villas-at-lakestone.

Kilmer, R., & Kilmer, W. O. (1992). *Designing interiors.* Orlando, Fla.: Holt, Reinhart and Winston.

Kim, S.-K., & Ahn, M. (2010). Residential technology for elderly Americans and Koreans aging at home. *Proceedings of the Housing Education and Research Association (HERA) Annual Conference,* 135–148. Portland, Ore., November 3–6, 2010.

Kim, S.-K., Ahn, M., & Tremblay, K. (2008). Contemporary kitchen and dining space design in urban multifamily housing in Korea. *Housing and Society, 35*(2), 117–138.

Kim, S.-K., & Lee, E. S. (2014). LEED for Homes Rating System and resident satisfaction with LEED-certified homes: Focusing on the U.S. cases. *Journal of Korean Housing, 25*(3), 25–34.

Kim, S.-K., Mrozowski, T., Harrell-Seyburn, A., Ehrlich, N., Hembroff, L., Lieburn, B., Mazor, M., Mclntyre, A., Mutton, C., Parsons, G., Syal, M., & Wilkinson, R. (2014). *Housing archetype analysis for home energy-efficient retrofit in the Great Lakes region.* Washington, D.C.: U.S. Department of Energy. Retrieved March 1, 2014, from http://www.nrel.gov/docs/fy14osti/60004.pdf.

Lee, E., & Kim, S.-K. (2012). Impact of green homes for low-income families: Post-occupancy evaluations of LEED-certified Habitat for Humanity homes in Michigan. *Proceedings of the 43rd Environmental Design and Research Association (EDRA) Conference,* 261–262. Seattle, Wash., May 30–June 2, 2012.

Marquit, A. (2013). *From Sears & Roebuck to skyscrapers: A history of prefabricated and modular housing.* New York: City of New York. Retrieved June 16, 2014, from http://www.nyc.gov/html/dob/downloads/pdf/history_of_prefabricated_and_modular_construction.pdf.

Mayberry Homes. (2016). Features floor plans. Retrieved March 20, 2016, from http://www.mayberryhomes.com/.

McAlester, V., & McAlester, L. (1984). *A field guide to American houses.* New York: Alfred A. Knopf.

McGuirk, J. (2014). Opinion: The perfect architectural symbol for an era obsessed with customization and participation. *Dezeen Magazine,* March 20, 2014. Retrieved November 20, 2014, from http://www.dezeen.com/2014/03/20/opinon-justin-mcguirk-le-corbusier-symbol-for-era-obsessed-with-customisation/.

Morris, E. W., & Winter, M. (1978). *Housing, family, and society.* New York: John Wiley & Sons.

National Association of Home Builders. (2016). ICC700 National Green Building Standards. Retrieved May 5, 2016, from http://www.nahb.org/en/research/nahb-priorities

/green-building-remodeling-and-development/icc-700-national-green-building-standard.aspx.

National Association of Home Builders Research Center. (2002). LifeWise home. Retrieved March 1, 2014, from http://homes-across america.org/search/details.cfm?who=102&Feature=all&action=showDetails&Query=MultiQuery.

Pile, J. F. (2007). *Interior design*. Upper Saddle River, N.J.: Pearson Prentice Hall.

Preiser, W. F., White, E., & Rabinowitz, H. (1988). *Post-occupancy evaluation*. New York: Van Nostrand Reinhold.

Rapoport, A. (1969). *House form and culture*. Upper Saddle River, N.J.: Prentice Hall.

Reichel, C. (n.d.). LaHouse building features. Retrieved January 20, 2016, from http://www.lsuagcenter.com/topics/family_home/home/la_house/about_lahouse/building_features/lahouse-building-features-throughout.

Riis, J. (1890). *How the other half lives: Studies among the tenements of New York*. New York: Charles Scribner's Sons.

U.S. Bureau of the Census. (n.d.a). Characteristics of new housing. Retrieved June 4, 2014, from https://www.census.gov/construction/chars/completed.html.

U.S. Bureau of the Census. (n.d.b). Historical census of housing tables. Retrieved June 4, 2014, from https://www.census.gov/hhes/www/housing/census/historic/units.html.

U.S. Bureau of the Census. (2014). New residential construction: Length of time. Retrieved February 28, 2016, from http://www.census.gov/construction/nrc/lengthoftime.html.

U.S. Department of Justice. (2010). *2010 ADA standards for accessible design*. Washington, D.C.: U.S. Department of Justice. Retrieved November 15, 2015, from http://www.ada.gov/regs2010/2010ADAStandards/2010ADAStandards_prt.pdf.

U.S. Green Building Council. (2013). LEED v4 for Home Design and Construction. Retrieved January 30, 2016, from https://www.usgbc.org/sites/default/files/LEED%20v4%20ballot%20version%20(Homes)%20-%2013%2011%2013.pdf. Working version released 2012.

U.S. Green Building Council. (2016). LEED version 4. Retrieved May 5, 2016, from http://www.usgbc.org/resources/leed-v4-building-design-and-construction-current-version.

Weidemann, S., & Anderson, J. (1985). A conceptual framework for residential satisfaction. In I. Altman & C. M. Werner (Eds.), *Home environments: Human behavior and environment, advanced in theory and research* (pp. 153–182). New York: Plenum Press.

Zeisel, J. (1984). *Inquiry by design: Tools for environment-behavior research*. Cambridge: Cambridge University Press.

Chapter 5   Multifamily Residential Design

BECKY L. YUST

WHY IS GOOD DESIGN OF MULTIFAMILY HOUSING IMPORTANT?

Multifamily housing, by definition, is a building with two or more dwelling units sharing a common wall. Although the term includes dwellings as small as duplexes and townhouses and as large as high-rise buildings, most people think of multifamily housing as a building with five or more units (Skobba, 2012). Every multifamily residential building is designed by someone, typically an architect, before it is built. But how does attending to design influence the success of the final product? Close attention to all of the design details can facilitate the development process by involving many perspectives, from the owner to the potential occupants. During the early stages of design, the purpose and mission for the structure are established. Phrased differently, who will be living in the building, what amenities are to be included, and what is the overall design concept of this building? Attention to design can help to ensure a high-quality product that will enhance the neighborhood, provide adequate features in the units, and be easy to manage after occupancy. In addition, well-designed structures can provide for the health, safety, and well-being of residents (see chapter 18) through the use of sustainable materials and finishes (see chapter 19), floor plan layouts that respect human behavior and provide for safety, and high satisfaction of both the residents and the community (Kowaltowski et al., 2006; see chapters 2, 12, and 13).

WHAT IS GOOD DESIGN?

Multifamily residences are homes for a variety of types of households, each of which has varying interpretations of good design. The building is typically owned by a company with preferences for particular design styles, and these choices are influenced by a number of factors, including profitability. In addition, the building is designed by an architect who brings his or her aesthetic orientation to the design of the building. Given these multiple perspectives, how can a multifamily residential building be considered well designed compared to other buildings? The U.S. Department of Housing and Urban Development (HUD) sponsored the establishment of a framework of four goals to evaluate the design of multifamily dwellings (Evans, 2001). Its focus tends to be on affordable housing (see chapter 10), but the criteria apply to any type of multifamily housing. The criteria do not establish a desired "style," but if the owner and architect attend to these criteria, the building is likely to be considered "good design."

The first criterion is that the building be designed to **meet the user's needs**. In the case of multifamily housing, the users are the individuals who will live there. A building that is designed with young families in mind may have different features than a building designed for elderly occupants (see chapters 6 and 17). For example, a family household will need more bedrooms, durable materials and finishes, and a larger kitchen than an elderly couple would need (Jiang & O'Neill, 2007). Today, many multifamily buildings are designed to accommodate a variety of household types (e.g., families and single individuals) so that they can remain economically viable and respond to changing demographics over time (Goodman, 1999). These demands require more variety in types of units within a building, making the design of the building more complex than, for example, a building of only studio apartments designed for single individuals. Households also have preferences for location based on their lifestyles (Lee, Beamish, & Goss, 2008). Providing for appropriate amenities can attract and serve residents (see chapter 2).

The second criterion is that the multifamily building **responds to the physical context** in which it is built. How the building is sited on a lot should be characteristic of other structures in the area in its setback and volume. If the building is a mid- or high-rise structure, is that typical of other adjacent structures? If not, the height could be disarming to passersby. A rule of thumb is that the front face of the building not exceed the width of the street. The overall shape of the structure should also respond to the design of neighboring structures (Stamps, 2013). If all of the roofs on the block are flat, a gabled roof could seem out of place, or vice versa. However, because advances in design occur over time, a building may be successful in its design when it does not replicate existing structures (see, e.g., Hanlon, 2014). Different but well-designed structures on a block can provide visual interest.

The third criterion addresses how the building **enhances the neighborhood**. While the direct users of the building are its occupants, people in the neighborhood are important to consider as well. If the building is not designed well, it will not enhance the neighborhood and will diminish the attractiveness of the neighborhood to future residents (Aiello, Ardone, & Scopelliti, 2010). Features such as the landscaping, sidewalks, and lighting need to be integrated with other amenities in the neighborhood (Kelly, 2009). The connection of the building to the neighborhood can welcome residents into the social fabric of the neighborhood (see chapters 12 and 13).

The fourth criterion is that the building be designed so that it is **built to last**. Materials and finishes of the highest quality possible will uphold their appearance and be easy to maintain. For example, the cost of replacing poor-quality windows after a few years of service can be prohibitive, especially for nonprofit housing developers. If priority is given to the use of high-quality and durable materials and finishes, they will not age as quickly and may be easier to repair. By using the best materials and finishes from the onset, the residents and the neighborhood benefit (see chapters 6, 18, and 19).

PRECEDENTS OF MULTIFAMILY HOUSING DESIGN

Multifamily housing dwellings have existed for centuries, just as single, detached dwellings have. Often multifamily housing is developed because the demand for housing is high and available land is limited (see chapters 1 and 2). An early example of multistory housing is the cliff dwellings in the southwestern United States of the Anasazi Indians (e.g., at Mesa Verde National Park). Building below the top of mesas into the sides of cliffs allowed families to live in a secure and safe environment and to share common facilities. The development was a cluster of attached single-family dwellings. There are still viable housing units developed in this way in European hill towns (Davis, 1995; see chapter 22) and, more recently, in the planning of cluster housing as an ecological housing alternative (Lenth, Knight, & Gilgert, 2006; see chapters 6, 18, and 19).

Over time, multifamily developments were purposefully planned to meet market demand, reduce housing costs for residents (see chapter 10), and increase the efficiency of use of building materials and utilities (see chapter 19). In the United States, the image of multifamily housing has been harmed by the evolution of buildings such as tenements on the Lower East Side of Manhattan (Riis, 1997). Built in the 1800s to accommodate large numbers of immigrant families, tenements lacked many amenities (e.g., toilet facilities and ventilation) and by the early 1900s were not considered adequate for habitation by local housing sanitation codes (Sante, 1991; see chapters 9 and 12).

As industrialization evolved, new concepts for building were explored at the Bauhaus in Germany in the early 1920s in Dessau, where a development for eight families was designed to integrate "into a light-colored, unsentimental, clean, and exceedingly wholesome setting for human existence and creative activity" (Wingler, 1969: 124). Ideas for mixed-unit types in housing developments were promoted, and multistory units were designed to reflect these same ideals. In the mid-1900s in the United States, low- and high-rise apartment blocks were built with acres of surrounding green space for residents, but the space was "not large enough to act as public parks, and not small enough to possess the intimate pleasure of the private garden" (Chermayeff & Alexander, 1963: 66). The context of a site and the housing needs to be planned holistically because integration with green space increases the satisfaction of residents (Odum, 2015; see chapters 2 and 19).

Design of multifamily housing can be done well. For example, in many cities in Europe, perimeter block housing has been developed. With parking provided underground or on the street, the housing units surround the perimeter of the block, allowing for the building to be one unit deep with at least two solar orientations for each unit. The central area is kept as common area for gardens, play areas, and so on (Hurd, 2014; see chapter 22). Some innovative developments have used this concept in the United States, but most often land costs and constraints of local parking requirements preclude it.

TYPES OF MULTIFAMILY HOUSING COMMUNITIES

Buildings with five or more units account for just over 16 percent of all housing units in the United States (U.S. Bureau of the Census, 2013). The tenure form accompanying multifamily housing may be renter- or owner-occupied. However, in the United States, it is more likely that single-family dwellings are owned (82 percent) and multifamily dwellings are rented (88 percent) (U.S. Bureau of the Census, 2013). Of those that are owned, forms of ownership are often through condominium and, to a lesser degree, cooperative ownership (see chapters 1, 2, and 8).

In the United States, the rental market served by multifamily dwellings has been characterized by three types: luxury, middle, and moderate/low-income, often labeled as affordable (Goodman, 1999). Multifamily housing communities that are owned by the residents can also be characterized in this way. The target market of potential residents influences the design, marketing, and management associated with the multifamily dwelling. The luxury multifamily housing market serves high-income households who have the resources to afford amenities such as a building management concierge and recreational facilities, among other services (Lee, Goss, & Beamish, 2007). The middle market, often termed market-rate housing, serves households that have an adequate income. If they rent in a multifamily building, they may be in transition, such as changing careers and therefore seeking to be more mobile or saving to eventually own a dwelling. Those who own a dwelling in this market, such as a townhouse, may do so because it is a less costly option than owning a single, detached dwelling. A common-interest community association usually takes care of maintenance, security, and so on (Langbein & Spotswood-Bright, 2004; see chapters 1, and 2, 7, 8, and 10).

Multifamily housing marketed to low- and moderate-income households is primarily rental units. Many of these households are housing cost burdened, meaning they pay over 30 percent of their income toward housing costs. Less than 24 percent of low-income households receive rental assistance (Joint Center for Housing Studies of Harvard University, 2013), so demand far exceeds the supply of affordable housing (see chapter 14). Additionally, low-income households often live in older housing units that are in poor condition, which affects the units' viability over time (Power, 2008; see chapters 9 and 10). Recently, there have been some multifamily dwellings designed for both low- and moderate-income renter and owner occupants in the United States. Via Verde in the Bronx in New York City is an example of a combined affordable owned- and rented-unit building (http://viaverdenyc.com/the_building). Of the 222 housing units at Via Verde, 71 (32 percent) are cooperative owner occupied by moderate-income households (earning 110 percent of the area median income [AMI]) and 151 (68 percent) are renter occupied by low-income households (earning between 30 and 90 percent of AMI). In some countries (e.g., China and the United Kingdom), government-owned and subsidized social housing estates that serve low-income households are being converted to private-sector ownership by allowing current low-income residents to purchase their dwelling units (Wang & Horner, 2012; see chapter 22). Unfortunately, these dwellings are old and may not have been well maintained over the years. The residents who assume ownership are not likely to have additional funds to improve their dwellings.

DESIGN CONSIDERATIONS ASSOCIATED WITH MULTIFAMILY HOUSING

The siting of multifamily housing can be crucial to its livability for residents and its acceptance in a community (see chapters 2, 12, and 13). There are many aspects involved in the design of a multifamily development. In addition to the layout of the housing unit and the building, the building shape, and the overall appearance, the relationship of the building to its environment includes consideration for how it is sited on the property, parking, open space, and landscaping. The following recommendations come primarily from the *Affordable Housing Design Advisor* (Evans, 2001), which provides guidelines for the design of affordable multifamily housing. However, these recommendations are applicable to the design of any type of multifamily housing.

Unit Layout

The individual housing unit is where residents spend most of their time. A sense of entry to the unit conveys a sense of home, especially if the resident is able to personalize the entry area. The size, shape, and number of rooms vary from studio-efficiency units—one large room for the kitchen and sleeping and a separate bathroom—to units with two or more stories with a number of rooms. Typically in multifamily housing developments designed for elderly persons, there will be a choice of one- or two-bedroom units with a kitchen, bathroom, and living room (see chapters 6 and 17). For other developments, a broad mix of unit types may be in the building so that the owner can respond to market demands over the life of the building (Peiser & Hamilton, 2012).

Because of the amount of time spent in the unit, windows are important

FIGURE 5.1
The Interior Hallway of a Double-Loaded Corridor Multifamily Building
Image credit: B. Yust.

to allow natural light and ventilation in all habitable rooms (see chapters 3, 6, and 18). In areas of the world that have harsh, cold winters, units may be designed to be entered from a common interior hallway, frequently called a double-loaded corridor because units are on either side of the corridor (see figure 5.1). These units have only one solar orientation, which can limit the amount of light that reaches into the rooms of the unit and prohibits cross-ventilation. In warmer climates, a building may be designed so that units can be entered from an exterior balcony, which allows for windows on two sides of the units, increasing the ability to use natural ventilation and natural light. The view from the windows in the main living area can bring a sense of nature indoors if the windows are low enough that a resident, when seated, is able to see out of them. This is particularly important for a sedentary resident population (Kaplan, 2001; see chapters 6, 17, and 19).

Many units are designed with an open floor plan between the kitchen, dining, and living rooms so that residents can use the space more flexibly (Friedman, 2007; see chapter 3). Hallways are usually kept at a minimum so that space is not wasted. However, for units with two or more residents, the relationship of the bedrooms, bathrooms, and living room is important to consider, allowing multiple uses within the unit while also providing privacy (see chapters 2, 6, and 17). Storage space within a unit can be minimal, so buildings will often have individual locked storage spaces in another part of the building for residents to use. Depending on the items stored, additional storage may be in the basement, in the parking garage, or on the same floor as the resident (Amole, 2009).

Renter-occupied multifamily buildings will have many more residents move in and out over time than those that are owner occupied (see chapters 1, 2, 9, and 10). Therefore, high-quality, easy-to-maintain flooring, walls, and cabinetry will last longer and not require premature capital investments. Environmentally safe materials will improve the indoor air quality (see chapter 18). Appliances and mechanical equipment for heating, cooling, and ventilation must be specified to meet user requirements and require minimal maintenance (see chapter 2). Regardless of whether the building owner or the resident pays directly for water and utilities, appliances and systems should be energy and water efficient, as they affect operating costs (Varady & Preiser, 1998; see chapter 19).

Building Layout

An inviting building entrance conveys a sense of security for residents and visitors (see chapter 6). Often the building manager's office is located so that it is visible from the entryway to provide supervision. Community rooms and lounges located where they are easily accessible for all residents, such as near the entryway and/or near elevators on upper floors, will ensure that they are used. Circulation through a building can provide opportunities for meeting other residents, but security and lighting are important in corridors so residents feel safe moving about the building. Buildings now include more amenities such as exercise rooms, extra storage units, and even art studios, which may be located in distant parts of the building, so security cameras monitored by management become more important to ensure residents' safety. Conveniently located trash and recycling facilities can encourage appropriate disposal (Ando & Gosselin, 2005; González-Torre & Adenso-Díaz, 2005).

FIGURE 5.2
An Articulated Façade
Such façades can mask the overall size of the structure.
Image credit: B. Yust.

Building Shape

The overall building shape is sometimes referred to as its scale or mass. Buildings that are large rectangular or square volumes may not be appropriate in lower-density neighborhoods. When a building is large because of the number of housing units in it, the upper floors of the building could be stepped back so that at the street it is only two or three stories and then the number of stories decreases away from the street. Breaking up the overall form of the building into various forms or articulating the façade can help to minimize the impact of its size (see figure 5.2; chapters 12 and 13).

Building Appearance

The appearance of a building is very important in how it fits within a neighborhood. Design decisions affecting the appearance include the type of building materials, the exterior color, the design of the façade, the design of the roof, the shape and size of windows, and the type of trim and details on the building. Neighbors may want a new development to be similar in character to current buildings in an area (O'Connor, 2006). Therefore, developers frequently use materials and colors typical of those used in a neighborhood rather than using something very different that might risk obtaining the approval of the city because of neighbors' objections (Farris, 2001; see chapters 12 and 13).

Location of Building on the Site

How the building is located on the site can affect its function for its residents and its relationship to neighboring properties (see chapters 12 and 13). The entry to the building should be obvious from the street, and sidewalks need to be planned to direct residents and visitors to the main entry. Zoning and building code requirements establish the distance of the building from its lot lines, referred to as setbacks (see chapter 9). Building siting can take advantage of natural light to reduce energy consumption and provide for the potential use of alternative energy, such as solar power (Edwards & Torcellini, 2002) (see chapters 18 and 19).

Parking

The local zoning code establishes the minimum number of parking spaces per unit, such as one space, one and a half spaces, or two spaces per dwelling unit. In some dense urban areas, less than one space per unit and even no parking spaces may be allowed because it is assumed that there are adequate public transportation options for residents (Guo & Ren, 2013). When zoning allows a reduced number of parking spaces, the land that would be devoted to parking can be used for an increased number of housing units or common green space instead. If a developer wants to provide fewer parking spaces than designated in the local zoning code, a zoning variance must be granted by the municipality (Stubbs, 2002). Such a request may be contested by neighbors on adjacent property because they may assume that the new residents will use the public streets for parking (see chapter 9).

In addition to the parking spaces provided, access from the public street to the parking spaces and vehicular movement on the site need to be designed to be safe and to minimize conflicts between vehicles, bicycles, and pedestrians. For example, children should not have to cross a driveway to get to a playground or other site amenities. Traffic-calming layouts can reduce vehicular speeds by breaking up large parking lots into smaller lots and using landscaping to influence driving behavior (Naderi, 2003).

Security is a necessary consideration for parking lots and underground parking. Adequate lighting and security cameras can help deter vandalism and assaults. Placing the parking where it is visible to people from their housing-unit windows can provide informal surveillance (Levy & Tartaro, 2010; Newman, 1972).

Open Space

Common outdoor areas on the site, designed to be shared and accessible to all residents, will enhance the livability of a development (see figure 5.3). However, it is important to delineate the common public open space from residents' private open spaces. Private open space is the outdoor area as-

FIGURE 5.3
An Example of Open Space
On the left, the building encompasses the open space for use by residents. On the right, the plantings and fencing denote separation of private space from the public sidewalk.
Image credit: B. Yust.

sociated with a particular housing unit, such as a porch or a small yard. Townhouse developments frequently separate the private outdoor area from the public open space with fencing and/or plantings. In multistory housing, upper-level units may have balconies to accommodate seating to enjoy the air and views. Many multifamily housing developments that have incorporated open space for residents do so through courtyards, community vegetable gardens, and play spaces (Huang, 2006; see chapters 3 and 19).

Landscaping

Well-designed landscaping is important for the appearance of a development and its sense of safety and can also reduce the environmental impact of the development. Plants that are indigenous to the area will generally require less maintenance over time, and many developments in arid communities may be required to use xeriscaping or hardscaping (the use of rocks and pavers that do not require water) (Hayden, Casenaasasi, Haver, and Oki, 2015). In all communities, too much or too little water can create environmental problems, and landscaping can help to mitigate the problems. Water runoff during a storm carries surface pollutants and can contaminate lakes and rivers. Today developments are incorporating permeable pavers to avoid runoff and rain gardens to capture excess water and allow it to be slowly absorbed into the ground (see chapter 19). Plants should be selected and placed so that people cannot hide from view among them. The Crime Prevention through Environmental Design approach (CPTED) (Carter, Carter, & Dannenberg, 2003; Jeffrey, 1971) and the book *Defensible Space* (Newman, 1972) identify how to plan and maintain the physical environment to increase residents' safety and deter criminals.

CONCERNS REGARDING MULTIFAMILY HOUSING

Residents living in multifamily housing have the same concerns as those who live in single-family housing. Foremost is that the housing is affordable (see chapter 10). Residents also need to feel safe, secure, and protected from fire danger. In one's home, a sense of privacy, limited noise transmission, and adequate ventilation for air quality are important (see chapter 3). Because of the proximity of others within a multifamily building, and the limitations on modifications that residents can make to their units, particularly among renters, the concerns discussed here tend to be essential for multifamily housing residents (see chapter 9).

Affordability

As defined by HUD, residents of any housing unit are "housing cost burdened" when their housing costs exceed 30 percent of their income. Residents in multifamily dwellings are disproportionately renters, and renters are more likely to be housing cost burdened because their incomes tend to be lower than incomes of homeowners. Renters do not have control over the rent charged to them, which can increase at the end of each lease period. Over the past decade, with the new household formation of millennials, increased numbers of households of color, and foreclosures, the latter accelerated by the Great Recession, the number and proportion of renters in the

United States has increased across all age groups except for those seventy-five years of age and older (Joint Center for Housing Studies of Harvard University, 2013; see chapters 1, 2, 9, and 10, 15, and 16).

In contrast to renting, an owner of a unit in a multifamily condominium development is responsible for securing a private mortgage to purchase the individual unit (see chapter 8). Additionally, the owner, as a member of the common interest community (homeowners') association, is obligated to pay a monthly fee to the association to cover maintenance and improvement costs for common areas of the building and grounds. Should the individual owner lapse in payment of the association fee, the owner can be foreclosed and lose his or her housing unit, just as he or she can for nonpayment of a mortgage (Giantomasi, 2003; see chapter 15).

Safety and Security

Because multifamily housing developments have multiple residents by definition, it is common for residents not to know one another, especially in rental buildings where the turnover is high (see chapter 9). Residents also invite friends who are typically unknown to other residents and the management to visit. Thus a secure entryway is extremely important for everyone to feel safe while still being convenient for residents. There could be as many as three doors to unlock to gain entry to an actual unit—an exterior door from the street, an interior vestibule door, and the door to the unit—and a balance needs to be crafted between safety and convenience. Because a lock or a keyless entry system can fail, or because someone coming through a door may let others through at the same time, security cameras are more common in larger buildings to monitor those entering (Yuen et al., 2006; see chapter 3).

Fire

Multifamily buildings are designed to meet more stringent fire and smoke resistance, fire protection, and egress codes than single-family dwellings (see chapter 9). Nevertheless, should a fire erupt in a multifamily dwelling, it will affect a greater number of people. New buildings have extensive sprinkler systems to extinguish a fire as close to its source as possible. However, the water used, in addition to the smoke, can create extensive damage and require that many residents find alternative locations to live while repairs are made. Because so many fires start from cooking, some building owners supply small fire extinguishers that attach with a magnet to the underside of an exhaust hood over a range. The extinguisher emits sodium bicarbonate powder, a nontoxic chemical that puts out grease fires immediately. In this way, the fire is contained and damage beyond the range is minimized (e.g., StoveTop FireStop, 2013; see chapter 3).

Privacy

Living in close proximity to others can limit one's anonymity among neighbors. When inside a unit, unless the windows are oriented appropriately, residents may be able to see into other units in adjacent parts of the building. Even though a unit may have private outdoor space, it may be immediately next to another resident's private outdoor space and may not provide desired privacy when using it. Additionally, in most rental buildings, state law provides the property manager the right, and under some funding programs the responsibility, to enter the unit at least once a year to conduct an inspection. In many states, only a twenty-four-hour notice is required by law.

Noise

Noise can best be addressed during the design and construction phases of the building. Party walls, that is, walls shared by two units, can be designed and constructed to minimize noise transmission between all shared walls, floors, and ceilings. For example, wall studs can be staggered so that there is a break from one side of the wall to the other, and insulation in all walls, ceilings, and floors mitigates noise transmission between units and between the unit and the common corridors of the building. Multifamily buildings designed for families with children would especially benefit from sound mitigation so that natural outbursts of children do not create tension between neighbors. The quality of windows specified for the building can help to mitigate noise from outdoor traffic (Thalheimer, 2000; see chapter 18).

Odors

All occupied buildings must manage air quality to avoid problems with excess moisture and mold. In housing, this is done through active ventilation in bathrooms, where a low-volume fan is always on and the capacity increases when a light is turned on, and in kitchens, with ventilation hoods over ranges. However, in multifamily buildings, odors that develop from cooking can permeate the corridors of the building. If residents are of differing cultural backgrounds, they may have different culinary perspectives and may object to odors created by ingredients considered common to other residents. Also, management needs to ensure that the collection area for trash and recyclables is frequently emptied and cleaned to minimize odors that could develop. Another odor problem can occur if the elevator for the building extends from an underground parking garage to the residents' floors. If air quality in the garage is not managed, exhaust odors and contaminants can waft throughout the building (Spengler & Chen, 2000; see chapter 18).

DESIGN TRENDS IN MULTIFAMILY HOUSING

Square Footage

There is a trend today to broaden the range of sizes of units in multifamily housing—both a push to decrease and one to increase the size (James, 2007; see chapter 1). The two impulses are driven by different reasons because larger and smaller units serve different market demands (see chapter 2). In markets where housing is in high demand, particularly for single adults, and the cost is high, such as in San Francisco and Manhattan, reducing the minimum unit square footage allowed in zoning codes is being tested. The problem in both of these markets, however, is that as land and buildings are devoted to single-person units, affordable housing options for families with low incomes become scarcer. Additionally, of all rented housing units, just over 30 percent have three or more bedrooms, whereas of all owner-occupied housing units, over 80 percent have three or more bedrooms.

Communities in the United States experiencing in-migration of families from other countries are experiencing a need for large, affordable rental housing (Clark, Deuloos, & Dieleman, 2000).

Sustainability

Whether by legislation or by owner intent, green building practices are increasing. Owners generally pay for all common utilities, such as electricity for lighting in corridors, so it is to their advantage to select energy- and water-efficient equipment. As these common costs are incorporated into rents, sustainable design elements can benefit renters as well. Some owners are also working with residents to engage in green living practices to increase rates of recycling (Ando & Gosselin, 2005) and reduce overall water and energy use (see chapter 19).

Location

The community context of multifamily housing is important to the well-being of all of the residents in the community. In communities that have limited zoning classifications, such as only single-family dwellings, there may not be sufficient multifamily housing choices for single persons, especially older persons and young adults (Chakraborty, Knaap, Nguyen, & Shin, 2010). Many communities are diversifying their zoning codes so that a mix of housing options is available, allowing a wide variety of household types and income levels to own or rent (Schmitz et al., 2005; see chapters 1, 2, 7, 9, and 10, and 17).

As communities invest in mass-transportation systems, they need a high number of riders to ensure the viability of the systems. Promoting the building of multifamily dwellings along transit corridors can provide the density necessary for ridership and reduce the need for automobile ownership. Transit-oriented development (TOD) encourages linking housing and transportation through planning and incentives for development. In recent years, the opportunity to walk to local commercial areas has been examined as a health benefit as well as a housing benefit. Planning multifamily housing to enable residents to walk or bike to stores, services, and adjacent developments improves livability (Larco, Stockard, Steiner, & West, 2013). Understanding the culture of a community can help to identify the most important connections (Al-Hormoud, 2003).

Mixed Developments

There are at least four types of mixed developments: (1) developments with a variety of income requirements for units within the building, (2) developments with spaces for residential and commercial purposes within the building, (3) developments that combine permanent housing units with a hotel setting, and (4) developments that allow different uses of space within the unit. All of these types attempt to attract a diverse market and serve community needs (Tong & Wong, 1997; see chapter 2).

A great deal of work has been done on increasing the diversity of socioeconomic levels of households in communities, and the same trend is occurring in multifamily buildings (see chapter 16). Rent subsidies for some residents and market-rate rents for others diversify the income range of

FIGURE 5.4

An Example of Mixed Use
This building, containing only forty-nine apartment homes, most of them affordable to low-income families, was designed to include a retail establishment on the first floor. After the space was marketed for a number of years, a childcare center leased it. It is open seven days a week and until 11:00 p.m. on weekdays to help families who must work late shifts.
Image credit: B. Yust.

households living in proximity to one another (see chapter 14). This diversity is viewed as an advantage to the owners of buildings because they can market the property to a variety of households. Also, residents have the potential to meet a wider variety of households than they might otherwise encounter (Joseph, Chaskin, & Webber, 2007).

Historically, commercial corridors in neighborhoods consisted of buildings with retail establishments on the first level and residential units on upper floors. Over time, communities enacted zoning that limited mixed uses in buildings (see chapters 9 and 12). Recently, cities and their residents have come to understand the advantages of allowing for mixed uses within the same structure and have adopted zoning that reflects how cities traditionally developed. Retail businesses on the ground floor can serve the residents of the neighborhood as well as those living in the building (see figure 5.4). Financing can be more complicated for these developments, but there are many successful models (Gyourko & Rybczynski, 2000).

A recent trend has been to combine the housing and hospitality industries into one structure. Hotels serve individuals on a temporary basis but also have amenities that can be too expensive to provide in a multifamily housing building. By combining hotel rooms and housing units in the same building, all residents benefit from, for example, concierge services, restaurants, airport transportation service, shops, business services, and fitness centers, to name a few. Either renting the housing units or selling them as condominiums with a monthly association fee can provide a stable base of monthly income for the building owner, limiting the effect of times when hotel rooms are undersold (Rutes, 2001).

Finally, accelerated by the most recent economic downturn (see chapter 15), individuals may desire to work for income in their homes. In a multifamily building, some types of work could create concerns for other residents. Work that is best suited for this arrangement is that which does not require clients to visit the person in the unit, does not involve hazardous materials, and does not create noise. Individuals have worked in their homes for centuries, but in multifamily housing there may be restrictions, such as explicit prohibitions on commercial activity, that could violate one's lease.

Alternatively, there are developments that are designed to encourage living and working in the dwelling unit (Dolan, 2012). The most common of these is artists' lofts, and in successful artist developments, large studios for painting, sculpture, and dance are provided in common areas of the building. In addition to local zoning codes, the International Building Code (International Code Council, 2012) includes standards for designing and building live-work dwellings to ensure safety for all of the residents.

DESIGN CONCERNS FOR SPECIAL POPULATIONS

Many people with special needs may benefit from living in multifamily housing. Housing built specifically for low-income elderly persons has been funded under the federal Section 202 program since 1959, and market-rate age-segregated cooperatives are a popular option for elderly persons who wish to be in a community of other elders. Assisted-living housing for elderly persons offers a menu of services selected and paid for by the individual elder. Multifamily housing brings elders together, which can improve their social interactions and subsequent quality of life. In the design of these units, providing for gathering spaces on each floor, such as near the elevator, and community spaces on the ground floor can promote interactions and limit the isolation of elders (Kweon, Sullivan, & Wiley, 1998; see chapter 17).

Based on funding sources, multifamily housing may be required to provide a certain percentage of units that meet accessibility requirements. These units are designed so that residents can fully utilize the kitchen and bath in their units. Ideally, all housing units would employ universal design so that should a resident experience a mobility disability, he or she would not have to move in order to continue to live independently (Crews & Zavotka, 2006; see chapters 3 and 17).

Individuals with mental health disabilities may require supportive social services to maintain their ability to live independently. Also, older youth who are no longer eligible for foster care often need services to transition to work and educational programs while living independently. The design of multifamily housing for these populations will require private office space for service providers and possibly space on each floor for residents (Nelson, Aubry, and Lafrance, 2007).

BEYOND DESIGN

Development of multifamily residential structures requires market analysis, site selection and entitlement, funding, construction, and marketing. The design of a building must respond to each of these elements. Because the predominant housing structure in the United States is the single-family detached home, opposition to multifamily housing is common in some neighborhoods as well as in small towns and rural areas (Obrinsky & Stein, 2007). Multifamily housing can meet the need for affordable housing (see chapter 9), especially when new industries locate in small towns, and good design can help to assuage opposition. However, design alone may not quell opposition toward affordable multifamily housing, so involvement with the community early on in a project is critical to its ultimate success (Schmitz et al., 2005).

Whether the housing units are owned or rented, a management structure is required for multifamily housing developments. Management practices and policies can help achieve a positive experience for residents or can result in a negative experience even when the design of the building is of the highest quality. Resident satisfaction in both market-rate and affordable developments and owned and rented developments is affected directly by management through, for example, resident selection policies, enforcement of rules, effective communication with residents, responsiveness and dependability of staff, and maintenance and cleanliness of common areas (Paris & Kangari, 2005).

CONCLUSION

Multifamily housing is an important housing option for households at all income levels and across the lifespan. A community with a diversity of housing types and price points can meet a variety of housing needs. Citizens can remain in the same community as their needs change due to family formation, aging, or changing income (see chapters 10 and 17). Also, because by definition multifamily housing is at a higher density than single-family detached dwellings, the increased number of people can provide an expanded base for economic development and public transportation demand in the community.

Well-designed developments improve the quality of life for their residents as well as for the community in which they are located. The markets served by multifamily housing are broad, from renters by choice, to high-end condominium owners, to live-work residents, to low-income elderly residents. A development team that has common goals can ensure that the development will meet residents' needs, will fit within the context of the site and the neighborhood, and will be sustainable (see chapters 12, 13, 18, and 19).

REFERENCES

Aiello, A., Ardone, R. G., & Scopelliti, M. (2010). Neighbourhood planning improvement: Physical attributes, cognitive and affective evaluation and activities in two neighbourhoods in Rome. *Evaluation and Program Planning, 33*(3), 264–275.

Al-Hormoud, M. (2003). Functional distance effect on social interactions in multifamily housing in Jordan. *Housing and Society, 30*(2), 165–188.

Amole, D. (2009). Residential satisfaction in students. *Journal of Environmental Psychology, 29*(1), 76–85.

Ando, A. W., & Gosselin, A. Y. (2005). Recycling in multifamily dwellings: Does convenience matter? *Economic Inquiry, 43*(2), 426–439.

Carter, S. P., Carter, S. L., & Dannenberg, A. L. (2003). Zoning out crime and improving community health in Sarasota, Florida: "Crime prevention through environmental design." *American Journal of Public Health, 93*(9), 1442–1445.

Chakraborty, A., Knaap, G.-J., Nguyen, D., & Shin, J. H. (2010). The effects of high-density zoning on multifamily housing construction in the suburbs of six U.S. metropolitan areas. *Urban Studies, 47*, 437–451.

Chermayeff, S., & Alexander, C. (1963). *Community and privacy*. New York: Doubleday.

Clark, W. A., Deurloo, M. C., & Dieleman, F. M. (2000). Housing consumption and residential crowding in U.S. housing markets. *Journal of Urban Affairs, 22*(1), 49–63.

Crews, D. E., & Zavotka, S. (2006). Aging, disability, and frailty: Implications for universal design. *Journal of Physiological Anthropology, 25*(1), 113–118.

Davis, S. (1995). *The architecture of affordable housing*. Berkeley: University of California Press.

Dolan, T. (2012). *Live-work planning and design: Zero-commute housing*. Hoboken, N.J.: John Wiley & Sons.

Edwards, L., & Torcellini, P. A. (2002). *A literature review of the effects of natural light on building occupants*. Golden, Colo.: National Renewable Energy Laboratory.

Evans, D. (2001). *Affordable housing design advisor*. Newark, N.J.: Center for Building Knowledge, New Jersey Institute of Technology. Retrieved June 15, 2016, from www.designadvisor.org.

Farris, J. T. (2001). The barriers to using urban infill development to achieve smart growth. *Housing Policy Debate, 12*(1), 1–30.

Friedman, A. (2007). The use of architectural flexibility for achieving affordability in housing. In W. M. Rohe & H. L. Watson (Eds.), *Chasing the American dream: New perspectives on affordable homeownership* (pp. 146–168). Ithaca, N.Y.: Cornell University Press.

Giantomasi, G. (2003). A balancing act: The foreclosure power of homeowners' associations. *Fordham Law Review, 72*, 2503–2542.

González-Torre, P. L., & Adenso-Díaz, B. (2005). Influence of distance on the motivation and frequency of household recycling. *Waste Management, 25*(1), 15–23.

Goodman, J. (1999). The changing demography of multifamily rental housing. *Housing Policy Debate, 10*(1), 31–57.

Guo, Z., & Ren, S. (2013). From minimum to maximum: Impact of the London parking reform on residential parking supply from 2004 to 2010? *Urban Studies, 50*(6), 1183–1200.

Gyourko, J. E., & Rybczynski, W. (2000). Financing new urbanism projects: Obstacles and solutions. *Housing Policy Debate, 11*(3), 733–750.

Hanlon, B. (2014). Suburban challenges. In L. Benton-Short (Ed.), *Cities of North America: Contemporary challenges in U.S. and Canadian cities* (pp. 273–296). Plymouth, UK: Rowman and Littlefield.

Hayden, L., Cadenasso, M. L., Haver, D., & Oki, L. R. (2015). Residential landscape aesthetics and water conservation best management practices: Homeowner perceptions and preferences. *Landscape and Urban Planning, 144*, 1–9.

Huang, S. C. L. (2006). A study of outdoor interactional spaces in high-rise housing. *Landscape and Urban Planning, 78*(3), 193–204.

Hurd, A-P. (2014). How outdated parking laws price families out of the city. CityLab. Retrieved January 26, 2017, from http://www.citylab.com/housing/2014/08/how-outdated-parking-laws-price-families-out-of-the-city/375646/.

International Code Council. (2012). *International building code*. Brea, Calif.: Author.

James, R. N. (2007). Multifamily housing characteristics and tenant satisfaction. *Journal of Performance of Constructed Facilities, 21*(6), 472–480.

Jeffrey, C. R. (1971). *Crime prevention through environmental design (CPTED)*. Beverly Hills, Calif.: Sage.

Jiang, L., & O'Neill, B. C. (2007). Impacts of demographic trends on U.S. household size and structure. *Population and Development Review, 33*(3), 567–591.

Joint Center for Housing Studies of Harvard University. (2013). *America's rental housing: Evolving markets and needs*. Boston, Mass.: Author.

Joseph, M. L., Chaskin, R. J., & Webber, H. S. (2007). The theoretical basis for addressing poverty through mixed-income development. *Urban Affairs Review, 42*(3), 369–409.

Kaplan, R. (2001). The nature of the view from home: Psychological benefits. *Environment and Behavior, 33*(4), 507–542.

Kelly, E. (2009). *Practical apartment management*. Chicago: Institute of Real Estate Management.

Kowaltowski, D. C., da Silva, V. G., Pina, S. A., Labaki, L. C., Ruschel, R. C., & de Carvalho Moreira, D. (2006). Quality of life and sustainability issues as seen by the population of low-income housing in the region of Campinas, Brazil. *Habitat International, 30*(4), 1100–1114.

Kweon, B. S., Sullivan, W. C., & Wiley, A. R. (1998). Green common spaces and the social integration of inner-city older adults. *Environment and Behavior, 30*(6), 832–858.

Langbein, L., & Spotswood-Bright, K. (2004). Efficiency, accountability, and private government: The impact of residential community associations on residential property values. *Social Science Quarterly, 85*(3), 640–659.

Larco, N., Stockard, J., Steiner, B., & West, A. (2013). Trips to strips: Walking and site design in suburban multifamily housing. *Journal of Urban Design, 18*(2), 281–303.

Lee, H-J., Beamish, J. O., & Goss, R. C. (2008). Location preferences of multifamily housing residents. *Housing and Society, 35*(1), 41–58.

Lee, H-J., Goss, R. C., & Beamish, J. O. (2007). Influence of lifestyle on housing preferences of multifamily housing residents. *Housing and Society, 34*(1), 11–30.

Lenth, B. A., Knight, R. L., & Gilgert, W. C. (2006). Conservation value of clustered housing developments. *Conservation Biology, 20*(5), 1445–1456.

Levy, M. P., & Tartaro, C. (2010). Auto theft: A site-survey and analysis of environmental crime factors in Atlantic City, N.J. *Security Journal, 23*(2), 75–94.

Naderi, J. R. (2003). Landscape design in clear zone: Effect of landscape variables on pedestrian health and driver safety. *Transportation Research Record: Journal of the Transportation Research Board, 1851*(1), 119–130.

Nelson, G., Aubry, T., & Lafrance, A. (2007). A review of the literature on the effectiveness of housing and support, assertive community treatment, and intensive case management interventions for persons with mental illness who have been homeless. *American Journal of Orthopsychiatry, 77*(3), 350–361.

Newman, O. (1972). *Defensible space: Crime prevention through urban design.* New York: Macmillan.

Obrinsky, M., & Stein, D. (2007). *Overcoming opposition to multifamily rental housing.* (White paper.) Washington, D.C.: National Multifamily Housing Council.

O'Connor, Z. (2006). Bridging the gap: Façade colour, aesthetic response, and planning policy. *Journal of Urban Design, 11*(3), 335–345.

Odum, C. O. (2015). Residents' satisfaction with integration of the natural environment in public housing design. *International Journal of Housing Markets and Analysis, 8*(1), 73–96.

Paris, D. E., & Kangari, R. (2005). Multifamily affordable housing: Residential satisfaction. *Journal of Performance of Constructed Facilities, 19*(2), 138–146.

Peiser, R., & Hamilton, D. (2012). *Professional real estate development.* Washington, D.C.: Urban Land Use Institute.

Power, A. (2008). Does demolition or refurbishment of old and inefficient homes help to increase our environmental, social, and economic viability? *Energy Policy, 36*(12), 4487–4501.

Riis, J. A. (1997). *How the other half lives: Studies among the tenements of New York.* New York: Penguin.

Rutes, W. A. (2001). *Hotel design: Planning and development.* New York: W. W. Norton.

Sante, L. (1991). *Low life: Lures and snares of old New York.* New York: Farrar, Straus, and Giroux.

Schmitz, A., Corcoran, S., Gournay, I., Kuhnert, M., Pyatok, M., Retsinas, N., & Scully, J. (2005). *Affordable housing: Designing an American asset.* Washington, D.C.: Urban Land Institute.

Skobba, K. (2012). Multifamily housing. In A. Carswell (Ed.), *The encyclopedia of housing* (2nd ed.) (pp. 489–493). Thousand Oaks, Calif.: Sage.

Spengler, J. D., & Chen, Q. (2000). Indoor air quality factors in designing a healthy building. *Annual Review of Energy and the Environment, 25*(1), 567–600.

Stamps, A. (2013). *Psychology and the aesthetics of the built environment.* Heidelberg: Springer Science & Business Media.

StoveTop FireStop. (2013). Housing Authority to install StoveTop FireStop. Retrieved January 26, 2017, from http://www.stovetopfirestop.com/2013/10/news/housing-authority-to-install-stovetop-firestop.

Stubbs, M. (2002). Car parking and residential development: Sustainability, design and planning policy, and public perceptions of parking provision. *Journal of Urban Design, 7*(2), 213–237.

Thalheimer, E. (2000). Construction noise control program and mitigation strategy at the Central Artery/Tunnel Project. *Noise Control Engineering Journal, 48*(5), 157–165.

Tong, C. O., & Wong, S. C. (1997). The advantages of a high density, mixed land use, linear urban development. *Transportation, 24*(3), 295–307.

U.S. Bureau of the Census. (2013). *General housing data: All occupied units, Table C-01-AO*. Retrieved January 26, 2017, from http://www.census.gov/programs-surveys/ahs/data.2013.html.

Varady, D. P., & Preiser, W. F. (1998). Scattered-site public housing and housing satisfaction: Implications for the new public housing program. *Journal of the American Planning Association, 64*(2), 189–207.

Wang, N., & Horner, R. M. W. (2012). Is privatization the answer for social housing? A comparative study of China and the United Kingdom. *Housing and Society, 39*(1), 99–124.

Wingler, H. M. (1969). *The Bauhaus*. Boston: MIT Press.

Yuen, B., Yeh, A., Appold, S. J., Earl, G., Ting, J., & Kurnianingrum Kwee, L. (2006). High-rise living in Singapore public housing. *Urban Studies, 43*(3), 583–600.

Chapter 6

Universal Design in Housing

SANDRA C. HARTJE, HEIDI H. EWEN,
AND KENNETH R. TREMBLAY

Universal design (UD), also called inclusive design, lifespan design, or design-for-all, may be conceptualized as a paradigm, a social movement, an example, a prototype, or an approach to design (McGuire & Scott, 2006; Scott, McGuire, & Shaw, 2003). Perceptions of product designs, the built environment, and human ability have evolved, and will continue to evolve, as researchers expand their understanding and as building technologies are developed. Increasingly, social reformers are integrating UD into action plans and standards, including the Convention on the Rights of Persons with Disabilities, passed in 2009 (Ostroff, 2011). Architects, contractors, and interior designers have operationalized UD in practice, regarding it as an approach to design (see figures 6.1 and 6.2).

In the most functional sense, UD is a design approach that recognizes the wide range of human abilities (physical, cognitive, and sensory) and accommodates the changes most people experience over their lifespan. L. Young (2011) argues that this design approach strives to make practical, day-to-day tasks possible and safer for the global population. When a product cannot be used as intended, or when a setting is incompatible with a person's abilities, it is a failure of the design, not the individual (Moore, 2001). The Center for Universal Design (CUD) at North Carolina State University (CUD, n.d.: n.p.) formally defines UD as the design of products and environments that are "usable by all people, to the greatest extent possible, without the need for adaptation or specialized design." The intentions and results of integrating UD are to simplify life for everyone by adjusting the built environment to make products more usable by as many people as possible at little or no extra cost. Therefore, UD benefits people of all ages, sizes, heights, abilities, and limitations (Pilarski & Rath, 2013).

UD benefits people through all life stages, including children, seniors, and those inconvenienced by a temporary or permanent injury or a progressive medical condition. In doing so, it respects human diversity, allows for mastery over the environment, and promotes inclusion of all people in all activities of life (Story, Mueller, & Mace, 1998). For example, a person pushing a baby stroller will appreciate a nonstep entrance (see chapter 17). A child or seated person can help prepare meals in a kitchen with varying-

FIGURE 6.1
Baldwin Residence, Seattle, Washington
The nonstep entrance shows a gently sloping path into the front entry, which makes it easy for anyone using wheels, from strollers to bicycles to rolling suitcases, as well as anyone using a wheelchair or scooter. The exterior door is 3 ft. wide, and the threshold is level. The house numbers are large and visible from a distance.
Image credit: Dale Lang, NW Architectural Photography (http://www.nwphoto.net). Reprinted with permission.

FIGURE 6.2
Baldwin Residence, Seattle, Washington, Back Side of Building
Image credit: Dale Lang, NW Architectural Photography (http://www.nwphoto.net). Reprinted with permission.

height countertops (see chapter 3). Movers, paramedics, and firefighters will appreciate wider doors and hallways on moving day or in emergencies, when there will be more flexibility for navigating the space or helping people.

UD also benefits people who would like to age in place. The AARP Home and Community Preferences of the 45+ Population survey showed that most adults age forty-five and older want to age in place rather than relocate to a different home or community. Seventy-eight percent of respondents stated that they would like to stay in their current residence as long as possible, while 80 percent stated that they would like to remain in their local community for as long as possible (AARP Research and Strategic Analysis, 2014). Incorporating UD into homes can help older adults achieve these goals (see chapter 17).

UD in housing supports social, economic, and environmental sustainability. Social sustainability is reflected in a person's ability to live in his or her home and neighborhood through his or her lifespan. Additionally, the individual is able to move about safely inside the home and feel comfortable, secure, and independent in his or her home (see chapter 18). Economic sustainability, or cost efficiency, is achieved in newly built homes partially by reducing extensive remodels and expensive retrofitting and delaying moves to long-term care facilities (see chapter 17). Finally, environmental sustainability is enabled through the efficient use of resources, such as construction materials, water, waste, and energy (see chapter 19). In terms of a bigger picture, UD makes connections among housing characteristics, the neighborhood, transportation choices, and community to ensure a healthy, sustainable community (L. Young, 2011; see chapters 2, 12, and 13).

This chapter discusses (a) the conceptualization, evolution, and foundations of UD; (b) the benefits of UD in housing; (c) the integration of UD into the overall design of the home; and (d) the design principles of a universally designed home. The chapter then provides a case study of a universally designed home in Seattle, Washington. Finally, we discuss policies and programs to implement UD in housing and conclude with a discussion on the expansion of the implementation of UD in housing.

CONCEPTUALIZING UNIVERSAL DESIGN

Within the human population, there is a range of physical and psychological abilities. Individuals vary in age, size, height, ability, and physical and psychological task limitations. Therefore, understanding these variations is critical for designing effectively. Physical human abilities include proprioception (i.e., sensing where one's bodily limbs are with one's eyes closed), muscle function and mobility, vision, hearing, and touch. Psychological abilities include interpreting bodily sensations, mental acuity, problem solving, and executive functioning (e.g., managing time, maintaining attention, and planning). Variation in any of these areas may affect design usability, the types of people who may use a design, and ways to test a product or environment to assess its broad usability (Story et al., 1998).

The benefits of UD may be experienced by all populations but may be essential for those who have limits in their abilities to perform daily tasks. Most people are able to perform the most basic tasks essential for living independently. Activities of daily living (ADLs) include dressing, bathing, and using the toilet (Palmer & Harley, 2011). Instrumental activities of daily living (IADLs) are more complex and include keeping track of appointments and managing finances (e.g., balancing a checkbook). A considerable proportion (13 percent) of adults over the age of sixty-five experience cognitive impairments (Mebane-Sims, 2009) and an even higher proportion (22 percent) of persons with developmental disabilities experience difficulties with ADLs and IADLs (Fisher & Kettl, 2005; Kottorp, Bernspang, & Fisher, 2003). Over time, due to normal aging, disease, or disability, many people experience declines in their abilities to perform ADLs and IADLs. Typically, the greater the number of activity limitations, the greater the disability (see chapter 17). Although UD is not design for people with disabilities, they receive significant benefits from UD.

EVOLUTION OF UNIVERSAL DESIGN

UD is a relatively young approach to design that has evolved over the past four decades. It began with the assistive technology, barrier-free design, and architectural accessibility movements of the 1940s and 1950s, when thousands of disabled veterans returned from World War II and the Korean War

(Story et al., 1998). Thus, in the 1940s and 1950s, efforts to improve prosthetics and orthotics intensified. In the 1960s and 1970s rehabilitation engineering research centers were established to address technological problems of rehabilitation, including communication, mobility, and transportation. Rehabilitation engineering became a specialty that applied scientific principles and engineering methodologies to these challenges. The label *assistive technology* was applied to devices for personal use created specifically to enhance the physical, sensory, and cognitive abilities of people with disabilities and to help them function more independently in environments incompatible with their needs (Story et al., 1998).

In the 1970s, Michael Bednar, an American architect, introduced the idea that removing barriers in the built environment enhanced the functional capacity of not only disabled but also nondisabled people. He suggested that a broader, more universal concept beyond accessibility was needed (Bednar, 1977). Thus the UD movement emerged from the recognition that many features that were attractive and marketable, yet less expensive, could be commonly provided.

Ron Mace, a U.S. architect who used a wheelchair and a ventilator as a result of post-polio syndrome, began using the term *universal design* in the 1980s and worked to define it in relation to accessible design (Institute for Human Centered Design, 2016a). Mace argued that UD is "not a new science, a style or unique in any way. It requires only an awareness of need and market and a commonsense approach to making everything we design and produce usable by everyone to the greatest extent possible" (Institute for Human Centered Design, n.d.: n.p.). In sum, UD is an approach in which designers strive to incorporate features that make each design more universally usable. The principles of UD were developed further in 1997 by a working group of designers, architects, engineers, and researchers (Connell et al., 1997). These principles are discussed further in the next section.

FOUNDATIONS OF UNIVERSAL DESIGN

Understanding foundations that support UD assists both professionals and consumers in understanding and applying this approach to design. The Institute for Human Centered Design (IHCD), *The Principles of Universal Design* (Connell et al., 1997), and the cornerstones of UD provide examples of foundational concepts. The Institute for Human Centered Design (n.d.) has two core convictions that drive the perspective that UD must become intrinsic to good design. The first is that design influences people's daily lives, sense of control, and comfort and therefore is powerful. The second is that variability in human capabilities is truly ordinary. Previously, UD was a way of conceptualizing design based on four premises: first, good design understands that varying ability is a common characteristic of being human; second, good design works for all individuals, regardless of presence or absence of a disability; third, good design includes both aesthetics and usability, which are not mutually exclusive; and fourth, good design shows that physical and emotional well-being are influenced by a sense of comfort and safety and our ability to master our environment (Institute for Human Centered Design, 2016b).

The Principles of Universal Design were developed in 1997 by the CUD to guide the design of environments, products, and communications. The

Principle 1: Equitable Use	
Definition:	The design is useful and marketable to people with diverse abilities.
Guidelines:	1a. Provide the same means of use for all users: identical whenever possible; equivalent when not. 1b. Avoid segregating or stigmatizing any users. 1c. Provisions for privacy, security, and safety should be equally available to all users. 1d. Make the design appealing to all users.
Principle 2: Flexibility in Use	
Definition:	The design accommodates a wide range of individual preferences and abilities.
Guidelines:	2a. Provide choice in method of use. 2b. Accommodate right- or left-handed access and use. 2c. Facilitate the user's accuracy and precision. 2d. Provide adaptability to the user's pace.
Principle 3: Simple and Intuitive Use	
Definition:	The use of the design is easy to understand, regardless of the user's experience, knowledge, language skills, or current concentration level.
Guidelines:	3a. Eliminate unnecessary complexity. 3b. Be consistent with user expectations and intuition. 3c. Accommodate a wide range of literacy and language skills. 3d. Arrange information consistent with its importance. 3e. Provide effective prompting and feedback during and after task completion.
Principle 4: Perceptible Information	
Definition:	The design communicates necessary information effectively to the user, regardless of ambient conditions or the user's sensory abilities.
Guidelines:	4a. Use different modes (pictorial, verbal, tactile) for redundant presentation of essential information. 4b. Maximize "legibility" of essential information. 4c. Differentiate elements in ways that can be described (i.e., make it easy to give instructions or directions). 4d. Provide compatibility with a variety of techniques or devices used by people with sensory limitations.
Principle 5: Tolerance for Error	
Definition:	The design minimizes hazards and the adverse consequences of accidental or unintended actions.
Guidelines:	5a. Arrange elements to minimize hazards and errors: most-used elements, most accessible; hazardous elements eliminated, isolated, or shielded. 5b. Provide warnings of hazards and errors. 5c. Provide fail-safe features. 5d. Discourage unconscious action in tasks that require vigilance.
Principle 6: Low Physical Effort	
Definition:	The design can be used efficiently and comfortably and with a minimum of fatigue.
Guidelines:	6a. Allow user to maintain a neutral body position. 6b. Use reasonable operating forces. 6c. Minimize repetitive actions. 6d. Minimize sustained physical effort.
Principle 7: Size and Space for Approach and Use	
Definition:	Appropriate size and space is provided for approach, reach, manipulation, and use regardless of user's body size, posture, or mobility.
Guidelines:	7a. Provide a clear line of sight to important elements for any seated or standing user. 7b. Make reach to all components comfortable for any seated or standing user. 7c. Accommodate variations in hand and grip size. 7d. Provide adequate space for the use of assistive devices or personal assistance.

FIGURE 6.3
The Principles of Universal Design, Version 2.0
Source: Connell et al., 1997.

principles have been used to evaluate existing designs, guide the design process, and educate people about the characteristics of more usable products and environments. Although the principles address the usable aspect of design, the actual practice of design and the application of the design process may also consider economics, engineering, culture, gender, and environmental concerns. These principles offer designers guidance to better integrate design features that meet the needs of as many users as possible. Figure 6.3 presents the seven principles of UD, with the definition and guidelines developed by the CUD.

More recently, Null (2014) has posited, based on the underlying principles developed by Mace, that four cornerstones should be considered essential for creating UD:

1. **Supportive:** the design should "provide a necessary aid to function, and it must not, in providing such aid, create any undue burden on any user";
2. **Adaptable:** "a product or environment should serve a majority of individuals who have a variety of changing needs";
3. **Accessible:** attitudinal and physical barriers are removed;
4. **Safety oriented:** the design promotes health and well-being and is corrective and preventative (Null, 2014: 13–16).

According to Null, these four interrelated aspects of a design provide useful standards for the measurement and evaluation of new and existing products and environments.

BENEFITS OF UNIVERSAL DESIGN IN HOUSING

Residents of UD housing enjoy advantages over those who reside in traditional housing. Most homes are designed for an average person with average physical abilities. According to the CUD, "living spaces have long been designed for use by one 'average' physical type—young, fit, male and adult" (CUD, 2000: 4). However, "average" does not accurately represent the majority of people, including children, women, older adults, or people with permanent physical disabilities. Functioning at peak ability is often a temporary state of being, given that the aging process slows sensory and motor systems (Null, 2014). In addition, many people may experience temporary disabilities, such as a broken limb or a serious illness, or conditions such as pregnancy. The composition of the population is changing. Many people survive permanently disabling accidents and illnesses, and even more are living longer (see chapter 17). It would seem logical that spaces built to accommodate the population must, by necessity, change.

INTEGRATION OF UNIVERSAL DESIGN INTO THE OVERALL DESIGN OF THE HOME

UD uses a range of attitudinal, design, and construction adjustments to create improved living spaces that benefit everyone, yet it is flexible enough to be adapted to specific needs as circumstances change in people's lives. UD is not a particular housing type or style. From the outside, a universally designed home will look similar to a traditionally designed one. Incorporating UD features and products during the design and construction phase of housing results in an integrated housing design that is safe and easy to use (Joines, 2009).

Integrating UD features and products in new home construction results in a design that is both functional and aesthetically pleasing. By contrast, features and products added in a renovation or remodel may look like add-ons, with the design features standing out and giving the home an institutional appearance. For example, navigating steps is often difficult and unsafe for individuals who experience problems walking, for individuals pushing strollers, or for movers (Greiman & Ravesloot, 2016; Shaikh, Kauppi, & Pallard, 2013). A solution is to berm the entrance (i.e., grading the yard to create a gently sloping walk to one or more entries to the home). A bermed entrance can be incorporated into a newly constructed home or accomplished as a renovation to existing housing (L. C. Young, 2006). Unlike many ramped entries added later on, bermed entrances do not carry the risk of a stigmatizing appearance, do not look temporary or added on, and are often landscaped to become an attractive entry to a home (Steinfeld & Maisel, 2012).

Safety and Ease of Use

As safety is of utmost concern in utilizing design features and products, a key goal of UD is to minimize the possibility of accidents by making features easier and more convenient to use. For example, lever handles on faucets or hands-free faucets can be operated with a closed fist or a hand motion. Electric outlets installed at a height of eighteen inches, rather than the standard of fifteen inches, make it easier to plug in an electrical cord and may prevent problems related to balance or vision and potentially prevent a fall. Installing door handles instead of doorknobs allows people to open a door with an elbow or arm when their hands are full. Therefore, UD results in safety, convenience, and ease of use (Null, 2014; see chapter 17).

Emotional Support

UD offers emotional support by creating homes usable throughout the lifespan. UD may minimize and even eliminate the traumatic experience of older adults needing to leave the comfort and security of familiar surroundings and a community of neighbors and friends because they are no longer able to climb stairs in their own homes (Young and Pace, 2001). There is a vast body of scholarly literature on the importance of aging in place and the role of home as an expression, or continuation, of self (Mallet, 2004; Oswald & Werner-Wahl, 2005; Taylor, 2009) (see chapter 17).

Cost-Effectiveness

Universally designed housing is financially cost-effective both in the short and long term. In the short term there are the initial costs for design and construction, and in the long term there are the saved costs of future remodeling or moving. Consideration could also be given to cost savings in terms of minimizing human costs and not changing the design of housing.

Designing and building a home with UD features and products may cost slightly more than building a conventional home. Many variables influence the cost of new housing construction, including the site costs, the hard costs

TABLE 6.1
UD Features, Cost to Household, Post versus Ante Construction

UD feature	Cost to household post construction	Cost to household ante construction
Widen the hallway to accommodate a wheelchair	$4,500 (if increasing the hallway at the expense of the bedrooms and living rooms); or $10,000 (if maintaining the same living area and moving the external walls)	$1,200 to allow for the extra floor area, or no cost if the design was carefully considered
Widen the internal and external doors	$4,000	$300
Ramp to the front door	$700	$0 (the house would be designed with level thresholds)

Source: Queensland Government, Department of Housing, 2015.

for building and interiors (i.e., materials, construction, and labor), and the soft costs (i.e., design fees, taxes, and insurance) (American Institute of Architects, n.d.). The cost difference for interior design components such as lever door handles instead of knobs, 3-foot-wide doors, wider hallways, and placement of electrical outlets and switches may be minimal. Some estimates of cost for UD features approximate 1–3 percent for new construction and up to 10–15 percent for renovation of an existing home (Plough Foundation, 2015). Other estimates state that the costs of essential UD housing features add 0–5 percent to the otherwise equivalent typical home built without UD features (Richard Duncan, personal communication, 2015). However, costs can actually range considerably higher if many additional features or higher-cost products and fixtures are used. Incorporating a shaft for an eventual elevator in a multistory home can be expensive at the time of construction but may save money if the elevator is needed later. The single biggest costs are design and engineering challenges for the entrance, as access can involve the close consideration of site selection, orientation, grading, and foundation styles. However, altering an existing home to accommodate changing abilities or lifestyles can cost up to three times more than including the same features during the initial design and build stage, as the footprint of the home needs to be altered. Table 6.1 compares and contrasts costs to a household post versus ante construction for the case of the state of Queensland in Australia.

Costs notwithstanding, basic UD features are achievable in homes of any size, although affordable housing developers and market-rate builders state that the smaller the size of the home, the greater the challenges associated with achieving a universal outcome (Duncan, personal communication, 2015). However, the experiences of affordable homebuilders, such as Habitat for Humanity, have shown that basic UD can be achieved even in extremely modest-sized homes, such as a 1,200-square-foot home with three bedrooms. In the future, the cost of UD planning and products will decrease as this design approach becomes more established and standardized, as professionals in the construction industry become more knowledgeable and experienced, and as products are increasingly available (Null, 2014).

DESIGN PRINCIPLES OF A UNIVERSALLY DESIGNED HOME

A universally designed home is comprehensive and holistic, incorporating UD features, materials, and products at all levels, from site selection, to space planning and room arrangements, to materials, individual products, and appliances. The difference between incorporating some UD features and products into housing (partial) and designing and building a universally designed home (whole) will be influenced by the scope of the project and by many levels of consideration, such as

1. The housing type, whether
    a. new construction or home modification/retrofit;
    b. new construction, custom, or speculative housing and single unit or part of a development; and
    c. single-family or multifamily.
2. The scope of the plan's
    a. interior and/or exterior spaces of the housing unit; and
    b. the relationship between the housing unit, the site, the neighborhood, and the community.
3. The phase of design or construction when decisions are being made regarding UD features and/or product characteristics'
    a. planning;
    b. selection of materials/products; and/or
    c. during construction.
4. The application of building codes and laws to the project
    a. local;
    b. state; or
    c. national.

Housing producers and consumers may begin a discussion of the design features and products to be incorporated into housing to make it universal by applying the principles of UD to housing design and products. The examples presented in figure 6.4 are neither exhaustive nor exclusive. For some principles an explanation of the benefits is provided.

Examples of UD features and products are available from a range of sources and in a variety of formats for housing consumers and industry professionals. The examples may include ideas and concepts that contribute to or can be components of UD or lists of design features and product characteristics. The examples may be presented (1) by the location, either interior or exterior; (2) by the room or space in which they are to be located, such as the bathroom or entrance; (3) in the categories of structural or nonstructural elements (structural elements are most cost-effectively incorporated in the design phase of new construction but may also be incorporated in major remodels, while nonstructural features are incorporated into a finished housing unit); and (4) in tiers, such as essential or advanced design features, or as silver, gold, and platinum. There are many checklists that may be used as a guide in the design phase or for postconstruction verification (Sandler, 2009; U.S. Department of Housing and Urban Development, 1996).

FIGURE 6.4
Examples of the Principles of UD Applied to Housing
Source: Authors, based on National Association of Home Builders Research Center and Barrier Free Environments, 1996; and CUD, 2006.

Principle 1: Equitable Use
■ Multiple-height countertops ■ Cutting boards ■ Wider interior doorways ■ Side-by-side refrigerator
Principle 2: Flexibility in Use
■ Full-extension pull-out pantries and drawers ■ Railings on both sides of the stairs ■ Curbless shower, adjustable-height movable hand-held showerhead or a 60–72 in. flexible hose that allows easy use by people of varying heights ■ 48 in. work aisles ■ Multiple counter heights ■ D-shaped pulls ■ Rocker light switches
Principle 3: Simple and Intuitive Use
■ Step-less entrance ■ Offset water controls in the shower and tub allow for easy access from outside the tub/shower, which reduces reaching and bending, without inconvenience when inside the tub ■ Single-lever faucets
Principle 4: Perceptible Information
■ Large dial on a thermostat or telephone ■ Use of color contrast (for example, between countertop and floor or between sink and countertop)
Principle 5: Tolerance for Error
■ Crank- or power-operated counter system or lever handles that can be texturized to communicate to those with low vision that the door should not be opened ■ Magnetic induction cooktop that is not hot to the touch
Principle 6: Low Physical Effort
■ Lever door handles or loop handle pulls on drawers and cabinets that make it easier to operate with the elbow or the knee when one's hands are full ■ Light switches at 44–48 in. high and thermostats 48 in. above the floor, which makes them easier to operate with one's elbow when one's hands are full ■ Electrical outlets placed at 18 in. minimum height so they are easy to reach without bending or from a seated position ■ Removable cabinet fronts at sink with insulated pipes that improve access to these areas and protect legs from hot pipes ■ Varied-height counters that reduce bending and back strain ■ Front-loading washer and dryer with front controls that reduce the need to bend, stoop, or lean over to reach clothes ■ D-shaped pulls on cabinets
Principle 7: Space and Size for Approach
■ Entry doors of 36 in. minimum width, interior doors with 32 in. clearance, and hallway widths of a minimum 42 in. ■ Knee space under sinks

CASE STUDY: THE BALDWIN RESIDENCE IN SEATTLE, WASHINGTON

The Baldwin Residence, a universally designed single-family home, is located on a small (forty-four hundred square feet), narrow (33.5 feet) urban infill lot in the Green Lake neighborhood of Seattle, Washington, and built by its owner Emory Baldwin, an architect, in 2006. Baldwin had several objectives in mind when designing his family home: first, to demonstrate the principles of UD, lifespan design, and flexibility that allow for the changing needs of people over time; second, to show that these principles could be implemented economically and aesthetically; third, to demonstrate that a typical contractor could easily build this type of home; and fourth, to educate other designers, owners, and builders.

The home is a three-story residence with thirty-three hundred square feet, including a finished basement with an accessible mother-in-law apartment. The main floor is accessible from the front sidewalk, and the basement is accessible from the rear via an alley. The main floor has an open layout. Figures 6.5 through 6.9 show both accessible and UD features that are flexible and adaptable to accommodate changing family needs. This home received the 2009 American Institute of Architects Small Project Award for Accessible Residential Design and was featured in many publications. Emory Baldwin states,

> We believe the finished house is a good example of an urban solution for an "aging-in-place" home. Our family uses all of the spaces well, and as they were intended. Some of the things that we like particularly best about the house are features that may seem intended for a person with a disability, but that make our lives easier as well. For instance, the gently sloping path to our front door (and the low threshold there) make it easy to push our children's strollers inside, and also makes it easier for my wife's grandparents to visit. The stacking closets are currently used as extra deep storage, and work well for stowing strollers without needing to collapse them. The upper level of the stacking closets is used as a "reading nook" for bedtime stories, and has been designed to be semi-open until the elevator is needed in the future (Age-in-Place at Home, n.d.: n.p.).

FIGURE 6.5
Baldwin Residence, Seattle, Washington, The Entrance
The main level has smooth wood flooring, which reduces tripping and makes it easier to use wheeled objects. Adequate space is provided for turning wheeled objects. Storage is provided at multiple levels to accommodate all family members. To the right is a powder bath—also with a 3-ft.-wide door.
Image credit: Dale Lang, NW Architectural Photography (http://www.nwphoto.net). Reprinted with permission.

FIGURE 6.6
Baldwin Residence, Seattle, Washington, The Kitchen
UD features in the kitchen include wide clearance space between island and counter (5 in. width), loop handles on cabinets that are easy to open with a closed fist, pull-out drawers in cabinets and pantry, most kitchen storage in base cabinets (in drawers and pull-out shelves), wall oven at accessible height with racks lining up with countertop (and controls within reach range), smooth surfaces for easy movement of pots and pans, a sink with a pull-out spray near the stove for filling pots, and a smooth, glass energy-efficient induction cooktop that allows for easy transfer of pots and pans and is safe for children because it does not get too hot. The controls of the cooktop are lockable and are located along the front so that the user does not need to reach across the burners to adjust the heat level.
Image credit: Dale Lang, NW Architectural Photography (http://www.nwphoto.net). Reprinted with permission.

FIGURE 6.7
Baldwin Residence, Seattle, Washington, Circulation—Stairs and Elevator Shaft
The short run of stairs reduces injuries from falls, which is good for everyone, especially toddlers and elderly persons. The stairs wrap around three stacked closets, which are sized and wired for a future elevator should the need arise someday. Currently, the extra-deep closet space provides deep storage for strollers and tricycles. The upstairs section of the closet is used as a reading nook for bedtime stories. The door has lever handles, which are easy to open with a closed fist or while holding keys, bags, or children. In addition, the floor structure of closets is removable and, independent from the rest of the floor, an elevator pit has been built into the foundation.
Image credit: Dale Lang, NW Architectural Photography (http://www.nwphoto.net). Reprinted with permission.

FIGURE 6.8
Baldwin Residence, Seattle, Washington,
Master Bathroom Shower
The shower is curbless, which allows someone using a wheelchair to roll in and someone with balance limitations to walk in, eliminating a potential tripping hazard. The shower controls are offset so the water can be adjusted before getting into the shower and getting wet. The hand-held shower unit has a long, flexible hose and is attached to an adjustable glide bar. The walls have blocking for the future addition of grab bars.
Image credit: Dale Lang, NW Architectural Photography (http://www.nwphoto.net). Reprinted with permission.

FIGURE 6.9
Baldwin Residence, Seattle, Washington,
Future Flexibility and Adaptability
The dining room is open to the second floor. The structure has been sized to allow a future room to infill the open space above the dining room.
Image credit: Dale Lang, NW Architectural Photography (http://www.nwphoto.net). Reprinted with permission.

POLICIES AND PROGRAMS TO IMPLEMENT UNIVERSAL DESIGN IN HOUSING

Policies and programs that encourage or require the adoption of UD, accessibility, and/or visibility criteria can ensure that single-family homes not covered by existing federal laws (i.e., the Architectural Barriers Act of 1968, Section 504 of the Rehabilitation Act of 1973, and the Fair Housing Act) are accessible to people of all physical abilities. Federal policies have the potential to require visitability or UD criteria in new homes. For example, the proposed Inclusive Home Design Act of 2002, H.R. 5683, required "new covered dwellings (certain residences designed, constructed, commissioned, or contracted with Federal financial assistance) to include at least one entrance that is accessible to, and usable by, people with disabilities. It exempts buildings from that and other entrance requirements on account of the terrain or due to unusual physical limitations. It further requires of covered dwellings pertaining to: (1) accessible interior doors; (2) accessible environmental controls; and (3) accessible habitable space and an accessible bathroom" (U.S. Congress, 2002: n.p.). The bill has been reintroduced in subsequent sessions of Congress, the most recent being H.R. 3260, the Eleanor Smith Inclusive Home Design Act of 2015. This act

> Requires newly constructed, federally assisted single family houses and town houses to include at least one level that complies with the Standards for Type C (Visitable) Units of the American National Standards Institute (ANSI) Standards for Accessible and Usable Buildings and Facilities (1005-ICC ANSI A117.1 –2009) and any future revisions.
>
> Requires: (1) each applicant for federal financial assistance to submit compliance assurances to the relevant federal agency, and (2) each person who arranges for design or construction of a covered dwelling to submit architectural and construction plans for state or local approval. Prohibits federal financial assistance to a state or local government unit unless the recipient is taking certain enforcement actions with regard to covered dwellings. (U.S. Congress, 2015: n.p.)

As of this writing, this bill has been referred to the House Committee on Financial Services.

Several state and local governments have implemented policies and programs to incorporate UD into new and existing housing, either through regulations or incentives. More specifically, three categories of local and state policies and programs, discussed below, mainly address accessibility in single-family homes (Hartje, 2004). The first category discusses builder requirements for subsidized housing, the second category covers builder requirements or incentives for unsubsidized housing, and the third category discusses voluntary incentives for consumers.

Regulated or incentivized design features vary, depending on whether the purpose is to meet visitability, full accessibility, or UD guidelines. Visitability has the smallest number of accessibility features, full accessibility has a moderate number of additional features to support long-term use by people with mobility limitations, and UD provides the highest number and broader range of features that improve usability, safety, and health for a more diverse group of people and abilities.

Category 1: Builder Requirements for Subsidized Housing

Government-subsidized public housing provides living units through local housing authorities and the U.S. Department of Housing and Urban Development to economically disadvantaged individuals and households (see chapter 14). Similar to other housing discussed in this chapter, aspects of subsidized housing may be unsupportive to individuals of varied abilities (Pynoos, Nishita, Cicero, & Caraviello, 2008). Many policies assist individuals in their ability to remain in their apartments in public housing developments. However, it was not until the Fair Housing Amendments Act (FHAA) of 1988 was instituted that attention was given to changes in design prospects (Fair Housing Amendments Act, 2006). The FHAA created improvements yet left gaps in policy coverage that have resulted in the formation of two movements to address the problems of visitability and UD (Pynoos et al., 2008).

UD features in housing are represented at the most basic level by the concept of visitability, or basic accessibility, which represents a limited set of features and minimum standards for access and is an important, albeit small, component of UD. The purpose of visitability is to allow persons in wheelchairs or with other mobility problems the ability to visit residents of subsidized housing. Visitability in public housing has been conceptualized as a civil rights approach under the Section 504 statute (Nishita, Liebig, Pynoos, Perelman, & Spegal, 2007). Although visitability seeks to increase the supply of accessible housing through the inclusion of three basic structural features at the time of home construction, it is often implemented in local ordinances that generally require, at a minimum, four or five features on the main level of the home. These features include a nonstep entrance, wider interior doorways (thirty-two-inch clear opening) and hallways (forty-two inches wide), basic access to a bathroom, raised electrical outlets and lowered switches, and wall reinforcements in the bathrooms (Pynoos et al., 2008; Pynoos & Nishita, 2007).

Throughout the United States, many cities have passed visitability ordinances for subsidized housing since the FHAA of 1988, including Atlanta, Georgia (1992); Austin, Texas (1998); and Urbana, Illinois (2000). In St. Louis, Missouri, the minimum UD requirements for new construction using affordable housing trust funds from the city were revised in 2008.

The term *visitability* originated with the concept of basic home access within the Atlanta, Georgia, area (Vaughn & Pound, 2010) and was voluntarily incorporated into new Habitat for Humanity construction projects. Similarly, other cities saw voluntary incorporation of visitability accommodations. Using a UD checklist, the design component was implemented to verify UD requirements during the design phase of a project, while the construction component was implemented to aid in verifying UD construction tolerances and other requirements in both the predrywall construction phase and the substantial completion phase of a project. In 2014 Westchester County, New York, adopted an act for fair housing rights under the Section 504 statute that prohibits discrimination based upon disability (Westchester County Board of Legislators, 2014). The level of accessibility required by Section 504 is greater than the requirements of the Fair Housing Act (Morris, 2014). This act required the inclusion of several UD features in a minimum of 50 percent of new fair and affordable residential housing developments that receive support from programs funded by the county. Specifically, inclusive design features of step-free entrances, accessible toilet facilities, and wide doorways and hallways were recommended and enacted by the Board of Legislators of Westchester County.

The purpose of the design features was to make a housing unit more accessible for persons with mobility disabilities and promote independent aging. Some of the design features were nonstep entries, one-story living spaces, wider doorways and hallways, turnaround floor space, grab bars, removable cabinets, and reachable switches and controls.

Category 2: Builder Requirements or Incentives for Unsubsidized Housing

Vermont was the first state to establish a set of visitability features for almost all housing, even conventionally financed (i.e., unsubsidized) housing. As of 2002, the Vermont law required any speculatively built single-family or multifamily housing unit to adhere to a number of construction standards that closely follow the visitability legislation. In the case of Georgia, the EasyLiving^{cm} Home program is a voluntary certificate program designed to encourage builders of single-family homes, duplexes, and triplexes to include EasyLiving^{cm} Home features in the design and construction of new homes. Among the features are easy access for entry, easy passages through the doors and hallways, and easy use or open floor plans (EasyLiving, 2012).

In January 2013 Delaware's New Castle County Council approved a universal design ordinance that requires age-restricted housing construction (or those substantially renovated) to include the option of six UD features for the buyer. The developer must offer the following options to consumers as part of the construction: first, nonstep main entry; second, offset tub/shower controls with adjacent clear floor space; third, wide blocking installed in walls around the tub/shower and toilet for future grab bars; fourth, lever-type door handles; fifth, single-lever faucets; and sixth, utilization of minimum and maximum heights for switches and outlets. The ordinance also contains language encouraging all new construction to incorporate UD elements.

Category 3: Tax or Fee Incentives for Consumers

Examples of tax and fee incentives include reduced building permit fees for new construction with accessibility features in Freehold Borough, New Jersey, and cash rebates from the city after passing compliance inspections in Escanaba, Michigan. The Michigan ordinance offers a financial incentive for voluntarily meeting a list of at least ten visitability or accessibility features. A noteworthy example is the program in Irvine, California, where consumers can select and pay for UD features of their choice. Features range from lever-style door hardware, a standard feature at no cost, to thirty-two-inch-wide interior doors and a curbless shower in lieu of a standard tub or shower, as optional features for additional costs. The city of Irvine was awarded the 2002 Accessible America Award from the National Organization on Disability for this program (Kochera, 2002; Spegal & Liebig, n.d.).

CONCLUSION

UD is an approach to design that recognizes and accommodates ordinary changes people experience over their lives due to aging and life circumstances by addressing the range of human abilities: physical, cognitive, and sensory. UD benefits people through all life stages, including children and adults, older adults experiencing age-related changes, and people of all ages experiencing a temporary or permanent disease or disability (Golant, 2015; Story et al., 1998; see chapter 17). UD supports one of the most important goals of good design, namely, that it should meet the needs of as many users as possible, at present and in the future (Pynoos et al., 2008). Ideally, UD will be applied at all scales of design related to housing: community, neighborhood, site, housing unit, and appliances/products/materials (American Institute of Architects, n.d.; see chapters 2, 12, and 13).

Given the nature of housing and UD as an approach, there will not be one single method that is effective for all housing but rather a combination of various methods appropriate to different housing types and situations. These methods will include mandatory standards and voluntary incentives, the use of prescriptive and performance criteria, and other policies and programs, as previously discussed, with the goal not only of housing being more usable for residents but also of designing for social inclusion, health and wellness, and equity (Steinfeld, 2014; see chapters 12, 13, 18, and 19).

As more people experience the benefits of UD, it could very well expand across housing markets through policies that both require and encourage it. Changing the way housing is designed and built to extend UD will require that most stakeholders participate in the process from conceptual design to policy to practice. These stakeholders are housing producers (architects, developers, builders), financial institutions, housing consumers, the planning community, and government officials at the local, state, and national levels, among others (Kochera, 2002).

Awareness, education, and advocacy are critical for expanding the UD approach so that when it is applied to housing, it will include all persons and create inclusion through the integration of design features, product characteristics, and services. Universally designed housing will thus be connected to social, economic, and environmental sustainability (see chapter 19).

Although progress has been made, there is still much to be done to extend UD beyond the dominant role of designing for accessibility and into the mainstream of practice for designing and building housing that is universal. Richard Duncan, executive director of the RL Mace Universal Design Institute, states, "From the perspective of more usable and supportive environments, the U.S. remains principally focused on accessibility: developing regulations, codes, standards, policies and procedures to provide societal inclusion to people with disabilities" (Duncan, 2014: n.p.). Edward Steinfeld, director of the Center for Inclusive Design and Environmental Access (IDEA), echoes that sentiment about UD in general, not just related to housing, by suggesting that the public has limited knowledge and interest in UD due to not seeing the personal relevance, while builders do not see it as something that can increase property values and manufacturers do not see that it can improve the competitiveness of their products. However, there are good examples of the value of UD for all stakeholders (Steinfeld, 2014). Finally, Salmen (2011: 6.6) states that "most building designers, developers, and construction professionals lack an understanding of the changing needs and abilities of our society, and thus of how to develop appropriate UD solutions." He goes on to explain that further regulation will never resolve the challenges, and that the only long-term solution is appropriately targeted educational materials and programs. He concludes by writing, "Once developed and disseminated, there will be more widespread accessibility, and, eventually, a demand by consumers for the superior performance of UD will overtake the need for prescriptive standards" (Salmen, 2011: 6.6).

REFERENCES

AARP Research and Strategic Analysis. (2014). *Home and community preferences of the 45+ population*. Washington, D.C.: AARP.

Age-in-Place at Home. (n.d.). The Baldwin house: Additional information. Retrieved July 12, 2016, from http://www.aipathome.com/showcases/aip-homes-communities/baldwin-house/additional-information/.

American Institute of Architects. (n.d.). Construction costs. Retrieved July 12, 2016, from http://www.aia.org/aiaucmp/groups/aia/documents/pdf/aiab097618.pdf.

Bednar, M. J. (Ed.). (1977). *Barrier-free environments*. Stroudsburg, Pa.: Dowden, Hutchinson & Ross.

CUD (Center for Universal Design). (n.d.). *About UD*. Retrieved July 12, 2016, from www.ncsu.edu/ncsu/design/cud/about_ud/about_ud.htm.

CUD (Center for Universal Design). (2000). *Housing for the lifespan of all people.* Raleigh: North Carolina State University. Retrieved July 12, 2016, from https://www.ncsu.edu/ncsu/design/cud/pubs_p/docs/housing%20for%20lifespan.pdf.

CUD (Center for Universal Design). (2006). *Universal design in housing.* Raleigh: Center for Universal Design, North Carolina State University.

Connell, B. R., Jones, M., Mace, R., Mueller, J., Mullick, A., Ostroff, E., Sanford, J., Steinfeld, E., Story, M., & Vanderheiden, G. (1997). *The principles of universal design.* Version 2.0. Retrieved July 23, 2016, from https://www.ncsu.edu/ncsu/design/cud/about_ud/udprinciplestext.htm.

Duncan, R. (2014). *Universal design.* Retrieved July 19, 2016, from http://universaldesign.ie/What-is-Universal-Design/Conference-Proceedings/Universal-Design-for-the-21st-Century-Irish-International-Perspectives/#Background.

EasyLiving. (2012). *EasyLiving[cm] home program.* Retrieved July 13, 2016, from http://elhomes.org/.

Fair Housing Amendments Act of 1988. (2006). Pub. L. No. 100–430, 102 Stat. 1619 (codified as amended at 28 U.S.C 2341–2412, 42 U.S.C. 3601–3619).

Fisher, K., & Kettl, P. (2005). Aging with mental retardation: Increasing population of older adults with MR require health interventions and prevention strategies. *Geriatrics, 60,* 26–29.

Golant, S. M. (2015). *Aging in the right place.* Baltimore: Health Professions Press.

Greiman, L., & Ravesloot, C. (2016). Housing characteristics of households with wheeled mobility device users from the American Housing Survey: Do people live in homes that facilitate community participation? *Community Development, 47,* 63–74.

Hartje, S. C. (2004). Developing an incentive program for universal design in new, single-family housing. *Housing and Society, 31,* 195–212.

Institute for Human Centered Design. (n.d.). *Universal design.* Retrieved July 27, 2015, from http://www.humancentereddesign.org/.

Institute for Human Centered Design. (2016a). *The Baldwin residence.* Retrieved July 12, 2016, from http://www.dev.ihcdstore.org/?q=print/129.

Institute for Human Centered Design. (2016b). *Universal design is good design.* Retrieved July 16, 2016, from http://www.humancentereddesign.org/projects/universal-design-good-design.

Joines, S. (2009). Enhancing quality of life through universal design. *NeuroRehabilitation, 25,* 313–326.

Kochera, A. (2002). *Accessibility and visitability features in single-family homes: A review of state and local activity.* Washington, D.C.: AARP Public Policy Institute.

Kottorp, A., Bernspang, B., & Fisher, A. G. (2003). Validity of a performance assessment of activities of daily living for people with developmental disabilities. *Journal of Intellectual Disability Research, 47,* 597–605.

Mallett, S. (2004). Understanding home: A critical review of the literature. *Sociological Review, 52,* 62–89.

McGuire, J. M., & Scott, S. S. (2006). Universal design for instruction: Extending the universal design paradigm to college instruction. *Journal of Postsecondary Education and Disability, 19,* 124–134.

Mebane-Sims, I. (2009). 2009 Alzheimer's disease: Facts and figures. *Alzheimer's Disease and Dementia, 5,* 234–270.

Moore, P. (2001). *Universal accessibility is the reason for design.* Retrieved July 12, 2016, from www.asaging.org.

Morris, L. L. (2014). *Accessibility for all: Fair housing rights in the Lower Hudson Valley.* White Plains, N.Y.: Westchester Residential Opportunities.

National Association of Home Builders Research Center and Barrier Free Environments. (1996). *Residential remodeling and universal design: Making homes more comfortable and accessible.* Retrieved July 12, 2016, from https://www.huduser.gov/portal//Publications/PDF/remodel.pdf.

Nishita, C. M., Liebig, P. S., Pynoos, J., Perelman, L., & Spegal, K. (2007). Promoting basic accessibility in the home: Analyzing patterns in the diffusion of visitability legislation. *Journal of Disabled Political Studies, 18,* 2–13.

Null, R. (2014). *Universal design principles and models.* Boca Raton, Fla.: CRC Press.

Ostroff, E. (2011). Universal design: An evolving paradigm. In W. Preiser & K. H. Smith (Eds.), *Universal design handbook* (pp. 1.3–1.11). New York: McGraw-Hill.

Oswald, F., & Werner-Wahl, H. (2005). Dimensions of the meaning of home in later life. In G. Rowles & H. Chaudhury (Eds.), *Home and identity in late life: International perspectives* (pp. 21–45). New York: Springer.

Palmer, M., & Harley, D. (2011). Models and measurement in disability: An international review. *Journal of Health Policy and Planning, 27*, 357–364.

Pilarski, C., & Rath, J. F. (2013). Moving beyond accessibility accommodations to a more inclusive environment for everyone. *Spotlight on Disability Newsletter.* Washington, D.C.: American Psychological Association.

Plough Foundation. (2015). *Aging in place and universal design: Making your home accessible, no matter your age or ability.* Retrieved July 12, 2016, from http://www.plough.org/assets/2012/plough_aginginplace_booklet-f_web.pdf.

Pynoos, J., & Nishita, C. (2007). Aging in place. In S. Carmel, C. A. Morse, & F. M. Torres-Gil (Eds.), *Lessons on aging for three nations: Vol. 1. The art of aging well* (pp. 185–198). Amityville, N.Y.: Baywood.

Pynoos, J., Nishita, C., Cicero, C., & Caraviello, R. (2008). Aging in place, housing, and the law. *Elder Law Journal, 16,* 77–106.

Queensland Government, Department of Housing. (2015). *Smart housing: Towards sustainable housing: Cost-efficiency.* Retrieved July 12, 2016, from http://www.hpw.qld.gov.au/SiteCollectionDocuments/SmartHousingCostEfficiencyBooklet.pdf.

Salmen, J. P. S. (2011). U.S. accessibility code and standards: Challenges for universal design. In W. Preiser & K. H. Smith (Eds.), *Universal design handbook* (pp. 6.1–6.7). New York: McGraw Hill.

Sandler, L. A. (2009). *Universal design and green home survey checklist.* Iowa City: University of Iowa Clinical Law Programs.

Scott, S. S., McGuire, J. M., & Shaw, S. F. (2003). Universal design for instruction: A new paradigm for adult instruction in postsecondary education. *Remedial and Special Education, 24,* 369–379.

Shaikh, A., Kauppi, C., & Pallard, H. (2013). Development of supportive housing for seniors in Iroquois Falls, Canada. *OIDA International Journal of Sustainable Development, 6*(3), 11–22.

Spegal, K., & Liebig, P. (n. d.). *Visitability: Trends, approaches, and outcomes.* Retrieved July 17, 2016, from California Department of Housing and Community, http://www.hcd.ca.gov/codes/state-housing-law/amercitystatelaws_attach_1b.doc.

Steinfeld, E. (2014). *The future of universal design: From accessibility to inclusion.* Retrieved July 12, 2016, from https://usodep.blogs.govdelivery.com/2014/02/04/the-future-of-universal-design/.

Steinfeld, E., & Maisel, J. L. (2012). Public accommodations. In E. Steinfeld & J. Maisel (Eds.), *Universal design: Creating inclusive environments* (pp. 187–220). New York: Wiley.

Story, M. F., Mueller, J. L., & Mace, R. (1998). *The universal design file: Designing for people of all ages and abilities.* Raleigh: Center for Universal Design, North Carolina State University.

Taylor, S. (2009). *Narratives of identity and place.* New York: Routledge.

U.S. Congress. (2002). Summary: H.R. 5683 Inclusive Home Design Act of 2002. 107th Congress (2001–2002). Retrieved July 12, 2016, from https://www.congress.gov/107/bills/hr5683/BILLS-107hr5683ih.pdf.

U.S. Congress. (2015). Summary: H.R. 3260 Eleanor Smith Inclusive Home Design Act of 2015. 114th Congress (2015–2016). Retrieved July 12, 2016, from https://www.congress.gov/114/bills/hr3260/BILLS-114hr3260ih.pdf.

U.S. Department of Housing and Urban Development. (1996). *Residential remodeling and universal design: Making homes more comfortable and accessible.* Washington, D.C.: U.S. Department of Housing and Urban Development.

Vaughn, J. R., & Pound, P. (2010). *The state of housing in America in the 21st century: A disability perspective.* Washington, D.C.: National Council on Disability.

Westchester County Board of Legislators. (2014). Westchester legislators adopt universal design standards for county residential housing. Retrieved July 12, 2016, from http://

westchesterlegislators.com/district-14/34-news/media-center/1928-westchester-legislators-adopt-universal-design-standards-for-county-residential-housing.html.

Young, L. (2011). Universal housing: A critical component of a sustainable community. In W. Preiser & K. H. Smith (Eds.), *Universal design handbook* (pp. 24.3–24.13). New York: McGraw-Hill.

Young, L., & Pace, R. (2001). The next-generation universal home. In W. Preiser & E. Ostroff (Eds.), *Universal design handbook* (pp. 34.3–34.21). New York: McGraw-Hill.

Young, L. C. (2006). *Residential rehabilitation, remodeling and universal design*. Raleigh: Center for Universal Design, North Carolina State University.

SECTION III
HOMEOWNERSHIP

Chapter 7   Home Buying and Homeownership

MARILYN J. BRUIN AND
DEBORAH MITCHELL

Many factors influence how a household is housed, including household size, the age of household members, household preferences and resources, and market opportunities and constraints (Morris & Winter, 1975). In the United States, 63.7 percent of housing units are owner occupied as of this writing, compared to 69.2 percent in the first quarter of 2005 (U.S. Bureau of the Census, n.d.). Historically, young adults forming households have driven entry-level home buying. However, due to the Great Recession and the tightening of underwriting guidelines, many millennials have postponed or foregone homeownership (Prevost, 2015). Nevertheless, the American Dream, the aspiration to own a home, has remained strong despite the national house price crash (Belsky, 2013; Federal Reserve Bank, 2014; Mantel, 2012; Quercia, Freeman, & Ratcliffe, 2011; see chapters 1, 2, 8, 10, and 15, and 17).

In the United States, housing on privately owned land has historical underpinnings (Rohe, 2012). In the mid-1700s, Thomas Jefferson proposed that each colonist reside in his own home on a plot of his own land (Rohe, 2012). This aspiration has consistently been supported by public policy (Immergluck, 2012). For example, the Homestead Act of 1882 provided opportunities for pioneers to build on 160 acres of farmland. The Federal Housing Administration (FHA) mortgage insurance program, an outcome of the Housing Act of 1934, made long-term affordable mortgage financing accessible. Following World War II, the loan insurance program of the U.S. Department of Veterans Affairs began guaranteeing mortgages for veterans, reservists, National Guard members, and certain surviving spouses, to acknowledge military service (Schwartz, 2015). Since 1913, and especially after World War II, the most enduring financial incentive has been through the federal tax system, which allows the deduction of mortgage interest and property tax expenses and excludes capital gains from taxation on the majority of home sales (Rohe, 2012; Roskey & Green, 2006; Schwartz, 2015), as discussed below (see chapters 2, and 8, and 10).

The purpose of this chapter is to describe and discuss characteristics associated with home buying and homeownership, as well as factors associated with securing a preapproved mortgage, searching for a home, owning a home, and fulfilling postpurchase responsibilities, followed by a conclusion.

CHARACTERISTICS ASSOCIATED WITH HOME BUYING AND HOMEOWNERSHIP

Status and Control

Homeownership is regarded as part of the American Dream; it signals accomplishment, conveys social status, and is equated with "family virtue, political stability, and civic responsibility" (Kelly, 1993: 149). Compared to renters, homeowners tend to have more freedom to adapt their surroundings and more access to tax savings, although they also face more responsibilities for home maintenance (Cullen, 2003; Mantel, 2012; Quercia et al., 2011; Reid, 2014). Homeowners may feel that they have control over their housing expenses. In the case of a fixed-rate mortgage, premium and interest payments are stable, although expenses for insurance and property taxes are likely to increase over time (see chapters 1 and 2).

Tax Benefits

The U.S. tax code incentivizes homeownership by allowing borrowers to deduct the interest portion of mortgage payments as well as property taxes from state and federal income taxes (Schwartz, 2015). However, only taxpayers who itemize deductions, rather than take the standard deduction, benefit from this incentive (Herbert, McCue, & Sanchez-Moyano, 2014). At the beginning of the mortgage term the majority of the monthly payment covers interest expenses, which are deductible on income tax returns. Toward the end of the mortgage term the majority of the monthly payment covers the principal, which is not deductible on income tax returns.

Homeowners who sell residential property may be protected from paying capital gains tax, defined as the appreciation of an asset. For example, if a property was purchased for $200,000 and sold ten years later for $400,000, there is $200,000 in appreciation or increase in equity value. In the United States federal capital gains tax rates, which differ from income tax rates, range from 0 percent for taxpayers in a low tax bracket to 20 percent for taxpayers in a high tax bracket; some states also tax capital gains. However, if the seller has lived in the property for at least two of the previous five years and if the profit on the sale is less than $250,000 for a single filer or $500,000 for joint filers, the capital gain is not taxed by the Internal Revenue Service (Manzi & Michael, 2014; McClure, 2012; Perez, 2015).

Home Equity

Monthly mortgage payments can be considered a form of forced savings designed to build equity, which includes the cash amount of the down payment and the amount that has been paid on the principal. Paying more than the required monthly payment and designating the additional payment toward the principal, called "prepaying," may also increase equity by decreasing interest expenses and reducing the principal balance. Thus the borrower may be able to pay off the mortgage before the end of the original mortgage term (Freddie Mac, 2011a). The process of repaying a mortgage helps a household build equity over time, which becomes available when the property is sold. Mortgage equity may also help in establishing a line of credit or a home equity loan, which allows households to finance expenditures such as remodeling or rehabilitation projects or other large expenditures, including paying college tuition or large medical bills, establishing a small business, or buying another home (Freddie Mac, 2011b).

However, wealth in the form of home equity is not liquid (i.e., it is typically not easily and quickly converted into cash). Furthermore, as the national house price crash and the ensuing foreclosure crisis illustrated, home equity can be negatively impacted when local home values decrease. Following the rapid escalation of house prices in the 1990s and early 2000s, in part triggered by social pressure to be part of the "ownership society," some borrowers either failed to recognize or ignored the risks associated with homeownership (Esswein, 2015). When house prices plummeted in 2006 some borrowers realized that their mortgage debt exceeded the value of the property, called "being underwater," and thus were prevented from refinancing their mortgages, resulting in increased interest payments and sometimes eventual foreclosure (Esswein, 2015; see chapter 15).

In sum, for some borrowers, especially those with few resources, the combination of market risk and long-term financial debt, in addition to the responsibilities of caring for a property, may be stressful and outweigh the financial, personal, and social advantages of homeownership (Freddie Mac, 2014; Herbert et al., 2014; Lubell, 2014; Rohe, Van Zandt, & McCarthy, 2002; see chapter 2). For some who do buy homes, as evidenced during the national foreclosure crisis, this combination can be financially and personally devastating (Rohe, 2012; see chapter 15).

SECURING A PREAPPROVED MORTGAGE

A mortgage is a long-term loan secured by real estate (Immergluck, 2012). As of this writing, almost 77 percent of home buyers used mortgage financing to secure residential property (RealtyTrac, 2015). Some home buyers will search for financing on their own, turn to a lender, use a mortgage broker, or rely on a realtor, family, or friends for referrals. Others turn to professional financial or housing counselors, who may help determine financial readiness to purchase, calculate an affordable mortgage amount and thus an affordable property value, and evaluate mortgage products to determine the best fit for a household (see chapter 10). The U.S. Department of Housing and Urban Development (HUD) funds housing counselors in nonprofit and governmental agencies through multiple homeownership programs. Prospective home buyers can find a list of HUD-approved counselors on the HUD website (U.S. Department of Housing and Urban Development, n.d.b). Before seeking preapproval for a mortgage, prospective buyers assemble financial records with a housing or financial counselor for a mortgage application. Lenders ask for pay statements, W-2 forms for the past two years, debt amounts and payment schedules, and information about financial obligations, as well as bank account information and investment statements (Freddie Mac, 2011a). Applicants are also asked to provide copies of previous tax returns and proof of supplemental income. A counselor also helps prospective buyers check credit scores, develop a household budget, and create a savings plan for the down payment and for meeting expected housing-related and other household expenses (Agarwal, Amromin, Ben-David, Chomsisengphet, & Evanoff, 2014; U.S. Department of Housing and Urban Development, n.d.b).

Because mortgage financing has long-term implications, borrowers typically evaluate mortgage products to select the product that best fits their needs (Freddie Mac, 2011a; Kiplinger's, 2006). The total cost of repaying a mortgage includes the total monthly payments over the life of the mortgage, which are determined by the interest rate, the terms or the length of the loan, the down payment, and the type of loan. The annual percentage rate (APR) may include these total financing costs, thus making a comparison among mortgage products from different lenders possible. However, not every lender includes all items in their APR, making it difficult to compare APRs across products (Rascoff & Humphries, 2015).

Lenders charge interest, fees, and points to cover their costs and profit for making money available over a long period of time. Points are the amount of cash borrowers pay the lender beyond the down payment when they take out a loan. One point typically equals 1 percent of the mortgage amount. Paying points allows borrowers to substitute up-front fees for lower monthly payments over the life of the loan.

Mortgage lenders also require borrowers to document their ability to comply with both front-end and back-end qualifying ratios. The first step is to determine and document the combined gross monthly income(s) of the borrower(s). To meet the front-end ratio, no more than 28 percent of the total gross monthly household income is expected to be spent on the mortgage principal and interest, property taxes, homeowner's insurance, and, if applicable, mortgage insurance. To meet the back-end ratio, no more than 36 percent of total gross household income is expected to cover the housing costs in addition to other long-term debt payments.

Down Payment

A down payment is defined as the proportion of upfront cash paid toward the price of the property (Freddie Mac, 2011b; Kiplinger's, 2006). In the mortgage industry, a 20 percent down payment is considered the benchmark for a prime mortgage (i.e., a mortgage with a favorable interest rate) (Sheldon, 2014). Depending on the availability of mortgage funds and programs to incentivize home buying, benchmarks for down payments can fluctuate. At the time of this writing borrowers paying less than 20 percent as a down payment are typically required to purchase private mortgage insurance (U.S. Department of Housing and Urban Development, 2015a). This insurance protects the lender if the borrower defaults on the mortgage (Bray, Schroeder, & Stewart, 2015; Federal Housing Administration, 2015). The borrower typically deposits monthly payments in an escrow account until the premium is due.

However, home buyers who are unable or unwilling to contribute cash for a 20 percent down payment may still become homeowners. For example, the FHA currently requires a down payment of 3.5 percent for FHA-insured mortgages (Federal Housing Administration, 2015). The U.S. Department of Veterans Affairs does not require a down payment for eligible service members, veterans, and members of the National Guard (U.S. Department of Veterans Affairs, n.d.). Eligible low- and moderate-income borrowers in rural markets may apply for the Single Family Housing Guaranteed Loan Program provided by Rural Development, U.S. Department of Agriculture (Sheldon, 2014; U.S. Department of Agriculture, n.d.). The Rural Development and FHA low-down-payment options require mortgage insurance,

TABLE 7.1
Monthly Housing Costs for 30- and 15-Year Mortgages with a 20 Percent Down Payment

Mortgage	Interest rate	Purchase price	Loan amount	Down payment	Monthly components interest	Total monthly payment
30-year mortgage	3.0%	$197,000	$157,600	$39,400	$664	$992
	4.5%				$799	$1,127
	5.0%				$846	$1,174
15-year mortgage	3.0%	$197,000	$157,600	$39,400	$1,088	$1,416
	4.5%				$1,206	$1,534
	5.0%				$1,246	$1,574

Source: Authors, based on Bluejay, n.d.

which adds to the expense of the loan (Federal Housing Administration, 2015; U.S. Department of Agriculture, n.d.).

Down payment assistance programs, which borrowers may have to navigate, are available to eligible borrowers and implemented at the federal, state, and local levels through governmental and nonprofit organizations. Information about access to state and community down payment assistance programs is often available through housing counselors. As the vast majority of programs have limited funding, funds may be depleted by the time a borrower applies for them (see chapters 8 and 10).

The Interest Rate

The interest rate on mortgages is influenced by the terms and the type of the mortgage. For example, the total interest expense for a $197,000 mortgage at 4.5 percent over thirty years is $162,341; the same $197,000 financed at 4.5 percent over fifteen years has a total interest expense of $74,264 (HomePath .com, n.d.a, n.d.b). While the total interest expense for the fifteen-year-long mortgage is lower, the monthly payment is higher because of the shorter repayment period. Table 7.1 compares monthly payments of thirty-year and fifteen-year mortgages at three different interest rates.

Figures 7.1 and 7.2 compare the interest and principal by the number of payments for a thirty-year and a fifteen-year mortgage with an interest rate of 4.5 percent. These figures illustrate the interplay between interest and principal, comparing mortgages with different terms but the same interest rate (Minnesota Homeownership Center, 2011).

Mortgage interest rates are influenced by the U.S. prime lending interest rate, determined by the Federal Reserve Bank (Federal Reserve Bank, 2014; Mantel, 2012).

Prepayment Penalties

Mortgage terms may define prepayment penalties that may apply if the borrower pays off the mortgage before the end of the mortgage term. This may happen if the property is sold or the borrower refinances the mortgage. Prepayment fees may be substantial during the early years of the mortgage (Consumer Financial Protection Bureau, n.d.). Some states have eliminated prepayment penalties or set limits on the amount lenders can specify in the mortgage contract for penalties (Consumer Financial Protection Bureau, n.d.).

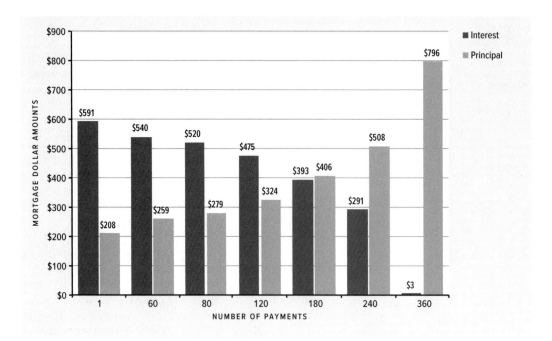

FIGURE 7.1
Simulated Monthly Mortgage Payments

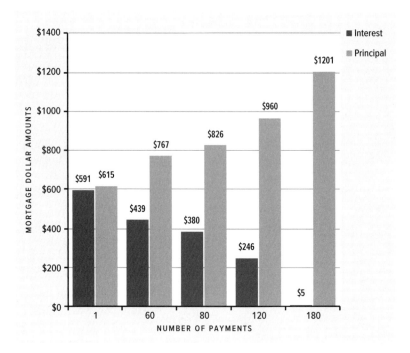

FIGURE 7.2
Simulated Monthly Mortgage Payments

Credit Score

A borrower's credit score, one of several factors reviewed to estimate the likelihood that he or she will make timely payments, influences the interest rate he or she is offered on a mortgage. In the United States three national credit reporting companies, Equifax, Experian, and TransUnion, collect and summarize information on individuals' credit accounts, repayment histories, and records of liens, judgments, and bankruptcies (MyFICO.com, n.d.). Ninety percent of lenders use a FICO credit score developed by Fair Issac & Company as well as other credit bureaus to rank consumer creditworthiness (Consumer Financial Protection Bureau, n.d.). This score ranges from 300 to 850, where higher scores indicate good credit management and thus predict a borrower who is a good (i.e., low) credit risk, resulting in a relatively low mortgage interest rate. In turn, lower scores indicate historical issues with credit management and predict a borrower who is a poor (i.e., high) credit risk, resulting in a relatively high mortgage interest rate.

Mortgage Types

There are two types of mortgages, fixed-rate and adjustable-rate (Furlong, Lang, & Takhtamanova, 2014). A borrower with a fixed-rate mortgage has stable monthly payments over the life of the mortgage, whereas a borrower with an adjustable-rate mortgage (ARM) may experience a change in payments over the life of the mortgage. If interest rates are relatively high, borrowers may initially choose an adjustable-rate mortgage with the thought that the interest rate will subside in the ensuing years. The initial interest rate of an adjustable-rate mortgage is typically lower than the rate for a fixed-rate mortgage. As a comparison, in 2017 an average initial interest rate for a thirty-year adjustable-rate mortgage was 3.87 percent and the annual percentage rate for a thirty-year fixed-rate mortgage was 4.05 percent (Bankrate, n.d.). With an adjustable-rate mortgage, the lower initial interest rate can mean the home buyer qualifies for a larger mortgage. However, a small difference in interest rate also means a small difference in the amount of the mortgage. Over time the interest rate increases or decreases at predetermined intervals, typically in one, two, three, or five years, to "adjust the interest" to reflect changes in the cost of borrowing money (McWhiney, 2017). The mortgage terms specify the reset amount of the ARM interest rate, which is tied to an index, for example, the Cost of Funds Index (COFI) or the London Interbank Offered Rate (LIBOR), to which the lender typically adds a certain percentage. The mortgage terms also specify two types of caps. First, the lifetime cap specifies the maximum to which the interest rate may increase or decrease over the length of the mortgage. Second, periodic caps limit increases in the interest rate from one adjustment period to the next. For example, if the initial interest rate is 3 percent and the lifetime cap is 3.5 percent, the maximum interest rate would not exceed 6.5 percent. If the initial interest rate is 3 percent and the periodic cap is 0.5 percent, the maximum interest rate after the first adjustment period would not exceed 3.5 percent. By the same token, the most that the interest rate could fall after the first adjustment period would be to 2.5 percent. Borrowers may also have the opportunity to convert an ARM to a fixed-rate mortgage.

MORTGAGE APPLICATION DECISION

If a mortgage application is rejected, the reason for rejection must be explained to the applicant. Because underwriting guidelines vary across institutions, it is possible that a factor that results in a rejection from one lender will not result in a rejection from another lender (Freddie Mac, 2011b; Kiplinger's, 2006). For example, if an insufficient down payment is a reason for a rejected application, an applicant may decide to postpone applying for a mortgage until he or she has secured a higher down payment. The applicant may also apply for a down payment assistance program or may apply to a lender with different criteria for the down payment. In general, understanding the process of qualifying for a mortgage and a lender's specific requirements regarding the down payment, credit scores, and qualifying ratios can help a borrower understand his or her likelihood of obtaining a mortgage from a specific lender. If an applicant is unable to meet the qualifying ratio for a fixed-rate mortgage, he or she may qualify for an ARM with a lower initial monthly payment.

BUYING A HOME

Searching for a home in a desired neighborhood, making an offer, and closing on the purchase can be intimidating, especially for first-time buyers, as this process is quite complicated. Thus many home buyers work with several professionals who are bound to uphold fair housing regulations. These regulations require real estate agents not to steer clients to specific properties or a particular neighborhood. In other words, agents must ensure equal access to members of protected classes (i.e., a person cannot be targeted for discrimination due to race, color, religion, national origin, age [forty or over], gender, pregnancy, citizenship, familial status, disability, veteran status, or genetic characteristics). Lenders are also required to provide equitable terms and qualifying criteria.

A real estate agent will help home buyers access information about properties, prices, and neighborhood amenities (Robertson, 2013). Home buyers may work with housing counselors to learn about the home-buying process and to prepare for the mortgage application. They may work with lenders or mortgage brokers to secure a preapproval letter for the mortgage application. Throughout the home-buying process they may also work with a home inspector, an appraiser, insurance agents, a representative from a title agency, and possibly attorneys.

Real estate agents or associates are a key conduit between the buyer and the seller of a property. They are licensed by their respective state government and belong to a multiple listing service (MLS). The MLS is a database of properties available for sale shared by several real estate agents who are active in a certain geographical area. Most real estate agents or associates earn a commission based on the sales price of a home. Thus there is a financial incentive to sell a home for a price as high as possible. However, some agents or associates earn a flat fee (Kiplinger's, 2006). Some real estate professionals may ask a prospective buyer to sign an exclusive buyer-broker agreement, which means that a buyer cannot work with other agents or brokers when looking at properties or making offers to purchase during a stated timeframe (Freddie Mac, 2011b). However, an exclusive agreement does not prevent a prospective buyer from searching on his or her own for properties online, through print media, or by word of mouth.

Once a desired property is selected, a prospective buyer may want to find out as much as possible about the property, the neighborhood, and, if applicable, the municipality, the school district, and amenities. A buyer may also want the real estate agent to provide an overview of recently sold properties in the neighborhood in order to understand the current market value of homes before beginning negotiations with a seller.

An estimate of the market value or an appraisal may help the buyer and agent determine a reasonable offer amount. The appraisal is a professional valuation of the property used to calculate the qualifying ratios and to determine the final approval of mortgage financing. If an appraisal is lower than the purchase price or mortgage amount, the borrower may not meet the qualifying ratios nor receive final approval for a mortgage. The final approval contingency gives a home buyer the option to void the offer or renegotiate the purchase price (Bray et al., 2015; Freddie Mac, 2011b; Kiplinger's, 2006).

A buyer may want to inspect and review municipal records, neighborhood crime statistics, and insurance rates in the respective zip code. Finally, a buyer may want to tour the neighborhood at various times of the day, including rush hour and evenings, and different days of the week, including the weekend, to learn about noise and traffic patterns (Kiplinger's, 2006; Rascoff & Humphries, 2015).

A buyer may ask the seller and the seller's agent questions about the property, including requesting copies of utility bills. In many states sellers are required by law to disclose major physical defects and incidents of water damage in a home, and in all states sellers must disclose the presence of lead-based paint hazards in units built before 1978 (NOLO, n.d.b).

Home Inspection

Many buyers make an offer contingent on an assessment by a professional home inspector. The home inspector assesses the integrity of the structure as well as the life cycle of the major systems and advises the buyer. If the home inspector identifies major concerns regarding repairs or replacements, the buyer with a home inspection contingency in the purchase offer may withdraw the offer, make the purchase of the home contingent upon the seller making repairs, or renegotiate the purchase price. It is important for the buyer to walk through the property with the inspector and/or receive a written report of the estimated life cycle of major components and systems, as well as to receive advice on operation and maintenance of them (Bruss, 2002; Freddie Mac, 2011b; Kiplinger's, 2006). In addition to the home inspection, many lenders in some parts of the country require a termite inspection prior to approving the mortgage financing.

The Purchase Offer

A purchase offer is a legally binding contract issued by a home buyer and his or her realtor to purchase a desired property. When a seller accepts a home buyer's purchase offer, both parties enter into a commitment called a purchase agreement. This agreement includes a deposit, sometimes called "earnest money," of about 1–5 percent of the purchase price, depending on the particular situation, which demonstrates a serious intention to purchase the property (Fannie Mae, 2015). Earnest money is held in escrow until the end of the closing process, when it is applied to the down payment and closing costs. In addition to earnest money, a buyer may want to have additional cash on hand to demonstrate his or her ability to buy and maintain a home and to pay off a mortgage. The acceptance of the purchase offer begins the escrow period, when the property is not on the market any longer and the lender completes the final approval of the mortgage and begins processing the paperwork for the closing. If the buyer backs out of the sale, the earnest money is typically forfeited to the seller (Freddie Mac, n.d.; Kiplinger's, 2006).

A purchase offer should clearly state the types of fixtures or tangible assets on the property, the date for a final walk-through of the vacant unit by the buyer, the closing date, and the possession date. A purchase offer should also list any contingencies that may trigger the need to withdraw or renegotiate the offer. For example, a common contingency is final mortgage approval by the lender.

The Closing or Settlement

The closing or settlement meeting is the final step in the home-buying process. In this meeting, the buyer, the seller (who may not be physically present), or their representatives (who also may not be physically present), and representatives of the lender and the title company process agreements and forms (Bray et al., 2015; Gill, n.d.; Minnesota Homeownership Center, 2011). Typically the buyer pays fees, depending on state and local regulations and practices and on the mortgage, including loan costs (i.e., processing and underwriting fees); appraisal, certification, service, and recording fees; credit report costs; closing and escrow fees; title insurance fees; city, county, and state tax stamps; and numerous escrow payments. In some states buyers also pay for the title search and insurance and for the recording of the sale with the local tax assessor (Freddie Mac, 2011b).

At the closing, the buyer must also provide proof of homeowner's or hazard insurance and prepay the interest and the property taxes for the first month(s) of the mortgage. Buyers, especially first-time buyers, who move from another state or longtime homeowners who are not familiar with current practices may want to review the itemized list of charges and fees with an attorney. Then all agreements, including a deed, which is a notarized statement that transfers the real property from the seller to the buyer and confirms the sale; the mortgage, which is the loan secured by the property; and declarations to transfer tax obligations are signed and fees are paid. Finally, the homeowner receives the keys to his or her new home.

OWNING A HOME

Homeownership has many privileges and responsibilities. This section discusses monthly mortgage payments, forms of homeownership, and select postpurchase responsibilities. Postpurchase considerations include planning for home maintenance, repairs, and improvements; refinancing options; and foreclosure prevention. These issues influence the house's market value and home equity, which in turn influence household wealth (Freddie Mac, 2011b; Kiplinger's, 2006).

Monthly Mortgage Payment

The amount of the monthly mortgage payment is influenced by several factors: first, the principal or the amount of the mortgage; second, the interest rate; and third, the terms and the type of the mortgage (Fannie Mae, 2000; Freddie Mac, 2011a). Most lenders require or encourage homeowners to set up an escrow account in order to save on a monthly basis for the annual or biannual payments of property taxes, homeowner's/hazard insurance, and mortgage insurance, if applicable. The mortgage lender then pays the annual tax and insurance expenses from the escrow account.

Forms of Ownership

Individuals or couples own most single-family homes and the lots on which they sit. A single individual typically purchases residential property in his or her own name. Married couples typically own residential property through joint tenancy with the right of survivorship (i.e., if one spouse dies, the other spouse becomes the sole owner). Unmarried couples may choose to hold residential property in joint tenancy or tenancy in common or to form a legal partnership to own property (NOLO, n.d.a). The latter two forms of ownership do not include the right of survivorship. However, when an individual dies, his or her will may include instructions about how to transfer property upon death. Forms of ownership may vary in community-property states such as Arizona, California, Idaho, Louisiana, Nevada, New Mexico, Texas, Washington, and Wisconsin. In these states assets are co-owned by default and pass directly to the surviving spouse unless a will states differently (Federal Housing Administration, 2015; NOLO, n.d.a).

Condominium ownership includes a housing unit, either attached or detached, and an undivided interest in common areas such as yards, elevators, hallways, parking spaces, and recreational areas. A condominium owner typically finances a unit through a mortgage and typically becomes a member of the condominium association. An owner agrees to abide by covenants, conditions, and restrictions of the condominium association and is entitled to review governing documents of the association, which define common elements and maintenance expectations, before the purchase is completed. Members of the association typically pay a monthly assessment fee, which covers expenses for building and yard maintenance, improvements to the common areas, and a reserve fund that covers larger renovation and rehabilitation projects (Barber & Gaskill, 2008; HOA-USA, 2010). Members may also be subject to special assessments to cover large, unplanned expenses (Barber & Gaskill, 2008; HOA-USA, 2010).

Cooperative ownership differs from single-family or condominium ownership (Bray et al., 2015; Federal Housing Administration, 2015; Rascoff & Humphries, 2015; Silver, 2012). A cooperative owner purchases a share in a corporation, which typically holds a mortgage on the development, including all the units and common spaces. The nonprofit cooperative corporation, rather than cooperative owners, is responsible for paying taxes and insurance, supervising maintenance, and planning for routine care and improvements. A cooperative owner has a share in the corporation, a right to live in a specific unit as a tenant stockholder, and the right to elect members to a governing board that makes decisions on behalf of the residents or co-operative owners, all based on the governing document (Barber & Gaskill, 2008).

SELECT POSTPURCHASE RESPONSIBILITIES

Maintenance, Repairs, and Improvements

Borrowers, regardless of the form of ownership, are responsible for maintaining their property (Minnesota Homeownership Center, 2011). Deferred maintenance and neglect in the form of cracked sidewalks, peeling paint, crumbling masonry, a leaky roof, or broken fixtures, for example, detract from a property's value, may lead to disagreements between neighbors, and may ultimately lead to municipal code violations. The goal of regular preventative maintenance is to avoid an expensive crisis and repair and to extend the life of expensive systems such as the heating, ventilation, and air conditioning (Beals, 2012).

Maintenance and replacement needs of housing components increase with the age of the building and are typically not evenly spread over time. For example, kitchen appliances have an expected life cycle of ten years. New homeowners may need to replace several appliances within the first few years. Wise homeowners plan for routine maintenance as well as the replacement of expensive systems such as a furnace. As a general rule of thumb, owners of a new $172,000 property (the average property value in the United States as of this writing) should budget about $1,720 (or 1 percent) per year for routine maintenance. Owners of a thirty-year-old property should budget about $6,500 (or almost 4 percent) per year (Beals, 2012). Households may want to establish a specific account for maintenance and regularly deposit funds for repairs and replacements. The accumulation of funds will allow a homeowner to meet maintenance or replacement expenditures without financial trauma or stress (Rascoff & Humphries, 2015).

Over time, many homeowners remodel or change their home to meet their specific needs. Homeowners may want to consider the value of other properties in the neighborhood and whether they expect to recoup the costs of improvements and additions if and when they sell the property. To protect their home equity, they may also need to carefully assess their skills and resources to complete a do-it-yourself project. Alternatively, many homeowners avoid home modifications because they do not know how to find reliable, skilled contractors, electricians, and plumbers (Mitchell et al., 2014). Poor workmanship by unskilled homeowners or careless professionals may diminish the quality and value of the home (Bray et al., 2015).

Refinancing Options

When mortgage interest rates are relatively low, many homeowners may refinance their mortgage to secure more favorable mortgage terms or to liquidate equity and replace their previous mortgage. In some cases the new mortgage may also offer the long-term predictability of monthly mortgage payments. For example, borrowers who refinance from an adjustable-rate to a fixed-rate mortgage gain the advantage of being able to predict future mortgage payments (Fannie Mae, 2015). When it comes to refinancing there are as many considerations as when purchasing a mortgage (Federal Reserve Bank, 2014). Borrowers go through application, approval, and closing processes and may incur expenses (Fannie Mae, 2015). When considering costs to refinance, decision points include the interest rates of the current and future mortgage, fees and closing costs, the length of time the household expects to own the property, and possible tax advantages (Brady, Canner, & Maki, 2000; Canner, Dynan, & Passmore, 2002). Borrowers who maintain a solid credit history, make timely mortgage payments, and have equity in the property are likely to obtain an approval of their request to refinance, from either their current or an alternative lender (Fannie Mae, 2015).

Homeowners over the age of sixty-two with home equity may convert their home equity into cash, an income stream, or a line of credit through a reverse mortgage, formally called a Home Equity Conversion Mortgage (HECM) (Jaffe, 2012). Unlike a refinanced conventional mortgage, borrowers with a reverse mortgage are not required to repay the loan until they move or their estate is settled (Carswell, Seay, & Polanowski, 2013; Davidoff, Gerhard, & Post, 2015). Reverse mortgages are intended to convert equity on a primary residence. The mortgage is collateralized by the property and must be paid before the equity is accessed. The first reverse mortgage was originated in 1961. Congress authorized a reverse mortgage demonstration program in 1987 as an FHA insurance program, and in 1988 HUD gained authority to insure reverse mortgages (American Advisors Group, n.d.). The HECM program is currently administered by the U.S. Department of Housing and Urban Development to insure lenders against loss on reverse mortgages (U.S. Department of Housing and Urban Development, 2015b). Overall, the majority of home-owning seniors are aware of reverse mortgages, although only a small proportion of these seniors understand the specific benefits (Davidoff et al., 2015). A requirement of the HECM program is that homeowners must meet with a HUD-approved counselor to be informed about the financial implications and costs before they can refinance with a reverse mortgage (U.S. Department of Housing and Urban Development, 2015b).

Foreclosure Prevention

Mortgages are long-term financial contracts secured by real property that allow lenders to foreclose on or take back the property if borrowers become delinquent. However, borrowers who become delinquent due to an unexpected financial hardship, have a history of timely payments, and can demonstrate the ability to bring the mortgage current within six months may be able to work out an agreement with their lender. There are a variety of loss-mitigation tools to prevent a mortgage foreclosure, and these tools help keep a homeowner in his or her home and help the lender recover the balance of the mortgage. They include:

1. A special forbearance that reduces or suspends monthly payments for a period of time.
2. A partial release that requires principal payments but reduces or suspends the interest payments.
3. A loan modification changing one or more of the terms to make the mortgage manageable for the homeowner. For example, extending the length of the mortgage to lower the amount of the monthly payment (Minnesota Homeownership Center, 2011).

In 2009 the FHA introduced the Home Affordable Refinance Program (HARP) program, which was designed to help borrowers who have made on-time payments over the most recent twelve months yet have little or no equity (Home Affordable Refinance Program, n.d.b). HARP enables homeowners with mortgages owned by Fannie Mae or Freddie Mac to refinance their mortgage into a fixed-rate product without an appraisal or new or additional mortgage insurance (Home Affordable Refinance Program, n.d.b). Several aspects of HARP can make it advantageous for homeowners who have stayed current on their payments. Not requiring an appraisal limits closing costs; lowering or eliminating mortgage insurance and lower interest rates translate into decreased monthly payments. HARP has been extended by the federal government several times and is currently scheduled to sunset on December 31, 2018 (Home Affordable Refinance Program, n.d.a, n.d.b).

With any loss-mitigation tool, the past-due amount and fees may be added to the end of the life of the loan (Minnesota Homeownership Center, 2011). If it is not possible to bring the mortgage current, the borrower may need to sell the property and pay off the mortgage. The lender or mortgage insurer may agree to a short sale that pays off the mortgage even if the proceeds are less than the mortgage balance (Minnesota Homeownership Center, 2011). A homeowner considering loss-mitigation tools or a short sale to resolve a delinquent mortgage may want to obtain advice from a housing counselor, accountant, and/or attorney regarding the short- and long-term financial implications of these strategies. For example, a homeowner may want to understand the tax implications if a portion of the mortgage is discharged or forgiven and how a short sale may impact his or her credit score. Although foreclosure prevention can be complicated, intimidating, and time-consuming, working out a solution is typically less damaging than a foreclosure for the long-term financial well-being of a household (see chapter 15).

CONCLUSION

Despite the national house price crash following the Great Recession (see chapter 15), home equity has remained the largest single financial asset for most households (DeGiovanni & McCarthy, 2011; Quercia et al., 2011; Reid, 2014). The majority of households continue to pursue homeownership as a means to financial wealth and access to neighborhoods perceived to have good schools, amenities, and social networks. Homeownership "embodies the ideals of upward mobility and achievement and . . . renting is seen as an inferior housing choice" (Reid, 2014: 153).

Financing the purchase of a residential property with a mortgage is a complicated legal process and implies a borrower's long-term commitment to make on-time payments to the lender, the local government, and an insurance company (Fannie Mae, 2015; see chapter 8). Housing tenure is one of the most important decisions households make, with implications for the household's short- and long-term financial well-being and quality of life (see chapter 2). The Great Recession has left many homeowners in foreclosure or with mortgage debt exceeding their property's local market value. The majority of future home buyers will be first-generation homeowners who may avoid devastating negative financial outcomes by educating themselves about the home-buying process, developing informed expectations, and critically evaluating professional advice, including information about mortgage finance (see chapter 15). In the United States, federal, state, and local governments support homeownership through public policy, financial assistance programs, and outreach education and counseling that prepare home buyers to make informed decisions (Agarwal et al., 2014).

REFERENCES

Agarwal, S., Amromin, G., Ben-David, I., Chomsisengphet, S., & Evanoff, D. (2014). *The effectiveness of mandatory mortgage counseling: Can one dissuade borrowers from choosing risky mortgages?* (Working Paper). Retrieved August 16, 2015, from http://www.nber.org/papers/w19920.

American Advisors Group. (n.d.). *The history of the reverse mortgage.* Retrieved March 24, 2016, from https://www.aag.com/news/history-reverse-mortgage.

Bankrate. (n.d.). Mortgage center. http://www.bankrate.com/mortgage-center.

Barber, S. R., & Gaskill, V. (2008). *Community associations: A guide to successful management.* Chicago: Institute of Real Estate Management.

Beals, R. K. (2012, May 29). Look at maintenance costs before leaping into homeownership. *U.S. News & World Report.* Retrieved August 16, 2015, from http://money.usnews.com/money/personal-finance/articles/2012/05/29/look-at-maintenance-costs-before-leaping-into-homeownership.

Belsky, E. S. (2013). *The dream lives on: The future of homeownership in America.* Cambridge, Mass.: Joint Center for Housing Studies of Harvard University.

Bluejay, M. (n.d.). Figuring the monthly payment on a mortgage. *How to Buy a House.* Retrieved January 26, 2017, from http://michaelbluejay.com/house/figurepayment.html.

Brady, P. J., Canner, G. B., & Maki, D. M. (2000). The effects of recent mortgage refinancing. *Federal Reserve Bulletin, 87*(7), 441–450. Retrieved August 16, 2015, from http://web.b.ebscohost.com.ezp2.lib.umn.edu/ehost/pdfviewer/pdfviewer?vid=2&sid=c810e16f-e1bb-426e-acbd-16a8160db7ec%40sessionmgr198&hid=110.

Bray, I., Schroeder, A., & Stewart, M. (2015). *Nolo's essential guide to buying your first home.* Berkeley, Calif.: Nolo.

Bruss, R. (2002, August 16). Make purchase offer contingent on inspection. *Chicago Tribune.* Retrieved March 24, 2016, from http://articles.chicagotribune.com/2002-08-16/business/0208160021_1_home-defect-professional-home-inspector-home-inspectors.

Canner, G., Dynan, K., & Passmore, W. (2002). Mortgage refinancing in 2001 and early 2002. *Federal Reserve Bulletin.* Retrieved August 16, 2015, from http://www.federalreserve.gov/pubs/bulletin/2002/1202lead.pdf.

Carswell, A. T., Seay, M. C., & Polanowski, M. (2013). Reverse mortgage fraud against seniors: Recognition and education of a burgeoning problem. *Journal of Housing for the Elderly, 27,* 147–160.

Consumer Financial Protection Bureau. (n.d.). *Shopping for a mortgage: What you can expect under federal rules.* Retrieved September 10, 2015, from http://files.consumerfinance.gov/f/201401_cfpb_mortgages_consumer-summary-new-mortgage.pdf.

Cullen, J. (2003). *The American dream: A short history of an idea that shaped a nation.* New York: Oxford University Press.

Davidoff, T., Gerhard, P., & Post, T. (2015). *Reverse mortgages: What homeowners (don't) know and how it matters.* Retrieved August 16, 2015, from http://papers.ssrn.com/sol3/Papers.cfm?abstract_id=2528944.

DeGiovanni, F. F., & McCarthy, G. (2011). Foreword. In R. G. Quercia, A. Freeman, & J. Ratcliffe (Eds.), *Regaining the dream: How to renew the promise of homeownership for America's working families* (pp. vii–xii). Washington, D.C.: Brookings Institution Press.

Esswein, P. M. (2015). Home price hikes take a breather. *Kiplinger's Personal Finance, 46*(1), 68–73.

Fannie Mae. (2000). *Achieving homeownership: A resource for housing educators and counselors.* Washington, D.C.: Fannie Mae.

Fannie Mae. (2015). *Know your options*. Retrieved November 16, 2015, from http://www.knowyouroptions.com.

Federal Housing Administration. (2015). *FHA requirements: Mortgage insurance for FHA insured loan*. Retrieved August 16, 2015, from http://www.fha.com/fha_requirements_mortgage_insurance.

Federal Reserve Bank. (2014). *A consumer's guide to refinancing*. Retrieved August 16, 2015, from http://www.federalreserve.gov/pubs/refinancings/default.htm#consider.

Freddie Mac. (n.d.). *My home: Glossary of terms*. Retrieved September 10, 2015, from http://myhome.freddiemac.com/resources/glossary.html.

Freddie Mac. (2011a). *Choosing the mortgage option for you*. Retrieved August 16, 2015, from http://www.freddiemac.com/homeownership/pdf/choosing_the_mortgage_option.pdf.

Freddie Mac. (2011b). *Your step-by-step mortgage guide: From application to closing*. Retrieved August 16, 2015, from http://www.freddiemac.com/homeownership/pdf/step-by-step_mortgage_guide.pdf.

Freddie Mac. (2014). *Perceptions of renting and homeownership*. Retrieved September 10, 2015, from http://www.freddiemac.com/multifamily/pdf/mf_renter_profile.pdf.

Furlong, F., Lang, D., & Takhtamanova, Y. (2014). *Drivers of mortgage choices by risky borrowers*. (FRBSF Economic Letter 2014-01). Retrieved August 16, 2015, from http://www.frbsf.org/economic-research/publications/economic-letter/2014/january/factors-lower-credit-rating-borrowers-adjustable-rate-mortgage/el2014-01.pdf.

Gill, E. B. (n.d.). *Home buyers: What documents to expect at your close of escrow*. Retrieved February 4, 2016, from http://www.nolo.com/legal-encyclopedia/home-buyers-what-documents-expect-your-close-escrow.html.

Herbert, C. E., McCue, D. T., & Sanchez-Moyano, R. (2014). Is homeownership still an effective means to build wealth for low-income and minority households? In E. S. Belsky, C. E. Herbert, & J. H. Molinsky (Eds.), *Homeownership built to last: Balancing access, affordability, and risk after the housing crisis* (pp. 50–98). Washington, D.C., and Cambridge, Mass.: Brookings Institution Press and Joint Center for Housing Studies of Harvard University.

HOA-USA. (2010). *Guide to understanding homeowner associations*. Retrieved August 16, 2015, from https://docs.google.com/viewerng/viewer?url=http://www.traditionsinpinevillehoa.com/HOA/assn23341/images/hoa_usa_guide_to_understanding_homeowner_associations.pdf.

Home Affordable Refinance Program. (n.d.a). *About HARP*. Retrieved August 16, 2015, from http://www.harp.gov/About.

Home Affordable Refinance Program. (n.d.b). *Your best route to a better mortgage*. Retrieved August 16, 2015, from http://www.harp.gov/Default.aspx?Page=1.

HomePath.com. (n.d.a). *Monthly payment calculator*. Retrieved August 16, 2015, from https://www.homepath.com/calculators_pop/index.html?type=homeloan&ht=875.

HomePath.com. (n.d.b). *Mortgage affordability calculator*. Retrieved August 16, 2015, from https://www.homepath.com/calculators_pop/index.html?type=affordability&ht=900.

Immergluck, D. (2012). Mortgage finance. In A. T. Carswell (Ed.), *The encyclopedia of housing* (pp. 466–471). Thousand Oaks, Calif.: Sage.

Jaffe, A. J. (2012). Reverse-equity mortgage. In A. T. Carswell (Ed.), *The encyclopedia of housing* (pp. 636–638). Thousand Oaks, Calif.: Sage.

Kelly, B. M. (1993). *Expanding the American dream: Building and rebuilding Levittown*. Albany: State University of New York Press.

Kiplinger's. (2006). *Buying and selling a home*. Washington, D.C.: Kaplan.

Lubell, J. (2014). Filling the void between homeownership and rental housing: A case for the use of shared equity homeownership. In E. S. Belsky, C. E. Herbert, & J. H. Molinsky (Eds.), *Homeownership built to last: Balancing access, affordability, and risk after the housing crisis* (pp. 203–227). Washington, D.C., and Cambridge, Mass.: Brookings Institution Press and Joint Center for Housing Studies of Harvard University.

Mantel, B. (2012). Future of homeownership: Should government do more to help homeowners? *CQ Researcher, 22*(44). Retrieved August 16, 2015, from http://library.cqpress.com/cqresearcher/document.php?id=cqresrre2012121400.

Manzi, N., & Michael, J. (2014). *Capital gains taxation: Federal and state*. Minneapolis:

Minnesota House of Representatives. Retrieved January 28, 2016, from http://www.house.leg.state.mn.us/hrd/pubs/ss/sscapgain.pdf.

McClure, K. (2012). Tax incentives. In A. T. Carswell (Ed.), *The encyclopedia of housing* (pp. 729–732). Thousand Oaks, Calif.: Sage.

McWhinney, J. E. (2017). Mortgages: Fixed-rate versus adjustable-rate. http://www.investopedia.com/articles/pf/05/031605.asp.

Minnesota Homeownership Center. (2011). *Path to successful homeownership*. Retrieved August 16, 2015, from http://www.hocmn.org/wp-content/uploads/2013/01/PathSuccessfulHO_Dec20111.pdf.

Mitchell, D., Rafshit, S., Knoblauch, K., Morton, V., Wilson, B., & Bruin, M. (2014). *Aging and housing in North Saint Paul*. Minneapolis, Minn.: Center for Urban and Regional Analysis.

Morris, E. W., & Winter, M. (1975). A theory of family housing adjustment. *Journal of Marriage and the Family, 37*(1), 79–88.

MyFico.com. (n.d.). *Glossary of credit terms*. Retrieved March 24, 2016, from http://www.myfico.com/CreditEducation/Glossary.aspx.

NOLO. (n.d.a). *Marriage and property ownership: Who owns what?* Retrieved August 16, 2015, from http://www.nolo.com/legal-encyclopedia/marriage-property-ownership-who-owns-what-29841.html.

NOLO. (n.d.b). *Nolo's plain-English law dictionary: Disclosure*. Retrieved April 30, 2016, from http://www.nolo.com/dictionary/disclosure-term.html.

Perez, W. (2015). *Sale of your home: Capital gains taxes*. Retrieved August 16, 2015, from http://taxes.about.com/od/taxplanning/qt/home_sale_tax.htm.

Prevost, L. (2015, March 8). Millennials on the homeownership path. *New York Times*, n.p. Retrieved February 11, 2016, from http://www.nytimes.com/2015/03/08/realestate/millennials-on-the-homeownership-path.html?_r=0.

Quercia, R. G., Freeman, A., & Ratcliffe, J. (2011). *Regaining the dream: How to renew the promise of homeownership for America's working families*. Washington, D.C.: Brookings Institution Press.

Rascoff, S., & Humphries, S. (2015). *The new rules of real estate*. New York: Grand Central.

RealtyTrac. (2015, July 22). *FHA buyer share of home sales at two-year high in Q2 2015 as all-cash buyer share drops to 82-month low in June*. Retrieved November 16, 2015, from http://www.realtytrac.com/news/foreclosure-trends/realtytrac-june-and-midyear-2015-u-s-home-sales-report/.

Reid, C. (2014). To buy or not to buy? Understanding tenure preferences and the decision-making process of lower-income households. In E. S. Belsky, C. E. Herbert, & J. H. Molinsky (Eds.), *Homeownership to last: Balancing access, affordability, and risk after the housing crisis*. (pp. 143–171). Washington, D.C., and Cambridge, Mass.: Brookings Institution Press and Joint Center for Housing Studies of Harvard University.

Robertson, C. (2013). *Tips for first-time home buyers*. Retrieved September 10, 2015, from http://www.thetruthaboutmortgage.com/tips-for-first-time-homebuyers/.

Rohe, W. (2012). Homeownership. In A. T. Carswell (Ed.), *The encyclopedia of housing* (pp. 293–298). Thousand Oaks, Calif.: Sage.

Rohe, W. M., Van Zandt, S., & McCarthy, G. (2002). Social benefits and costs of homeownership. In N. P. Retsinas & E. S. Belsky (Eds.). *Low-income homeownership: Examining the unexamined goal* (pp. 99–140). Washington, D.C.: Brookings Institution Press.

Roskey, C. B., & Green, M. S. (2006). Federal government housing policies. In J. L. Merrill, S. R. Crull, K. R. Tremblay, L. L. Tyler, & A. T. Carswell (Eds.), *Introduction to housing* (pp. 139–165). Upper Saddle River, N.J.: Pearson Prentice Hall.

Schwartz, A. F. (2015). *Housing policy in the United States*. New York: Routledge.

Sheldon, S. (2014). *How much of a down payment do you really need to buy a house?* Retrieved August 16, 2015, from http://blog.credit.com/2014/08/how-much-of-a-down-payment-do-you-really-need-to-buy-a-house-93579/.

Silver, H. (2012). Cooperative housing. In A. T. Carswell (Ed.), *The encyclopedia of housing* (pp. 101–107). Thousand Oaks, Calif.: Sage.

U.S. Bureau of the Census. (n.d.). *Quarterly homeownership rates for the U.S. and regions:*

1965 to present, table 14. Retrieved August 16, 2015, from http://www.census.gov/housing/hvs/data/histtabs.html.

U.S. Department of Agriculture. (n.d.). *Single Family Housing Guaranteed Loan Program*. Retrieved September 17, 2015, from http://www.rd.usda.gov/programs-services/single-family-housing-guaranteed-loan-program.

U.S. Department of Housing and Urban Development. (n.d.a). *Frequently asked questions about HUD's reverse mortgages*. Retrieved February 4, 2016, from http://portal.hud.gov/hudportal/HUD?src=/program_offices/housing/sfh/hecm/rmtopten.

U.S. Department of Housing and Urban Development (n.d.b). *HUD Office of Housing counseling*. Retrieved September 17, 2015, from http://www.hud.gov/offices/hsg/sfh/hcc/hcs.cfm.

U.S. Department of Housing and Urban Development. (2015a). *Buying a home*. Retrieved August 16, 2015, from http://portal.hud.gov/hudportal/HUD?src=/topics/buying_a_home.

U.S. Department of Housing and Urban Development. (2015b). *Consumer fact sheet for Home Equity Conversion Mortgages (HECM)*. Retrieved August 16, 2015, from http://portal.hud.gov/hudportal/documents/huddoc?id=DOC_13006.pdf.

U.S. Department of Veterans Affairs. (n.d.). *Federal benefits for veterans, dependents and survivors*. Retrieved August 16, 2015, from http://www.va.gov/opa/publications/benefits book/benefits chap06.asp.

Chapter 8 The Housing Finance Industry

KATRIN B. ANACKER

Over the past two centuries, the U.S. housing finance industry has evolved from a set of informal, local arrangements to a formal, well-developed, international infrastructure based on partnerships between public and private participants that specialize in funding, lending, and servicing (Aalbers, 2012a, 2012b; Bernanke, 2015; Blinder, 2014; Dymski, 2012a, 2012b; Forrest, 2011; Gotham, 2012; Ho, 2009; Integrated Financial Engineering, Inc., 2006; Johnson & Kwak, 2010; Paulson, 2013; Rajan, 2010; Ronald & Dol, 2011; Sassen, 2012; H. Schwartz, 2012; Sveinsson, 2011; Wainwright, 2012; Williams, 2011). The evolution of the housing finance industry has been influenced by private-sector innovations in the form of mortgage products, mortgage-related securities, specialized institutions, risk management tools, and public-sector responses to economic shocks in the form of public policies. However, this evolution has not been linear (i.e., public policies are not necessarily established after economic shocks) (Integrated Financial Engineering, Inc., 2006).

The U.S. housing finance system was world class in its size, scope, and efficiency (Integrated Financial Engineering, Inc., 2006) until the start of the national crisis related to subprime lending (i.e., lending at higher interest rates and foreclosures in the first quarter of 2007, when most lenders reduced mortgage availability (Li and Goodman, 2014). At that time researchers discovered that some subprime borrowers could have qualified for prime loans (Lee, 2007) and that some mortgage products were toxic and designed to explode, despite the good repayment intentions and behavior of many borrowers (Carr, 2009). They also discovered that the private mortgage recording system Mortgage Electronic Registration Systems, Inc. (MERS) (Mortgage Electronic Registration Systems, n.d.), which has increasingly replaced the public mortgage recording system at the county courthouse, had not been without flaws (Brown, 2014; see chapter 15). This chapter discusses select actors and infrastructures in the U.S. housing finance industry, including building and loan societies (B&Ls), mortgage banks, the Federal Housing Administration (FHA), the Federal National Mortgage Association (Fannie Mae), and the Federal Home Loan Mortgage Corporation (Freddie Mac).

BUILDING AND LOAN SOCIETIES

Building and loan societies were established in the United States in the 1830s (Bodfish, 1931; Dexter, 1889; Wright, 1894) and served as the initial providers of home loans.[1] These lenders provided a well-functioning savings infrastructure with savings contracts for down payment for homeowners until the 1950s (Mason, 2004). A typical historic B&L was a small mutual fund into which all members made weekly or monthly dues payments. The pooled dues were invested in mortgage loans that the association made to the subset of members who chose to purchase new or existing homes (Bodfish, 1931; Mason, 2004; Snowden, 2003). B&Ls had a cooperative character that might remind some of local fraternities (Banerjee, Besley, & Guianne, 1994; Dexter, 1889).

The contractual foundation of B&Ls was the share accumulation plan, in which each nonborrowing member, after having paid an entrance fee in some cases, pledged to buy shares in the association by paying regular weekly or monthly dues until his or her investment reached a predetermined maturity value. Once a certain amount was reached, a nonborrowing member became a borrowing member who could take out a mortgage based on a mortgage contract. These mortgages had a life cycle of only a few years (Bodfish, 1931; Dexter, 1889). Nonborrowers and borrowers fully shared the risks and rewards of the association's mortgage portfolio (Snowden, 1997, 2003). Unlike bank customers, who could immediately withdraw their deposits, potentially leading to bank runs, B&L members were the legal owners of the thrift and thus could not immediately withdraw money (Mason, 2004).

The first B&L in the United States was the Oxford Provident Building Association, which was established in January 1831 in Frankford, an independent borough that later became incorporated into Philadelphia (Bodfish, 1931; Dexter, 1889; Mason, 2004; Piquet, 1930; Teck, 1968; Wright, 1894). The first B&Ls gradually benefited from the movement of people to cities and the westward migration (Bodfish, 1931; Mason, 2004; Riegel & Doubman, 1927; Teck, 1968). The number of B&Ls remained very small in the first five decades, including during the Civil War, and then increased in the 1880s, during a period of rapid urbanization (Bodfish, 1931; Mason, 2004; Riegel & Doubman, 1927; Teck, 1968). In the 1880s urban home building activity and then mortgage lending increased rapidly, although annual building volumes fluctuated, partly due to the national economy and partly due to a collapse in local real estate markets that also negatively impacted the respective B&Ls (Mason, 2004; Snowden, 1988, 2003; Weiss, 2002). During the same time, B&Ls became more popular and were the primary providers of residential mortgage financing for single-family homes until the 1930s. They eventually declined when most of them were ultimately transformed into savings and loan societies (S&Ls) in the 1950s (Mason, 2004; Snowden, 1997, 2003).

During the time of the early B&Ls, banking institutions primarily dis-

---

1. Alternative names for B&Ls were cooperative savings and loan associations, building and loan associations, building associations, mutual loan associations, mutual savings and loan associations, homestead aid associations, savings fund and loan associations, cooperative banks, cooperative savings and loan associations, building societies, and building clubs, among others (Bodfish, 1931; Clark & Chase, 1927; Dexter, 1889; Riegel & Doubman, 1927; Wright, 1894). Also, there are many variations among these associations (Riegel & Doubman, 1927; Wright, 1894).

counted commercial paper (i.e., sold certificates of deposit or bonds below face value) and made business loans. Before 1900 national banks were discouraged by custom and prohibited by regulation from lending on real estate of any kind (Snowden, 2003). Thus many prospective homeowners in the United States saved to buy their homes, informally arranged loans through relatives or friends, or applied for mortgages with individual conventional lenders such as nonnational banks (Weiss, 2002).

B&Ls' share of the institutional mortgage market was 14 percent in 1893, 24 percent in 1905, around 36 percent in the early 1920s, and just under 50 percent between 1925 and 1930 (Bodfish, 1931; Mason, 2004; Snowden, 2003). However, these market shares substantially declined between 1929 and 1933, partly due to the Great Depression and refinancing activities through the Home Owners' Loan Corporation (HOLC).

The majority of B&Ls had fewer than two hundred members, while a few had more than five hundred (Mason, 2004; Snowden 1997, 2003). Many B&L members might have had preexisting social connections, as they all resided in the same city and possibly in the same neighborhood (Besley, Coate, and Loury, 1993). Many sources stress the importance of community and its social sanctions in sustaining nonopportunistic behavior among participants (Banerjee et al., 1994). Thus many cooperatives were sustained by repeated interactions among the participants, enabling peer monitoring, as some neighbors may have had more and better information about borrowers than lenders did (Banerjee et al., 1994; Besley, 1993; Stiglitz & Weiss, 1981).

Members were interested in earning relatively high dividends for their shares (i.e., higher rates than in the conventional market) and relatively low interest rates on their mortgages (i.e., lower rates than in the conventional market). Within this setup, B&Ls were able to make loans and pay premiums on time if nonborrowing members paid their dues and borrowing members paid their payments on time. Whenever a member wanted to leave the B&L, he or she could do so after a thirty- to ninety-day grace period, paying an early withdrawal penalty (Bodfish, 1931; Dexter, 1889), although courts ruled against these withdrawal penalties. Also, penalties and statutes prohibited total withdrawals in excess of 50 percent of current association earnings (Mason, 2004; Snowden, 1997, 2003). These early withdrawal fees, however, relieved the associations from maintaining higher reserves and liquidity, thus making them less vulnerable to economic and financial shocks (Mason, 2004; Snowden 1997, 2003).

B&Ls were typically mutually owned (i.e., owned and run by members for the benefits of members). They were typically local, so members were able to monitor each other and convene in frequent membership meetings (Bodfish, 1931; Snowden, 1997; Stiglitz, 1990). Organizational schemes differed slightly. In terminating associations, first established in the 1830s, every member joined when the association was established and each was required to attend meetings and to borrow during the life of the association, which was typically short lived. In serial associations, first established in the 1850s, members could join at certain points in time over the life of the association, and funds could be shifted across saving and borrowing cohorts. In permanent (or Dayton) plan associations, first established well after the 1850s, business was not conducted at membership meetings but in offices that were open several hours each day to collect members' dues and interest payments (Bodfish, 1931; Clark & Chase, 1927; Dexter, 1889; Piquet, 1930; Riegel & Doubman, 1927; Snowden, 1997; Teck, 1968). In 1893, 14 percent of B&Ls were organized as terminating associations, 58 percent were organized as serial associations, and 28 percent were organized as permanent plan associations, although the spatial distribution was uneven (Snowden, 1997; Wright, 1894).

A typical B&L was managed by its secretary, president, and directors (Bodfish, 1931). The secretary dealt directly with the members and also recruited members, collected fees at meetings, collected loan applications, prepared mortgage papers, kept the association's accounts, and reported on the status of the B&L to the directors and stockholders. The president headed the association and all of its meetings, signed documents, and led the board of directors. The board of directors, consisting of at least three to five rotating directors who were elected by the members at the annual meetings for term-limited positions, managed the B&L, approved loan applications at monthly board meetings, and monitored the secretary (Piquet, 1930; Riegel & Doubman, 1927; Snowden, 1997). The appraisal committee was instrumental to the safety and soundness of a B&L (Dexter, 1889; Riegel & Doubman, 1927; Snowden, 2003). It examined loans presented to the association, viewed and appraised properties, and made recommendations for mortgages (Riegel & Doubman, 1927).

Often, the officers and the director served on a voluntary or part-time basis while the president typically served without pay and the secretary received moderate pay (Bodfish, 1931; Mason, 2004; Piquet, 1930; Riegel & Doubman, 1927). Others typically involved in a B&L were local people who worked in closely related real estate specialties, including surveyors, title specialists, attorneys, real estate and insurance agents, homebuilders, and building material suppliers, among others (Piquet, 1930). B&Ls were typically promoted by the so-called building and loan men, who worked on a part-time and voluntary basis. Obviously, with real estate professionals involved in B&Ls, conflicts of interest could arise within the organization. For example, Snowden (1997) points out that a secretary who ran the day-to-day operations earned fees and commissions for each loan the B&L made.

The vast majority of B&Ls were local organizations, although in the mid-1880s to mid-1890s a few regional or national B&Ls were founded, culminating in 1893 with the establishment of the U.S. League of Local Building and Loans, a forerunner of the U.S. Savings and Loan League (Bodfish, 1931). However, the national B&L movement ended quickly in 1896 due to national economic and foreclosure crises (Bodfish, 1931; Mason, 2004; Snowden, 1997). Local members of B&Ls had tried to prevent the formation of a national B&L (Mason, 2004), stressing localization due to its perceived soundness and safety (Snowden, 1997). These members generally feared competition, wanted to protect the good reputation of the local B&Ls, and did not want to be subject to close supervision by the national B&Ls (Bodfish, 1931).

The national B&Ls had several advantages, but they also had disadvantages over the typical local B&L. In terms of advantages, national B&Ls had a geographically more diverse loan portfolio, potential higher earnings due to an increased market size, and lower administrative expenses in theory due to efficiencies of scale (Bodfish, 1931; Snowden, 2003). In terms of disadvantages, they had to maintain centralized, full-time staffs along with field staff and local loan boards, thus requiring an entrance fee for new members and a fixed proportion of regular dues to fund these expenses, resulting in higher operating expenses than local B&Ls.

In the 1930s and 1940s, the local and regional B&L movement gradually transitioned into the regional and national savings and loan (S&Ls) society industry. During the same time the federal S&L charter, the Federal Home Loan Bank (FHLB) system of federal deposit insurance, and associated regulations were established, enabling S&Ls to become a national industry until their decline in the 1980s and 1990s (Mason, 2004).

MORTGAGE BANKS

Mortgage banks originate mortgages, which they typically pool and sell to an institutional investor on the so-called secondary mortgage market (i.e., Wall Street, Fannie Mae, or Freddie Mac) through a process called mortgage securitization, where several mortgages are bundled and then sold in one package, thus spreading risk (Corgel, Ling, & Smith, 2001). Alternatively, mortgage banks may keep each originated mortgage in their portfolio. Mortgage securitization was started in 1968 after Congress created Ginnie Mae to insure FHA loans, as discussed below. It gained popularity after 1970, when Fannie Mae securitized and bundled mortgages originated by banks and Freddie Mac securitized and bundled mortgages originated by savings and loans. Over time, government-sponsored securitization led to private-sector securitization (Immergluck, 2012).

Until the mid-2000s, most mortgage banks seemed to lend somewhat liberally. However, this changed in reaction to the house price, subprime, and foreclosure crises, as illustrated by the Mortgage Bankers Association's (MBA) Mortgage Credit Availability Index (MCAI). This index is calculated based on several factors related to borrower eligibility, including credit score, loan type, loan-to-value ratio (i.e., the relationship between the mortgage amount and the house price), and so on (see figure 8.1). A decrease in the MCAI indicates tightening lending standards while an increase indicates loosening lending standards. The MCAI was set to 100 in March 2012; it

FIGURE 8.1
Total Mortgage Credit Availability Index (MCAI), June 2004–June 2017
Source: Mortgage Bankers Association, 2015; powered by Ellie Mae's AllRegs® Market Clarity®. Reprinted with permission.

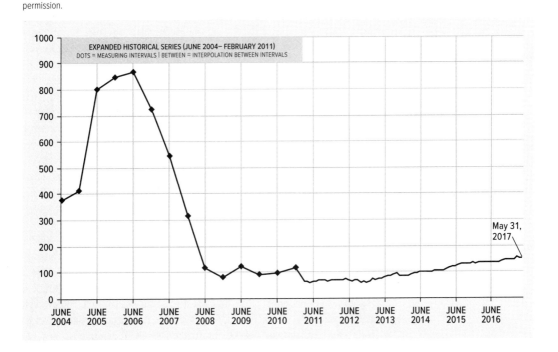

reached almost 900 points in June 2006 and has been hovering around 100 since early 2010 (as of this writing).

Over the next few years mortgage credit availability is not expected to improve due to pending housing finance reform measures, including the proposed winding down of Fannie Mae and Freddie Mac, general risk aversion based on the somewhat recent foreclosure crisis, and increased legal litigation risks based on recently adjusted liability and lending standards (Carr & Anacker, 2014; Goodman, Zhu, & George, 2015). More specifically, for mortgages guaranteed either implicitly (by Fannie Mae and Freddie Mac) or explicitly (by the FHA, the Department of Veterans Affairs, and the U.S. Department of Agriculture) and bundled into securities, the "government retains the right to put the credit risk back on the lender if the agency finds a mistake in the underwriting of the loan. Because a great deal of uncertainty has existed over how government agencies enforce this right" (Goodman et al., 2015: 2), mortgage banks and other lenders have reduced their lending activities in the recent past. For example, Goodman et al. (2015) estimate that 4.2 million more loans would have been made between 2009 and 2013 if lending standards had been similar to 2001 levels. This trend may impact homeownership and wealth-building opportunities in the near and distant future, especially for millennials, who might become first-time home buyers at some point in time.

FEDERAL HOUSING ADMINISTRATION

The Federal Housing Administration, established in 1934 to insure mortgages, is an important component of the U.S. housing finance system. The FHA does not originate mortgages; only lenders do. FHA-insured mortgages were the first guaranteed mortgages in the United States, backed by the full faith and credit of the U.S. government. They were a major contributor to the post–World War II housing boom, particularly in the suburbs, and they accelerated the spread of homeownership (Goodman & Nichols, 1997; Gramlich, 2007; Quercia & Park, 2012; Santiago, Galster, Tucker, Santiago-San Roman, & Kaiser, 2011; U.S. Department of Housing and Urban Development, 2014). Over the past eight decades the FHA has insured forty million mortgages (Carr, 2013) and has provided three main benefits to the U.S. housing market. First, the agency has provided and continues to provide regional and countercyclical stabilization (Galante, 2013). In other words, when conventional lenders scale down their activities during an economic crisis, the FHA scales up. Second, the FHA initially provided and keeps providing mortgage credit to borrowers, especially to first-time home buyers (U.S. Department of Housing and Urban Development, 2014) and, later, neighborhoods underserved by the private mortgage market (Immergluck, 2011). Third, it tests and standardizes new types of mortgages (Pennington-Cross & Yezer, 2000).

The FHA was established by the National Housing Act of 1934. A year earlier, in 1933, the Home Owners' Loan Corporation had been established to help refinance single-family home mortgages that were delinquent or had been defaulted on during the Great Depression (Crossney & Bartelt, 2005; Metzger, 1998). Four years later, in 1938, President Franklin D. Roosevelt established the Federal National Mortgage Association, discussed below (Newton, 1998). While the HOLC refinanced mortgages near or in foreclosure until 1936 (Metzger, 1998), both the FHA and Fannie Mae have continued to facilitate the flow of credit to home buyers, homebuilders, and financial institutions to the present day (Jakle & Wilson, 1992).

Prior to the establishment of the FHA, down payment requirements were large, often more than 50 percent; repayment schedules were short, typically five years; and balloon payments (i.e., a payment in one large sum at the end of the loan term) were also large (Schwartz, 2015). One of the biggest financial innovations of the FHA was the development of the long-term, twenty- to thirty-year standardized low-interest fixed-rate amortizing mortgage for single-family homes. Also, the FHA instituted layout, construction, and underwriting standards and required a relatively low down payment with the borrower also paying an insurance premium in proportion to the outstanding loan amount to the FHA to protect the HUD-approved mortgage lender (Baxandall & Ewen, 2000; Howard, 2014; Jackson, 1985; Johnson, 1996; Levy, 1997; Mason, 2004; Oliver & Shapiro, 2006; Roskey & Green, 2006; Weiss, 2002). This mortgage design still remains the norm throughout the government-backed and private mortgage lending industry. If the borrower defaults on the mortgage, the FHA pays the lender and repossesses the home (Morrow-Jones, 1998).

Over time, the FHA's market share of mortgages has fluctuated greatly. FHA insurance volume typically increases during weaker economic periods such as recessions, when the private mortgage market largely retracts from lending. In turn, that volume decreases during stronger economic periods, when the private lending market shows more signs of vitality and is more willing to originate mortgages (U.S. Government Accountability Office, 2007; U.S. Department of Housing and Urban Development, 2014). As shown in figure 8.2, the FHA proportion of all mortgages was 1.8 percent in 2005 and 2006, 3.3 percent in 2007, 16.9 percent in 2008, 20.4 percent in 2009, 18.3 percent in 2010, 13.7 percent in 2011, and 11.5 percent in 2012).

The decrease of the FHA's market share in the early 2000s illustrates the crowding out of the FHA by the private mortgage market, with its many

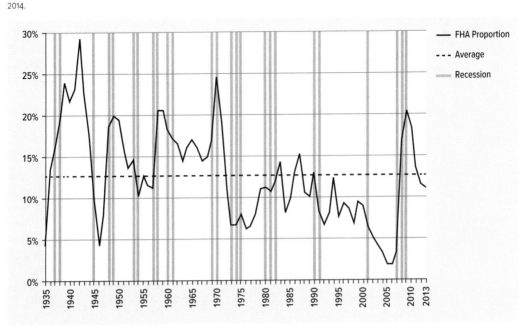

FIGURE 8.2
FHA Proportion of U.S. Mortgage Market, 1935–2013
Source: Author, based on Golding, Szymanoski, and Lee, 2014.

poorly underwritten and unsustainable high-cost loans and its many aggressive independent mortgage brokers (Anacker & Crossney, 2013; Bradford & Shlay, 1996; Pinto, 2014; Shiller, 2008). During that time, FHA insurance almost sank into oblivion. In turn, the increase in the FHA's market share in the late 2000s, after the private mortgage market had largely abandoned lending, has reinforced the FHA's core mission (Berenbaum & Forrest, 2013). In sum, "when conventional lending falters, the FHA picks up the slack" (A. Schwartz, 2014: 666).

The impact of the FHA's countercyclical role on property values and the economy has been analyzed in recent research. If there had been no FHA-insured mortgages during the Great Recession, which took place from December 2007 to June 2009, it has been estimated that property values would have declined an additional 25 percent. This would have resulted in over $3 trillion in lost housing equity, three million additional lost jobs and an unemployment rate of 12 percent, and a loss of half a trillion dollars in economic output (Carr, 2013; Griffith, 2012).

From 1934 to the early to mid-1960s, the FHA almost exclusively benefited non-Hispanic white borrowers who bought new single-family detached homes in non-Hispanic white communities. These communities occasionally included racial covenants and were typically located in suburbs that had not changed in their racial and social composition and were not predicted to do so in the future (Bratt, Stone, & Hartman, 2006; Crossney & Bartelt, 2005; Dreier, Mollenkopf, & Swanstrom, 2014; Immergluck, 2009; Kleniewski, 1997; Wiese, 2004). In other words, "the FHA . . . redlined the cities [i.e., it did not lend in cities], speeding the migration of the white middle class out of the older central cities" and contributing to residential racial and ethnic segregation (Dreier et al., 2014: 121; powell, 2012). The FHA's practices were based on historic mortgage underwriting ratios and risk-rating systems adopted from the HOLC, which had previously adopted them from the real estate industry; these practices were based on attitudes and predictions about the trajectory of property values in communities (Pendall, Nelson, Dawkins, & Knaap, 2005; Peterson, 2013; Rosenbaum & Friedman, 2007; see chapters 7, 10, and 15).

Although the U.S. Supreme Court ruled in 1948 in *Shelley v. Kraemer* that state courts were prohibited from enforcing racial covenants, and the FHA revised its underwriting manual in 1950 to factor in Shelley v. Kraemer, the FHA nevertheless continued to favor racial segregation and to refrain from challenging racial steering and redlining for many years (Dreier, 2013; Harris, 2013; Squires & Hartman, 2013). In the mid-1950s, the FHA began to soften its exclusionary stance and made substantial investments toward expanding black/African American homeownership (Wiese, 2004).

From the early to mid-1960s through the mid-2000s, the FHA continued to disproportionately benefit non-Hispanic white borrowers but also increasingly benefited borrowers of color (Perry, 1995). Since the mid-2000s, the FHA has insured and refinanced proportionately more conventional mortgages held by borrowers of color than those held by whites (Quercia & Park, 2012). For example, in 2009 about 60 percent of black/African American and Hispanic/Latino borrowers obtained an FHA-insured mortgage, compared to about 35 percent of non-Hispanic white borrowers (U.S. Department of Housing and Urban Development, 2011). Since then these proportions have decreased, possibly reflecting an increase in other racial and ethnic groups taking out FHA-insured mortgages (U.S. Department of Housing and Urban Development, 2014; see chapter 16).

Over the past decades, some factors of the lending requirements for FHA-insured mortgages have been eased. For example, the absolute maximum loan size of FHA-insured mortgages has increased due to increasing house prices. In 2015 the limit was $271,050 in all markets and up to $729,750 in high-cost markets (Van Order & Yezer, 2014). Over time, some factors of the lending requirements for FHA-insured mortgages have been eased while others have been tightened. For example, the down payment requirement for these mortgages changed from typically 10 percent in the 1930s to 3.5 percent at present, although borrowers with relatively low credit scores now face increased down payment requirements (Carr, 2013; Immergluck, 2009; Peterson, 2013; U.S. Department of Housing and Urban Development, 2014).

Similarly, over time the average maximum loan-to-value (LTV) ratio of FHA-insured mortgages has increased from 80 percent of the property value (i.e., 20 percent down payment) to the current 96.5 percent (i.e., 3.5 percent down payment) (U.S. Department of Housing and Urban Development, n.d.). Furthermore, FHA-insured mortgages now require increased insurance premiums (Denton, 2006; Urban Institute, 2014). Moreover, insurance requirements for FHA-insured mortgages now apply for the entire life cycle of the mortgage, unlike conventional mortgages, where the insurance requirement ends when the LTV has reached 80 percent, and former FHA-insured mortgages, where the insurance requirement ended once the LTV had reached 78 percent (Gordon, 2013; see chapters 7 and 10).

FANNIE MAE AND FREDDIE MAC

The Federal National Mortgage Association (Fannie Mae) and the Federal Home Loan Mortgage Corporation (Freddie Mac) are two government-sponsored enterprises (GSEs) that are part of the U.S. housing finance industry (Carr & Anacker, 2014). In 1938 President Franklin D. Roosevelt established Fannie Mae to encourage the flow of credit to home buyers, homebuilders, and financial institutions (Reingold & Bolinger, 2012), just four years after the FHA had been established (Newton, 1998). The establishment of Fannie Mae and the FHA made homeownership affordable for millions of U.S. households by lowering such down payment requirements substantially (Johnson, 1996).

Three decades later, in 1968, Congress split Fannie Mae into two units. One unit bought government-issued loans and would remain a government entity, called Ginnie Mae (Congressional Budget Office, 1991), and one became the privatized Fannie Mae, from then on owned by stockholders, although its public mission continued (Brandlee, 2011). Congress had become concerned about Fannie Mae's increased debt, a potential government liability, and about increasing interest rates, which indicated a decrease in housing construction and housing finance activity (Hagerty, 2012).

In 1970 Congress, in response to a request by the savings and loan industry, passed a law that became part of the Federal Home Loan Bank System, then the regulator of the savings and loan industry (Stanton, 2012). As a result, Fannie Mae continued to securitize and bundle mortgages originated by banks, while Freddie Mac securitized and bundled mortgages originated by savings and loans, expanding the secondary market for mortgages (Wallison, 2011).

Securitization revolutionized home mortgage finance by connecting Wall Street with Main Street. It tapped huge new pools of capital across the nation and abroad to finance home mortgages in the United States. Lenders, in a continuous cycle, could make loans, sell those loans for securitization, and then invest the sales proceeds into a new batch of loans, which in turn could be securitized. Securitization also solved an age-old problem for banks. In the past, banks had held home mortgages until they were paid off, which meant that banks were financing long-term mortgage loans with short-term demand deposits. This "lending long and borrowing short" pattern destabilized banks. Securitization solved that problem by allowing banks to move mortgages off their books in exchange for upfront cash, which in turn added liquidity to the lending market (Engel & McCoy, 2011).

Fannie Mae and Freddie Mac were granted several advantages (Calabria, 2011; Howard, 2014; Reiss, 2011; Stanton, 2007), including an implicit federal guarantee (Baily, 2011), in other words a potential bailout. Also, Fannie Mae and Freddie Mac were granted exemption from state and local taxes (Pozen, 2011), relatively low minimum capital requirements compared to most banks (Engel & McCoy, 2011; Zandi, 2009), and the commitment of the U.S. Treasury to buy up to $2.25 billion of their debt securities if the need arose (Dynan & Gayer, 2011), among many other advantages (Carr & Anacker, 2014).

In return for preferential or special treatment by the government, Fannie Mae and Freddie Mac were tasked to support housing finance by lowering the cost of mortgage credit for many borrowers (Johnson, 1996); purchasing conforming mortgages, pooling and insuring them against default, and then issuing bonds or securitized claims to the public (Immergluck, 2009); and absorbing some risk in the mortgage market (Johnson & Kwak, 2010; see chapters 7 and 10).

In addition to these tasks, Fannie Mae and Freddie Mac were also required to meet affordable housing goals set by the U.S. Department of Housing and Urban Development, first established in the Federal Housing Enterprise Financial Safety and Soundness Act (FHEFSSA) of 1992 and later modified (Engel & McCoy, 2011). The three statutory goals were

- The Low- and Moderate-Income Housing Goal: loans to borrowers with incomes at or below the median income for the market area in which they live;
- The Special Affordable Goal: loans to very low-income borrowers (i.e., those with incomes at or below 60 percent of the area median income), or to low-income borrowers living in low-income areas (i.e., borrowers with incomes at or below 80 percent of the area median income, living in census tracts in which the median income of households is at or below 80 percent of the area median income);
- The Underserved Areas Goal: loans to borrowers living in low-income census tracts (tracts in which the median income of residents is at or below 90 percent of the area median income) or tracts with a high proportion of residents of color (tracts in which residents of color make up at least 30 percent of residents, and the median income of

residents in the tracts does not exceed 120 percent of the area median income (Weicher, 2010: 3).

The subprime, foreclosure, and economic crises, which started in 2007, placed enormous additional pressures on Fannie Mae and Freddie Mac. The GSEs were not at the forefront with respect to the purchase and securitization of subprime loans that were at the center of attention during the foreclosure crisis. However, eventually they did purchase bundled mortgages backed by poorly underwritten subprime loans and later they securitized high-risk Alternative-A prime mortgages (i.e., mortgages originated to borrowers who did not provide full documentation, had relatively low credit scores and relatively high LTV values, and in some cases held investment properties), which would eventually contribute to hemorrhaging losses for both GSEs (Howard, 2014; Scharfstein & Sunderam, 2011). The result was that both GSEs, similar to most Wall Street companies, required substantial financial support from the government to continue operating.

In September 2008 the U.S. Department of the Treasury and the Federal Housing Finance Agency (FHFA) placed Fannie Mae and Freddie Mac into conservatorship (National Commission on the Causes of the Financial and Economic Crisis in the United States, 2011), "a process in which the government holds a failed financial institution with the purpose of restoring the firm to solvency" (Stanton, 2012: 245). Thus the implicit federal guarantee became explicit when the federal government guaranteed principal and interest payments on the two GSEs' debt- and mortgage-backed securities (Engel and McCoy, 2011). Since then, policy makers have discussed the role of Fannie Mae and Freddie Mac in the housing and homeownership market. Although many earlier proposals suggested a reduced role for both GSEs, later proposals suggested eliminating them (McLean & Nocera, 2011; U.S. Department of the Treasury and U.S. Department of Housing and Urban Development, 2011; Housing Commission, 2013).

For example, in May 2014 the U.S. Senate Banking Committee approved legislation to reform the nation's housing finance system. The justification for the termination of Fannie Mae and Freddie Mac is that greater levels of private capital in the housing finance system will protect U.S. taxpayers from future bailouts (U.S. Senate Banking Committee, 2014). Although Fannie Mae and Freddie Mac received $187.4 billion from the government after 2008, they have paid the Treasury $192.0 billion as of February 2014 (Prior, 2014). In other words, both firms have started generating profits and have repaid the government more in dividends than they received in bailout funds, which has led some to conclude that because Fannie Mae and Freddie Mac have turned profitable, they should be taken out of conservatorship and be allowed to operate again as shareholder-owned, quasi-government institutions.

Nevertheless, the number of housing finance reform proposals that have called for the elimination of Fannie Mae has increased (Corker, 2013; Griffith, 2012; Hensarling, n.d.; Stein & Johnson, 2013; U.S. Senate Banking Committee, 2014; U.S. Senate Committee on Banking, Housing, and Urban Affairs, 2014; Waters, 2014). Winding down parts of the housing finance infrastructure that were established as far back as the Great Depression would mean that the seventy-year-long era of relatively high homeownership rates could come to an end (see chapter 15).

CONCLUSION

The FHA, Fannie Mae, Freddie Mac, and mortgage banks, along with the Federal Home Loan Banks (not discussed in this chapter due to space constraints), are a major reason that the United States became a nation of homeowners. However, over the past several decades, Fannie Mae and Freddie Mac have increasingly become targets for private firms. Before 2008 most arguments launched against the two GSEs were technocratic and small scale (Carr & Anacker, 2014). After 2008 the number of critics who launched ideological, broad-brush arguments against Fannie Mae and Freddie Mac increased (Meyer, 2008; Pollock, 2014). Interestingly, the FHA has been spared in discussions on housing finance reform (Housing Commission, 2013).

Most suggested legislation has focused on channeling Fannie Mae's and Freddie Mac's business and profits to private financial firms. Interestingly, based on a memorandum from December 2010 (released in February 2014) and on the amended senior preferred stock agreement from August 2012, Fannie Mae's common equity stockholders will not have access to any positive earnings in the future (Garrison, 2014). Instead, Fannie Mae is now required to remit to the Treasury Department all of its retained earnings in excess of the respective capital reserve amount (Howard, 2014).

For the past seventy years, homeownership has been the cornerstone of the American Dream, serving as the single-largest and most sustainable source of wealth building, pride, and accomplishment for many Americans, assisted by the U.S. housing finance industry (Carr & Anacker, 2014). Winding down Fannie Mae and Freddie Mac will not solve the current dearth in mortgage lending. Indeed, estimates conclude that mortgages will become more, not less, costly with enactment of any of the suggested bills that include the elimination of Fannie Mae and Freddie Mac, causing the homeownership rate to remain steady or possibly decrease in the short term and midterm (Timiraos, 2014; see chapter 15).

REFERENCES

Aalbers, M. B. (2012a). European mortgage markets before and after the financial crisis. In M. B. Aalbers (Ed.), *Subprime cities: The political economy of mortgage markets* (pp. 120–150). Malden, Mass.: Wiley-Blackwell.

Aalbers, M. B. (2012b). Subprime cities and the twin crises. In M. B. Aalbers (Ed.), *Subprime cities: The political economy of mortgage markets* (pp. 3–22). Malden, Mass.: Wiley-Blackwell.

Anacker, K. B., & Crossney, K. B. (2013). Analyzing CRA lending during the tsunami in subprime lending and foreclosure in the Philadelphia MSA. *Housing Studies, 28,* 529–552.

Baily, M. N. (2011). *The future of housing finance: Restructuring the U.S. residential mortgage market.* Washington, D.C.: Brookings Institution Press.

Banerjee, A. V., Besley, T., & Guianne, T. W. (1994). Thy neighbor's keeper: The design of a credit cooperative with theory and a test. *Quarterly Journal of Economics, 109,* 491–515.

Baxandall, R., & Ewen, E. (2000). *Picture windows: How the suburbs happened.* New York: Basic Books.

Berenbaum, D., & Forrest, K. S. (2013). Onward and upward: The fight to ensure equal access to credit via the Federal Housing Administration. In C. Hartman & G. D. Squires (Eds.), *From foreclosure to fair lending* (pp. 41–54). New York: New Village Press.

Bernanke, B. S. (2015). *The courage to act: A memoir of a crisis and its aftermath*. New York: W. W. Norton.

Besley, T., Coate, S., & Loury, G. (1993). The economics of rotating savings and credit associations. *American Economic Review, 83*, 792–810.

Blinder, A. S. (2014). *After the music stopped: The financial crisis, the response, and the work ahead*. New York: Penguin.

Bodfish, H. M. (Ed.) (1931). *History of building and loan in the United States*. Chicago: U.S. Building and Loan League.

Bradford, C., & Shlay, A. B. (1996). Assuming a can opener: Economic theory's failure to explain discrimination in FHA lending markets. *Cityscape, 2*, 77–87.

Brandlee, K. (2011). *Promoting homeownership in the United States: The rise and fall of Fannie Mae and Freddie Mac*. Iowa City: University of Iowa.

Bratt, R. G., Stone, M. E., & Hartman, C. (2006). Why a right to housing is needed and makes sense: Editors' introduction. In R. G. Bratt, M. E. Stone, & C. Hartman (Eds.), *A right to housing: Foundation for a new social agenda* (pp. 1–19). Philadelphia: Temple University Press.

Brown, E. (2014, July 8). The looming foreclosure crisis: As the Fed runs out of bullets, local governments step in. *Huffington Post*. Retrieved from http://www.huffingtonpost.com/ellen-brown/the-looming-foreclosure-c_b_5561871.html.

Calabria, M. (2011, May 7). Fannie, Freddie, and the subprime mortgage market. *CATO Institute Briefing Papers*.

Carr, J. (2013). *Rethinking the Federal Housing Administration*. Washington, D.C.: Center for American Progress.

Carr, J. H. (2009). *Home foreclosure: Will voluntary modifications help families save their homes?* [Testimony]. Washington, D.C.: U.S. House of Representatives: Committee on the Judiciary. Retrieved February 13, 2015, from http://judiciary.house.gov/_files/hearings/pdf/Carr090709.pdf.

Carr, J. H., & Anacker, K. B. (2014). The past and current politics of housing finance and the future of Fannie Mae, Freddie Mac, and Homeownership in the United States. *Banking and Financial Services Policy Report: A Journal of Trends in Regulation and Supervision 33*, 1–10.

Clark, H. F., & Chase, F. A. (1927). *Elements of the modern building and loan associations*. New York: MacMillan.

Congressional Budget Office. (1991). *Controlling the risks of government-sponsored enterprises*. Washington, D.C.: Congress of the United States.

Corgel, J. B., Ling, D. C., & Smith, H. C. (2001). *Real estate perspectives: An introduction to real estate*. Boston: McGraw-Hill Irwin.

Corker, B. (2013, June 25). *Housing Finance Reform and Taxpayer Protection Act*. Washington, D.C.: Sen. Bob Corker.

Crossney, K. B., & Bartelt, D. W. (2005). Residential security, risk, and race: The Home Owners' Loan Corporation and mortgage access in two cities. *Urban Geography, 26*(8), 707–736.

Denton, N. A. (2006). Segregation and discrimination in housing. In R. G. Bratt, M. E. Stone, & C. Hartman (Eds.), *A right to housing: Foundation for a new social agenda* (pp. 61–81). Philadelphia: Temple University Press.

Dexter, S. (1889). Co-operative savings and loan associations. *Quarterly Journal of Economics, 3*, 315–335.

Dreier, P. (2013). Building a movement for fair lending, foreclosure relief, and financial reform. In C. Hartman & G. D. Squires (Eds.), *From foreclosure to fair lending: Advocacy, organizing, occupy, and the pursuit of equitable access to credit* (pp. 287–321). New York: New Village Press.

Dreier, P., Mollenkopf, J., & Swanstrom, T. (2014). *Place matters: Metropolitics for the twenty-first century*. Lawrence: University Press of Kansas.

Dymski, G. A. (2012a). The reinvention of banking and the subprime crisis: On the origin of subprime loans, and how economists missed the crisis. In M. B. Aalbers (Ed.), *Subprime cities: The political economy of mortgage markets* (pp. 151–184). Malden, Mass.: Wiley-Blackwell.

Dymski, G. A. (2012b). Subprime crisis and urban problematic. In M. B. Aalbers (Ed.),

Subprime cities: The political economy of mortgage markets (pp. 293–314). Malden, Mass.: Wiley-Blackwell.

Dynan, K., & Gayer, T. (2011). Government's role in the housing finance system: Where do we go from here? In M. N. Baily (Ed.), *The future of housing finance: Restructuring the U.S. residential mortgage market* (pp. 66–91). Washington, D.C.: Brookings Institution Press.

Engel, K. C., & McCoy, P. A. (2011). *The subprime virus: Reckless credit, regulatory failure, and next steps.* Oxford: Oxford University Press.

Forrest, R. (2011). Households, homeownership and neoliberalism. In R. Forrest and Ngai-Ming Yip (Eds.), *Housing markets and the global financial crisis: The uneven impact on households* (pp. 1–19). Northampton, Mass.: Edward Elgar.

Galante, C. (2013). *Written testimony of Assistant Secretary for Housing and Federal Housing Administration Carol Galante: Hearing before the House Financial Services Committee.* Washington, D.C.: U.S. Department of Housing and Urban Development.

Garrison, T. (2014, February 18). Paying Fannie and Freddie investors was never part of the plan. Investors: This is government confiscation of private property. Housingwire.com.

Golding, E. L., Szymanoski, E. J., & Lee, P. P. (2014). *FHA at 80: Preparing for the future.* Washington, D.C.: U.S. Department of Housing and Urban Development.

Goodman, J. L., & Nichols, J. B. (1997). Does FHA increase home ownership or just accelerate it? *Journal of Housing Economics, 6*, 184–202.

Goodman, L., Zhu, J., & George, T. (2015). *The impact of tight credit standards on 2009–13 lending.* Washington, D.C.: Urban Institute.

Gordon, J. (2013). *Examining the proper role of the Federal Housing Administration in our mortgage insurance market.* Testimony before the House Committee on Financial Services. Washington, D.C.: Center for American Progress.

Gotham, K. F. (2012). Creating liquidity out of spatial fixity: The secondary circuit of capital and the restructuring of the U.S. housing finance system. In M. B. Aalbers (Ed.), *Subprime cities: The political economy of mortgage markets* (pp. 25–52). Malden, Mass.: Wiley-Blackwell.

Gramlich, E. M. (2007). *Subprime mortgages: America's latest boom and bust.* Washington, D.C.: Urban Institute Press.

Griffith, J. (2012). *The Federal Housing Administration saved the housing market.* Washington, D.C.: Center for American Progress.

Hagerty, J. (2012). *The fateful history of Fannie Mae: New Deal birth to mortgage crisis fall.* Mount Pleasant, S.C.: History Press.

Harris, D. (2013). *Little white houses: How the postwar home constructed race in America.* Minneapolis: University of Minnesota Press.

Hensarling, J. (n.d.). *Reforming Fannie Mae and Freddie Mac.* Washington, D.C.: Rep. Jeb Hensarling.

Ho, K. (2009). *Liquidated: An ethnography of Wall Street.* Durham, N.C.: Duke University Press.

Housing Commission. (2013). *Housing America's future: New directions for national policy.* Washington, D.C.: Bipartisan Policy Center.

Howard, T. (2014). *The mortgage wars: Inside Fannie Mae, big-money politics, and the collapse of the American Dream.* New York: McGraw Hill.

Immergluck, D. (2009). *Foreclosed: High-risk lending, deregulation, and the undermining of America's mortgage market.* Ithaca, N.Y.: Cornell University Press.

Immergluck, D. (2011). From minor to major player: The geography of FHA lending during the U.S. mortgage crisis. *Journal of Urban Affairs, 33*, 1–20.

Immergluck, D. (2012). Mortgage finance. In A. T. Carswell (Ed.), *The encyclopedia of housing* (pp. 467–471). Thousand Oaks, Calif.: Sage.

Integrated Financial Engineering, Inc. (2006). *Evolution of the U.S. housing finance system: A historical survey and lessons for emerging mortgage markets.* Washington, D.C.: U.S. Department of Housing and Urban Development.

Jackson, K. T. (1985). *Crabgrass frontier: The suburbanization of the United States.* Oxford: Oxford University Press.

Jakle, J. A., & Wilson, D. (1992). *Derelict landscapes: The wasting of America's built environment.* Savage, Md.: Rowman and Littlefield.

Johnson, J. A. (1996). *Showing America a new way home: Expanding opportunities for home ownership*. San Francisco: Jossey-Bass.

Johnson, S., & Kwak, J. (2010). *13 bankers: The Wall Street takeover and the next financial meltdown*. New York: Pantheon Books.

Kleniewski, N. (1997). *Cities, change, and conflict: A political economy of urban life*. Belmont, Calif.: Wadsworth.

Lee, M. (2007). *Subprime mortgages: A primer*. National Public Radio. Retrieved February 13, 2015, from http://www.npr.org/templates/story/story.php?storyId=9096735.

Levy, J. M. (1997). *Contemporary urban planning*. Upper Saddle River, N.J.: Prentice Hall.

Li, W., & Goodman, L. (2014). *A better measure of mortgage application denial rates*. Washington, D.C.: Urban Institute.

Mason, D. L. (2004). *From buildings and loans to bail-outs: A history of the American savings and loan industry*. Cambridge: Cambridge University Press.

McLean, B., & Nocera, J. (2011). *All the devils are here: The hidden history of the financial crisis*. New York: Portfolio/Penguin.

Metzger, J. T. (1998). Home Owners' Loan Corporation. In W. van Vliet (Ed.), *The encyclopedia of housing* (pp. 232–233). Thousand Oaks, Calif.: Sage.

Meyer, D. (2008, July 17). *Fannie's lesson: The real scandals are legal*. National Public Radio.

Morrow-Jones, H. A. (1998). Federal Housing Administration. In W. van Vliet (Ed.), *The encyclopedia of housing* (pp. 181–183). Thousand Oaks, Calif.: Sage.

Mortgage Bankers Association. (2015). *Mortgage credit availability increases in April*. Washington, D.C.: Mortgage Bankers Association.

Mortgage Electronic Registration Systems, Inc. (n.d.). About us. Reston, Va.: Mortgage Electronic Registration Systems.

National Commission on the Causes of the Financial and Economic Crisis in the United States. (2011). *The financial crisis inquiry report*. New York: PublicAffairsReports.

Newton, L. Q. (1998). Fannie Mae. In W. van Vliet (Ed.), *The encyclopedia of housing* (pp. 171–172). Thousand Oaks, Calif.: Sage.

Oliver, M. L., & Shapiro, T. M. (2006). *Black wealth/White wealth*. New York: Routledge.

Paulson, H. M. (2013). *On the brink: Inside the race to stop the collapse of the global financial system*. New York: Business Plus.

Pendall, R., Nelson, A. C., Dawkins, C. J., & Knaap, G. J. (2005). Connecting smart growth, housing affordability, and racial equity. In X. de Souza Briggs (Ed.), *The geography of opportunity: Race and housing choice in metropolitan America* (pp. 219–246). Washington, D.C.: Brookings Institution Press.

Pennington-Cross, A., & Yezer, A. M. (2000). The Federal Housing Administration in the new millennium. *Journal of Housing Research, 11*, 357–372.

Perry, V. (1995). Research findings: Who are FHA borrowers? *Secondary Mortgage Markets, 11*, 13.

Peterson, S. J. (2013). *Planning the home front: Building bombers and communities at Willow Run*. Chicago: University of Chicago Press.

Pinto, E. J. (2014). *Homeownership and the state of the union: Creating a straight, broad highway to debt-free ownership*. Washington, D.C.: American Enterprise Institute.

Piquet, H. S. (1930). *Building and loan associations in New Jersey*. Princeton, N.J.: Princeton University Press.

Pollock, A. J. (2014, April 7). Plan C: A simple fix for Fannie and Freddie. *Congress Blog: The Hill's Forum for Lawmakers and Policy Professionals*.

powell, j. a. (2012). *Racing to justice: Transforming our conceptions of self and other to build an inclusive society*. Bloomington: Indiana University Press.

Pozen, R. C. (2011). Toward a three-tier market for U.S. home mortgages. In M. N. Baily (Ed.), *The future of housing finance: Restructuring the U.S. residential mortgage market* (pp. 26–65). Washington, D.C.: Brookings Institution Press.

Prior, J. (2014, February 21). Fannie and Freddie to pay back taxpayers. *Politico*.

Quercia, R. G., & Park, K. A. (2012). *Sustaining and expanding the market: The public purpose of the Federal Housing Administration*. Chapel Hill: University of North Carolina Center for Community Capital.

Rajan, R. G. (2010). *Fault lines: How hidden fractures still threaten the world economy*. Princeton, N.J.: Princeton University Press.

Reingold, D., & Bolinger, J. (2012). Federal government. In A. T. Carswell (Ed.), *The encyclopedia of housing* (pp. 211–216). Thousand Oaks, Calif.: Sage.

Reiss, D. (2011). *Fannie Mae, Freddie Mac, and the future of federal housing finance policy: Regulatory failure, and next steps.* Oxford: Oxford University Press.

Riegel, R., & Doubman, J. R. (1927). *The building-and-loan association.* New York: John Wiley & Sons.

Ronald, R., & Dol, K. (2011). Housing in the Netherlands before and after the global financial crisis. In R. Forrest and Ngai-Ming Yip (Eds.), *Housing markets and the global financial crisis: The uneven impact on households* (pp. 93–112). Northampton, Mass.: Edward Elgar.

Rosenbaum, E., & Friedman, S. (2007). *The housing divide: How generations of immigrants fare in New York's housing market.* New York: New York University Press.

Roskey, C. B., & Green, M. S. (2006). Federal government housing policies. In J. L. Merrill, S. R. Crull, K. R. Tremblay, Jr., L. L. Tyler, & A. T. Carswell (Eds.), *Introduction to housing* (pp. 139–165). Upper Saddle River, N.J.: Pearson Prentice Hall.

Santiago, A. M., Galster, G. C., Tucker, C. M., Santiago-San Roman, A. H., & Kaiser, A. A. (2011). Be it ever so humble, there's no place like home: The experiences of low-income, minority homebuyers. In R. M. Silverman & K. L. Patterson (Eds.), *Fair and affordable housing in the U.S.: Trends, outcomes, future directions* (pp. 289–342). Leiden: Brill.

Sassen, S. (2012). Expanding the terrain for global capital: When local housing becomes an electronic instrument. In M. B. Aalbers (Ed.), *Subprime cities: The political economy of mortgage markets* (pp. 74–96). Malden, Mass.: Wiley-Blackwell.

Scharfstein, D., & Sunderam, A. (2011). The economics of housing finance reform. In M. N. Baily (Ed.), *The future of housing finance: Restructuring the U.S. residential mortgage market* (pp. 146–198). Washington, D.C.: Brookings Institution Press.

Schwartz, A. (2014). Commentary: The essential if problematic role of FHA mortgage insurance. *Housing Policy Debate, 24,* 666–669.

Schwartz, A. (2015). *Housing policy in the United States.* New York: Routledge.

Schwartz, H. (2012). Finance and the state in the housing bubble. In M. B. Aalbers (Ed.), *Subprime cities: The political economy of mortgage markets* (pp. 53–73). Malden, Mass.: Wiley-Blackwell.

Shiller, R. J. (2008). *The subprime solution: How today's global financial crisis happened, and what to do about it.* Princeton, N.J.: Princeton University Press.

Snowden, K. A. (1988). Mortgage lending and American urbanization. *Journal of Economic History, 48,* 273–285.

Snowden, K. A. (1997). Building and loan associations in the U.S., 1880–1893: The origins of localizations in the residential mortgage market. *Research in Economics, 51,* 227–250.

Snowden, K. A. (2003). The transition from building and loan to savings and loan, 1890–1940. In S. L. Engerman, P. T. Hoffman, J.-L. Rosenthal, & K. L. Sokoloff (Eds.), *Finance, intermediaries, and economic development* (pp. 157–206). Cambridge: Cambridge University Press.

Squires, G. D., & Hartman, C. (2013). Occupy Wall Street: A new wave of fair housing activism? In C. Hartman & G. D. Squires (Eds.), *From foreclosure to fair lending: Advocacy, organizing, occupy, and the pursuit of equitable access to credit* (pp. 1–17). New York: New Village Press.

Stanton, T. H. (2007). The life cycle of the government-sponsored enterprise: Lessons for design and accountability. *Public Administration Review, 67,* 837–845.

Stanton, T. H. (2012). Government-sponsored enterprises. In A. T. Carswell (Ed.), *The encyclopedia of housing* (pp. 247–250). Thousand Oaks, Calif.: Sage.

Stein, E., & Johnson, C. (2013). *Framework for housing finance reform: Fixing what went wrong and building on what works.* Durham, N.C.: Center for Responsible Lending.

Stiglitz, J. E. (1990). Peer monitoring and credit markets. *World Bank Economic Review, 4,* 351–366.

Stiglitz, J. E., & Weiss, A. (1981). Credit rationing in markets with imperfect information. *American Economic Review, 71,* 393–410.

Sveinsson, J. R. (2011). Housing in Iceland in the aftermath of the global financial crisis.

In R. Forrest and Ngai-Ming Yip (Eds.), *Housing markets and the global financial crisis: The uneven impact on households* (pp. 57–73). Northampton, Mass.: Edward Elgar.

Teck, A. (1968). *Mutual savings banks and savings and loan associations: Aspects of growth.* New York: Columbia University Press.

Timiraos, N. (2014, April 28). How much will mortgage rates rise in Fannie, Freddie overhaul? *Wall Street Journal.*

Urban Institute. (2014, August). *Housing finance at a glance: A monthly chartbook.* Washington, D.C.: Urban Institute, Housing Finance Policy Center.

U.S. Department of Housing and Urban Development. (n.d.). *Regulatory impact of implementing "Helping Families Save Their Homes" Act.* Washington, D.C.: U.S. Department of Housing and Urban Development. Retrieved February 13, 2015, from http://archives.hud.gov/initiatives/hopeforhomeowners/h4heconomicanalysis.cfm.

U.S. Department of Housing and Urban Development. (2011). *U.S. housing market conditions.* Washington, D.C.: U.S. Department of Housing and Urban Development.

U.S. Department of Housing and Urban Development. (2014). *FHA at 80: Preparing for the future.* Washington, D.C.: U.S. Department of Housing and Urban Development.

U.S. Department of the Treasury and U.S. Department of Housing and Urban Development. (2011). *Reforming America's housing finance market: A report to Congress.* Washington, D.C.: U.S. Department of the Treasury and U.S. Department of Housing and Urban Development.

U.S. Government Accountability Office. (2007). *Federal Housing Administration: Decline in the agency's market share was associated with product and process developments of other mortgage market participants.* Washington, D.C.: U.S. Government Accountability Office.

U.S. Senate Banking Committee. (2014). *Section-by-section of Senate Banking Committee Leaders' bipartisan housing finance reform draft.* Washington, D.C.: Congress of the United States.

U.S. Senate Committee on Banking, Housing, and Urban Affairs. (2014, March 28). *Johnson, Crapo announce housing finance reform markup.* Washington, D.C.: U.S. Senate Committee on Banking, Housing, and Urban Affairs.

Van Order, R., & Yezer, A. (2014). FHA: Recent history and future prospects. *Housing Policy Debate, 24,* 644–650.

Wainwright, T. (2012). Building new markets: Transferring securitization, bond-rating, and a crisis from the U.S. to the U.K. In M. B. Aalbers (Ed.), *Subprime cities: The political economy of mortgage markets* (pp. 97–119). Malden, Mass.: Wiley-Blackwell.

Wallison, P. J. (2011). Eliminating the GSEs as part of comprehensive housing finance reform. In M. N. Baily (Ed.), *The future of housing finance* (pp. 92–110). Washington, D.C.: Brookings Institution Press.

Waters, M. (2014, March 27). *Waters unveils housing finance reform legislation.* Washington, D.C.: Rep. Maxine Waters.

Weicher, J. C. (2010, November 17). The affordable housing goals, homeownership and risk: Some lessons from past efforts to regulate the GSEs. Paper presented at the conference The Past, Present, and Future of the Government-Sponsored Enterprises, Federal Reserve Bank of St. Louis, St. Louis, Mo. Retrieved July 15, 2012, from http://research.stlouisfed.org/conferences/gse/Weicher.pdf.

Weiss, M. A. (2002). *The rise of community builders. The American real estate industry and urban land planning.* Washington, D.C.: BeardBooks.

Wiese, A. (2004). *Places of their own: African American suburbanization in the twentieth century.* Chicago: University of Chicago Press.

Williams, P. (2011). The credit crunch in the U.K.: Understanding the impact on housing markets, policies, and households. In R. Forrest and Ngai-Ming Yip (Eds.), *Housing markets and the global financial crisis: The uneven impact on households* (pp. 41–56). Northampton, Mass.: Edward Elgar.

Wright, C. D. (1894). *Ninth annual report of the commissioner of labor: Building and loan associations.* Washington, D.C.: Government Printing Office.

Zandi, M. (2009). *Financial shock: Global panic and government bailouts—How we got here and what must be done to fix it.* Upper Saddle River, N.J.: FT Press.

Chapter 9   Renting

CHERIE STUEVE, MARTIN C. SEAY,
AND ANDREW T. CARSWELL

Renting provides a vital housing solution for many households. The decision to rent can be highly personal, as it tends to be based on personal preferences, employment, financial circumstances, and sometimes uncertainty about a householder's personal and professional future (see chapter 2). While renting is an attractive housing option for many households, not all households are able to find affordable rental units. Many local housing markets have an insufficient number of affordable housing units, resulting in many low- and moderate-income households spending a high percentage of their budget on housing-related expenses. Many households adapt to these costs by finding roommates, choosing a smaller unit than desired, and living farther away from metro areas, where housing is less expensive (Stone, 2006; see chapter 10).

Consequently, past and present local, state, and national policy discussions have focused on the lack of affordable housing and the underfunding of rental housing assistance programs to support eligible low- and moderate-income households (National Low Income Housing Coalition, 2014b). Currently, only 25 percent of eligible renter households receive some form of assistance (Bipartisan Policy Center, 2013; see chapter 14). The inability to afford rental housing has been partially spurred by long-term real wage stagnation or decline (Kusisto, 2015). Between 2013 and 2015 there were only minimal increases in real wages while housing costs increased, creating affordability issues for many households (Anacker & Li, 2016; Anderson, 2015; Sparshott, 2015). In 2015 a household with one full-time minimum-wage worker could not afford a modest two-bedroom rental unit anywhere in the country (National Low Income Housing Coalition, 2015; see chapter 10). This chapter discusses several aspects of renting: the historical social status of renters, the demand for and characteristics of rental housing, the supply and characteristics of rental housing, and the demographic and socioeconomic drivers of rental housing. Then the chapter discusses the government's role in rental housing through health and housing codes, zoning ordinances, height restrictions, eviction laws, rent control, and select federal programs, such as rental housing assistance vouchers, the Low-Income Housing Tax Credit (LIHTC), and nondiscrimination in rental housing.

HISTORIC SOCIAL STATUS OF RENTERS

In the United States, landlord-tenant relations have a long and checkered past filled with conflicts. The early colonial period was marked by stark differences in class and economic status between renters and owners. For several decades, many areas did not even allow tenants the right to vote (Dreier, 1982; Krueckeberg, 1999). Because of the difference in standing between renters and landowners, tenants staged collective protests that sometimes resulted in physical conflict and damage to landowners' properties (Countryman, 1976). As the United States transitioned from an agrarian, rural society to an industrialized, urban one, conflicts between tenants and landlords continued due to overcrowded, unhealthy living environments in low-quality rental housing in many major cities. In response to these issues, activists such as Lawrence Veiller and Jacob Riis dedicated themselves to improving urban workers' housing situations not only as a societal and moral imperative but also as a way of improving the health and welfare of the workforce through improved living conditions (Goss & Campbell, 2008; Howe, 2012; Riis, 1971; Veiller, 1910; see chapter 18).

During the twentieth century, many state and local governments enacted tenants' rights laws and ordinances, partly triggered by the demands of tenants' organizations, enabling renters and their organizations to exercise more power and authority in landlord-tenant conflicts (Heskin, 1981; Marcuse, 1981). Through these tenants' organizations, disgruntled renters waged numerous rent strikes. These strikes saw tenants collectively refusing to pay their rent until certain concessions had been met by the landlords, such as making repairs to the property, improving neighborhood conditions, establishing a grievance process, and preventing ad hoc evictions (Gilderbloom, 2012; Marcuse, 1981). Tenants' organizations also fought for long-term goals, such as housing affordability and rent control in cities considered unaffordable (Block, 2008; Cohen, Wardip, & Williams, 2013; see chapter 10).

ADVANTAGES AND DISADVANTAGES OF RENTING

While there have been struggles between tenants and landlords throughout American history, modern-day renters enjoy many more liberties than the generations of renters before them. Renting provides several advantages compared to homeownership. First, renting translates into relatively predictable monthly costs over the life of a lease, although these costs may change once the end of the lease has been reached, possibly making the unit unaffordable. Second, renting allows the renter to defer the vast majority of repairs and routine maintenance to the landlord. Third, renting provides flexibility to change housing with relatively small costs within a relatively short time frame. Fourth, rental housing may be located in neighborhoods or developments that are characterized by a good sense of community. In upscale neighborhoods or developments, this sense of community may be enhanced by amenities such as swimming pools, playground areas, clubhouses, fitness facilities, on-site maintenance personnel, twenty-four-hour security, and concierge services for pet care and dry cleaning (Davis, 2012).

Renting also comes with several disadvantages. First, renters are unable to use their rent payments to reduce their federal tax liability, unlike homeowners with mortgages, who are able to claim mortgage interest and property taxes paid as itemized deductions on their tax returns, offsetting a portion of the ownership costs. Second, renting does not act as a forced savings vehicle that results in rent-free living at the end of the mortgage term. Thus renting does not result in decreased monthly housing expenses, which might be especially appreciated after retirement, when a householder's income typically decreases while medical expenses typically increase (Joint Center for Housing Studies of Harvard University, 2014). Third, renting may restrict an individual's ability to customize his or her living environment by improving efficiencies, such as upgraded windows, insulation, and energy-efficient appliances, or to make other structural additions or changes. Fourth, some rental housing may be located in dense neighborhoods or developments, translating into a lack of privacy and an inability to control noise from neighbors (Davis, 2012; see chapter 2).

DEMAND FOR AND CHARACTERISTICS OF RENTAL HOUSING

Over the past decade the proportion of renter households has grown from 31 percent of all households in 2005 (about thirty-four million) to 37 percent of all households in 2015 (about forty-three million). This increase will most likely continue, as an additional 4.0 to 4.7 million renter households are expected to enter the market over the next decade, with immigration being the biggest driver of this trend (Joint Center for Housing Studies of Harvard University, 2013).

While household composition can be a factor in the decision about whether to rent or buy, income remains one of the driving factors in determining tenure status. Whereas only 13 percent of all U.S. households earn less than $15,000 annually, roughly 25 percent of all renters are in that income category. This pattern is reversed for households with incomes over $75,000, with only 17 percent of these households renting (Joint Center for Housing Studies of Harvard University, 2013; see chapter 1). Wealth is another factor in determining tenure status. While the down payment requirement of conventional loans is 20 percent, the current down payment requirement of the Federal Housing Administration is 3.5 percent. Either of these down payment amounts may be an insurmountable barrier for many low- and moderate-income renters (Joint Center for Housing Studies of Harvard University, 2013; see chapters 7, 8, and 10).

Characteristics of rental housing range from very small units in multifamily developments (sometimes called studios, efficiencies, single-room occupancies [SROs], microunits, or Accessory Dwelling Units [ADUs] with basic or minimalist features; to buildings with two units, typically called duplexes or duets, each with its separate entrance; to very large freestanding units with high-end, luxury furnishings and amenities, such as a pool or workout facilities (Chapple, Nemirow, Wegmann, & Dentel-Post, 2013; see chapter 17). Over 30 percent of occupied rental units are single-family homes, and nearly 20 percent of occupied rental units are in buildings that have two to four units, based on estimates of the American Housing Survey for 2011 (Joint Center for Housing Studies of Harvard University, 2013). Indeed, only 29 percent of occupied rental units are in buildings with ten or more units (Joint Center for Housing Studies of Harvard University, 2013).

Renter households are more commonly located in metropolitan areas, with 43 percent of all renters living in urban areas and 40 percent in suburban areas but only 17 percent in rural areas (Joint Center for Housing Studies of Harvard University, 2013). In rural areas, single-family units and mobile homes make up 60 percent of the rental unit supply because apartment buildings are not as common (Joint Center for Housing Studies of Harvard University, 2013; see chapter 1).

SUPPLY OF RENTAL HOUSING

Rental housing represents a dynamic sector of the overall housing market, with an economic impact of approximately $1 trillion (Fuller, 2013). Throughout the twentieth century, companies and well-off individuals primarily owned rental properties. In the late 1990s and early 2000s the notion of individual ownership of rental properties gained a foothold, driven by an abundance of investment capital, the economic boom (interrupted by a small recession from March to November 2001), the presence of tax incentives for developers, and perceptions of low risks in real estate investments. Thus the real estate market heated up and investment in rental properties soared, resulting in about 5 percent of households investing in rental housing (National Bureau of Economic Research, n.d.; Seay, Carswell, Nielsen, & Palmer, 2013; see chapter 8).

The foreclosure crisis of the mid- to late 2000s also contributed to changes in the investor ownership structure in rental housing. About three million single-family owner-occupied homes transitioned to rental properties between 2007 and 2011 (Joint Center for Housing Studies of Harvard University, 2013). This vast increase occurred partially due to a large number of institutional investors strategically purchasing these properties (Edelman, Gordon, & Sanchez, 2014; Weise, 2013). While this process may have increased the rental housing supply, some critics have concerns over how investor landlords will maintain the properties and about the impact on the respective local housing markets when these investors sell the homes in the future (Edelman et al., 2014; Joint Center for Housing Studies of Harvard University, 2014). Additional concerns include how long these homes will remain on the rental market, which creates uncertainty among renters (Edelman et al., 2014; see chapter 15).

While investments in rental properties during the economic boom and the transition from owner-occupied to rental units during the foreclosure crisis have increased the number of available rental units, the rental housing supply, especially of affordable units, has nevertheless been a concern for decades (see chapter 15). Existing affordable rental units are at risk of being removed from the rental market, regardless of whether they are subsidized or unsubsidized. In some cases, units are upgraded or converted to condominium ownership, with prices that are unaffordable for many low- and moderate-income households. Older rental buildings are at risk of being demolished due to their condition or the cost of compliance with current housing codes. Long wait lists provide evidence of the affordable housing shortage for subsidized rental units. These wait lists often stretch on for years or decades. Some communities even close their wait lists to new applicants (Bratt, 2012; see chapter 10).

The private housing sector is typically not able or willing to produce and maintain a sufficient number of rental units that are affordable to low- or moderate-income households because the cost of new construction and land exceeds the level of monthly rent affordable for such households. In 2011 only 34 percent of newly constructed rental units in the United States were affordable to median-income households (National Low Income Housing Coalition, 2014a). Without sufficient funding for rental assistance programs that provide subsidies to bridge the gap between affordable and market rents, low- and moderate-income households must compete for housing within the existing rental unit supply (National Low Income Housing Coalition, 2014a; see chapters 10 and 14).

RENTAL HOUSING OVER THE HOUSEHOLDER'S LIFE CYCLE

Renter households are diverse and composed of individuals in all stages of the life cycle. Historically, most Americans have followed a fairly stable trajectory in their housing status over their life cycle, with transition points based on age, relationship status, and household income. Most young Americans enter the housing market as renters, leaving their childhood home for college or entry-level employment. At this point in the life cycle, renting is often preferred given the flexibility in rental terms, the ability to change roommates, and more predictable monthly housing costs. Most often young adults will remain renters through graduation and for a number of years after entering the workforce. Over time, many people cohabitate or marry, have children, obtain stable employment, and then become homeowners. Such a move to homeownership provides not only housing stability but also a wealth-building opportunity that renters typically do not experience. Moves from homeownership to renting typically occur with empty-nest households or in the case of retirement or foreclosure (Clark, Deurloo, & Dieleman, 2003; Cook, Bruin, & Yust, 2012; Skobba & Goetz, 2012; see chapters 1, 2, 10, 15, and 17).

DEMOGRAPHIC AND SOCIOECONOMIC DRIVERS OF RENTAL HOUSING

While the traditional trajectory of housing over the life cycle has remained strong, there is some evidence that it may have started to shift based on the somewhat recent Great Recession and foreclosure crisis (Joint Center for Housing Studies of Harvard University, 2013; see chapter 15). For young adults, limited employment opportunities and relatively high student debt levels have impacted household formation and marriage rates, delaying the transition away from the childhood home to renting and, ultimately, to owning (Casselman, 2016; see chapters 1 and 2). Economic challenges for many young households have had lingering negative effects on homeownership, as building and rebuilding credit to qualify for a mortgage in a tight credit environment and building and rebuilding lost wealth are both difficult (National Low Income Housing Coalition, 2014a; Woluchem & George, 2014; see chapters 7, 8, 10, and 15). This shift toward renting has also occurred among blacks/African Americans, Hispanics/Latinos, and low- and middle-income people who lost their homes due to foreclosure (Joint Center for Housing Studies of Harvard University, 2013; see chapters 10 and 15).

GOVERNMENT'S ROLE IN RENTAL HOUSING

Over the past several decades, local governments have established many policies that are intended to increase the physical and mental well-being of residents, including renters, such as health and housing codes, zoning ordinances, height restrictions, eviction laws, landlord-tenant laws, rent control, and nondiscrimination policies (see chapter 14).

Health and Housing Codes

In the late nineteenth and the beginning of the twentieth centuries, tenement buildings that were common in major urban areas such as New York City brought about severe health concerns for their residents (Riis, 1971; Veiller, 1910). Severe overcrowding and poor air circulation often resulted in the spread of illnesses such as cholera, typhoid, smallpox, yellow fever, and tuberculosis (Dreier, 1982; Novick & Morrow, 2001). In response to these outbreaks, citizen activists helped establish a series of housing codes that eventually became standard for many urban areas throughout the United States. These regulations address a broad array of issues, including proper light and ventilation, adequate plumbing and drainage, mandatory sewage disposal, fire protection, and regular maintenance schedules (Bauman, Biles, & Szylvian, 2000). These types of housing codes have persisted and are usually considered standard operating procedure for apartment communities, although modifications and upgrades to housing codes are made by public officials (Krieger & Higgins, 2002; see chapter 14).

Zoning Ordinances

Municipal planning departments designate certain land uses for certain parcels through a process called zoning, with the aim of improving health and safety and sometimes resulting in land being put to its highest and best use (see chapter 19). Zoning may entail minimum lot and unit sizes, parking lot restrictions, and maximum household sizes, among other restrictions. Some restrictions have resulted in a decreased supply of rental properties in certain locations, thus increasing rents and producing a de facto environment of "Not In My Back Yard" (NIMBY) that disenfranchises renters (Boudreaux, 2011; Galster, Tatian, Santiago, Pettit, & Smith, 2003; Glaeser, Gyourko, & Saks, 2005; Magliocca, McConnell, Walls, & Safirova, 2012; see chapter 10).

Height Restrictions

Many localities place restrictions on the height of buildings, including rental buildings. There are several reasons for these ordinances, such as preserving the character of a neighborhood, maintaining residential safety, preserving views and the beauty of the landscape, and maintaining or even increasing social interactions (Bertaud & Brueckner, 2005; Kim, 2012; Krieger & Higgins, 2002). Negative consequences of height restrictions may be increased land and property values, causing some to take advantage of lower land and property values at the urban or suburban fringe (Bertaud & Brueckner, 2005; Boudreaux, 2011; see chapters 12 and 13).

Tenant Eviction Laws

A typical lease is a formal contract between a landlord and a renter that spells out specific responsibilities of both. If a tenant breaks the lease or violates the rental agreement, a landlord may terminate the agreement. Violations include late payment of rent, disturbing the neighbors, or keeping an unauthorized pet on the premises. In the case of an eviction, a household loses the right to reside in a unit. In some cases a household's possessions may be placed on the street or adjoining yard, causing devastating effects for the household involved (Desmond, 2016; Scherer, 2012). If a tenant chooses to fight the eviction, the landlord may be compelled to file an eviction lawsuit to carry the process through to its completion. Eviction laws usually allow for such an action to occur in cases of nonpayment of rent, although during the foreclosure crisis some paying renters were evicted when their landlords failed to make mortgage payments (Furman Center for Real Estate and Urban Policy, 2009). Some jurisdictions require proof of a legal concept known as "just cause" in order to proceed with an eviction. Just cause may include the nonpayment of rent, a breach of the rental agreement, or substantial damage to a unit (Stewart, Warner, & Portman, 2016; see chapter 11).

Rent Control

Rent control is a policy that stabilizes rent levels for existing residents in rental housing, aiming to increase housing affordability. It exists in a few cities, such as New York or San Francisco, that have seen high growth in rents (Beyer, 2015; Matthews, 2014). Economists have debated the advantages and disadvantages of rent control for decades. While some scholars bemoan the detrimental aspects of rent control, such as deferred maintenance and market inefficiencies (Block, 2008), others suggest that rent control has an overall benign effect on markets and enhances social welfare (Grant, 2012; see chapter 10).

Nondiscrimination Policies

Historically, many landlords evaluated applicants for rental housing based on their personal criteria, which often resulted in housing discrimination. The Civil Rights Act of 1968 explicitly banned housing discrimination against protected classes, taking into account race, color, religion, national origin or ancestry, sex, and age. In 1988 the Fair Housing Amendments Act added disability and familial status to the list of protected classes (Galster, 2012). Racial and ethnic discrimination may be detected through a set of testers, who have similar characteristics to each other yet differ by race and ethnicity (Riach & Rich, 2002). While discrimination in rental housing has continued, it has become more subtle over the years (Galster, 2012; Ondrich, Stricker, & Yinger, 1999; Turner et al., 2013). Fair housing law provides individuals with a process and remedy if they experience discrimination in the housing market (see chapters 14 and 16).

Landlord-Tenant Statutes

Because there is potential for conflict between a landlord and a tenant on a variety of issues, many states and the District of Columbia have established laws regarding the proper resolution of matters related to the fulfillment of residential lease agreements (Stewart et al., 2016). These councils and statutes were largely originated during the second half of the twentieth century as a way of redressing some of the imbalances that existed among tenants who felt disenfranchised in dispute situations; they are usually considered to be a result of both the civil rights movement and the overall consumer rights revolution of the 1970s and 1980s (Widrow, 2005). While it is important that renters know that they have such rights available to them, outside of federally assisted housing landlord-tenant laws may differ in scope across states (Stewart et al., 2016; see chapter 14).

CONCLUSION

At some point in their lives, almost all individuals rent a home. Renting may be an appropriate and viable housing option for many individuals and households. The flexibility and features of renting may be attractive to people in many different stages of life (see chapters 1 and 2). While homeownership has remained a goal for many Americans, it may be out of reach for some households. The lack of affordable rental housing for low- and moderate-income households has been an ongoing problem in the United States that will persist in the near and distant future (see chapter 10). Local, state, and national housing assistance programs help bridge the gap between income and housing costs for some eligible households, but funding and support still lag behind the growing need for affordable housing, which could be partially addressed by a broader understanding that renting remains a viable, respectable, and honorable option for many people (see chapter 14).

Meanwhile, many recent changes have caused ripple effects throughout the rental housing sector that may have long-term impacts. For example, the initiation of several state legislative bills advocating a minimum-wage increase to nearly fifteen dollars per hour during the 2016 legislative session has several potential implications for the rental housing industry in terms of improving affordability (Morath, Orden, & Lazo, 2016). Several booming metropolitan areas have experienced increased demand for smaller, more affordable micro or studio apartment units, particularly among millennials (Barrionuevo, 2016; Cook et al., 2012). Various federal, state, regional, and local initiatives have been developed to promote the construction of green and sustainable rental housing units to address affordability issues (Carswell & Smith, 2009; Linstroth, 2013; U.S. Department of Housing and Urban Development, n.d.). These changes may be a good first step when it comes to increasing housing affordability, which will be needed as the demand for rental housing increases in the near and distant future (see chapters 1, 2, 10, 15, and 19).

REFERENCES

Anacker, K. B., & Li, Y. (2016). Analyzing housing affordability of U.S. renters during the Great Recession, 2007 to 2009. *Housing and Society, 43*(1), 1–17.

Anderson, B. (2015, September 8). Apartment rents grow faster than incomes. *National Real Estate Investor.* Retrieved April 18, 2016, from http://nreionline.com/multifamily/apartment-rents-grow-faster-incomes.

Barrionuevo, A. (2016). High-tech millennial lifestyle inspires micro apartment boom. *Curbed.* Retrieved April 15, 2016, from http://www.curbed.com/2016/3/15/11235986/micro-apartments-tech-industry-millennials.

Bauman, J. F., Biles, R., & Szylvian, K. M. (2000). *From tenements to the Taylor Homes: In search of an urban housing policy in twentieth-century America*. Harrisburg: Pennsylvania State University Press.

Bertaud, A., & Brueckner, J. K. (2005). Analyzing building-height restrictions: Predicted impacts and welfare costs. *Regional Science and Urban Economics, 35*, 109–125.

Beyer, S. (2015, April 24). How ironic: America's rent-controlled cities are its least affordable. *Fortune*. Retrieved June 10, 2016, from http://www.forbes.com/sites/scottbeyer/2015/04/24/how-ironic-americas-rent-controlled-cities-are-its-least-affordable/#147659f47e36.

Bipartisan Policy Center (2013). Housing America's future: New directions for national policy. Retrieved June 10, 2016, from http://bipartisanpolicy.org/sites/default/files/BPC_Housing%20Report_web_0.pdf.

Block, W. (2008). Rent control. In D. Henderson (Ed.), *The concise encyclopedia of economics*. Indianapolis: Library of Economics and Liberty.

Bratt, R. G. (2012). Public housing. In A. T. Carswell (Ed.), *The encyclopedia of housing* (pp. 569–574). Thousand Oaks, Calif.: Sage.

Carswell, A. T., & Smith, S. (2009). The greening of the multifamily residential sector. *Journal of Engineering, Design & Technology, 7*(1), 65–80.

Casselman, B. (2016, May 27). *Stuck in your parents' basement? Don't blame the economy*. Retrieved May 31, 2016, from http://fivethirtyeight.com/features/stuck-in-your-parents-basement-dont-blame-the-economy/.

Chapple, K., Nemirow, A., Wegmann, J., & Dentel-Post, C. (2013). *The potential for second units in the East Bay*. Berkeley: University of California Center for Community Innovation. Retrieved May 25, 2016, from http://escholarship.org/uc/item/4hg2z73w#page-1.

Clark, W. A., Deurloo, M. C., & Dieleman, F. M. (2003). Housing careers in the United States, 1968–93: Modelling the sequencing of housing states. *Urban Studies, 40*, 143–160.

Cohen, R., Wardip, K., & Williams, L. (2013). *Rental housing affordability: A review of current research*. Washington, D.C.: Center for Housing Policy. Retrieved June 10, 2016, from http://www.nhc.org/media/files/RentalHousing.pdf.

Cook, C., Bruin, M., & Yust, B. L. (2012). Housing adjustment theory. In A. T. Carswell (Ed.), *The encyclopedia of housing* (pp. 336–338). Thousand Oaks, Calif.: Sage.

Countryman, E. (1976). Out of the bounds of the law: Northern land rioters in the eighteenth century. In A. F. Young (Ed.), *The American revolution* (pp. 37–70). DeKalb: Northern Illinois University Press.

Davis, J. E. (2012). Tenure sectors. In A. T. Carswell (Ed.), *The encyclopedia of housing* (pp. 741–744). Thousand Oaks, Calif.: Sage.

Desmond, M. (2016). *Evicted: Poverty and profit in the American city*. New York: Crown.

Dreier, P. (1982). The status of tenants in the United States. *Social Problems, 30*(2), 179–198.

Edelman, S., Gordon, J., & Sanchez, D. (2014). *When Wall Street buys Main Street: The implications of single-family rental bonus for tenants and housing markets*. Washington, D.C.: Center for American Progress. Retrieved June 10, 2016, from http://cdn.americanprogress.org/wp-content/uploads/2014/02/WallStMainSt_Report.pdf.

Fuller, S. (2013). *The trillion dollar apartment industry*. Washington, D.C.: National Multi Housing Council.

Furman Center for Real Estate and Urban Policy. (2009). *The impacts of foreclosure on renters*. New York: Furman Center for Real Estate and Urban Policy.

Galster, G. C. (2012). Discrimination. In A. T. Carswell (Ed.), *The encyclopedia of housing* (pp. 137–142). Thousand Oaks, Calif.: Sage.

Galster, G. C., Tatian, P., Santiago, A. M., Pettit, K. L. S., & Smith, R. (2003). *Why Not In My Backyard? Neighborhood impacts of deconcentrating assisted housing*. New Brunswick, N.J.: Center for Urban Policy Research/Transaction Publishers.

Gilderbloom, J. (2012). Rent strikes. In A. T. Carswell (Ed.), *The encyclopedia of housing* (pp. 597–599). Thousand Oaks, Calif.: Sage.

Glaeser, E. L., Gyourko, J., & Saks, R. (2005). Why is Manhattan so expensive? Regulation and the rise in housing prices. *Journal of Law and Economics, 48*(2), 331–369.

Goss, R. C., & Campbell, H. L. (2008). The evolution of residential property management: From caretaker to income maximization managers. *Housing and Society, 35*(1), 5–20.

Grant, H. (2012). Rent control. In A. T. Carswell (Ed.), *The encyclopedia of housing* (pp. 596–599). Thousand Oaks, Calif.: Sage.

Heskin, A. D. (1981). The history of tenants in the United States, struggle and ideology. *International Journal of Urban and Regional Research, 5*(2), 178–204.

Howe, D. (2012). Housing codes. In A. T. Carswell (Ed.), *The encyclopedia of housing*. Thousand Oaks, Calif.: Sage.

James, R. N., Carswell, A. T., & Sweaney, A. (2009). Sources of discontent: Residential satisfaction of tenants from an Internet ratings site. *Environment and Behavior, 41*(1), 43–59.

Joint Center for Housing Studies of Harvard University. (2013). *America's rental housing: Evolving markets and needs*. Cambridge, Mass.: Harvard University.

Joint Center for Housing Studies of Harvard University. (2014). *Housing America's older adults: Meeting the needs of an aging population*. Cambridge, Mass.: Harvard University.

Kim, S.-K. (2012). High-rise housing. In A. T. Carswell (Ed.), *The encyclopedia of housing* (pp. 262–265). Thousand Oaks, Calif.: Sage.

Krieger, J., & Higgins, D. L. (2002). Housing and health: Time again for public health action. *American Journal of Public Health, 92*(5), 758–768.

Krueckeberg, D. A. (1999). The grapes of rent: A history of renting in a country of owners. *Housing Policy Debate, 10*(1), 9–30.

Kusisto, L. (2015, May 19). Minimum wage in U.S. cities not enough to afford rent, report says. *Wall Street Journal*. Retrieved May 25, 2016, from http://blogs.wsj.com/developments/2015/05/19/report-minimum-wage-in-u-s-cities-not-enough-to-afford-rent/.

Linstroth, T. (2013). *Moving on up: The growth of green affordable housing*. Washington, D.C.: U.S. Green Building Council. Retrieved April 15, 2016, from http://www.usgbc.org/articles/moving-growth-green-affordable-housing.

Magliocca, N., McConnell, V., Walls, M., & Safirova, E. (2012). Zoning on the urban fringe: Results from a new approach to modeling land and housing markets. *Regional Science and Urban Economics, 42*(1), 198–210.

Marcuse, P. (1981). The rise of tenant organizations. In J. Pynoos, R. Schaffer, and C. M. Hartman (Eds.), *Housing urban America* (pp. 49–54). Chicago: Aldine.

Matthews, C. (2014, July 10). America's housing affordability crisis is getting worse. *Fortune*. Retrieved April 15, 2016, from http://fortune.com/2014/07/10/us-housing-affordability/.

Morath, E., Orden, E., & Lazo, A. (2016, March 31). Push for $15 minimum wage heats up. *Wall Street Journal*. Retrieved April 15, 2016, from http://www.wsj.com/articles/race-for-15-minimum-wage-heats-up-1459451862.

National Bureau of Economic Research. (n.d.). *U.S. business cycle expansions and contractions*. Cambridge, Mass.: National Bureau of Economic Research.

National Low Income Housing Coalition (2014a). *National housing trust fund*. Washington, D.C.: National Low Income Housing Coalition. Retrieved June 10, 2016, from http://nlihc.org/issues/nhtf.

National Low Income Housing Coalition (2014b). *Out of reach: Twenty-five years later, the American housing crisis continues*. Washington, D.C.: National Low Income Housing Coalition. Retrieved June 10, 2016, from http://nlihc.org/sites/default/files/oor/2014OOR.pdf.

National Low Income Housing Coalition (2015). *Out of reach: Low wages and high rents lock renters out*. Washington, D.C.: National Low Income Housing Coalition. Retrieved July 9, 2016, from http://nlihc.org/sites/default/files/oor/OOR_2015_FULL.pdf.

Novick, L. F., & Morrow, C. B. (2001). Defining public health: Historical and contemporary developments. In L. F. Novick & G. Mays (Eds.), *Public health administration: Principles for population-based management* (pp. 3–33). Gaithersburg, Md.: Aspen.

Ondrich, J., Stricker, A., & Yinger, J. (1999). Do landlords discriminate? The incidence and causes of racial discrimination in rental housing markets. *Journal of Housing Economics, 8*(3), 185–204.

Riach, P. A., & Rich, J. (2002). Field experiments of discrimination in the market place. *Economic Journal, 112*(483), F480–F518.

Riis, J. A. (1971). *How the other half lives*. New York: Dover.

Scherer, A. (2012). Eviction. In A. T. Carswell (Ed.), *The encyclopedia of housing* (pp. 193–195). Thousand Oaks, Calif.: Sage.

Seay, M. C., Carswell, A. T., Nielsen, R., & Palmer, L. (2013). Rental real estate ownership prior to the Great Recession. *Family and Consumer Sciences Research Journal, 41*(4), 363–374.

Skobba, K., & Goetz, E. G. (2012). Housing careers. In A. T. Carswell (Ed.), *The encyclopedia of housing* (pp. 342–344). Thousand Oaks, Calif.: Sage.

Sparshott, J. (2015, July 28). Rising rents outpace wages in wide swaths of the U.S. *Wall Street Journal*. Retrieved April 18, 2016, from http://www.wsj.com/articles/rising-rents-outpace-wages-in-wide-swaths-of-the-u-s-1438117026.

Stewart, M., Warner, R., & Portman, J. (2016). *Every landlord's legal guide*. Berkeley, Calif.: Nolo.

Stone, M. E. (2006). Housing affordability: One-third of a nation shelter poor. In R. G. Bratt, M. E. Stone, & C. Hartman (Eds.), *A right to housing: Foundation for a new social agenda* (pp. 38–60). Philadelphia: Temple University Press.

Turner, M. A., Santos, R., Levy, D. K., Wissoker, D., Aranda, C., & Pitingolo, R. (2013). *Housing discrimination against racial and ethnic minorities 2012*. Washington, D.C.: U.S. Department of Housing and Urban Development.

U.S. Department of Housing and Urban Development. (n.d.). *Energy-efficient and Green HOME housing*. Washington, D.C.: Author. Retrieved April 15, 2016, from http://portal.hud.gov/hudportal/HUD?src=/program_offices/comm_planning/affordablehousing/programs/home/greenhome.

Veiller, L. (1910). *Housing reform: A hand-book for practical use in American cities*. New York: Charities Publication Committee.

Weise, K. (2013, February 11). Investors turn Atlanta's foreclosed homes into rentals. *Bloomberg Businessweek*. Retrieved April 15, 2016, from http://www.bloomberg.com/news/articles/2013-02-11/investors-turn-atlanta-s-foreclosed-homes-into-rentals.

Widrow, W. (2005, November/December). The tenant movement and housers. *Shelterforce Online*. Issue 144. Washington, D.C.: National Housing Institute. Retrieved July 14, 2016, from http://shelterforce.com/online/issues/144/tenantsandhousers.html.

Woluchem, M., & George, T. (2014). Is student debt hindering homeownership? *Metro Trends*. Retrieved June 10, 2016, from http://blog.metrotrends.org/2014/07/student-debt-hindering-homeownership/.

Chapter 10 Housing Affordability

CHRISTINE C. COOK, MARILYN J. BRUIN, AND BECKY L. YUST

It is critical that communities create and preserve housing that is affordable and available to low- and moderate-income families. The inability to find affordable housing increases the strain on a household's overall household budget, leaving too little for other necessities, like food, health care, transportation to work, and child care (Viveiros & Sturtevant, 2014). For households, affordable housing fosters self-sufficiency, encourages family stability, and improves life chances for children (Millennial Housing Commission, 2002; Newman & Holupka, 2015). Financial strain associated with high housing costs also has been linked to limitations in children's reading and math skills, poor health outcomes, overcrowding, and homelessness (Cohen, 2011; Mueller & Tighe, 2007; National Low Income Housing Coalition, 2014a; Pollack, Griffin, & Lynch, 2010; see chapter 2). A shortage of affordable housing affects the fabric of neighborhoods by limiting socioeconomic diversity (see chapters 12, 13, and 16). The search for affordable housing can cause disruption in children's schooling and a household's access to health care, health resources, and informal and formal social networks (Brennan, 2011; Miller, Pollack, & Williams, 2011; see chapter 18).

The need for and pursuit of affordable housing has been characterized as a "silent crisis" (U.S. Department of Housing and Urban Development, 2014). Cost-burdened renters struggle to pay rent and utilities. Cost-burdened owners may have problems keeping up with property maintenance as well as holding on to home equity (Schwartz & Wilson, 2008). Absent affordable housing, households may be forced to live far from job centers, which increases transportation costs and traffic congestion and causes unemployment, underemployment, or the departure from the labor force altogether (Viveiros & Sturtevant, 2014; see chapter 1).

Community planners, housing professionals, and human service providers understand that a lack of affordable housing constitutes a crisis for communities and individual households. The development of affordable housing can be a tool in community revitalization (Krigman, 2010). To be effective, "affordable housing [provision]... must be combined with other neighborhood improvements such as schools, retail shops, and parks" (Krigman, 2010: 233). This approach not only contributes to economic growth but is a necessary component in attracting and keeping employment opportunities (Oakley & Tsao, 2006).

Despite the evidence that affordable housing is important, not everyone agrees that a mix of low- and moderate-cost housing is needed in communities. Resistance by neighbors to this type of housing has been characterized as NIMBYism (Not In My Back Yard), which can impact the development of affordable housing (National Low Income Housing Coalition, 2003). Thus one of the major challenges policy makers and housing advocates face is how to build a constituency in favor of affordable housing (Dolbeare, 2001). On a larger scale, in the past decade or so, tensions among community growth management strategies, land use regulations, and smart growth plans have sometimes derailed the provision of affordable housing (Addison, Zhang, & Coomes, 2013). When competing for limited community resources, affordable housing advocates often engage in urban and regional collaborations and coalitions to implement strategies and meet housing goals (Addison et al., 2013; Krigman, 2010). The result of these collaborative efforts may be mixed-income housing developments with a substantial number of affordable units, for example (Goetz, 2013; see chapters 12 and 13).

The goal of this chapter is to discuss housing affordability issues. We begin by defining and measuring housing affordability. Next we examine rental housing affordability challenges. We then discuss rental housing affordability solutions. We end the chapter with our observations on the kind of support needed to meet the challenges of housing affordability for low-income households.

DEFINING AND MEASURING HOUSING AFFORDABILITY

The definition of housing affordability has been debated and has changed over time. The standard first set in 1955 by the U.S. Department of Agriculture was that households should not spend more than one-third of their income on housing costs (Kutty, 2005). In 1965 the U.S. Department of Housing and Urban Development (HUD) lowered the standard to no more than 25 percent of a household's income, in order to leave enough for other needs (Mimura, 2008). In 1981 HUD set a standard that a household should not spend more than 30 percent of its total gross income on housing costs, including mortgage or rent payments and utilities (National Low Income

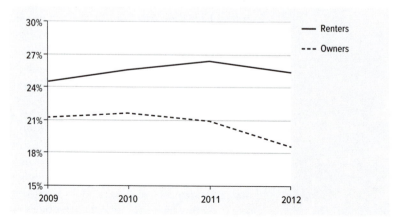

FIGURE 10.1
Comparison of Proportions of Working Renter and Homeowner Households Severely Cost Burdened, 2009–12
Source: Viveiros & Sturtevant, 2014.

Housing Coalition, 2014b). A household that spends more is considered to be housing cost burdened. If the household spends more than 50 percent of its gross income on housing costs it is considered to be severely housing cost burdened (U.S. Department of Housing and Urban Development, 2013). There is widespread agreement that renters with low incomes experience the worst housing affordability problems (Joint Center for Housing Studies of Harvard University, 2013; National Low Income Housing Coalition, 2014b). As shown in figure 10.1, working-renter households are more likely to be severely cost burdened than homeowners (see chapters 1, 2, 7, and 9).

Over the past few years various indices have been developed to measure and compare housing affordability on national, regional, and local levels. The National Association of Home Builders (NAHB) and the National Association of Realtors (NAR) provide indices on the affordability of new and existing homes. These indices allow comparisons among locations and can be used to influence local, state, and federal housing policies (see chapter 14). Figure 10.2 illustrates the Housing Opportunity Index (HOI), a measure of affordability for median-priced new and existing homes for sale in selected years, calculated by the NAHB.

As shown in figure 10.2, in 1993 the median price of homes sold in the United States was $112,000, compared to $205,000 in 2013, an increase of 83 percent over two decades. Median family income grew from $39,700 in 1993 to $64,400 in 2013, an increase of 62 percent over two decades. In other words, median family incomes have not kept pace with median house prices. If the increase in the price of housing had matched inflation since 1993, in 2013 the median price of homes sold would have been $180,561, almost $25,000 less than the actual median price in 2013.[1] A value of 100 on the HOI means that 100 percent of median-priced homes sold in the area were affordable to those with the median family income. The HOI fluctuated from 66.8 in 1993 to 58.9 in 2003. In 2005 the HOI had a value of 41, indicating that only about 40 percent of homes sold were affordable to families with the median income. In 2011 the HOI reached a high of 75.9 (National Association of Home Builders, 2016).

Similarly, figure 10.3 illustrates the Housing Affordability Index (HAI), based on data assembled by the NAR, showing the change in housing affordability from 1993 through 2013. A value of 100 on the Composite HAI means that a household with the median income meets the income threshold to qualify for a mortgage on a median-priced home, assuming a 20 percent down payment. An index above 100 signifies that the household earning the median income surpasses this threshold. For example, figure 10.3 shows that in 2006 the HAI was 107.6, meaning that a household earning the median family income had 107.6 percent of the income necessary to qualify for a conventional loan, assuming a 20 percent down payment. While the HAI has always ranked above 100, the 2006 index illustrates low affordability when the national house price bubble was at its peak (National Association of Realtors, 2014).

Transportation costs can be a major factor impacting housing affordability (Center for Housing Policy, 2012). Thus the U.S. Department of Housing and Urban Development has developed the Location Affordability Index (LAI), which estimates the combined cost of housing and transportation

---

1. The inflationary change in the value of homes was determined by using the U.S. Bureau of Labor Statistics' Consumer Price Index inflation calculator at http://data.bls.gov/cgi-bin/cpicalc.pl.

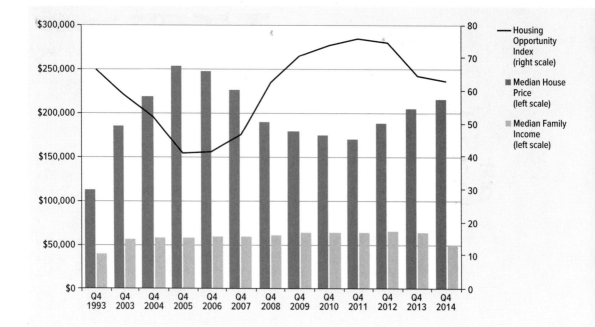

FIGURE 10.2
Housing Opportunity Index (HOI) in the United States, 1993, 2003–14
Source: Derived from National Association of Home Builders, 2016.
Note: The HOI for a given area is defined as the share of homes sold in that area that would have been affordable to a family earning the local median income, based on standard mortgage underwriting criteria.

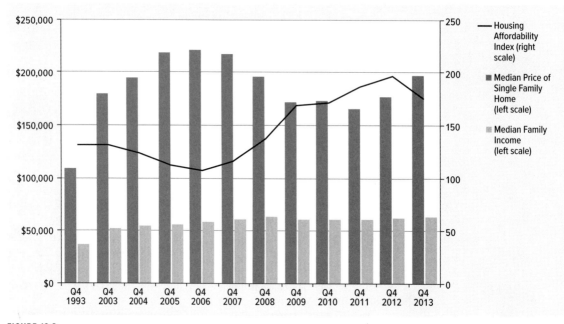

FIGURE 10.3
Housing Affordability Index (HAI) in the United States, 1993, 2003–13
Source: National Association of Realtors, http://www.realtor.org/topics/housing-affordability-index.

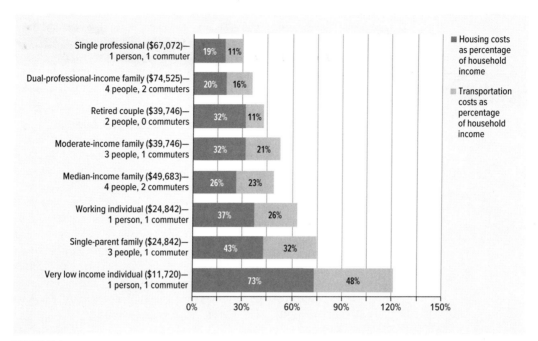

FIGURE 10.4
Location Affordability for Ames, Iowa, for Eight Household Profiles, Differentiated by Household Size and Number of Commuters (annual income in parentheses)
Source: Derived from "Location Affordability Portal," http://www.locationaffordability.info/default.aspx.

for owners and renters in every census block in the United States (U.S. Department of Housing and Urban Development, 2015a). Figure 10.4 provides an example of the LAI for eight different household profiles in Ames, Iowa. The profiles are based on household income, household size, and number of commuters. The LAI ranges from 30 percent of income (19 percent housing costs plus 11 percent transportation costs) for a single professional to 121 percent of income (73 percent housing costs plus 48 percent transportation costs) for a very low income, single-person household. While the former household does not have affordability issues, the latter household does. Households with a calculated LAI greater than their income illustrate that some households would need to rely on additional sources of support, such as government assistance programs, savings, family assistance, and so on. In sum, location does make a difference in affordability when considering housing and transportation costs.

Beyond these indices, there continues to be considerable debate about housing affordability and the appropriate calculations to reflect a household's ability to pay for its housing and other needs (Burke, Stone, & Ralston, 2011; Gan & Hill, 2009; Pelletiere, 2008; Stone, 1993, 2006). The failure of many indices to account for nonhousing needs has led to an alternative method of measuring affordability called the residual income measure. As discussed above, the current ratio measure for calculating housing affordability specifies that a household should not spend more than 30 percent of its total gross income on housing costs, including mortgage or rent payments and utilities. The residual income measure takes into account the cost of nonshelter necessities first, ahead of housing expenses, and also reflects differences in household size and income. The most fully developed and extensively applied version of the residual income measure was initially formulated by Stone (1993), although support for this method has waxed and waned (Stone, 2012). A major drawback to this method is that expenditure data from diverse household configurations are required but not always easily derived. Using the residual measure, Stone concludes that about 30 percent of all households are shelter poor, as they are left with too little money to pay for food, health care, transportation to work, and child care after paying housing costs (Stone, 1993, 2012).

The annual report *Out of Reach*, published by the National Low Income Housing Coalition (NLIHC), discusses housing affordability by calculating the housing wage (i.e., the hourly wage a full-time worker must earn to afford a two-bedroom rental home at HUD-estimated fair market rent [FMR] while spending no more than 30 percent of his or her income on housing costs) (National Low Income Housing Coalition, 2014b). The NLIHC found that the national housing wage for a rental unit with two bedrooms was $18.92 in 2014, far greater than the federal minimum wage of $7.25 that year. According to the NLIHC, there is no state in the United States where a full-time minimum-wage worker can afford a one- or two-bedroom rental unit at FMR. Perhaps not surprisingly, the highest housing wages for a two-bedroom FMR unit are in Hawaii ($31.54), the District of Columbia ($28.25), California ($26.04), Maryland ($24.94), and New Jersey ($24.92); the lowest are in South Dakota ($13.09), West Virginia ($12.80), Kentucky ($12.69), Arkansas ($12.56), and Puerto Rico ($10.19) (see chapters 1, 2, 7, and 9).

HOUSING AFFORDABILITY CHALLENGES

The past and present shortage of affordable rental housing is a result of a failure both to preserve existing affordable units and to build a sufficient number of new affordable housing units. Policy makers, housing advocates, and public policy analysts further maintain that local, state, and federal officials have not achieved enough in terms of affordable housing assistance for low- and moderate-income households (Housing Assistance Council, 2012; U.S. Department of Housing and Urban Development, 2013; National Low Income Housing Coalition, 2012a, 2012b, 2013a, 2014b, 2014c). For example, one of the ways that communities fail to preserve the existing affordable rental housing stock is by removing older, poorer quality, and often less expensive housing units from their inventories. Other barriers to affordable housing may be zoning and land use restrictions, along with impact fees (Listokin & Hattis, 2005; National Association of Home Builders, 2014; Quigley & Rosenthal, 2005; Somerville & Mayer, 2003; U.S. Department of Housing and Urban Development, 2008). Rehabilitating older buildings can cost more than the value of the buildings or constructing new units because they may have structural and maintenance issues that must be brought up to current code requirements (Feldman, 2002). Thus many older units are ultimately lost to decay or demolition (Duany, 2001; National Association of Home Builders, 2014; see chapters 9 and 14).

With little revenue to cover operating and maintenance costs and the potential of landlords prioritizing their own income over maintaining quality housing, the low-rent affordable housing stock has been especially vulnerable to removal (Joint Center for Housing Studies of Harvard University, 2013). According to the Joint Center for Housing Studies of Harvard University (2013: 19), "Of the 34.8 million rentals that existed in 2001, some 1.9 million were demolished by 2011—a loss rate of 5.6 percent. Losses of units renting for less than $400, however, were nearly twice as high at 12.8 percent. Although making up only a small share of the overall rental supply, homes renting for less than $400 thus accounted for more than a third (650,000) of total removals. Removal rates for units with rents between $400 and $600 were also relatively high: 6.7 percent." The loss rate of rental units is lower for units with higher rents. Units with rents of $800 per month or higher have a loss rate of only 3 percent (Joint Center for Housing Studies of Harvard University, 2013; see chapter 9).

Another contributor to the affordable rental housing shortage is the loss of affordable units to gentrification, the "transformation of a working-class or vacant area of the city to middle-class residential and/or commercial uses" (Lees, Slater, & Wyly, 2008: xv; see chapters 1 and 2). This process results in the rehabilitation of the housing stock in previously decayed and decaying inner-city neighborhoods (Newman & Wyly, 2006). Due to rent and property tax increases, respectively, many renting and owning low-income families can no longer afford to live in these neighborhoods and need to move to other neighborhoods (Brown-Saracino, 2010; Freeman, 2006; Lees et al., 2008; Slater, 2006; see chapter 9).

Finally, high-income households may choose to rent low-cost units in an effort to limit their housing expenses, which puts them in competition with lower-income households for available housing. For example, in 2011, 2.6 million affordable rental units were occupied by high-income households (Joint Center for Housing Studies of Harvard University, 2013).

Overall, 18.1 million households in the United States spent more than 50 percent of their income on housing in 2012, making them severely housing cost burdened (Viveiros & Sturtevant, 2014). Extremely low income (ELI) households (i.e., households earning up to 30 percent of the area median income [AMI]) continue to be a subject of particular concern among policy makers, housing advocates, and public policy analysts, as the vast majority are housing cost burdened (National Low Income Housing Coalition, 2014b; U.S. Department of Housing and Urban Development, 2013; see chapters 9 and 14).

Five groups of extremely low income renters have been identified as especially affected by shortages of affordable housing: the elderly and the disabled; people of color; female-headed households, regardless of whether they have children; veterans; and rural households (Housing Assistance Council, 2012; Viveiros & Sturtevant, 2014). Individuals or households that fall into more than one of these groups have an increased likelihood of a housing affordability problem. Households that possess multiple risk factors are often termed "precariously housed" and may be in danger of becoming homeless (see chapters 9 and 11).

In summary, the supply of low-cost rental housing units has been insufficient for the demand for this type of housing. In the near and distant future, the demand for affordable rental housing is expected to increase dramatically due to the increase in population in general and the increase in the proportion of the population that is low- and moderate-income (Joint Center for Housing Studies of Harvard University, 2013; see chapters 1, 2, and 15).

HOUSING AFFORDABILITY SOLUTIONS

Building and maintaining affordable housing has always been a challenge. Because housing development requires a substantial amount of investment and because not many investors are willing and/or able to fund the entire development, developers, nonprofit organizations, and the government typically collaborate to expand or maintain the stock of affordable housing (Krigman, 2010). Strategies for solving housing affordability problems can be referred to broadly as either reducing the cost of housing construction and rehabilitation or increasing resources available for housing. Examples of reducing costs include employing alternative and sometimes nontraditional land use strategies; utilizing new building materials or systems, such as manufactured housing or modular building components; and/or decreasing management and finance costs by providing low- or no-interest loans and tax credits to developers in order to reduce costs for low-income owners and renters (see chapter 14).

Land Use Strategies

Promoting higher density and mixed-use development is one method of reducing the cost of housing and thus potentially increasing housing affordability. When land prices are high, building more housing units and/or smaller units on the available land or relaxing design standards reduces the cost of each unit. Some municipalities may offer a density bonus, allowing not only more units in the development but also a certain number or proportion of units that are affordable for eligible households, achieving inclusionary zoning (Katz, 2000). Also, if housing units are built above an income-producing business, housing costs may be lower. Implementing legislation at the state or federal level that would require communities to have sufficient amounts of land zoned for multifamily or manufactured housing also has the potential to improve the number of affordable housing options in a community (Boudreaux, 2011).

Another land use strategy is establishing a Community Land Trust (CLT) (Davis, 2010a, 2010b). The CLT, typically a nonprofit organization, purchases community lands with the intention of retaining ownership of the parcels to preserve the affordability of housing on these lands in perpetuity. The cost to the buyer is for the home only, not the land. If the homeowner ever chooses to sell, he or she and the CLT share any appreciated equity (Davis, 2010b). When the home is sold, the CLT has the right of first refusal to ensure that the home is sold to another low- or moderate-income buyer and the property remains affordable (Skobba & Carswell, 2014; see chapter 14).

Limited equity cooperatives "have a strong record of providing high-quality, safe, affordable housing for low- and moderate-income populations" (Thaden, Greer, & Saegert, 2013; Davis, 2010a, 2010b; Saegert & Benitez, 2005: 427). In this model, residents collectively own the building instead of each member owning a single apartment or home (Thaden et al., 2013). Limited equity cooperative ownership agreements often allow owners to pass their shares on to their heirs; however, at the time of sale of the shares to new owners, the value may be restricted, keeping the shares affordable (Saegert & Benitz, 2005; see chapters 1, 2, and 7).

Building-Cost Strategies

Costs for materials and labor make up a large proportion of overall building costs. In addition to these factors, builders argue that increased and increasing standards and codes, along with design standards, constrain the supply of new affordable housing (National Association of Home Builders, 2014;

Span, 2001). For instance, some municipalities prohibit the use of vinyl siding as a building material and may require the use of more expensive building materials, such as brick (Duany, 2001; see chapter 5).

Factory-built housing includes manufactured and modular housing, which offers economies in the manufacturing process that can significantly reduce costs. In 1974 Congress declared that manufactured housing plays a vital role in meeting the national housing need and provides a significant resource for affordable homeownership and rental housing. Thus it established the HUD Code, which has provided construction and safety standards for manufactured housing since that time (U.S. Department of Housing and Urban Development, n.d., 2001).

Manufactured housing has advantages and disadvantages. With regard to advantages, manufactured housing is typically less expensive than site-built homes, as it is produced in a factory off site, its average square footage is typically smaller, and the building materials are typically less expensive. Also, manufactured homes are assembled more quickly than traditional construction. Many homes assembled on site, regardless of whether they are manufactured or not, suffer from vandalism and materials theft during construction. As manufactured homes are assembled much more quickly, they are exposed to these issues for a shorter time frame (Manufactured Housing Institute, 2014a, 2014b).

With regard to disadvantages, manufactured homes continue to suffer an image problem. This negative image may contribute to NIMBYism (National Low Income Housing Coalition, 2003). Furthermore, manufactured homes are typically constructed by low-skilled construction workers, compared to highly skilled workers who work in traditional construction trades. Thus high-skilled craftsmanship is replaced by low-skilled factory work processes (Olsen, 1997; see chapters 5 and 19).

Another strategy to reduce building costs, regardless of whether the home is manufactured or not, is using donated labor and materials, a strategy used by many faith-based organizations such as Habitat for Humanity. In such projects volunteers donate their labor to build modest site-built homes for low-income households (Habitat for Humanity, n.d.b). Volunteer labor is also used in urban homesteading programs to attract households to move to inner-city neighborhoods and in self-help housing, used in some rural communities through the Housing Assistance Council (Sullivan & Ward, 2012). These strategies allow people to reduce costs by building or rehabilitating their own homes. Funders may recognize the in-kind contributions of the owners, also called "sweat equity," as contributing to the financial resources available for construction and rehabilitation (Habitat for Humanity, n.d.a). Some self-help housing programs require that several households work together to build and complete homes for all involved households before everyone can move in (Habitat for Humanity, n.d.a; see chapter 7).

Finance-Cost Strategies

The cost of borrowing money is an important component of the cost of housing. Low-interest loans to developers, builders, landlords, or home buyers for constructing or rehabilitating affordable housing may reduce the cost of housing. Money for construction and permanent loans, whether borrowed by the developer, builder, landlord, or home buyer, is usually issued at a rate of interest that is factored into the cost of the housing unit. Programs providing below-market interest rate (BMIR) loans, that is, a loan with either no interest or interest charged at a rate below the applicable federal rate (Internal Revenue Service, 2015), may be available to eligible individuals or developers. HUD offers the Section 221(d)(3) and (4) program, through which landlords with income-eligible housing can apply for BMIR loans and then offer housing units for a reduced rent to eligible residents (U.S. Department of Housing and Urban Development, 2007). Another example of finance-cost strategies is the Low-Income Housing Tax Credit (LIHTC) Program (see chapters 8 and 14).

PUBLIC POLICY

Hundreds of federal, state, and municipal programs address affordable housing, either on the supply or the demand side. In the case of the former, programs subsidize developers, builders, landlords, and home buyers. In the case of the latter, programs subsidize eligible home buyers and renters. Although federal rental assistance programs support the nation's most vulnerable families and individuals, "more than three-quarters of the $270 billion in federal housing spending in 2012 (including both federal outlays and the costs of tax expenditures) went to homeowners, who make up less than two-thirds of American households. Renters make up more than one-third of households but received less than one-fourth of federal housing spending" (Sard & Fischer, 2013: 4). Table 10.1 provides an overview of major federal rental housing programs, income-target requirements, and national funding levels.

Despite the abundance of programs, housing assistance is not an entitlement (i.e., not everyone eligible for assistance receives it). Thus waiting lists are typically long and sometimes even closed due to the large demand for affordable housing. Despite the variety of programs and approaches, the number of assisted households declined for the first time ever in 1994 and has been dropping ever since (Schwartz, 2015).

In 2011 approximately 4.8 million eligible rental households in the United States received housing assistance through programs administered by HUD, representing about 4 percent of all households and 12 percent of all U.S. renter households (National Low Income Housing Coalition, 2012b). Despite rental assistance, about 60 percent of extremely low income renters and about 30 percent of very low income renters did not have access to affordable and available housing units in 2011. In 2013 there were 1.6 very low income households with worst-case needs for every very low income household with rental assistance (U.S. Department of Housing and Urban Development, 2015b). In 2011 a record high of 8.48 million households in the United States did not receive government housing assistance and either paid more than 50 percent of their income on rent and/or lived in severely inadequate conditions (e.g., in a housing unit that lacked adequate maintenance and services such as heat during winter). These households are labeled "worst case needs" households (U.S. Department of Housing and Urban Development, 2013, 2015b).

An example of a public policy focused on addressing housing affordability is the National Housing Trust Fund (NHTF), which is a major policy initiative for the production, rehabilitation, and preservation of affordable rental housing (National Low Income Housing Coalition, 2013b). The NHTF

TABLE 10.1
Overview of Major Federal Rental Housing Programs, Income Target Requirements, and National Funding Levels

Rental housing program	Income target requirements	National funding levels
Public housing	At least 40% of units are for households with incomes less than 30% of AMI, with the remainder for households earning up to 80% of AMI	$6.4 billion (FY 2016 HUD appropriation)
Housing vouchers	At least 75% of vouchers are for households with incomes less than 30% of AMI, with the remainder for households earning up to 80% of AMI	$19.6 billion (FY 2016 HUD appropriation)
Project-based rental assistance	At least 40% of units are for households with incomes less than 30% of AMI, with the remainder for households earning up to 80% of AMI	$10.6 billion (FY 2016 HUD appropriation)
Section 202 and Section 811	All units are for households with incomes less than 50% of AMI	$584 million (FY 2016 HUD appropriation)
HOME Investment Partnerships	If used for rental, at least 90% of units assisted throughout the jurisdiction must be for households under 60% AMI, with the remainder for households up to 80% AMI; if there are more than 5 HOME-assisted units in a building, then 20% of the HOME-assisted units must be for households under 50% AMI; all assisted homeowners must be below 80% of AMI	$950 million (FY 2016 HUD appropriation)
Community Development Block Grant (CDBG)	At least 70% of households served must have low or moderate incomes, less than 80% AMI; remaining funds can serve households of any income group	$3 billion (FY 2016 HUD appropriation)
McKinney-Vento Homeless Assistance Grants	All assistance is for participants who meet HUD's definition of homeless (those who lack a fixed, regular, and adequate nighttime residence)	$2.2 billion (FY 2016 HUD appropriation)
Housing Opportunities for People with AIDS (HOPWA)	All housing is for households with incomes less than 80% of AMI	$335 million (FY 2016 HUD appropriation)
Low-Income Housing Tax Credit (LIHTC)	All units are for households with incomes less than 50% or 60% of AMI (depending on how the development was financed)	$7.8 billion (FY 2016 estimated tax expenditure)
Federal Home Loan Banks' Affordable Housing	All units are for households with incomes less than 80% of AMI; for rental projects, 20% of units are for households earning less than 50% of AMI	$328 million (2014 FHLB assessment)
Section 515, rural rental housing	All units are for households with incomes less than $5,500 above 80% of AMI. Priority is first for households in substandard housing and second for households earning less than 50% of AMI	$28 million (FY 2016 USDA appropriation)
Section 521, rural rental assistance	In new projects, 95% of units are for households with incomes less than 50% of AMI; in existing projects, 75% of units are for households earning less than 50% of AMI	$1.4 billion (FY 2016 USDA appropriation)
National Housing Trust Fund	At least 90% of funds must be for rental housing, and at least 75% of rental housing funds must benefit households with incomes below 30% of AMI or at poverty level, whichever is greater; remaining funds can assist households with incomes below 50% of AMI; up to 10% may be for homeowner activities benefiting households with income below 50% of AMI	$186.6 million (first-time funding estimate for the National Housing Trust Fund [NHTF], established as a provision of the Housing and Economic Recovery Act of 2008)

Source: Authors, based on National Low Income Housing Coalition, 2016b.
Note: Extremely low income: income less than 30 percent of AMI; very low income: income less than 50 percent of AMI; low income: income less than 80 percent of AMI.

was established in 2008 but was only recently funded, in 2016. It provides a supply of rental housing that low-income people can afford. Instead of land held in perpetuity, as in the CLT model described above, a housing trust fund establishes a means for housing—rented or owned—to be available to eligible community residents to "begin to close the gap between supply and demand for truly affordable housing" (National Low Income Housing Coalition, 2013b: 4). The legislation requires both rental and homeowner units to be affordable for at least thirty years, and there is a campaign that is urging HUD to set a fifty-year affordability period (National Low Income Housing Coalition, 2013b). The NHTF is funded by an assessment of 0.042 percent of the business volume of the government-sponsored enterprises Freddie Mac and Fannie Mae (National Low Income Housing Coalition, 2016a; see chapters 7, 9, and 14).

NONPROFIT HOUSING ORGANIZATIONS

Other important rental housing affordability solutions are offered through state and local nonprofit housing organizations (Housing Assistance Council, 2012; Krigman, 2010). While some nonprofit organizations operate at the state or regional level, others operate at the municipal or the neighborhood level. Nonprofit housing organizations are committed to making housing affordable for residents through, for example, development, management, education, and advocacy. These organizations may provide homeownership opportunities, low-rent housing, and assistance for clients to secure a living wage (i.e., the minimum income needed to meet basic needs in a community) and access to medical and social services. These local nonprofit organizations provide important resources in addition to those provided by government entities (see chapters 7 and 9).

Some nonprofit organizations administer special savings programs called Individual Development Accounts (IDAs), in which eligible low-income households' savings are matched by the organization, often tied to financial literacy training (Housing Assistance Council, 2012). Funds can only be used for specific purposes, including down payment for a home. Financially literate buyers are generally considered to have a lower risk of mortgage default than others. Some states offer reduced-cost loan terms for home buyers who complete financial literacy training. Some faith-based organizations even offer no-interest loans for eligible low-income buyers, providing a rental housing affordability solution (see chapter 7).

CONCLUSION

How can the persistent and increasing housing affordability problem be solved? Reducing the cost of housing and increasing resources for housing have been discussed above as essential to maintaining and increasing the availability of affordable housing, particularly for eligible very low and extremely low income renters. Despite the fact that there are many programs already in existence, there is still not enough affordable housing. To garner the support needed to solve the affordability problem, the public must become aware of the critical need for affordable housing and be willing to provide the necessary support for it. However, negative public perceptions of subsidized housing and housing-assisted households persist, and NIMBY-ism remains a significant national problem (Clark & Viveiros, 2014; National Low Income Housing Coalition, 2003, 2012a; Tighe, 2012; see chapter 14). The first step in solving the affordability problem must be to address misperceptions of housing programs and replace them with more positive images.

Finding ways to do this are critical and should be considered in all discussions of housing policy (Dolbeare, 2001). Only then will we be able to solve the housing affordability challenge.

Once the public embraces the need for affordable housing and is willing to provide the necessary support, the question becomes how best to meet the needs. As discussed above, the basic problem is the imbalance between the cost of housing and the resources of low- and moderate-income households. It follows that solutions could address either reducing the cost of housing or increasing the resources households can access to fulfill their housing needs. Some of these strategies may help builders and developers, both for-profit and not-for-profit, as they provide housing, while others target housing consumers directly. Other strategies may include financial counseling for low- and moderate-income households to achieve their housing goals (Fox, Bartholomae, & Lee, 2005; see chapters 7 and 9).

The importance of housing is greater than the sum of individual housing units. As the largest component of most household budgets, housing that is affordable is indispensable to households and their communities. As discussed above, the current minimum wage, even with a full-time job, is insufficient to afford modest rental housing, regardless of whether it is located in an urban or a rural area in the United States.

Programs addressing the need for affordable housing have come and gone throughout the history of the United States, but it is clear that there will always be a part of the population that the market does not or cannot serve. Some government-supported production will always be needed for purposes of neighborhood stabilization, for people with special needs, and for cushioning low-income housing from inflationary price pressures (National Low Income Housing Coalition, 2012a, 2012b; see chapter 14). Surveys show that Americans have become increasingly concerned about the availability of affordable housing, and yet housing tends to be low on most policy agendas (National Low Income Housing Coalition, 2012a; Nelson, 2003). In some communities, public-service employees, including police officers, schoolteachers, librarians, and other valuable community employees, are paid less than the area median income. Thus they have difficulties finding affordable housing and are forced to live somewhere else. Comprehensive housing assessments should be a part of every community's future plan so that a dialogue to meet future housing needs can occur, protecting the interests of all of a community's citizens.

REFERENCES

Addison, C., Zhang, S., & Coomes, B. (2013). Smart growth and housing affordability: A review of regulatory mechanisms and planning practices. *Journal of Planning Literature, 28*(3), 215–257.

Boudreaux, P. (2011). *The housing bias: Rethinking land use laws for a diverse America.* New York: Palgrave Macmillan.

Brennan, M. (2011). The impacts of affordable housing on education: A research summary. *Insights from Housing Policy Research.* Washington, D.C.: Center for Housing Policy.

Brown-Saracino, J. (Ed.). (2010). *The gentrification debate: A reader.* New York: Routledge.

Burke, T., Stone, M., and Ralston, L. (2011). *The residual income method: A new lens on housing affordability and market behaviour.* AHURI Final Report No. 176. Melbourne: Australian Housing and Urban Research Institute.

Center for Housing Policy. (2012). *Losing ground: The struggle of moderate income house-*

holds to afford the rising costs of housing and transportation. Washington, D.C.: Center for Housing Policy and Center for Neighborhood Technology.

Clark, A. E., & Viveiros, J. (2014). *Building support for affordable communities: A summary of research on opinion and messaging.* Washington, D.C.: National Housing Conference and Center for Housing Policy.

Cohen, R. (2011). *The impacts of affordable housing on health: A research summary: Insights from housing policy research.* Washington, D.C.: Center for Housing Policy.

Davis, J. E. (2010a). More than money: What is shared in shared equity homeownership? *Journal of Affordable Housing & Community Development Law* 19(3/4), 259–277.

Davis, J. E. (2010b). *Origins and evolution of the Community Land Trust in the United States.* Cambridge, Mass.: Lincoln Institute of Land Policy.

Dolbeare, C. N. (2001). Housing affordability: Challenge and context. *Cityscape: A Journal of Policy Development and Research,* 5(2), 111–130.

Duany, A. (2001). Three cheers for gentrification. *American Enterprise,* 12(3), 36–40.

Feldman, R. (2002). The affordable housing shortage: Considering the problem, causes and solutions. *The Region,* 16(3), 7–14.

Fox, J., Bartholomae, S., & Lee, J. (2005). Building the case for financial education. *Journal of Consumer Affairs,* 39(1), 195–214.

Freeman, L. (2006). *There goes the hood: Views of gentrification from the ground up.* Philadelphia: Temple University Press.

Gan, Q., & Hill, R. J. (2009). Measuring housing affordability: Looking beyond the median. *Journal of Housing Economics,* 18(2), 115–125.

Goetz, A. (2013). Suburban sprawl or urban centres: Tensions and contradictions of smart growth approaches in Denver, Colorado. *Urban Studies,* 50(11), 2178–2195.

Habitat for Humanity. (n.d.a). *Answering tough questions: What is "sweat equity"?* Retrieved July 14, 2015, from http://www.habitat.org/youthprograms/act-speak-build-week/answering-tough-questions.

Habitat for Humanity. (n.d.b). *Habitat for Humanity international mission statement and principles.* Retrieved July 14, 2015, from http://www.habitat.org/how/mission_statement.aspx.

Housing Assistance Council. (2012). *Taking stock 2012: Rural people, poverty and housing in the 21st century.* Washington, D.C.: Housing Assistance Council.

Internal Revenue Service. (2015). *Below market interest loans* (Publication 535). Retrieved June 10, 2016, from http://taxmap.ntis.gov/taxmap/pubs/p535-017.htm.

Joint Center for Housing Studies of Harvard University. (2013). *America's rental housing: Evolving markets and needs.* Cambridge, Mass.: Joint Center for Housing Studies of Harvard University.

Katz, B. (2000, November 29). *The need to connect smart growth and affordable housing.* Speech before the Vermont Affordable Housing Conference.

Krigman, Y. (2010). The role of community development corporations in affordable housing. *Journal of Affordable Housing & Community Development Law,* 19(2), 231–253.

Kutty, N. K. (2005). A new measure of housing affordability: Estimates and analytical results. *Housing Policy Debate,* 16(1), 113–142.

Lees, L., Slater, T., & Wyly, E. (2008). *Gentrification.* New York: Routledge.

Listokin, D., & Hattis, D. B. (2005). Building codes and housing. *Cityscape,* 8(1), 21–68.

Manufactured Housing Institute. (2014a). *Quick facts: Trends and information about the manufactured housing industry.* Retrieved July 14, 2015, from http://www.manufacturedhousing.org/media_center/default.asp.

Manufactured Housing Institute. (2014b). *Understanding today's manufactured housing.* Retrieved July 14, 2015, from www.manufacturedhousing.org/lib/forcedownload.asp?filepath=/admin/template/brochures/925temp.pdf.

Millennial Housing Commission. (2002). *Meeting our nation's housing challenges: Report of the bi-partisan Millennial Housing Commission.* Retrieved August 15, 2003, from http://www.mhc.gov.

Miller, W. D., Pollack, C. E., & Williams, D. R. (2011). Healthy homes and communities: Putting the pieces together. *American Journal of Preventative Medicine,* 40(1S1), S48–S57.

...MONTGOMERY, AND CULHANE

...nelessness within academia is a relatively new phe-...t has been a persistent social problem in American ...oos, struggles over income and housing have posed ...Americans living in poverty. In the nineteenth cen-...ng to find work, those with disabilities, or those too ...on the generosity of charities for shelter and food. ...ouses and almshouses traditionally housed people ...ider "homeless" (Katz, 1996).

...ness was increasingly discussed in academic, advo-...s, although there was no common definition of the ...issues sound trivial, they carry great consequences ...many people are identified as homeless, how many ...ervices from federal, state, and local governments ...es of services they may receive.

...gh the mid-1980s, American sociologists, the first ...ness as its own domain, employed a wide range of ...ness, from anyone with inadequate housing—those ...bers or in nonhomeless institutions like jails, hos-...enters—to individuals and households sleeping in ...or places not meant for habitation, like the streets ...Hopper, 2002; Jencks, 1994; Lee, Tyler, & Wright, ...on homelessness evolved, so did the definition of ...e U.S. Department of Housing and Urban Develop-...people experiencing homelessness as those who, "in ...alternative but to obtain it from a private or public ...nt of Housing and Urban Development, 1984: 127). ...the scope of services in the first piece of federal leg-...lelessness, the Housing Homeless Act of 1986, and ...ermanently in the landmark 1987 McKinney-Vento ...federal funding for homelessness services (Jencks, ...d 14).

Some in the advocacy community—most notably Mitch Snyder of the Community for Creative Nonviolence—pushed for broader rules that included the "unstably housed," or people who are on the brink of losing their housing, who are doubling up or "couch surfing" with friends, or who are staying with family as temporary shelter (Hopper, 2002; Jencks, 1994; Snyder & Hombs, 1986). Snyder argued that, although not literally homeless, unstably housed individuals and households were still despairingly poor and needed essentially the same services as those who met the government's definition for homelessness. While the latter group may have had places where they could stay, these shelters were often in states of disrepair. A tenant of a single-room occupancy (SRO) unit on Manhattan's Bowery Street, a family staying at a relative's home, or a person sleeping on his friend's couch generally lacks a consistent, adequate place to stay and, according to this definition, is technically homeless.

Despite objections from the advocacy community, prominent scholars in the area of homelessness and poverty research subscribed to HUD's early definition by either explicitly endorsing similar definitions or confining their studies and estimates of homelessness to those sleeping in shelters or places not meant for human habitation (Hopper, 2002; Jencks, 1994; Rossi, 1991). Even though unstably housed people were in need, they argued, literally homeless individuals had qualitatively different and more severe challenges. This group, therefore, should be the recipient of funds and services geared toward "the homeless." Also, this was the group that could be counted. The earliest estimates of this group, arrived at by consulting experts in a few cities, were between two and three million people; however, no one could explain exactly what population that count represented or to what degree it was accurate (Jencks, 1994).

COUNTING THE HOMELESS POPULATION

Earnest estimates of homelessness began in 1980 and have evolved from extremely limited and rudimentary guesses to rigorous, if imperfect, scientifically based methods. As part of the 1980 decennial census, the U.S. Bureau of the Census counted twenty-three thousand people who indicated a shelter as their permanent address on a census form. Although this count excluded those who did not complete a census form or reported an address other than a shelter, it was the first step toward officially endorsed counts (Jencks, 1994). In 1984 HUD attempted to improve this estimate by calling shelter directors in large cities and U.S. homelessness experts and asking for local estimates. This approach produced an estimated range between 320,000 and 340,000 persons experiencing homelessness in the United States. Both the National Bureau of Economic Research (NBER) and staff at ICF, Inc., a research and technical assistance firm, examined HUD's methods and came to similar conclusions (Burt & Cohen, 1989).

Soon after HUD released its range in 1984, academics sought to improve on the federal government's methods. Burt and the Urban Institute developed the next estimate (Burt & Cohen, 1989). Burt selected a sample of twenty cities with populations over one hundred thousand, chose 381 providers of shelter and meals in these sites, and interviewed seventeen hundred people who were receiving services related to housing. She produced a high estimate, concluding that there were between five hundred thousand

and six hundred thousand literally homeless people on a given night in the United States in 1987 (Burt & Cohen, 1989).

Rather than developing a national estimate, Rossi (1991) concentrated on improving local estimates of the unsheltered homeless population. Using Chicago as a laboratory, he and his team concluded that the most accurate assessment was the result of a stratified random sample. Thus Rossi divided the city into areas of high, medium, and low likelihood of finding a homeless person, and within each section he would canvass a random sample of blocks. Rossi also suggested that, rather than categorizing people as homeless or not homeless based on their appearance, canvassers should ask everyone they encounter about their housing in order not to let stereotypes bias results (Rossi, 1991).

Academics continued to refine estimation methods through the 1990s. For example, Link et al. (1994) used phone surveys of individual households to develop homelessness prevalence rates, an estimation of how many people were homeless over a period of time. They found that 3.1 percent of respondents had been literally homeless at some point over the previous five years, and 7.4 percent had been homeless at some point during their lifetime (Link et al., 1994). Culhane et al. (1994) used shelter data to estimate homelessness rates in New York City and Philadelphia and found point-in-time rates ranging from 0.11 to 0.25 percent of the population and annual prevalence rates of 1 percent for both cities (Culhane, Dejowski, Ibanez, Needham, & Macchia, 1994). They also found a five-year rate of 3.2 percent in New York City, akin to the Link et al. (1994) estimate.

Efforts to count the homeless population advanced in the early 2000s as cities like New York began instituting their own official counts that built on previous methods. Beginning in 2007, the federal government mandated that all municipalities receiving federal funding through the McKinney-Vento Act provide biennial estimates of their homeless population and provided guidance on how those counts should be conducted (U.S. Department of Housing and Urban Development, 2008; see chapters 10 and 14).

Counts of homeless populations are conducted by Continuums of Care (CoCs), the local networks through which shelters and other homeless service providers have applied for and receive federal funding through the McKinney-Vento and HEARTH Acts. The unsheltered population is estimated by the CoC based on methods advanced by Burt and Rossi and recommended by HUD. Sheltered homeless individuals are counted using data that shelters enter into the local Housing Management Information System (HMIS), a database tracking shelter stays and other client-level information and collected by CoCs (U.S. Department of Housing and Urban Development, 2008, 2014c).

These data are aggregated by the CoC and submitted to HUD, which releases national estimates of homelessness through the Annual Homelessness Assessment Report (AHAR), which is released in two versions every year. First, there is a point-in-time (PIT) count that estimates the number of sheltered and unsheltered people experiencing homelessness on a single night in January. The second part of the report provides a count of people using shelter and transitional housing over the course of a federal fiscal year, from October 1 through September 30 of the following year (U.S. Department of Housing and Urban Development, 2014a, 2014b, 2014c).

The latest figures, from 2013 and 2014, respectively, estimate that approximately 1.4 million people were homeless between October 2011 and September 2012, and approximately 580,000 people were homeless on a given night in January 2014 in the United States (U.S. Department of Housing and Urban Development, 2014a, 2014b). Both estimates are significant decreases (10.5 and 13 percent, respectively) from the first official counts in 2007. These counts indicate that most homeless families and approximately half of homeless single adults are sheltered and that most shelter users are single adults, about 10 percent of whom identify as veterans.

ANALYZING CHARACTERISTICS OF THE HOMELESS POPULATION

Official homeless counts, the broader homelessness literature, and shelter operations generally divide people experiencing homelessness into two groups: unaccompanied single adults and families with children. Single adults, who comprised 63 percent of the overall homeless population over the course of 2013, are those whom the general public most frequently associates with homelessness. Homeless individuals are generally and disproportionately male (72 percent), of color (55 percent), and older than forty years, with significantly higher rates of behavioral health problems compared with nonhomeless adults (U.S. Department of Housing and Urban Development, 2014a).

While many (52 percent) single adults experiencing homelessness stayed in homeless shelters or transitional housing at the time of the PIT count, singles made up 86 percent of unsheltered homeless households (U.S. Department of Housing and Urban Development, 2014b). The divergent methods of tracking sheltered and unsheltered homelessness precipitate wide disparities in available data on the two groups. While the findings are limited, researchers have studied unsheltered homelessness by collecting primary data at social service agencies for people experiencing homelessness or through outreach at outdoor places where people experiencing homelessness may congregate, including parks and encampments. Persons experiencing unsheltered homelessness tend to be chronically homeless (i.e., experiencing at least one year of continuous homelessness or four or more episodes of homelessness during the three previous years), to be unemployed, and to have a low level of education (Shern et al., 2000). They have higher rates of behavioral health issues than their sheltered counterparts—more than half of a sample of people experiencing unsheltered homelessness had been diagnosed with a serious mental illness (O'Toole, Gibbon, Hanusa, & Fine, 1999; Shern et al., 2000). Another study found that individuals with substance abuse disorders were more likely be unsheltered (Tsai, Kasprow, Kane, & Rosenheck, 2014). Finally, people living in unsheltered situations also tend to have higher rates of physical health issues (Shern et al., 2000; Tsai et al., 2014).

Family homelessness is represented by a starkly different demographic. These are typically households led by single women of color between their early twenties and late thirties with young children. Of all people in sheltered families, more than 60 percent were younger than eighteen years, with 52 percent of them under the age of five in 2012 (U.S. Department of Housing and Urban Development, 2014a). In general, homeless families resemble other low-income families, although many have fewer resources on which to rely in difficult circumstances. They have similar education levels but are less likely to be employed at a given moment and, when employed, have generally lower incomes. They are also slightly more likely to have suffered recent physical or mental abuse and to have a smaller social support network on which they can rely, contributing to higher rates of residential instability, even preceding literal homelessness (Bassuk, Weinreb, Dawson, Perloff, & Buckner, 1997).

The heads of household of homeless families face significant physical and behavioral health barriers as well, although the evidence is mixed on the extent to which their difficulties exceed those of other low-income families. The most comprehensive review of these differences suggests that women experiencing homelessness are more likely than other low-income women, but less likely than single men experiencing homelessness, to have substance abuse and serious mental illness diagnoses; they also experience acute and chronic health problems—notably anemia, asthma, ulcers, and dental care deficiencies—more than the general population of women (Bassuk et al., 1997; Rog & Buckner, 2007).

ANALYZING REASONS FOR HOMELESSNESS

In the United States, a complex interaction among broad economic and personal factors places people at risk for homelessness. Since Shlay and Rossi (1992) examined the relative importance of each factor in 1992, researchers have come to some consensus on a model that incorporates both micro- and macro-level contributors to homelessness (Jencks, 1994; Main, 1998; O'Flaherty & Wu, 2006; Shlay & Rossi, 1992), with the bulk of research on the former. Early quantitative research about factors that contribute to homelessness suggested that individual-level variables are the best predictors, and most research over the past two decades has focused on them (Early, 1999, 2004; Early & Olsen, 2002).

There is no set of characteristics that accurately predicts future homelessness, but researchers have identified contributing factors. Residential instability and prior shelter use are consistently among the best predictors of future homelessness, and households facing imminent eviction are also most likely to enter a homeless shelter (Byrne, Treglia, Kuhn, Kane, & Culhane, 2016; Shinn et al., 1998; Shinn, Greer, Bainbridge, Kwon, & Zuiderveen, 2013). Black/African American families and families in which the head of household is young or pregnant are generally more likely to become homeless (Shinn et al., 1998; Shinn, Baumohl, & Hopper, 2001; Shinn et al., 2013; see chapter 16). Access to less social capital—the extent and depth of social networks—is associated with increased rates of homelessness (Toohey, Shinn, & Weitzman, 2004), as is veteran status (Fargo et al., 2012; O'Flaherty, 2009; see chapter 12).

Mental illness and substance abuse, often perceived by the general public as pervasive causes of homelessness, play a much smaller role than is often assumed. In general, rates of serious mental illness and substance abuse are higher among homeless than nonhomeless populations but constitute a percentage far less prevalent than is generally perceived (Montgomery, Metraux, & Culhane, 2013). Among families in New York City, substance abuse and mental health indicators were not significant predictors of subsequent homelessness (Shinn et al., 2013).

Macro-level narratives of homelessness examine a lack of affordable housing, changing community-level demographics, and broad economic conditions like the unemployment rate (see chapters 1, 2, 12, and 13). Repeated examinations across metropolitan areas find that homelessness rates are higher in areas with more constrained housing markets, demonstrated by higher rents and fewer vacancies (Byrne, Munley, Fargo, Montgomery, & Culhane, 2013; Lee, Price-Spratlen, & Kanan, 2003; Quigley & Raphael, 2001; see chapters 2 and 9). This is corroborated by the perceptions of city officials across the country, 72 percent of whom cite a lack of affordable housing as a primary cause of homelessness for families with children (U.S. Conference of Mayors, 2008). O'Flaherty and Wu (2006) focused on non-housing-specific factors of homelessness and found increases in the homelessness rate in response to decreases in economic health, as determined by a composite economic indicator compiled by the New York Federal Reserve tracking employment, real earnings, and average weekly hours of work (O'Flaherty & Wu, 2006).

Even after identifying all individual and macro-level factors that pose risk for homelessness, predicting imminent homelessness remains onerous. Homelessness is a classic "needle in a haystack" problem: less than 1 percent of low-income people in U.S. cities and less than 3 percent of individuals with serious mental illness were homeless on a given night (Early & Olsen, 2002; Frank & Glied, 2006; O'Flaherty, 2009; Shinn et al., 1998). In their study predicting homelessness among families receiving cash assistance in New York City, Shinn and her colleagues found that their best model, using a breadth of household characteristics, correctly identified 66 percent of subsequent shelter users, with a false positive rate—the proportion of people who are incorrectly predicted to enter shelter—of 10 percent (Shinn et al., 1998). In a subsequent effort to improve risk detection, Shinn et al. developed a screening tool administered to families seeking homelessness prevention services; their final model improved the earlier model's sensitivity, detecting 75 percent of homeless families, but also increased the false positive rate to 37 percent (Shinn et al., 2013).

The same difficulty holds true for predicting shelter patterns among those who have already become homeless. Kuhn and Culhane (1998) and Culhane et al. (2007) grouped homeless households into three typologies of shelter use based on the number and duration of homelessness episodes. Transitional shelter users comprise 60 to 80 percent of people in shelters; they use shelters once or twice for short periods of time. Episodic shelter users have three or more distinct shelter stays and constitute approximately 10 percent of shelter users. Finally, chronically homeless shelter users generally have a small number of stays but each stay lasts at least six months (Culhane, Metraux, Park, Schretzman, & Valente, 2007; Kuhn & Culhane, 1998). Among other predictors, the likelihood of a household being episodically or chronically homeless increases with a black/African American head of household and as the head of household's age increases. While helpful for describing group characteristics, these are not predictive or specific enough to make predictive categorizations of shelter use.

The literature also explores factors that affect a household's likelihood of ending a particular shelter episode or returning to shelter, with similar limitations. Young families of color leave shelters quickly but return at higher than average rates (see chapter 16). Screening positive for mental illness and substance abuse are also indicative of longer and repeat shelter stays. Greater financial and social supports, on the other hand, lead to exit and reduced recidivism. Those who exit a shelter with a rental subsidy are much less likely to return to homelessness than those who do not have a subsidy (Allgood & Warren, 2003; Byrne et al., 2016; Shinn et al., 1998; Wong, Culhane, & Kuhn, 1997).

ENDING HOMELESSNESS

Over the past twenty-five years there has been a policy shift from passively managing homelessness to an active agenda to end it with a new set of tools. Traditional models relied heavily on emergency shelter and transitional housing to address social service needs and stabilize clients before transitioning them to permanent housing. In many cases, permanent housing options did not become available until clients completed assigned tasks like demonstrating sobriety from drugs or alcohol or showing improvement in mental health status.

The new paradigm is a prevention-driven approach that seeks to eliminate or minimize the need for shelter. It builds on a progressive engagement model used extensively in public health that classifies services into three types of prevention: primary prevention for those at risk of homelessness; secondary prevention, targeting those who have recently become homeless; and tertiary prevention, addressing the needs of people experiencing chronic homelessness (Burt, Pearson, & Montgomery, 2005; Culhane, Metraux, & Byrne, 2011).

Primary and secondary prevention are increasingly addressed through programs collectively termed "homelessness prevention and rapid rehousing" that provide short-term, highly flexible assistance that addresses the cause of an imminent or recent housing crisis. It can include funding to cover rental assistance, security deposits, move-in costs, and utility payments as well as more traditional casework such as connecting clients to mainstream social services like Medicaid and cash assistance. These approaches were first developed at the local and state levels, including in New York City; Hennepin County, Minnesota; Philadelphia; Columbus, Ohio; and the Commonwealth of Massachusetts, and then codified at the federal level in the American Recovery and Reinvestment Act (ARRA) of 2009 (Byrne et al., 2016; National Alliance to End Homelessness, 2014; Wong et al., 1999).

The ARRA allocated $1.5 billion over three years to the Homelessness Prevention and Rapid Re-housing Program (HPRP) to mitigate an increase in homelessness during the Great Recession (see chapter 15). The program gained more permanent status in the 2009 HEARTH Act. In the amendment and reauthorization of the McKinney-Vento Act, the Emergency Shelter Grant was renamed the Emergency Solutions Grant and the list of eligible activities was expanded to include more flexible prevention and rapid rehousing services (Byrne et al., 2016; Culhane et al., 2011; National Alliance to End Homelessness, 2014).

Homelessness prevention and rapid rehousing programs have been launched and expanded without strong evidence of their effectiveness, although recent evaluation results are promising. Only one study has used an experimental design to evaluate a homelessness prevention program in New York City, finding that families who received an intervention were less likely than a control group to subsequently enter emergency shelter (Rolston, Geyer, & Locke, 2013). Other nonexperimental work has been encouraging. An observational study tracked the homeless service use of participants in the Department of Veterans Affairs' homelessness prevention and rapid rehousing program, Supportive Services for Veteran Families, and work has been done in Georgia and Philadelphia to evaluate housing outcomes of prevention and rapid rehousing of clients (Byrne et al., 2016; Rodriguez, 2013; Taylor, 2014). These studies show low rates of homelessness during the year after exiting the program; between 2 and 5 percent of those who received homelessness prevention services and between 5 and 15 percent of those who received rapid rehousing became homeless within a year of receiving services.

Permanent supportive housing (PSH), on the other hand, is a widely accepted tool for ending homelessness for medically vulnerable and chronically homeless individuals (Caton, Wilkins, & Anderson, 2007). Begun in the mid-1980s, PSH programs differ from other living arrangements by providing a combination of flexible, voluntary supports for maintaining housing and access to individualized support services. Although implementation varies across programs and sites, a set of core principles unifying PSH programs includes

- residents have rights of tenancy;
- the housing is not time-limited;
- the housing is affordable; and
- accommodations are made for tenants' housing preferences (Rog et al., 2014).

One increasingly popular version of PSH is Housing First, an evidence-based approach for addressing chronic homelessness primarily among individuals with serious mental illness, substance abuse disorders, and co-occurring conditions (Gilmer et al., 2014; Montgomery, Hill, Kane, & Culhane, 2013; Rog et al., 2014). Developed by Tsemberis at Pathways for Housing, Housing First provides immediate housing without any requirement of sobriety or service enrollment. The model, as explained by Tsemberis (2010: 43), "is based on a belief that housing is a basic human right rather than something . . . the person has to earn or prove that they deserve."

Beyond Rog et al.'s principles of PSH, there are four additional tenets of Housing First. First, consumers must play an active role in choosing all aspects of their housing—neighborhood, apartment, whether to have roommates, and the timing and type of treatment they receive. Second, there is a separation between housing and social services. Housing is not contingent on receipt of services, and should the consumer be evicted for a lease violation, he or she maintains access to social services. Third, there is a recovery orientation; service plans are dictated by consumers' goals rather than the assessment of a clinician. Fourth, there is community integration, which means that consumers rent ordinary apartments, from a landlord, alongside other, nonhomeless renters and homeowners. The placement and social interactions encouraged by program staff help instill and sustain societal norms among consumers (Tsemberis, 2010; Tsemberis, Gulcur, & Nakae, 2004).

The thirty-year history of PSH permits a more robust body of evaluation research than that of homelessness prevention and rapid rehousing. Most studies suggest significant improvements in housing retention and decreases in homelessness among individuals and families placed in PSH (Montgomery et al., 2013; Rog et al., 2014). A meta-analysis by Leff et al. (2009) suggests that PSH has the largest effect on housing stability, with PSH housing retention rates ranging from 75 to 88 percent (Martinez & Burt, 2006; Rog et al., 2014; Tsemberis, 2010; Tsemberis et al., 2004). The relevant literature has become robust, substantiated by multiple studies with varied methodologies over the past decade, with at least four Randomized Controlled Trials (RCT) and several quasi-experimental studies (i.e., evaluations not subject to randomization) evaluating program impacts. One such trial of PSH in five Canadian cities, for example, found that over two years PSH participants were housed for more than twice the number of days as those in the control group (73 compared to 32 percent), and 62 percent were housed for the entirety of the six months prior to the follow-up period (Mental Health Commission of Canada, 2014).

Recent years have seen the emergence and rapid growth of a body of research examining the direct and peripheral costs of homelessness, focusing on the utilization of health, criminal justice, emergency department, and other acute public services by homeless persons (Kuno, Rothbard, Averyt, & Culhane, 2000; Kushel, Vittinghoff, & Haas, 2001; Salit, Kuhn, Hartz, Vu, & Mosso, 1998). The majority of studies find reductions in emergency department and inpatient hospital utilization (Basu, Kee, Buchanan, & Sadowski, 2012; Culhane, Metraux, & Hadley, 2002; Larimer et al., 2009; Martinez & Burt, 2006; Srebnik, Connor, & Sylla, 2013), as well as criminal justice involvement (Culhane et al., 2002; New York City Department of Health and Mental Hygiene, 2013) once consumers find stable housing. All studies on the subject show that the costs of permanent supportive housing are to some degree offset by the savings in peripheral services, and most report a net cost savings.

CONCLUSION

This chapter highlights the progress of homelessness research over the past three decades: empirical estimates now guide the understanding of the scope, characteristics, and needs of the homeless population, and these advances have been essential for developing and refining policies attributed to recent decreases in homelessness. As budget-strapped federal and state agencies, municipal governments, and nonprofit, academic, and advocacy organizations seek to eliminate homelessness while reducing expenditures, research evaluating intervention strategies and matching them to appropriate populations is needed.

While early evidence of the effectiveness of HPRP is encouraging, it is sparse, particularly given the recent proliferation of this intervention. Future research is needed to assess the model's applicability to broader populations and geographies. These efforts must be conducted in tandem with the development of tools to accurately predict homelessness risk and effectively assign households to appropriate interventions. Prevention is inefficient when provided to households who would not otherwise become homeless, and the light touch of rapid rehousing services provided to a household requiring more intensive PSH might be considered a wasted resource. The prevention screening tool developed by Shinn et al. has demonstrated promise with families who are at high risk of homelessness in New York City, but replication studies with other populations and in diverse geographies should assess the model's broader applicability. A method of predicting chronic homelessness is similarly needed.

The tools addressing homelessness are aimed at a moving target. Demographic and social circumstances of those facing a housing crisis reflect broader population and economic trends. The aging of the baby boomers, for example, is likely to precipitate an increase in the share of homeless adults in their sixties and seventies over the next twenty years and a concomitant rise in the health care needs and costs of homeless adults.

The homeless services system must be adaptive to these changes but need not be reinvented. The prevention-based paradigm, which outlines a progressive model of engagement without prescribing specific interventions, should continue to frame the policy response. Policy makers and social workers alike have room to innovate within the framework—to take relevant pieces of existing approaches and match them with services most appropriate for emerging populations. Resources must respond to, or even precede, changes in the needs of those facing housing loss if homelessness is ever to approach an end.

REFERENCES

Allgood, S., & Warren, R. S. (2003). The duration of homelessness: Evidence from a national survey. *Journal of Housing Economics, 12*, 273–290.

Bassuk, E. L., Weinreb, L. F., Dawson, R., Perloff, J. N., & Buckner, J. C. (1997). Determinants of behavior in homeless and low-income housed preschool children. *Pediatrics, 100*(1), 92–100.

Basu, A., Kee, R., Buchanan, D., & Sadowski, L. S. (2012). Comparative cost analysis of housing and case management program for chronically ill homeless adults compared to usual care. *Health Services Research, 47*, 523–543.

Burt, M. R., & Cohen, B. E. (1989). *America's homeless: Numbers, characteristics, and programs that serve them*. Washington, D.C.: Urban Institute.

Burt, M. R., Pearson, C. L., & Montgomery, A. E. (2005). *Strategies for preventing homelessness*. Washington, D.C.: Urban Institute. Retrieved August 4, 2015, from http://www.urban.org/UploadedPDF/1000874_preventing_homelessness.pdf.

Byrne, T., Munley, E. A., Fargo, J. D., Montgomery, A. E., & Culhane, D. P. (2013). New perspectives on community-level determinants of homelessness. *Journal of Urban Affairs, 35*(5), 607–625.

Byrne, T., Treglia, D., Kuhn, J., Kane, V., & Culhane, D. P. (2016). Predictors of homelessness following exit from homelessness prevention and rapid re-housing programs: Evidence from the Department of Veterans Affairs Supportive Services for Veteran Families Program. *Housing Policy Debate, 26*(1), 252–275.

Caton, C. L., Wilkins, C., & Anderson, J. (2007). People who experience long-term homelessness: Characteristics and interventions. In D. P. Culhane, G. Locke, & J. Khadduri (Eds.), *Toward understanding homelessness: The 2007 National Symposium on Homelessness Research* (pp. 4-1–4-44). Washington, D.C.: U.S. Department of Housing and Urban Development.

Culhane, D. P., Dejowski, E. F., Ibanez, J., Needham, E., & Macchia, I. (1994). Public shelter admission rates in Philadelphia and New York City: The implications of turnover for sheltered population counts. *Housing Policy Debate, 5*(2), 107–140.

Culhane, D. P., Metraux, S., & Byrne, T. (2011). A prevention-centered approach to homelessness assistance: A paradigm shift? *Housing Policy Debate, 21*(2), 295–315.

Culhane, D. P., Metraux, S., & Hadley, T. (2002). Public service reductions associated with placement of homeless persons with severe mental illness in supportive housing. *Housing Policy Debate, 13*(1), 107–163.

Culhane, D. P., Metraux, S., Park, J. M., Schretzman, M., & Valente, J. (2007). Testing a typology of family homelessness based on patterns of public shelter utilization in four U.S. jurisdictions: Implications for policy and program planning. *Housing Policy Debate, 18*(1), 1–28.

Early, D. W. (1999). A microeconomic analysis of homelessness: An empirical investigation using choice-based sampling. *Journal of Housing Economics, 8*(4), 312–327.

Early, D. W. (2004). The determinants for homelessness and the targeting of housing assistance. *Journal of Urban Economics, 55*, 195–214.

Early, D. W., & Olsen, E. O. (2002). Subsidized housing, emergency shelters, and homelessness: An empirical investigation using data from the 1990 census. *Advances in Economic Analysis & Policy, 2*(1), 1–34.

Fargo, J., Metraux, S., Byrne, T., Munley, E., Montgomery, A., & Jones, H. (2012). Prevalence and risk of homelessness among U.S. veterans. *Preventing Chronic Disease, 9*, E45.

Frank, R. G., & Glied, S. (2006). Changes in mental health financing since 1971: Implications for policymakers and patients. *Health Affairs, 25*(3), 601–613.

Gilmer, T. P., Stefancic, A., Katz, M. L., Sklar, M., Tsemberis, S., & Palinkas, L. A. (2014). Fidelity to the Housing First model and effectiveness of permanent supported housing programs in California. *Psychiatric Services 65*(11), 1311–1317.

Hopper, K. (2002). *Reckoning with homelessness.* Ithaca, N.Y.: Cornell University Press.

Jencks, C. (1994). *The homeless.* Cambridge, Mass.: Harvard University Press.

Katz, M. B. (1996). *In the shadow of the poorhouse.* New York: Basic Books.

Kuhn, R., & Culhane, D. P. (1998). Applying cluster analysis to test a typology of homelessness by pattern of shelter utilization: Results from the analysis of administrative data. *American Journal of Community Psychology, 26*(2), 207–232.

Kuno, E., Rothbard, A. B., Averyt, J., & Culhane, D. (2000). Homelessness among persons with serious mental illness in an enhanced community-based mental health system. *Psychiatric Services, 51*(8), 1012–1016.

Kushel, M. B., Vittinghoff, E., & Haas, J. S. (2001). Factors associated with the health care utilization of homeless persons. *Journal of the American Medical Association, 285*(2), 200–206.

Larimer, M. E., Malone, D. K., Garner, M. D., Atkins, D. C., Burlingham, B., Lonczak, H. S., . . . Marlatt, G. A. (2009). Health care and public service use and costs before and after provision of housing for chronically homeless persons with severe alcohol problems. *Journal of the American Medical Association, 301*, 1349–1357.

Lee, B. A., Price-Spratlen, T., & Kanan, J. W. (2003). Determinants of homelessness in metropolitan areas. *Journal of Urban Affairs, 25*, 335–355.

Lee, B. A., Tyler, K. A., & Wright, J. D. (2010). The new homelessness revisited. *Annual Review of Sociology, 36*, 501–521.

Leff, H. S., Chow, C. M., Pepin, R., Conley, J., Allen, I. E., & Seaman, C. A. (2009). One size fit all? What we can and can't learn from a meta-analysis of housing models for persons with mental illness. *Psychiatric Services, 60*(4), 473–482.

Link, B. G., Susser, E., Stueve, A., Phelan, J., Moore, R. E., & Struening, E. (1994). Lifetime and five-year prevalence of homelessness in the United States. *American Journal of Public Health, 84*(12), 1907–1912.

Main, T. (1998). How to think about homelessness: Balancing structural and individual causes. *Journal of Social Distress and the Homeless, 7*(1), 41–54.

Martinez, T. E., & Burt, M. R. (2006). Impact of permanent supportive housing on the use of acute care health services by homeless adults. *Psychiatric Services, 57*, 992–999.

Mental Health Commission of Canada. (2014). *National final report: Cross-Site at Home/Chez Soi Project.* Retrieved August 4, 2015, from http://www.mentalhealthcommission.ca.

Montgomery, A. E., Hill, L. L., Kane, V., & Culhane, D. P. (2013). Housing chronically homeless veterans: Evaluating the efficacy of a Housing First approach to HUD-VASH. *Journal of Community Psychology, 41*(4), 975–991.

Montgomery, A. E., Metraux, S., & Culhane, D. (2013). Rethinking homelessness prevention among persons with serious mental illness. *Social Issues and Policy Review, 7*(1), 58–82.

National Alliance to End Homelessness. (2014). *Rapid re-housing: A history and core components.* Washington, D.C.: National Alliance to End Homelessness.

New York City Department of Health and Mental Hygiene. (2013). *New York/New York III supportive housing evaluation: Interim utilization and cost analysis*. Retrieved August 4, 2015, from http://www.nyc.gov/html/doh/downloads/pdf/mental/housing-interim-report.pdf\nhttp://www.nyc.gov/html/doh/html/pr2013/pr048-13.shtml.

O'Flaherty, B. (2009). *Homeless in the United States*. New York: Columbia University Press.

O'Flaherty, B., & Wu, T. (2006). Fewer subsidized exits and a recession: How New York City's family homeless shelter population became immense. *Journal of Housing Economics, 15*(2), 99–125.

O'Toole, T. P., Gibbon, J. L., Hanusa, B. H., & Fine, M. J. (1999). Utilization of health care services among subgroups of urban homeless and housed poor. *Journal of Health Politics, Policy and Law, 24*, 91–114.

Quigley, J. M., & Raphael, S. (2001). The economics of homelessness: The evidence from North America. *European Journal of Housing Policy, 1*(3), 323–336.

Rodriguez, J. (2013). *Homelessness recurrence in Georgia*. Atlanta: Georgia Department of Community Affairs.

Rog, D. J., & Buckner, J. C. (2007). Homeless families and children. In D. P. Culhane, G. Locke, & J. Khadduri (Eds.), *Toward understanding homelessness: The 2007 national symposium* (pp. 4:5-1–5-33). Washington, D.C.: U.S. Department of Health and Human Services.

Rog, D. J., Marshall, T., Dougherty, R. H., George, P., Daniels, A. S., Ghose, S. S., & Delphin-Rittmon, M. E. (2014). Permanent supportive housing: Assessing the evidence. *Psychiatric Services, 65*, 287–294.

Rolston, H., Geyer, J., & Locke, G. (2013). *Final report: Evaluation of the Homebase Community Prevention Program*. Bethesda, Md.: Abt Associates.

Rossi, P. H. (1991). *Down and out in America: The origins of contemporary homelessness*. Chicago: University of Chicago Press.

Salit, S. A., Kuhn, E. M., Hartz, A. J., Vu, J. M., & Mosso, A. L. (1998). Hospitalization costs associated with homelessness in New York City. *New England Journal of Medicine, 338*, 1734–1740.

Shern, D. L., Tsemberis, S., Anthony, W., Lovell, A. M., Richmond, L., Felton, C. J., . . . Cohen, M. (2000). Serving street-dwelling individuals with psychiatric disabilities: Outcomes of a psychiatric rehabilitation clinical trial. *American Journal of Public Health, 90*(12), 1873–1878.

Shinn, M., Baumohl, J., & Hopper, K. (2001). The prevention of homelessness revisited. *Analyses of Social Issues and Public Policy, 1*, 95–127.

Shinn, M., Greer, A. L., Bainbridge, J., Kwon, J., & Zuiderveen, S. (2013). Efficient targeting of homelessness prevention services for families. *American Journal of Public Health, 103*, 324–330.

Shinn, M., Weitzman, B. C., Stojanovic, D., Knickman, J. R., Jiménez, L., Duchon, L., . . . Krantz, D. H. (1998). Predictors of homelessness among families in New York City: From shelter request to housing stability. *American Journal of Public Health, 88*, 1651–1657.

Shlay, A., & Rossi, P. H. (1992). Social science research and contemporary studies of homelessness. *Annual Review of Sociology 18*, 129–160.

Snyder, M., & Hombs, M. E. (1986). *Homelessness in America*. Washington, D.C.: Community for Creative Nonviolence.

Srebnik, D., Connor, T., & Sylla, L. (2013). A pilot study of the impact of Housing First–supported housing for intensive users of medical hospitalization and sobering services. *American Journal of Public Health, 103*(2), 316–321.

Taylor, J. (2014). *Housing assistance for households experiencing homelessness*. Paper presented at the National Conference on Family and Youth Homelessness.

Toohey, S. M., Shinn, M., & Weitzman, B. C. (2004). Social networks and homelessness among women heads of household. *American Journal of Community Psychology, 33*(1–2), 7–20.

Tsai, J., Kasprow, W. J., Kane, V., & Rosenheck, R. A. (2014). Street outreach and other forms of engagement with literally homeless veterans. *Journal of Health Care for the Poor and Underserved, 25*(2), 694–704.

Tsemberis, S. (2010). Housing First: Ending homelessness, promoting recovery, and reducing costs. In B. O'Flaherty & I. G. Ellen (Eds.), *How to house the homeless* (pp. 37–56). New York: Russell Sage Foundation.

Tsemberis, S., Gulcur, L., & Nakae, M. (2004). Housing First, consumer choice, and harm reduction for homeless individuals with a dual diagnosis. *American Journal of Public Health, 94*(4), 651–656.

U.S. Conference of Mayors. (2008). *A status report on hunger and homelessness in America's cities*. Washington, D.C.: U.S. Conference of Mayors.

U.S. Department of Housing and Urban Development. (1984). The extent of homelessness in America: A report to the secretary on the homeless and emergency shelters. In J. Erickson & C. Wilhelm (Eds.), *Housing the homeless* (pp. 127–143). New Brunswick, N.J.: Transaction.

U.S. Department of Housing and Urban Development. (2008). *A guide to counting the unsheltered homeless population*. Washington, D.C.: U.S. Department of Housing and Urban Development.

U.S. Department of Housing and Urban Development. (2014a). *Annual homelessness assessment report: 2013, part II*. Washington, D.C.: U.S. Department of Housing and Urban Development.

U.S. Department of Housing and Urban Development. (2014b). *Annual homelessness assessment report: 2014, part I*. Washington, D.C.: U.S. Department of Housing and Urban Development.

U.S. Department of Housing and Urban Development. (2014c). *Point in time count methodology guide*. Washington, D.C.: U.S. Department of Housing and Urban Development.

Wong, Y.-L. I., Culhane, D. P., & Kuhn, R. (1997). Predictors of exit and reentry among family shelter users in New York City. *Social Service Review, 71*(3), 441–462.

Wong, Y.-L. I., Koppel, M., Culhane, D. P., Metraux, S., Eldridge, D. E., Hillier, A., & Lee, H. R. (1999). *Help in time: An evaluation of Philadelphia's community-based homelessness prevention program*. Retrieved August 4, 2015, from http://works.bepress.com/dennis_culhane/83.

SECTION IV
HOUSING POLICY

Chapter 12   Housing and Community

KATHRYN HOWELL

The way in which poor communities have been viewed by scholars, planners, and policy makers has been a function of the way each community has been defined for theoretical, planning, or policy purposes, the value that has been placed on communities by these professionals, and the way each group acknowledges and regards the voices of the community (Friedman, 1987; Massey, 2008). The presumed ability and capacity of communities to organize and make decisions about their futures impacts the way that policy and planning decisions are conceptualized and put into practice in low-income communities. This has particularly been the case in urban housing and redevelopment policy in the past century (N. Davidson, 2009; Davis, 1991; see chapter 14).

Housing policy has been both an explicit social policy and an implicit community policy. From tenement reform, settlement houses, and urban renewal at the turn of the twentieth century to public housing, mobility, and urban redevelopment programs, the ways in which communities are approached and housing is built, funded, and managed have determined how a community looks and who resides in the community (Hall, 2014; K. Jackson, 1985; Vale, 2000; see chapters 1, 2, 9, 10, 15, and 16). Housing policy has further determined how the residents of each community interact, what opportunities and amenities they have access to, and how they are represented politically (Duneier, 1999; Goetz, 2013; Vale, 2013; see chapter 13). More importantly, housing policy and planning interventions have determined who has a voice in the community. These interventions have often defined community as a geographic space, delineated by particular streets, census tracts, or zip codes, and as a social space, defined by the interactions and relationships between and among residents (Crenson, 1983; Davis, 1991).

Historically, the poor, like the communities in which they live, have been thought to embody threats to the moral and physical health and safety of the city (Riis, 1890; Vale, 2000). More recently, scholars and activists have argued that the neighborhoods themselves can be toxic for the residents who live in them (DeLuca & Dayton, 2009; Massey & Denton, 1998). They argue that low-income residents can benefit from living in proximity to higher-income neighbors who can expose them to middle-class norms, wider job networks, and improved educational outcomes (Briggs, Popkin, & Goering, 2010; Massey & Denton, 1998). Conversely, research on HOPE VI and Moving to Opportunity programs has called into question the benefits of mixed-income communities (Kleit, 2005). The arguments supporting mixed-income development have justified policy responses that redevelop and disperse low-income communities in the name of improvements in the health, safety, and welfare of not just the residents of the redeveloped communities but future neighborhood residents and cities themselves (Goetz, 2013; Vale, 2013).

This chapter examines ways neighborhoods have been defined and represented by residents, policy makers, and advocates. It further outlines the ways in which housing and planning policies in the United States over the past century have affected those definitions. These policies will be discussed in terms of their stated policy goals and the outcomes that have resulted. Finally, it explores historical changes in the discourse of community and how that has affected the way that residents interact within those communities.

DEFINING AND REPRESENTING COMMUNITY

Conflicts over defining neighborhoods for the purposes of representation and development are rooted in contrasting views of neighborhoods as primarily physical places versus communities (Davidson, 2009). Community, in turn, has been defined in both geographic and social terms by residents, policy makers, theorists, and advocates (Harvey, 2008; Leventhal, Brooks-Gunn, & Kamerman, 2000). Boundaries are sometimes assumed to overlap with official neighborhood boundaries designated by city governments, while at other times they are assumed to be defined by demographic or social groups, classes, and races and ethnicities without regard to location (Crenson, 1983; Davis, 1991). These conflicting conceptions of community, as well as the dominant perceptions of low-income communities specifically, have impacted the way community development and community control have been approached by city governments and developers (M. Jackson, 2008; Manzo, Kleit, & Couch, 2008). The demise of legal segregation, ongoing international immigration, including from the developing world (see chapter 25), and gentrification pressures on central city neighborhoods have also created neighborhoods that are less homogeneous than the segregated communities of the past, leading to greater conflict both within and outside communities (Leventhal et al., 2000; Peterman, 2000).

Although planning and policy practice and research have defined communities as geographic places that contain residents, scholars have debated whether neighborhoods are geographically bounded spaces or communities of people (Crenson, 1983; Davis, 1991). Neighborhoods rarely fit specific geographic boundaries and are typically more than a physical space. Leventhal et al. (2000: 192) argue that "viewing communities as places—as neighborhoods or as geographical or bureaucratic locales—suggests that communities are manageable units around which to organize and deliver services," implying a certain level of control over the space by those defining it. Further, neighborhoods may also be considered as a "face," or a community with a system of social supports and relationships, or as a "space," defined as "built places for activity—living, working and political organizing" (Leventhal et al., 2000: 198). To these authors, it is the interaction of space, place, and face that determines neighborhood strength and identity (Leventhal et al., 2000; Peterman, 2000). Brown and Richman argue for a place-based definition that includes a social component and contend that neighborhoods are spaces of continuous social interaction with meaning for the residents (Brown & Richman, 2000).

However, these conflicting definitions of community frequently lead to debates among residents about the spatial and symbolic boundaries of neighborhoods. Crenson (1983) discovered differences in residential conceptions of communities based on race and income in his exploration of Baltimore neighborhoods. Further, not only is the definition of community contested, it also has to be defended fiercely to be maintained, meaning that not only is representation at stake in a more formal sense, but the day-to-day control of neighborhood space is disputable as communities change (Crenson, 1983; Cresswell, 1996).

The meanings of neighborhood spaces have been particularly challenging as neighborhoods change and the value and meaning of communities are contested by new and longtime residents. Neighborhood residents generally retain a parochial focus on maintaining or improving the conditions in their neighborhoods and may face conflict among diverse goals. However, elected officials are also pressured to increase income, property, and sales tax revenue through the attraction of high-income residents and high-grossing businesses at a citywide level. These divergent goals often come into sharp relief in decisions about issues such as zoning and increases in density, tax incentives for business development, and parking. The relative power of communities across the city and resident groups within the neighborhood may mean that groups such as homeowners or higher-income residents have more power to influence citywide decisions, suggesting, as Fainstein does, that "deliberative democracy operates poorly in situations of social and economic inequality." Fainstein and others propose that the voices of low-income residents may get lost as cities change and inequality both within and among urban neighborhoods increases (Fainstein, 2010: 29; Crenson, 1983; Davis, 1991; Freeman, 2006).

TURN-OF-THE-CENTURY HOUSING AND COMMUNITY INTERVENTIONS

The conflicting physical and geographic definitions of community and the voice that communities have had in processes of change became a growing part of the redevelopment landscape as cities urbanized during the Industrial Revolution. The growth in industrialization, southern and eastern European immigration, and black/African American migration from the South resulted in a rapid densification of housing and congested housing conditions in central city neighborhoods close to industry (see chapter 16). This growth in employment-based urbanization "unleashed a set of social, economic and technological changes that dramatically altered the urban environment" (Massey, 2008: 39). At the close of the nineteenth century, Riis (1890) and his counterparts in London presented images of depravity and public health threats, such as cholera, in urban tenements that shocked upper- and middle-class Victorians. In cities like New York, Washington, D.C., and London, the state of the slums reflected the fears of disease and moral contagion held by many outside the slums (Hall, 2014; see chapter 18).

Rising fears about the spread of disease and moral depravity, as well as growing awareness of the deplorable conditions in which the working class lived, led to a move to reform housing codes and to intervene in the lives of the immigrants living in these communities. Social reformers hoped to remedy the threats to physical and moral health through changes in the communities in which these residents lived, thereby "saving the immigrant from his (and, especially her) own errors and excesses" (Hall, 2014: 42) and elevating "the moral tone of the segregated populations" (Park, 1984: 9). To accomplish this, they developed settlement houses that provided education, clubs for seniors, and "fallen women" programs for the working-class poor of the industrialized cities. The objectives were to encourage immigrant assimilation, if possible, or to coerce those who did not assimilate into leaving and to improve the city by improving public spaces (Hall, 2014). Some social reformers argued for neighborhood revitalization to improve the life of the residents. This geographic determinism encouraged the belief that "the city's physical appearance would symbolize its moral purity" (Hall, 2014: 46). The activism led city governments to intervene in housing for the first time by requiring basic building standards to improve health and sanitation, as well as creating a system of parks in many cities across America. City governments also improved municipal services by providing water and sewer services more broadly across cities (see chapters 13 and 18). However, communities of color remained underserved in many cities (K. Jackson, 1985; see chapter 16).

Increasingly, wealthy city dwellers escaped the disease, crime, and moral decay of the growing cities through moves to new suburbs just outside the city limits. From there, they could avoid daily interactions with the working class, immigrants, and blacks/African Americans but still access managerial positions using the new streetcars that had become a staple of modern cities. Instead, suburbanites could live in open, healthy communities, reflecting the commonly held belief that individuals were shaped and formed by the communities in which they lived. This suburbanization of non-Hispanic white, middle-class residents kicked off the racial and ethnic segregation that is common in the modern American city (K. Jackson, 1985; Massey, 2008).

Ernest Burgess and Robert Park, researchers at the Chicago School of Urban Sociology, argued that the growth in racial segregation in U.S. cities was a natural economic process that reflected the desire for blacks/African Americans to self-segregate (Massey & Denton, 1998). Burgess and Park believed that the concentration of new immigrants and poor residents in substandard housing conditions was part of a natural succession of urban neighborhoods. Reflecting both contemporary thought about the natural and desirable state of single-family ownership and open space for quality of life, as well as the "natural" state of market capitalism, they argued that the worst neighborhoods were in the center of the city and neighborhoods improved outward from there. The poorest and newest migrants, they argued, would naturally assimilate, moving up socioeconomically and out geographically, leaving the poorest housing for the next wave of immigrants (Park, 1984).

Until the rise of industrialization, many cities had residential blocks that were racially and economically integrated. However, new immigrant communities were not as concentrated or segregated in immigrant ghettos as Park and Burgess suggested, even after industrialization. Ghettos in this context refer to "a set of neighborhoods inhabited exclusively by members of one group and within which virtually all members of that group live" (Massey, 2008: 39). Instead, individual nationalities were rarely the majority in any given community but were part of larger immigrant and working-class areas located near employment (Hall, 2014; Massey, 2008). Conversely, blacks/African Americans remained highly segregated over the next century, while immigrant communities tended to represent a step on the road to upward mobility (Massey, 2008; see chapter 16).

LEGAL SUPPORT FOR COMMUNITY-BASED CONTROL

Although planners and others involved in urban policy in the first half of the twentieth century argued that decisions about where to live were rational ones based on market preferences, the structurally defined housing options for low-income households—particularly people of color—were limited by both legal and social confines (Schwartz, 2014). Although there was significant de facto segregation based on intimidation, legal structures assisted in de jure segregation of communities and engendered significant and persistent socioeconomic segregation (K. Jackson, 1985). As urban areas began to change and wealthy professionals moved to suburbs, restrictive covenants and zoning were used to prevent people of color from buying homes and to bar the construction of multifamily housing units as a means of maintaining a particular demographic, social, and architectural look and feel in suburban communities (Massey & Denton, 1998; see chapter 16).

In 1926 the village of Euclid, Ohio, using Standard State Zoning Enabling legislation, which gave local jurisdictions power to institute zoning, determined a division of uses, including the prohibition of apartment buildings in single-family residential neighborhoods. When this zoning decision was challenged, the Supreme Court ruled that zoning was a legitimate use of local police powers to support the health, safety, and moral and physical welfare of the public. The Supreme Court further argued that apartment buildings prevented single-family development and should be classified as commercial buildings. Specifically, the court stated "that the development of detached house sections is greatly retarded [sic] by the coming of apartment houses, which has sometimes resulted in destroying the entire section for private house purposes; that, in such sections, very often the apartment house is a mere parasite [sic], constructed in order to take advantage of the open spaces and attractive surroundings created by the residential character of the district" (*Village of Euclid v. Ambler Realty Co.*, 1926: n.p.). This decision opened the door to use zoning as a means of creating high-income neighborhoods with single-family homes located far from apartments and industrial areas (see chapter 13).

Newly formed all-non-Hispanic white neighborhood associations developed restrictive deed covenants attached to each neighborhood property that prohibited the sale or lease to or residence by blacks/African Americans. While 75 percent of neighborhood owners were required to agree to the covenants before they were enforceable, many were pressured into signing once their neighbors agreed (Massey, 2008). Although the Supreme Court made restrictive covenants unenforceable in 1948, restrictive covenants remained part of deeds (K. Jackson, 1985). While covenants regarding property-related attributes such as the sales price, exterior appearance, and uses are still instituted by neighborhood associations, covenants based on characteristics of the occupants of the property were made illegal in the Fair Housing Act of 1968 (K. Jackson, 1985; Schwartz, 2014; see chapter 16).

In addition to the restrictive covenants that kept blacks/African Americans out of non-Hispanic white communities, lending practices institutionalized by the federal government highly rated newly built suburban, all-non-Hispanic white communities and prevented lending in communities of color. The Home Owners Loan Corporation (HOLC) institutionalized this practice, called redlining, in 1933. The HOLC created a system of neighborhood appraisals based on normative value judgments about the density, race, and age of the neighborhood to evaluate the risk of lending in these areas. Non-Hispanic white, professional communities with new housing stock were rated the highest (with an A rating, marked in blue), while black/African American communities with old housing stock were rated the lowest (with a D rating, marked in red) and deemed definitely declining. The HOLC system standardized and legitimized the practice of discriminatory lending, effectively encouraging the relocation of upper-income and non-Hispanic white homeowners while preventing homeownership for blacks/African Americans, who were typically unable to obtain a mortgage to purchase a home (Crossney, 2005; K. Jackson, 1985; Massey, 2008; see chapters 8 and 16).

URBAN RENEWAL, CIVIL RIGHTS, AND COMMUNITY DEVELOPMENT

The focus on rational and technical professional planning and market-driven, natural succession of neighborhood conditions, combined with the broader definition of neighborhoods as spatial rather than social places, legitimized the wave of urban renewal that followed World War II. Planners regarded urban development as a technical function requiring specific skills and a knowledge base that disregarded local knowledge and individual needs in favor of experts who, they believed, could rationally evaluate the available options and discern the best strategy to address challenges as planners defined them (Brooks, 2002). Neighborhoods were seen as physical spaces that had declining relevance as non-Hispanic white families continued their migration to growing suburbs in order to escape the desegregation of their schools and neighborhoods (see chapter 2). The federal government supported these moves through the discriminatory lending practice of redlining, as discussed above (see chapter 8). Meanwhile, continued housing discrimination, zoning, and the lingering effects of restrictive covenants kept poor black/African American families from leaving inner city neighborhoods. Many of these predominantly black/African American neighborhoods were located adjacent to downtowns and suffered from crowding, distressed conditions, and increasing poverty (Hall, 2014; K. Jackson, 1985; M. Jackson, 2008; Massey, 2008; see chapter 16).

Federal and local government officials hoped to prevent further deterioration and irrelevance of the city through urban renewal projects. Originally focused on clearing black/African American slums and building new housing for working poor residents, urban renewal became largely about slum clearance and commercial redevelopment, which local governments used to acquire properties and spur commercial development in declining downtowns (Vale, 2013). Typically, local governments acquired land by designating it blighted under broad federal guidelines and then razed the buildings. By defining neighborhoods as blighted, local governments could justify the clearance of low- and moderate-income communities in the name of progress and modernity without substantive review or consideration by the community impacted by this redevelopment. Thus urban renewal was referred to as "Negro Removal" by many blacks/African Americans, and it became synonymous with displacement of entire communities in cities across the United States (Briggs et al., 2010; Goetz, 2013; M. Jackson, 2008). N. Davidson (2009: 2) argues that urban renewal "not only ignored existing urban fabric, but also paid far too little heed to those living in the communities targeted by that renewal." It further reinforced the idea that neighborhoods, particularly low-income communities of color, are primarily places within the city without the capacity to act on their own behalf (see chapters 14 and 16).

The civil rights movement, as well as the community destruction caused by urban renewal, generated strong critiques of the "belief that planners, using the rational planning model, could articulate goals for and speak on behalf of a community without the direct involvement of the community" (Peterson, 1991: 38). The power to speak for one's own community and have a role in the way it changed became a key piece of housing policy and urban planning during the civil rights movement (Peterman, 2000). Advocacy planners argued that to remedy the exclusion of marginalized groups, especially people of color, professional technical assistance, such as organizing neighborhood residents and articulating planning goals, should be available to help these groups navigate urban planning and policy processes and articulate their needs to city planners. Further, advocacy planners such as Davidoff argued that planning is inherently value laden and that those values cannot be removed from the process. Rather than being detached and neutral in planning processes, advocacy planners were encouraged to engage with marginalized groups to bridge gaps between city agencies and the communities impacted by their plans (Brooks, 2002; Checkoway, 1994; Davidoff, 1965; Peterman, 2000).

As federal policies for housing and community development changed during the late 1960s and early 1970s, advocacy planners and community groups bypassed or minimized the role and autonomy of local governments in decision making about local redevelopment (M. Jackson, 2008; Slessarev, 1988). Beginning in the late 1960s, as the effects of urban renewal became visible and the civil rights movement gained strength, federal funds often went directly to community organizations in neighborhoods that were low income or of color, helping to build a cohort of grassroots leaders (N. Davidson, 2009; Peterman, 2000; Twelvetrees, 1989). The results of these efforts included the creation of community development corporations (CDCs) and mobilization within communities to "oppose threats to their physical integrity or to take advantage of federal programs" (Gittel & Vidal, 1998: 34; Erikson, 2009). These groups assisted with job creation, small business development, and the development of affordable housing, as well as providing "a political voice for poor and racialized minorities previously excluded from decision-making" (Newman & Lake, 2006: 45). Further, after the passage of the Civil Rights Act of 1964 and the Voting Rights Act of 1965, housing and community development interventions "sought to break down remaining discriminatory barriers as well as to compensate African-Americans for past inequalities by providing programs especially designed to uplift the inner city poor" (Slessarev, 1988: 369; see chapter 16).

Initially, CDCs were intended to be based and staffed within the neighborhood itself and focused on neighborhood areas. They were intended to be a source of neighborhood empowerment, with the ultimate goal of community control through community organizing (Peterman, 2000). CDCs see themselves as representatives of the communities in which they work. Outside agencies and organizations, such as local and state governments and lenders, often accept their authority as community leaders (Gittel & Vidal, 1998; Peterman, 2000). However, many critics have raised concerns about whether those CDCs that are governed and staffed by nonresidents can adequately represent the interests of the community (Stoecker, 2003). Kelly (1976) provided evidence that increased community control leads to better performance of CDCs. On the other hand, critics argue that "community development corporations reproduce inequality since they help government evade its responsibilities as well as making very little positive differences to ghettos" (Twelvetrees, 1989: 189–190). However, CDCs are generally believed to be necessary to provide equitable housing development (Schwartz, 2014; Twelvetrees, 1989; see chapter 8).

Conversely, community-based organizations (CBOs) are governed and staffed by members of a particular community in which they are located and are organized to serve, mobilize, and advocate for that community. CBOs are often less professionalized than their CDC counterparts and are more focused on community organizing and oppositional politics. Therefore, they are less likely than CDCs to access government resources such as grants, technical assistance, and political influence. CDCs and CBOs are necessary for communities to be effective and equitable in redevelopment efforts due to the focus of the former on development of physical units and the latter on advocacy and ensuring equity in redevelopment (Gittel & Vidal, 1998; Stoecker, 2003).

Community development corporations have reacted to the changes in the political and funding environment. Their heavy dependence on federal and foundation funding has caused them to focus on physical redevelopment and thus less on services or oppositional politics through community organizing. Further, redevelopment and organizing are often conflicting goals because of the necessity of maintaining good relationships with funding organizations. This challenge of balancing the need to maintain funding for housing and community development against the need for community organizing has led some community advocates to question whether the mainstreaming of service provision through federally funded organizations has meant that community leaders have actually made progress toward equity or whether the inclusion of protest movements into mainstream organizations is actually counterproductive in terms of moving their agendas forward (Fainstein, 1995; Piven, 1977; Stoecker, 2003; see chapters 8 and 14).

In practice, community control by residents who are low income and of color, consistent with the Right to the City, or the right to be an active and equal citizen within the community, as advocated by Harvey (2008), relies on radical and insurgent planners who work with and listen to residents left out of the mainstream of economic development and social interaction in order to ensure that they are not left out of processes. These practices are rooted in a tradition of social mobilization and social theory. Unlike social reform planning, which "would ameliorate, through social welfare programs, urban design and land controls, the worst effects of unfettered economic growth" (Friedman, 1987: 297), as was typically seen in the Victorian and urban renewal eras, social mobilization seeks to change the basic political economic structures that produce marginalization. Its focus is on grassroots, community-based action rather than state action. Social mobilization is based in the Marxist tradition that stresses dialectical relationships, class struggle, and the relationships of workers to modes of production. It also has roots in social anarchism, which rejects state authority and focuses on communal organization from the ground up in a classless society (Castells, 1979, 1985; Friedman, 1987; see chapter 16).

Although federal funding to community organizations was short lived in the 1960s and 1970s, these groups have remained empowered and have continued to organize to provide services when the government and private sectors fail (Rubin, 2000; Twelvetrees, 1989), to protest destructive redevelopment schemes (Gittel & Vidal, 1998; M. Jackson, 2008; Peterman, 2000), and to advocate for greater redistribution of resources to low-income households (Newman & Lake, 2006; Peterman, 2000). However, as cities changed, "attempts, even successful ones, to exert power and to gain control of neighborhoods seemed to be futile in places where resources had fled, disinvestment was rampant, and those responsible for decline were, often as not, located outside the neighborhood and were well insulated from advocacy organizing tactics" (Peterman, 2000: 49). Conversely, the growth in the number of neighborhood groups spread to middle- and high-income neighborhoods, resulting in a growth in NIMBY (Not In My Back Yard) activism that built and reinforced growing racial, ethnic, and socioeconomic segregation in communities (Fisher, 1984; Kruse, 2007).

In the late 1960s, the increasingly segregated ghettos across the United States erupted in violence as "the planet as building site collided with the 'planet of slums'" (Harvey, 2008: 428), particularly in Watts, Detroit, and other neighborhoods and cities from 1965 to 1967 and following the assassination of Dr. Martin Luther King Jr. in April 1968. Efforts to redesign cities and marginalize the poor through urban renewal, combined with continued race-based disparity and discrimination, resulted in rising frustration among blacks/African Americans in segregated communities. The Kerner Commission report, issued shortly before the 1968 civil rights riots, "concluded that the riots [of 1967] stemmed from the persistence of racial discrimination and a historical legacy of disadvantages . . . but one factor was clearly identified by the commissioners as underlying all other social and economic problems: segregation" (Massey & Denton, 1998: 59). The report recommended policies to remediate that issue, including using federal housing programs to desegregate communities and passing legislation prohibiting housing discrimination (Hall, 2014). In spite of the passage of the Fair Housing Act shortly after Martin Luther King Jr.'s assassination, which banned discrimination in the rental or sale of housing, "not only did the ghetto fail to disappear; in many ways its problems multiplied. As segregation persisted, black isolation deepened, and the social and economic problems that had long plagued African American communities worsened" (Massey & Denton, 1998: 61). Although the Fair Housing Act was broad in its prohibition of discrimination in the housing market, it legally relies on the victim of discrimination to prove the discrimination. It also did not give the U.S. Department of Housing and Urban Development (HUD) the power to enforce the act through proactive investigation in housing markets. Amendments in 1988 strengthened the act, gave HUD more enforcement powers, and expanded the classes protected under the law (Schwartz, 2014).

At the same time, state and local governments had grown frustrated with the lack of local discretion over the use of federal funding and the complexity of federal categorical grants. Thus, shortly after his election, Richard Nixon led the fight to pass the Community Development Act of 1974. This act, which, among other things, created the Community Development Block Grant (CDBG) Program, gave more power and flexibility to state and local jurisdictions in redevelopment. Previously, local governments had to apply for one project at a time within a narrow scope. CDBG combined eight federal community development programs, including urban renewal, in one program (Hayes, 1995; Schwartz, 2014; Twelvetrees, 1989).

Although CDBG has had significant success, its discretionary nature has resulted in complaints and conflicts between HUD and state governments. In Texas, for example, CDBG funds were intended for disaster recovery after Hurricane Ike in 2008. After statewide nonprofits filed a complaint, HUD found that the state of Texas had not used funds to assist low-income communities of color, as was required. The state was required to repay some of the funds through appropriations to low-income communities (Poverty and Race Research Action Council, 2013). CDBG was the start of a trend of devolution of responsibility away from the federal government to state and local housing and community development departments and local planning departments. While local jurisdictions are required to create a consolidated plan that explains both the needs and uses for the federal allocation of funds, the jurisdictions are not required to follow the plan (Schwartz, 2014).

Similar to the way that public housing policies during the New Deal era allowed for local norms and planning practices to dominate equity concerns, since the 1970s, devolution of federal funds has fueled the existing regime-based politics of local political landscapes. Stone defines regime politics as "informal arrangements that surround and complement the formal workings of governmental authority" (1989: 3), often centered on a pro-growth agenda with an emphasis on the central business district over neighborhoods. Due to the local nature of capital and development, state and local governments face particular pressure in the implementation of federal and local housing policies. Because land regulations are largely local or state-controlled, real estate developers lobby at the local and state levels for zoning changes, beneficial regulation, or support for particular land deals. Local governments are also pressured through NIMBY concerns and the pressure to attract businesses and residents, meaning that affordable housing, equity concerns, and community control remain highly politicized and personal at the local level (Basolo, 1999; Harvey, 1996; Hayes, 1995; M. Jackson, 2008; Stone, 1989; Sugrue, 2005; see chapters 14 and 16).

NEIGHBORHOOD EFFECTS, RESIDENTIAL MOBILITY, AND REDEVELOPMENT IN THE 1990S AND 2000S

The toxicity of poor neighborhoods for those who live in them is an idea dating back to the early twentieth century, when Riis and others revealed the conditions in the slums of Western cities, reinforcing the belief that neighborhoods defined the people who lived in them (Hall, 2014; Riis, 1890; Vale, 2000). This idea of toxic neighborhoods was advanced further as researchers began examining the impact that structural racism (Massey & Denton, 1998), chronic unemployment (Wilson, 1996), and concentrated poverty have on family and child outcomes (Briggs et al., 2010; see chapter 18). To address these issues, policy makers and researchers have advocated enabling poor people to move to high-opportunity neighborhoods using Housing Choice Vouchers (HCVs) and redevelopment of public housing and the built environment to integrate poor households into mixed-income communities (Briggs et al., 2010; Day, 2003; Julian & McCain, 2009; Kleit, 2005; see chapters 14 and 16).

By the end of the 1970s, after decades of neighborhood abandonment by middle-class, non-Hispanic whites and blacks/African Americans, "the image of poor, minority families mired in an endless cycle of unemployment, unwed childbearing, illiteracy, and dependency had coalesced into a compelling and powerful concept: the urban underclass" (Massey & Denton, 1998: 4). Moreover, the concept of the urban underclass has been characterized by extreme detachment from the labor force, social isolation, and persistent poverty. Four theoretical explanations have been offered for the persistence of the urban underclass: a culture of poverty, racism, larger economic restructuring, and welfare dependency, either for incentivizing poverty or for its lack of comprehensive efforts (Briggs et al., 2010; Massey & Denton, 1998; Peterson, 1991).

The structural concentration of poverty, it is argued, "deprive[s] residents not only of resources and conventional role models, but also of cultural learning from mainstream social networks that facilitate social and economic advancement in industrial society" (Sampson & Morenoff, 2000: 19). The effects of social isolation, according to Wilson and others, are distinct from those described as resulting from membership in a culture of poverty because such isolation is argued to provoke adaptive responses to the structural constraints and opportunities of concentrated poverty rather than an internalization of norms (Briggs et al., 2010; Sampson & Morenoff, 2000; Wilson, 2009). The structural view of poverty led researchers to argue that neighborhoods themselves were toxic, contributing to poor family and child outcomes. In recent years, this argument also provided the justification for physical and social overhauls of communities, including public housing communities, in a wave of gentrification (Freeman, 2006; Goetz, 2013; see chapter 16).

The literature on neighborhood effects of poverty argues that persistently poor neighborhoods have broken social relations, including high levels of anger, demoralization, fear, diminished interaction, and informal cooperation, as well as diminution of responsibility for neighborhood safety and quality (Brown & Richman, 2000). Wilson's classic argument was that the "movement of black middle class and high-wage industrial jobs away from historically black urban communities had created a new and isolated 'urban underclass' defined by concentrated minority poverty in inner city neighborhoods" (Briggs et al., 2010: 36). By the end of the 1970s, this migration removed the social networks and organizations vital to social control and advancement. High levels of social organization, measured by the level of weak and strong ties (discussed in detail below), institutions, formal organizations, and social control, are necessary for the success and flourishing of neighborhood stability, mobilization, and advancement (Crenson, 1983; Granovetter, 1983; M. Jackson, 2008; Wilson, 1996), or more specifically in the development of social capital, the "networks, norms, and trust that facilitate coordination and cooperation for mutual benefit" (Brown & Richman, 2000: 171). Researchers believed that the lack of such control, as evidenced by physical signs of disorder, lead to a further breakdown in control. In the early 1980s, Kelling and Wilson (1982) introduced the broken windows theory, which suggests that disorder in communities is a cause of crime. Further, small amounts of disorder, such as a broken window, will indicate a breakdown of community control, increasing neighborhood fear and engendering further disorder. However, in a later experiment, Sampson and Raudenbush (1999) found little evidence that physical disorder leads to crime. Nevertheless, policies based on the previous argument have remained standard practice in maintaining order and were, for example, a centerpiece of former New York City mayor Rudolph Giuliani's urban policing policy (Duneier, 1999; see chapter 16).

Researchers such as Mayer and Jencks (1989) and Wilson (1996), who focus on neighborhood effects, suggest that because the environment in which a person lives has an impact on his or her educational outcomes, social mobility, and job opportunities, households that are low-income or of color should move to mixed-income communities that will help them build social capital. Social capital is defined in many ways but is broadly described as the "features of social organization, such as networks, norms, and trust, that facilitate coordination and cooperation for mutual benefit" (Putnam, 1993: 36). There are two types of social bonds thought to produce social capital: strong ties and weak ties (Granovetter, 1983). Strong ties are the family and close social relationships that facilitate a household's survival through assistance such as child care, transportation, or short-term loans (Dawkins, 2006; Kleit, 2010; Manzo, Kleit, & Couch, 2008; Stack, 1974). Weak ties, such as those between neighbors, provide access to networks and information that help residents to access better jobs, better schools, and other advancement opportunities. In other words, weak ties are used to "navigate a wider middle-class world and provide entry to someone attempting to break into that world" (Freeman, 2006: 149). The idea of weak ties is based on Bourdieu's (1986) concept of *habitus*, or collective cultural competency and behavioral expectations that signify inclusion into a class and create a lens through which that class views and acts in the world. These competencies may include public behavior, knowledge of negotiating educational or employment structures, or "appropriate" ways to access governmental or neighborhood organizations and resources (Lin, 1999; Weininger, 2005). Through weak ties, it is assumed that low-income households residing in mixed-income communities might acquire middle-class cultural habits that expand job and social networks. Although strong ties are important for daily survival, researchers point to the advancement potential from weak ties as one of the most important benefits of mixed-income communities (Briggs et al., 2010; Goetz, 2002; Rosenbaum, 2000; see chapter 16).

Based on these theories, mobility and redevelopment programs were developed to help low-income households build weak ties by changing the environments in which they live. The first of these programs, Gautreaux, resulted from the court-ordered desegregation of public housing in Chicago in 1976 after the Supreme Court found that the Chicago Housing Authority and HUD had used race as a basis for siting public housing, resulting in the segregation of low-income black/African American households. The Gautreaux program created a lottery that allowed seventy-one hundred families living in public housing to receive vouchers that included individual counseling to help them move to non-Hispanic white communities in the suburbs before the program concluded in 1998 (Rosenbaum, 2000).

Following Gautreaux, HUD created the Moving to Opportunity (MTO) demonstration program between 1993 and 2003. The program had an experimental design to determine whether residents gained access to jobs and education by leaving their highly segregated communities in the inner city. While Gautreaux focused on racial desegregation and income as factors for improving outcomes, MTO only required households to find low-poverty neighborhoods, regardless of racial or ethnic composition, in which to use their vouchers (Goetz, 2013; Schwartz, 2014).

At the same time, the federal government was investigating the state of public housing (Cisneros, 2009). The Commission on Severely Distressed Public Housing found that a small percentage of public housing was severely distressed and crime ridden, creating negative outcomes for the residents who lived in it. The state of high-rise buildings was particularly notable. Since the 1960s, public housing had been notorious for mismanagement, poor conditions, and concentrations of poverty and crime. It had also faced significant political pressure from conservatives who felt that the government should not intervene in the housing market and provide social services to low-income households (Cisneros, 2009; Goetz, 2013).

Throughout the middle of the twentieth century, local mismanagement, institutionalized racism, and perennial funding cuts for operating expenses contributed heavily to the challenges faced by many public housing authorities. At the same time, urban housing markets softened as more suburbs grew and industrial decline left many cities with fractions of their former populations. The often-cited example of these combined challenges is St. Louis's Pruitt-Igoe, a twenty-eight-hundred-unit development that opened in 1954 and was built on land formerly occupied by strong black/African American neighborhoods with poor physical housing conditions. The Pruitt-Igoe development was much anticipated but was quickly plagued by high crime rates and poor management, and thus high vacancy rates. Soon Pruitt-Igoe—and its demolition in 1974—became a symbol of the failure of public housing in the media and political debates (Goetz, 2013; K. Jackson, 1985; Schwartz, 2014).

To address the concentration of poverty, race and ethnicity, housing conditions, and the sustainability of funding, the National Commission on Severely Distressed Public Housing released a report in 1992 (National Commission on Severely Distressed Public Housing, 1992), which led to the creation of the HOPE VI program in 1993. HOPE VI utilized public-private partnerships and a mixed-income model to redevelop the communities in which public housing residents lived. Goetz (2013) argues that a "discourse of disaster" was created to justify significant demolition of all public housing, rather than just the outliers that had been part of the National Commission on Severely Distressed Public Housing's list of approximately eighty-six thousand distressed units.

Initially, the program required a one-for-one replacement of public housing units. However, that requirement was quickly removed as a cost-containing measure. Thus fewer new units were built, and many public housing residents were permanently displaced. Although the commission found that only 6 percent (or approximately 86,000 units) of the public housing stock was "severely distressed," roughly 250,000 units have been demolished through HOPE VI (Cisneros, 2009). More generally, there has been significant debate about the role of HOPE VI for public housing residents. Goetz (2013) found that HOPE VI has been largely beneficial for cities hoping to redevelop key real estate near gentrifying neighborhoods—particularly in cities with high concentrations of blacks/African Americans.

Although there have been significant improvements in maternal mental health and the health outcomes of girls as a result of these efforts, boys' outcomes have been worse than they might have been in their previous neighborhoods. This may be due to the fact that many of these families, particularly in MTO and HOPE VI, remain in the same schools or schools of similarly poor quality compared to the schools they attended before the intervention (Briggs et al., 2010; DeLuca & Dayton, 2009). In other words, the results of the mobility and redevelopment programs have been mixed. Indeed, little evidence has been found of strong or weak ties between different social groups in studies of mobility such as Gautreaux and MTO, HOPE VI, or gentrifying neighborhoods (Briggs et al., 2010; Freeman, 2006; Kleit, 2005; Rosenbaum, 2000; see chapters 14 and 16).

REDEVELOPMENT AND NEIGHBORHOOD CHANGE AFTER 2000

Over the past two decades, as cities have become places where non-Hispanic white, middle-class residents want to live, the cost, production, and preservation of affordable housing have all been critical issues for determining the direction of communities. Federal, state, and local housing policies have largely focused on building and preserving affordable housing, defined in terms of units preserved, rather than on preserving the communities and cultural institutions that predated each neighborhood's redevelopment. This focus implicitly allows future low-income renters to benefit from the new amenities brought by new, affluent residents, such as improved infrastructure, parks, retail, and services. Notably missing from policy and planning discussions in redevelopment is how remaining low-income residents will be affected by changing demographics and community norms. As balances of power and interests in changing communities shift within neighborhood organizations, public discourse, and city government, new and old residents increasingly come into conflict, and often, long-term residents are no longer able to take an active role in their communities (Crenson, 1983; Davis, 1991; Freeman, 2006; see chapter 14).

Considerable research has found evidence of conflict between income groups in changing neighborhoods. In Freeman's work on gentrifying neighborhoods in New York City, he found conflict around neighborhood expectations of behavior as newcomers, accustomed to one set of neighborhood rules, questioned the legitimacy of the existing norms into which they moved, including uses of public space, relationships with police, and quiet hours in the neighborhood (Freeman, 2006). Research on neighborhoods in Baltimore, New Orleans, and London found similar outcomes, with low-income residents experiencing increased tension and conflicting expectations as neighborhoods changed (Crenson, 1983; M. Davidson, 2010; Parekh, 2008). Ethnographic research on homelessness has found strong evidence for the formal and informal enforcement of social norms of the community (Dooling, 2009; Duneier, 1999; Mitchell, 2003).

These tensions are manifested in the misunderstandings and misreadings of social norms between non-Hispanic white residents and residents of color around family structure, street life and activity, employment, and informal economies. Anderson argues that "alienation from mainstream society and its institutions" has created "a kind of institutionalized oppositional culture, a reaction to a history of prejudice and discrimination that now finds its way into schools and other institutions" (1999: 323). While race and ethnicity may not be the only factors impacting relationships between new and long-term residents, the presence of race exacerbates divisions in norms of behavior in gentrifying neighborhoods (Anderson, 1999; Duneier, 1999; Kirschenman, 1991; Park, 1984; Schwartz, 2014; Venkatesh, 2006; Wilson, 1996).

These symbolic boundaries between groups are reinforced by the decades of social and spatial segregation that have resulted in both ignorance of the city and fear of its residents because of the socioeconomic and racial and ethnic isolation of almost a century of segregation (Goldsmith, 2002). As a result, many non-Hispanic whites have grown up with limited interaction with cities and the urban poor. Segregation and white flight that concentrated poverty, race, and ethnicity in the urban core on the one hand and non-Hispanic white and Asian middle- and upper-class households in the suburbs on the other hand changed the expectations and social norms of suburban middle-class residents (Goldsmith, 2002; Kruse, 2007), although this division is softening, according to Anacker (2015).

These conflicting norms may help to explain why, contrary to research that argues that the proximity of low-income residents to higher-income residents would lead to increased access to social networks, there has been little social interaction in mixed-income neighborhoods (Freeman, 2006; Kleit, 2005). Moreover, conflicting definitions of the community as place based, rather than person based, have been expressed through contradictory narratives of the neighborhood past and present by different groups of residents as well as outside actors. This loss of control of space by low-income residents decreases political power for low-income residents and residents of color in their neighborhoods to define the community's history, a situation that has been exacerbated through the redevelopment of urban neighborhoods in the past decade. As neighborhoods change and low-income households are increasingly in the minority in a community, their interests may not be adequately represented (Davis, 1991; Kleit, 2005; Freeman, 2006; Newman & Lake, 2006; see chapter 16).

CONCLUSION

Housing and community are inextricably linked. In the first half of the twentieth century, housing policy was used to address threats to moral and physical contagion (Riis, 1890; see chapter 18), segregate blacks/African Americans out of non-Hispanic white neighborhoods (Hall, 2014; K. Jackson, 1985), and address poverty (Goetz, 2013; Mayer & Jencks, 1989; Vale, 2013; see chapter 16). These efforts were typically instituted from the top down as a rational planning response to a social problem (K. Jackson, 1985). Historic policies such as redlining continue to define the way in which cities and suburbs develop as well as the people who have access to high-opportunity neighborhoods (Massey, 2008; see chapter 14).

In the 1960s and 1970s there were interludes of community-based control and planning as the federal government funded local organizations to build housing, organize tenants, provide job training, and assist small, local businesses (Fainstein & Hirst, 1995; Fisher, 1984). These efforts by organizations created an infrastructure for community empowerment that focused on existing neighborhood residents' needs and strengths. However, the direct funding of community-based organizations ended with the creation of CDBG and the increasing devolution of responsibility from the federal government to state and local agencies (Twelvetrees, 1989; see chapter 14).

More recently, demand for dense, walkable neighborhoods near the urban core by young, educated, and affluent new residents has rebounded (Leinberger & Alfonzo, 2012). Cities are undertaking large-scale redevelopment efforts aimed at attracting a larger tax base and additional investments (Goetz, 2013). Housing and redevelopment policy is once again framed by planners and policy makers as a "bricks and mortar" intervention, with vibrant future communities thought to be an organic output of that intervention, often without addressing the existing needs of the community (Hyra, 2008). As a result of redevelopment in many cities, the built environment, social life, and culture of formerly disinvested communities have changed to reflect the needs and demands of the more affluent population of young, educated, and often non-Hispanic white residents (Freeman, 2006; Hyra, 2008; see chapters 1, 2, and 7, and 18).

Housing has been used to protect communities from outsiders, provide empowerment for communities, and improve opportunities for interaction among residents. It has also been used to prevent low-income households and communities of color from accessing opportunities such as schools, careers, and safe neighborhoods (Massey, 2008; see chapter 16). Housing has more recently been used to offer residents in high-poverty neighborhoods the opportunity to move to new neighborhoods (Cisneros, 2009; Rosenbaum, 2000). However, the benefits of those moves have been questioned by researchers, who find that movers are not attending better schools (Briggs et al., 2010) or benefiting from new, strong ties that might offer them the chance for upward socioeconomic mobility (Kleit, 2005). Regardless of how they have been used, housing and community have been inextricably linked in policy and planning in the past century of U.S. policy (see chapter 14).

REFERENCES

Anacker, K. B. (2015). Introduction. In K. B. Anacker (Ed.), *The new American suburb: Poverty, race and the economic crisis* (pp. 1–11). Farnham, UK: Ashgate.

Anderson, E. (1999). *Codes of the street*. New York: Norton.

Basolo, V. (1999). Passing the housing policy baton in the U.S.: Will cities take the lead? *Housing Studies, 14*(4), 433–452.

Bourdieu, P. (1986). The forms of capital. In J. Richardson (Ed.), *Handbook of theory and research for the sociology of education* (pp. 241–258). New York: Greenwood Press.

Briggs, X., Popkin, S., & Goering, J. (2010). *Moving to opportunity: The story of an American experiment to fight ghetto poverty*. Oxford: Oxford University Press.

Brooks, M. P. (2002). *Planning theory for practitioners*. Chicago: Planners Press.

Brown, P., & Richman, H. A. (2000). Neighborhood effects and state and local policy. In G. Duncan, L. Aber, & J. Brooks-Gunn (Eds.), *Neighborhood poverty: Vol. 2. Policy implications in studying neighborhoods* (pp. 164–181). Thousand Oaks, Calif.: Sage.

Castells, M. (1979). *The urban question: A Marxist approach*. Cambridge, Mass.: MIT Press.

Castells, M. (1985). *The city and the grassroots: A cross-cultural theory of urban social movements*. Berkeley: University of California Press.

Checkoway, B. (1994). Paul Davidoff and advocacy planning in retrospect. *Journal of the American Planning Association, 60*(2), 139–143.

Cisneros, H. G. (2009). A new moment for people and cities. In H. G. Cisneros and

Laura Engdahl (Eds.), *From despair to HOPE: HOPE VI and the new promise of public housing in America's cities* (pp. 3–14). Washington, D.C.: Brookings Institution Press.

Crenson, M. (1983). *Neighborhood politics*. Cambridge, Mass.: Harvard University Press.

Cresswell, T. (1996). *In place/out of place: Geography, ideology, and transgression*. Minneapolis: University of Minnesota Press.

Crossney, K. B. (2005). The legacy of the Home Owners' Loan Corporation. *Housing Policy Debate, 16*(3/4), 547–574.

Davidoff, P. (1965). Advocacy and pluralism in planning. *Journal of the American Institute of Planning, 31*(4), 331–338.

Davidson, M. (2010). Love thy neighbor? Social mixing in London's gentrification frontiers. *Environment and Planning, 42*, 524–544.

Davidson, N. M. (2009). Reconciling people and place in housing and community development policy. *Georgetown Journal on Poverty Law & Policy, 26*(1), 1–10.

Davis, J. E. (1991). *Contested ground: Collective action and the urban neighborhood*. Ithaca, N.Y.: Cornell University Press.

Dawkins, C. J. (2006). Are social networks the ties that bind families to neighborhoods? *Housing Studies, 21*(6), 867–881.

Day, K. (2003). New urbanism and the challenges of designing for diversity. *Journal of Planning Education and Research, 23*, 83–95.

DeLuca, S., & Dayton, E. (2009). Switching social contexts: The effects of housing mobility and school choice programs on youth outcomes. *Annual Review of Sociology, 35*, 457–491.

Dooling, S. (2009). Ecological gentrification: A research agenda exploring justice in the city. *International Journal of Urban and Regional Affairs, 33*(3), 621–639.

Duneier, M. (1999). *Sidewalk*. New York: Farrar, Strauss, and Giroux.

Erikson, D. (2009). *The housing policy revolution: Networks and neighborhoods*. Washington, D.C.: Urban Institute Press.

Fainstein, S. (1995). Urban social movements. In D. Judge, G. Stoker, & H. Wolman (Eds.), *Theories of urban politics* (pp. 181–204). Thousand Oaks, Calif.: Sage.

Fainstein, S. (2010). *The just city*. Ithaca, N.Y.: Cornell University Press.

Fainstein, S., & Hirst, C. (1995). Urban social movements. In D. Judge, G. Stoker, & H. Wolman (Eds.), *Theories of urban politics* (pp. 181–204). Thousand Oaks, Calif.: Sage.

Fisher, R. (1984). *Let the people decide: Neighborhood organizing in America*. New York: Twayne.

Freeman, L. (2006). *There goes the hood: Views of gentrification from the ground up*. Philadelphia: Temple University Press.

Friedman, J. (1987). *Planning in the public domain: From knowledge to action*. Princeton, N.J.: Princeton University Press.

Gittel, R., & Vidal, A. (1998). *Community organizing: Building social capital as a development strategy*. Thousand Oaks, Calif.: Sage.

Goetz, E. G. (2002). Forced relocation vs. voluntary mobility: The effects of dispersal programs on households. *Housing Studies, 17*(1), 107–123.

Goetz, E. G. (2013). *New Deal in ruins: Race, economic justice, and public housing policy*. Ithaca, N.Y.: Cornell University Press.

Goldsmith, W. W. (2002). From the metropolis to globalizations: The dialectics of race and urban form. In S. F. Fainstein & S. Campbell (Eds.), *Readings in urban theory* (pp. 129–149). Malden, Mass.: Blackwell.

Granovetter, M. (1983). The strength of weak ties: A network theory revisited. *Sociological Theory, 1*, 201–233.

Hall, P. (2014). *Cities of tomorrow*. Malden, Mass.: Blackwell.

Harvey, D. (1996). *Justice, nature, and the geography of difference*. Malden, Mass.: Blackwell.

Harvey, D. (2008). *Social justice and the city*. Athens: University of Georgia Press.

Hayes, R. A. (1995). *The federal government and urban housing: Ideology and change in public policy*. Albany: State University of New York Press.

Hyra, D. S. (2008). *The new urban renewal: The economic transformation of Harlem and Bronzeville*. Chicago: University of Chicago Press.

Jackson, K. T. (1985). *Crabgrass frontier: The suburbanization of the United States*. New York: Oxford University Press.

Jackson, M. (2008). *Model city blues: Urban space and organized resistance in New Haven.* Philadelphia: Temple University Press.

Julian, E. K., & McCain, D. L. (2009). Housing mobility: A civil right. In C. Hartman & G. D. Squires (Eds.), *The integration debate: Competing futures for American cities* (pp. 85–98). New York: Routledge.

Kelling, G. L., & Wilson, J. Q. (1982). Broken windows: The police and neighborhood safety. *Atlantic Magazine, 249*(3), 29–38.

Kelly, R. M. (1976). *Community participation in directing economic development.* Cambridge, Mass.: CCED.

Kirschenman, J. A. (1991). "We'd love to hire them, but . . .": The meaning of race for employers. In C. A. Jencks (Ed.), *The urban underclass* (pp. 203–232). Washington, D.C.: Brookings Institution.

Kleit, R. (2005). HOPE VI new communities: Neighborhood relationships in mixed-income housing. *Environment and Planning, 37*, 1413–1441.

Kleit, R. G. (2010). Draining ties: Tie quality versus content in low-income women's social networks when displaced by redevelopment. *Journal of Social and Personal Relationships, 27*(4), 573–588.

Kruse, K. M. (2007). *White flight: Atlanta and the making of modern conservatism.* Princeton, N.J.: Princeton University Press.

Leinberger, C. B., & Alfonzo, M. (2012, May 25). *Walk this way: The economic promise of walkable places in metropolitan Washington, D.C.* Washington, D.C.: Brookings Institution. Retrieved from http://www.brookings.edu/research/papers/2012/05/25-walkable-places-leinberger.

Leventhal, T., Brooks-Gunn, J., & Kamerman, S. B. (2000). Communities as place, face, and space: Provision of services to poor urban children and their families. In G. Duncan, J. Brooks-Gunn, & L. Aber (Eds.), *Neighborhood poverty: Contexts and consequences for children* (pp. 182–305). Thousand Oaks, Calif.: Sage.

Lin, N. (1999). Building a network theory of social capital. *Connections, 22*(1), 28–51.

Manzo, L. C., Kleit, R. G., & Couch, A. D. (2008). "Moving three times is like having your house on fire once": The experience of place and impending displacement among public housing residents. *Urban Studies, 45*(9), 1855–1878.

Massey, D. (2008). Origins of economic disparities. In J. H. Carr & N. K. Kutty (Eds.), *Segregation: The rising costs for America* (pp. 39–80). New York: Routledge.

Massey, D., & Denton, N. A. (1998). *American apartheid: Segregation and the making of the underclass.* Cambridge, Mass.: Harvard University Press.

Mayer, S., & Jencks, C. (1989). Growing up in poor neighborhoods: How much does it matter? *Science, 234* (4897), 1441–1445.

Mitchell, D. (2003). *The right to the city: Social justice and the fight for public space.* New York: Guilford Press.

National Commission on Severely Distressed Public Housing. (1992). *Final report of the National Commission on Severely Distressed Public Housing.* Washington, D.C.: National Commission on Severely Distressed Public Housing.

Newman, K., & Lake, R. (2006). Democracy, bureaucracy and difference in community development politics since 1968. *Progress in Human Geography, 30*(1), 44–61.

Parekh, T. (2008). *Inhabiting Tremé: Gentrification, memory and racialized space in a New Orleans neighborhood.* Austin: University of Texas Press.

Park, R. A. (1984). *The city: Suggestions for the investigation in the urban environment.* Chicago: University of Chicago Press. (Original work published 1925).

Peterman, W. (2000). *Neighborhood planning and community-based development: The potential and limits of grassroots action.* Thousand Oaks, Calif.: Sage.

Peterson, P. (1991). Urban underclass and the poverty paradox. In C. Jencks & P. E. Peterson (Eds.), *The urban underclass* (pp. 3–27). Washington, D.C.: Brookings Institution Press.

Piven, F. F. (1977). *Poor people's movements: Why they succeed, how they fail.* New York: Vintage Books.

Poverty and Race Research Action Council. (2013). *Affirmatively furthering fair housing at HUD: A first term report card.* Washington, D.C.: Poverty and Race Research Action Council.

Putnam, R. (1993). The prosperous community: Social capital and community life. *American Prospect, 13*, 35–42.

Riis, J. (1890). *How the other half lives: Studies among the tenements of New York*. Boston: St Martin's Press.

Rosenbaum, L. S. (2000). *Crossing the class and color lines: From public housing to white suburbia*. Chicago: University of Chicago Press.

Rubin, H. J. (2000). *Renewing hope within neighborhoods of despair: The community-based development model*. Albany: State University of New York Press.

Sampson, R. J., & Morenoff, J. D. (2000). Ecological perspectives on the neighborhood context of urban poverty. In J. Brooks-Gunn, G. Duncan, & L. Aber (Eds.), *Neighborhood poverty: Contexts and consequences for children* (pp. 1–22). Thousand Oaks, Calif.: Sage.

Sampson, R. J., & Raudenbush, S. W. (1999). Systematic social observation of public spaces: A new look at disorder in urban neighborhoods. *American Journal of Sociology, 105*, 603–651.

Schwartz, A. F. (2014). *Housing policy in the United States*. New York: Routledge.

Slessarev, H. (1988). Racial tensions and institutional support: Social programs during a period of retrenchment. In M. Weir, A. S. Orloff, & T. Skocpol (Eds.), *The politics of social policy in the United States* (pp. 357–379). Princeton, N.J.: Princeton University Press.

Stack, C. (1974). *All our kin: Strategies for survival in a black community*. New York: Basic Books.

Stoecker, R. (2003). Understanding the development-organizing dialectic. *Journal of Urban Affairs, 25*(4), 493–513.

Stone, C. (1989). *Regime politics governing Atlanta, 1946–1988*. Lawrence: University Press of Kansas.

Sugrue, T. (2005). *The origins of the urban crisis: Race and inequality in postwar Detroit*. Princeton, N.J.: Princeton University Press.

Twelvetrees, A. (1989). *Organizing for neighborhood development*. Brookfield, Vt.: Avebury.

Vale, L. (2000). *From the Puritans to the projects: Public housing and public neighbors*. Cambridge, Mass.: Harvard University Press.

Vale, L. (2013). *Purging the poorest: Public housing and the design politics of twice-cleared communities*. Chicago: University of Chicago Press.

Venkatesh, S. A. (2006). *Off the books: The underground economy of the urban poor*. Cambridge, Mass.: Harvard University Press.

Village of Euclid v. Ambler Realty Co., 272 U.S. 365 (1926).

Weininger, E. B. (2005). Foundations of Pierre Bourdieu's class analysis. In E. O. Wright, *Approaches to class analysis* (pp. 82–118). Cambridge: Cambridge University Press.

Wilson, W. J. (1996). *When work disappears: The world of the new urban poor*. New York: Vintage.

Wilson, W. J. (2009). *More than just race: Being black and poor in the inner city*. New York: Norton.

Chapter 13   Neighborhood Amenities

ELIZABETH MUELLER

Where we live determines the quality of public and private services available to us, our individual or family economic stability, our ability to build wealth, and our exposure to environmental conditions that can affect our health (powell, 2002; see chapters 2, 7, 8, 9, 10, 12, 14, and 18). These positive or negative features, called amenities and disamenities, have been studied in many disciplines and fields (Newburger, Birch, & Wachter, 2011). They may be real or perceived (Marans, 1979). While the concept of amenities originated in the field of economics and was focused on how neighborhood characteristics shape property values (Kain & Quigley, 1970; Krumm, 1980), thinking about how neighborhood context benefits residents has evolved over time to incorporate social and physical benefits in addition to financial ones (Chaskin, 1997; see chapters 7, 8, and 12). The meaning and causal explanations linked to the associations among various features of residential neighborhoods and a variety of measures of the quality of life have been used to justify a wide range of public policies, many aimed at correcting inequalities (see chapters 12, 14, and 16). This chapter traces the evolution of thinking about the benefits to residence in a particular place.

NEIGHBORHOOD CONTEXT AND HOME VALUES: THE STARTING POINT

Kain and Quigley (1970) built on earlier hedonic models of home prices and incorporated the characteristics of both homes and the neighborhood where they were located into their model of home prices in St. Louis (Kain & Quigley, 1970; Rosen, 1974). Their finding that factors beyond the home itself had about as much effect on prices as features of the home was considered pathbreaking. The dimensions of neighborhood context that they introduced (i.e., describing the social and natural environment and the location within the regional market) foreshadowed many of the key questions that continue to animate current housing policy and urban planning discussions: What are the demographic and socioeconomic characteristics of the neighborhood's residents? What is the quality of public spaces? Do surrounding uses of property or conditions expose residents to environmental hazards? What is the quality of the schools? What is the level of crime? How close are potential workplaces? Within the bundle of "residential services" that Kain and Quigley found collectively influential, they also found one feature—school quality—to be significantly and positively linked to home prices.

Currently there is great interest in defining and understanding the way that neighborhood amenities relate to resident well-being across a range of fields (see chapter 2). These features have always been of interest to those who make their living developing, selling, or buying real estate and to urban economists (see chapters 7 and 8). Thinking about the role of place, however, has now expanded to include the ways it shapes a broader set of life chances and experiences, and the range of interested disciplines and fields has broadened. Researchers in various social science disciplines and fields are concerned with understanding the mechanisms that foster and maintain patterns of inequality (see chapter 16). Scholars and professionals in fields of practice that shape neighborhood physical or social environments, including urban planners, public health professionals, and social workers, are interested in understanding the role of various spatial characteristics in reproducing patterns of socioeconomic inequality (see chapters 14 and 18). Armed with this information, practitioners might avoid deepening or reproducing such patterns through public actions and identify ways to improve current and future outcomes (see chapter 12). Policy makers concerned with urban inequality and the revitalization of poor communities are interested in using policy levers to increase place-based access to opportunity (see chapters 12, 14, and 16). Finally, community residents are interested in pushing for improvement in amenities that will improve the quality of their lives and for fairness in provision of services across city neighborhoods (see chapter 12).

THE UNEVEN LANDSCAPE OF NEIGHBORHOOD AMENITIES

Neighborhoods vary in terms of the number and quality of available amenities (or disamenities) that together help determine their desirability as places to live. For some researchers, this variation is seen as a benefit, allowing many residents to select communities that offer the mix of services and amenities that they desire and that meet their budgets (see chapters 2 and 7). This idea was expressed formally by economist Charles Tiebout in his 1956 article "A Pure Theory of Local Expenditures," where he argued that individuals or households will move from one jurisdiction to another ("voting with their feet") in order to meet their preferences for government services and for tax rates (Tiebout, 1956). Similarly, economist William Fischel argues that homeowners, or "homevoters," choose their residence with local services in mind, since these services enhance or detract from the value of their homes (Fischel, 2001). Both models assume that information on service quality and tax levels are readily available and that households are easily able to move between jurisdictions.

However, considerable evidence challenges the assumption of a real estate marketplace in which all households are free to choose any neighborhood. Instead, the idea that who lives in an area is related to the quality of local services and other amenities was established early in urban history. Kain and Quigley's study (1970) in St. Louis found that the same home value was associated with a lower level of amenities in neighborhoods of color, introducing the possibility that home buyers of color pay higher prices for the same home or neighborhood amenities than their white counterparts. More recent studies continue to document the premium paid by black/African American home buyers (Myers, 2004). Others have found evidence that the availability of public goods and services is related to the absence of low-income households (Crane & Manville, 2008). Economic homogeneity is linked to willingness to pay for neighborhood goods and services (Fischel, 2001). Together these findings suggest connections between the level of affluence and both racial and ethnic exclusion and neighborhood amenities, particularly services supported by residents' taxes.

The historical factors producing separate real estate markets for blacks/African Americans in U.S. cities in the twentieth century are well documented and include private land use and development restrictions, zoning and planning practices, federal mortgage-lending policies (discussed below), and public housing and urban renewal programs (Gotham, 2000; Hirsch, 1983; Jackson, 1985; Massey & Denton, 1993). Restrictions attached to private property deeds established patterns in many cities as early as the late nineteenth century and played an important role in blocking access to high-amenity urban and suburban neighborhoods for low-income residents, particularly blacks/African Americans (Fogelson, 2005). Private restrictive covenants were intended to both exclude undesirable neighbors (by explicitly forbidding the sale of property to nonwhites) and prevent owners from doing anything to their properties thought to threaten community property values. Such restrictions established racially and ethnically divided patterns still discernible in many cities (Gotham, 2000; Silver, 1997; Tretter, 2012). These restrictions were viewed as so critical to property values that they were prominently featured in marketing for new developments (Fogelson, 2005). While racially restrictive covenants were struck down by the Supreme Court in 1948 (*Shelley v. Kraemer*, 1948), restrictions on allowable uses and on lot size and property characteristics ensured that property values in wealthy (i.e., non-Hispanic white) areas of cities would remain high, while the lack of such restrictions undermined home values in low-income, nonwhite neighborhoods (Tretter, 2012). Many cities later codified these patterns through land use and zoning regulations in early comprehensive plans. Since the 1920s, zoning and land use controls have replaced property covenants in most cities as the vehicle for protection of property values and—potentially—for the exclusion of "undesirable" people or forms of development. In particular, residential land use controls that limit density have produced what Pendall has labeled "the chain of exclusion," whereby the resulting limited housing choices effectively exclude low-income households, often of color, from certain jurisdictions (Pendall, 2000). Such practices remain quite common: large lot zoning, Not In My Back Yard (NIMBY) attitudes, and economies of scale encourage development of homogeneous neighborhoods of single-family detached residences, while land available for multifamily affordable or subsidized housing is limited or isolated (Pendall, Puentes, & Martin, 2006; Schill, 2004; see chapters 8, 9, and 10).

Federal housing policies further strengthened these patterns. Federal mortgage insurance, introduced during the Great Depression but most influential in the post–World War II era, reinforced the patterns established by private restrictions and codified in early city plans through the use of underwriting criteria that rated the riskiness of mortgage lending and favored greenfield development, particularly in areas that were uniformly single-family construction and where nonwhites were absent (Jackson, 1985; Massey & Denton, 1993). Satter's detailed account of the exploitation of black/African American home buyers through the contract-sales system in Chicago during this period makes clear how the resulting lack of access to mortgage loans led buyers to purchase poor-quality homes in neighborhoods with inadequate and poor-quality public services at inflated prices (Satter, 2009). Sugrue (1996) describes the struggle over economic restructuring, racial strife, and open housing in Detroit and the shifting color lines between neighborhoods. Black/African American suburbanization also segregated residents, who then faced higher-than-average property taxes, financially strapped public schools, and lower and more slowly increasing property values than residents of non-Hispanic white suburbs (Wiese, 2004). The long-term consequences of this exclusion, in terms of home values and the accumulation of wealth by black/African American homeowners, has been profound: nearly two thirds of black/African American households had no net financial assets in 1988, twenty years after the passage of the Fair Housing Act had outlawed housing discrimination (Oliver & Shapiro, 1995).

Federal affordable housing programs, beginning with the creation of local housing authorities and the siting of the first public housing developments, favored locating affordable housing in low-income neighborhoods. This practice reflected both a desire to replace dilapidated housing in such neighborhoods and local social norms regarding race. However, the combined effects of urban renewal and public housing policy exacerbated rather than alleviated central city crowding in neighborhoods of color as the scale of slum clearance overshadowed construction of public housing for those displaced (Hirsch, 1983; Jackson, 1985; Massey & Denton, 1993; see chapters 7, 8, 9, 10, 11, and 14).

By the mid-twentieth century a fairly durable pattern of income and racial segregation had been established in most cities. By the early 1970s, overt forms of racial and ethnic discrimination in lending and real estate practices were no longer legal. Since that time, justifications for racial and ethnic exclusion have shifted from open racial and ethnic prejudice, to arguments based on threats to property values (Freund, 2007), to more nuanced discriminatory practices (Turner, 2005; Turner et al., 2013; Yinger, 2000). However, planning practices linked to both income and racial and ethnic exclusion have continued (Pendall, 2000; Pendall et al., 2006; Rothwell & Massey, 2009; Talen, 2005). Also, evidence suggests that economic segregation has increased over the past forty years (Abramson, Tobin, & VanderGoot, 1995; Fischer, 2003; Massey, 2001; Massey & Eggers, 1990). Thus, rather than reflecting a broader set of choices, evidence suggests that the variation in amenities offered across neighborhoods should instead be seen as indicative of a lack of choice for households that are low income or nonwhite (see chapters 9, 10, and 16).

INCOME AND RACIAL SEGREGATION AND THE EFFECTS OF LIVING IN A POOR NEIGHBORHOOD

The connection between home values and neighborhood amenities, and the increase in measures of economic segregation, suggests a widening gap between the types of places where low- and high-income residents live. In addition, evidence suggests a strong connection between race/ethnicity and residence in a high-poverty neighborhood (Bischoff & Reardon, 2013). Seventy-eight percent of high-poverty census tracts (i.e., those where at least 40 percent of residents are poor) are predominantly nonwhite (U.S. Department of Housing and Urban Development, 2014: 9; see chapters 10 and 16). At the other end of the spectrum, high-income households are increasingly likely to live in majority upper-income neighborhoods: by 2010, 18 percent of households with incomes above $104,000 lived in majority upper-income census tracts—twice the rate compared to 1980 (Fry & Taylor, 2012). Such neighborhoods are also racially homogeneous: in 2010, 85 percent of residents of census tracts with median incomes above $145,073 were white (Solari, 2012). Income segregation is increasing most rapidly in fast-growing regions where growth is fed by in-migration (Fry & Taylor, 2012). This increase suggests that the patterns of new development in these areas are highly segmented, where new neighborhoods are accessible (and perhaps marketed) to a fairly homogeneous set of buyers or renters (see chapters 2, 7, and 17).

Since the 1980s, scholars have explored the consequences for residents of living in a poor neighborhood. Initially this was framed primarily in terms of the effects on poor people—particularly children—of having poor neighbors. What were the "neighborhood effects," scholars asked, of living in a neighborhood of concentrated poverty (Ellen & Turner, 1997)? How do the effects of living in a particular neighborhood relate to individual family circumstances? Does neighborhood context help create a separate culture, making it more difficult for residents to escape poverty (Jencks & Peterson, 1991; see chapters 9, 10, and 11)?

A great deal of scholarly evidence has linked neighborhood conditions, particularly concentrated poverty, to poor quality of life for residents. Such neighborhood conditions, in combination with individual or family characteristics, present a richer explanation of the poor performance of children in schools or of adults in the labor market (Sampson, Sharkey, & Raudenbush 2007; Trent, 1997; Wilson, 1996) than earlier approaches. The evidence was strongest in two areas thought to be important determinants of health: education and future socioeconomic mobility. Crime and delinquency, education outcomes, psychological distress, and health problems, among other things, were all exacerbated by living in a neighborhood with a high poverty rate (Ellen & Turner, 2003; see chapter 12). Tipping points were identified by scholars studying these patterns. The relationships between poverty and crime and leaving school and the length of time in poverty were strongest in neighborhoods with poverty rates above 20 percent and rose as poverty increased until reaching a threshold at around 40 percent (Galster, 2012). During the 1990s home values were found to decline rapidly in neighborhoods with poverty rates above 10 percent in the nation's largest metropolitan areas (Galster, Cutsinger, & Malega, 2008; see chapter 7).

However, the mechanisms through which the factors were linked, and thus the appropriate solutions, were more difficult to determine. Two competing approaches were suggested, one emphasizing the ways that interactions with more affluent neighbors might benefit low-income residents and the other focusing on the ways that lack of access to key resources, like high-quality schools, undermined low-income residents. Of course, the two are related—attendance at a high-performing school may also mean interacting with children from more affluent, highly educated households, for example. The dominant hypothesis initially centered on the ways that the isolation of the residents of poor neighborhoods cut them off from social networks important to their quality of life and chances for upward mobility. In a sense, certain types of neighbors were seen as neighborhood "amenities." William Julius Wilson emphasizes the way that the "spatial mismatch" created by the shift toward suburban employment centers away from central city neighborhoods of color magnified these challenges (Wilson, 1996). In particular, the movement of middle-class blacks/African Americans out of central city neighborhoods, closer to job growth in the suburbs, was one factor in the creation of concentrated-poverty neighborhoods whose residents, disproportionately of color, were isolated from the social networks that might help them find jobs (Wilson, 1996, 2012; see chapters 12 and 16).

An additional hypothesized consequence of the loss of middle-class neighbors was a decline in residents' social capital. Two forms of social capital were identified by scholars, based on the strength of ties among members of networks and the purposes of networks. Networks of strong ties were more common among individuals of similar social status and, for poor people, were most useful for meeting daily needs—what Briggs (1998) labels "bonding capital" (Stack, 1974). Lang and Hornburg describe this same idea as "the stock of social trust, norms, and networks that people can draw upon in order to solve common problems" (Lang & Hornburg, 1998: 4). Ties between people of different status, or between residents of poor communities and outsiders, were labeled "weak ties" (Granovetter, 1973) or "bridging capital" (Briggs, 1998) and were thought to be especially important in countering the social and economic isolation of the poor. Such ties might bring resources and information important for obtaining a job or access to other forms of information or resources important for community improvement and individual mobility. However, social capital is strongly linked to power, with marginalized communities possessing both little power and few socially organized assets to build upon (DeFilippis, 2001). For critics, building fruitful relationships is about both building relationships and having the power to leverage them (Saegert, 2012; see chapter 12).

Sharkey (2009, 2012) emphasizes how neighborhood effects are compounded when children who grow up in poor neighborhoods then raise their own children in such circumstances. Comparing educational outcomes for children whose own parents grew up in either poor or middle-class neighborhoods, he finds that the child of a parent raised in a poor neighborhood does markedly poorer on standardized tests. He concludes that "the parent's environment during childhood may be more important than the child's own environment" (Sharkey, 2012: 130–131). His analysis of neighborhood mobility from one generation to the next reveals that blacks/African Americans are much more likely to remain in poor neighborhoods across generations: 67 percent of black/African American families from poor neighborhoods a generation ago remain in such areas, compared to only 40 percent of similar non-Hispanic white families. Indeed, 48 percent of black/African American families have lived in poor neighborhoods for at least two generations, compared to only 7 percent of non-Hispanic white families (Sharkey, 2012: 39). Thus, leaving poor places appears to be much more difficult for blacks/African Americans. Multigenerational exposure to neighborhood poverty affects school performance and also family income, labor force participation, occupational status, and wealth (Sharkey, 2009; see chapters 12 and 16).

Moving from a focus on neighbors to the quality of various neighborhood assets has brought its own challenges. As noted above, school quality was highlighted in Kain and Quigley's study (1970) and has consistently been at the center of discussions of neighborhood amenities. A legion of researchers has attempted to disentangle the interactions between neighborhood and individual and school characteristics that are most strongly linked to disadvantage. Evidence of the role neighborhoods play in educational attainment is contradictory in terms of the specific neighborhood characteristics that matter most and which adolescents may be most vulnerable to neighborhood effects (Card & Krueger, 1992; Ellen & Turner, 1997; Ginther, Haveman & Wolfe, 2000; Harding, 2003: Wodtke, Harding, & Elwert, 2011). It has proven challenging to separate the effects of neighborhoods from those of families and parenting, although research is increasingly connecting the two (Sampson et al., 2007; Schellenberg, 1998; Trent, 1997). Sharkey's (2012) longitudinal research suggests that the influence of neighborhood and family characteristics are intertwined over time. Recent studies link child and maternal health to achievement gaps in education and focus attention on the connections between neighborhood context and health (Currie, 2005). On the whole, evidence is strong on the costs of segregating poor people into highly poor neighborhoods. The challenge has become defining the characteristics of places—in terms of both tangible physical characteristics and less tangible social ones—that will reverse the consequences of this segregation for the poor (see chapter 12).

RECASTING OPPORTUNITIES AS NEIGHBORHOOD AMENITIES

If the mechanisms explaining the problems associated with living in a poor neighborhood have been difficult to tease out, one clear conclusion has nevertheless emerged: leaving a poor neighborhood should remove the source of the negative "neighborhood effects" that poor residents experience. As the result of a series of legal battles concerning the racial and ethnic segregation of public housing, a framework began to emerge for judging what type of neighborhoods residents of concentrated poverty neighborhoods should move to—in essence, a way of thinking about which neighborhood amenities matter most. In a 1976 suit against the Chicago Housing Authority, in response to claims that the housing authority had segregated its units in poor neighborhoods of color, the court ruled that local public housing authorities could not locate subsidized housing only in nonwhite areas (*Gautreaux v. Chicago Housing Authority*, 1974; Tein, 1992). Instead, housing authorities were directed to provide additional housing in predominantly nonwhite areas (Rubinowitz, 1992). The program adopted by the Chicago Housing Authority was regional in scale and enabled the use of housing vouchers (then called Section 8 certificates) throughout a six-county area.

The rise in emphasis on the use of housing vouchers in federal housing policy coincided with Wilson's work on the connection between racial segregation and isolation from social and economic networks important to mobility (Wilson, 1996). Special housing mobility programs were established, structured by legal settlements emanating from legal challenges to segregated public housing practices. The most prominent program was based on the Gautreaux lawsuit and the subsequent court-mandated remedy in Chicago. This program required participants to use their vouchers to move to neighborhoods with poverty rates below 10 percent and where fewer than 30 percent of residents were black/African American. Participants were provided with counseling and other assistance to enable them to locate and move to homes in qualifying suburban neighborhoods (Goetz, 2003). Early studies of Gautreaux voucher holders found dramatic improvements for children: children moving to predominantly non-Hispanic white suburbs were significantly less likely to drop out of school, more often in college-track courses, and more likely to enroll in four-year colleges (Rosenbaum, 1995). However, confidence in these findings was undercut by methodological problems. Studies were based on small, nonrandom samples of program participants and did not include information on residents who had left the suburbs, since they could not be located. Finally, factors used to screen residents, and the fact that participation in the program required considerable persistence, biased comparisons of self-selected participants and nonparticipants (Popkin, Buron, Levy, & Cunningham, 2000).

In 1992 the focus of mobility programs shifted from racial and ethnic to economic inclusion. The Moving to Opportunity Program (MTO) was a demonstration program targeted at families living in high-poverty neighborhoods (defined as at least 40 percent of the area population in poverty). The program tested the impact of moving these families to areas with poverty rates below 10 percent. Families moving to low-poverty areas were found to be more satisfied with their neighborhood and less afraid of crime (Goering et al., 1999). Results on other factors that were expected based on assumptions regarding the benefits of interacting with nonpoor neighbors, such as school performance or obtaining a job, were mixed. Program participation was significantly but modestly linked with the characteristics of schools attended and did result in a large drop in the share of female youth working and out of school, but it yielded no significant effects on measures of educational performance (Goering & Feins, 2003; Orr et al., 2003).

Despite the mixed results of the MTO experiment, the idea of neighborhood-based access to opportunity began to take hold. Similar arguments were made regarding the benefits of redeveloping public housing to include nonpoor households. However, gaining access to opportunity-rich neighborhoods—or including housing for low-income residents alongside market-rate housing—requires pushing against many factors that have helped produce homogeneous middle-class neighborhoods in the first place. Middle-class or affluent neighborhoods are often designed to exclude multifamily housing, thus preventing access by low-income renters (McClure, 2010). Similarly, such neighborhoods, particularly in the suburbs, are often auto oriented and lack adequate public transportation services for low-income households that cannot afford to commute by car (Levine, 2006).

To illustrate the overlapping problems of poor neighborhoods, and to contrast them with the characteristics of more affluent neighborhoods, fair housing advocates developed a set of metrics to assess the sorts of opportunities that living in different types of neighborhoods can offer. Data on related issues are collected at the census-tract level and grouped together into indices that are scored relative to the region so that neighborhoods in a region can be compared to each other. Finally, a composite overall index of opportunity is created from these topical indices and used to map the landscape of opportunity in the community (Reece, Norris, Olinger, Holley, & Martin, n.d.). Opportunity maps shade neighborhoods according to their score on indices measuring "indicators of community health and of individual and family financial, educational, health, and vocational well-being" (Reece et al., n.d.: 4). One of the components of the overall index—the Neighborhood Quality Index—incorporates assumptions about the negative impact of living among concentrations of renters or poor people (powell, Reece, & Gambhir, 2007: 34).

Opportunity maps and similar metrics assessing neighborhood conditions are increasingly referenced in housing policy discussions. Several states have adopted rules for allocation of federal tax credits for construction of affordable housing that are based on the concept of access to high-opportunity areas (Bookbinder et al., 2008). Similarly, some cities are using opportunity maps to guide the selection of appropriate sites for development of affordable housing (City of Austin, Texas, 2014). Finally, opportunity mapping has been employed by communities planning for transit-oriented sustainable development (Kirwan Institute & Puget Sound Regional Council, 2012; see chapters 9, 10, 12, and 16).

Yet again, discerning how proximity relates to access, and what other forces come into play, is difficult. When is spatial proximity essential or a determinant of access and when is it necessary but insufficient condition for such access? For example, living near a clinic may not indicate access to the clinic, which may be based on insurance coverage or program rules regarding eligibility for service. Critics raise concerns that scoring neighborhoods using such metrics implies that outcomes for families will correlate with incremental improvements in neighborhood conditions (Ludwig et al., 2008). Similarly, others raise concerns that the rhetoric of "escaping to opportunity" portrays low-income neighborhoods in an overly simplistic, negative way (Axel-Lute, 2014). Finally, the scoring process relies heavily on metrics related to the poverty of residents, consistent with arguments about the ills associated with concentrated poverty. As a result, the policy solutions advocated, in addition to enabling low-income people to move to more affluent areas, may have the perverse effect of incentivizing efforts to keep low-income people out of an area or to steer investment out of high-poverty areas (Kriesberg, 2011; see chapter 12).

LINKING AMENITIES TO A BROADER DEFINITION OF WELL-BEING

In recent years, conversations about neighborhood character have returned to a more holistic view of the relationship between physical and social characteristics of neighborhoods and quality of life, emphasizing a wide range of neighborhood amenities. This approach has renewed emphasis on the physical character of neighborhoods and has broadened this emphasis to include the health impacts of neighborhood form and access to public and private goods and services that contribute to health. The focus is on identifying the components of "healthy neighborhoods."

The current discussion resonates with visions of neighborhoods integrating physical and social features to promote health at the beginning of the twentieth century. The settlement house movement emphasized the need for playgrounds for children and for public spaces and services in crowded immigrant neighborhoods of industrial cities (Spain, 2001). Perry's early twentieth-century conception of the ideal "neighborhood unit" emphasized the physical design of the neighborhood in order to create a community-centric lifestyle,

FIGURE 13.1
Neighborhood-Unit Principles
Source: Perry, 1929.

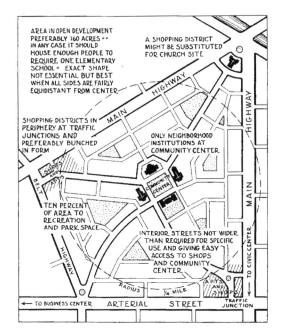

protected from the smoke and ugliness of the industrial city (Perry, 1929; see figure 13.1). Neighborhoods were to be designed to protect residential areas, with community life focused on schools and playgrounds and traffic and shopping areas kept on the periphery. Such designs were promoted as a way of protecting the safety and welfare of residents. Neighborhood units were promoted as the building blocks of larger regional communities (Mumford, 1954). Present-day New Urbanism harkens back to many of these concepts, emphasizing the design of public spaces and human-scaled, pedestrian-oriented streetscapes (Duany & Plater-Zyberk, 1994; see chapter 12).

The negative effects of the industrial city environment on property values, health, and social welfare were motivating factors in the formation of the fields of urban planning, social work, and public health (Corburn, 2009; Sclar & Northridge, 2001). While initially united behind efforts to pave streets and install public sewers and safe drinking-water systems, three separate fields eventually emerged, with social work and public health more focused on the establishment of social and health services and urban planning focused on the physical design of cities and the regulation of development. Public health and medicine adopted a biomedical view of health, focused on the individual, with little consideration for his or her environment. Social work turned toward individual case management, and urban planning focused on land and economic development. This disconnect from the original shared mission of these fields and from the interrelated physical, social, and environmental nature of their concerns was perhaps most visible in the post–World War II era, and it has had profound and lasting consequences (see chapter 18).

In recent years, the fields of urban planning and public health have reengaged around the influence of the built environment on health (Corburn, 2013; Lopez, n.d.). In urban planning, attention to the connection between environment, planning, and health was galvanized by the environmental justice movement more than twenty-five years ago (see chapter 18). In 1987 the United Church of Christ Commission for Racial Justice published the report *Toxic Wastes and Race in the United States*, which "found race to be the most potent variable in predicting where commercial hazardous waste facilities were located in the U.S., more powerful than household income, [or] the value of homes" (Bullard, Mohai, Saha, & Wright, 2007). While public awareness of the impact of exposure to environmental hazards has grown dramatically since that time, along with federal regulations meant to protect citizens, recent research has found that such racial and ethnic disparities remain common (Bullard et al., 2007; Maantay, 2001; see chapter 16).

Recent findings link sprawling development patterns to health problems, thus broadening the discussion of the connection between environment and urban planning to include suburban, middle-class neighborhoods. In 2003 a national study found that people living in sprawling counties weighed significantly more than residents of more compact counties and were more likely to suffer from chronic diseases, including hypertension and high blood pressure (Ewing, Schmid, Killingsworth, Zlot, & Raudenbush, 2003). Researchers concluded that the explanation for the differences was the level of physical activity residents engaged in as part of their daily lives (Ewing et al., 2003). These findings have reinforced the importance of facilitating development patterns that give residents easy access to sites important to their daily activities—work, home, and shops and services—by foot or by transit.

Urban planning practice has turned toward encouraging alternatives to driving, including walking, bicycling, and use of public transit, with improved sidewalk networks, mixed-use development that places shops, apartments, and offices in close proximity, and greater residential density near transit stations (American Planning Association, 2012). Researchers have documented the impact that transit use can have on obesity (MacDonald, Stokes, Cohen, Kofner, & Ridgeway, 2010) and are emphasizing the potential of land use changes to produce such outcomes (Lyons, Peckett, Morse, Khurana, & Nash, 2012). Planners and New Urbanists are also encouraging other land uses and urban design features thought to contribute to health and quality of life, including parks and open spaces, playgrounds, sidewalks, community gardens, tree canopy, shaded transit stops and walkways, and the mix of fast food outlets, farmers' markets, supermarkets, and so on (Congress for the New Urbanism, n.d.; Ricklin & Kushner, n.d.). Planners now speak of "complete streets" that offer safe travel for pedestrians, cyclists, and transit users by separating sidewalks, bike lanes, and transit stops from automobile traffic. Similarly, planning processes that integrate transportation, land use, and community design aim to create "complete communities." Such concepts are increasingly being incorporated into comprehensive plans (McCann & Rynne, 2010; Pivo, 2005).

However, the turn to New Urbanism has also raised the same tensions about the connection between physical and social aspects of neighborhoods. Interestingly, social aspects of behavioral change are not yet well understood. Emerging research on transit use suggests that the demographics and socioeconomics of the nearby population are strongly linked to use, challenging the focus on density and land use without paying attention to who lives there. Researchers find, in particular, that renters and low-income households are more likely to use nearby transit, while homeowners are more likely to continue to rely on cars (Chu, 2012; Chu & Polzin, 2007). Others fear that environmental improvements, if capitalized into home values, will result in a resegregation of places (Mueller & Dooling, 2011). To date, there has been less attention to the social aspects of neighborhoods that might reinforce physical activity—an area where rebuilding the link to social work may be especially important.

In public health, the tremendous increases in obesity, asthma rates (particularly for black/African American children), and other factors leading to a shorter life expectancy for today's children than for their parents have motivated researchers to investigate a broad set of social determinants of health (Marmot & Vilkinson, 2005). However, public health researchers are more intentional in their focus on the connection between social and physical features of neighborhoods linked to health and how these relate to individual or household characteristics. They group the social determinants of health into two broad categories: local stressors linked to health (e.g., violent crime, financial insecurity, environmental toxins) and social integration and social support (e.g., social networks and resources available through networks). They are increasingly interested in understanding how land use policies, in combination with other efforts, can be a tool for health (Northridge, Sclar, & Biswas, 2003). The urban planning and public health fields have collaborated on the development of health impact assessment tools for focusing attention on the health consequences of development patterns (American Public Health Association, n.d.). However, such tools have proven difficult to integrate into the planning process. Debates center on whether the creation of a separate process, rather than integration of health into existing environmental impact reviews, makes more sense (Salkin & Ko, 2011). Regardless, at the neighborhood scale, health impact assessment offers the potential to bridge the divide between physical and social aspects of neighborhoods (see chapter 18).

CONCLUSION

While public policy and practices related to neighborhood quality have changed over time by incorporating lessons from past mistakes, the fundamental elements and tensions identified at the beginning of this chapter remain the same. In brief, conceptions of neighborhood amenities continue to include both tangible physical characteristics and less tangible social aspects. While researchers' thinking regarding the physical aspects of neighborhoods has seemingly advanced, the connection between neighborhood amenities and social exclusion has remained strong, as evidenced by the increasing income segregation in many neighborhoods. By contrast, high-amenity neighborhoods remain affluent, by and large.

Efforts to value the quality of neighborhood amenities in public programs, particularly those that affect the poor, have often fallen short for two main reasons. First, it is difficult to define and measure what makes a neighborhood work for poor residents. Second, we lack understanding of when proximity to services or opportunities provides meaningful access to them for poor residents. While the quest for better measures continues, and has been useful in highlighting the cumulative impact of past practices on poor neighborhoods, it has been less helpful in identifying the way forward. In this regard, the turn toward consideration of the connection between the built environment and health is especially promising. It offers urban planners and policy makers, as well as developers and community organizations, the opportunity to reintegrate consideration of social aspects of neighborhood life into our conception of what constitutes a good neighborhood.

REFERENCES

Abramson, A. J., Tobin, M. S., & VanderGoot, M. R. (1995). The changing geography of metropolitan opportunity: The segregation of the poor in U.S. metropolitan areas, 1970 to 1990. *Housing Policy Debate, 6,* 45–72.

American Planning Association. (2012). *Policy guide on smart growth.* American Planning Association. Retrieved January 26, 2017, from https://www.planning.org/policy/guides/pdf/smartgrowth.pdf.

American Public Health Association. (n.d.). *Promoting health impact assessment to achieve health in all policies.* Retrieved January 26, 2015, from http://apha.org/policies-and-advocacy/public-health-policy-statements/policy-database/2014/07/11/16/51/promoting-health-impact-assessment-to-achieve-health-in-all-policies.

Axel-Lute, M. (2014, August 13). The dangerous rhetoric of escaping to opportunity. *Shelterforce.* Retrieved January 26, 2017, from http://www.rooflines.org/3812/the_dangerous_rhetoric_of_escaping_to_opportunity/.

Bischoff, K., & Reardon, S. F. (2013). Residential segregation by income, 1970–2009. In J. R. Logan (Ed.), *The lost decade? Social change in the U.S. after 2000.* New York: Russell Sage Foundation. Retrieved January 26, 2017, from http://www.s4.brown.edu/us2010/Projects/Reports.htm.

Bookbinder, S., Buchanan, A., Daniel, T., Hooks, J., Parker, S., & Tegeler, P. (2008). *Building opportunity: Civil Rights best practices in the Low Income Housing Tax Credit Program.* Poverty and Race Research Action Council. Retrieved January 26, 2017, from http://www.prrac.org/pdf/BuildingOpportunity.pdf.

Briggs, X. de S. (1998). Brown kids in white suburbs: Housing mobility and the multiple faces of social capital. *Housing Policy Debate, 9*(1), 177–221.

Bullard, R. D., Mohai, P., Saha, R., & Wright, B. (2007). *Toxic wastes and race at twenty, 1987–2007.* United Church of Christ Justice & Witness Ministries. Retrieved January 26, 2017, from http://d3n8a8pro7vhmx.cloudfront.net/unitedchurchofchrist/legacy_url/491/toxic-wastes-and-race-at-twenty-1987-2007.pdf?1418423933.

Card, D., & Krueger, A. B. (1992). Does school quality matter? Returns to education and the characteristics of public schools in the United States. *Journal of Political Economy, 100,* 1–40.

Chaskin, R. J. (1997). Perspectives on neighborhood and community: A review of the literature. *Social Service Review, 71*(4), 521–547.

Chu, X. (2012). *An assessment of public transportation markets using NHTS data.* Tampa, Fla.: National Center for Transit Research. Retrieved January 26, 2017, from http://www.nctr.usf.edu/wp-content/uploads/2013/01/77920.pdf.

Chu, X., & Polzin, S. E. (2007). *Development of alternative measures of transit mode share* (No. NCTR-77708). Tampa, Fla.: National Center for Transit Research. Retrieved January 26, 2017, from http://www.nctr.usf.edu/pdf/77708.pdf.

City of Austin, Texas. (2014, September 26). Rental housing development assistance application and scoring criteria. Retrieved January 26, 2017, from http://www.austintexas.gov/page/housing-application-center.

Congress for the New Urbanism. (n.d.). *Health districts—Project overview.* Retrieved January 26, 2017, from http://www.cnu.org/healthdistricts.

Corburn, J. (2009). *Toward the healthy city.* Cambridge, Mass.: MIT Press.

Corburn, J. (2013). *Healthy city planning: From neighborhood to national health equity.* New York: Routledge.

Crane, R., & Manville, M. (2008, July). People or place? Revisiting the who versus the where of urban development. *Land Lines,* 2–7.

Currie, J. (2005). Health disparities and gaps in school readiness. *Future of Children, 15*(1), 117–138.

DeFilippis, J. (2001). The myth of social capital in community development. *Housing Policy Debate, 12,* 781–805.

Duany, A., & Plater-Zyberk, E. (1994). The neighborhood, the district and the corridor. In P. Katz (Ed.), *The New Urbanism: Toward an architecture of community* (pp. xvii–xx). New York: McGraw-Hill. Retrieved January 26, 2017, from http://www.csus.edu/indiv/s/shawg/courses/154/articles/TNU2.pdf.

Ellen, I., & Turner, M. (1997). Does neighborhood matter? Assessing recent evidence. *Housing Policy Debate, 8*(4), 833–866.

Ellen, I. G., & Turner, M. A. (2003). Do neighborhoods matter and why? In J. Goering & J. D. Feins (Eds.), *Choosing a better life? Evaluating the Moving to Opportunity social experiment* (pp. 313–338). Washington, D.C.: Urban Institute Press.

Ewing, R., Schmid, T., Killingsworth, R., Zlot, A., & Raudenbush, S. (2003). Relationship between urban sprawl and physical activity, obesity and morbidity. *Journal of Health Promotion, 18*(1), 47–57.

Fischel, W. A. (2001). *The homevoter hypothesis: How home values influence local government taxation, school finance, and land-use policies*. Cambridge, Mass.: Harvard University Press.

Fischer, M. J. (2003). The relative importance of income and race in determining residential outcomes in U.S. urban areas, 1970–2000. *Urban Affairs Review, 38*, 669–696.

Fogelson, R. M. (2005). *Bourgeois nightmares: Suburbia, 1870–1930*. New Haven, Conn.: Yale University Press.

Freund, D. M. P. (2007). *Colored property: State policy and white racial politics in suburban America*. Chicago: University of Chicago Press.

Fry, R., & Taylor, P. (2012). *The rise of residential segregation by income*. Washington, D.C.: Pew Research Center.

Galster, G. (2012). The mechanisms of neighbourhood effects: Theory, evidence, and policy implications. In M. van Ham, D. Manley, N. Bailey, L. Simpson, & D. Maclennan (Eds.), *Neighbourhood effects research: New perspectives* (pp. 23–56). Dordrecht, Netherlands: Springer.

Galster, G., Cutsinger, J., & Malega, R. (2008). The social costs of concentrated poverty: Externalities to neighboring households and property owners and the dynamics of decline. In E. S. Belsky & N. P. Retsinas (Eds.), *Revisiting rental housing: Policies, programs, and priorities* (pp. 93–113). Washington, D.C.: Brookings Institution Press.

Gautreaux v. Chicago Housing Authority, 503 F.2d 1974.

Ginther, D., Haveman, R., & Wolfe, B. (2000). Neighborhood attributes as determinants of children's outcomes: How robust are the relationships? *Journal of Human Resources, 35*, 603–642.

Goering, J., & Feins, J. D. (Eds.). (2003). *Choosing a better life? Evaluating the Moving to Opportunity social experiment*. Washington, D.C.: Urban Institute Press.

Goering, J., Kraft, J., Feins, J., McInnis, D., Holin, M. J., & Elhassan, H. (1999). *Moving to Opportunity for Fair Housing Demonstration Program: Current status and initial findings*. Washington, D.C.: U.S. Department of Housing and Urban Development. Retrieved January 26, 2017, from http://www.huduser.org/portal//Publications/pdf/mto.pdf.

Goetz, E. G. (2003). Housing dispersal programs. *Journal of Planning Literature, 18*(3), 3–16.

Gotham, K. F. (2000). Urban space, restrictive covenants and the origins of racial residential segregation in a U.S. city, 1900–50. *International Journal of Urban and Regional Research, 24*(3), 616–633.

Granovetter, M. S. (1973). The strength of weak ties. *American Journal of Sociology, 78*(6), 1360–1380.

Harding, D. J. (2003). Counterfactual models of neighborhood effects: The effect of neighborhood poverty on dropping out and teenage pregnancy. *American Journal of Sociology, 109*(3), 676–719.

Hirsch, A. (1983). *Making the second ghetto: Race and housing in Chicago, 1940–1960*. Chicago: University of Chicago Press.

Jackson, K. (1985). *Crabgrass frontier: The suburbanization of the United States*. New York: Oxford University Press.

Jencks, C., & Peterson, P. E. (1991). *The urban underclass*. Washington, D.C.: Brookings Institution Press.

Kain, J. F., & Quigley, J. M. (1970). Measuring the value of housing quality. *Journal of the American Statistical Association, 65*(330), 532–548.

Kirwan Institute, & Puget Sound Regional Council. (2012). *Equity, opportunity, and sustainability in the Central Puget Sound Region*. Columbus, Ohio: Kirwan Institute for the Study of Race and Ethnicity, The Ohio State University.

Kriesberg, J. (2011, October 14). *Will opportunity mapping take us in the wrong direction?* Massachusetts Association of Community Development Corporations. Retrieved January 26, 2017, from http://www.macdc.org/2011/10/will-opportunity-mapping-take-us-in-the-wrong-direction.

Krumm, R. J. (1980). Neighborhood amenities: An economic analysis. *Journal of Urban Economics, 7*(2), 208–224.

Lang, R., & Hornburg, S. (1998). What is social capital and why is it important to public policy? *Housing Policy Debate, 9*(1), 1–16.

Levine, J. (2006). *Zoned out: Regulation, market, and choice in transportation and metropolitan land-use*. Washington, D.C.: Resources for the Future.

Lopez, R. (n.d.). *Building American public health: Urban planning, architecture, and the quest for better health in the United States*. New York: Palgrave Macmillan.

Ludwig, J., Liebman, J. B., Kling, J. R., Duncan, G. J., Katz, L. F., Kessler, R. C., & Sanbonmatsu, L. (2008). What can we learn about neighborhood effects from the Moving to Opportunity experiment? *American Journal of Sociology, 114*(1), 144–88.

Lyons, W., Peckett, H., Morse, L., Khurana, M., & Nash, L. (2012). *Metropolitan area transportation planning for healthy communities* (No. FHWA-HEP-13-006). Washington, D.C.: U.S. Department of Transportation, Federal Highway Administration. Retrieved January 26, 2017, from http://www.planning.dot.gov/documents/Volpe_FHWA_MPOHealth_12122012.pdf.

Maantay, J. (2001). Zoning, equity and public health. *American Journal of Public Health, 91*, 1033–1041.

MacDonald, J. M., Stokes, R. J., Cohen, D. A., Kofner, A., & Ridgeway, G. K. (2010). The effect of light rail transit on body mass index and physical activity. *American Journal of Preventive Medicine, 39*(2), 105–112.

Marans, R. W. (1979, March). *The determinants of neighborhood quality: An analysis of the 1976 Annual Housing Survey*. Washington, D.C.: U.S. Department of Housing and Urban Development, Office of Policy Development and Research.

Marmot, M., & Vilkinson, R. (2005). *Social determinants of health*. Oxford: Oxford University Press.

Massey, D. S. (2001). Residential segregation and neighborhood conditions in U.S. metropolitan areas. In N. J. Smelser, W. J. Wilson, & F. Mitchell (Eds.), *America becoming: Racial trends and their consequences* (pp. 391–434). Washington, D.C.: National Academy Press.

Massey, D. S., & Denton, N. A. (1993). *American apartheid: Segregation and the making of the underclass*. Cambridge, Mass.: Harvard University Press.

Massey, D. S., & Eggers, M. L. (1990). The ecology of inequality: Minorities and the concentration of poverty, 1970–1980. *American Journal of Sociology, 95*, 1153–1188.

McCann, B., & Rynne, S. (2010). *Complete streets: Best policy and implementation practices* (Planning Advisory Service No. PAS 559). Chicago: American Planning Association.

McClure, K. (2010). The prospects for guiding Housing Choice Voucher households to high-opportunity neighborhoods. *Cityscape, 12*(3), 101–122.

Mueller, E. J., & Dooling, S. (2011). Sustainability and vulnerability: Integrating equity into plans for central city redevelopment. *Journal of Urbanism: International Research on Placemaking and Urban Sustainability, 4*(3), 201–222.

Mumford, L. (1954). The neighbourhood and the neighbourhood unit. *The Town Planning Review, 24*(4), 256–270.

Myers, C. K. (2004). Discrimination and neighborhood effects: Understanding racial differentials in U.S. housing prices. *Journal of Urban Economics, 56*(2), 279–302.

Newburger, H. B., Birch, E. L., & Wachter, S. M. (2011). *Neighborhood and life chances: How place matters in modern America*. Philadelphia: University of Pennsylvania Press.

Northridge, M. E., Sclar, E. D., & Biswas, P. (2003). Sorting out the connections between the built environment and health: A conceptual framework for navigating pathways and planning healthy cities. *Journal of Urban Health, 80*(4), 556–568.

Oliver, M. L., & Shapiro, T. M. (1995). *Black wealth, white wealth: A new perspective on racial inequality*. New York: Routledge.

Orr, L., Feins, J., Beecroft, E., Sanbonmatsu, L., Katz, L., Liebman, J., & Kling, J. (2003).

Moving to Opportunity interim impacts evaluation. Washington, D.C.: U.S. Department of Housing and Urban Development.

Pendall, R. (2000). Local land use regulation and the chain of exclusion. *Journal of the American Planning Association, 66*(2), 125–142.

Pendall, R., Puentes, R., & Martin, J. (2006). *From traditional to reformed: A review of the land use regulations in the nation's 50 largest metropolitan areas*. Washington, D.C.: Brookings Institution. Retrieved January 26, 2017, from http://sarasota.ifas.ufl.edu/Sustain/BasicsToBigPicture/site/d/brookings_institute.pdf.

Perry, Clarence Arthur (1929). The neighborhood unit. In *Regional survey of New York and its environs*. New York: Regional Plan of New York and Its Environs.

Pivo, G. (2005). *Creating compact and complete communities: Seven propositions for success*. Chicago: AICP.

Popkin, S. J., Buron, L. F., Levy, D. K., & Cunningham, M. K. (2000). The Gautreaux legacy: What might mixed-income and dispersal strategies mean for the poorest public housing tenants? *Housing Policy Debate, 11*(4), 911–42.

powell, j. a. (2002). Opportunity-based housing. *Journal of Affordable Housing & Community Development Law, 12*(188), 188–228.

powell, j. a., Reece, J., & Gambhir, S. (2007). *The geography of opportunity, Austin region*. Columbus, Ohio: Kirwan Institute for the Study of Race and Ethnicity, The Ohio State University.

Reece, J., Norris, D., Olinger, J., Holley, K., & Martin, M. (n.d.). *Place matters: Using mapping to plan for opportunity, equity, and sustainability*. Columbus, Ohio: Kirwan Institute for the Study of Race and Ethnicity, The Ohio State University.

Ricklin, A., & Kushner, N. (n.d.). *Healthy plan-making: Integrating health into the comprehensive planning process: An analysis of seven case studies and recommendations for change*. Chicago: American Planning Association. Retrieved January 26, 2017, from https://www.planning.org/research/publichealth/pdf/healthyplanningreport.pdf.

Rosen, S. (1974). Hedonic prices and implicit markets: Product differentiation in pure competition. *Journal of Political Economy, 82*(1), 34–55.

Rosenbaum, J. E. (1995). Housing mobility strategies for changing the geography of opportunity. *Housing Policy Debate, 6*(1), 231–270.

Rothwell, J., & Massey, D. S. (2009). The effect of density zoning on racial segregation in U.S. urban areas. *Urban Affairs Review, 44*(6), 779–806.

Rubinowitz, L. S. (1992). Metropolitan public housing desegregation remedies: Chicago's privatization program. *Northern Illinois University Law Review, 12*(3), 590–669.

Saegert, S. (2012). Building civic capacity in urban neighborhoods: An empirically grounded analysis. In J. DeFilippis & S. Saegert (Eds.), *The community development reader* (2nd ed., pp. 220–227). New York: Routledge.

Salkin, P., & Ko, P. (2011, October). The effective use of health impact assessment (HIA) in land-use decision making. *Zoning Practice*. Retrieved January 26, 2017, from http://papers.ssrn.com/sol3/papers.cfm?abstract_id=1937412.

Sampson, R. J., Sharkey, P., & Raudenbush, S. W. (2007). Durable effects of concentrated disadvantage on verbal ability among African-American children. *Proceedings of the National Academy of Sciences, 105*(3), 845–852.

Satter, B. (2009). *Family properties: Race, real estate, and the exploitation of black urban America*. New York: Metropolitan Books.

Schellenberg, S. J. (1998). *Hard work for good schools: Facts not fads in Title I reform*. Cambridge, Mass.: Harvard University.

Schill, M. H. (2004). *Regulations and housing development: What we know and what we need to know*. U.S. Department of Housing and Urban Development, Conference on Regulatory Barriers to Affordable Housing. Retrieved January 26, 2017, from http://www.huduser.org/rbc/pdf/regulations_housing_development.pdf.

Sclar, E., & Northridge, M. E. (2001). Property, politics, and public health. *American Journal of Public Health, 91*, 1013–1015.

Sharkey, P. (2009). *Neighborhoods and the black-white mobility gap*. Philadelphia: Pew Charitable Trusts.

Sharkey, P. (2012). *Stuck in place: Urban neighborhoods and the end of progress toward racial equality*. Chicago: University of Chicago Press.

Shelley v. Kraemer, 334 U.S. 1 (1948).

Silver, C. (1997). The racial origins of zoning in American cities. In J. M. Thomas & M. Ritzdorf (Eds.), *Urban planning and the African-American community: In the shadows* (pp. 23–42). Thousand Oaks, Calif.: Sage.

Solari, C. D. (2012). Affluent neighborhood persistence and change in U.S. cities. *City & Community, 11*(4), 370–388.

Spain, D. (2001). *How women saved the city*. Minneapolis: University of Minnesota Press.

Stack, C. B. (1974). *All our kin: Strategies for survival in a black community*. New York: Basic Books.

Sugrue, T. J. (1996). *The origins of the urban crisis: Race and inequality in postwar Detroit*. Princeton, N.J.: Princeton University Press.

Talen, E. (2005). Land use zoning and human diversity: Exploring the connection. *Journal of Urban Planning and Development, 131*(4), 214–232.

Tein, M. (1992). The devaluation of nonwhite community in remedies for public housing discrimination. *University of Pennsylvania Law Review, 140*, 1463–1503.

Tiebout, C. M. (1956). A pure theory of local expenditures. *Journal of Political Economy, 64*(5), 416–424.

Trent, W. J. (1997). Why the gap between black and white performance in school? A report on the effects of race on student achievement in the St. Louis public schools. *Journal of Negro Education, 66*(3), 320–329.

Tretter, E. (2012). *Austin restricted: Progressivism, zoning, private racial covenants, and the making of a segregated city*. Austin: Institute for Urban Policy Analysis, University of Texas. Retrieved January 26, 2017, from http://hdl.handle.net/2152/21232.

Turner, M. A. (2005). *Discrimination against persons with disabilities: Barriers at every step*. Washington, D.C.: U.S. Department of Housing and Urban Development. Retrieved January 26, 2017, from http://www.huduser.org/portal/publications/hsgspec/dds.html.

Turner, M. A., Santos, R., Levy, D. K., Wissoker, D., Aranda, C., & Pitingolo, R. (2013). *Housing discrimination against racial and ethnic minorities 2012*. Washington, D.C.: U.S. Department of Housing and Urban Development. Retrieved January 26, 2017, from http://www.huduser.org/portal/Publications/pdf/HUD-514_HDS2012.pdf.

U.S. Department of Housing and Urban Development. (2014, Spring/Summer). Expanding opportunity through fair housing choice. *Evidence Matters*, 1–11.

Wiese, A. (2004). *Places of their own: African American suburbanization in the twentieth century*. Chicago: University of Chicago Press.

Wilson, W. J. (1996). *When work disappears: The world of the new urban poor*. New York: Knopf.

Wilson, W. J. (2012). *The truly disadvantaged: The inner city, the underclass and public policy* (2nd ed.). Chicago: University of Chicago Press.

Wotke, G. T., Harding, D. J., & Elwert, F. (2011). Neighborhood effects in temporal perspective. *American Sociological Review, 76*(5), 713–736.

Yinger, J. (2000). Housing discrimination and residential segregation as causes of poverty. *IRP Focus, 21*(2), 51–55.

Chapter 14

Federal Housing Policy

KIRK MCCLURE

THE ROLE OF THE FEDERAL GOVERNMENT IN HOUSING

In the housing sector, the federal government, with some exceptions, engages other entities to do the work. The federal government is not in the job of owning housing, but it will subsidize other entities to own and manage housing for the poor. These entities can be other units of government or they can be for-profit or nonprofit entities acting under the condition that the owner will serve those who are eligible and who have a defined housing need. The federal government is not in the job of lending money, but it will subsidize lenders under the condition that they will lend to those who are eligible and who have a defined housing need. The federal government is not in the job of developing housing, but it provides subsidies to developers who will develop housing serving those households who are eligible and who have a defined housing need. While the federal government does not generally own, finance, or create housing, it does play a vital role in ensuring that these three activities occur.

The housing sector is made up of actors operating in many roles. Builders and developers acquire land, subdivide it, add the necessary infrastructure, and then construct housing. Investors or homeowners own properties and manage them themselves or through professional property managers. Lenders loan money to investors or borrowers to provide the funds needed to pay for the development or acquisition of housing (see chapter 8).

The federal government could operate in any of these roles, but it has chosen to adopt a more hands-off position (Erickson, 2009). Rather than use federal employees to work as builders, developers, investors, property managers, or lenders, the federal government uses its considerable influence to cause other organizations, whether for-profit, nonprofit, or even other governmental units, to do the work.

This approach has, by many measures, succeeded well, but many problems remain. The United States enjoys the benefits of a very large housing stock that is generally in good physical condition. It is a nation of about 116 million households living in about 132 million housing units. Thus the housing industry is capable of producing more than enough units. More than half of these units were built after 1975. In a typical year the industry adds 1.8 to 2.1 million units, which is much higher than the rate at which we add households. Finally, only 1.8 percent of households report severe physical problems with their homes and only 3.7 percent report moderate problems (U.S. Bureau of the Census, 2014; see chapter 1).

The detached approach of the federal government does, however, have its shortcomings. Despite the surplus of housing units, homelessness has remained a problem (see chapter 11). Despite the adequate supply of good-quality housing, many households must allocate more than 30 percent of their income toward housing costs. Thus these households have a high housing cost burden, indicating affordability problems. Twenty-nine percent of owners and 55 percent of renters suffer from a high housing cost burden. What these shortcomings mean is that the current role of the government is more focused on maintaining the flow of housing into the already ample supply of units and addressing the many and varied forms of housing affordability problems found within these markets (see chapter 10). The government does not, however, take any active steps to control the price of housing.

The federal government typically addresses housing problems by working through other organizations, leaving itself in the role of funding these initiatives (see chapter 12). Many of the programs implemented by the federal government are designed to help low-income renter households consume good-quality housing at affordable prices (see chapter 10). The government generally contracts with builders, developers, investors, and lenders to run these programs. Many of the programs implemented by the federal government are designed to help home buyers purchase a home. For many of these buyers a home might not be affordable otherwise. Very few of the programs for home buyers provide direct assistance (see chapter 7). More commonly, these programs work indirectly by insuring the mortgage lender against loss, making the lender more willing to originate a mortgage loan with a low-income, first-time home buyer. A few of the programs are even more indirect, operating in the secondary mortgage market. The federal government sponsors secondary markets to purchase loans from lenders so that they will have money available to originate additional loans, ensuring an adequate supply of mortgage credit. The federal government also monitors where and to whom mortgage lenders make loans, ensuring that all neighborhoods and all racial and ethnic groups have access to mortgages (see chapter 8).

THE GOALS OF FEDERAL HOUSING POLICY

The goals of federal housing policy are many and varied. Katz, Turner, Brown, Cunningham, and Sawyer (2003) offer the following list of goals:

1. Preserve and expand the supply of good-quality housing units.
2. Make existing housing more affordable and more readily available.
3. Promote racial and economic diversity in residential neighborhoods.
4. Help households build wealth.
5. Strengthen families.
6. Link housing with essential supportive services.
7. Promote balanced metropolitan growth.

These goals articulate the notion that it is the job of the federal government to make sure that the housing stock is able to grow sufficiently given the expansion of the population and that additions to the stock are of good quality and affordably priced. Even with the successes of the quantity of housing produced, the premise of these goals is that it takes continuous federal intervention to perpetuate these successes. This issue is not trivial. Some have argued that the housing industry does not need any government intervention and that it could operate better with less or no intervention at all (American Enterprise Institute, 2014; Husock, 2009). However, there is a widely held opinion that if the nation is to successfully meet the housing challenges of the future, the federal government will need to act, although it will need to act differently than it has in previous decades, given the knowledge gained from the boom-and-bust cycle of the first decade of this century (Been & Ellen, 2012; see chapters 1, 2, 7, 8, 9, and 10, 15).

The goals listed above go far beyond the quantity, quality, and price of housing; they seek to make housing a platform for accomplishing additional national goals. Generally, housing is fixed in location, which means that where a household chooses to consume housing determines much more than shelter itself. The location establishes the neighborhood where the household will live, with its inventory of services, schools, institutions, and amenities (see chapter 13). Neighborhoods offer very different opportunities for residents to lead safe and happy lives with access to good schools, gainful employment, and services not otherwise available (see chapters 12 and 13). Housing location can be instrumental in breaking down patterns of racial and ethnic separation as well as poverty concentration. Increasingly, the federal government is looking for ways to make its housing efforts serve broader goals of dismantling racial and ethnic barriers to economic progress and breaking the cycle of poverty (U.S. Department of Housing and Urban Development, 2014i; see chapters 11 and 16).

Finally, the goal of promoting balanced metropolitan growth speaks to the way metropolitan areas expand. The house price bubble from 2000 to 2008 was more than just a price bubble; it was a production bubble as well. Housing markets across the nation built more housing than population growth required, especially in Florida, Arizona, Nevada, and California (McClure, 2013). The surpluses were not distributed evenly. They attracted households into new subdivisions, pulling them out of older neighborhoods, which hastened the demise of those neighborhoods. The housing industry should help metropolitan areas pursue balanced growth (see chapters 8 and 15). Sprawl, neighborhood decline, and affordability are all concerns of growth management, which aims to determine the right number, price, and location for housing growth (Downs, 2003; see chapter 10). The federal government has a role to play in this process.

Interestingly, the goals listed above do not include homeownership, yet homeownership is often mentioned as a federal goal (Landis & McClure, 2010). Homeownership is often equated with the American Dream, and thus it is often assumed that the federal government has established homeownership as a goal (see chapters 1, 2, 8, and 10). Many federal programs exist to promote homeownership, but they may have been established less as policy instruments aimed at homeownership and more as a means to accomplish other objectives such as full employment (Carliner, 1998; see chapter 10).

Beyond specific goals held by the federal government for housing, the housing industry plays a very active role in achieving other federal goals.

The housing construction industry, which caters to housing consumption, is a very large segment of the economy, and the federal government has an interest in maintaining economic stability by slowing the economy down when it grows too fast (periods when inflation is high) and stimulating it when it is sluggish (periods when unemployment is high). The government will often use the housing industry to try to stabilize the economy. The housing sector tends to lead economic cycles, slowing down first when the economy is about to contract and starting up quickly when the economy is beginning to expand (Leamer, 2007). Thus speeding up and slowing down housing construction and purchasing are strategies the federal government uses to stabilize the economy. The American Recovery and Reinvestment Act of 2009 (ARRA) is an example. It pumped about $14 billion into the housing sector to stimulate the overall economy during the Great Recession (U.S. Department of Housing and Urban Development, 2014f; see chapters 7, 8 and 15).

STRATEGIES THE FEDERAL GOVERNMENT USES TO PERFORM ITS ROLE IN HOUSING

The federal government has adopted many and varied strategies to achieve its housing goals. Some focus on the entire economy, whereas others focus on helping specific populations find and afford good-quality housing. These strategies can be differentiated as direct versus indirect subsidy programs and then further by the nature of the subsidy delivery mechanism (i.e., whether it is attached to the intended household or to the housing unit).

Direct Subsidies: Project Based

The federal government directly subsidizes developments built and operated to serve eligible low-income people, which is probably the most widely recognized form of federal intervention into the housing market. The oldest intervention of this type is public housing, a program created in 1937 in which a federal subsidy funds a specific housing project directly or, more commonly, through another entity such as a Public Housing Authority (PHA). The PHA, a branch of local government, owns and operates such housing for eligible renters, who are usually extremely low income (Mitchell, 1985). Public housing has been evaluated favorably and unfavorably, and the debate over its future remains unresolved. There are calls for its replacement with mixed-income, mixed-ownership housing (Popkin et al., 2004). At the same time, there are also calls for its continuation and revitalization (Goetz, 2013).

The subsidy can also flow directly to a privately owned housing development from the U.S. Department of Housing and Urban Development (HUD). The Section 8 New Construction/Substantial Rehabilitation Program attaches a subsidy to units through a long-term lease. This approach was created in 1974 as part of the Section 8 Program, which came into being with the landmark Housing and Community Development Act. The Section 8 Program was very active under the Carter administration, but the Reagan administration brought it to a halt. With this program, the federal government agrees to pay a portion of the rent of a unit for up to forty years with the condition that the unit be rented to eligible low-income tenants. This program funds a large portfolio of developments, and a version of this program is being revived through the use of what are now called project-based vouchers (U.S. Department of Housing and Urban Development, 2014h).

The subsidy can also flow to a development in the form of a loan with a below-market interest rate. An example of this approach is found in the former Section 236 Program. By offering low-interest-rate loans, the program brought about the new construction or rehabilitation of existing housing for eligible low- and moderate-income households. While many Section 236 developments still exist, this program is no longer producing units (Comptroller General of the United States, 1978).

The Low-Income Housing Tax Credit (LIHTC) Program was created in 1986, perhaps in response to the Reagan administration ending the Section 8 New Construction/Substantial Rehabilitation Program. The LIHTC attaches a subsidy to a development in a more indirect manner, with the federal government giving tax credits to investors in specific low-income developments. This program allocates tax credits to states, which competitively award a limited number of credits to newly built or rehabilitated developments for occupancy by low-income households (McClure, 2000; see chapters 9 and 10).

Generally, project-based housing seems to be evaluated as expensive and ineffective, generating concentrations of poverty (Newman & Schnare, 1997; Turner, 1998; Wallace, 2000). However, the currently active LIHTC program has been found, in certain circumstances, to be cost-effective and capable of producing affordable housing in low-poverty suburban markets where prior programs could not make entry (Deng, 2005; McClure, 2006).

Direct Subsidies: Tenant Based

The federal government helps eligible low-income households consume housing in the marketplace through income transfers that flow through a Public Housing Authority. Thanks to this setup, the tenant has considerable choice of where to live. This approach was created in 1974, also as part of the Section 8 Program. Originally called the Section 8 Existing Housing Certificate Program, it has evolved into the Housing Choice Voucher (HCV) Program.

The federal government contracts with a local housing authority to administer the HCV Program, with the federal government paying for the costs of the program in addition to an administrative fee to the local housing authority. The housing authority maintains a waiting list of eligible renter households who are considered extremely low income (i.e., households that have an income that is below 30 percent of the annual median family income, as determined by HUD for each metropolitan and nonmetropolitan area).

As funds become available, they are allocated to households on the list in the form of a voucher. The tenant seeks an apartment in the private market that is offered at rent that is below a set threshold, passes a physical inspection, and is owned by a landlord who is willing to accept partial payment of rent from the PHA. If the unit is acceptable, the tenant pays at least 30 percent (but not more than 40 percent) of his or her income toward the costs of rent plus utilities while the PHA pays the remainder of the rent and utilities (McClure, 2005).

Tenant-based assistance offers choice to the assisted household, and this choice is viewed as the strength of the strategy, especially where housing markets are soft with ample stocks of units (Turner, 1998). There has been a long debate among housing policy analysts over the relative merits of project-based versus tenant-based housing programs. There seems to be general agreement, however, that tenant-based programs should make up the bulk of federal efforts to assist low-income households (Galster, 1997; Winnick, 1995; see chapters 9 and 10).

Direct Subsidies: Place Based

Federal subsidies to housing can also be place based in that the funds must be used in a particular location but may be directed either to a household or to a development within that location. In the past, categorical grants were competitively awarded by the federal government to specific projects; however, the distribution of these grants was normally uneven. While some communities were very successful at winning grants, others were not. President Nixon brought this funding approach to a halt through a moratorium, effectively forcing Congress to pass the Housing and Community Development Act of 1974. This act brought about the Section 8 housing programs discussed above, and it brought into being the Community Development Block Grant (CDBG) Program. With the CDBG Program, the allocation of funds shifted from competitive categorical grants to block grants allocated by formula, with each eligible city receiving its share of the overall funds. Nevertheless, there are some constraints on the use of the funds. For example, they must be used in low-income neighborhoods and serve certain federal goals, but otherwise each recipient community has a great deal of discretion in how to use the funds (Orlebeke & Weicher, 2014).

The CDBG Program is broadly focused, including community development, neighborhood revitalization, economic development, and the rehabilitation of housing. Even with its broad range of permissible uses, most communities use their CDBG funds to promote housing affordability and preservation (Rich, 2014). A similar block grant program was created as part of the Affordable Housing Act of 1990. The HOME Investment Partnerships Program (HOME) is more narrowly focused on housing with the express purpose of "building, buying, and/or rehabilitating affordable housing for rent or homeownership or providing direct rental assistance to low-income people" (U.S. Department of Housing and Urban Development, 2014c: n.p.; see chapters 7, 9, and 10).

Taken together, the CDBG and HOME Programs provide a significant amount of annual funding from the federal government to local communities to use in the neighborhoods of participating cities to promote community development and affordable housing. These programs have a long list of both successes and failures. Improvements are needed in these programs to enhance their effectiveness, and they are threatened by reduced funding levels (Rohe & Galster, 2014).

Direct Subsidies: Special Needs Populations

Some programs of the federal government are designed to provide grants or development assistance to particular housing projects that serve populations with special needs. Examples of this type of program include homeless shelters, shelters for people with AIDS, and projects with nonprofit sponsors who own projects for the poor elderly. The assistance can also take the form of special set-asides of tenant-based assistance. For example, the Housing Choice Voucher (HCV) Program contains the Veterans Affairs Supportive Housing Program (VASH), a special set-aside of funds to serve veterans (U.S. Department of Housing and Urban Development, 2014e). There are numerous evaluations of these programs, and their findings vary widely in terms of the performance of each (U.S. Department of Housing and Urban Development, 2014d). HUD provides access to this literature through its HUD-USER website (U.S. Department of Housing and Urban Development, 2014d).

Indirect Subsidies: Loan Insurance

The federal government intervenes in housing markets through various indirect mechanisms. The most common versions of these indirect subsidies are the various loan insurance programs. Private, for-profit lenders are, understandably, reluctant to make loans that carry a high risk. The federal government can help lenders accommodate that risk by insuring some or all of the potential loss that could result from a risky loan failing. Thanks to the insurance, lenders are now willing to make the loan.

The federal government operates the Federal Housing Administration (FHA), which is effectively an agency offering insurance to lenders under a variety of programs. The FHA insures loans made to eligible low-income, first-time home buyers. It also insures loans on multifamily developments, including rentals, single-room occupancy projects, cooperative developments, and manufactured home parks. The housing units in the developments with the insured loans shelter eligible households, and FHA insurance helps developers to obtain loans that they would not otherwise be able to leverage in the private capital markets. The agency is largely self-funded in that borrowers pay insurance premiums to the FHA to provide a pool of funds that the FHA uses to cover losses. However, the federal government is in a backstop role. If a sudden downturn in the economy causes an unexpected drawdown of the FHA's funds, the federal government is under considerable pressure to augment FHA funds to cover those losses. In 2013 the FHA drew $1.7 billion to bolster its insurance funds, the first time that it needed federal government assistance (Puzzangher, 2013).

The FHA has survived, and even thrived, over its long life due to its ability to transform itself as the mortgage market has changed. It began as an insurance carrier for lenders when none existed. As private insurance has succeeded in the marketplace, the FHA has invented new programs serving the needs of special populations (Pennington-Cross & Yezer, 2000). After the collapse of the housing market in 2008, the FHA's share of loans increased dramatically, although many of these loans are performing poorly (Shriver, 2013; see chapter 8).

Indirect Subsidies: Tax Breaks

It is frequently argued that the federal government's biggest housing program is the Mortgage Interest Deduction (MID), which subsidizes middle- and upper-income borrowers by allowing deductions from their income tax that are greater than the standard deduction. Thus itemizing borrowers enjoy a significant tax break (Schwartz, 2014). In 2014 the standard deduction was $6,200 for single individuals and $12,400 for married couples filing jointly. Generally, if the taxpayer has mortgage interest expenses and property tax payments exceeding the standard deduction, he or she is allowed to deduct the excess while not having to claim the imputed rental income value of the property. In other words, the homeowner is allowed to deduct some of the expenses of buying the home but is not required to report as income the rental income that the owner would receive were it not for the fact that the owner occupies the home. In addition to the MID, homeowners enjoy reduced capital gains taxation. If the taxpayer sells the home, the first $250,000 for single individuals or $500,000 for couples in profit on the sale is exempt from capital gains taxation. These tax breaks may be causing households to purchase more housing than they need and to delay downsizing when their household size changes over time (Glaeser & Shapiro, 2002).

Tax breaks also come in other forms. The federal government makes the interest paid to holders of certain bonds exempt from federal income taxation. States can issue bonds at relatively low interest rates because of this exemption. The proceeds from these bonds are allocated, usually through each state's housing finance agency, to lenders who originate loans with eligible low-income, first-time home buyers who are purchasing modestly priced homes as their primary residence. This approach is used with mortgage revenue bonds (MRBs). Because of the low interest rate, MRBs are beneficial to eligible home buyers, permitting them to obtain more favorable loan terms than they would in the conventional mortgage loan market. While this program can be helpful to eligible home buyers, if it is implemented poorly, home prices can rise (McClure, 1989; see chapter 8).

As an alternative to MRBs, the federal government also operates a Mortgage Credit Certificate (MCC) Program. Rather than issuing MRBs and loaning the proceeds to eligible low-income home buyers, a state will sometimes opt to exchange its MRB capacity for MCCs. The state then allocates MCCs to eligible low-income home buyers, who can deduct the tax credits on their federal income tax returns, with the credits being a percentage of the interest payments that the home buyer made on a conventional mortgage loan. The MCC program can be helpful as an alternative to the MRB program when mortgage interest rates are very low, rendering the MRB program ineffective (Greulich & Quigley, 2009).

Regulation

The federal government leaves most building codes and inspections to local governments. It does not operate as an overseer of local housing markets, but there are a few exceptions. The biggest exception is that the federal government is active in the area of fair housing, which has evolved over time. Fair housing legislation prohibits discrimination against a list of protected classes in virtually all housing transactions. These protected classes include people defined by race, color, national origin, religion, sex, familial status, or handicap, among others (U.S. Department of Housing and Urban Development, 2014b). Some critics argue that this role is too passive and reactive. It is passive in that the government does not take active steps to prevent discrimination. It is reactive in that it waits until discrimination occurs, often with little chance to implement a meaningful remedy (Silverman, 2011). HUD seems to be taking steps to take a more active role in its published rule to strengthen the efforts of communities receiving federal housing funds to affirmatively further fair housing. More specifically, HUD is building a data tool for communities called an assessment of fair housing (AFH), which states,

> The AFH focuses program participants' analysis on four primary goals: a) improving integrated living patterns and overcoming historic patterns of segregation; b) reducing racial and ethnic concentrations of poverty; c) reducing disparities by race, color, religion, sex, familial status, national origin, or disability in access to community assets such as education, transit access, and employment, as well as exposure to environmental health hazards and other stressors that harm a person's quality of life; and d) responding to disproportionate housing needs by protected class. (U.S. Department of Housing and Urban Development, 2014a: n.p.)

It will be interesting to see if this new tool becomes the proactive mechanism that has been missing in the fair housing process. While discrimination against protected classes of people is illegal in housing, the political will to stop it has remained weak. The success of HUD's new fair housing initiative will depend upon its ability to overcome political resistance (Tighe, 2011).

The federal government is also active in enforcing antidiscriminatory actions by lenders through the Community Reinvestment Act (CRA), which mandates that most lenders report the actions taken on each home loan application. The CRA was adopted in 1977 as a reaction to redlining, a practice in which lenders would draw a red line on a map indicating that no loans would be made inside the areas bounded by the red line, usually an area with a high proportion of people of color. The CRA places the weight of federal bank regulators to bear on lenders to ensure that the banks are meeting the credit needs of all neighborhoods.

Secondary Mortgage Market

Among the many strategies adopted by the federal government in the housing arena is its effort to create and maintain a secondary market for mortgages. A secondary market is a place for banks and other mortgage originators to sell mortgage-backed loans so that they have more money available to originate additional loans. In the 1930s the federal government became concerned that borrowers were unable to gain access to adequate supplies of mortgage credit. Lenders willing to originate mortgages were limited by the amount of deposits they held; thus they could grant relatively few loans. To resolve this problem, the federal government created the Federal National Mortgage Association (Fannie Mae). The agency was later privatized, with the government retaining one component of the secondary mortgage activity, the mortgages insured by the FHA through the Government National Mortgage Association (Ginnie Mae). The other component was the privatized Fannie Mae, from then on owned by stockholders, although its public mission continued (Carr & Anacker, 2014). A sister agency to Fannie Mae was created in 1970, the Federal Home Loan Mortgage Corporation (Freddie Mac). It is also a private corporation with a public mission. Together, these agencies are part of a group of agencies called government-sponsored enterprises, or GSEs (Stanton, 2012). They attract funds to the mortgage industry by selling insured bonds to investors. Fannie Mae and Freddie Mac use the proceeds from the sale of these bonds to purchase loans from mortgage lenders. The lenders service the loans and have new resources to originate additional mortgages. The investors who purchase bonds from the GSEs do so with an unwritten understanding that the bonds, in the event of failure, will be backed by the federal government. The collapse of the financial market during the Great Recession tested this notion, and the federal government acted upon that unwritten guarantee, making the implicit guarantee explicit (Carr & Anacker, 2014). Thus Fannie Mae and Freddie Mac were brought under conservatorship in 2008. As of this writing their fate is uncertain (see chapter 8).

TIMELINE AND CHANGES IN EMPHASIS OF SELECT HOUSING PROGRAMS

Table 14.1 traces the various types of programs pursued by the federal government over the past eighty years. It is useful as a means to understand the evolution of federal policies in housing.

The federal role in housing began during the Great Depression. The federal government's first significant foray into the private housing market was part of the Hoover administration's efforts to bring the nation out of the Depression. This effort created the Federal Housing Administration to insure loans for home buyers, but this program was not passed until 1934, after Franklin Delano Roosevelt was elected. Because of the insurance the FHA offered to lenders, they were—for the first time—willing to make long-term,

TABLE 14.1
Timeline of Select Federal Legislation and Housing Programs

1934	Federal Housing Administration created
1937	Housing Act passed, creating public housing
1938	Fannie Mae chartered
1949	Housing Act uncoupled public housing from slum clearance and began a separate urban renewal program
1959	Section 202 direct loans authorized
1961	Section 221(d)(3 and 4) authorized
1965	HUD created as a cabinet-level department
1968	Fannie Mae privatized and Ginnie Mae created
1968	Section 236 authorized
1969	Brooke Amendment to the Housing Act of 1937 passed, changing public housing
1970	Freddie Mac created
1974	Housing and Community Development Act adopted, creating the CDBG and Section 8 Programs and ending the Urban Renewal Program
1975	Home Mortgage Disclosure Act passed
1977	Community Reinvestment Act passed
1986	Low-Income Housing Tax Credit (LIHTC) Program created
1990	National Affordable Housing Act passed and HOME Program created
1993	HOPE VI Program created
2008	Housing and Economic Recovery Act passed
2008	Fannie Mae and Freddie Mac brought into conservatorship
2009	American Recovery and Reinvestment Act passed, creating the Neighborhood Stabilization Program

Source: Author, adapted from U.S. Department of Housing and Urban Development, 2014i.

level-payment, self-amortizing home purchase loans. This action is credited with being an important force in shifting the United States from a nation of renters to a nation of homeowners, although the FHA was very slow to extend the same assistance to borrowers of color that it initially extended only to whites (Mitchell, 1985; see chapter 8).

The next major milepost, the creation of public housing as part of the Housing Act of 1937, came after the formation of the FHA. This act still stands as the framework for federal housing programs for eligible low-income households. Public housing was created initially to serve the working poor rather than the poorest of the poor and may owe its initial passage by Congress as much to a desire to stimulate the construction industry as to house the poor (Mitchell, 1985). However, public housing struggled with the problem of having to charge rents beyond the means of the poor. The Brooke Amendment in 1969 linked the rent in public housing to the income level of the tenant and provided for additional subsidy funds to help local housing authorities cover costs of operation that could not be covered through rent (Mitchell, 1985; see chapter 9).

In 1938 the federal government recognized that lenders were not able to provide a steady supply of credit for mortgage loans. To resolve this issue, the federal government chartered the Federal National Mortgage Association, as discussed above (see chapter 8).

The Housing Act of 1949 was another major milepost in federal housing policy. With this act, the government pledged itself to the goal of providing "a decent home and suitable living environment for all Americans" (Housing Act of 1949: n.p.). The Housing Act of 1949 also establishes as a national objective the achievement as soon as feasible of a decent home and a suitable living environment for every American family (Truman, 1949). With the act, Congress authorized construction of 810,000 public housing units over a six-year period, to bring the total to 1 million public housing units (Mitchell, 1985). Prior to this act, for each public housing unit built, one slum unit had to be demolished. The act uncoupled public housing from demolition and created the urban renewal program, which took over the role of slum clearance. Sadly, urban renewal is routinely viewed as a source of troubles in urban areas rather than a source of solutions. It became widely misused, contributing to a decade of riots and protests in ghetto communities (Weiss, 1980). Thus the urban renewal program was finally halted in 1974.

During the turbulent 1960s, the federal government searched for new strategies to help resolve the problems of urban unrest in general and housing inadequacy and unaffordability in particular. To solve these problems, the federal government began to turn away from publicly owned and operated housing, which was the model for public housing, and toward privately owned and operated housing to serve the needs of eligible low- and moderate-income households. In 1959 the Section 202 Program was created. This approach provides 100 percent of the development financing needed for a nonprofit sponsor to develop housing for eligible poor elderly households. In 1961 the government authorized the FHA to expand its insurance operations to promote the development of more multifamily rental properties. The Section 221(d)(3) Program insured public, nonprofit, and cooperative mortgagors, while the Section 221(d)(4) Program insured mortgages with for-profit sponsors. In 1964 Section 312 direct rehabilitation loans were created and Section 235 subsidized mortgages for homebuyers were established. These programs were followed in 1968 by the Section 236 Program, which provided below-market-rate-interest loans for multifamily rental properties serving eligible moderate-income households.

With all these new programs, it became clear that the issues of housing and urban development needed a cabinet-level department within the federal government. In 1965 HUD was created to serve as the administrative home of these many different programs and initiatives. The FHA and the many housing and urban development programs were brought under HUD's leadership, including nominal oversight of the GSEs.

In the 1960s and 1970s the government's approach to housing evolved. The federal government turned its attention to the practices of lenders. In 1975 the Home Mortgage Disclosure Act (HMDA) mandated that lenders report on the location, race, and gender of applicants for loans, making it possible for bank examiners to uncover patterns of discrimination in lending. In 1977 the Community Reinvestment Act (CRA) gave even more strength to the reporting process, allowing federal regulators to sanction lenders found not to be serving the credit needs of the local communities where the banks accept deposits.

During this decade the concern over housing became less an issue of quantity and more an issue of affordability. Over the preceding decades, the number of housing units became sufficient to meet the needs of the population and the quality of housing improved. Unfortunately, these increases in quantity and quality were typically accompanied by higher rents and house prices. While the nation still needed more housing units to meet the demands of a growing population, it also needed strategies to help low-income people consume the housing that existed without imposing an undue burden upon these households' income. The Housing and Community Development Act of 1974 reflected this change in direction and was an important turning point for federal housing policy. The act brought the urban renewal program to an end. It consolidated several categorical grant programs into the Community Development Block Grant (CDBG) Program. It marked the slowdown in the various production programs that had been previously established, and it initiated the Section 8 Programs.

Section 8 programs came in two forms. The first adopted the housing allowance approach to rental assistance. With this approach, an eligible household is given a certificate, which is now called a voucher. The tenant seeks out a unit in the private market, paying 25 (and later 30) percent of a household's income toward rent; the landlord accepts the voucher for the remainder of the rent, which is paid by the Section 8 Program through a local Public Housing Authority. The second form of the Section 8 Program gave contracts to developers to either build new units or perform substantial rehabilitation of existing units for occupancy by eligible low-income renter households. As with the certificate program, each tenant in these newly built or rehabilitated units would pay 30 percent of household income toward rent, with the program paying the remainder of the rent. This guaranteed rent made it possible for developers to leverage the loans that they needed to fund the development.

Currently, the Section 8 certificate program lives on in the form of the HCV Program. The Section 8 New Construction and Substantial Rehabilitation Program survived for only about ten years. The Reagan administration effectively stopped the program by seeking no new funds for it. Thus in the early 1980s the nation was, for the first time since 1937, without a major housing production program that added units to the housing stock.

In 1986 Congress responded to this situation with the creation of the LIHTC Program as part of the Tax Reform Act, which instituted many changes to the federal income tax treatment of real estate investments, including housing. The LIHTC was a new tax credit, modeled on the historic rehabilitation tax credit. Investors would join in the ownership of housing built or rehabilitated for low-income rental occupancy. The investors would receive tax credits for ten years, so long as the property remained in low-income occupancy for at least fifteen years. The LIHTC Program differs from the Section 8 production program in a very important manner. Whereas the Section 8 Program sets rents at 30 percent of the eligible low-income tenant's income, the LIHTC program sets rents based upon what typical moderate-income households in the area can afford. As such, the LIHTC tends to serve the least worst off of the low-income renter population, while its predecessor, the Section 8 project-based program, served the poorest of the low-income renter population.

The Section 8 certificate program evolved into the HCV Program as the nation's major tenant-based approach to assisted rental housing, while the LIHTC replaced the Section 8 New Construction and Substantial Rehabilitation Program as the nation's major project-based approach. The HCV Program and the LIHTC remain today as the two principal strategies used by the federal government to serve the housing needs of the poor.

The 1990s brought a few more adjustments in the way the federal government implements its housing policies. The National Affordable Housing Act of 1990 instituted new, more rigorous, local planning requirements for communities making use of federal funds. The federal government commonly requires communities receiving federal funds to conduct various planning exercises. The 1990 act imposed an additional planning requirement. Each community was to prepare a Comprehensive Housing Affordability Strategy Plan, which replaced many of the individual plans required earlier. This plan, later renamed the Consolidated Plan, was straightforward. It called for communities to assess the supply and demand conditions in their respective local housing markets. This assessment directed communities to identify the form and scale of the mismatches between the supply of housing of various types and at various price levels and the demand for that housing across households of different income levels. After the community had identified mismatches through this assessment, it was to develop a multiyear strategy to address these mismatches using federal and other resources. In addition to this assessment of needs and development of strategies, the Consolidated Plan also requires that communities address a variety of other housing issues, including an analysis of any impediments to fair housing, an analysis of barriers to affordable housing, and an examination of the extent to which homes in the community pose threats based on lead-based paint.

The 1990 act also created the HOME Investment Partnerships Program, a new block grant program. Unlike the CDBG Program, which can be used for housing as well as community and economic development, HOME Program funds could only be used to address problems of housing affordability. With the adoption of the Consolidated Plan and the HOME Program, the federal government recognized that housing problems differ from one community to another and that each community can and should be responsible for identifying the type of problems that exist within its jurisdiction and for designing appropriate strategies to resolve these problems.

The 1990s also brought a change in the federal government's approach to public housing. Growing recognition of the problems with many severely distressed public housing projects led to a need for change. The HOPE VI Program was designed to address these problems. Local housing authorities were asked to prepare plans for redevelopment of their most distressed public housing projects and compete for HOPE VI funds to implement these plans, which were expected to include demolition of some or all public housing units and redevelopment of the sites with mixed-income housing at a lower density. The plans are also expected to reach beyond the individual public housing development and include community and supportive services to improve the conditions within the neighborhood. This approach has evolved into the Choice Neighborhoods Program, which addresses the same needs but can be applied more broadly than just to neighborhoods with the most distressed public housing (see chapters 7, 9, and 10).

A price bubble is a condition in which prices for a good rise faster than the underlying fundamental drivers of demand. In housing, this means that house prices rise much faster than household income. The first decade of the new millennium witnessed both a huge house price bubble and a huge growth in the supply of housing. House prices and rents were rising much faster than household incomes for most renters and owners (Roubini & Mihm, 2011). Housing units were being built much faster than the population could form new households. The house price bubble burst in 2007, putting many homeowners "underwater," meaning that their mortgage had an outstanding balance greater than the home's market value (McClure, 2013). The bubble never really burst in the rental market, as rents have continued to increase faster than the average household income of renters. After 2007, the production bubble slowed its expansion, but only a very imperfect housing recovery has occurred, as units continued to be added to the already bloated stock even after the price bubble burst in 2007 (McClure, 2013). The house price bubble and its collapse caused the federal government to respond in a variety of ways, including placing Fannie Mae and Freddie Mac in conservatorship, passing the ARRA, and initiating a variety of other programs to address defaults and foreclosures (see chapters 1, 7, 8, 15).

SCALE OF THE FEDERAL PROGRAMS

Federal Portfolio of Assisted Units

HUD struggles in its attempts to determine how many units it assists and where they are located. This is because HUD depends upon the reporting of the many different agencies and developers who work with it, and these reports often contain errors and incomplete information. These problems lead to both undercounting and overcounting in HUD's programs. Undercounting occurs because not every agency reports accurately. Overcounting results from adding the various programs together, causing an overlap in numbers. It is known that some households in the HCV Program reside in units assisted by the LIHTC Program, for example. This overlap is probably about 18 percent (Williamson, 2011). Thus, if 18 percent of all LIHTC units have voucher holders, the overcount could be as much as 360,000 units.

Table 14.2 shows how the portfolio of federally assisted housing has changed over time. The stock of public housing has contracted, as has the stock of Section 8 project-based housing. However, the HCV and the LIHTC Programs have expanded. The former is now over twice the size of

TABLE 14.2
Number of Federally Assisted Rental Housing Units by Program, 1997 and 2012

Program name	Number of housing units, 1997	Number of housing units, 2012	Change in number of housing units, 1997–2012
PROJECT-BASED PROGRAMS			
Publicly owned developments			
Public housing	1,321,717	1,156,839	−164,878
Privately owned developments			
Section 8 new const./sub. rehab	894,684	776,984	−117,700
Section 236	447,606	121,795	−325,811
Miscellaneous HUD multifamily	402,088	498,635	96,547
LIHTC	699,461	1,974,163	1,274,702
TOTAL PROJECT-BASED	3,765,556	4,528,416	762,860
TENANT-BASED PROGRAMS			
Housing choice voucher	1,433,191	2,339,198	906,007
TOTAL ASSISTED UNITS, ALL PROGRAMS	5,198,747	6,867,614	1,668,867

Source: U.S. Department of Housing and Urban Development, 2014g.

the public housing program portfolio, while the latter has become the nation's largest production program of rental units for eligible low-income households. These two programs reflect the advice of Downs (1990) that the federal government should help the poorest of the poor with voucher-style assistance and, to the extent that the government chooses to sponsor any production programs, it should target a higher income stratum in programs to leverage public investment through rents that tenants can afford to pay (see chapters 9 and 10).

Budget for Assisted Housing

The stock of assisted housing is 6.8 million units and growing, comprising about one in six of all rental units. This number seems like a very large supply of units. However, the American Community Survey (ACS) reports that in 2010, even with all of the assisted units in the supply, over 10.1 million renter households still paid more than 30 percent of their income for housing. This population of renters suffering from a high housing cost hardship indicates that there is a large unmet need, and sadly, the affordability problem is growing.

When housing is built, it tends to last a long time. Independent of the life span of a housing unit, contracts for assisted housing, which last for twenty, thirty, or even forty years, do come to an end. Budget authority is a commitment by the government to spend money over the life of the subsidy contract. A budget outlay is the annual expenditure on that contract, and spending in any one year may reflect past commitments. Thus if the stock of assisted housing is to meet the growing demand for affordable housing, new budget authority is needed (Schwartz, 2014). HUD, whose budget is about $40 billion, has found itself a victim of the sequestration process, which is a set of automatic budget cuts mandated by the Budget Control Act of 2011. The prospects for a significant increase in HUD's budget authority in order to address the large and growing need for additional affordable housing assistance seem dim at the current time (see chapters 9 and 10).

Nonbudget Programs

Some programs, such as the MID, do not show up in the federal budget. Such tax breaks amount to over $100 billion of deductions for tens of millions of homeowners, nearly all of whom are middle- and upper-income households (Glaeser & Shapiro, 2002). The U.S. Office of Management and Budget (OMB) (2005) estimates that for 2006 the MID cost the government about $76 billion, while that year the entire HUD discretionary budget was only $35 billion (U.S. Department of Housing and Urban Development, 2004). It is not entirely clear whether the federal government would experience an increase in revenues for the full amount if the tax breaks to homeowners were eliminated. Upper-income households would probably rearrange their finances to avoid paying taxes through other means, yielding less than the full value of these tax breaks (Poterba & Sinai, 2008). Even with that caveat, it is clear that more federal resources are expended on middle- and upper-income homeowners than on low-income households (see chapter 7).

The LIHTC Program is also a nonbudget program, given that it is funded through a tax break rather than a direct expenditure. This program is now the primary affordable housing production program, and it offers tax credits in two forms. The first form is a 9 percent credit, which is the standard credit allocated through a competitive process managed by state housing finance agencies. These 9 percent credits comprise about 60 percent of all tax credits allocated annually. The second form is a 4 percent credit utilized when the development is financed through the use of private-activity tax-exempt bonds. These 4 percent credits make up the remaining 40 percent of all the credits. As of this writing, there is a tax reform bill before the House of Representatives Ways and Means Committee that would end all private-activity bond financing and thus repeal all of the 4 percent credits. If passed, the reduction in credits could mean a dramatic reduction in the number of affordable rental units produced (see chapters 8, 9, 10, and 11).

GSEs

As of 2008, Fannie Mae and Freddie Mac owned or guaranteed about half of the nation's $12 trillion mortgage market (Duhigg, 2008). Even in conservatorship, they continue to back a considerable portion of all loan originations. Beekman Advisors (2013) reports the two entities purchasing over 60 percent of all single-family originations and just under 60 percent of multifamily originations in 2012. It is unclear what form these GSEs will take if and when reform takes shape. Any major changes in the GSEs could influence the availability, pricing, and terms of the home mortgage loans that home buyers will be able to leverage (see chapter 8).

CONCLUSION

Housing market conditions nationwide suggest that the dual strategy of supporting both a tenant-based voucher program and a project-based production program will remain the preferred approach for federal assistance in providing affordable housing. Some local housing markets suffer from tight market conditions, making project-based programs necessary; other markets are soft, making tenant-based programs the more cost-effective solution. However, the nation is generally facing a condition that favors an expanded use of voucher programs and a reduced use of production programs. While there is a shortage of affordable housing in most markets, there is—at the same time—a surplus of housing units in the moderate price categories. Thus it makes little sense to add units to a stock of housing that is already bloated. However, it does make sense to help eligible low-income households consume the stock of housing that already exists, and this is what vouchers do well.

Research shows that vouchers are less expensive per household served compared to project-based programs (Deng, 2005). Generally, this cost savings means that the federal government can help a larger number of low-income households consume existing housing for the same level of expenditure that building and operating units for their occupancy would require. Given the cost-effectiveness of vouchers and the surpluses of housing found in so many of the nation's markets, the future of project-based rental housing is uncertain.

Changes in the portfolio of assisted housing suggest that the era of public housing is slowly drawing to a close. The portfolio of public housing has contracted and will probably continue to do so. Across all public housing, the estimated capital needs to return the units to good condition total about $26 billion (Abt Associates, 2010). It is unlikely that the federal government will want to spend this amount of money to replenish this aging stock. It is more likely that the federal government will follow the path of the HOPE VI and Choice Neighborhoods Programs in the future, replacing older, high-density projects occupied entirely by eligible low-income households with new, lower-density, mixed-income developments. The mixed-income developments will probably have mixed public and private, shared ownership as well.

The LIHTC remains the government's favored production program. Although it may not continue to produce units at the same pace in the future, it is very likely to remain an important tool in the progression toward the use of mixed-income developments.

The HCV Program will probably be the primary affordable housing program of the future, but it too will probably see a change in focus. For this tenant-based housing program, the federal government is looking to do more than make housing affordable. The government wants to provide housing assistance so that renters can live in neighborhoods free of any fear of crime and be able to gain access to good schools and gainful employment. At the same time, the federal government hopes to deconcentrate poverty and promote racial and ethnic integration. We can expect to see increasing initiatives in which the HCV Program calls for PHAs to do more than provide affordable shelter. The PHAs will be expected to guide HCV households away from high-poverty, racially and ethnically concentrated neighborhoods and toward high-opportunity, economically, racially, and ethnically integrated neighborhoods (see chapters 9 and 10).

The future of federal housing policy in mortgage finance is very uncertain. The GSEs may be fully privatized with little or no federal governmental oversight. They may serve a much smaller role in guaranteeing the flow of mortgage credit in the future. The cost and availability of mortgage loans may change as a result, especially for low- or moderate-income home buyers (Carr & Anacker, 2014; see chapters 7, 8, and 15).

Federal housing policy has changed its emphasis over time. It has moved from augmenting the supply of units to augmenting the buying power of households. The programs have shifted from resolving a shortage of units to resolving the ability of households to afford units in the marketplace. It is easy to project more of the same for the future, but the politics of austerity suggest that a retreat by the federal government from the area of housing may be in store. The participation of philanthropic and nonprofit organizations may rise, at least partially, to replace decreased or lost federal resources. The federal programs will exist, but their funding is threatened. Sequestration means fewer dollars for these housing programs, and a sluggish economy offers little hope for any significant change in the total federal resources allocated to housing. The need is expanding, but the federal commitment is not.

REFERENCES

Abt Associates, Inc. (2010). *Capital needs in the Public Housing Program.* Prepared for the U.S. Department of Housing and Urban Development. Accessed at http://portal.hud.gov/hudportal/documents/huddoc?id=PH_Capital_Needs.pdf.

American Enterprise Institute. (2014). *The government mortgage complex.* Accessed at http://www.aei.org/module/1/the-government-mortgage-complex.

Beekman Advisors. (2013). *The new housing finance system: Are we there yet?* The Federal Reserve Bank of Cleveland 2013 Policy Summit, September 19, 2013. Accessed at http://www.clevelandfed.org/community_development/events/ps2013/pres_opening_narasimhan_ballroom.pdf.

Been, V., & Ellen, I. G. (2012). *Challenges facing housing markets in the next decade: Developing a policy-relevant research agenda.* Washington, D.C.: Urban Institute. Accessed at http://www.urban.org/publications/412556.html.

Carliner, M. S. (1998). Development of federal homeownership "policy." *Housing Policy Debate, 9*(2), 229–321.

Carr, J. H., & K. B. Anacker (2014). The past and current politics of housing finance and the future of Fannie Mae, Freddie Mac, and homeownership in the United States. *Banking and Financial Services Policy Report, 33*(7), 1–10.

Comptroller General of the United States. (1978). *Section 236 rental housing: An evaluation with lessons for the future.* Report to Congress PAD-78-13. Washington, D.C.: Office of the Comptroller General of the United States.

Deng, L. (2005). The cost-effectiveness of the low-income housing tax credit relative to vouchers: Evidence from six metropolitan areas. *Housing Policy Debate, 16*(3/4), 469–511.

Downs, A. (1990). A strategy for designing a fully comprehensive national housing policy for the federal government of the United States. In D. Dipasquale & L. Keyes (Eds.), *Building foundations* (pp. 61–112). Philadelphia: University of Pennsylvania Press.

Downs, A. (2003). *Growth management, smart growth and affordable housing.* Washington, D.C.: Brookings Institution.

Duhigg, C. (2008, July 11). Loan-agency woes swell from a trickle to a torrent. *New York Times.* Retrieved August 24, 2017, from http://www.nytimes.com/2008/07/11/business/11ripple.html?ex=1373515200&en=8ad220403fcfdf6e&ei=5124&partner=permalink&exprod=permalink.

Erickson, D. J. (2009). *The housing policy revolution: Networks and neighborhoods.* Washington, D.C.: Urban Institute Press.

Galster, G. C. (1997). Comparing demand-side and supply-side housing policies: Sub-market and spatial perspectives. *Housing Studies, 12*(4), 561–577.

Glaeser, E. L., & Shapiro, J. M. (2002). *The benefits of the home Mortgage Interest Deduction.* (Working Paper 9284). Cambridge, Mass.: National Bureau of Economic Research.

Goetz, E. G. (2013). *New Deal ruins: Race, economic justice, and public housing policy.* Ithaca, N.Y.: Cornell University Press.

Greulich, E., & Quigley, J. M. (2009). Housing subsidies and tax expenditures: The case of mortgage credit certificates. *Regional Science and Urban Economics, 39*(6), 647–657.

Housing Act of 1949, Public Law 81-171 (1949).

Husock, H. (2009). *Public housing and rental subsidies: Downsizing the federal government*. Washington, D.C.: Cato Institute. http://www.downsizinggovernment.org/hud/public-housing-rental-subsidies.

Katz, B., Turner, M. A., Brown, K. D., Cunningham, M., & Sawyer, N. (2003). *Rethinking local affordable housing strategies: Lessons from 70 years of policy and practice*. Washington, D.C.: Brookings Institution Center on Urban and Metropolitan Policy and the Urban Institute.

Landis, J., & McClure, K. (2010). Rethinking federal housing policy. *Journal of the American Planning Association, 76*(3), 319–348.

Leamer, E. E. (2007). *Housing IS the business cycle*. (Working Paper 13428). Cambridge, Mass.: National Bureau of Economic Research.

McClure, K. (1989). A research note on the capitalization of mortgage revenue bond benefits. *National Tax Journal, 42*(1), 85–88.

McClure, K. (2000). The low-income housing tax credit as an aid to housing finance: How well has it worked? *Housing Policy Debate, 11*(1), 91–114.

McClure, K. (2005). Rent burden in the Housing Choice Voucher Program. *Cityscape, 8*(2), 5–20.

McClure, K. (2006). The low-income housing tax credit program goes mainstream and moves to the suburbs. *Housing Policy Debate, 17*(3), 419–446.

McClure, K. (2013). *The American housing bubble: Lessons for planners*. Paper presented at the Joint Conference of the Association of Collegiate Schools of Planning and the Association of European Schools of Planning.

Mitchell, J. P. (1985). *Federal housing policy & programs: Past and present*. New Brunswick, N.J.: Center for Urban Policy Research, Rutgers University.

Newman, S. J., & Schnare, Ann B. (1997). "And a suitable living environment": The failure of housing programs to deliver on neighborhood quality. *Housing Policy Debate, 8*(4), 703–741.

Orlebeke, C. J., & Weicher, J. C. (2014). How CDBG came to pass. *Housing Policy Debate, 24*(1), 14–45.

Pennington-Cross, A., & Yezer, A. M. (2000). The Federal Housing Administration in the new millennium. *Journal of Housing Research, 11*(2), 357–372.

Popkin, S. J., Katz, B., Cunningham, M. K., Brown, K. D., Gustafson, J., & Turner, M. A. (2004). *A decade of HOPE VI: Research findings and policy challenges*. Washington, D.C.: Urban Institute.

Poterba, J., & Sinai, T. (2008). Tax expenditures for owner-occupied housing: Deductions for property taxes and mortgage interest and exclusion of imputed rental income. *American Economic Review, 98*(2), 84–99.

Puzzangher, J. (2013, September 28). FHA to get $1.7 billion in its first taxpayer-funded bailout. *Los Angeles Times*.

Rich, M. J. (2014). Community Development Block Grants at 40: Time for makeover. *Housing Policy Debate, 24*(1), 3–13.

Rohe, W. M., & Galster, G. C. (2014). The Community Development Block Grant Program turns 40: Proposal for program expansion and reform. *Housing Policy Debate, 24*(1), 3–13.

Roubini, N., & Mihm, S. (2011). *Crisis economics: A crash course in the future of finance*. New York: Penguin.

Schwartz, A. F. (2014). *Housing policy in the United States*. New York: Routledge.

Shriver, S. (2013). Strategies for defending foreclosures of FHA-insured mortgages. *Clearinghouse Review: Journal of Poverty Law and Policy, 46*, rev. 484.

Silverman, R. M. (2011). Fair housing in the U.S. real estate industry: Perceptions of black real estate professionals. In R. N. Silverman & K. L. Patterson (Eds.), *Fair and affordable housing in the U.S.: Trends, outcomes, future directions* (pp. 67–88). Leiden, Netherlands: Brill.

Stanton, Thomas H. (2012). Government-sponsored enterprises. In A. T. Carswell (Ed.), *The encyclopedia of housing* (pp. 245–250). Los Angeles: Sage.

Tighe, J. R. (2011). Barriers to fair housing policy implementation: Finance, regulation, and public opinion. In R. M. Silverman & K. L. Patterson (Eds.), *Fair and affordable housing in the U.S.: Trends, outcomes, future directions* (pp. 91–123). Leiden, Netherlands: Brill.

Truman, Harry S. (1949, July 15). Statement by the president upon signing the Housing Act of 1949. In G. Peters and J. T. Woolley (Eds.), *The American presidency project*. Retrieved August 24, 2017, from http://www.presidency.ucsb.edu/ws/?pid=13246.

Turner, M. A. (1998). Moving out of poverty: Expanding mobility and choice through tenant-based housing assistance. *Housing Policy Debate, 9*(2), 373–394.

U.S. Bureau of the Census. (2014). American FactFinder. 2012 American Community Survey 1-year estimates.

U.S. Department of Housing and Urban Development. (2004). *HUD's FY 2005 budget*. Retrieved August 24, 2017, from http://archives.hud.gov/budget/fy05/index.cfm.

U.S. Department of Housing and Urban Development. (2014a). *Affirmatively furthering fair housing proposed rule*. Retrieved August 24, 2017, from http://www.huduser.org/portal/affht_pt.html.

U.S. Department of Housing and Urban Development. (2014b). *Fair housing—It's your right*. Retrieved August 24, 2017, from http://portal.hud.gov/hudportal/HUD?src=/program_offices/fair_housing_equal_opp/FHLaws/yourrights.

U.S. Department of Housing and Urban Development. (2014c). *HOME investment partnership program*. Retrieved August 24, 2017, from http://portal.hud.gov/hudportal/HUD?src=/program_offices/comm_planning/affordablehousing/programs/home/.

U.S. Department of Housing and Urban Development. (2014d). *Housing and supportive services for people with special needs and the homeless*. Retrieved August 24, 2017, from http://www.huduser.org/portal/taxonomy/term/38.

U.S. Department of Housing and Urban Development. (2014e). *Housing Choice Voucher-related PIH notices*. Retrieved August 24, 2017, from http://portal.hud.gov/hudportal/HUD?src=/program_offices/public_indian_housing/programs/hcv/forms/notices.

U.S. Department of Housing and Urban Development. (2014f). *HUD implementation of the Recovery Act*. Retrieved August 24, 2017, from http://portal.hud.gov/hudportal/HUD?src=/recovery/about.

U.S. Department of Housing and Urban Development (2014g). *Picture of subsidized households*. Retrieved August 24, 2017, from http://www.huduser.org/portal/datasets/assthsg.html.

U.S. Department of Housing and Urban Development. (2014h). *Project-based vouchers*. Retrieved August 24, 2017, from http://portal.hud.gov/hudportal/HUD?src=/program_offices/public_indian_housing/programs/hcv/project.

U.S. Department of Housing and Urban Development. (2014i). *Timeline 1930 to 2010*. Retrieved August 24, 2017, from http://archives.huduser.org/about/hud_timeline/index.html.

U.S. Office of Management and Budget. (2005). *Analytical perspectives: Budget of the United States government*. Washington, D.C.: U.S. Government Printing Office.

Wallace, J. E. (2000). Financing affordable housing in the United States. *Housing Policy Debate, 6*(4), 785–814.

Weiss, M. A. (1980). The origins and legacy of urban renewal. In J. P. Mitchell (Ed.), *Federal housing policy & programs: Past and present* (pp. 253–285). New Brunswick, N.J.: Center for Urban Policy Research, Rutgers University.

Williamson, A. R. (2011). Can they afford the rent? Resident cost burden in low-income housing tax credit developments. *Urban Affairs Review, 47*(6), 775–799.

Winnick, L. (1995). The triumph of housing allowance programs: How a fundamental policy conflict was resolved. *Cityscape, 1*(3), 95–121.

Chapter 15 The Great Recession

KATRIN B. ANACKER

For the past several decades the United States has been characterized by long-term economic and social changes, such as the loss of blue-collar jobs that paid well and came with good benefits and the creation of new jobs in the service industry that are characterized by low or stagnant wages with few or no benefits (Bartlett & Steele, 2012). The reasons for these developments are globalization and offshoring, automation, the dearth of public and private investment in infrastructure and in new productive facilities, the dramatic decline in worker unionization, the reduction in the progressiveness of the tax code, and the "Great Risk Shift," in which governments and corporations have shifted economic risk to households (Hacker, 2008; Krueger, 2012).

In the most recent recession, from December 2007 to June 2009, also called the Great Recession, gross domestic product (GDP) began to fall in the fourth quarter of 2007, the unemployment rate began to increase in January 2008, and both factors deteriorated greatly in the third quarter of 2008 (Zandi, 2012b). While the economy began to improve gradually in the third quarter of 2009, the unemployment rate continued to increase through December 2009 (Zandi, 2012b). The unemployment rate decreased to 6.7 percent by November 2013, but it had not reached precrisis levels as of this writing (Bureau of Labor Statistics, n.d.; Shierholz, 2014). These occurrences combined greatly affected the housing market (see chapter 1).

Recessions are defined as a "significant decline in economic activity spread across the economy, lasting more than a few months, normally visible in production, employment, real income, and other indicators" (National Bureau of Economic Research, n.d., n.p.). They have been triggered by many factors, including interest rates, the behavior of oil prices, or the unemployment rate (Labonte, 2010; Lewis, 2014; Zandi, 2012b). The Great Recession was somewhat unique, as it was primarily triggered by housing-related factors that have been in place for years, if not decades.

Apart from the increase and decrease in the unemployment rate and the increase in underemployment rates during and after the Great Recession, the United States has also witnessed an increase in other indicators of economic ill-being, including increased Supplemental Nutrition Assistance

Program (SNAP) participation rates (U.S. Department of Agriculture, n.d.), relatively low household formation rates (Paciorek, 2013), low housing construction rates (U.S. Bureau of the Census, n.d.), and low mortgage origination rates combined with high mortgage refinance rates (Carr, Anacker, & Hernandez, 2013), among other factors. At the household level, the Great Recession has impacted credit scores (Bovino, 2014; Brevoort & Cooper, 2013; Molloy & Shan, 2013) and assets (Bricker, Kennickell, Moore, & Sabelhaus, 2012), including property values (Shiller, 2012) and retirement account balances (Butrica, 2013; see chapters 1, 2, 7, 8, 9, 10, and 17). It might take the United States decades, and possibly more than an entire generation, to reach a point where well-being is restored, opportunities are plentiful, and wealth-building potential is again within reach.

This chapter takes a look at the Great Recession through the housing lens with a special focus on homeownership. Despite the Great Recession and its impacts on homeownership, the United States is still a country of homeowners, given its relatively high homeownership rate. The sections below are about homeownership and housing policy in the United States, followed by a discussion about the national foreclosure crisis, the national (housing) policy response to the Great Recession and the national foreclosure crisis, and the road ahead in terms of homeownership.

HOMEOWNERSHIP AND HOUSING POLICY IN THE UNITED STATES

Homeownership has been deemed important in the United States because many consider it an indicator of middle-class status and good citizenship for individuals and an indicator of economic and social stability of neighborhoods due to the historical importance of the ownership of land and the fact that at the nation's founding only landowners could vote (Quercia, Freeman, & Ratcliffe, 2011). Thus homeownership has become a central component of the American Dream, encouraged and supported by public policy, real estate interest groups, and the housing finance industry (Rohe, 2012; see chapters 7 and 8).

The outcomes of homeownership for both individuals and society have been discussed for many years. Some aspects of these outcomes that have been analyzed include household mobility; labor force behavior; housing maintenance and property improvements; urban form, environment, and segregation; local political, social, and crime activity; child and teenage outcomes; residents' health; and the elderly, although selection bias and data issues have been acknowledged (Dietz & Haurin, 2003; see chapters 1, 2, 7, 8, 9, 10, 17, and 18).

At the societal level, homeownership may result in the stimulation of commodity, job, and financial markets. For example, constructing, repairing, and furnishing a home require the purchase of building materials, tools, and durable goods, such as furniture and appliances. Housing generates jobs in construction, manufacturing, professional services, and other sectors. Mortgage lending and secondary market activity constitute a large proportion of domestic and international financial markets, as witnessed in the foreclosure crisis (Financial Crisis Inquiry Commission, 2011). Homeowners tend to take better care of their properties than landlords and are more likely to participate in elections and voluntary organizations, as they have an economic and emotional stake in their community. Homeowners also typically stay longer in their homes than renters, contributing to neighborhood stability (Rohe, 2012). As the Great Recession has shown, homeownership may also negatively impact commodity, job, and financial markets and mortgage lending and may negatively impact domestic and international financial markets. Vacant and foreclosed homes may negatively impact adjacent property values and neighborhood stability and security (Immergluck, 2009; see chapter 7).

U.S. housing policy has consistently favored homeownership over rental housing. Recent estimates suggest that the federal government provides six dollars in support of homeownership for every one dollar in support of rental housing (Rohe, 2012). While some housing policies were unintended and indirect, many later policies were intended and direct. In regard to the former, the United States has allowed the deduction of interest since 1913, including interest on mortgages. As the homeownership rate was relatively low in the 1910s and 1920s, not many taxpayers took advantage of this deduction (Dolbeare, 1998). This changed in the 1950s, however, when homeownership rates increased rapidly and taxpayers who itemized their business-related expenses began to take advantage of this deduction (Lewis, 2014). The Office of Management and Budget (OMB) projects the Mortgage Interest Deduction (MID) to be the second-largest of all tax expenditures of the federal government for the 2012 to 2016 fiscal years (FYs) (Wandling, 2012). In FY 2013 the MID totaled about $70 billion (Toder, 2013). While some have considered the MID to be a homeownership policy, others argue that it favors those homeowners who itemize their expenses, those with higher household incomes, and those with larger mortgages (Wandling, 2012). As of this writing, the MID is being reconsidered, and several alternatives have been suggested (Harris, Steuerle, & Eng, 2013, among others; see chapters 7 and 14).

Government involvement in intended and direct housing policies started during the Great Depression, when the United States faced a housing crisis; both housing production and demand for housing had been somewhat low since the late 1920s. The Great Depression had a severe negative impact on the housing finance and home-building industries, among other actors. President Franklin D. Roosevelt's New Deal instituted several domestic economic stimulus programs, including housing programs, in the early to late 1930s.

First, in 1932 President Hoover signed the Federal Home Loan Bank Act, which led to the creation of the Federal Home Loan Bank (FHLB) system. This action was triggered by massive mortgage defaults and foreclosures that led to bankruptcies of many borrowers as well as bankruptcies of many saving and loan (S&L) institutions after the stock market crash in 1929. Modeled after the Federal Reserve System, the FHLB system had twelve regional banks that would supervise member institutions that purchased stock in their respective FHLB (Federal Home Loan Banks, n.d.; Keating, 1998). For the past eight decades FHLBs have supplied credit to local and regional lending institutions to finance housing and economic development in their communities, although they are not dependent on taxpayers (Federal Home Loan Banks, n.d.; Stanton, 2012).

In 1933 President Roosevelt increased the federal role in the housing finance market by establishing the Home Owners' Loan Corporation (HOLC) to issue $2 billion in government-backed long-term federal bonds to refinance short-term mortgages in default or in foreclosure and to fund the purchase of nonperforming loans. Mortgages in default were converted into fifteen-year loans with lower monthly payments due to long-term repayment schedules and lower interest rates, preventing borrowers from losing their homes. These actions stabilized local housing markets and improved the viability of lenders (Immergluck, 2009; Metzger, 1998; Shiller, 2008). By the time is was liquidated in 1954, HOLC had refinanced 1.8 million delinquent mortgages (Keating, 1998).

In 1934 President Roosevelt established the Federal Housing Administration (FHA), primarily to stimulate the residential lending and home-building industries in the short term and to improve housing in the long term. Prior to the creation of the FHA, down payment requirements were large, repayment schedules were short, and balloon payments at the end of the life cycle of a mortgage were large. Thus homeownership had been unaffordable for many until the FHA was established (Immergluck, 2009).

In 1965 the FHA was subsumed under the U.S. Department of Housing and Urban Development when that department was established. As the largest mortgage insurer in the world, the FHA provides insurance products for single-family and multifamily homes, manufactured homes, and hospitals, operating entirely from self-generated income (Steggell, 2012). Since 1934 the FHA has insured more than forty million mortgages, making the United States a nation of homeowners after World War II (Galante, 2013c; Steggell, 2012).

FHA-insured mortgages currently require a down payment of 3.5 percent (previously 3 percent), a repayment period of thirty years (up from twenty years in the 1950s), and full amortization (Shiller, 2008). The FHA does not originate mortgages but insures them against borrower default for premiums that are ultimately paid by the borrower, benefiting approved lenders, subject to minimum property standards and maximum mortgage limits. FHA insurance reduces risk, which translates into lower mortgage interest rates that in turn translate into increased borrowing (Steggell, 2012).

The FHA's market share increased to a peak of 21.1 percent in 2010 from 3.1 percent of loan originations in 2005 (Galante, 2013a). As of the third quarter of 2013, the FHA's market share was 12.2 percent for all loans, including purchase and refinance loans (U.S. Department of Housing and Urban Development, 2013). This relatively low market share was due to a decrease in the overall size of the mortgage market rather than to exceptionally high FHA loan volumes (Galante, 2013a).

Early on the FHA was criticized for refusing to insure mortgages in neighborhoods that had a moderate or high proportion of borrowers of color, partially contributing to residential racial, ethnic, and economic segregation. However, this practice changed with passage of the Fair Housing Act in 1968. Currently the FHA offers insurance for mortgages to those who have been excluded from the private conventional mortgage market, including first-time home buyers. Seventy-eight percent of home-purchase loans insured by the FHA went to first-time home buyers (Galante, 2013a, 2013b, 2013c).

In 1938 President Roosevelt established the Federal National Mortgage Association, or Fannie Mae, to encourage the flow of credit to residential housing and financial institutions. In 1968 Fannie Mae was privatized (i.e., shifted to ownership by stockholders), although the federal government continued to support Fannie Mae by implicitly backing its borrowings, and the Federal Reserve allowed Fannie Mae to take advantage of the discount window (i.e., lower interest rates). In 1970 Congress established the Federal Home Loan Mortgage Corporation, or Freddie Mac. Both Fannie Mae and Freddie Mac supported the secondary mortgage market through purchasing, bundling, insuring, and selling residential mortgages, standardizing mortgage documentation, and creating a more integrated national mortgage market. Liquidity of the mortgage market increased over time, which fueled the market but at the same time indicated vulnerability when toxic products increasingly entered the system, despite risk diversification (Pozen, 2010).

Another unintended and indirect housing policy was the Servicemen's Readjustment Act of 1944, also called the GI Bill of Rights, introduced by President Roosevelt. This bill provided unemployment benefits, job training and placement benefits, subsidized or even free college tuition, and low-interest, zero down payment mortgages for homes or businesses (McKenna, 2008). The GI Bill subsidized home purchases for seventeen million people (Shiller, 2005). From 1945 to 1956 Veterans Administration (VA) mortgages accounted for 35 percent of net new mortgage flows, compared to 14 percent through the FHA (Immergluck, 2009).

In sum, these policies, the economic boom times of the 1950s and 1960s, and other factors caused the national homeownership rate to increase from 43.6 percent in 1940, to 55 percent in 1950, to 61.9 percent in 1960, to 62.9 percent in 1970, and then to 64.4 percent in 1980 (U.S. Bureau of the Census, n.d.; see also chapters 8 and 14).

THE NATIONAL FORECLOSURE CRISIS

Foreclosure is a "situation in which a homeowner is unable to make full principal and interest payments on his or her mortgage" (investopedia, n.d., n.p.). After ninety days, the lender seizes the property, evicts the homeowner, and eventually sells the home, based on the mortgage contract. Until recently foreclosures were a rare occurrence. National foreclosure rates on conventional mortgages were about 0.3 to 0.4 percent in the early 1980s and around 1 percent in the remainder of that decade. They exceeded 1.1 percent in the late 1990s and reached 1.3 percent in late 2003, although there were regional exceptions (Li & Morrow-Jones, 2010). In the following years, national foreclosure rates increased partially due to high-risk mortgage lending, especially the use of subprime mortgages (Engel & McCoy, 2011; Financial Crisis Inquiry Commission, 2011; Immergluck, 2012). In 2010, the year with the highest proportion of foreclosures, 2.23 percent of housing units received at least one foreclosure filing; in 2012, 1.39 percent of units did; and in 2013, 1.04 percent of units received at least one filing (RealtyTrac, 2014; see chapter 8). Figure 15.1 shows the number of foreclosure starts and completions in the United States from 2008 to 2015.

The most recent foreclosure crisis was caused by the burst of a house price bubble that had been ongoing from 2000 to 2006 (Glaeser, Gyourko, & Saiz, 2008). House price bubbles and crashes, especially regional and local ones, have continued to appear in the United States (Shiller, 2005, 2008, 2012). In economic terms, a bubble is "a situation in which the market prices of certain assets (such as stocks or real estate) rise far above the present value of the anticipated cash flow from the asset" (Smith & Smith, 2006: 3). In this

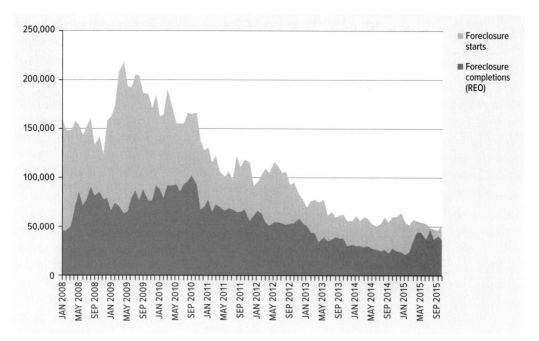

FIGURE 15.1
Number of Foreclosure Starts and Completions in the United States, 2008–15
Source: RealtyTrac, n.d. Reprinted with permission.

case, the market price of housing rose far above its actual value. When the bubble burst, homes were worth far less than what had been paid for them. Most recently, between mid-2006 and March 2012 national house prices fell by 35 percent, although there has been much variation (Bovino, 2014; see chapter 7).

Long-Term Factors Driving the National Foreclosure Crisis

The national foreclosure crisis that led to the Great Recession was partially fueled by the lending boom that occurred in the late 1990s and the early to mid-2000s. This lending boom occurred due to regulation, policy, and market factors.

From the early 1980s up to the late 2000s, regulation benefited lenders and thus increased lending volume. Before the 1980s, mortgage applicants, based on then-current mortgage underwriting practices and standards, either qualified for a mortgage or did not. The mortgage could be a conventional, an FHA, or a VA mortgage (Schwartz, 2010). In 1980 the Depository Institutions Deregulation and Monetary Control Act gave banks the flexibility to set rates and fees for mortgages, and the 1982 Alternative Mortgage Transaction Parity Act allowed banks to make variable-rate mortgages and mortgages with balloon payments (Ludwig, Kamihachi, & Toh, 2009). Thus in the mid-1980s lenders introduced risk-based pricing (i.e., in exchange for higher risk of predicted default, borrowers would pay higher interest rates and fees). These subprime, adjustable-rate, or high-cost mortgages would become common in the 1990s and 2000s (Financial Crisis Inquiry Commission, 2011). In 1999 North Carolina tried to curb high-cost mortgages through the North Carolina Predatory Lending Law, Senate Bill 1149 (General Assembly of North Carolina, 1999), but this and other state laws were superseded in February 2004 when the Office of the Comptroller of the Currency (OCC) officially preempted all state laws regulating the lending practices of national banks and their subsidiaries, stating that national institutions should be subject only to federal law (Engel & McCoy, 2011; Immergluck, 2009). In 1999 the Gramm-Leach-Bliley Act, also known as the Financial Services Modernization Act, allowed commercial banks, investment banks, securities firms, and insurance companies to consolidate, removing barriers among them and allowing them to become "too big to fail" (Financial Crisis Inquiry Commission, 2011). These developments fostered the increase of innovative mortgage products, some of which would become toxic, while the stringency of underwriting standards of some lenders decreased (Immergluck, 2009).

Policy factors also fueled the lending boom, driven by a push for homeownership for multiple reasons. For example, emphasis increased on owning for the sake of owning and to show patriotism post-9/11, exemplified by President George W. Bush's Ownership Society label (Engel & McCoy, 2011). Another reason was rising income and wealth inequality, exemplified on the low end by stagnant or decreasing real incomes and increasing job insecurity (Rajan, 2010). Another policy factor that fueled the lending boom was the very low interest rates set by the U.S. Federal Reserve in the 2000s (Zandi, 2012b).

Among market factors, rating agencies such as Standard & Poor's, Moody's Investor Service, and Fitch Ratings continued to issue stellar ratings for mortgage-backed securities that were of much lower quality than they were rated and that would ultimately crash (Engel & McCoy, 2011; Immergluck, 2009; Lewis, 2014; Pozen, 2010; Prins, 2009). Also, mortgage securitization was practiced not only by the government-sponsored enterprises (GSEs) but also by Wall Street, facilitating the increase in mortgage lending (see chapters 8 and 14).

Short-Term Factors Driving the National Foreclosure Crisis

The Great Recession was primarily triggered by the national foreclosure crisis, although many other contributing factors had been in place for years. Foreclosures occur when homeowners are forced to stop making payments on their mortgages for multiple reasons. In the foreclosure crisis of the mid-2000s these reasons included, first, unplanned personal emergencies, such as medical expenses, divorce, or the death of a spouse or relative, among others (Brevoort & Cooper, 2013); second, the expense of adjustable-rate mortgages (ARMs) or subprime mortgages in the context of the bursting of the house price bubble (Financial Crisis Inquiry Commission, 2011); third, unplanned professional emergencies, such as a reduced paycheck or the loss of a job (Warren & Tyagi, 2005); and fourth, underwater status and strategic default (Brevoort & Cooper, 2013).

The first category, unplanned personal emergencies, has triggered foreclosures since the beginning of the use of mortgages, although during the recent crisis the passage of the Affordable Care Act (ACA) might have reduced the number of people forced into foreclosure due to medical expenses (Warren & Tyagi, 2005).

The second and third categories, toxic products in times of the bursting house price bubble and unplanned professional emergencies, have primarily triggered foreclosures during the Great Recession and beyond. Whereas many foreclosures in 2007 and 2008 were triggered by resetting mortgage interest rates for ARMs, in 2008 and 2009 many were triggered by employment-related financial difficulties as the economy deteriorated (Financial Crisis Inquiry Commission, 2011; Zandi, 2012a). Both types of triggers were caused by the bursting of the house price bubble, although Shiller points to unrealistic public expectations of future price increases and especially the social contagion of boom thinking (Shiller, 2005, 2008, 2012).

The national house price bubble burst in early 2006, when the supply of new homes began to outstrip demand (Roubini & Mihm, 2011). The growing housing oversupply led to a slowdown of the national house price increase and the ultimate collapse of house prices beginning in April 2006 (CoreLogic 2013), which in turn prevented borrowers with subprime mortgages from refinancing their loans when their rates reset upward in late 2006 and early 2007 (Engel & McCoy, 2011; Financial Crisis Inquiry Commission, 2011; Immergluck, 2009; Schwartz 2012), resulting in the national foreclosure crisis.

The fourth category, underwater status (negative home equity) and strategic default (a decision by the borrower to stop making mortgage payments by choice, not necessity), has been analyzed through quantitative and qualitative methods (Foote, Gerardi, & Willen, 2008). The overall projected proportion of homeowners with negative home equity is estimated to be 16.6 percent (Wolff, 2010). This proportion not only indicates that borrowers purchased properties in metropolitan areas and neighborhoods that disproportionately lost value due to the foreclosure crisis but also could indicate that some home values might have been inflated upon origination, which is corroborated by the literature (National Association of Home Builders, 2012; see chapter 8).

Consequences of the National Foreclosure Crisis

The total equity lost by households with recently foreclosed properties is estimated at more than $7 trillion (Raskin, 2012). In addition, as of 2009, an estimated $502 billion in property value has been lost due to nearby foreclosures (Center for Responsible Lending, n.d., based on CRL, Credit Suisse, Moody's Economics.com, MBA). The decrease in property values has affected not only households themselves but also adjacent properties and entire neighborhoods, with losses ranging from about $10,000 in Minneapolis–St. Paul (Moreno, 1998) to about $159,000 in Cook County, Illinois (Campbell, Giglio, & Pathak, 2011; Immergluck & Smith, 2006; see chapter 7).

Homeowners who are foreclosed upon not only lose their home but might be on a path to unstable housing in the future. Their credit ratings decrease, making it difficult or impossible for them to purchase or rent another home (Brevoort & Cooper, 2013; Molloy & Shan, 2013). Many have used up their financial reserves during the foreclosure process, making it difficult to provide down payments or deposits. Some renters whose landlords are foreclosed upon may be forced to move in with family or friends or to live in their cars; only a few stay in homeless shelters (Pettit & Comey, 2012). Many foreclosed homeowners seem to remain in their neighborhood, but they do not move to less desirable neighborhoods or more crowded living conditions, instead preferring to rent in the neighborhood in which they previously owned (Molloy & Shan, 2013). In addition to these issues, people who go through foreclosure, regardless of their tenure status, may also suffer socially, emotionally, and psychologically, especially those with children (Been, Ellen, Schwartz, Stiefel, & Weinstein, 2011; see chapters 7 and 8).

Many neighborhoods have been negatively impacted by the national foreclosure crisis through vacant, boarded-up, or abandoned housing, which might invite criminal activities. Municipalities have faced increased policing costs due to vandalism and other crimes; increased firefighting costs due to arson; demolition costs; costs for removing trash, mowing lawns, and clearing snow, as many mortgage holders, including banks, do not conduct these maintenance activities; record-keeping costs during the foreclosure process; and decreasing tax revenues as some owners or borrowers stop paying taxes and as property values decrease (Immergluck, 2009, 2012a). Thus some cities, such as Richmond, California, have considered the use of eminent domain to seize abandoned properties (Schafran & Feldstein, 2013; see chapters 7, 8, 12, and 13).

The Great Recession also caused a breakdown of financial markets for asset-backed securities, commercial paper, and interbank lending and the failure of several large, established financial firms that, in some cases, the government was unwilling to rescue (Labonte, 2010). Since 2007 the proportion of mortgages originated through private mortgage lending has declined, while the proportion of mortgages securitized and insured through the GSEs and the FHA has increased (Engel & McCoy, 2011; see chapter 8).

THE NATIONAL (HOUSING) POLICY RESPONSE TO THE GREAT RECESSION AND THE FORECLOSURE CRISIS

After the start of the national foreclosure crisis in early 2007, the financial system and the broader economy started to decline, although the stock market continued to rally for a few months, as indicated by its peak in October 2007 (Zandi, 2012a). During the first months of the Great Recession, many economists and some policy makers and government officials argued that the housing market should be allowed to work itself out of its crisis and that the government should not intervene (Jackson, 2007). Over time, however, many realized that the Great Recession was more severe than previously assumed (Zandi, 2012a). For example, hundreds of banks and mortgage lenders went bankrupt, among them Countrywide Financial, Bear Stearns Companies, Lehman Brothers Holding, Merrill Lynch, Washington Mutual, Wachovia, Citigroup, and American International Group (Barofsky, 2012; Engel & McCoy, 2011; Financial Crisis Inquiry Commission, 2011; Immergluck, 2011; Pozen, 2010; Prins, 2009). Government intervention was essential to prevent the complete collapse of the U.S. financial system and, potentially, the U.S. economy (Zandi, 2012a). Interestingly, although housing-related factors triggered the Great Recession, initial government interventions primarily focused on sectors other than housing.

Government intervention for the financial sector occurred through the Emergency Economic Stabilization Act (EESA), passed in October 2008, which included the Troubled Assets Relief Program (TARP), for an initial price tag of $700 billion (although by April 2013 only $428 billion had been disbursed, and the subsidy costs were estimated to be $21 billion [Lerner et al., 2013]). Originally, TARP was designed to buy up toxic assets, but it ended up being a program that disbursed funds to banks and the auto industry in exchange for dividend-paying preferred stock (Prins, 2009; Zandi, 2012a). Thanks to TARP, the banking system survived the crisis. Also, in 2008 the Federal Deposit Insurance Corporation (FDIC) launched an initiative that mass-modified loans in the portfolio of the failed thrift institution IndyMac, which resulted in a projected $1.5 million in avoided foreclosure costs (Engel & McCoy, 2011).

Government intervention for consumers occurred through the Economic Stimulus Act of 2008, which was signed into law in February 2008. This $152 billion stimulus provided tax rebates to low- and middle-income U.S. taxpayers and tax incentives to stimulate business investment and it increased limits on conforming mortgages eligible for government insurance and GSE purchase to stimulate the economy (Zandi, 2012a). Later, the Housing and Economic Recovery Act (HERA), passed in July 2008, introduced the Hope for Homeowners (H4H) Program, in which lenders could write down existing mortgages and refinance borrowers into loans for less than 90 percent of their current property value. Only 340 loans were originated through the program (Immergluck, 2011, 2012a). HERA also provided a tax credit for eligible first-time home buyers (later this included those who had not owned a home in the past three years) of up to $8,000 from 2008 to 2010 (Immergluck 2011; Internal Revenue Service, n.d.; Pozen, 2010).

Another massive public policy response in the form of economic stimulus was the American Recovery and Reinvestment Act (ARRA), which was signed into law in February 2009 and for which about $830 billion was allocated (Reichling et al., 2013). This economic recovery program was among the biggest in U.S. history (Zandi, 2012a). ARRA stimulated the purchase of goods and services by funding construction and other investment activities that could take several years to complete; it provided funds to states and localities and increased aid for education and transportation projects; it supported people in need by extending and expanding unemployment benefits and increasing benefits under the Supplemental Nutrition Assistance Program; and it provided temporary tax relief for individuals and businesses by raising exemption amounts for the alternative minimum tax, adding a new Making Work Pay tax credit, and creating enhanced deductions for depreciation of business equipment (Reichling et al., 2013; Zandi, 2012a).

Whereas the Great Depression triggered the establishment of many institutions that favored homeownership, the Great Recession has led to the dismantling of many such institutions, affecting opportunity and wealth building. During the Great Depression, the federal government established HOLC, the FHA, and the GSEs. While HOLC was wound down in 1936, the FHA and the GSEs were established, supporting opportunity and wealth building for decades. Interestingly, and perhaps ironically, the Great Recession has caused some to question the need for the FHA and the GSEs (Gyourko, 2011; Pinto, 2011; Pollock, 2013; see chapters 8 and 14).

The FHA has played a countercyclical role, offering liquidity to the mortgage finance system whenever the private financial sector retrenched (Galante, 2013c). The contribution of the FHA to the housing recovery has not been without stress, however. The fiscal year (FY) 2012 actuarial independent review, conducted by Integrated Financial Engineering (IFE), evaluated FHA's Mutual Mortgage Insurance (MMI) Fund, which covers FHA's single-family programs. In that year, the capital reserve ratio of the fund fell below zero to negative 1.44 percent, and the fund's economic value stood at negative $16.3 billion against an active portfolio of $1.13 trillion (Galante, 2013c).

Over the past several years, the Obama administration increased FHA insurance premiums four times, to the highest levels in FHA's history. It tightened underwriting requirements that required borrowers with relatively low credit scores to furnish higher down payments and to present the source of down payments. The administration also overhauled the process through which lenders review loan applications and increased efforts to minimize losses on delinquent loans (Griffith, 2012).

The actuary evaluating the FHA projected that the MMI Fund capital reserve ratio would be positive by FY 2014 and reach 2.0 percent during FY 2017 under its base-case estimate, assuming no changes in policy or other actions by the FHA. However, policy changes that were announced when the actuarial report was released are expected to accelerate the time to the fund's recovery (Galante, 2013c).

Fannie Mae and Freddie Mac were taken into conservatorship in 2008, "a process in which the government holds a failed financial institution with the purpose of restoring the firm to solvency and returning it to private hands" (Stanton, 2012: 245). Most recently, conversations have focused on the future of Fannie Mae and Freddie Mac and how to replace them (Barth et al., 2013). The GSE Reform Act of 2013, introduced by Senators Bob Corker (R-Tenn.) and Mark Warner (D-Va.) on June 25, 2013, is a bipartisan legislative initiative that advocates a new Federal Mortgage Insurance Corporation (FMIC) that would be an independent government agency insuring mortgage-backed securities issued by private financial institutions. Under the proposed legislation, the federal government would provide catastrophic insurance for the mortgage market, guaranteeing mortgages only after private investors have absorbed the first 10 percent of losses (Corker, 2013).

Government interventions for foreclosed homeowners and communities have consisted of several initiatives and programs, although many economists and politicians have been critical of the impacts. The first such program was the FHA Secure Program, announced in August 2007, through which the FHA refinanced delinquent homeowners into more affordable loans to prevent foreclosure; fewer than two thousand homeowners at risk of foreclosure were assisted (Swarns, 2008). FHA Secure was followed by the Hope Now Alliance, announced in October 2007, which was an alliance of lenders, NeighborWorks, and nonprofit organizations that provided foreclosure prevention counseling to homeowners over the phone free of charge.

In December 2007 the National Foreclosure Mitigation Counseling (NFMC) Program was launched and funded with over $500 million, which was awarded to local housing counseling organizations to advise homeowners in or at risk of foreclosure. Mayer et al. (2012) found that after the Home Affordable Modification Program was established, a loan modification through NFMC resulted in an average additional reduction of $176 in monthly payment and a reduction of 36 percent in foreclosure completions, among many other findings.

HERA, passed in July 2008, provided $7 billion in funding for local governments and nonprofit organizations to buy and renovate foreclosed properties through the Neighborhood Stabilization Programs (NSP1, NSP2, NSP3) to stabilize communities ravaged by the foreclosure crisis (Schwartz, 2012; U.S. Department of Housing and Urban Development, 2011).

The passage of the Financial Stability Act of 2009 resulted in the Making Home Affordable (MHA) initiative, for which $29.9 billion was allocated (Carr, Anacker, & Mulcahy, 2011). MHA has many components, among them the Home Affordable Modification Program (HAMP) and the Home Affordable Refinance Program (HARP). HAMP was conducted in two steps. First, the program encouraged lenders to reduce mortgage payments of eligible borrowers to 38 percent of the borrower's income; second, the federal government helped to further reduce mortgage payments to 31 percent of the borrower's income (Immergluck, 2012). HARP is intended to help eligible homeowners refinance their mortgages under more affordable terms through the GSEs (Schwartz, 2012).

From January 1, 2008, until the end of the third quarter of 2013, servicers conducted almost 3.3 million modifications through the HAMP program (Office of the Comptroller of the Currency, 2013). From April 1, 2009, to September 30, 2013, HARP refinanced almost three million loans (Federal Housing Finance Agency, 2013). While both programs have had significant design and implementation issues, they have nevertheless prevented many foreclosures and helped with many refinances.

Another outcome of the Great Recession was the passage of the Dodd-Frank Wall Street Reform and Consumer Protection Act, commonly referred to as Dodd-Frank, in 2010, which led to numerous financial reforms, including the establishment of the Consumer Financial Protection Bureau (CFPB) in 2011, an independent federal agency that regulates financial products and services regardless of the type of institution (Engel & McCoy, 2011; see chapter 8).

While a series of economic stimuli have been passed, these acts may have been insufficient in the context of the magnitude of the crisis. Moreover, many subsidies have disproportionately aided major corporations and, by extension, their executives and shareholders. The result is that public policy may have contributed to an increase in economic and social inequality while failing to address fundamental challenges facing the economy. The unwillingness of Congress to pass legislation that invests in America's infrastructure and green technologies may have consequences for years. Attempts to achieve a massive deficit reduction without a view toward investments in the economy threaten to put the nation back on the road to another recession.

CONCLUSION

The Great Recession seems to have put a damper on homeownership as a strategy of wealth building (Joint Center for Housing Studies of Harvard University, 2009). While some have questioned the value of homeownership in general, suggesting the new label Rentership Society (Florida, 2010), others still consider homeownership key to asset accumulation in the long run (Belsky, 2013; Quercia et al., 2011; see chapters 7 and 9).

Interestingly, survey analyses show that economically advantaged respondents still aspire to homeownership, but this is not necessarily the case for economically disadvantaged ones, although there are exceptions (Bracha & Jamison, 2012; Collins & Choi, 2010; Drew & Herbert, 2012; see chapter 16). The question remains if and how the Great Recession has impacted economically advantaged respondents, also called "the middle class," and what this means for the future of homeownership in the United States. Until the

Great Recession, many considered a college degree the ticket to moving into or remaining in the middle class. However, increasing college tuition, decreasing public support for institutions of secondary education and for students, increasing unaffordability of student loans, relatively high unemployment rates among the young, even after graduation from college, and the high proportion of young people in involuntary part-time jobs or in jobs they were not trained for have caused many to question the value of a college education. Concomitantly, household formation rates among the young have decreased due to their remaining at home or moving back in with their parents (Paciorek, 2013; see chapters 1 and 2).

Also, mortgages have become more difficult to obtain, especially because relatively high credit scores are needed to obtain a loan. For example, as of November 2013, the tenth percentile of FICO scores on new originations stood at 660, compared to the low 600s prior to the Great Recession. Also, down payment requirements have remained high relative to the early 2000s (Urban Institute, 2014; see chapters 7 and 8).

In the short and mid-run, unemployment and underemployment rates for many young people will not decrease, and median and mean real incomes probably will not increase much. Thus, many young people will postpone or might even forego homeownership altogether (see chapters 1, 2, and 7).

However, many consider homeownership in order to access high-quality education, rewarding and well-paying jobs, convenient transportation, valuable social networks, and high-quality physical and mental health and recreational centers (Carr & Kutty, 2008). For many, especially those with low and moderate incomes, homeownership seems to be one of the few, if not the only, wealth-accumulation strategies in the long run. Some have pointed out alternatives, such as participating in secondary or tertiary education, establishing and owning a business, or investing in the stock or other markets, but in the current day and age these investments tend to be somewhat risky and require a substantial investment of resources, either money or time and effort. Future research should compare and contrast these investment alternatives with homeownership (see chapters 7 and 8).

REFERENCES

Barofsky, N. (2012). *Bailout: An inside account of how Washington abandoned Main Street while rescuing Wall Street*. New York: Free Press.

Barth, C. M., Bond, C. S., Brady, E., Cisneros, H., Couch, R. M., DelliBovi, A. A. . . . Zigas, B. (2013). *Housing America's future: New directions for national policy*. Washington, D.C.: Bipartisan Policy Center. Retrieved February 13, 2014, from http://bipartisanpolicy.org/sites/default/files/BPC_Housing%20Report_web_0.pdf.

Bartlett, D. L., & Steele, J. B. (2012). *The betrayal of the American Dream*. New York: PublicAffairs.

Been, V., Ellen, I. G., Schwartz, A. E., Stiefel, L., & Weinstein, M. (2011). Does losing your home mean losing your school?: Effects of foreclosures on the school mobility of children. *Regional Science and Urban Economics, 41*, 407–414.

Belsky, E. S. (2013). *The dream lives on: The future of homeownership in America*. Cambridge, Mass: Joint Center for Housing Studies of Harvard University. Retrieved February 13, 2013, from http://jchs.harvard.edu/sites/jchs.harvard.edu/files/w13-1_belsky_0.pdf.

Bivens, J., & Shierholz, H. (2010). *For job seekers, no recovery in sight: Why prospects for job growth and unemployment remain dim*. Washington, D.C.: Economic Policy Institute. Retrieved February 13, 2014, from http://s2.epi.org/files/page/-/bp259/bp259.pdf.

Bovino, B. A. (2014, January). Remarks given at the conference "A 2014 Economic Forecast and What it Means for Housing," Bipartisan Policy Center, Washington, D.C.

Bracha, A., & Jamison, J. C. (2012). *Shifting confidence in homeownership: The great recession* (Public Policy Discussion Paper 12-4). Boston: Federal Reserve Bank of Boston. Retrieved February 13, 2014, from http://www.bostonfed.org/economic/ppdp/2012/ppdp1204.pdf.

Brevoort, K. P., & Cooper, C. R. (2013). Foreclosure's wake: The credit experiences of individuals following foreclosure. *Real Estate Economics, 41*, 747–792.

Bricker, J., Kennickell, A. B., Moore, K. B., & Sabelhaus, J. (2012). Changes in U.S. family finances from 2007 to 2010: Evidence from the Survey of Consumer Finance. *Federal Reserve Bulletin, 98*(2), 1–80.

Bureau of Labor Statistics (n.d.). *Labor force statistics from the Current Population Survey.* Retrieved February 13, 2014, from http://data.bls.gov/timeseries/LNS14000000.

Butrica, B. A. (2013). *Retirement plan assets*. Washington, D.C.: Urban Institute. Retrieved February 13, 2014, from http://www.urban.org/UploadedPDF/412622-Retirement-Plan-Assets.pdf.

Campbell, J. Y., Giglio, S., & Pathak, P. (2011). Forced sales and house prices. *American Economic Review, 101*, 2108–2131.

Carr, J. H., Anacker, K. B., & Hernandez, I. (2013). *The state of the U.S. economy and homeownership for Americans.* Arlington, VA: Schar School of Policy and Government, George Mason University. Retrieved February 13, 2014, from http://policy.gmu.edu/wp-content/uploads/State_of_Housing_In_Black_America_Final.pdf.

Carr, J. H., Anacker, K. B., & Mulcahy, M. L. (2011). *The foreclosure crisis and its impact on communities of color: Research and solutions.* Arlington, VA: Schar School of Policy and Government, George Mason University. Retrieved February 13, 2014, from http://policy.gmu.edu/wp-content/uploads/ncrc_foreclosurewhitepaper_2011.pdf.

Carr, J. H., & Kutty, N. (2008). The new imperative for equality. In J. H. Carr & N. K. Kutty (Eds.), *Segregation: The rising costs for America* (pp. 1–37). New York: Routledge.

Center for Responsible Lending. (n.d.). *Snapshot of a foreclosure crisis: 15 fast facts.* Retrieved February 13, 2014, from http://www.responsiblelending.org/mortgage-lending/research-analysis/snapshot-of-foreclosure-crisis.pdf.

Collins, J. M., & Choi, L. (2010). *The effects of the real estate bust on renter perceptions of homeownership* (Working Paper 2010-01). San Francisco: Federal Reserve Bank of San Francisco. Retrieved February 13, 2014, from http://www.frbsf.org/community-development/files/wp2010-01.pdf.

CoreLogic (2013). *Home price index report*. Retrieved February 13, 2014, from http://www.corelogic.com/research/hpi/corelogic-hpi-may-2013.pdf.

Corker, R. (2013). *Banking committee senators introduce legislation to modernize and reform America's broken housing finance system.* [Press release.] Retrieved February 13, 2014, from http://www.corker.senate.gov/public/index.cfm/news?ContentRecord_id=df5abc5a-fdd4-4ddb-91b5-55559281c644.

Dietz, R. D., & Haurin, D. R. (2003). The social and private micro-level consequences of homeownership. *Journal of Urban Economics, 54*, 401–450.

Dolbeare, C. N. (1998). Tax expenditures. In W. van Vliet (Ed.), *The encyclopedia of housing* (pp. 575–577). Thousand Oaks, Calif.: Sage.

Drew, R. B., & Herbert, C. (2012). *Post-recession drivers of preferences for homeownership.* Cambridge, Mass.: Joint Center for Housing Studies of Harvard University. Retrieved February 13, 2014, from http://www.jchs.harvard.edu/sites/jchs.harvard.edu/files/w12-4_drew_herbert.pdf.

Engel, K. C., & McCoy, P. A. (2011). *The subprime virus: Reckless credit, regulatory failure, and next steps.* Oxford: Oxford University Press.

Federal Home Loan Banks (n.d.). *The federal home loan banks: The basics.* Retrieved February 13, 2014, from http://www.fhlbanks.com/assets/pdfs/sidebar/FHLBanks_TheBasics_4_2012.pdf.

Federal Housing Finance Agency (2013). *Refinance report. Third quarter 2013.* Retrieved February 13, 2014, from http://www.fhfa.gov/webfiles/25886/3Q2013RefiReportF.pdf.

Financial Crisis Inquiry Commission (2011). *The financial crisis inquiry report: Final report of the National Commission on the Causes of the Financial and Economic Crisis in the United States.* New York: Public Affairs.

Florida, R. (2010). *The great reset: How new ways of living and working drive post-crash prosperity*. New York: Harper.

Foote, C. L., Gerardi, K., & Willen, P. S. (2008). Negative equity and foreclosure: Theory and evidence. *Journal of Urban Economics, 64*, 234–245.

Galante, C. (2013a, June 4). Federal Housing Administration's fiscal year 2014 budget request: Written testimony of Carol Galante, assistant secretary for housing/Federal Housing Administration commissioner, U.S. Department of Housing and Urban Development (HUD). Retrieved February 13, 2014, from http://portal.hud.gov/hudportal/HUD?src=/press/testimonies.

Galante, C. (2013b, July 24). Proposed FHA Solvency Act of 2013: Written testimony of Carol Galante, assistant secretary for housing/Federal Housing Administration commissioner, U.S. Department of Housing and Urban Development (HUD). Retrieved February 13, 2014, from http://portal.hud.gov/hudportal/HUD?src=/press/testimonies.

Galante, C. (2013c, February 13). Written testimony of Carol Galante, assistant secretary for housing/Federal Housing Administration commissioner, U.S. Department of Housing and Urban Development (HUD). Retrieved February 13, 2014, from http://portal.hud.gov/hudportal/HUD?src=/press/testimonies.

General Assembly of North Carolina (1999). *Session Law 1999-332. Senate Bill 1149*. Retrieved February 13, 2014, from http://www.responsiblelending.org/north-carolina/nc-mortgage/policy-legislation/SB_1149_PDF.pdf.

Glaeser, E. L., Gyourko, J., & Saiz, A. (2008). *Housing supply and housing bubbles* (Working Paper 14193). Cambridge: Mass: National Bureau of Economic Research. Retrieved February 13, 2014, from http://www.nber.org/papers/w14193.

Griffith, J. (2012). *The Federal Housing Administration saved the housing market*. Washington, D.C.: Center for American Progress. Retrieved February 13, 2014, from http://www.americanprogress.org/wp-content/uploads/2012/10/Griffith_FHA.pdf.

Gyourko, J. (2011). *Is FHA the next housing bailout?* Washington, D.C.: American Enterprise Institute. Retrieved February 13, 2014, from http://www.aei.org/papers/economics/financial-services/housing-finance/is-fha-the-next-housing-bailout/.

Hacker, J. S. (2008). *The great risk shift: The new economic insecurity and the decline of the American Dream*. Oxford: Oxford University Press.

Harris, B., Steuerle, C. E., & Eng, A. (2013). *Beyond mortgage interest subsidies: New perspectives on tax incentives for homeownership*. Unpublished manuscript.

Immergluck, D. (2009). *Foreclosed: High-risk lending, deregulation, and the undermining of America's mortgage market*. Ithaca, N.Y.: Cornell University Press.

Immergluck, D. (2011). *Too little, too late and too timid: The federal response to the foreclosure crisis at the 5-year mark*. Retrieved February 13, 2014, from http://papers.ssrn.com/sol3/papers.cfm?abstract_id=1930686.

Immergluck, D. (2012). Foreclosures. In A. T. Carswell (Ed.), *The encyclopedia of housing* (pp. 231–236). Thousand Oaks, Calif.: Sage.

Immergluck, D., & Smith, G. (2006). The external costs of foreclosure: The impact of single-family mortgage foreclosures on property values. *Housing Policy Debate, 17*, 57–79.

Internal Revenue Service (n.d.). *First-time homebuyer credit*. Retrieved February 13, 2014, from http://www.irs.gov/uac/First-Time-Homebuyer-Credit-1.

investopedia.com (n.d.). *Foreclosure—(FCL) Definition*. Retrieved July 10, 2014, from http://www.investopedia.com/terms/f/foreclosure.asp.

Jackson, A. (2007, November). Remarks given at the International Housing Finance Policy Roundtable, U.S. Department of Housing and Urban Development, Washington, D.C.

Joint Center for Housing Studies of Harvard University (2009). *The state of the nation's housing*. Retrieved February 13, 2014, from http://www.jchs.harvard.edu/sites/jchs.harvard.edu/files/son2009_bw.pdf.

Keating, W. D. (1998). Federal Home Loan Bank system. In W. van Vliet (Ed.), *The encyclopedia of housing* (pp. 179–180). Thousand Oaks, Calif.: Sage.

Krueger, A. B. (2012). *The rise and consequences of inequality in the United States*. Remarks delivered at the Center for American Progress, Washington, D.C. Retrieved

February 13, 2014, from http://www.whitehouse.gov/sites/default/files/krueger_cap_speech_final_remarks.pdf.

Labonte, M. (2010). *The 2007–2009 recession: Similarities to and differences from the past* (Report R40198). Washington, D.C.: Congressional Research Service. Retrieved February 13, 2014, from http://www.fas.org/sgp/crs/misc/R40198.pdf.

Lerner, A., Fontaine, P., Gullo, T., & Holland, J. (2013). *Report on the Troubled Asset Relief Program—May 2013*. Washington, D.C.: Congressional Budget Office. Retrieved February 13, 2014, from http://www.cbo.gov/sites/default/files/cbofiles/attachments/44256_TARP.pdf.

Levine, L. (2009). *Countercyclical job creation programs*. (Report 92-939). Washington, D.C.: Congressional Research Service. Retrieved February 13, 2014, from http://assets.opencrs.com/rpts/92-939_20090115.pdf.

Lewis, M. (2014). *Liar's poker: Rising through the wreckage on Wall Street*. New York: W. W. Norton.

Li, Y., & Morrow-Jones, H. (2010). The impact of residential mortgage foreclosure on neighborhood change and succession. *Journal of Planning Education and Research, 30*, 22–39.

Ludwig, E. A., Kamihachi, J., & Toh, L. (2009). The CRA: Past successes and future opportunities. In P. Chakrabarti, D. Erickson, R. S. Essene, I. Galloway, & J. Olson (Eds.), *Revisiting the CRA: Perspectives on the future of the Community Reinvestment Act* (pp. 84–104). Boston: Federal Reserve Bank of Boston; San Francisco: Federal Reserve Bank of San Francisco.

Mayer, N., Tatian, P. A., Temkin, K., & Calhoun, C. A. (2012). *Has foreclosure counseling helped troubled homeowners? Evidence from the evaluation of the National Foreclosure Mitigation Counseling Program*. Washington, D.C.: Urban Institute. Retrieved February 13, 2014, from http://www.urban.org/UploadedPDF/412492-has-foreclosure-counseling-helped-troubled-homeowners.pdf.

McKenna, C. (2008). *The homeownership gap: How the post–World War II GI Bill shaped modern day homeownership patterns for Black and White Americans*. Unpublished master's thesis. Massachusetts Institute of Technology. Cambridge.

Metzger, J. T. (1998). Home Owners' Loan Corporation. In W. van Vliet (Ed.), *The encyclopedia of housing* (pp. 232–233). Thousand Oaks, Calif.: Sage.

Molloy, R., & Shan, H. (2013). The postforeclosure experience of U.S. households. *Real Estate Economics, 41*, 225–254.

Moreno, A. (1998). *Effectiveness of mortgage foreclosure prevention: Summary of findings*. Minneapolis: Family Housing Fund. Retrieved February 13, 2014, from http://www.fhfund.org/_dnld/reports/MFP_1995.pdf.

National Association of Home Builders (2012). *A comprehensive framework for housing finance system reform*. Retrieved February 13, 2014, from https://www.nahb.org/assets/docs/files/NAHBHousingFinanceWhitePaperFeb2012_20120302094029.pdf.

National Bureau of Economic Research (n.d.). *U.S. business cycle expansions and contractions*. Retrieved February 13, 2014, from http://www.nber.org/cycles.html.

Office of the Comptroller of the Currency (2013). *OCC mortgage metrics report: Disclosure of national bank and federal savings association mortgage loan data. Third quarter 2013*. Retrieved February 13, 2014, from http://www.occ.gov/publications/publications-by-type/other-publications-reports/mortgage-metrics-2013/mortgage-metrics-q3-2013.pdf.

Paciorek, A. (2013). *The long and the short of household formation*. Washington, D.C.: Board of Governors of the Federal Reserve System. Retrieved February 13, 2014, from http://www.frbatlanta.org/documents/news/conferences/13pre_speakerseries_householdFormations.pdf.

Pettit, K. L. S., & Comey, J. (2012). *The foreclosure crisis and children: A three-city study*. Washington, D.C.: Urban Institute. Retrieved February 13, 2014, from http://www.urban.org/UploadedPDF/412517-The-Foreclosure-Crisis-and-Children-A-Three-City-Study.pdf.

Pinto, E. J. (2011, December). Remarks given at the conference "Is FHA the Next Housing Bailout?," American Enterprise Institute, Washington, D.C.

Pollock, A. J. (2013). *An American housing finance dilemma: What to do with Fannie Mae and Freddie Mac?* Washington, D.C.: American Enterprise Institute. Retrieved February 13, 2014, from http://www.aei.org/article/economics/financial-services/housing-finance/an-american-housing-finance-dilemma-what-to-do-with-fannie-mae-and-freddie-mac/.

Pozen, R. (2010). *Too big to save? How to fix the U.S. financial system.* New York: John Wiley & Sons.

Prins, N. (2009). *It takes a pillage: Behind the bailouts, bonuses, and backroom deals from Washington to Wall Street.* Hoboken, N.J.: John Wiley & Sons.

Quercia, R. G., Freeman, A., & Ratcliffe, J. (2011). *Regaining the dream: How to renew the promise of homeownership for America's working families.* Washington, D.C.: Brookings Institution Press.

Rajan, R. G. (2010). *Fault lines: How hidden fractures still threaten the world economy.* Princeton, N.J.: Princeton University Press.

Raskin, S. B. (2012). *Creating and implementing an enforcement response to the foreclosure crisis.* Remarks delivered at the Association of American Law Schools, Washington, D.C. Retrieved February 13, 2014, from http://www.federalreserve.gov/newsevents/speech/raskin20120107a.pdf.

RealtyTrac (n.d.). *Number of foreclosure starts and completions in the United States.* Irvine, Calif.: RealtyTrac.

RealtyTrac (2014). *1.4 million U.S. properties with foreclosure filings in 2013 down 26 percent to lowest annual total since 2007.* Retrieved February 13, 2014, from http://www.realtytrac.com/Content/foreclosure-market-report/2013-year-end-us-foreclosure-report-7963.

Reichling, F., Edelberg, W., Page, B., Brewster, J., Lasky, M., & Shakin, J. (2013). *Estimated impact of the American Recovery and Reinvestment Act on employment and economic output from October 2012 through December 2012.* Washington, D.C.: Congressional Budget Office. Retrieved February 13, 2014, from http://www.cbo.gov/sites/default/files/cbofiles/attachments/43945-ARRA.pdf.

Rohe, W. (2012). Homeownership. In A. T. Carswell (Ed.), *The encyclopedia of housing* (pp. 293–298). Thousand Oaks, Calif.: Sage.

Roubini, N., & Mihm, S. (2011). *Crisis economics: A crash course in the future of finance.* New York: Penguin Books.

Schafran, A., & Feldstein, L. M. (2013). Black, brown, white, and green: Race, land use, and environmental politics in a changing Richmond. In C. Niedt (Ed.), *Social justice in diverse suburbs: History, politics, and prospects* (pp. 155–171). Philadelphia: Temple University Press.

Schwartz, A. (2012). U.S. housing policy in the age of Obama: From crisis to stasis. *International Journal of Housing Policy, 12,* 227–240.

Schwartz, A. F. (2010). *Housing policy in the United States.* New York: Routledge.

Shierholz, H. (2014). *Six years from its beginning, the Great Recession's shadow looms over the labor market.* Washington, D.C.: Economic Policy Institute. Retrieved February 13, 2014, from http://www.epi.org/publication/years-beginning-great-recessions-shadow/.

Shiller, R. J. (2005). *Irrational exuberance.* New York: Currency/Doubleday.

Shiller, R. J. (2008). *The subprime solution: How today's global financial crisis happened, and what to do about it.* Princeton, N.J.: Princeton University Press.

Shiller, R. J. (2012). *Finance and the good society.* Princeton, N.J.: Princeton University Press.

Smith, M. H., & Smith, G. (2006). *Bubble, bubble, where's the housing bubble?* (Papers on Economic Activity, 2006-1). Washington, D.C.: Brookings Institution.

Stanton, T. H. (2012). Government sponsored enterprises. In A. T. Carswell (Ed.), *The encyclopedia of housing* (pp. 245–250). Thousand Oaks, Calif.: Sage.

Steggell, C. (2012). Federal Housing Administration. In A. T. Carswell (Ed.), *The encyclopedia of housing* (pp. 216–221). Thousand Oaks, Calif.: Sage.

Swarns, R. L. (2008, April 30). Federal mortgage plan falls short, critics say. *New York Times.* Retrieved February 13, 2014, from http://www.nytimes.com/2008/04/30/business/30fha.html?_r=0.

Toder, E. J. (2013). *Options to reform the home Mortgage Interest Deduction.* Unpublished manuscript.

Urban Institute. (2014). *Housing finance at a glance: A monthly chartbook.* Retrieved February 13, 2014, from http://www.urban.org/UploadedPDF/412993_Housing-Finance-At-A-Glance-January-2014.pdf.

U.S. Bureau of the Census (n.d.). *Quarterly starts and completions by purpose and design.* Retrieved February 13, 2014, from http://www.census.gov/construction/nrc/.

U.S. Department of Agriculture (n.d.). *Program data: Supplemental Nutrition Assistance Program.* Retrieved February 13, 2014, from http://www.fns.usda.gov/pd/snapmain.htm.

U.S. Department of Housing and Urban Development (2011). *Neighborhood Stabilization Program grants.* Retrieved February 13, 2014, from http://portal.hud.gov/hudportal/HUD?src=/program_offices/comm_planning/communitydevelopment/programs/neighborhoodspg.

U.S. Department of Housing and Urban Development (2013). *National housing market summary.* Retrieved February 13, 2014, from http://www.huduser.org/portal/periodicals/ushmc/pdf/NationalSummary_3q13.pdf.

Wandling, R. A. (2012). Tax expenditures. In A. T. Carswell (Ed.), *The encyclopedia of housing* (pp. 725–729). Thousand Oaks, Calif.: Sage.

Warren, E., & Tyagi, A. W. (2005). *All your worth: The ultimate lifetime money plan.* New York: Free Press.

Wolff, E. N. (2010). *Recent trends in household wealth in the United States: Rising debt and the middle-class squeeze—an update to 2007* (Working Paper 589). Annandale-on-Hudson, N.Y.: Levy Economics Institute of Bard College. Retrieved February 13, 2014, from http://www.levyinstitute.org/pubs/wp_589.pdf.

Zandi, M. (2012a, September 28). Obama policies ended housing free fall. *Washington Post.* Retrieved February 13, 2014, from http://www.washingtonpost.com/realestate/obama-policies-ended-housing-free-fall/2012/09/27/20635604-0372-11e2-9b24-ff730c7f6312_print.html.

Zandi, M. (2012b). *Paying the price: Ending the Great Recession and beginning a new American century.* Upper Saddle River, N.J.: FT Press.

SECTION V
SPECIAL TOPICS IN HOUSING

Chapter 16

Housing and Racial and Ethnic Diversity

KATRIN B. ANACKER

Over the next few decades, the United States will gradually become a society in which non-Hispanic whites will be in the minority and people of color will be in the majority. Whereas 61.75 percent of the total resident population in the United States (of one race only) was non-Hispanic white in 2015, only 42.58 percent is projected to fall into this category in 2060 (Frey, 2013). In the near and distant future the proportion of people of color will increase (Frey, 2015). In other words, the United States will become a "majority-minority" nation in a few decades, although Texas, New Mexico, and California are already "majority-minority" states (Frey, 2013). Figure 16.1 illustrates these developments.

The increase in the proportion of people of color can be attributed to several developments. One is the relatively high fertility rates of Hispanics/Latinos (Frey, 2015; Monger & Yankay, 2014; Passel, Livingston, & Cohn, 2012). Another is the increase in the proportion of people of two or more races due to the increase in racial and ethnic intermarriage rates (Frey, 2015; U.S. Bureau of the Census, 2012; Wang, 2012). A further reason is the somewhat high immigration rates of Hispanics/Latinos and Asians (Frey, 2015; Passel et al., 2012). Finally, the number of deaths among non-Hispanic whites is higher than those among any other racial and ethnic group (Frey, 2013, 2015).

In 2011, 50.4 percent of the nation's population younger than age one was of color (Passel et al., 2012). In two to three decades the vast majority of these very young people will form households, which typically occurs when people are in their twenties and thirties (Paciorek, 2013; see chapters 1, 2, and 9). Thus the majority of newly formed households will be of color (Joint Center for Housing Studies of Harvard University, 2014). The majority of these newly formed households will begin as renters, and some will eventually become homeowners (see chapters 7 and 9). This chapter discusses housing in the context of racial and ethnic diversity for renters and homeowners in the United States. Macroeconomic, public policy, and individual factors that influence homeownership will also be discussed in greater detail.

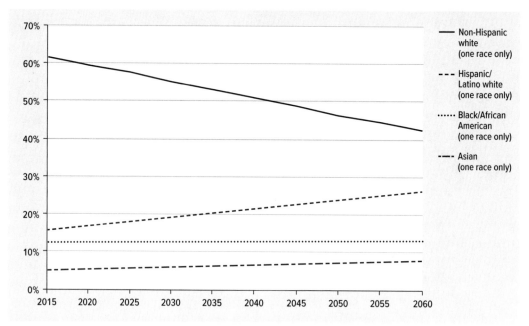

FIGURE 16.1
Proportion Distribution of the Projected Population by Race and Ethnicity, United States, 2015–60
Source: U.S. Bureau of Census, 2012.

RENTERS IN THE UNITED STATES BY RACE AND ETHNICITY

Many consider the United States to be a nation of homeowners (Editors of New Strategist Publications, 2011). This statement is probably most fitting for many non-Hispanic whites, since they have a relatively high homeownership rate (see chapter 7). This statement is less fitting for many blacks/African Americans or Hispanics/Latinos, however, since those groups have a relatively low homeownership rate (see chapter 9).

Many policy makers are concerned with the relatively high housing cost burden of many renters, who have lower household incomes and lower wealth compared to most homeowners (Joint Center for Housing Studies of Harvard University, 2014). Renters of color tend to have lower household incomes and lower wealth compared to renters as a whole (Joint Center for Housing Studies of Harvard University, 2014; see chapter 10).

A moderate rental housing cost burden (having rental housing costs higher than 30 percent of a renter's pretax [Schwartz, 2015] or adjusted [Pelletiere, 2008] income) might result in overcrowding, doubling up, or difficulties meeting expenses related to food, transportation, education, and health care, among other expenses, or saving for retirement. A severe rental housing cost burden (having rental housing costs higher than 50 percent of a renter's income) might also potentially result in eviction and eventual homelessness (Joint Center for Housing Studies of Harvard University, 2013; Schwartz and Wilson, n.d.). Many low-income renters affected by a moderate or severe rental housing burden are unable to draw from resources such as a savings account or a support network that is able and willing to provide sustained financial assistance in the mid- and long run (Bratt, 2006; Joint Center for Housing Studies of Harvard University, 2012, 2013; Tilly, 2006).

TABLE 16.1
Proportions of Renters with No, Moderate, and Severe Housing Cost Burdens by Race and Ethnicity, 2001, 2007, and 2011

Race/ethnicity	2001: no burden	2001: moderate burden	2001: severe burden	2007: no burden	2007: moderate burden	2007: severe burden	2011: no burden	2011: moderate burden	2011: severe burden
Non-Hispanic White	63.10%	18.89%	18.00%	58.27%	20.58%	21.15%	53.98%	21.45%	24.56%
Black/African American	52.22%	21.84%	25.94%	45.53%	23.86%	30.62%	40.90%	24.25%	34.84%
Hispanic/Latino	54.02%	23.59%	22.40%	47.34%	26.05%	26.60%	42.53%	26.35%	31.12%
Asian/other	58.09%	18.83%	23.08%	54.12%	21.40%	24.48%	51.36%	20.89%	27.75%

Source: Author, based on Joint Center for Housing Studies of Harvard University, 2013.

Table 16.1 illustrates the proportions of renters with no, moderate, and severe housing cost burdens by race and ethnicity. This table shows that the proportion of renters who face severe housing cost burdens has increased from 2001 to 2011 for each racial and ethnic group but in particular for blacks/African Americans and Hispanics/Latinos (see chapter 10).

HOMEOWNERS IN THE UNITED STATES BY RACE AND ETHNICITY

Homeownership has been associated with higher social status since the beginning of the history of the United States. In the distant past only male, non-Hispanic white landowners could vote (Quercia, Freeman, & Ratcliffe, 2011). Currently many consider homeownership an indicator of economic and social stability for neighborhoods and an indicator of good citizenship and middle-class status for individuals (Rohe, 2012). Homeownership has been utilized to access or leverage funds for attending college, starting businesses, weathering financial emergencies, or preparing for retirement, among other purposes (Chang, 2010). Many consider homeownership a good strategy for building wealth over time, especially for low- and moderate-income people, including people of color (Belsky & Retsinas, 2005).

Figure 16.2 illustrates developments in the homeownership rate from 1995 to 2013, differentiated by race and ethnicity. Non-Hispanic white and black/African American homeownership rates peaked in 2004 at 76.0 and 49.7 percent, respectively. The Asian/other homeownership rate peaked in 2006 at 60.8 percent, and the Hispanic/Latino homeownership rate peaked in 2006 and 2007 at 49.7 percent (see chapter 7).

While the non-Hispanic white homeownership rate peaked in 2004, the foreclosure rate for this group gradually and then rapidly increased in 2009 (Reid, n.d.), as illustrated in figure 16.3. Thus the temporal gap between the decrease in the non-Hispanic white homeownership rate and the increase of the non-Hispanic white foreclosure rate may be attributed to the decrease in the non-Hispanic white proportion of the population and thus decreased household formation rates among non-Hispanic whites, followed by economic uncertainty and then the Great Recession.

The decrease in the black/African American homeownership rate after 2004 can be explained by the rather early and rapid increase in the foreclosure rate among blacks/African Americans in 2006 (Gottesdiener, 2013;

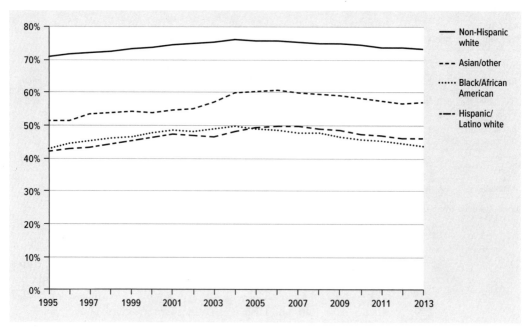

FIGURE 16.2
Homeownership Rates by Race and Ethnicity, 1995–2013
Source: U.S. Bureau of Census, 2012.

FIGURE 16.3
Proportion of Mortgages in Foreclosure or Real Estate Owned (REO) by Race and Ethnicity, 2006–11
Source: Reid, n.d.

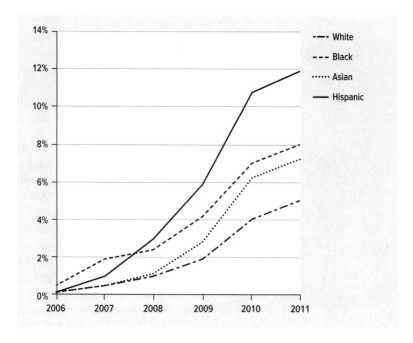

Reid, n.d.), well before the increase in the national foreclosure rate in 2007. Blacks/African Americans have been disproportionately affected by the foreclosure crisis. For example, nearly 8 percent of this population group has been foreclosed upon since early 2007, compared to 4.5 percent of non-Hispanic whites, controlling for differences in incomes among the two groups (Bocian, Li, & Ernst, 2010). Elevated foreclosure rates among blacks/African Americans were partially triggered by their relatively low household incomes, their relatively low credit ratings (Traub, n.d.), and their increased exposure to subprime and other toxic mortgages (Jayasundera, Silver, Anacker, & Mantcheva, 2010).

The peak in the Asian/other homeownership rate in 2006 may be attributed to the mortgage lending frenzy, partially fueled by this group's relatively high household incomes and their relatively high credit ratings. These factors may also explain the lagged onset of foreclosures among them in 2008 (Reid, n.d.).

Finally, the peak in the Hispanic/Latino homeownership rate may be explained by the mortgage lending frenzy and the increase in population and thus relatively high household formation rates of Hispanics/Latinos, which superseded the onset of foreclosures among this ethnic group in 2007 (Reid, n.d.; see chapter 15).

The homeownership rate is influenced by many factors at the national and individual levels. The sections below will focus on individual and then macroeconomic factors that influence U.S. homeownership, followed by public policy factors. All sections focus on race and ethnicity.

INDIVIDUAL FACTORS THAT INFLUENCE HOMEOWNERSHIP BY RACE AND ETHNICITY

While many people face hurdles to homeownership, blacks/African Americans and Hispanics/Latinos face elevated hurdles, as they have higher unemployment and underemployment rates, lower household incomes, lower wealth, lower credit scores, and higher loan-to-value and debt-to-income ratios than non-Hispanic whites and Asians (Bhutta and Canner, 2013). In addition to these factors, many people of color are affected by racial and ethnic discrimination (Turner et al., 2013).

Unemployment influences homeownership. Mortgage applicants who are unemployed have very low odds of obtaining a loan in the first place. Borrowers who become unemployed or experience pay cuts often struggle to make their monthly mortgage payments (NeighborWorks America, 2013). While the unemployment rate peaked at 9.2 percent for non-Hispanic whites in October and November 2009, it peaked at 16.9 percent for blacks/African Americans in March 2010, at 8.4 percent for Asians in December 2009 and January and February 2010, and at 13.1 percent for Hispanics and Latinos in August 2009 (U.S. Bureau of Labor Statistics, n.d.b). However, by May 2014 the unemployment rate had decreased to 5.4 percent for non-Hispanic whites, 11.5 percent for blacks/African Americans, 5.3 percent for Asians, and 7.7 percent for Hispanics and Latinos (U.S. Bureau of Labor Statistics, n.d.b; see chapter 7). Figure 16.4 illustrates these patterns by race and ethnicity from January 2004 to May 2014.

While the decrease in the unemployment rate might be cause for celebration, it masks the fact that the underemployment rate has increased. The underemployment rate counts jobless workers who report that they are actively seeking work, who work part time but want and are available to work full time ("involuntary" part timers), and who want and are available to work and have looked for work in the last year but have given up actively seeking work ("marginally attached" workers) (Shierholz, 2013). The national underemployment rate was 13.4 percent, regardless of race or ethnicity, averaged for the second quarter of 2013 through the first quarter of 2014 (U.S. Bureau

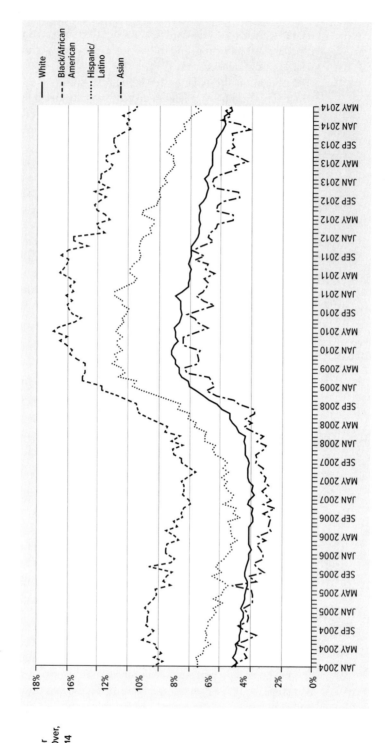

FIGURE 16.4
Unemployment Rate for Workers 16 Years and Over, January 2004–May 2014
Source: Bureau of Labor Statistics, n.d.b.

of Labor Statistics, n.d.a, n.d.b), although it was lower for whites and higher for blacks/African Americans and Hispanics/Latinos (Economic Policy Institute, 2014). The high underemployment rates for blacks/African Americans and Hispanics/Latinos relative to non-Hispanic whites and Asians indicates that the effects of the Great Recession on the labor market have been deep, and they have been more severe for people of color (see chapter 15). Figure 16.5 illustrates these patterns for whites, blacks/African Americans, and Hispanic/Latinos from 2000 to 2013.

Income and wealth levels are also drivers of homeownership. While the median household income for non-Hispanic white households was $57,952 for the period 2008–2012,[1] it was $35,564 for black/African American households, $71,709 for Asian households, and $41,994 for Hispanic/Latino households (U.S. Bureau of the Census, n.d.), not controlling for any other factors. Wealth influences homeownership, as it determines the size of the down payment. A higher down payment reduces the debt burden assumed by a home buyer. While the median net worth for non-Hispanic white households was $113,149 in 2009, it was $5,677 for black/African American households, $78,066 for Asian households, and $6,325 for Hispanic/Latino households (Kochhar, Fry, & Taylor, 2011; see chapter 15).

In addition to these factors, credit scores influence homeownership by affecting access to a mortgage. Credit scores are proprietary data gathered by credit scoring companies, including FICO (Fair, Isaac and Company), as briefly mentioned above. Whereas researchers have published credit scores differentiated by select demographic factors based on databases of credit scoring companies (Austin, 2012; Barenstein, Ruparel, & Thompson, 2007; Board of Governors of the Federal Reserve System, 2007), credit scores differentiated by race and ethnicity are difficult to find. Surveys on credit scores serve as a good proxy, revealing a racial and ethnic gap. Fifty-nine percent of non-Hispanic white households with credit card debt reported credit scores of 700 or above, indicating at least good credit, compared to only 24 percent of black/African American households (Rice & Swesnik, 2014; Traub, n.d.). Loan-to-value (LTV) and debt-to-income (DTI) ratios also influence homeownership by affecting access to mortgages. Similar to the discussion above, these ratios are more favorable for non-Hispanic whites and Asians compared to blacks/African Americans and Hispanics/Latinos (Haughwout, Mayer, & Tracy, 2009; see chapters 7, 8, and 15).

Finally, discrimination influences homeownership. While blatant acts of housing discrimination faced by home buyers of color have continued to decline, more subtle forms of housing denial have stubbornly persisted. Compared to non-Hispanic whites, black/African American home buyers who contact real estate agents about recently advertised homes for sale learn about 17 percent fewer available homes and are shown 18 percent fewer units. These proportions are 15 and 19 percent for Asian home buyers, respectively. Interestingly, there is no statistically significant difference between non-Hispanic white and Hispanic/Latino home buyers (Turner et al., 2013).

In sum, racial and ethnic gaps in the homeownership rate between non-Hispanic whites and Asians on the one hand and blacks/African Americans and Hispanics/Latinos on the other are influenced by many factors, including unemployment and underemployment rates, household incomes and wealth, credit scores, and racial and ethnic discrimination. These and

1. American Community Survey (ACS) five-year averages, 2008–2012.

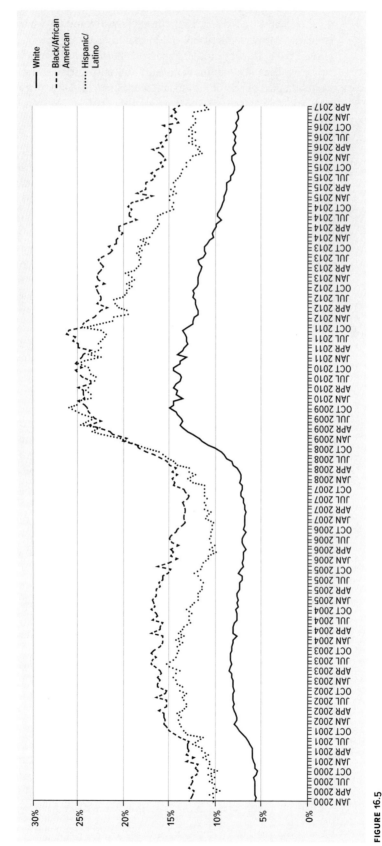

FIGURE 16.5
Underemployment Rate of Workers Age 16 and Older by Race and Ethnicity, January 2000–April 2017
Source: Shierholz, 2013.
Note: Data for Asians not provided.

other factors determine the mortgage type and amount available to potential homeowners. These factors also influence the type, size, age, and amenities of the home, the type of neighborhood, and, finally, opportunities such as well-being and wealth building, which in turn determine the individual factors that influence homeownership (see chapters 1, 2, 7, 8, and 15).

MACROECONOMIC FACTORS THAT INFLUENCE HOMEOWNERSHIP BY RACE AND ETHNICITY

Over the past two or three decades incomes have remained stagnant or declined for many Americans, causing income inequality to increase. "The political response to rising inequality—whether carefully planned or an unpremeditated reaction to constituent demands—was to expand lending to households, especially low-income ones" (Rajan, 2010: 9). Macroeconomic public strategies have been to cut interest rates or to maintain relatively low interest rates, as determined by the Federal Reserve. Low interest rates have kept inflation and mortgage interest rates relatively low (Rajan, 2010), partially fueling homeownership (see chapter 7). Figure 16.6 illustrates the overall decline of thirty-year fixed mortgage rates from 1993 to 2013.

Macroeconomic private strategies aimed at including people of color within the mortgage lending process have included practices such as implementing risk-based pricing and developing new mortgage products. Before the 1980s, mortgage applicants, based on then-current underwriting practices and standards, either qualified for a mortgage or did not. At that point in time, mortgages were either conventional or a Federal Housing Administration (FHA) or Veterans Administration (VA) mortgage (Schwartz, 2015). This situation changed in the early 1980s, when the Depository Institutions Deregulation and Monetary Control Act gave banks the flexibility to set rates for mortgages and the Alternative Mortgage Transaction Parity Act allowed banks to offer variable-rate mortgages with balloon payments (Lud-

FIGURE 16.6
Interest Rates of 30-Year Fixed Mortgages, 1993–2013
Source: Freddie Mac, http://www.freddiemac.com/pmms/pmms30.htm.

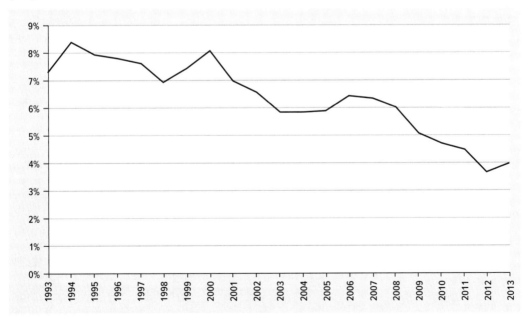

wig, Kamihachi, & Toh, 2009). Lenders then introduced risk-based pricing (i.e., in exchange for a higher risk of predicted default, borrowers would pay higher interest and fees) in the mid-1980s (Immergluck, 2009).

In the mid- to late 1990s product innovation caught on, including nontraditional mortgages such as hybrid adjustable-rate mortgages (ARMs), interest-only loans, pay-option ARMs, or loans with negative amortization (Engel & McCoy, 2011).

> Historically, subprime had referred to features of borrowers. Typically, subprime borrowers had been people with blemished credit histories, often with significant amounts of equity in their homes. In the second iteration of subprime lending, the word *subprime* shifted to describe the type of loan, not the features of borrowers. These new products were also referred to as Alt-A or nonprime loans; prime loans were called A loans. (Engel & McCoy, 2011: 34)

Subprime loans have higher interest rates than prime loans and are targeted to borrowers who do not qualify for prime loans because they are considered risky borrowers. Interestingly, many studies have shown that subprime and nontraditional mortgages are more heavily concentrated in neighborhoods of color, even after controlling for many demographic, socioeconomic, and mortgage-related factors (Bocian, Ernst, & Li, 2006; Center for Responsible Lending, 2007; Mayer & Pence, 2008; see chapters 7 and 8).

PUBLIC POLICY FACTORS THAT INFLUENCE HOMEOWNERSHIP BY RACE AND ETHNICITY

U.S. public policy has directly and indirectly supported homeownership for decades, based on the assumption that homeownership has positive consequences, although some of the consequences did not turn out to be positive and many of these assumptions have not been researched to a large degree (Dietz & Haurin, 2003). Public policies and public institutions have included the Mortgage Interest Deduction (since 1913), the Federal Home Loan Bank (FHLB) system (since 1932), the Home Owners' Loan Corporation (HOLC, from 1933 to 1954), the Federal Housing Administration (FHA, since 1934), the Federal National Mortgage Association (Fannie Mae, since 1938), the Servicemen's Readjustment Act (since 1944), the Government National Mortgage Association (Ginnie Mae, since 1968), the Federal Home Loan Mortgage Corporation (Freddie Mac, since 1970), and the Federal Housing Enterprises Financial Safety and Soundness Act (FHEFSSA, since 1992) (Anacker, 2015).

While these public policies benefit many, regardless of race and ethnicity, the FHA and the FHEFSSA seem to disproportionately benefit borrowers of color. In 1934 President Roosevelt established the FHA primarily to stimulate the residential lending and home-building industries in the short run and to improve the housing stock in the long run. Prior to the establishment of the FHA, down payment requirements were large, repayment schedules were short, and balloon payments at the end of the life cycle of the mortgage were large (Carr & Anacker, 2014). Thus homeownership had been unaffordable for many until the FHA was established (Immergluck, 2009). The FHA, operating under the U.S. Department of Housing and Urban Development since 1965, provides insurance products for borrowers of approved mortgage lenders for single-family, multifamily, and manufactured homes and hospitals. It operates entirely from self-generated income (Steggell, 2012; see also chapters 7 and 8).

Over the past few decades, the FHA has played a countercyclical role that again became apparent during and especially after the Great Recession. While the FHA's market share was 3.1 percent of all mortgage originations in 2005, its market share was 21.1 percent in 2010 and 12.2 percent in the third quarter of 2013 (U.S. Department of Housing and Urban Development, 2013). The FHA's low market share in 2005 can be explained by the many borrowers of FHA-insured loans who refinanced their mortgages through subprime and nontraditional mortgages. Its high market share in 2010 can be explained by the agency's continued insurance efforts. Since 2008, most private lenders have sharply reduced mortgage availability, partly due to tighter standards for down payments, credit scores, and debt-to-income ratios (Fratantoni, Khater, Li, & Goodman, 2015; Li & Goodman, 2014). The relatively low market share in 2013 can be explained by the decrease in the overall size of the mortgage market, not only due to the continuation of reduced mortgage availability but also to the general continued economic uncertainty. Also, many households are overleveraged and millennials have postponed and possibly discarded interest in the notion of homeownership (Galante, 2013a; Parrott & Zandi, 2013; Vague, 2014). Figure 16.7 illustrates the proportion of FHA versus non-FHA mortgages from 1993 to 2012.

Reduced mortgage availability is illustrated by recently increased mortgage insurance premium (MIP) and down payment requirements (U.S. Department of Housing and Urban Development, 2012). The MIP, to be paid by the borrower, changed to 1.75 percent as of April 9, 2012, from 1 percent as of October 4, 2010 (U.S. Department of Housing and Urban Development, 2012). FHA-insured loans to borrowers with a FICO score of 579 or lower require a minimum down payment of 10 percent, and loans to borrowers with a FICO score of 580 or above require a minimum down payment of 3.5 percent. While the minimum FICO score for an FHA-insured loan is 500,

FIGURE 16.7
Proportion of FHA versus Non-FHA Mortgages, 1993–2012
Source: Original information based on data from the National Association of Realtors, the U.S. Census Bureau, and HUD, http://portal.hud.gov/hudportal/documents/huddoc?id=fhamkt0712.pdf.

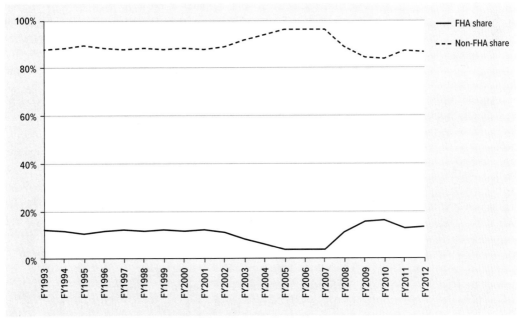

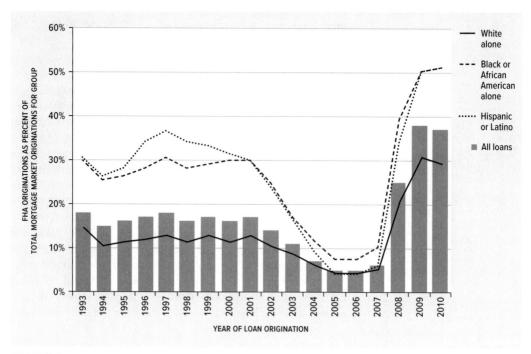

FIGURE 16.8
FHA Originations as Proportion of Total Mortgage Market Originations by Race and Ethnicity, 1993–2010
Source: U.S. Department of Housing and Urban Development, n.d.
Note: Data for Asians not provided.

current FHA borrowers have an average credit score above 700, about fifty points higher than in normal times (Parrott & Zandi, 2013).

Over the past two decades, the FHA has disproportionately benefited borrowers of color. During the national mortgage lending frenzy the proportion of borrowers of color who obtained an FHA-insured mortgage decreased, as many refinanced their mortgages with subprime and nontraditional mortgages. After 2007 the proportion of FHA borrowers of color increased, as many refinanced their subprime and other nontraditional loans that had reset to higher rates through FHA-insured mortgages. Figure 16.8 illustrates the increase in these proportions.

In 2011, 50.1 percent of all black/African American and 48.5 percent of Hispanic/Latino home buyers obtained a mortgage insured by the FHA, according to HMDA data, representing a large shift back to the FHA for this population group (Galante, 2013a, 2013b, 2013c; U.S. Department of Housing and Urban Development, 2012; see also chapters 7, 8, and 15).

Other policies that have disproportionately benefited borrowers of color are the affordable housing goals established by the U.S. Department of Housing and Urban Development in 1992 and codified in the Federal Housing Enterprises Financial Safety and Soundness Act (FHEFSSA) for the government-sponsored enterprises (GSEs) Fannie Mae and Freddie Mac. In return, the GSEs were exempted from state and local taxes, which made mortgages more affordable (Engel & McCoy, 2011; see also chapters 7 and 8).

The three statutory goals were as follows:

- The Low- and Moderate-Income Housing Goal: loans to borrowers with incomes at or below the median income for the market area in which they live;
- The Special Affordable Goal: loans to very low income borrowers (those with incomes at or below 60 percent of the area median

income), or to low-income borrowers living in low-income areas (borrowers with incomes at or below 80 percent of the area median income, living in census tracts in which the median income of households is at or below 80 percent of the area median income);

- The Underserved Areas Goal: loans to borrowers living in low-income census tracts (tracts in which the median income of residents is at or below 90 percent of the area median income) or high-minority tracts (tracts in which minorities make up at least 30 percent of residents, and the median income of residents in the tracts does not exceed 120 percent of the area median income) (Weicher, 2010: 3).

Table 16.2 shows the established affordable housing goals by type and by market share from 1993 to 2008. The table illustrates that for underserved areas the market share of the GSEs increased from 34 percent in 1995 to 44 percent in 2005 and 2006 and then decreased to 42 percent in 2008. The increase in the market share is also reflected in the increase in the black/African American and Hispanic/Latino homeownership rates, which peaked in 2004 and 2006–7, respectively, as shown in Figure 16.2. Interestingly, mortgages insured by the GSEs perform better than mortgages owned by servicers, as they contain a higher proportion of prime loans (Office of the Comptroller of the Currency, 2014; see chapter 10).

Since 2008, the benchmarks for the affordable housing goals have been reduced by the Federal Housing Finance Agency (FHFA). Examples of programs and initiatives that address the impact of the national foreclosure cri-

TABLE 16.2
Affordable Housing Goals of the GSEs Compared to Market Shares

Year	Low- and moderate-income goal	Low- and moderate-income market	Special affordable goal	Special affordable market	Underserved areas goal	Underserved areas market
1993	30.0%	NR	NA	NA	30.0%	NR
1994	30.0%	NR	NA	NA	30.0%	NR
1995	30.0%	57.0%	NA	29.0%	30.0%	34.0%
1996	40.0%	57.0%	12.0%	29.0%	21.0%	33.0%
1997	42.0%	57.5%	14.0%	29.0%	24.0%	34.0%
1998	42.0%	54.0%	14.0%	26.0%	24.0%	31.0%
1999	42.0%	58.0%	14.0%	29.0%	24.0%	34.0%
2000	42.0%	59.0%	14.0%	30.0%	24.0%	35.0%
2001	50.0%	55.0%	20.0%	26.5%	31.0%	33.0%
2002	50.0%	50.0%	20.0%	23.5%	31.0%	34.0%
2003	50.0%	53.0%	20.0%	24.5%	31.0%	34.0%
2004	50.0%	58.0%	20.0%	28.0%	31.0%	42.0%
2005	52.0%	57.0%	22.0%	28.0%	37.0%	44.0%
2006	53.0%	55.0%	23.0%	27.5%	38.0%	44.0%
2007	55.0%	52.0%	25.0%	24.7%	38.0%	40.0%
2008	56.0%	54.0%	27.0%	26.5%	39.0%	42.0%

Source: Weicher, 2010. Reprinted with permission.
Note: Market shares are reported to the nearest percentage, except where the share is halfway between two percentage points (e.g., 57.5%) or where the market share is within 1 percent of the goal;
NA: Goals were set in dollar amounts rather than percentages for each GSE; NR: Market shares not reported.

sis are the FHA Secure Program, through which the FHA refinanced delinquent homeowners into more affordable mortgages to prevent foreclosure; the Hope Now Alliance, which provided foreclosure-prevention counseling to homeowners over the phone free of charge; the National Foreclosure Mitigation Counseling (NFMC) Program, which awarded funding to local housing counseling organizations to advise homeowners in or at risk of foreclosure; HERA, which provided funding for local governments and nonprofit organizations to buy and renovate foreclosed properties through the Neighborhood Stabilization Programs (NSP1, NSP2, NSP3) in order to stabilize communities impacted by the foreclosure crisis; and the Making Home Affordable (MHA) initiative, which includes the Home Affordable Modification Program (HAMP) and the Home Affordable Refinance Program (HARP) (Carr & Anacker, 2013). While HAMP seeks to reduce the debt-service costs of eligible homeowners at risk of foreclosure, HARP helps eligible homeowners refinance their mortgages under more affordable terms through the GSEs (Schwartz, 2012).

The NFMC and HAMP Programs have disproportionately benefited borrowers of color. The NFMC Program was established in December 2007 to increase the availability of foreclosure counseling by strengthening the capacity of various housing counseling agencies, such as HUD-approved housing counseling intermediaries, State Housing Finance Agencies, and NeighborWorks organizations. Since the program's start, Congress has made seven appropriations, totaling over $695 million. In 2008 and 2009 this program helped save local governments, lenders, and borrowers approximately $920 million. The NFMC Program has provided foreclosure prevention counseling to more than 1.5 million homeowners, resulting in an average mortgage modification of $176 per month, representing $372 million in annual savings to these homeowners (NeighborWorks America, 2013).

Many of the beneficiaries of the NFMC program are of color. Whereas non-Hispanic whites comprise 84 percent of all homeowners, they make up only 57 percent of all NFMC Program clients. Interestingly, blacks/African Americans comprise 8 percent of all homeowners, but they make up 26 percent of all NFMC Program clients. Similarly, Hispanics/Latinos also comprise 8 percent of all homeowners, but they make up 19 percent of all NFMC Program clients. These percentages illustrate that many borrowers of color have been impacted by the subprime and foreclosure crises (NeighborWorks America, 2013).

HAMP has also disproportionately benefited borrowers of color. As illustrated in Table 16.3, while 56.5 percent of borrowers who were both seriously delinquent and in foreclosure were non-Hispanic white, 51.4 percent of borrowers who entered the HAMP application process were non-Hispanic white. For blacks/African Americans, these proportions were 15.1 versus 17.8 percent, respectively; for Asians, 4.9 versus 4.8 percent; and for Hispanics, 21.4 versus 23.2 percent (Mayer & Piven, 2012).

On a broader scale, the federal government also established the Consumer Financial Protection Bureau (CFPB) in 2011, based on the Dodd-Frank Wall Street Reform and Consumer Protection Act of 2010. The CFPB provides information to consumers so they better understand the terms of their agreements with financial companies. The agency is broadly empowered to purge unfair, deceptive, and abusive lending practices from the financial markets as well as promote consumer financial education, monitor

TABLE 16.3
Comparison of Homeowners with Troubled Mortgages (Seriously Delinquent or Foreclosed) with HAMP Applicants, by Race and Ethnicity

Race/ethnicity	Proportion of borrowers seriously delinquent (60+ days)	Proportion of borrowers with completed foreclosures	Proportion of borrowers seriously delinquent or in foreclosure	Proportion of borrowers who entered HAMP application process
Non-Hispanic White	57.3%	55.4%	56.5%	51.4%
Black/African American	15.9%	14.2%	15.1%	17.8%
Asian	4.6%	5.3%	4.9%	4.8%
Hispanic	20.3%	22.8%	21.4%	23.2%
Non-Hispanic other	1.8%	2.2%	2.1%	2.8%
TOTAL	100.0%	100.0%	100.0%	100.0%

Source: Mayer & Piven, 2012. Reprinted with permission.

financial markets, and recommend improvements to financial services delivery (Carr & Anacker, 2013); it has also disproportionately benefited consumers of color (see chapters 7, 8, 10, and 15).

CONCLUSION

This chapter discussed housing in the context of racial and ethnic diversity for renters and homeowners in the United States, focusing on individual factors, differentiated by race and ethnicity, macroeconomic factors, and public policy, all of which influence homeownership. Over the next few decades the proportions of Hispanics/Latinos, blacks/African Americans, and Asians will increase. Thus the United States will become a nation of people of color.

Over the past decades, many black/African American and Hispanic/Latino communities, compared to many non-Hispanic white and Asian communities, have faced challenges that have had and will continue to have vast effects on the opportunities, well-being, and wealth-building potential of current and future generations. Despite the Great Recession, homeownership will likely continue to be the number-one wealth-building tool for most households, especially households of color (see chapters 7 and 15). However, households of color have faced elevated hurdles to homeownership. The planned housing finance reform and the intended elimination of Fannie Mae and Freddie Mac will most likely impact affordable homeownership and possibly increase the hurdles to it, especially for home buyers of color (Carr & Anacker, 2014; see chapters 8 and 15). Thus future generations of blacks/African Americans and Hispanics/Latinos will be excluded from opportunities, well-being, and wealth building. Ironically this exclusion might occur in a nation some have called the "world's wealthiest country" (Leef, 2013, n. p.), and one that has prided itself on providing equal opportunities for all.

REFERENCES

Anacker, K. B. (2015). Saving while black: From the Freedman's Savings Bank, to public policy missing in action, to a new downpayment savings product and policy. *Banking and Financial Services Policy Report 34*, 11–17.

Austin, A. (2012). *A good credit score did not protect Latino and Black borrowers*. Washington, D.C.: Economic Policy Institute. Retrieved July 22, 2014, from http://www.epi.org/publication/latino-black-borrowers-high-rate-subprime-mortgages/.

Barenstein, M., Ruparel, A., & Thompson, R. K. (2007). *Credit-based insurance scores: Impacts on consumers of automobile insurance*. Report to Congress by the Federal Trade Commission. Retrieved July 22, 2014, from http://www.ftc.gov/sites/default/files/documents/reports/credit-based-insurance-scores-impacts-consumers-automobile-insurance-report-congress-federal-trade/p044804facta_report_credit-based_insurance_scores.pdf.

Belsky, E. S., & Retsinas, N. P. (2005). New paths to building assets for the poor. In N. P. Retsinas & E. S. Belsky (Eds.), *Building assets, building credit* (pp. 1–9). Cambridge, Mass.: Joint Center for Housing Studies of Harvard University; Washington, D.C.: Brookings Institution Press.

Bhutta, N., & Canner, G. B. (2013). Mortgage market conditions and borrower outcomes: Evidence from the 2012 HMDA data and matched HMDA-credit record data. *Federal Reserve Bulletin 99*, 1–58.

Board of Governors of the Federal Reserve System (2007). *Report to the Congress on credit scoring and its effects on the availability and affordability of credit*. Retrieved July 22, 2014, from http://www.federalreserve.gov/boarddocs/rptcongress/creditscore/creditscore.pdf.

Bocian, D. G., Ernst, K. S., & Li, W. (2006). *Unfair lending: The effect of race and ethnicity on the price of subprime mortgages*. Durham, N.C.: Center for Responsible Lending. Retrieved July 18, 2014, from http://www.responsiblelending.org/mortgage-lending/research-analysis/rr011-Unfair_Lending-0506.pdf.

Bocian, D. G., Li, W., & Ernst, K. S. (2010). *Foreclosures of race and ethnicity: The demographics of a crisis*. Durham, N.C.: Center for Responsible Lending. Retrieved July 23, 2014, from http://www.responsiblelending.org/mortgage-lending/research-analysis/foreclosures-by-race-executive-summary.pdf.

Bratt, R. G. (2006). Housing and economic security. In R. G. Bratt, M. E. Stone, & C. Hartman (Eds.), *A right to housing: Foundation for a new social agenda* (pp. 399–426). Philadelphia: Temple University Press.

Carr, J. H., & Anacker, K. B. (2013). Five lessons offered by but not learned from the recent collapse of the U.S. economy and the housing market. In C. Hartman, & G. D. Squires (Eds.), *From foreclosure to fair lending: Advocacy, organizing, occupy, and the pursuit of equitable credit* (pp. 55–82). New York: New Village Press.

Carr, J. H., & Anacker, K. B. (2014). The past and current politics of housing finance and the future of Fannie Mae, Freddie Mac, and homeownership in the United States. *Banking and Financial Services Policy Report, 33*, 1–10.

Center for Responsible Lending (2007). *Subprime lending: A net drain on homeownership*. Retrieved July 18, 2014, from http://www.responsiblelending.org/mortgage-lending/research-analysis/Net-Drain-in-Home-Ownership.pdf.

Chang, M. L. (2010). *Shortchanged: Why women have less wealth and what can be done about it*. Oxford: Oxford University Press.

Dietz, R. D., & Haurin, D. R. (2003). The social and private micro-level consequences of homeownership. *Journal of Urban Economics, 54*, 401–450.

Economic Policy Institute (2014). *All races hurt by recession, racial and ethnic disparities persist: Underemployment rate of workers age 16 and older by race and ethnicity, 2000–2014*. Retrieved July 23, 2014, from http://stateofworkingamerica.org/charts/underemployment-by-race-and-ethnicity/.

Editors of New Strategist Publications (2011). Introduction. In New Strategist Publications (Eds.), *Americans and their homes: Demographics of homeownership* (pp. 1–3). Amityville, N.Y.: New Strategist Publications.

Engel, K. C., & McCoy, P. (2011). *The subprime virus: Reckless credit, regulatory failure, and next steps*. Oxford: Oxford University Press.

Fratantoni, M., Khater, S., Li, W., & Goodman, L. (2015). *Measuring mortgage credit availability*. Housing Finance Policy Center lunchtime data talk, Urban Institute, Washington, D.C.

Freddie Mac (n.d.). *30-year fixed-rate mortgages since 1971*. Retrieved July 17, 2014, from http://www.freddiemac.com/pmms/pmms30.htm.

Frey, W. H. (2013, June 19). *Shift to a majority-minority population in the U.S. happening faster than expected*. Washington, D.C.: Brookings Institution. Retrieved July 5, 2014, from http://www.brookings.edu/blogs/up-front/posts/2013/06/19-us-majority-minority-population-census-frey.

Frey, W. H. (2015). *Diversity explosion: How new racial demographics are remaking America*. Washington, D.C.: Brookings Institution Press.

Galante, C. (2013a, June 4). Federal Housing Administration's Fiscal Year 2014 budget request: Written testimony of Carol Galante, assistant secretary for housing/Federal Housing Administration commissioner, U.S. Department of Housing and Urban Development (HUD). Retrieved February 13, 2014, from http://portal.hud.gov/hudportal/HUD?src=/press/testimonies.

Galante, C. (2013b, February 13). Written testimony of Carol Galante, assistant secretary for housing/Federal Housing Administration commissioner, U.S. Department of Housing and Urban Development (HUD). Retrieved July 23, 2014, from http://portal.hud.gov/hudportal/HUD?src=/press/testimonies.

Galante, C. (2013c, July 24). Written testimony of Carol Galante, assistant secretary for housing/Federal Housing Administration commissioner, U.S. Department of Housing and Urban Development (HUD. Retrieved July 23, 2014, from http://portal.hud.gov/hudportal/HUD?src=/press/testimonies.

Gottesdiener, L. (2013). *A dream foreclosed: Black America and the fight for a place to call home*. Westfield, N.J.: Zuccotti Park Press.

Haughwout, A., Mayer, C., & Tracy, J. (2009). *Subprime mortgage pricing: The impact of race, ethnicity, and gender on the cost of borrowing* (Staff Report 368). New York: Federal Reserve Bank of New York. Retrieved July 23, 2014, from http://www.newyorkfed.org/research/staff_reports/sr368.pdf.

Immergluck, D. (2009). *Foreclosed: High-risk lending, deregulation, and the undermining of America's mortgage market*. Ithaca, N.Y.: Cornell University Press.

Jayasundera, T., Silver, J., Anacker, K. B., & Mantcheva, D. (2010). *Foreclosure in the nation's capital: How unfair and reckless lending undermines homeownership*. Washington, D.C.: National Community Reinvestment Coalition. Retrieved July 22, 2014, from http://www.ncrc.org/images/stories/pdf/research/ncrc_foreclosure_paper_final.pdf.

Joint Center for Housing Studies of Harvard University (2012). *The state of the nation's housing 2012*. Retrieved July 22, 2014, from http://www.jchs.harvard.edu/sites/jchs.harvard.edu/files/son2012.pdf.

Joint Center for Housing Studies of Harvard University (2013). *America's rental housing: Evolving markets and needs*. Retrieved July 23, 2014, from http://www.jchs.harvard.edu/sites/jchs.harvard.edu/files/jchs_americas_rental_housing_2013_1_0.pdf.

Joint Center for Housing Studies of Harvard University (2014). *The state of the nation's housing 2014*. Retrieved July 23, 2014, from http://www.jchs.harvard.edu/sites/jchs.harvard.edu/files/sonhr14_txt_bw-full.pdf.

Kochhar, R., Fry, R., & Taylor, P. (2011). *Wealth gaps rise to record highs between whites, blacks and Hispanics*. Washington, D.C.: Pew Research Center. Retrieved July 23, 2014, from http://www.pewsocialtrends.org/files/2011/07/SDT-Wealth-Report_7-26-11_FINAL.pdf.

Leef, G. (2013, November 1). America is the world's wealthiest country—Here is why that's a problem. *Forbes*. Retrieved July 23, 2014, from http://www.forbes.com/sites/georgeleef/2013/11/01/america-is-the-worlds-wealthiest-country-heres-why-thats-a-problem/.

Li, W., & Goodman, L. (2014). *Measuring mortgage credit availability using ex-ante probability of default*. Washington, D.C.: Urban Institute. Retrieved January 6, 2015, from http://www.urban.org/UploadedPDF/2000018-Measuring-Mortgage-Credit-Availability-Using-Ex-Ante-Probability-of-Default.pdf.

Ludwig, E. A., Kamihachi, J., & Toh, L. (2009). The CRA: Past successes and future opportunities. In P. Chakrabarti, D. Erickson, R. S. Essene, I. Galloway, & J. Olson (Eds.), *Revisiting the CRA: Perspectives on the future of the Community Reinvestment Act* (pp. 84–104). Boston: Federal Reserve Bank of Boston; San Francisco: Federal Reserve Bank of San Francisco.

Mayer, C., & Pence, K. (2008). *Subprime mortgages: What, where, and to whom?* Washington, D.C.: Federal Reserve Board. Retrieved July 18, 2014, from http://www.federalreserve.gov/pubs/feds/2008/200829/200829pap.pdf.

Mayer, N., & Piven, M. (2012). *Experience of people of color, women, and low-income homeowners in the Home Affordable Modification Program.* Washington, D.C.: Urban Institute. Retrieved July 21, 2014, from http://www.urban.org/UploadedPDF/412597-Experience-of-People-of-Color-Women-and-Low-Income-Homeowners.pdf.

Monger, R., & Yankay, J. (2014). *U.S. lawful permanent residents: 2013.* Retrieved July 4, 2014, from http://www.dhs.gov/sites/default/files/publications/ois_lpr_fr_2013.pdf.

NeighborWorks America (2013, October 22). *National Foreclosure Mitigation Counseling Program: Congressional update.* Retrieved July 22, 2014, from http://www.nw.org/network/foreclosure/nfmcp/documents/2013NFMCReport.pdf.

Office of the Comptroller of the Currency (2014). *OCC mortgage metrics report: Disclosure of National Bank and Federal Savings Association mortgage loan data: First quarter 2014.* Retrieved July 21, 2014, from http://www.occ.gov/publications/publications-by-type/other-publications-reports/mortgage-metrics-2014/mortgage-metrics-q1-2014.pdf.

Paciorek, A. D. (2013). *The long and the short of household formation.* Washington, D.C.: Federal Reserve Board. Retrieved July 4, 2014, from http://www.federalreserve.gov/pubs/feds/2013/201326/201326pap.pdf.

Parrott, J., & Zandi, M. (2013). *Opening the credit box.* Washington, D.C.: Urban Institute. Retrieved July 18, 2014, from http://www.urban.org/UploadedPDF/412910-Opening-the-Credit-Box.pdf.

Passel, J. S., Livingston, G., & Cohn, D. (2012). *Explaining why minority births now outnumber white births.* Washington, D.C.: Pew Research Center. Retrieved July 4, 2014, from http://www.pewsocialtrends.org/2012/05/17/explaining-why-minority-births-now-outnumber-white-births/.

Pelletiere, D. (2008). *Getting to the heart of housing's fundamental question: How much can a family afford?* Washington, D.C.: National Low Income Housing Coalition.

Quercia, R. G., Freeman, A., & Ratcliffe, J. (2011). *Regaining the dream: How to renew the promise of homeownership for America's working families.* Washington, D.C.: Brookings Institution Press.

Rajan, R. G. (2010). *Fault lines: How hidden fractures still threaten the world economy.* Princeton, N.J.: Princeton University Press.

Reid, C. (n.d.). *Addressing the disparate impact of foreclosures on communities of color.* Retrieved July 17, 2014, from http://www.ncg.org/s_ncg/bin.asp?CID=18222&DID=47517&DOC=FILE.PDF.

Rice, L., & Swesnik, D. (2014). Discriminatory effects of credit scoring on communities of color. *Suffolk University Law Review 46*, 935–966.

Rohe, W. (2012). Homeownership. In A. T. Carswell (Ed.), *The encyclopedia of housing* (pp. 293–298). Thousand Oaks, Calif.: Sage.

Schwartz, A. F. (2012). U.S. housing policy in the age of Obama: From crisis to stasis. *International Journal of Housing Policy 12*, 227–240.

Schwartz, A. F. (2015). *Housing policy in the United States.* New York: Routledge.

Schwartz, M., & Wilson E. (n.d.). *Who can afford to live in a home?: A look at data from the 2006 American Community Survey.* Washington, D.C.: U.S. Bureau of the Census.

Shierholz, H. (2013). *Roughly one in five Hispanic and black workers are "underemployed."* Washington, D.C.: Economic Policy Institute. Retrieved July 3, 2014, from http://www.epi.org/publication/roughly-hispanic-black-workers-underemployed/.

Steggell, C. (2012). Federal Housing Administration. In A. T. Carswell (Ed.), *The encyclopedia of housing* (pp. 216–221). Thousand Oaks, Calif.: Sage.

Tilly, C. (2006). The economic environment of housing: Income inequality and insecurity. In R. G. Bratt, M. E. Stone, & C. Hartman (Eds.), *A right to housing: Foundation for a new social agenda* (pp. 20–37). Philadelphia: Temple University Press.

Traub, A. (n.d.). *Discredited: How employment credit checks keep qualified workers out of a job.* New York: Demos. Retrieved July 18, 2014, from http://www.demos.org/sites/default/files/publications/Discredited-Demos.pdf.

Turner, M. A., Santos, R., Levy, D. K., Wissoker, D., Aranda, C., & Pitingolo, R. (2013).

Housing discrimination against racial and ethnic minorities 2012. Washington, D.C.: U.S. Department of Housing and Urban Development. Retrieved July 10, 2014, from http://www.huduser.org/portal//Publications/pdf/HUD-514_HDS2012.pdf.

U.S. Bureau of Labor Statistics (n.d.a). *Alternative measures of labor underutilization for states, second quarter of 2013 through first quarter of 2014 averages*. Retrieved June 30, 2014, from http://www.bls.gov/lau/stalt.htm.

U.S. Bureau of Labor Statistics (n.d.b). *Labor force statistics from the Current Population Survey*. Retrieved June 30, 2014, from http://data.bls.gov/timeseries/LNS14000003 &series_id=LNS14000006&series_id=LNU04032183&series_id=LNS14000009.

U.S. Bureau of the Census (n.d.). *Table 16: Quarterly homeownership rates by race and ethnicity of householder: 1994 to present (histtab16)*. Retrieved July 17, 2014, from http://www.census.gov/housing/hvs/data/histtabs.html.

U.S. Bureau of the Census (2012). *Table 6: Percent of the projected population by race and Hispanic origin for the United States: 2015 to 2060 (NP2012-T6)*. Retrieved July 4, 2014, from http://www.census.gov/population/projections/data/national/2012/summarytables.html.

U.S. Department of Housing and Urban Development (2012). *Annual report to Congress: Fiscal year 2012 financial status FHA mutual mortgage insurance fund*. Retrieved July 18, 2014, from http://portal.hud.gov/hudportal/documents/huddoc?id=F12MMIFundRepCong111612.pdf.

U.S. Department of Housing and Urban Development (2013). *National housing market summary*. Retrieved July 18, 2014, from http://www.huduser.org/portal/periodicals/ushmc/pdf/NationalSummary_3q13.pdf.

Vague, R. (2014). *The next economic disaster: Why it's coming and how to avoid it*. Philadelphia: University of Pennsylvania Press.

Wang, W. (2012). *The rise of intermarriage: Rates, characteristics vary by race and gender*. Washington, D.C.: Pew Research Center. Retrieved July 5, 2014, from http://www.pewsocialtrends.org/files/2012/02/SDT-Intermarriage-II.pdf.

Weicher, J. C. (2010). *The affordable housing goals, homeownership and risk: Some lessons from past efforts to regulate the GSEs*. Paper presented at conference on "The Past, Present, and Future of the Government-Sponsored Enterprise," Federal Reserve Bank of St. Louis, St. Louis, Mo. Retrieved July 8, 2014, from http://research.stlouisfed.org/conferences/gse/Weicher.pdf.

Chapter 17   Housing and Aging

DEIRDRE PFEIFFER

The United States has been in the throes of a dramatic demographic shift—aging. In 2012, 14 percent of people living in the United States were seniors, which in this chapter means being age sixty-five or older. By 2030 an estimated 20 percent of people living in the United States will be seniors (Ortman, Velkoff, & Hogan, 2014; see chapters 1 and 2). How does aging affect housing needs? What can practitioners, policy makers, and researchers do to help Americans remain independent and engaged in their communities as they age?

This chapter answers these questions. The first half will review demographic trends in aging in the United States and address how seniors are reshaping their homes and communities (see chapters 1 and 2). Older adults are more likely to live alone or in multigenerational households (Taylor et al., 2010). Older adults also are more likely to live in suburbs (Frey, 2007) and rural communities (Kirschner, Berry, & Glasgow, 2009), and they have a strong desire to stay where they have existing social networks (Harrell, Lynott, Guzman, & Lampkin, 2014; see chapter 12). Additionally, this population is more likely to have fixed incomes and have difficulty paying for other expenses, such as health care, after housing costs are met (Hayutin, 2012; see chapter 10).

The second half of this chapter will explore diverse strategies to help seniors age in places that are affordable, nurturing, and well matched to their capacities. Secondary dwelling units and universal design modifications are promising ways to make housing more flexible for seniors (Greenhouse, 2012; Hare, 1991; Howe, 1990; Litchfield, 2011; Null & Cherry, 1996). Publicly subsidized affordable rental housing and reverse mortgages can help make senior housing more affordable (Harrell, Brooks, & Nedwick, 2009; Haurin, Ma, Moulton, Schmeiser, and Seligman, 2016; Perl, 2010; see chapters 10 and 14). Retrofitting naturally occurring retirement communities (NORCs) to be livable for seniors and providing age-restricted and supportive housing offer older adults needed community choice (Durrett, 2009; Harrell et al., 2014; Pynoos, Liebig, Alley, & Nishita, 2004). Together, these strategies can help keep seniors supported and socially integrated in the remaining years of their life (see chapter 12).

AN AGING AMERICA

The United States' older population is increasing at a rapid rate. In demographic terms, this means that seniors are starting to outnumber children. From 2012 to 2050, the number of seniors is projected to almost double, from forty-three to eighty-four million, which will increase their share of the population from 14 to 21 percent (Ortman et al., 2014). Shortly after 2050, seniors are expected to account for a greater proportion of the population than children under age eighteen (Ortman et al., 2014; see chapters 1 and 2).

One driver of this trend is the aging of the baby boom generation. Baby boomers were born in the two decades immediately after World War II, 1946 to 1964, a period marked by elevated fertility rates. Baby boomers' age group, fifty-five- to sixty-four-year-olds, was the fastest growing age group in the 2000s (Lipman, Lubell, & Salomon, 2012). Currently, there are about seventy-seven million baby boomers, representing just less than one-quarter of the population (Colby & Ortman, 2014). Baby boomers are beginning to transition from middle to older age—the first baby boomers became seniors in 2011.

Advances in health care also contribute to the aging of the United States. Both life span and health span are lengthening. Life expectancy increased markedly during the twentieth century. While Americans born in 1900 were expected to live to age forty-seven, this had increased to sixty-eight by 1950 and seventy-eight by 2010 (Carstensen, 2012; Centers for Disease Control and Prevention, 2013; Hayutin, 2012). A person's health span is the number of years that he or she is expected to be relatively free from chronic illness and disease (National Academy of Sciences, 2008). Americans are not only living longer but also functioning at a higher level over a longer period of time compared to several decades ago, in spite of the increasing prevalence of chronic disease. The country is experiencing a "compression of morbidity," a term Fries (1980) suggested to refer to the trend of people being able to stay mobile and relatively healthy until the end of their life. Advancements in medical technology such as organ replacement and regeneration, which entails stimulating a person's body to repair his or her own organs, gene therapy, nanotechnology, and fast, daily disease screening may help to stall and potentially reverse bodily decline. For instance, in the future, seniors may start their day by spitting into a box in their bathroom, which would be able to quickly detect signs of impending disease, enabling them to treat it long before symptoms appear (Garreau, 2013b). If health care costs and the emerging epidemics of obesity, heart disease, and diabetes can be kept in check, living to (and past) one hundred may become commonplace (Arrison, 2011; Garreau, 2013a; Vaupel, 2010). Despite these possibilities, the prevalence of these epidemics remains high, and they are partly responsible for rising health care costs (Centers for Disease Control and Prevention, 2014a, 2014b, 2014c).

The changing composition of the elderly and advancements in medical technology are helping to redefine the culture of aging. The life cycle stages that compose the second half of life have diversified. No longer are Americans going from working adulthood to retirement. A new, transitional stage called "active retirement" has emerged (Brooks, 2011). Active retirement spans the fifties, sixties, and seventies. Active retirees tend to be empty nesters who are scaling down their careers. This gives them more time and flexibility to travel and have fun. This stage is often defined by having new experiences, moving to new places, and meeting new people (Brooks, 2011; see chapter 2).

SENIORS' HOUSING TRENDS

Aging brings about wide-reaching physiological, social, and economic changes. Physiological changes include declines in body function, such as lung capacity, bone density, memory, and information processing, and a tempering of emotions. Some of these occur as a normal part of the aging process, while others are a result of chronic disease (see chapter 6). Social changes include a narrowing and deepening of social relationships (Carstensen, 2012; see chapter 12). Economic changes primarily include changes in employment. Seniors who have the resources and desire to leave the labor market are retiring. Every day, about ten thousand baby boomers retire (Bethell, 2011; see chapter 2). Of this group, some stay engaged in their communities by becoming volunteers and taking on other roles (see chapter 12). Other seniors do not have the resources or desire to retire and continue to work full time or part time (Thayer, 2007; see chapter 2). Diminished home values and personal savings in the aftermath of the Great Recession have postponed the retirement of many baby boomers (Kochhar, Fry, & Taylor, 2011; Lusardi & Mitchell, 2013; see chapters 2 and 15).

These interlocking transformations lead seniors to rely on their relatives and friends more and use their homes and communities differently than other age groups (see chapter 6). Suburban and rural places are bearing the brunt of these changes. More than 50 percent of senior-headed households are suburban (Lipman et al., 2012). Just over 20 percent of senior-headed households are rural (Housing Assistance Council, 2011; U.S. Bureau of the Census, 2010). Communities in these types of places are struggling to overcome barriers to meeting aging residents' changing needs, which include a lack of walkable or transit-accessible services and amenities and visitable housing, among other conditions (see chapter 13).

Living Alone

Seniors, particularly women, are increasingly likely to live alone. Almost 30 percent of all adults living alone and not in an institution in the United States are seniors (Klinenberg, 2012). The proportion of seniors living alone has increased from 10 percent to over 30 percent since 1950 (Klinenberg, 2012). Living alone often results from unexpected changes in family circumstances, such as the death of a spouse or a divorce. In the past, these events were associated with impoverishment, particularly for women, and led older adults to move in with family (Ruggles, 2007). At the turn of the twentieth century, for instance, only 10 percent of senior widows lived alone. Today, 62 percent of senior widows live alone (Klinenberg, 2012).

Other older adults prefer to live alone rather than with family or in an institutional setting, such as assisted living or a nursing home (Klinenberg, 2012). Living with family can mean taking on unwanted extra work, such as childcare or household chores, and enduring emotional strain (Newman, 2010). The freedom from responsibility toward others that comes with living alone can be rewarding for seniors, especially after decades of raising children and climbing the career ladder (Klinenberg, 2012). Moving into a nursing home, on the other hand, can lead to a loss of independence, privacy, and social networks (see chapter 2).

There are disadvantages to living alone as well. Living alone puts people, including older adults, at risk of social isolation, which is characterized by physical or emotional distance from other people (Elder & Retrum, 2012). Seniors who live alone are more likely to spend the majority of their time alone than married seniors—on average, ten hours a day compared to five hours a day for married seniors (Klinenberg, 2012). An estimated 16 percent of seniors experience social isolation because they live alone and speak a language other than English or have a disability that makes social interaction difficult (Elder & Retrum, 2012). Built environment characteristics, such as low-density housing, also can frustrate seniors' social interaction (Elder & Retrum, 2012). Social isolation can degrade older adults' physical and mental health (Elder & Retrum, 2012). Socially isolated seniors may lack social support networks that can help them adapt to and cope with stressful situations. Diseases such as diabetes, arthritis, hypertension, and emphysema may develop or progress faster for these seniors (Tomaka, Thompson, & Palacios, 2006). One reason for this may be that they do not receive the medical care that they need because no one is there to remind them about or transport them to doctors' appointments or the pharmacy (Hughes-Cromwick & Wallace, 2006). Social isolation may lead to chronic loneliness, depression, and, in rare cases, suicide (Elder & Retrum, 2012). Strategies to help seniors socialize and avoid becoming isolated include connecting them with volunteer visiting and companionship programs and virtual communities (Elder & Retrum, 2012; see chapter 12).

Living in Multigenerational Households

Seniors are also more likely than the general population to live in multigenerational households. Multigenerational households are those households that have two or more related adult generations under one roof, such as an adult daughter living with her mother or a married couple with children living with their elderly parents. While about 16 percent of people of all age groups residing in the United States live in a multigenerational household, about 20 percent of seniors do, an increase from about 17 percent in 1990 (Harrell, Kassner, & Figueiredo, 2011; Taylor et al., 2011). Still, current proportions of seniors living in multigenerational households are far lower than rates prior to the establishment of Social Security in 1935, when seniors were more reliant on family to survive. In 1900, for instance, 57 percent of seniors lived in multigenerational households (Taylor et al., 2010).

Multigenerational households including seniors may form when seniors' adult children move in with them or seniors move out of their homes and in with their adult children (Bethell, 2011; Newman, 2010). These living arrangements may benefit all household members. Seniors may have others to help with caretaking and household chores as their mobility and acuity deteriorate (Bethell, 2011; Newman, 2010). Adult children may value their parent's help with childcare, cooking, and other household tasks that are typically difficult to undertake in two-worker households (Bethell, 2011; Newman, 2010). Both groups may enjoy the daily socialization that comes from living with family (Bethell, 2011; Newman, 2010). Finally, the costs of living together may be significantly less than living apart. Combining resources may mean access to more amenities in the home and more money left over to pay for health care, education, and other expenses (Bethell, 2011).

Multigenerational living arrangements also have drawbacks. Seniors may struggle to find privacy within the home, especially if living with family results in overcrowding (Newman, 2010). Older adults may miss their independence. Quarrels may result when views about child rearing, financial management, cooking style, cleanliness, and other values diverge (Newman, 2010).

Over-Housed in the Suburbs

The aging of America is primarily a suburban phenomenon. Much of the growth in the senior population over the next several decades is expected to occur in the suburbs of metropolitan areas in the western and southern regions, such as Las Vegas, Phoenix, Raleigh, and Atlanta. These are places where baby boomers have moved and are planning to grow old (Frey, 2007; DeGood, 2011).

Regardless of their regional location, suburban seniors may be "over-housed." This means that they have at least one unused or underused room. Over-housed seniors may be "house rich but cash poor," that is, they may hold equity in their home but may not be able to access it to pay for maintenance and other costs. Being over-housed is also a condition experienced by older adult homeowners in rural communities and central cities. Whether they will be able to eventually benefit from their equity by selling their homes depends in part on whether the millennial generation that is entering adulthood in the 2000s will have the education and income needed to afford them (Myers, 2008) and be willing to live in suburbia. Some studies in the wake of the Great Recession have found that these young adults prefer to live in denser, more walkable central cities and suburban downtowns, which would put the equity of older adults living in lower-density, automobile-dependent suburbs at risk (e.g., Leinberger, 2011). This claim is hotly debated by journalists, housing scholars, and policy makers (e.g., Kotkin, 2011).

Isolated in Rural Areas

Rural places are aging much faster than urban places (Kirschner, Berry, & Glasgow, 2009). This is due in part to rural seniors' preference to stay in their communities, the continued outmigration of working-age adults to cities and suburbs, and the migration of seniors to rural areas with natural amenities (Kirschner, Berry, & Glasgow, 2009). Thus the proportion of older adults in rural areas has increased over time. Seniors currently head over 25 percent of rural households (Housing Assistance Council, 2013).

Rural seniors are vulnerable to social isolation, like suburban seniors, yet their access to fresh food, banking, and medical care is typically more limited than that of suburban seniors (Bailey, 2010; Elder & Retrum, 2012). The number of rural local grocery stores, for instance, plummeted during the 1990s and 2000s, requiring some seniors to travel long distances to access regional supercenter grocery stores, such as Walmart (Bailey, 2010). In 2010 about 20 percent of rural census tracts had low food access, meaning that at least five hundred people or one-third of residents lived over ten miles from a supermarket (U.S. Department of Agriculture, 2013). About 808,000 seniors lived in these communities (U.S. Department of Agriculture, 2013).

In about 43 percent of low-food-access rural communities, more than half of seniors lived at least ten miles away from a supermarket (U.S. Department of Agriculture, 2013). These issues are compounded by declines in rural bus service during the latter half of the 2000s. By 2010 over 10 percent of rural residents, approximately nine million people, had no access to rural bus service (Firestine, 2011; see chapter 13).

Older adults in rural communities have several defining housing conditions. Rural seniors are more likely to be homeowners than all seniors (83 percent compared to 79 percent of all seniors) (Housing Assistance Council, 2013; U.S. Bureau of the Census, 2012). Their housing is typically older; although only about 5 percent live in structures with moderate or severe physical issues, the cost of maintaining or upgrading them may be higher (Housing Assistance Council, 2013). Older adults living in rural areas are twice as likely to live in mobile homes compared to those in urban areas but less likely to live in mobile homes than rural residents of all ages. In turn, the proportion of rural seniors living in mobile homes is expected to increase as the baby boomer generation ages (George, Pinder, & Rose, 2003; see chapter 7).

Aging in Place

Regardless of where seniors live, most want to stay in their community and in their home as they age. About 90 percent of seniors surveyed in 2012 by the American Association of Retired Persons (AARP) wanted to continue living in their community for as long as possible (Harrell et al., 2014; see chapter 12).

The desire to age in place has practical and symbolic roots. On a practical level, seniors, compared to groups of a younger age, want to engage with people and places they already know and love—the itch for having new experiences is no longer as strong (Carstensen, 2006). On a symbolic level, seniors' homes and communities are not only places of shelter and points of access to services and amenities but also containers of memories and personal artifacts. They are deeply intertwined into seniors' sense of self (Csikszentmihalyi & Rochberg-Halton, 1981). For seniors, moving away from home may entail losing a part of oneself. Seniors who are able to age in place may be more socially engaged and have a higher sense of self-control, life satisfaction, and quality of life than those who age elsewhere (Kochera, Straight, & Guterbock, 2005; see chapter 12).

Historically, healthier and younger seniors (age sixty-five to seventy-four) tended to live at home until they experienced a disability or a severe, debilitating illness that left them unable to live independently (see chapter 6). Eventually they would move in with family or into assisted living or a nursing home (Pynoos & Liebig, 1995). Three emerging trends are helping frail seniors realize their desire to age in place. The first is the development of relatively affordable medical devices and services, including portable blood pressure or blood sugar monitors and oxygen tanks and local kidney dialysis centers. The second is the expansion of the home health care industry, which is driven in part by a redistribution of public funds away from nursing homes and into communities where seniors currently live. Rural seniors, however, have less access to home health care, in part because rural home health agencies tend to be smaller and more sparsely located than those in urban areas (Hutchinson, Hawes, & Williams, 2010). Rural seniors continue to rely disproportionately on institutions for long-term care, which constrains their ability to age in place (National Academy of Sciences, 2005). The third emerging trend is growing acceptance of universal design, which is explored later in the chapter (Pynoos & Liebig, 1995; see chapter 6).

Vulnerability to Shelter Poverty

Shelter poverty occurs when a household spends a large proportion of its income on housing so that few resources remain to meet their other needs (Stone, 1993). Seniors are at particular risk of shelter poverty because they are more likely to rely on fixed retirement and social welfare payments and have increasingly higher health care costs than other households. In the late 2000s, seniors were earning about $20,000 less annually than all age groups and spending a higher proportion of their income on housing and health care. The typical senior age seventy-five and older, for instance, spent 38 percent of his or her income on housing and 14 percent on health care, compared to rates of 35 percent and 4 percent among typical thirty-five to forty-four-year-olds (Hayutin, 2012).

Social Security Insurance income alone often falls short in paying for some expenses, including housing and medical care, with the average payment amounting to $14,000 annually. This is compounded by the fact that Medicare, a public health plan that covers most seniors, does not pay for many of the costs associated with long-term health care. For instance, Medicare only covers short-term nursing home stays and assisted living under certain circumstances, not the long-term receipt of these services (Benson & Aldrich, 2013). To receive subsidized long-term services and support, seniors must qualify for Medicaid (Benson & Aldrich, 2013). Impending federal budget cuts and deficit reduction plans may further limit the benefits of these programs in the future (Benson & Aldrich, 2013; see chapter 10).

Paying for housing comfortably into old age requires having private retirement savings. However, only about 30 percent of workers age fifty and older had saved at least $50,000 for retirement just prior to the start of the Great Recession in December 2007 (Thayer, 2007). Fluctuations in the financial and housing markets during the recession diminished many seniors' savings and home equity. Blacks/African Americans and Hispanics/Latinos, who lost 53 and 66 percent of their median net worth, respectively, during that time period, were particularly hard hit by declines in personal wealth; non-Hispanic whites, by comparison, experienced a loss of 15 percent (Kochhar et al., 2011; see chapters 10, 15, and 16).

The odds of experiencing shelter poverty vary by tenure. Seniors who own their homes without a mortgage are least at risk because they tend to have lower housing costs. More specifically, in 2009, about 60 percent of senior renters and 50 percent of senior homeowners with a mortgage paid 30 percent or more of their income on housing costs, compared to just fewer than 20 percent of seniors without a mortgage (Harrell, 2011). Because of their lower housing costs, seniors without a mortgage need fewer resources to cover all of their expenses. A healthy senior who is living alone and owns his or her home free and clear needs about $16,300 a year to support himself or herself. In comparison, seniors who rent or have a mortgage need about $20,250 and $24,000, respectively (Reno & Veghte, 2010; see chapters 7, 9, and 10).

The proportion of older adults paying a mortgage increased from 22 to 30 percent during the 2000s, which may mean that their risk of shelter poverty is increasing (Consumer Financial Protection Bureau, 2014). This trend is mostly due to differences in borrowing practices of the baby boomers compared to those of previous generations. Baby boomers, for instance, have tended to buy more expensive homes with lower down payments (Lusardi & Mitchell, 2013; see chapter 7). Increases in a variety of expenses prior to and in the wake of the recession also may have made it difficult for some older adults to pay off their mortgage and compelled others to refinance their mortgage or take out home equity loans to meet it (Consumer Financial Protection Bureau, 2014; Lusardi & Mitchell, 2013). These increased expenses include health care, property taxes, utility and maintenance costs, and college tuition (Harrell, 2011; see chapter 15).

SENIORS' HOUSING NEEDS

Seniors ideally need flexible housing as they age. Strategies such as secondary dwelling units and universal design can help them to adapt their homes and maintain their independence as their capacities change. Universally designed homes provide supportive features that allow older adults to maintain independence regardless of age, ability, or disability. Due to uncertainty in their health care and other costs, seniors who rent their home need greater certainty over their housing costs, and seniors who own their home need greater access to their home equity. Senior-oriented affordable rental housing complexes and reverse mortgages are promising ways of making sure older adults have the resources that they need to make ends meet. Finally, seniors have diverse preferences and physical and mental capabilities. Accommodating those differences requires allowing for community choice. Options include naturally occurring retirement communities (NORCs) and age-restricted and supportive housing (see chapter 6).

Flexible Housing

Ideally, older adults need access to flexible housing to age in place. Flexible housing is housing that can be adapted over the life course as needs and abilities change (Howe, 1990). Two strategies to make housing more flexible include secondary dwelling units and universal design.

SECONDARY DWELLING UNITS

Secondary dwelling units are known by many names, such as granny flats, guest houses, backyard cottages, casitas, Accessory Dwelling Units (ADUs), and in-law suites, among others. Secondary dwelling units are secondary living quarters on a single-family home property and may take many forms, such as adapted garages, attics, basements, or rooms, or even attached apartments or detached cottages (Litchfield, 2011). Older adults may move into secondary dwelling units built by others or construct their own. The occupants of the secondary dwelling unit may be part of or separate from the household in the main home. The relationship those living in the secondary unit have with occupants of the main home depends on whether they are related, the extent of separation between the secondary dwelling and the main home (e.g., through a separate entrance and kitchen), and whether the secondary dwelling is rented out (see chapter 2).

Secondary dwelling units help to sustain diverse seniors' financial, physical, and mental health. For seniors in multigenerational households, they enable "privacy with proximity" (Hare, 1991: 60). For senior homeowners, the rent from a secondary dwelling unit increases income and thus reduces potential shelter poverty. Those who live alone may also gain a needed helping hand for daily chores and transportation. For senior renters, the construction of secondary dwelling units by homeowners may increase the stock of affordable, smaller homes and broaden their housing options (see chapter 10). For all seniors, secondary dwelling units may reduce the risk of social isolation and enable them to age in place (see chapter 12).

Secondary dwelling units are usually financed and constructed by homeowners. At present, no federal public subsidies exist, so costs can be a barrier to their construction. Based on completed projects in the San Francisco Bay area, for instance, constructing a six-hundred-square-foot, two-bedroom secondary dwelling unit cost an estimated $250,000 in the early 2010s (New Avenue Blog, 2014; see chapter 7). Qualifying for a loan to cover these costs is difficult in the current tight lending market in general (Parrott & Zandi, 2013; see chapter 8) and in the absence of special public programs in particular. Although some localities provide technical assistance to homeowners and reduce their construction costs by waiving fees or allocating Community Development Block Grant (CDBG) funds if the unit will be rented at an affordable rate to a low-income family, public support is not widespread (Sage Computing, 2008). As a result, most homeowners will pay for construction out of pocket (see chapter 14). In the wake of the Great Recession, many seniors' retirement assets have decreased while their debt has increased, leaving them without savings to pay for a secondary dwelling unit (Lusardi & Mitchell, 2013). Thus most older adults or homeowners who construct a secondary unit will end up taking out a mortgage to finance it, thereby compounding their debt (see chapter 8).

Secondary dwelling units are built legally or extralegally, depending on the stipulations of the local zoning and building code (see chapter 9). Allowing for secondary dwelling units is becoming increasingly common (see figure 17.1). The estimated number of jurisdictions allowing for secondary dwelling units increased from 100 to 330 from 1989 to 2012 nationwide (Hare, 1989; Schafran, 2012). However, this is still only a fraction of the thousands of jurisdictions that exist. A fear of parking congestion, noise, crime, and social diversity leads many localities to prohibit them or impose strict setback and lot-size restrictions. Others may require that occupants of the secondary dwelling unit be part of the same household as those living in the main home by prohibiting them to be rented out or to have a separate kitchen, bathroom, mailbox, or entrance (Pfeiffer, 2015). These regulations limit the production of units and minimize the benefits for low-income senior renters. Concerns about aging and a lack of housing options to accommodate seniors, however, is leading suburbs in Phoenix and elsewhere to consider liberalizing their regulations (Pfeiffer, 2015). Limiting zoning for secondary dwelling units to parcels near transit may help lessen the potential negative impacts of increased population density on quality of life (Wegmann & Chapple, 2014; see chapters 9 and 12).

Tract home developers are also getting into the market of building secondary dwelling units to accommodate multigenerational families (Spivak, 2012). Multigenerational tract home subdivisions premiered across the Sunbelt during the 2000s and early 2010s in places such as Raleigh, North Caro-

FIGURE 17.1
The Secondary Unit Legalization Industry in Los Angeles
Image credit: D. Pfeiffer.

lina; Gilbert, Arizona; and Irvine, California. One of the most popular models is Lennar's NextGen home (Spivak, 2012).

UNIVERSAL DESIGN AND VISITABILITY

Homes are places where the basic activities of daily living (ADLs) occur. ADLs include bathing and showering, dressing, eating, getting in and out of bed and chairs, walking, and using the toilet. Navigating features such as stairs, doorways, bathtubs, and counters in undertaking these tasks can be challenging and, at worst, life threatening to seniors with disabilities. In 2007, close to 30 percent of seniors age sixty-five to seventy-four and over 50 percent of those age seventy-five and older had at least one disability (Torres-Gil & Hofland, 2012). A study of noninstitutionalized seniors receiving Medicare that same year found that over 25 percent had difficulty performing one or more activities of daily living (Greenberg, 2010). When a home has features that fit poorly with a senior's abilities, it may hasten his or her decline and reduce his or her independence (Greenhouse, 2012).

Universally designed homes help people of all ages, including seniors, live independently and in place even as they experience changes in abilities, mobility, and acuity. The universal design concept was first articulated in the 1970s by Ron Mace, an architect and disability advocate who founded the Center for Universal Design at North Carolina State University (Center for Universal Design, 2008). Universal design is design for all people, regardless of age, ability, or change in ability. It allows for mastery over the environment, even as abilities change. It entails building or modifying a home so that people of all ages, abilities, and life statuses can use it (Null & Cherry, 1996). To be usable for seniors, a home must be able to accommodate their reduced stamina, balance, vision, hearing, and response time, among other conditions (Greenhouse, 2012). Small-scale modifications include painting steps with contrasting colors, installing grab bars, placing chairs and other furniture to rest on throughout the home, and installing lever handles for faucets and doors. Large-scale modifications include removing curbs from showers, allowing for space for wheelchairs underneath kitchen and bathroom counters and appliances, smoothing steps into ramps, and widening doorways and hallways (Null & Cherry, 1996; see chapter 6).

Modifying housing using universal design principles can be expensive. Costs of installing ramps, retrofitting bathrooms, and widening doorways range from the low $1,000s to the $10,000s (MetLife Mature Market Institute, 2010). The additional cost of incorporating universal design into new construction is cheaper. According to one estimate, this ranges from $1,500 to $2,500 (MissouriUD, 2013). Private foundations and nonprofits such as Habitat for Humanity subsidize the costs of modifications in targeted communities on a small scale. Federal sources of funding that help to cover modifications include the U.S. Department of Housing and Urban Development's (HUD) CDBG, HOME, and Section 202 Supportive Housing for the Elderly Programs and the U.S. Department of Agriculture's (USDA) Section 504 Program (Cisneros, 2012). The U.S. Department of Veterans Affairs also offers a Home Improvements and Structural Alterations grant for disabled veterans (U.S. Department of Veterans Affairs, 2014). States and localities occasionally have tax credits, deferred or low-cost loans, and grants to aid modifications (Cisneros, 2012).

Focusing on making homes more visitable is an incremental and more pragmatic approach to enabling seniors to age in place in their homes. Visitability entails a minimal level of modifications that would enable seniors and others with physical disabilities to be able to use their homes. Common visitability requirements include having a zero-step entrance, thirty-two-inch doorways and hallways, and a ground-floor half bathroom. Incorporating visitability features when a home is first constructed costs an estimated additional $100 to $600, which is substantially less than the costs of modifying an existing home (Greenhouse, 2012).

Since 1991, all new multifamily buildings with four or more units have been required to have modifications to accommodate persons in wheelchairs, in accordance with the 1988 Fair Housing Amendments Act (H.R. 1158, 100th Cong., 1988). This includes having adequate space in entryways, kitchens, and bathrooms, as well as reachable light switches and outlets. Some jurisdictions go beyond federal standards in their visitability requirements (Null & Cherry, 1996). For example, since 2002, Pima County, Arizona, has required that all new single-family homes have visitability. In contrast, other places require only that homes subsidized by public funds include these features (Maisel, Smith, & Steinfeld, 2008; see chapter 6).

Affordable Housing

Seniors on fixed incomes need predictable housing costs that are low enough to allow them to cover their other expenses (see chapter 10). Renters stand to benefit from federal public subsidies used to stimulate the construction of low-rent senior-targeted housing. However, the expiration of affordability restrictions through these programs may limit their long-term usefulness to senior renters (see chapters 9 and 14). Homeowners stand to benefit from strategies that enable them to tap into their housing equity to help pay for their expenses (see chapter 7). A reverse mortgage can help to achieve this end, although so far only a small proportion of senior homeowners have taken advantage of one (Haurin et al., 2016; see chapter 8).

SUBSIDIZED HOUSING TARGETED TO LOW-INCOME SENIOR RENTERS

Building and maintaining subsidized housing targeted to eligible low-income senior renters is one way to relieve the housing burden of those who rent. Publicly subsidized senior housing has existed since the passage of the Senior Citizen's Housing Act in 1962. A large minority of subsidized housing constructed during the latter half of the twentieth century was targeted to seniors, in part because it is less contentious to site these developments than other subsidized housing (Pynoos & Redfoot, 1995). In 2003 about 45 percent of the residents of privately owned subsidized housing were seniors (U.S. Department of Housing and Urban Development, 2008; see chapters 9 and 14).

A handful of public programs currently support the construction, rehabilitation, or maintenance of housing for eligible low-income seniors. Most important on the federal level is the Section 202 Supportive Housing for the Elderly Program, which is run by HUD. Funds go toward the construction of rental housing for people age sixty-two and older who earn less than half of their region's median income. Nonprofits build and manage this housing. By the end of the 2000s, there were more than 250,000 Section 202 rentals nationwide (Harrell et al., 2009). In many regions, however, the waitlist for getting into them is either long or closed (Pynoos et al., 2004).

Additional HUD sources that support housing construction and preservation for low-income senior renters include the Section 811 Supportive Housing for People with Disabilities, Housing Choice Voucher or Section 8, HOME Investment Partnership, and public housing/HOPE VI Programs. Other important sources are the Internal Revenue Service's Low-Income Housing Tax Credit (LIHTC) Program and the USDA's Section 515 Program. Local and state housing bonds and housing trust funds also subsidize the construction and preservation of low-cost housing for seniors, working in concert with larger federal sources of funding. A 2006 survey of ninety-nine state and local housing trust funds found that over 10 percent prioritized senior-oriented projects in some way (Accius, 2009; see chapter 14).

A limitation of the Section 202 Program and others targeted to seniors is that units subsidized are not permanently affordable—once landlords have paid off their subsidized mortgage, they are free to rent their apartments at market rates (Perl, 2010). The aging of subsidized rentals targeted to seniors, and landlords' lack of resources to renovate them, may also lead to a loss of housing if apartments become uninhabitable (Perl, 2010). Combined, these factors may significantly reduce low-income seniors' housing options in the near future, particularly in places close to transit (Harrell, Brooks, & Nedwick, 2009; Perl, 2010). A study of all federally subsidized housing (not necessarily targeted to seniors) in twenty U.S. metropolitan areas in 2008 found that the affordability restrictions of more than two-thirds of the approximately 250,000 units located within a half mile of transit expired by the end of 2014 (Harrell et al., 2009). More funding and more flexible terms are needed to meet demand and rehabilitate properties for seniors as this proportion increases (Harrell et al., 2009; Pynoos et al., 2004; see chapters 13 and 14).

REVERSE MORTGAGES

A reverse mortgage is similar to a home equity line of credit (HELOC) in that it converts some of the equity that a homeowner has in his or her home into cash, freeing up needed resources to pay for other things, including long-term health care. It is different from a HELOC in that the borrower does not have to repay the loan as long as he or she continues to maintain the home as a primary residence. Rather, the borrower repays the loan from the proceeds when the home is sold, or his or her heirs repay the loan upon the borrower's death. The most common reverse mortgage product is HUD's Home Equity Conversion Mortgage (HECM) Program, which is targeted to homeowners age sixty-two and older and insured by the Federal Housing Administration (National Council on Aging, 2013).

Currently, less than 2 percent of seniors hold a reverse mortgage, and 95 percent of these participate in the HECM Program (Haurin et al., 2016). While this is a small percentage, the number of seniors participating in the program grew over the 2000s, with about 6,600 HECMs originated in 2000 and 115,000 originated in 2009 (Haurin et al., 2016). Seniors who took out reverse mortgages during the mid-2000s housing boom and the Great Recession tended to live in states with more volatile home prices, to be younger, and to be couples or men as compared to those who took out their mortgages in the early 2000s (Haurin et al., 2016). Reverse mortgage originations of all types have since declined, with only fifty-one thousand started in 2012 (Silver-Greenberg, 2014).

Homeowners may receive money from a reverse mortgage in various forms, ranging from fixed monthly payments to a line of credit to a one-time lump-sum payment. The older the homeowner, the more his or her home is worth, and the lower the prevailing interest rate, the bigger the mortgage he or she can receive. To mitigate risk, financial institutions often charge reverse mortgage borrowers a higher upfront and mortgage premium fee than they charge for traditional home equity loans (Miller, 2014; National Council on Aging, 2013).

A concern with financing one's retirement using a reverse mortgage is that it may put seniors (and their heirs) at risk of losing their home, putting into question whether this innovation can provide seniors greater financial security. Seniors must maintain their home and pay their property taxes and homeowner's insurance in order to keep their reverse mortgage. Close to 10 percent of participants in the HECM Program were in default on their taxes or insurance in 2012 (Moulton, Haurin, & Shi, 2014). The lower a borrower's credit score and the higher the percentage of funds withdrawn in his or her first month of the loan, the greater the likelihood of default (Moulton et al., 2014). New rules established by HUD in 2013, such as tightened underwriting criteria, a moratorium on lump-sum withdrawals, and a limit on withdrawals in the first year of the loan, may be helping to reduce default risk. Unfortunately, this move has also curtailed participation in the program (Moulton et al., 2014). Another concern is that heirs may have trouble repaying the loan after a borrower's death if the amount of the mortgage exceeds the value of the home. As of March 2014, an estimated 13 percent of reverse mortgages were underwater (i.e., the homeowner had withdrawn more funds than the home was worth) (Silver-Greenberg, 2014). Although the HECM Program offers heirs the option of paying 95 percent of the home's current appraised value in lieu of the loan amount, some lenders start foreclosure proceedings unless the loan is paid off in full upon the borrower's death (Silver-Greenberg, 2014; see chapter 8).

Community Choice

Housing innovations and adaptations alone are often not enough to meet the needs of most Americans as they age. Older adults also require community choice. One option is the traditional, age-diverse community with walkable and transit-accessible services and amenities (Harrell et al., 2014). Another option is an age-restricted community that consolidates services on site. Strategies to broaden seniors' community choices include retrofitting NORCs and building and maintaining age-restricted housing, cohousing, and assisted living and nursing facilities.

RETROFITTING NATURALLY OCCURRING
RETIREMENT COMMUNITIES

As previously mentioned, communities that naturally rather than intentionally include a high proportion of seniors are called NORCs (Hunt & Gunter-Hunt, 1985). The scale of a NORC can range from a single building to an entire neighborhood. In 2003 about 16 percent of households headed by a person age fifty-five and older were living in a non-age-restricted community where most of their neighbors were age fifty-five and older (Kochera et al., 2005).

Neighborhood retrofitting is needed to transform NORCs into livable communities for seniors (Dunham-Jones & Williamson, 2011). Retrofitting entails altering the existing built environment to meet seniors' needs. According to Harrell et al. (2009), a livable community is "safe and provides affordable, appropriate housing; adequate transportation; and supportive community features and services" (Harrell et al., 2009: 7). Just as universal design adapts a home to a senior's needs and abilities, neighborhood retrofitting does the same for a broader community (see chapters 6, 12, and 13).

Ensuring flexible, diverse, and supportive housing so that seniors can age in place is critical in the process of creating a livable community (see chapters 12 and 13). Strategies include encouraging secondary dwelling units, universal design, and affordable housing (see chapters 6 and 10). NORCs also need to be connected to health care, transportation, and other services. For multifamily NORCs, including on-site, supportive staff and services is an efficient method of meeting seniors' needs (Pynoos & Liebig, 1995). A variety of strategies exist to overcome organizational, financial, and regulatory barriers to providing services, including having service coordinators on site and clustering senior housing and adult day health and senior centers (Pynoos et al., 2004; see chapters 12 and 13).

Changing infrastructure and land use to enable greater walkability is also key. According to the Pew Research Center's 2014 Political Polarization Survey, 58 percent of seniors prefer to live in walkable communities compared to 48 percent of the general public (Dimock, Kiley, Keeter, & Doherty, 2014). This is in part because seniors are more likely to not drive (Kochera et al., 2005). A walkable environment also enables seniors to exercise, which may improve their health and prolong their independence (Frank, 2012). Conversely, a nonwalkable environment may make seniors prone to social isolation and injuries (Elder & Retrum, 2012; Farber, Shinkle, Lynott, Fox-Grage, and Harrell, 2011). In 2007 seniors were disproportionately represented in pedestrian fatalities (20 percent, despite being 13 percent of the population) (Lynott et al., 2009). Making their neighborhood more pedestrian-friendly was the third most often cited priority mentioned by seniors surveyed by the AARP in 2012, behind increasing police presence and improving school quality and performance (Harrell et al., 2014).

To be walkable, a community must have proximity and connectivity (Frank, 2012). Proximity means that services and amenities, such as public transportation, grocery stores, and health clinics, are within a half mile. This can be accomplished through rezoning to allow new mixed-use and transit-oriented development or the joint use or adaptive reuse of existing, underused buildings, such as schools, strip malls, and warehouses (Dunham-Jones & Williamson, 2011; Farber et al., 2011; Harrell et al., 2009). Connectivity means that there are direct and safe pathways between homes and these services and amenities. A walkability audit, where seniors, planners, and other community members walk through the community together, can help identify problem spots. Retrofits such as adding more benches to sidewalks, cutting ramps into curbs, narrowing streets, establishing more crosswalks, incorporating medians and other traffic-calming measures, and providing more comfortable transit shelters can help to more safely connect seniors to nearby services and amenities (Lynott et al., 2009; see chapters 12 and 13).

In rural NORCs, having comprehensive and reliable access to transportation is essential for aging in place. Investing in transportation networks that link small towns together is a promising option. Another is expanding liability protections for volunteer drivers, who transport seniors for free in their private vehicles (Farber et al., 2011). Creating trails along abandoned railroad lines and other unused infrastructure is also a way to make rural NORCs more livable for seniors by giving them space to exercise and enjoy nature.

There are a growing number of comprehensive approaches that state legislatures can adopt to retrofit NORCs into livable communities for seniors. One is a Complete Streets policy, which has the purpose of ensuring that roadways are accessible and safe to navigate for people of all ages, abilities, and modes. An example of an intervention that helps to meet these goals is widening the shoulders of roads, particularly on busy arterials. Wider shoulders make roads safer for bicyclists and seniors, who may need more room to make a turn (Farber et al., 2011). As of 2011, twenty-five states, Washington, D.C., and Puerto Rico had enacted a Complete Streets policy (Farber et al., 2011). Their terms vary widely (Farber et al., 2011). States like Oregon require that all roads comply with Complete Streets goals, while others, like New Jersey, require only those funded by state or federal funds to comply. Some states, like Connecticut, target only bicyclists, motorists, pedestrians, and transit users in their policy, while others, like California, include children, persons with disabilities, and seniors (Farber et al., 2011). Another approach is to pass state legislation to coordinate the retrofitting of neighborhoods to make them livable for seniors. In 2008, for instance, the Georgia legislature established the Georgia for a Lifetime Initiative, which in part has the purpose of helping communities make land use, infrastructure, and public service changes so seniors can age in place (Farber et al., 2011).

Localities can also respond to NORC neighborhood retrofitting in a comprehensive way. Establishing a Complete Streets policy is one option, as described above. Another approach is to establish a senior overlay district. This is a form of zoning that builds upon the existing zoning to alter land use in accordance with seniors' needs. Examples include allowing for secondary dwelling units, a public transit center, mixed-use development, and health care facilities and requiring buildings to meet visitability standards (Menkin, 2001; see chapters 12 and 13).

ENABLING SENIORS TO LIVE TOGETHER

Communities that have a high proportion of seniors by design include age-restricted, cohousing, assisted living, and nursing home communities (see chapters 12 and 13). These are planned to effectively and efficiently meet seniors' unique needs.

Age-restricted communities proliferated in the latter half of the twentieth century. These are places with deeds requiring that occupants be fifty-five years of age or older. They typically are planned, detached single-family-home subdivisions that incorporate amenities enjoyed by seniors, such as golf courses and pools (see chapters 12 and 13). Most are targeted to middle- and upper-income seniors and have few housing options for low-income seniors (see chapter 10). Age-restricted communities are common in Sunbelt regions where many seniors are moving to retire, such as Phoenix and Las Vegas. One of the oldest planned age-restricted communities is Del Webb's Sun City outside of Phoenix, which opened in 1960. By 2014 there were over sixty-five hundred communities oriented to active seniors nationwide (Active Adult Living, 2014).

Cohousing is an emerging housing model adapted from northern Europe. The concept was first coined and imported to the United States by Charles Durrett and Kathryn McCamant, California architects who run the Cohousing Company. Cohousing consists of individually occupied homes, typically twenty to thirty units, around a communal space. Homes may be owned, rented, or owned cooperatively or by nonprofits. Some include affordability restrictions. Most communities include a communal house with a kitchen and dining area, a sitting area, and laundry facilities. Other amenities targeted to seniors may include a caretaker or guest house and a meditation room. Homes and common areas often are built with New Urbanist and universal design features to enable socializing and aging in place (Durrett, 2009; see chapter 6).

Cohousing is not only a place to live but also a way of life. Residents take an active role in their community's development and each other's lives. Jointly, they oversee the planning, purchase, construction, and maintenance of the community. They periodically cook for each other and have meals together in the communal dining room. They may provide emotional support and help one another with daily chores or transportation. These features may reduce seniors' risk of social isolation and stress and increase their sense of safety (Glass & Vander Plaats, 2013; see chapter 12).

In 2012 there were about 120 cohousing communities in the United States and another 120 under development (Klinger, 2012). Most are multigenerational. Some of the handful of examples of senior-oriented cohousing are Glacier Circle in Davis, California; ElderSpirit in Abingdon, Virginia; and Silver Sage in Boulder, Colorado (Durrett, 2009).

Independent and assisted living and nursing home facilities are situated in places that may or may not be residential and senior oriented. Independent living facilities have private residences clustered around communal spaces. They allow seniors to live independently while partaking in group activities, such as meals in a dining hall. They are different from cohousing communities in that they are professionally developed and managed. Assisted living facilities are similar to independent living facilities but they also provide on-demand help with dressing, bathing, showering, and other activities of daily living. Assisted living was the fastest growing type of senior housing in the late 1980s and early 1990s (Pynoos et al., 2004; see chapter 2).

The bulk of the cost for independent and assisted living is paid out of pocket. In 2009 entry fees for extensive contracts ranged from $160,000 to $600,000. Monthly fees ranged from $2,400 to $5,400 (Barbour, 2013). Like age-restricted communities, they are primarily targeted to middle- and upper-income seniors. Low-income seniors have access to assisted living through HUD's Assisted Living Conversion Program, which gives grants to help apartment buildings currently receiving HUD subsidies become assisted-living facilities (Perl, 2010; see chapter 14).

Nursing homes provide hospital-grade private or semiprivate rooms and around-the-clock care for people with physical or cognitive impairments. In 2004 there were 16,600 nursing homes housing 1.5 million residents (Bercovitz, Decker, Jones, & Remsburg, 2008). One out of every five deaths occurred in a nursing home (Bercovitz et al., 2008). Entering into a nursing home is the choice of last resort for most seniors, as many facilities are sometimes regarded as being dirty, uncaring, and in some cases outright dangerous. These stereotypes are partly unfounded, as there is wide variety in the quality of these facilities (Bercovitz et al., 2008; Klinenberg, 2012). Some seniors have the option to move into a facility that is clean, caring, and safe (Klinenberg, 2012). Medicaid has historically subsidized nursing homes for eligible low-income seniors (Pynoos & Redfoot, 1995; see chapters 2 and 14).

Complexes that combine independent with assisted living and nursing home facilities are called continuing care retirement communities. They offer a gradient of housing options and care depending on seniors' needs and abilities. Seniors living in these communities typically move in when they are living independently and progress to assisted living and nursing home facilities as their health declines. These places may offer seniors a better match between their needs and abilities and housing and surrounding social networks, helping to prevent the social isolation that can occur for seniors at assisted-living facilities (Klinenberg, 2012; see chapter 12).

CONCLUSION

The aging of America creates diverse opportunities and challenges for housing practitioners, policy makers, and researchers. Seniors differ from those in other age groups in that they are more likely to be living alone, on fixed incomes, and experiencing disabilities. Most are concentrated in suburban and rural areas that lack walkable amenities and services and reliable and affordable public transit (Harrell et al., 2014). However, most seniors want to age in place in walkable communities (see chapters 12 and 13).

Making housing more flexible through secondary dwelling units and universal design modifications is one strategy to support aging in place (see chapter 2). Publicly subsidizing low-cost rental housing for seniors and enabling senior homeowners to take out reverse mortgages to access their housing wealth is another (see chapter 14). Above all, seniors need community choice. While retrofitting can help make NORCs livable for seniors, housing models such as age-restricted communities, cohousing, and independent assisted-living and nursing home facilities provide them opportunities to live together (see chapter 2).

The decreasing proportion of seniors who have saved for their retirement and the increasing proportion of seniors who have debt will limit their ability to pay for their housing needs out of pocket. These trends also put into question the practicality of solutions like reverse mortgages, which—without adequate controls—may serve as a disincentive toward saving, compound seniors' debt, and put their financial security at risk. A paradigm change is in order, one that both engenders greater financial responsibility among Americans across the life span and cultivates greater social responsibility for helping impoverished or indebted seniors who may fall between the cracks (see chapter 10).

Moving forward, many lingering questions about housing and aging still need answers. For one, how do the outcomes of seniors who age in place differ from those who move to cohousing, independent and assisted-living or nursing home facilities, or age-diverse communities in the same area? What are ways of reducing the costs of strategies to make housing more flexible, such as secondary dwelling units and universal design, so that seniors can pay for them despite their limited savings and debt? How can practitioners, advocates, and researchers convince local public officials, residents, and developers to embrace these strategies? More broadly, how should our society keep housing affordable as Americans age in the face of rising health care costs, reduced savings and delayed retirement, and a shrinking social safety net? These complex issues are ripe for exploration.

REFERENCES

Accius, J. (2009, September). Housing trust funds. *AARP Factsheet 139R*. Retrieved September 10, 2014, from http://assets.aarp.org/rgcenter/ppi/liv-com/fs-139r.pdf.

Active Adult Living. (2014). *Find your ideal active adult 55+ retirement community on Active Adult Living*. Online database. Retrieved November 21, 2014, from www.activeadultliving.com.

Arrison, S. (2011). *100+: How the coming age of longevity will change everything, from careers and relationships to family and faith*. New York: Basic Books.

Bailey, J. (2010). *Rural grocery stores: Importance and challenge*. Lyons, Nebr.: Center for Rural Affairs.

Barbour, C. A. (2013). Continuing care options: The next generation of care. In J. M. Blanchard (Ed.), *Aging in community* (pp. 153–163). Chapel Hill, N.C.: Second Journey Publications.

Benson, W. F., & Aldrich, N. (2013). The aging middle class and public policy. In J. M. Blanchard (Ed.), *Aging in community* (pp. 171–182). Chapel Hill, N.C.: Second Journey Publications.

Bercovitz, A., Decker, F. H., Jones, A., & Remsburg, R. E. (2008). End-of-life care in nursing homes: 2004 National Nursing Home Survey. *National Health Statistics Reports, 8*, 1–24.

Bethell, T. (2011). *Family matters: Multigenerational families in a volatile economy*. Washington, D.C.: Generations United.

Brooks, D. (2011). *The social animal*. New York: Random House.

Carstensen, L. L. (2006). The influence of a sense of time on human development. *Science, 312*, 1913–1915.

Carstensen, L. L. (2012). A hopeful future. In H. Cisneros, M. Dyer-Chamberlain, & J. Hickie (Eds.), *Independent for life: Homes and neighborhoods for an aging America* (pp. 21–31). Austin: University of Texas Press.

Center for Universal Design. (2008). *About the center: Ronald Mace*. Retrieved September 10, 2014, from http://www.ncsu.edu/ncsu/design/cud/about_us/usronmace.htm.

Centers for Disease Control and Prevention. (2013). Deaths: Final data for 2010. *National Vital Statistics Reports, 61*(4), 1–118.

Centers for Disease Control and Prevention. (2014a). *Adult obesity facts*. Atlanta: Centers for Disease Control and Prevention. Retrieved September 10, 2014, from http://www.cdc.gov/obesity/data/adult.html.

Centers for Disease Control and Prevention. (2014b). *Heart disease facts*. Atlanta: Centers for Disease Control and Prevention. Retrieved September 10, 2014, from http://www.cdc.gov/heartdisease/facts.htm.

Centers for Disease Control and Prevention. (2014c). *National diabetes statistics report: Estimates of diabetes and its burden in the United States, 2014*. Atlanta: U.S. Department of Health and Human Services.

Cisneros, H. (2012). New visions for aging in place. In H. Cisneros, M. Dyer-Chamberlain, & J. Hickie (Eds.), *Independent for life: Homes and neighborhoods for an aging America* (pp. 3–20). Austin: University of Texas Press.

Colby, S. L., & Ortman, J. M. (2014, May). The baby boom cohort in the United States: 2012 to 2060. *U.S. Census Current Population Reports*, 1–16.

Consumer Financial Protection Bureau. (2014). *Snapshot of older consumers and mortgage debt*. Washington, D.C.: Office for Older Americans, Consumer Financial Protection Bureau.

Csikszentmihalyi, M., & Rochberg-Halton, E. (1981). *The meaning of things: Domestic symbols and the self*. Cambridge: Cambridge University Press.

DeGood, K. (2011). *Aging in place, stuck without option: Fixing the mobility crisis threatening the baby boom generation*. Washington, D.C.: Transportation for America.

Dimock, M., Kiley, J., Keeter, S. & Doherty, C. (2014). *Political polarization in the American public*. Washington, D.C.: Pew Research Center.

Dunham-Jones, E., & Williamson, J. (2011). *Retrofitting suburbia: Urban design solutions for redesigning suburbs*. Hoboken, N.J.: John Wiley and Sons.

Durrett, C. (2009). *The senior cohousing handbook*. Gabriola Island, Canada: New Society Publishers.

Elder, K., & Retrum, J. (2012). *Framework for isolation in adults over 50*. Washington, D.C.: AARP Foundation.

Fair Housing Amendments Act of 1988, H.R. 1158, 100th Cong. (1988).

Farber, N., Shinkle, D., Lynott, J., Fox-Grage, W. & Harrell, R. (2011). *Aging in place: A state survey of livability policies and practices*. Washington, D.C.: National Conference of State Legislatures and AARP Public Policy Institute.

Firestine, T. (2011). *The U.S. rural population and scheduled intercity transportation in 2010: A five-year decline in transportation access*. Washington, D.C.: U.S. Department of Transportation.

Frank, L. D. (2012). Healthy communities. In H. Cisneros, M. Dyer-Chamberlain, & J. Hickie (Eds.), *Independent for life: Homes and neighborhoods for an aging America* (pp. 146–158). Austin: University of Texas Press.

Frey, W. (2007). *Mapping the growth of older America*. Living Cities Census Series. Washington, D.C.: Metropolitan Policy Program, Brookings Institution.

Fries, J. (1980). Aging, natural death, and the compression of morbidity. *New England Journal of Medicine, 303*, 130–135.

Garreau, J. (2013a, September 25). Drooling on your shoes or living long and prospering? Four visions of our future lifespans. *Slate*. Retrieved September 10, 2014, from http://www.slate.com/articles/technology/future_tense/2013/09/four_scenarios_for_our_future_lifespans.html.

Garreau, J. (2013b). *The Washington longevity scenarios for 2030*. Paper presented at "The Future of Longevity" conference, Washington, D.C., October 4. Retrieved September 10, 2014, from http://newamerica.net/events/2013/the_future_of_longevity.

George, L., Pinder, J., & Rose, A. L. (2003). *Rural seniors & their homes*. Washington, D.C.: Housing Assistance Council.

Glass, A. P., & Vander Plaats, R. S. (2013). A conceptual model for aging better together intentionally. *Journal of Aging Studies, 27*, 428–442.

Greenberg, S. (2010). *A profile of older Americans: 2010*. Washington, D.C.: U.S. Department of Health and Human Services.

Greenhouse, E. (2012). The home environment and aging. In H. Cisneros, M.

Dyer-Chamberlain, & J. Hickie (Eds.), *Independent for life: Homes and neighborhoods for an aging America* (pp. 87–97). Austin: University of Texas Press.

Hare, P. H. (1989). *Accessory units: The state of the art*. Cornwall, Conn.: Patrick Hare Planning and Design.

Hare, P. H. (1991). The echo housing/granny flat experience in the U.S. *Journal of Housing for the Elderly, 7*, 57–70.

Harrell, R. (2011). Housing for older adults: The impacts of the recession. *AARP Public Policy Institute Insight on the Issues, 53*, 1–12.

Harrell, R., Brooks, A., & Nedwick, T. (2009). *Preserving affordability and access in livable communities: Subsidized housing opportunities near transit and the 50+ population*. Washington, D.C.: AARP Public Policy Institute.

Harrell, R., Kassner, E., & Figueiredo, C. (2011). Multigenerational households are increasing. *AARP Public Policy Institute Fact Sheet, 221*, 1–3.

Harrell, R., Lynott, J., Guzman, S. & Lampkin, C. (2014). *What is livable? Community preferences of older adults*. Washington, D.C.: AARP Public Policy Institute.

Haurin, D., Ma, C., Moulton, S., Schmeiser, M., Seligman, J., and Shi, W. (2016). Spatial variation in reverse mortgages usage: House price dynamics and consumer selection. *Journal of Real Estate Finance and Economics, 53*(3), 392–417. Retrieved September 10, 2014, from http://papers.ssrn.com/sol3/papers.cfm?abstract_id=2458183.

Hayutin, A. M. (2012). Changing demographic realities. In H. Cisneros, M. Dyer-Chamberlain, & J. Hickie (Eds.), *Independent for life: Homes and neighborhoods for an aging America* (pp. 35–44). Austin: University of Texas Press.

Housing Assistance Council. (2011). *Rural seniors and their homes*. Washington, D.C.: Housing Assistance Council.

Housing Assistance Council. (2013). *Rural seniors and their homes*. Washington, D.C.: Housing Assistance Council.

Howe, D. A. (1990). The flexible house: Designing for changing needs. *Journal of the American Planning Association, 56*, 69–77.

Hughes-Cromwick, P., & Wallace, R. (2006). Executive summary: Cost benefit analysis of providing non-emergency medical transportation. *TCRP Research Results Digest, 75*, 1–5.

Hunt, M. E., & Gunter-Hunt, G. (1985). Naturally occurring retirement communities. *Journal of Housing for the Elderly, 3*(3/4), 3–21.

Hutchinson, L., Hawes, C., & Williams, L. (2010). Access to quality health services in rural areas—long-term care. In L. Gamm & L. Hutchinson (Eds.), *Rural healthy people 2010: A companion document to healthy people 2010* (pp. 5–14). College Station: Texas A & M University System Health Science Center, School of Rural Public Health, Southwest Rural Health Research Center.

Kirschner, A., Berry, E. H., & Glasgow, N. (2009). The changing demographic profile of rural areas. *Rural New York Minute, 25*. Retrieved September 10, 2014, from http://cardi.cornell.edu/cals/devsoc/outreach/cardi/publications/loader.cfm?csModule=security/getfile&PageID=437557.

Klinenberg, E. (2012). *Going solo: The extraordinary rise and surprising appeal of living alone*. New York: Penguin Press.

Klinger, C. (2012, August/September). Cohousing creates community. *Mother Earth News*. Retrieved September 10, 2014, from http://www.motherearthnews.com/nature-and-environment/cohousing-zmgz12aszphe.aspx?PageId=2#axzz34djjHTmJ.

Kochera, A., Straight, A., & Guterbock, T. (2005). *Beyond 50.05: A report to the nation on livable communities: Creating environments for successful aging*. Washington, D.C.: AARP Public Policy Institute.

Kochhar, R., Fry, R., & Taylor, P. (2011). *Twenty-to-one: Wealth gaps rise to record highs between whites, blacks, and Hispanics*. Washington, D.C.: Pew Research Center.

Kotkin, J. (2011, November 30). Is suburbia doomed? Not so fast. *Forbes*. Retrieved September 10, 2014, from http://www.forbes.com/sites/joelkotkin/2011/11/30/is-suburbia-doomed-not-so-fast/.

Leinberger, C. B. (2011, November 25). The death of the fringe suburb. *New York Times*. Retrieved September 10, 2014, from http://www.nytimes.com/2011/11/26/opinion/the-death-of-the-fringe-suburb.html?_r=0.

Lipman, B., Lubell, J., & Salomon, E. (2012). *Housing an aging population: Are we prepared?* Washington, D.C.: Center for Housing Policy.

Litchfield, M. (2011). *In-laws, outlaws, and granny flats: Your guide for turning one house into two homes.* Newtown, Conn.: Taunton Press.

Lusardi, A., & Mitchell, O. S. (2013). *Older adult debt and financial frailty* (Working Paper WP 2013-291). Ann Arbor: Michigan Retirement Research Center, University of Michigan. Retrieved September 10, 2014, from http://www.mrrc.isr.umich.edu/publications/papers/pdf/wp291.pdf.

Lynott, J., Haase, J., Nelson, K., Taylor, A., Twaddell, H., Ulmer, J., McCann, B., & Stollof, E. (2009). *Planning complete streets for an aging America.* Washington, D.C.: AARP Public Policy Institute.

Maisel, J. L., Smith, E., & Steinfeld, E. (2008). *Increasing home access: Designing for visitability.* Washington, D.C.: AARP Public Policy Institute.

Menkin, C. (2001). Senior citizen overlay districts and assisted living facilities: Different but the same. *Pace Law Review, 21,* 481–509.

Metlife Mature Market Institute. (2010). *The MetLife aging in place workbook.* New York: Metropolitan Life Insurance Company.

Miller, J. (2014, April 13). How reverse mortgages work in 2014. *Las Vegas Review Journal.* Retrieved September 10, 2014, from http://www.reviewjournal.com/life/how-reverse-mortgages-work-2014.

MissouriUD. (2013). *What is UD?* Presentation at workshop on best practices in universal design. Jefferson City Missouri Department of Mental Health. Retrieved November 18, 2014, from http://dmh.mo.gov/docs/housing/UniversalDesign-Colleen Starkloff.pptx.

Moulton, S., Haurin, D. T., & Shi, W. (2014). *An analysis of default risk in the Home Equity Conversion Mortgage (HECM) program* (working paper). Columbus: John Glenn School of Public Affairs, The Ohio State University. Retrieved September 10, 2014, from http://ssrn.com/abstract=2468247.

Myers, D. (2008). *Immigrants and boomers: Forging a new social contract for the future of America.* New York: Russell Sage Foundation.

National Academy of Sciences. (2005). *Quality health care through collaboration: The future of rural health care.* Washington, D.C.: National Academies Press.

National Academy of Sciences. (2008). *Keck Futures Initiative: The future of human healthspan: Demography, evolution, medicine, and bioengineering, task group summaries.* Washington, D.C.: National Academies Press.

National Council on Aging. (2013). *Use your home to stay at home.* Washington, D.C.: National Council on Aging.

New Avenue Blog. (2014, September 23). What are the true costs of an accessory dwelling? *New Avenue.* Retrieved November 18, 2014, from http://blog.newavenuehomes.com/index.php/2014/09/23/what-are-the-true-costs-of-an-accessory-dwelling/.

Newman, S. (2010). *Under one roof again: All grown up and (re)learning to live together happily.* Guilford: Conn.: Globe Pequot Press.

Null, R. L., & Cherry, K. F. (1996). *Universal design: Creative solutions for ADA compliance.* Belmont, Calif.: Professional Publications.

Ortman, J. M., Velkoff, V. A., & Hogan, H. (2014). An aging nation: The older population in the United States. *Current Population Reports, P25-1140,* 1–28.

Parrott, J., & Zandi, M. (2013). *Opening the credit box.* New York: Moody's Analytics; Washington, D.C.: Urban Institute. Retrieved September 10, 2014, from http://www.urban.org/UploadedPDF/412910-Opening-the-Credit-Box.pdf.

Perl, L. (2010). *Section 202 and other HUD rental programs for low-income elderly.* Washington, D.C.: Congressional Research Service.

Pfeiffer, D. (2015). Retrofitting suburbia through second units: Lessons from the Phoenix region. *Journal of Urbanism, 8*(3), 279–301.

Pynoos, J., & Liebig, P. S. (1995). Housing policy for frail elders: Trends and implications for long-term care. In J. Pynoos & P. Liebig (Eds.), *Housing frail elders: International policies, perspectives, and prospects* (pp. 3–16). Baltimore: Johns Hopkins University Press.

Pynoos, J., Liebig, P., Alley, D., & Nishita, C. M. (2004). Homes of choice: Towards more effective linkages between housing and services. *Journal of Housing for the Elderly, 18*(3/4), 5–49.

Pynoos, J., & Redfoot, D. L. (1995). Housing frail elders in the United States. In J. Pynoos & P. Liebig (Eds.), *Housing frail elders: International policies, perspectives, and prospects* (pp. 187–210). Baltimore: Johns Hopkins University Press.

Reno, V. P., & Veghte, B. (2010). *Economic status of the elderly in the United States*. Washington, D.C.: National Academy of Social Insurance.

Ruggles, S. (2007). The decline of intergenerational coresidence in the United States, 1850 to 2000. *American Sociological Review, 72*(6), 964–989.

Sage Computing. (2008). *Accessory Dwelling Units: Case study*. Washington, D.C.: U.S. Department of Housing and Urban Development.

Schafran, A. (2012). *The politics of Accessory Dwelling Units in the United States*. Report prepared for Project de Recherché BIMBY. Obtained from the author.

Silver-Greenberg, J. (2014, March 26). Pitfalls of reverse mortgage may pass to borrower's heirs. *New York Times*. Retrieved September 10, 2014, from http://dealbook.nytimes.com/2014/03/26/pitfalls-of-reverse-mortgages-may-pass-to-borrowers-heirs/?_php=true&_type=blogs&_r=0.

Spivak, J. (2012, October). Making room for mom and dad. *Planning*, 8–13.

Stone, M. E. (1993). *Shelter poverty: New ideas on housing affordability*. Philadelphia: Temple University Press.

Taylor, P., Kochhar, R., Cohn, D., Passel, J. S., Velasco, G., Motel, S., & Patton, E. (2011). *Fighting poverty in a tough economy, Americans move in with their relatives*. Washington, D.C.: Pew Research Center.

Taylor, P., Passel, J., Fry, R., Morin, R., Wang, W., Velasco, G., & Dockterman, D. (2010). *The return of the multi-generational family household*. Washington, D.C.: Pew Research Center.

Thayer, C. (2007). *Preparation for retirement: The haves and have-nots*. Washington, D.C.: AARP Knowledge Management.

Tomaka, J., Thompson, S., & Palacios, R. (2006). The relation of social isolation, loneliness, and social support to disease outcomes among the elderly. *Journal of Aging and Health, 18*(3), 359–384.

Torres-Gil, F., & Hofland, B. (2012). Vulnerable populations. In H. Cisneros, M. Dyer-Chamberlain, & J. Hickie (Eds.), *Independent for life: Homes and neighborhoods for an aging America* (pp. 221–232). Austin: University of Texas Press.

U.S. Bureau of the Census. (2010). *2009 American Community Survey*. Washington, D.C.: U.S. Bureau of the Census.

U.S. Bureau of the Census. (2012). *2011 American Community Survey 5-year estimates*. Washington, D.C.: U.S. Bureau of the Census.

U.S. Department of Agriculture. (2013). *Food access research atlas data file*. Calculations made by author. Washington, D.C.: Economic Research Services, U.S. Department of Agriculture.

U.S. Department of Housing and Urban Development. (2008). *Characteristics of HUD-assisted renters and their units in 2003*. Washington, D.C.: U.S. Department of Housing and Urban Development.

U.S. Department of Veterans Affairs. (2014). Home improvements and structural alterations (HISA). *Rehabilitations and Prosthetic Services*. Retrieved September 10, 2014, from http://www.prosthetics.va.gov/psas/HISA2.asp.

Vaupel, J. W. (2010). Biodemography of human ageing. *Nature, 464*, 536–542.

Wegmann, J., & Chapple, K. (2014, February 5). Hidden density in single-family neighborhoods: Backyard cottages as an equitable smart growth strategy. *Journal of Urbanism. Advance online publication*. Retrieved September 10, 2014, from http://dx.doi.org/10.1080/17549175.2013.879453.

Chapter 18

Home Environments and Health

KATHLEEN R. PARROTT AND
JORGE H. ATILES

This chapter presents an overview of the impact of the home on the health of the people who live within it, based on a systems approach (CDC, 2006; U.S. Department of Energy, 2014). The home is influenced by both the macro- and microenvironments in which it is situated (figure 18.1). The macroenvironment encompasses the external factors that influence the home and can include factors such as climate, building site, legal requirements of the community, or technological developments (see chapters 12, 13, 19, and 20). The home's microenvironment, including the building structure, heating and cooling equipment, construction materials, and furnishings, is also a major influence on the health of the occupants of the home (Office of the U.S. Surgeon General, 2009; see chapters 2, 3, 5, and 6). Overall, a home is where the residents live, and they influence the home-health system with the choices they make about the design, construction, management, and maintenance of the home as well as how they live in that space. In turn, the residents' health is impacted by the various components of the home's environment.

To present this systems view of the home-health interaction, this chapter begins from the outside of the home and works inward. The influences of climate and building site are examined first; followed by building materials and practices; then furnishings, finishes, and household products; and finally occupant lifestyle issues. The concept of building practices is defined broadly to include issues of importance to healthy buildings such as ventilation, moisture control, and air and water quality. Lifestyle issues discussed include tobacco smoke and household pests. While this chapter does not exhaustively cover all factors influencing people's health in their homes, a broad spectrum of issues is introduced (see chapters 3 and 19).

Finally, the focus of this chapter is the house, within its macro- and microenvironments, and the *potential* influences on residents' health. Individual residents vary in their reactions to these influences and their specific health effects. This chapter does not provide detailed medical information and is not intended to be a diagnostic tool. Rather, it is designed to provide information on individual home hazards and building science principles as-

The authors recognize and acknowledge the contributions of Michael P. Vogel to the first draft of this chapter.

FIGURE 18.1
A Systems Approach to Home-Health Interaction
Source: Authors.

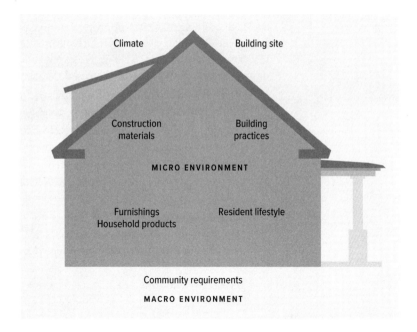

sociated with home environments and health. The goal of the chapter is to create an awareness of the possible health effects of various housing choices and decisions and suggest alternatives to minimize negative health consequences.

UNDERSTANDING THE HOME ENVIRONMENT–HEALTH INTERACTION

To most, a house is simply an assembly of building materials and furnishings. However, a home, if not properly designed, constructed, and operated, can create health risks for its occupants (Chiras, 2000). Young children and older adults, who have developing or weakening immune systems, respectively, are more susceptible to harmful products in the home than people of other ages. Past research has focused on the effects of contaminants such as lead, secondhand smoke, and roach feces on small children (CDC, 2006). Recently more emphasis has been placed on how environmental pollutants affect older adults (Office of the U.S. Surgeon General, 2009; see chapters 3, 6, and 20).

People with temporarily or permanently weakened immune systems due to severe allergies, asthma, or chronic illnesses or people on medications that suppress their immune systems are also more at risk of suffering the side effects of indoor contaminants. These individuals and their families should be especially aware of the issues highlighted in this chapter (Parrott, Atiles, & Vogel, 2006; see chapter 17).

Risk Factors

Many factors influence the environment of a home and the health of those who occupy the building. Some of the factors occur naturally, such as the radioactive gas radon. Other risk factors are human caused, created by poor choice of building materials, improper building practices, incorrect installation of mechanical equipment, or lack of timely maintenance (Office of the U.S. Surgeon General, 2009). Without careful attention to these natural and human-caused factors, there is increased risk of health concerns, such as

- allergy and asthma triggers from excessive *moisture* and *molds* (U.S. Environmental Protection Agency, 2008);
- irritation to eyes, nose, throat, lungs, and skin; headaches; drowsiness; damage to the nervous system, liver, and kidneys; and cancer from *volatile organic compounds (VOCs)*;
- flu-like symptoms, nervous system problems, rapid heart rate, fetus damage, and even death from *combustion gases*;
- lung cancer from *radon gas* and *asbestos-containing materials*;
- damage to the nervous system, kidneys, and reproductive system from *lead-based paint, lead-contaminated soils,* and *lead in drinking water*;
- blue-baby syndrome (methemoglobinemia) from *nitrate in drinking water*;
- nervous system damage, headaches, and cancer from *pesticides*; and
- gastrointestinal illnesses from *contamination of groundwater or surface water* and *faulty septic systems* (Office of the U.S. Surgeon General, 2009).

A basic principle of a healthy home is that a house works as a system and all things are connected; that is, for each design and construction decision made, there is an outcome, whether positive, neutral, or negative. From the climate where the house is located, to the specific building site, to the thousands of parts and pieces used for the actual construction, all factors have the potential to affect the home and the health of those who occupy the home. Creating and maintaining a healthy home begins with a holistic understanding of how home design, construction, and operational elements interact to create a dynamic system.

The systems approach to the study of the home environment–health interaction emphasizes that it is a dynamic relationship (U.S. Department of Energy, 2014). The factors in the system can vary, which can increase the risk for health effects. In particular, there is concern about

- toxicity of the pollutant or contaminant that has been introduced into the home environment;
- exposure or dosage, including quantity, length of time, and repetition of exposure;
- individual susceptibility, which can be influenced by age, general health, previous exposure, and other conditions; and
- synergistic effects that can increase risk, such as smoking or occupational exposure to other pollutants.

These factors illustrate that the health risks are situational and can be greater or lesser for different people in the household (CDC, 2006).

Despite the desire to make a home environmentally healthy, not all environmental hazards can be eliminated. The priority should be to focus on those hazards that present the greatest risk to the resident(s) of a particular home. In addition, the emphasis needs to be on having the greatest benefit for the cost and effort invested in reducing the greatest risks (Dadd, 2005).

Maintaining a healthy home usually means having an environmentally friendly home as well. Decisions that are good for the health of a home's occupants are generally also beneficial for the environment. Keeping a home healthy can also make it less polluting and more resource efficient (California Department of Housing and Community Development, 2009; CDC, 2006; World Health Organization, 2014; see chapters 3, 5, 6, and 19).

Climate Variables

In all climates, a basic criterion of home design and construction is to protect occupants from outdoor elements. Without adequate and well-managed air exchange, a home can have trapped and elevated levels of pollutants and moisture—an unhealthy environment for occupants (see chapters 3, 5, 6, and 19).

The United States is a large country with varying climatic regions. Climate zones are determined by many factors, including range and duration of air temperature levels, precipitation, and humidity, and can be influenced by geographic features such as mountains and bodies of water. Climate zones have a major impact on energy use, building construction, and landscaping of residential buildings. The Building America Program of the Department of Energy has identified eight U.S. climate zones: subarctic, very cold, cold, mixed-humid, mixed-dry, hot-humid, hot-dry, and marine (Baechler et al., 2010). The International Energy Conservation Code, part of the model International Residential Code, which is the basis of the building code for many municipalities in the United States, has eight zones and is similar to the Building America climate zone system (Baechler et al., 2010).

Climate zones are complex. Within climate zones are microclimates that vary within a region. Therefore, for this chapter we will use a broad perspective of four zones that focus on the climate impact on the building:

- **Cold**—heating-predominant climate
- **Temperate**—mixed heating and cooling climate
- **Hot-arid**—cooling-predominant climate
- **Hot-humid**—cooling- and dehumidification-predominant climate
  (U.S. Department of Energy, 2012)

In heating-predominant climates, the emphasis is on reducing home heat loss to the cold outdoors. Efficient homes located in a heating-predominant climate are typically constructed with greater amounts of insulation and utilize high-performance windows, doors, appliances, and heating systems. Special consideration is also given to preventing unwanted air leakage while providing healthy air exchange levels. In cooling-predominant climates, the emphasis is to reduce heat gain and, if necessary, control higher levels of relative humidity (CDC, 2006; Parrott et al., 2006).

Regardless of the type of climate, home design, material selection, and home maintenance are a balancing act of site-specific climate factors that include the following:

- **Solar quantity and quality.** The sun's position in the sky is described by its altitude and azimuth (the position of the sun with respect to north or south), which vary according to geographic location. Orientation of window openings, roof design, and landscape elements will play a major role in optimizing the benefits of the sun, such as solar gain, or in reducing unwanted solar heating in cooling-predominant climates.

- **Air temperature.** On a daily and seasonal basis, the air temperature is dependent on the sky's condition. During days with clear skies, solar radiation passes through the atmosphere freely and heats up surfaces and the air. During nights with clear skies, the heat from the earth's surface passes back through the sky, causing earth cooling. This diurnal cycle creates a large temperature variation. In climates with generally overcast skies, there is less variation.
- **Air movement around the home.** Breezes and winds can provide beneficial cooling around the house. However, winds can also create excessive air leakage and heat loss, driving rain, and damage to building materials. Predominant wind direction and speeds are factors in planning the building orientation and placement of windows and doors.
- **Precipitation amounts.** Snowfall, rain, fog, and thunderstorm patterns influence the selection of the best building design, style, and type and the strength requirements of building materials, the level of relative humidity and moisture in the home, and the potential growth of biological pollutants in and around the home (CDC, 2006; Parrott et al., 2006).

THE BUILDING SITE

Constructing a healthy home begins with proper siting of a building (Green Building Advisor, 2012). Building site considerations consist of three categories:

- the microclimate—site-specific prevailing climate conditions;
- natural site topographic factors that affect the microclimate; and
- human-caused factors.

Microclimate

The performance of every home is influenced by its own microclimate. The microclimate is the prevailing weather conditions of a specific building site—solar exposure, air movements, and so forth. Since the microclimate will affect the energy consumption, durability, and comfort performance of the building, factors such as these should be considered:

- Orientation of window openings to take advantage of solar benefits
- Orientation of the building to take advantage of cooling summer breezes or to avoid prevailing winter winds
- Design of the building to reduce the amount of surfaces exposed to outside air temperatures
- Selection and installation of building materials to avoid destructive elements of sun, wind, and moisture
- Creation of landscape, architectural, and plant elements such as windbreaks, fences, and earth mounds to direct or divert airflow and precipitation (CDC, 2006)

Natural Site Topographic Factors

The topography of a site can dramatically influence the daily air temperature, solar exposure, and moisture conditions. Topography defines the land and vegetation character, elevation difference, and water characteristics of the building site.

Topography also influences storm-water runoff, discussed in the next section, and the creation of wetlands on a building site, which can cause moisture, mold, and decay problems if not corrected when the house is built. Of any one hazard that is persistent in all climates, water and excessive moisture intrusion in buildings is the most likely to cause major damage to the building structure and serious health effects to occupants. Preventive or corrective building practices, as shown in sidebar 18.1, help to minimize water runoff to the building site and keep the structure dry. Overall drainage of the building site to keep foundation building materials dry is of particular importance.

Human-Caused Factors

From a simple look, a building site may appear to be the perfect location for a home. However, before proceeding with construction, any potential build-

---

SIDEBAR 18.1

Water Control

The following building practices and strategies maximize water control and should be considered during the planning and design of the lot, landscaping, and home.

- Roof overhangs should extend out to protect the building's exterior walls from excessive rainfall exposure. The best size for roof overhangs will depend on several factors, including the pitch of the roof, the style of the house, the latitude of the home's location (effect on winter and summer sun angles), the size and location of windows, and the construction of the roof.
- Gutters and extended downspouts should direct water away from the foundation.
- There should be a 5 percent ground slope away from the house foundation in all directions to direct water away from the foundation.
- Swales (ditches) are needed to redirect surface runoff on sloped sites.
- Backfill adjacent to the foundation to allow water to drain away from foundation walls. Drainage water can collect in perforated pipe (placed below the level of the floor slab) for a sump pump or outside drain.
- Include a below-grade waterproof wall barrier such as a membrane or mastic-type sealant to prevent water entry to foundation.
- Above-grade weatherproof materials and proper flashing can be used to resist water entry to building structure.
- Do not plant vegetation and landscaping immediately adjacent to the building foundation, as it may hold water and retain moisture in the building materials.
- Direct the drainage system around the foundation to a storm-water system.
- Put a membrane, such as plastic sheeting, over crawl space soil to control moisture.
- Put gravel covered with polyethylene membrane beneath floor slab to control moisture.
- Include a drainage screen between siding and sheathing in the walls in regions subject to wind-blown moisture.

Source: Dorman, 2005.

ing site and the surrounding area should be assessed to determine whether hazardous conditions are present that may potentially contaminate the soil and drinking water. While reclaimed industrial areas may be the most obvious areas of suspected hazards, the following issues may also affect a chosen building site:

- Brownfields, which are lands from abandoned, idled, or underused industrial and commercial facilities (such as a gas station, auto body shop, or dry cleaner), that may have hazardous substances, pollutants, or contaminants (U.S. Environmental Protection Agency, 2012b)
- Closed or abandoned dumps and landfills, especially those closed without proper engineering, groundwater monitoring, and guidance before the 1990s, when regulations were issued (U.S. Environmental Protection Agency, 2014b)
- Underground fuel or hazardous substance storage tanks left over from service stations, convenience stores, fleet service operators, and local governments, especially when the tanks are steel, common until the mid-1980s, which are likely to corrode and leak, leading to ground and water contamination (U.S. Environmental Protection Agency, 2015)
- Aboveground fuel or hazardous substance storage tanks, as might be used for heating or cooking fuel, especially if the tank caused spills or leakage onto the ground (U.S. Environmental Protection Agency, 2015)
- Agricultural operations, such as a feedlot, machine repair area, or pesticide/fertilizer/fuel storage area (U.S. Environmental Protection Agency, 2012b)

Before selecting a home or a site to construct a home, it is important to check with the local land use or planning department and investigate the history of the site to determine its previous uses and whether it is safe for development or construction. Liability for contamination of the site may pass to the current owner (U.S. Environmental Protection Agency, 2014a).

Storm-Water Runoff

Storm-water runoff is water that washes across land into nearby storm drains or directly into bodies of water. It can be a major factor influencing the location and construction of a healthy home. Water pollution also often occurs through storm-water runoff. Contaminated storm-water runoff that flows into storm drains is typically not treated before being emptied into the nearest body of water. Therefore, no matter where runoff appears to flow initially, the polluted water eventually reaches a water source. However, not all water runs off the land. Some of it seeps into the groundwater. If the water seeping down is contaminated, it will pollute the groundwater, which may feed drinking water wells and cause harm to users. Therefore, even if people live far from known water sources like oceans, lakes, ponds, rivers, and streams, their actions can still lead to pollution of the water supply (U.S. Environmental Protection Agency, 2014c).

The National Pollutant Discharge Elimination System (NPDES) Storm Water Program of the U.S. Environmental Protection Agency, under the authority of the Clean Water Act, began issuing regulations in the 1990s to address pollution from nonagricultural sources, specifically storm-water runoff. In 1990 Phase I was implemented, impacting primarily medium and large municipalities, while Phase II, affecting small municipalities, was developed in 1999 (U.S. Environmental Protection Agency, 2014b). As a result of this program, states and municipalities have been instituting new permitting requirements, fees, and taxes targeted to control storm-water runoff. For example, communities are conducting public education programs and promoting design ideas to minimize storm-water runoff, such as narrower streets, grass swales or drainage areas, and interlocking pavers with space to allow drainage (U.S. Environmental Protection Agency, 2014c). Homeowners may be required to pay a tax or fee related to the amount of their land that is covered by impervious (i.e., paved) surfaces or surfaces under a roof and thus is unable to absorb water.

Some common concerns about pollution of storm water are as follows:

- **Automotive waste.** Cars and other vehicles can cause contamination of water in several ways. Oil drips and fluid spills in driveways and parking areas can be picked up by runoff and carried into water sources. In addition, used oil and antifreeze are sometimes dumped into storm drains or ditches or simply onto the ground. Washing vehicles on paved surfaces, such as driveways and streets, causes potential problems because soapy and dirty water will run off into storm drains and water sources, causing groundwater to become contaminated (U.S. Environmental Protection Agency, 2014c).
- **Hazardous chemicals and products storage.** Many households store potentially hazardous chemicals and products, such as lawn and garden chemicals, home repair products, and paints, in outdoor sheds and buildings. See sidebar 18.2 (p. 332) for more information on safe storage of household, and potentially hazardous, chemicals and products.
- **Fertilizers and pesticides.** Failure to follow label directions and over-applying fertilizer and pesticides on lawns and gardens is not likely to have positive effects on a lawn or garden and increases the risks of water contamination. A soil test is recommended to determine the type and amount of fertilizer that is actually needed to benefit a lawn or garden (Rosen, Horgan, & Mugaas, 2015). Spills of fertilizers and pesticides can also quickly contaminate groundwater. Treating lawns up to forty-eight hours before rain will highly contaminate storm-water runoff because the rain will pick up the product before it can reach the root systems of plants. Similarly, excessive watering of lawns after treating with chemicals will interfere with the ability of the product to be effective and may pollute runoff. Using plants native to the area that can grow without much stimulation may be the most water-friendly approach to creating an environmentally sustainable yard (Krischik, Reed, & Willey, 2013).
- **Yard and garden waste.** Grass clippings and leaves are common examples of yard and garden waste. A harmful treatment of yard waste is to burn it along with household waste or garbage. Depending on what is in this waste, burning could release harmful gases and create air pollution. The ashes from such fires will settle on the ground and can seep down to contaminate surface and groundwater. Thus composting (i.e., the controlled decomposition of organic materials, such

as leaves, grass, and food scraps, by microorganisms) may be the best approach to handling yard waste. The result of this decomposition process is *compost* or *humus*, a crumbly, earthy-smelling, soil-like material that can be used to enrich the soil.

- **Improper landscaping.** A well-designed yard prevents excessive runoff and pollution problems. Scant landscaping, especially on hilly land, allows storm water to flow at increased rates and results in excess soil erosion. Short grass and lack of vegetation near sources of water are of particular concern because this increases the ability of runoff to carry pollutants directly into the water. To reduce water pollution and ground erosion, a buffer zone of vegetation could be left adjacent to water sources, although it should never be fertilized. Storm-water runoff, while typically associated with rain, is also produced artificially when people overwater their lawns. Excess water simply runs off the land, wasting an important resource. Native landscaping can reduce the need for applying additional water to yards and lawns. Homes in areas prone to wildfires or forest fires are of special concern when planning landscaping that controls erosion. Too many large shrubs and trees close to a home can create a fire hazard, so short grasses may be preferable (National Fire Protection Association, 2014).

- **Roof drainage.** Roof drainage should divert water away from a home's foundation walls to reduce the risk of interior moisture problems. Appropriate drainage, including the use of gutters, downspouts, and extension hoses, diverts roof water away from the house and driveway and allows it to filter through more permeable grounds such as a soakage trench system (a shallow, underground, gravel-filled trench, typically connected to a downspout) or grass swale. Downspouts that discharge onto paved surfaces cause concern for pollution since this water may carry automotive waste and other pollutants into storm drains (U.S. Environmental Protection Agency, 2014c).

BUILDING MATERIALS AND BUILDING PRACTICES

The impact of a home on its occupants has much to do with the materials and building practices used during the construction as well as the materials and furnishings added after the original construction, regardless of when a home was constructed (U.S. Environmental Protection Agency, 2013b). To evaluate the impact of building materials and practices on health, there are several areas to consider with respect to construction age and current building practices.

The age of a home may relate to occupants' health. Unless the house has undergone utility and material renovations since its original construction, an older home may contain hazardous materials, have utilities that do not meet codes, and utilize inefficient heating and air conditioning equipment that may produce pollutants. Table 18.1 shows possible hazards of older homes.

A new home may be designed and constructed to be more energy efficient. However, some newer homes are plagued with problems that can lead to health concerns, especially those related to poorly designed tight construction, including poor ventilation, excessive condensation leading to mold growth, back drafting of combustion appliances (that is, spillage of

TABLE 18.1
Possible Hazards of Older Homes

Hazard	Description and possible materials
Asbestos-containing materials	Homes built prior to 1980. Found in floor tiles, insulation materials like vermiculite, pipe and boiler wrap, exterior shingle siding, caulking compound, ceiling texture, and drywall compound. Poses a hazard if friable, damaged, or in poor condition.
Combustion gases such as carbon monoxide, nitrogen dioxide, carbon dioxide, and particulates	Any space- or water-heating equipment (furnace, range/oven, space heater, clothes dryer) that burns gas, oil, wood, coal, or kerosene. If not vented to the outside, or if flue or heat exchanger is not well maintained, a hazard exists. Back-drafting hazard is possible.
Drinking water contaminants (such as coliform bacteria, nitrate, or pesticides) in private water systems	Poorly maintained and shallow groundwater wells. Wells too close to septic systems, fuel and chemical storage areas, and agricultural feedlots.
Formaldehyde	Homes insulated with urea formaldehyde foam insulation (UFFI) during late 1970s–early 1980s. May lead to off-gassing of formaldehyde, a toxic volatile organic compound (VOC). Particleboard and MDF (medium-density fiberboard) used in kitchen cabinets, countertops, and furniture are also sources of formaldehyde.
Lead in water	Pre-1988 homes. Lead found in lead-based solder, brass well pumps and fixtures, and likely in homes with plumbing installed prior to 1930. Increased hazard with corrosive or acidic water.
Lead-based paint	Exterior and interior paints in homes built prior to 1978, most likely in homes built prior to 1950. Greater hazard if paint is in poor or damaged condition. The Lead Renovation, Repair and Painting Rule (2010) sets lead-safe work practices for all contractors working on housing built before 1978.
Molds	Can exist in any home with excessive moisture. May be present because of high relative humidity (>50%) and/or past flooding or water leaks. Poor home maintenance can contribute to mold growth.
Pressure-treated lumber (chromated copper arsenate [CCA], pentachlorophenol, and creosote)	Many exterior construction applications since 1900. Direct skin contact increases hazard. Extremely hazardous if burned. Today, CCA is approved only for exterior uses not in contact with food or drinking water, and pentachlorophenol and creosote are not approved for residential use (EPA, 2013).
Radon (naturally occurring radioactive gas)	A gas from soil and rock around foundations. Certain areas of the country are designated as high radon risk. During real estate transfers is the recommended time to test for radon if the home has not been previously tested.
Underground fuel-oil storage tank	Locations where fuel oil has been a predominant source of heating fuel prior to the 1980s. Leaking tanks can contaminate soil or groundwater.
Volatile organic compounds (VOCs)	A class of organic compounds that is easily evaporated into the air and used in the manufacturing, installation, and maintenance of many building products, including particleboard, cabinets, upholstered furniture, adhesives, carpet, fabric finishes, paints, paint strippers, wood finishes, and cleaning solvents. Many VOCs are toxic.

Source: Parrott, Atiles, and Vogel, 2006, slightly modified by authors.

combustion by-products into the home), and indoor air quality problems resulting from greater use of chemically based products, finishes, and furnishings). These issues are addressed in the following sections.

CURRENT BUILDING PRACTICES: VENTILATION

Good ventilation, a critical element in a healthy home, is necessary for moisture control as well as to remove airborne chemicals, particles, combustion by-products, and odors (U.S. Department of Energy, 2010). Residential ventilation systems are generally designed with the assumption that mixing or replacing indoor air with outside air improves indoor air. Although outdoor air is perceived to be fresher, depending on the location of the home, this may not always be true. If the outside air is polluted, special ventilation systems may be needed that provide additional air filtration and cleaning (U.S. Environmental Protection Agency, 2009).

Planning a home ventilation system usually focuses on sizing and locating exhaust fans. However, there must also be a way for adequate replacement air to be brought into the home, equalizing inside and outside air pressure. Ventilation systems for a home typically consist of local ventilation for problem areas such as kitchens and bathrooms and general ventilation for the whole house. Most building codes will specify only minimum ventilation requirements. Many professional and industry organizations involved with housing, such as the American Society of Heating, Refrigerating, and Air-Conditioning Engineers (ASHRAE), the Home Ventilating Institute (HVI), and the National Kitchen and Bath Association (NKBA), emphasize that mechanical ventilation is important for a healthy home and provide additional guidelines and recommendations for ventilation (American Society of Heating, Refrigerating, and Air-Conditioning Engineers, 2013; Beamish, Parrott, Emmel, & Peterson, 2013; Home Ventilating Institute, 2010; Parrott, Beamish, Emmel, & Peterson, 2013).

The most effective ventilation system for a home is usually a mechanical system that exhausts air to the outside. It is essential that ventilation is directed to the outdoors and not the basement, attic, or crawlspace. Selecting the right fan is important, but it is only part of the decision. Household ventilation must be considered as a system, including the fan, ducts, air intakes, controls, and installation (Home Ventilating Institute, 2010).

The simplest mechanical ventilation systems use separate, independently operating exhaust fans in each bathroom, the kitchen, and possibly in other areas such as the laundry room or a home workshop. The exhaust fans can operate by manual or automatic switches such as a humidistat or can be integrated into light switches (Parrott et al., 2013).

Many people resist using exhaust fans because of the noise associated with them (Parrott, Emmel, & Beamish, 2003). The noise level of fans is rated in sones, which is a measure of loudness. Generally, a fan rated less than 1.0 to 1.5 sones will be quiet enough to be considered only background noise (Parrott et al., 2013).

Kitchen Ventilation Fans

The choices in kitchens are usually between a fan mounted above the cooktop or range, usually with a hood (updraft), and a proximity system, installed in the cooktop or adjacent to the cooking surface (downdraft). Some kitchens may have a ceiling or wall-mounted exhaust fan, but that is generally not considered as effective as the updraft or downdraft systems. Kitchen ventilation systems are especially critical with gas cooking appliances to control combustion pollutants such as carbon monoxide and water vapor. Most codes, standards, or guidelines for residential ventilation specify a minimum amount of exhaust ventilation in the kitchen (Beamish et al., 2013).

Bathroom Ventilation Fans

Bathroom exhaust fans are usually installed near the shower or bathtub and are important to control excess moisture in the home. These fans should be turned on whenever the shower or tub is in use and run long enough to reduce the excess moisture from bathing activities. Humidistat controls can be used for an automated system. Typically, the bathroom door is undercut to ensure replacement air can enter the room. Most codes, standards, or guidelines for residential ventilation specify a minimum amount of exhaust ventilation for bathrooms, including the requirement for an operating window if no mechanical ventilation is installed (Parrott et al., 2013).

Whole-House Fans

An exhaust fan mounted in the attic of a home can be used to provide ventilation and fresh air to the entire home. Typically, a single large fan pulls air into the house through windows and doors and then exhausts it through vents in the attic. The air intake is often located in a hall or other central location in the home. This type of ventilation system is mostly used in the summer, typically in climates with hot days and cool nights. The whole-house fan exhausts heated air from the home and replaces it with cooler night air, providing a slight breeze at the same time (Home Ventilating Institute, 2010).

Fan Size

Exhaust fans are sized in CFM (cubic feet per minute) or L/s (liters per second). These terms describe the volume of air the fan can move in a period of time. Some ventilation recommendations are given in fan size only, which does not consider the size of the room and the efficiency of the installation. Other ventilation recommendations are made in ACH (air changes per hour), a measure of the number of times per hour a volume of air equivalent to the volume of the room should be exhausted.

The fan size determined by the ACH method is effective fan capacity, or how much air the fan can actually move. Effective fan capacity is not the same as the mechanical size of the fan. The effective fan capacity will depend on a number of factors, including:

- **Length of duct runs from the intake vent to the exhaust vent.** If the duct run is more than five feet, the size of the fan should be increased to compensate for the resistance of a longer duct run.
- **Elbows or bends in the ducts.** If there is more than one elbow or bend in the duct, the size of the fan should be increased to compensate for the greater resistance (Beamish et al., 2013; Home Ventilating Institute, 2010; Parrott et al., 2013).

Replacement Air and Back Drafting

An operating fan exhausting or removing air from a room is exhausting air not just from that room but from the entire home. Some of the replacement air may come from windows that are open, from people moving in and out of doors, or from leaks and cracks in the building envelope. However, in well-constructed, energy-efficient homes, there are limited places for replacement air to leak into the home. If replacement air is not provided through controlled ventilation, negative pressure can be created in the home, which can create problems with the operation of appliances that need to exhaust to the outside, such as a gas furnace or water heater. In this situation, called back drafting, dangerous combustion pollutants as well as excess moisture and radon gas can be pulled into the home. A simple solution to back-drafting problems, and to providing replacement air, can be opening a window when operating exhaust fans. However, this is not always a practical solution. Other solutions include a fresh air inlet into the home and a whole-house mechanical ventilation system that balances airflow into the home (Home Ventilating Institute, 2010).

A pressure diagnostic test, usually a blower door test, can be used both to evaluate the airtightness of the home and to identify unwanted air leaks (Holladay, 2010). This test can be useful for older homes as well as new construction. The results from the blower door test can be used to provide a plan for adequate and healthy ventilation of the home as well as to reduce energy-wasting air infiltration.

Whole-House Ventilation Systems

A balanced whole-house ventilation system is a more complex system that provides controlled, continuous ventilation to a home. Exhaust fan vents in one or more locations throughout the home pull air from the home and exhaust it to the outside. At the same time, fresh air is blown into the home through one or more inlets. The whole-house ventilation system can work through existing ductwork for heating and cooling systems or be entirely separate (Home Ventilating Institute, 2010).

Some whole-house ventilation systems are known as heat recovery ventilators (HRV). In these systems, the exhaust air from the home and the fresh air from outside are passed, simultaneously but separately, through a heat exchanger. In the wintertime, heat from the air in the home is recovered to preheat the fresh outdoor air. In the summertime, heat is removed from the incoming outside air. The net result is increased energy efficiency in the ventilation system. An energy recovery ventilator (ERV) is a similar system that also dehumidifies the incoming air from outside (Home Ventilating Institute, 2010).

The 2012 International Energy Conservation Code, which is incorporated into the 2012 International Residential Code (IRC), requires whole-house mechanical ventilation to provide adequate fresh air and moisture control, as needed for tightly constructed, energy-efficient homes (International Code Council, 2011). The IRC is a model code. Most states and municipalities use model codes as the basis for their mandatory building codes (Council of American Building Officials, 1997).

The American National Standard Institute and American Society of Heating, Refrigerating, and Air-Conditioning Engineers' ANSI/ASHRAE Standard 62.2-2013 is also a model ventilation standard that is incorporated into many state and municipal building codes (American Society of Heating, Refrigerating, and Air-Conditioning Engineers, 2013). Similar to the IRC, ASHRAE 62.2-2013 requires whole-house ventilation. The formula for calculating the required ventilation is based on the size of the building, the number of occupants, and the number of bedrooms. Given that major model ventilation codes like the IRC and ASHRAE require whole-house ventilation systems, the chapter authors believe that these systems will become more common in the future.

CURRENT BUILDING PRACTICES: MOISTURE CONTROL

The cycle of water evaporating and condensing in a room can lead to moisture problems, typically in a bathroom, kitchen, or laundry room. Many activities such as showering and cooking increase the air's temperature as well as its moisture level. However, materials and surfaces in these rooms tend to be cooler than the air, which leads to condensation.

Water vapor is present in the air in varying amounts. The maximum amount of water vapor depends on the temperature. The warmer the air, the more water vapor it will hold. Absolute humidity describes how much water vapor there is in the air. Relative humidity, expressed as a percentage, can be explained by the following formula:

$$\frac{\text{Amount of water vapor in the air}}{\text{Maximum amount of water vapor air can hold at a given temperature}} \times 100 = \text{Relative humidity}$$

Condensation is the opposite of evaporation and occurs when water vapor returns to a liquid state. As air cools it can no longer hold as much water vapor, so the vapor condenses into a liquid. The temperature at which condensation occurs is typically referred to as the dew point.

Excess moisture is a problem for both a building and its occupants' health and safety. Excess moisture in building materials leads to structural problems, such as peeling paint, rusting metal, and deterioration of joists and framing. Damp building materials tend to attract dirt and therefore require more cleaning and maintenance (U.S. Environmental Protection Agency, 2013b).

Damp spaces also make good environments for the growth of many biological pollutants. Bacteria, viruses, and pests, ranging from dust mites to cockroaches, thrive in moist spaces. Wet building materials can also harbor mold growth and wood-decaying fungi, which lead to further structural damage as well as pose a health threat for residents (CDC, 2006; National Center for Healthy Housing, 2008; U.S. Environmental Protection Agency, 2013b).

Hidden Condensation

The air temperature inside a bathroom or kitchen typically tends to be higher than the air temperature on the other side of the walls, floor, and ceiling. During the winter in a heating-dominant climate, this is especially true of exterior walls and a ceiling with an attic above it. As warm air rises, moving upward through walls and ceilings and meeting cool surfaces within the wall or ceiling cavities, it is lighter than cool air. At some point, the dew point temperature is reached and condensation occurs. This hidden condensation inside walls and attics can have harsh consequences for homeowners. As building materials get wetter, deterioration and mold growth can become extensive before the problem is noticed. In a cooling-dominant climate, the air moisture movement can also occur as air moves in the opposite direction, when warm, humid outside air moves toward cooler interior spaces, such as basements or air-conditioned rooms (Parrott et al., 2013).

Mold and Moisture

Molds are a natural part of the ecosystem and play an important role in digesting organic debris. Molds can grow on almost any organic matter, including skin cells, residues from shampoo, or textile fibers. Cellulosic building materials such as paper, wood, textiles, many types of insulation, carpet, wallpaper, and drywall make an excellent environment for mold growth. The cellulosic materials will absorb moisture, providing the right growth conditions, and the materials themselves will provide the food (U.S. Environmental Protection Agency, 2013b).

Molds, or fungi, reproduce through spores, which blow out into the air but can be dormant for years. With the right mix of nutrients, moisture, and oxygen, however, the spores can begin to grow. Most molds will start growing at a relative humidity of 70 percent or more, and most molds grow fast. If cellulosic building materials get wet, mold growth will begin in twenty-four to forty-eight hours. Mold growth on the surface of noncellulosic materials can start in the same time period as long as food and moisture are present (U.S. Environmental Protection Agency, 2013c).

There are no federal standards for mold in homes. Currently, there are no reliable do-it-yourself mold tests. Existing mold tests done by professionals may identify only species of mold. However, mold testing is not recommended. According to the U.S. Environmental Protection Agency, "In most cases, if visible mold growth is present, sampling is unnecessary" (U.S. Environmental Protection Agency, 2013b). Therefore, if there is evidence of mold, the best recommendation is to seek professional assistance from a reputable mold remediation company to begin appropriate remediation.

Molds can affect residents in different ways. For example, molds produce chemicals that irritate some people and can cause problems such as headaches, breathing difficulties, and skin, eye, and throat irritation. They can also aggravate other health conditions, such as asthma. In addition, some people are allergic to certain species of mold. Molds can also sensitize the body so that the person is more susceptible to health effects from exposure. Finally, some molds produce toxins. The likelihood of health effects increases with the amount of exposure to mold as well as the individual's sensitivity (Lankarge, 2003).

Preventing Moisture Problems

Preventing moisture problems involves many building and behavior-related items. Among them are water management to prevent infiltration through adequate landscaping, grading, and capillary breaks (a material or construction feature to prevent wicking of soil moisture into building materials). Indoors it is important to manage interior moisture sources such as HVAC (heating, ventilating, and air conditioning) equipment, duct leakages, and plumbing issues. Other sources of moisture can be controlled by adequate occupant behavior such as using exhaust ventilation when showering, bathing, cooking, and doing laundry. Good ventilation is necessary to prevent moisture problems and mold growth in the home. In new or remodeled homes, new building materials such as lumber, paint, concrete, and drywall can be a major source of moisture for a year or longer (Dorman, 2005; U.S. Environmental Protection Agency, 2013b).

The finish materials in a home can contribute to or help prevent moisture problems. After exposure to water and humidity, the more absorbent the materials, the longer they will stay damp, which supports mold growth. A hard surface or nonabsorbent material, such as glazed tile, solid surfacing, vitreous china, or engineered stone, reduces the likelihood of moisture absorption. Sealers applied to absorbent or porous materials such as clay tile, marble, or grout, can also reduce moisture absorption. Low-maintenance materials, fixtures, and fittings are also important for preventing mold growth. Materials that are kept clean are less likely to accumulate debris that can support mold growth (U.S. Environmental Protection Agency, 2013b; Parrott et al., 2013).

Vapor-retardant material such as plastic sheeting can be used in wall construction to block the flow of moist air into wall cavities or attics. There are special considerations about the placement and use of a vapor retarder, depending on whether the climate is heating or cooling dominant (U.S. Environmental Protection Agency, 2013b).

New products are becoming available with various types of antimicrobial finishes or additives. For example, paints are available with fungicides to prevent mold growth in the paint. In spite of this fungicide, particle matter that accumulates on top of the paint can become food for mold to grow under moist conditions. That is why it is important to keep painted surfaces clean and free of dust. There is some concern among health professionals about overexposure to some pesticides and antimicrobial products (Parrott et al., 2013).

CURRENT BUILDING PRACTICES: INDOOR AIR QUALITY

Good indoor air quality makes a space pleasant and healthy for the user. Providing good indoor air quality is a three-step process.

- **Source control.** This is the primary strategy for maintaining good indoor air quality (U.S. Environmental Protection Agency, 2013c). Sources of indoor air pollution in a room or building are minimized or prevented. Suggestions for minimizing indoor air pollutants such as radon, combustion pollutants (including carbon monoxide), lead dust, volatile organic compounds, and molds have been discussed (see table 18.1). Select household products will minimize the impact on indoor air quality and use the least amount necessary to complete a task (sidebar 18.2).
- **Ventilation.** Providing adequate air exchange through natural or mechanical ventilation dilutes the concentration of indoor air pollutants and ensures that the space has a supply of fresh air. Mechanical ventilation is discussed above.
- **Air cleaning.** This means, when necessary, using filters or other devices to remove potentially harmful indoor air pollutants (U.S. Environmental Protection Agency, 2012a).

SIDEBAR 18.2

Household Chemicals and Products: Best Practices

- Control home indoor air quality by the choices you make in using household chemicals and products.
- Use the least amount of a product that will get the job done.
- Read labels, follow safety precautions, and contact the manufacturer if you have questions.
- Use household chemicals and products only for their intended purpose.
- Choose product packaging that reduces the chance of spills and leaks and is childproof if children live in or visit the home.
- Keep household products in original containers so safety information, including accidental poisoning information, and directions for use are with the product.
- Always use household products in well-ventilated areas away from heat sources, living areas, and exploring children.
- Use storage areas designed to capture leaks and spills.

- Do not use a potentially hazardous chemical unless necessary.
- Request a Material Safety Data Sheet (MSDS) for potentially hazardous products so full safety and disposal information is available.
- Where possible, trade or donate any leftover products so that there is no product for disposal.
- If there is leftover product or chemical, follow label directions for disposal. Contact your local waste authority with any questions about disposal of potentially hazardous products.
- It is also a good idea to reduce the need for potentially hazardous household chemicals in the first place by practicing preventative maintenance.
- Clean spills and stains quickly.
- Remove food wastes promptly.
- Control excess moisture to reduce the likelihood of problems with mold or household pests.

Source: Centers for Disease Control and Prevention and U.S. Department of Housing and Urban Development, 2006; U.S. Environmental Protection Agency, 2012b, 2013d.

Air Cleaners

Choosing an air cleaner to improve air quality in a home is a complex task. Choices include various types of mechanical filtration, electrostatic, electronic, ion generating, and adsorption (such as activated charcoal) systems for air cleaning (U.S. Environmental Protection Agency, 2009, 2012a). According to the U.S Environmental Protection Agency, air cleaners that generate ozone are not recommended for use in occupied spaces, such as the home, as ozone is a respiratory irritant and can damage the lungs (U.S. Environmental Protection Agency, 2009, 2012a).

Air cleaners can be tabletop, freestanding, or integrated into heating, cooling, or ventilation systems. In addition to size, efficiency (the ability of the collecting medium to capture contaminants from the air stream) and effectiveness (the ability of the air cleaner to reduce contaminant concentrations in the room's air) must be considered. Cost to purchase and maintain the air cleaner, as well as the warranty involved, is among the other considerations (U.S. Environmental Protection Agency, 2009, 2012a).

Air cleaners are effective only on those contaminants that stay airborne long enough to reach the air cleaner. Appropriately selected and well-maintained air cleaners may reduce some contaminants in indoor air but should not be the primary method to improve air quality. The value of air cleaners in actually improving health is of considerable controversy, with the data being inconclusive and dependent on factors such as the type of air cleaner, the pollutants causing the health symptoms, and the sensitivities of the groups studied (U.S. Environmental Protection Agency, 2009, 2012a).

CURRENT BUILDING PRACTICES: MUNICIPAL VERSUS PRIVATE WATER SYSTEMS

Many Americans get their water from a public or municipal water system, whereas others use a private water source to tap directly into the groundwater or possibly surface water. Many people who are connected to public water systems do not understand that their water may come from groundwater, as would a private well-user's water. Public water sources also include local rivers and lakes. All of these sources of water may become contaminated in many ways and, therefore, affect consumers of municipal and private water alike. The differences between public and private water sources come in testing and treating the water (U.S. Environmental Protection Agency, 2002, 2005b).

Water Testing

Water from municipal systems is checked regularly for safety, according to guidelines established by the U.S. Environmental Protection Agency (EPA), by the local water authority, or by a similar agency. The presence of over ninety contaminants in public water supplies is regulated (U.S. Environmental Protection Agency, 2013a). If contaminants in the water supply are detected, the water must be treated. Therefore, consumers of such water can feel confident that the water coming into their home is safe to drink. However, there is still a potential for in-house pollution that may come from the plumbing itself (U.S. Environmental Protection Agency, 2002, 2005b, 2013a).

Consumers who obtain their water from a private source such as their own well, however, are responsible for testing their water, as routine EPA tests are not required for private water sources. In this case, tests should be conducted at least every year by a certified laboratory (U.S. Environmental Protection Agency, 2002, 2005b). Wells that are more than twenty years old should be tested more frequently. Basic tests to protect the safety and quality of the water include total coliform bacteria, nitrate, pH, and total dissolved solids. In addition, users of private water supplies have the same concerns as users of public water about the potential for in-house contamination (U.S. Environmental Protection Agency, 2002, 2005b, 2013a). In addition to following these guidelines, testing of both municipal and private water sources should be conducted whenever water changes in taste, smell, color or clarity, or there is a specific reason to believe that other contaminants such as pesticides or chemicals have entered the water supply (U.S. Environmental Protection Agency, 2002, 2005b).

Wells

All private well users should first ensure that they are properly using and protecting their well; this is the best approach to providing a quality water supply. Three basic principles will help well owners to ensure the safety of their well water.

- A well should be sited relatively high in the landscape and as far as possible from animal pens, septic tanks, dumps, and chemical storage areas. In addition, wells should not be located in areas that are prone to flooding.
- The well casing (the plastic or steel pipe that runs the depth of the well) should be sealed with a tight-fitting, vermin-proof cap and extend at least one foot above the ground. The area between the casing and the sides of the hole should be filled with grout.
- Devices designed to prevent backflow should be attached to the ends of faucets and hoses to prevent water-carrying pollutants from siphoning back into the water supply (U.S. Environmental Protection Agency, 2002).

In addition, abandoned wells, if not properly handled, present an opportunity for water contamination. Abandoned wells should be filled, sealed, and plugged. Such precautions will prevent the accidental seepage of pollutants into groundwater, as well as the intentional disposal of garbage or chemicals down the well (U.S. Environmental Protection Agency, 2002).

Water Treatment

Two facts about water contamination and treatment are commonly misunderstood. First, many potentially harmful water contaminants do not affect the taste or appearance of water. Second, simply boiling water may not make it safer, as some contaminants like nitrates actually become more concentrated with boiling. Unfamiliarity with these facts leads many Americans to assume that their water is safe when it could actually have short-term and/or long-term health effects on household members.

Over time, Americans have become more aware of the potentially hidden dangers in their water, and more products to improve water quality are available on the market. No one treatment device or method can remove all contaminants, bacteria, and minerals from water (U.S. Environmental Protection Agency, 2005a, 2005b, 2013a). Not only is such a task impossible, it is also undesirable—such pure water would be both bland and corrosive. Furthermore, the EPA does not test or register any water treatment system, so claims of such a status are deceptive (U.S. Environmental Protection Agency, 2005a).

Water treatment systems vary in approach, size, effectiveness, and cost. Household water should always be independently tested before making a choice of water treatment systems, especially more expensive equipment such as a water softener or iron filter. It is important to match any type of water treatment equipment to the water problem and the type and amount of pollutant to be removed. If more than one type of treatment device is needed, the order of installation may be critical (U.S. Environmental Protection Agency, 2005a).

Furnishings and Household Products

Some household furnishings may have finishes with chemicals that can affect the occupants' health. In particular, new items such as carpets, varnished woods, and textiles with special finishes have the potential to affect air quality in the home. Ventilation is important when new furnishings or finishes are introduced into a home. Environmentally friendly products with few or no VOCs reduce the risk. Consumers may want to choose products that are certified for low chemical emissions from organizations that use third-party, independent testing, such as the Greenguard Environmental Institute (www.greenguard.org) or the State of California Air Resources Board (www.arb.ca.gov).

Some potentially hazardous chemicals are also used in the manufacturing of household cleaning supplies, automotive products, hobby materials, and lawn and garden products that are used in and around the home. If not used and stored properly, these materials can evaporate, creating poor air quality, and can contaminate water supplies, posing long-term health risks for occupants (CDC, 2006; National Center for Healthy Housing, 2008; U.S. Environmental Protection Agency, 2012a, 2013d).

When selecting household products, it is important to read the ingredient label and look for warnings, such as *flammable, combustible, caution, warning, danger*, and *use in a ventilated area*, that indicate the presence of hazardous contents. Failure to follow label directions for safe use, storage, and disposal of chemical products creates a hazard in the home. Hazardous materials fall into one or more of four basic categories: corrosive materials, flammable materials, explosive or reactive materials, and toxic materials. For a more detailed assessment of a product, material safety data sheets (MSDSes) are available upon request from the product manufacturer. Most MSDSes are now available on the Internet (see chapters 3, 5, and 19).

Safe Storage and Disposal of Chemical Products

Improper storage and disposal of household chemicals can raise the risk of indoor air pollution, pose a threat to household members, and create a risk for the eventual contamination of groundwater. Refer to sidebar 18.2 for more information on safety with household products to protect indoor air quality.

RESIDENT LIFESTYLE

Concerns about creating and maintaining a healthy home are well founded. Without careful planning of the homesite and design, material selection, and maintenance, the home can become a hazardous place. Once the home is constructed, the residents have the opportunity to create and maintain a healthy environment with their activities and behaviors. Lifestyle choices that may affect the health of a home's residents include smoking, management of household pests, and pet ownership (see chapters 2, 3, 5, 6, and 19).

Environmental Tobacco Smoke

Environmental tobacco smoke (ETS), or secondhand smoke from cigarettes, pipes, or cigars, can affect the home and its residents (Office on Smoking and Health, 2006). Tobacco smoke is actually a mixture of gases and particles and is not easily removed from a home. Both the gaseous component and the particulate component have harmful effects on human health. Secondhand smoke is connected to many health problems. The U.S. Environmental Protection Agency (2011) estimates that three thousand nonsmokers die every year from lung cancer due to secondhand smoke. Secondhand smoke also causes other types of cancer, emphysema, and other chronic lung diseases and cardiovascular disease in nonsmokers. Less severe but still important consequences of ETS for nonsmokers are impaired breathing, a lowered immune system, and increased heart rate and blood pressure.

Many of the risks from ETS fall on children (Office on Smoking and Health, 2006). Infants and toddlers develop lower respiratory infections such as pneumonia, bronchitis, and bronchiolitis from exposure to secondhand smoke (U.S. Environmental Protection Agency, 2011). Children with asthma are particularly sensitive to secondhand smoke, as it can cause more frequent or more severe asthma attacks. The best solution to the problem of ETS in a home is to not allow smoking inside the home, especially if children are present. If someone is smoking inside the home, ventilate by opening windows or using an exhaust fan. However, it is important to know that no ventilation system can completely remove tobacco smoke from a home (Office on Smoking and Health, 2006).

Household Pests

A home is never completely pest free. It is important to know which bugs are to be expected occasionally in a home and which represent serious health risks. Roaches and dust mites are probably the most hazardous household pests commonly found in homes (Allergy and Asthma Foundation of America, 2005; Huss et al., 2001).

ROACHES

Roaches can get into food and spoil it. Roach feces can cause pollution of indoor air and can be a major trigger for asthma attacks, especially in children (Huss et al., 2001). Four basic principles will help get rid of roaches and protect the home.

- Both food particles and water attract roaches, but if roaches have nothing to eat they will look for somewhere else to live. Therefore, garbage should be sealed or thrown out every night. Neither dirty dishes nor pet food should be left out overnight. Food spills, crumbs, and water leaks should be cleaned up promptly.
- Roaches can be baited and trapped before they even have a chance to starve. Roach bait is available in premade traps and tubes. Traps should be placed in corners or against walls, out of reach of children. Low-toxicity pesticides such as boric acid may also be useful.
- In attempting to defeat roaches, outdoor pesticides should not be used inside the home, as they are unsafe in closed-in areas.

□ All pesticides should be tightly sealed and stored in their original containers in a cool, dry, locked cabinet, out of the reach of children (sidebar 18.2).

DUST MITES

Another type of household pest that often causes health problems, dust mites, lives all over people's homes—in carpets, upholstered furniture, bedding, and stuffed animals—but cannot be seen by the naked eye. Dust mites thrive in moist places and wherever they can feed on dead human skin cells. About twenty million people in the United States are allergic to the feces of dust mites, and for some people they serve as a trigger for asthma attacks (Allergy and Asthma Foundation of America, 2005).

One of the easiest places to guard against dust mites is in bedding. Zippered plastic mattress and pillow covers should be used underneath sheets to help protect sleepers from dust mites. In addition, all bedding (sheets, blankets, pillow covers, and mattress pads) should be washed in hot water or dried in a hot dryer (130°F) every week to kill any dust mites that might be living on them. Keeping the home's relative humidity level below 50 percent and limiting carpeted areas can help control dust mites (Allergy and Asthma Foundation of America, 2005; National Center for Healthy Housing, 2008).

PETS

Pets are welcome in many homes across the United States. However, indoor pets are potential health risks to some household members. Precautions should be taken to minimize these risks and ensure that a pet and its people can live healthily in a home together.

The health threat posed by pets comes primarily in the form of dander, which is skin flakes from furry animals. The most frequent types of problems triggered by pet dander in the air are allergic reactions and asthma attacks brought on by exposure to pet dander. Routine acts like making a bed and vacuuming can cause animal dander to get stirred up into the air. To help reduce the amount of dander in the air, pets should be kept out of carpeted areas, as walking across dander-infested carpets stirs up the dander. In addition, pets should be kept out of bedrooms to make the air in sleeping environments more healthy (CDC, 2006).

Indoor/outdoor pets present another possible health problem. They can bring outdoor particles such as pollen inside with them, which can further contaminate the indoor air of the home. Similar to pet dander, pollen often causes allergic reactions and is one of the suspected triggers or complicating factors of asthma (CDC, 2006).

CONCLUSION

The beginning of this chapter presented a systems approach for the study of the home-health interaction. The outdoors (or macroenvironment) in which the home is situated as well as the indoors (or microenvironment) of the home were presented as being part of that dynamic relationship. The residents, through their choices and decisions about design, construction, management, maintenance, and lifestyle, continuously influence the home's system and thus the health quality of the home's environment (see chapters

2, 3, 5, 6, and 19). This chapter detailed the opportunities, as summarized in the following paragraphs, that residents have to maintain their home as an environmentally healthy and friendly place to live.

The macroenvironment of the home includes the factors external to the building itself. Climate variables were presented and information on climate zones in the United States were discussed. A healthy home starts with a healthy building site, and this chapter presented information on the role of the microclimate of a site, natural topographic factors of the site, and possible human-caused factors. Storm-water runoff and its influence on the site, including possible controls through permits and taxes, concluded the sections of the chapter on the macroenvironment. The discussion of the macroenvironment of a healthy home began with information on building materials and building practices. This section also included information on the influence of construction age.

Current building practices that influence the development of a healthy home were presented in several sections of the chapter, on ventilation, moisture control, indoor air quality, and municipal versus private water systems. Two additional topics concluded the discussion of the microenvironment of the healthy home: furnishings and household products and resident lifestyle.

A home *can* be a healthy place to live. In order for this to happen, the residents of the home need to understand that their actions and choices will affect the quality and health of the indoor environment. The information in this chapter, while not exhaustive, introduces a framework for developing and maintaining a healthy home, as well as understanding the key issues and choices that are involved in making a home a safe and healthy place to live.

REFERENCES

Allergy and Asthma Foundation of America. (2005). *Dust mites*. Retrieved January 26, 2017, from http://www.aafa.org/display.cfm?id=8&sub=16&cont=48).

American Society of Heating, Refrigerating, and Air-Conditioning Engineers. (2013). *Ventilation and acceptable indoor air quality in low-rise residential buildings*. ANSI-ASHRAE Standard 62.2-2013.

Baechler, M. C., Williamson, J. L., Gilbride, T. L., Cole, P. C., Hefty, M. G., & Love, P. M. (2010). *Guide to determining climate regions by county*. Building America Best Practices Series, volume 7.1. Retrieved January 26, 2017, from http://apps1.eere.energy.gov/buildings/publications/pdfs/building_america/ba_climateguide_7_1.pdf.

Beamish, J. O., Parrott, K. R., Emmel, J., & Peterson, M. J. (2013). *Kitchen planning: Guidelines, codes, standards*. Hoboken, N.J.: John Wiley & Sons; Hackettstown, N.J.: National Kitchen and Bath Association.

California Department of Housing and Community Development. (2009). *Housing element policies and programs addressing climate change*. Retrieved January 26, 2017, from http://www.hcd.ca.gov/hpd/HE_PoliciesProgramsAddressingClimateChange.pdf.

CDC (Centers for Disease Control and Prevention) and U.S. Department of Housing and Urban Development. (2006). *Healthy housing reference manual*. (Revised). Atlanta: U.S. Department of Health and Human Services. Retrieved January 26, 2017, from http://www.cdc.gov/nceh/publications/books/housing/housing.htm.

Chiras, D. D. (2000). *The natural home*. White River, Vt.: Chelsea Green.

Council of American Building Officials. (1997). *An introduction to model codes*. Retrieved January 26, 2017, from http://www.codesusa.com/download/model%20codes.pdf.

Dadd, D. L. (2005). *Home safe home*. (2nd ed.). New York: Tarcher/Putnam.

Dorman, D. (2005). "Moisture control in homes." Part 3 of 3. *ASHI Reporter*, July 2005. Retrieved January 26, 2017, from http://www.ashireporter.org/HomeInspection/Articles/Moisture-Control-in-Homes/115.

Green Building Advisor. (2012). *Building lot and siting a house.* Retrieved January 26, 2017, from http://www.greenbuildingadvisor.com/green-basics/1-lot-and-neighborhood-overview-incomplete.

Holladay, M. (2010). *Blower door basics.* Green Building Advisor. Retrieved January 26, 2017, from http://www.greenbuildingadvisor.com/blogs/dept/musings/blower-door-basics.

Home Ventilating Institute. (2010). *Fresh ideas: The guide to home ventilation and indoor air quality.* Retrieved January 26, 2017, from http://www.hvi.org/publications/pdfs/HVI_FreshIdeaslores_31Dec09.pdf.

Huss, K., Adkinson, N. K., Eggleston, P. A., Dawson, C., Van Natta, M. L., & Hamilton, R. G. (2001). House dust mite and cock roach exposure are strong risk factors for positive allergy skin test response in the Childhood Asthma Management Program. *Journal of Allergy and Clinical Immunology, 107*(1): 48–54.

International Code Council. (2011). *2012 International residential code for one- and two-family dwellings.*

Krischik, V., Reed, C., & Willey, S. (2013). *Native plants for sustainable landscapes: Establishment and management of lakeshores and gardens.* Retrieved January 26, 2017, from http://www.extension.umn.edu/garden/yard-garden/landscaping/native-plants-for-sustainable-landscapes/.

Lankarge, V. (2003). *What every homeowner needs to know about mold.* New York: McGraw-Hill.

National Center for Healthy Housing. (2008). *What we do.* Retrieved January 26, 2017, from http://www.nchh.org/What-We-Do/Health-Hazards—Prevention—and-Solutions.aspx.

National Fire Protection Association. (2014). *The basics of defensible space and the "home ignition zone."* Retrieved January 26, 2017, from http://www.firewise.org/wildfire-preparedness/be-firewise/home-and-landscape/defensible-space.

Office of the U.S. Surgeon General. (2009). *The Surgeon General's call to action to promote healthy homes.* Retrieved January 26, 2017, from http://www.ncbi.nlm.nih.gov/books/NBK44192/.

Office on Smoking and Health. (2006). *The health consequences of involuntary exposure to tobacco smoke: A report of the Surgeon General.* Atlanta: Centers for Disease Control and Prevention. Retrieved January 26, 2017, from http://www.ncbi.nlm.nih.gov/books/NBK44318/.

Parrott, K. R., Atiles, J. H., & Vogel, M. P. (2006). Home environments and health. In Merrill, J. L., Crull, S. R., Tremblay, K. R., Jr., Tyler, L. L., & Carswell, A. T. (Eds.), *Introduction to housing* (pp. 55–86). Upper Saddle River, N.J.: Prentice Hall.

Parrott, K. R., Beamish, J. O., Emmel, J., & Peterson, M. J. (2013). *Bath planning: Guidelines, codes, standards.* Hoboken, N.J.: John Wiley & Sons; Hackettstown, N.J.: National Kitchen and Bath Association.

Parrott, K., Emmel, J. M., & Beamish, J. O. (2003). Use of kitchen ventilation: Impact on indoor air quality. *The Forum for Family and Consumer Issues 8*(1). Retrieved January 26, 2017, from http://www.ces.ncsu.edu/depts/fcs/pub/8(1)/forum.html.

Rosen, C. J., Horgan, P. P., & Mugaas, R. J. (2015). *Fertilizing lawns.* University of Minnesota Extension. Retrieved January 26, 2017, from http://www.extension.umn.edu/garden/yard-garden/lawns/fertilizing-lawns/.

U.S. Department of Energy. (2010). *Guide to home ventilation.* Retrieved February 22, 2017, from https://energy.gov/sites/prod/files/guide_to_home-ventilation.pdf.

U.S. Department of Energy. (2012). *Landscaping for energy efficiency.* Retrieved January 26, 2017, from http://energy.gov/energysaver/articles/landscaping-energy-efficient-homes.

U.S. Department of Energy. (2014). *Whole house systems approach.* Retrieved January 26, 2017, from http://energy.gov/energysaver/articles/whole-house-systems-approach.

U.S. Environmental Protection Agency. (2002). *Drinking water from household wells.* Retrieved January 26, 2017, from http://water.epa.gov/drink/info/well/upload/2003_06_03_privatewells_pdfs_household_wells.pdf.

U.S. Environmental Protection Agency. (2005a). *Filtration facts.* Retrieved January 26, 2017, from http://water.epa.gov/drink/info/upload/2005_11_17_faq_fs_healthseries_filtration.pdf.

U.S. Environmental Protection Agency. (2005b). *Home water testing*. Retrieved January 26, 2017, from water.epa.gov/drink/info/upload/2005_09_14_faq_fs_homewatertesting.pdf.

U.S. Environmental Protection Agency. (2008). *Mold remediation in schools and commercial buildings*. Retrieved January 26, 2017, from http://www.epa.gov/mold/mold_remediation.html#append_b.

U.S. Environmental Protection Agency. (2009). *Guide to air cleaners in your home*. Retrieved January 26, 2017, from http://www.epa.gov/iaq/pubs/airclean.html.

U.S. Environmental Protection Agency. (2011). *Health effects of exposure to secondhand smoke*. Retrieved January 26, 2017, from http://www.epa.gov/smokefree/healtheffects.html.

U.S. Environmental Protection Agency. (2012a). *The inside story: A guide to indoor air quality*. Retrieved January 26, 2017, from http://www.epa.gov/iaq/pubs/insidestory.html.

U. S. Environmental Protection Agency. (2012b). *Waste*. Retrieved January 26, 2017, from http://www.epa.gov/agriculture/twas.html.

U.S. Environmental Protection Agency. (2013a). *Basic information about regulated drinking water contaminants and indicators*. Retrieved January 26, 2017, from http://water.epa.gov/drink/contaminants/basicinformation/index.cfm.

U.S. Environmental Protection Agency (2013b). *A brief guide to mold, moisture and your home*. Retrieved January 26, 2017, from http://www.epa.gov/mold/moldguide.html.

U.S. Environmental Protection Agency. (2013c). *Care for your air*. Retrieved January 26, 2017, from http://www.epa.gov/iaq/pubs/careforyourair.html.

U.S. Environmental Protection Agency. (2013d). *Pesticides: Topical and chemical fact sheets: Health and safety fact sheets*. Retrieved January 26, 2017, from http://www.epa.gov/pesticides/factsheets/health_fs.htm#wood.

U.S. Environmental Protection Agency. (2014a). *Frequent questions about legal issues*. Region 7: Land reuse and revitalization. Retrieved January 26, 2017, from http://www.epa.gov/region7/land_revitalization/legal.htm#PurchaseSite.

U.S. Environmental Protection Agency. (2014b). *Municipal separate storm water sewer system (MS4) main page*. Retrieved January 26, 2017, from http://water.epa.gov/polwaste/npdes/storm water/Municipal-Separate-Storm-Sewer-System-MS4-Main-Page.cfm.

U.S. Environmental Protection Agency. (2014c). *National menu of stormwater best management practices*. Retrieved January 26, 2017, from http://www.epa.gov/npdes/stormwater/menuofbmps.

U.S. Environmental Protection Agency. (2015). *Cleaning up the nation's hazardous waste sites*. Retrieved January 26, 2017, from http://www.epa.gov/superfund/.

World Health Organization. (2014). *Household air pollution and health* (Fact Sheet 292). Retrieved January 26, 2017, from http://www.who.int/mediacentre/factsheets/fs292/en/.

Chapter 19 Sustainable Housing

JOSEPH LAQUATRA

Sustainability refers to use of resources by the current generation that does not reduce their availability for future generations (Shaharir & Alinor, 2013). Thus a community or society that practices sustainability can continue to do what it has been doing forever (Laquatra & Pierce, 2011b). However, current practices in many countries, including the United States, are not sustainable. Given the increasing global population, the currently expanding global economy, and thus the increasing global demand for resources, ways to imitate natural systems are optimally implemented when all resources are used in a process and there is no waste material. In such a system, materials are constantly recycled, and they serve as inputs to the human economy or nourishment to the ecosystem, thus ending the linear process currently used for material acquisition and use (Laquatra & Pierce, 2011b). The goal of this chapter is to cover various aspects of sustainable housing, including waste management at the construction site, energy efficiency, the use of renewable energy, green building, and sustainable communities.

SUSTAINABLE HOUSING

When the term *sustainability* is applied to housing, it refers to efficiencies in the use of materials to build homes and to the use of energy, water, and other utilities needed by those housing units throughout their existence (Laquatra & Pierce, 2011a). However, in U.S. housing construction, for example, current rates of raw material inputs and energy consumption required to construct and maintain buildings are not sustainable for any extended period of time (Laquatra & Pierce, 2014). Along the same lines, the widespread practice of simply burying construction and demolition materials, instead of using those materials to reduce the amounts of raw materials extracted from the environment, is a strategy that cannot be sustained indefinitely.

WASTE MANAGEMENT IN THE UNITED STATES

Dumping wastes into open pits (i.e., piles of waste open to the environment) was the most common method of disposal until well into the 1970s. Many of these dumps were located in wetland areas, known more commonly as swamps, gravel beds, ravines, and gullies. In 1972 the U.S. Environmental Protection Agency (EPA) estimated that almost all of the more than fourteen thousand municipalities across the country relied on open pits for waste disposal (Laquatra & Pierce, 2011b). As discussed by the EPA, none of the municipalities had implemented even the most basic landfill technology nor attempted to layer wastes or cover each day's accumulation of trash with fill, such as soil or an alternative, to reduce odors and limit vermin's access to food wastes. Even the best-managed landfills during that time had no linings to protect groundwater, or even surface water runoff, from leachate, which is water that has percolated through solid materials and retained components of those materials. This method of disposal continued to be the most widely used method across the country until the creation of the EPA in 1970 and its development of strict criteria for the construction and maintenance of sanitary landfills.

The Resource Conservation and Recovery Act of 1976 (RCRA), which amended the Solid Waste Disposal Act of 1965, forced the closure of open dumps across the country and developed regulations that dictated minimum standards for the construction and maintenance of sanitary landfills (Association of Science-Technology Centers Incorporated and Smithsonian Institution Traveling Exhibition Service, 1998). Current-day sanitary landfills require a liner system of compacted clay or high-density polyethylene. A leachate collection system is also required to collect the liquid that accumulates on the liner from the bottom of the reservoir. Methane gas collection wells are also required. Waste is placed over the liner and the leachate collection system and then covered at the end of each day with fill (National Solid Waste Management Association, 2008). In some cases, inert, or chemically inactive, types of construction and demolition materials are used as a daily cover material.

The closure of open dumps across the country and the expense of constructing engineered sanitary landfills significantly increased disposal costs of municipal solid waste. By the 1990s the increased cost of disposal began to make recycling of materials an economically viable option (Laquatra & Pierce, 2011b). Indeed, recovery of materials from the waste stream went from very small proportions to about 34.5 percent by 2012 (U.S. Environmental Protection Agency, 2014a).

WASTE MANAGEMENT IN CONSTRUCTION

The total amount of construction and demolition (C&D) debris was 233 million tons in the United States in 2011 (U.S. Environmental Protection Agency, 2016a). C&D debris includes wood, vinyl, asphalt, gypsum, and other materials and is generated when structures are built, repaired, and destroyed. In the United States, the construction of a single-family home typically produces between two and four tons of debris (Laquatra & Pierce, 2004). C&D debris typically does not contain putrescible wastes (i.e., wastes that are subject to decay, for which sanitary landfills are designed). Sanitary landfills are sites where materials are isolated from the environment until they have completely degraded (World Bank, 2000). In the 1990s, as a method to further reduce the demand for landfill space, some municipalities began to limit, and in some cases ban, C&D debris from their landfills (Laquatra & Pierce, 2004). Many materials in C&D debris can be recovered and recycled. Over the past few years efforts have been under way to raise awareness of this issue and to encourage sustainable building practices (U.S. Environmental Protection Agency, 2016b).

EFFICIENCY

Energy Efficiency

Basic features of a sustainable home include high levels of energy efficiency and healthy indoor air quality. A home with a high level of energy efficiency, alternatively called a "high performance house," includes high levels of insulation in the building enclosure, an uninterrupted air barrier, a drainage plane, and high-efficiency space conditioning and other mechanical systems (Memari et al., 2014). While a home with a high level of energy efficiency still needs energy, a net zero energy house is one that uses the energy it produces and has zero annual carbon emissions annually.

The Energy Star® Program is administered by the EPA. Since the start of this program in 1992, 1.3 million sustainable Energy Star® homes have been constructed in the United States (U.S. Environmental Protection Agency, 2014b). Homes qualify for the Energy Star® designation if they meet strict standards for energy efficiency, as set by the EPA (U.S. Environmental Protection Agency, 2013). This efficiency is achieved through an airtight building enclosure, high-efficiency heating and cooling systems, state-of-the-art measures to prevent water entry from the exterior, efficient lighting and appliances, and third-party verification.

Creating healthy indoor environments means avoiding hazards from mold and other allergens, combustion pollutants, volatile organic compounds, soil gases, lead, and asbestos. Ways of doing so include the use of water-managed building foundations, site drainage, adequate ventilation, informed selection of equipment for space conditioning and water heating, material choices, and sub-slab ventilation (Laquatra, Pillai, Singh, & Syal, 2008; see chapter 18).

Appliances, electronics, and lighting are responsible for 34.6 percent of a typical home's energy bill (U.S. Energy Information Administration, 2009). Table 19.1 provides a breakdown of a typical home's energy bill. However, energy consumption for each of these uses can be decreased substantially. Energy Star® appliances, including refrigerators, freezers, dishwashers, clothes washers, clothes dryers, room air conditioners, and others use between 10 and 50 percent less energy than less efficient products.

Lighting accounts for approximately 5 percent of a home's energy use, but it also represents an area where energy use can be substantially reduced. Incandescent lighting is the least efficient of residential choices, with only 10 percent of the energy that goes into an incandescent bulb being converted to light; the rest is given off as heat. While the 2007 Energy Independence and Security Act established improved energy efficiency requirements for light bulbs, incandescent, and even more efficient incandescents, are still the most inefficient of residential options. Compact fluorescent lamps (CFLs) use 25

TABLE 19.1
Breakdown of a Typical Home's Energy Bill

Component	Proportion of energy bill
Space heating and cooling	48%
Water heating	18%
Refrigeration	5%
Lighting	5%
Other (small appliances, electronics, etc.)	24%
TOTAL	100%

Source: Author, based on Plymouth Rock Energy, 2015.

to 35 percent of the energy used by incandescent bulbs and last ten times longer. Light-emitting diodes (LEDs) use 75 percent less energy than incandescent bulbs and last twenty-five times longer (U.S. Department of Energy, 2012b).

Advances in lighting efficiency have changed the way consumers compare and purchase lighting products. When incandescent bulbs represented the majority of lighting products that were used, consumers routinely compared them based on the amount of energy they consumed, or watts. Now bulbs are selected based on the amount of light they produce, or lumens, as well as cost. A sixty-watt incandescent bulb produces eight hundred lumens of light and, based on three hours of use per day, costs $8.02 per year. That same amount of lumens of light is produced by a ten-watt LED bulb and costs $1.34 per year (Natural Resources Defense Council, n.d.).

Heating and Cooling

For the average American home, heating and cooling expenses make up 54 percent of the home's annual energy costs (U.S. Department of Energy, 2012c). A typical heating system consists of a fuel, a device that converts that fuel to heat, a distribution system, and a venting system. A gas or oil furnace has a burner that ignites the fuel, a combustion chamber in which the fuel is burned, a heat exchanger through which home air passes to capture the heat from burning fuel, a venting system through which combustion products are directed to the outside, and ducts that direct heated air throughout the home. A boiler uses the same basic system, except that steam or heated water is directed throughout the home through pipes, radiators, or baseboard heaters (U.S. Department of Energy, 2013b).

In electric heating systems, production of the fuel takes place at a power plant. Electric resistance, through baseboard heaters, ceiling panels, or under-the-floor resistance systems, distributes heat. No venting system is required (U.S. Department of Energy, 2013b). Figure 19.1 shows types of home heating fuels typically used to heat American homes.

Recent advances in gas and oil central heating technology have resulted in highly efficient systems. However, in conventional furnaces and boilers, efficiency losses can be substantial and typically amount to thirty to forty-five cents of every heating dollar. These losses result from leaky or uninsulated ducts, clogged registers and filters, and, most substantially, from the use of heated air to maintain chimney draft and combustion (U.S. Department of Energy, 2013b).

FIGURE 19.1
Types of Home Heating Fuels
Source: U.S. Department of Energy, 2012b.

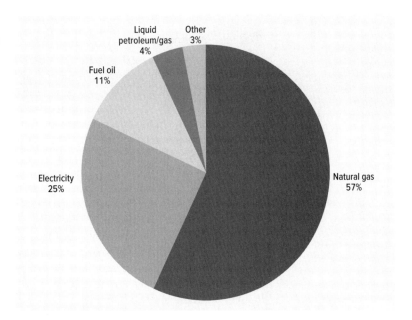

FIGURE 19.2
Combustion Air and System Venting
Source: Laquatra, 1999. Reprinted with permission.

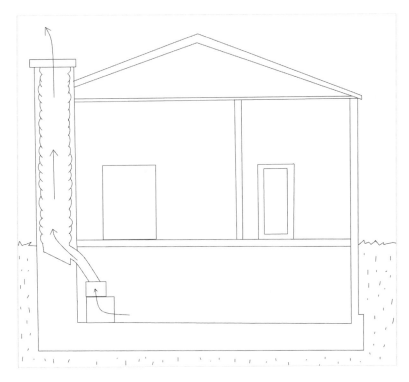

Conventional furnaces and boilers sacrifice some efficiency in order to vent unwanted combustion products from the home (see figure 19.2). By allowing flue gases to retain high temperatures, the natural force of rising hot air creates chimney draft, which exhausts water vapor, carbon dioxide, nitrogen oxides, sulfur dioxide, and carbon monoxide—all products of combustion. At the same time, air surrounding the heating unit is drawn into the burner to maintain combustion (Laquatra, 1999). In most cases, this is heated air, as shown in figure 19.2.

Heating System Efficiency

The efficiency of many existing furnaces or boilers can typically be improved. The correct match between a home and its heating equipment is like a balanced equation. A home's heating need is determined through heat loss calculations, which are based on local climatic conditions and thermal characteristics of the house, such as the amount and type of insulation, among other characteristics. The results of heat-loss equations are expressed in BTUs (British thermal units) per hour and refer to the rate at which heat must be supplied to a home during the coldest time of the year. As furnaces and boilers are categorized according to their heat-producing capacity in BTUs per hour, a close match between heat loss and heat production is optimal for efficiency. Competent heating technicians can calculate a home's heat loss and production with easily obtainable computer software.

Many homes are heated by systems with much larger heating capabilities than are needed to maintain a comfortable temperature. Thus these systems are oversized. The size of a furnace refers to how many BTUs it can generate in an hour. There are two issues with an oversized unit. First, it increases the operating cycle losses, mentioned above, and second, it results in high off-cycle losses.

With regard to the second point, whenever the thermostat sends the proper signal to the burner, the combustion process stops, essentially turning the system off. Hence the term *off-cycle*. However, even though the system is off, the heated combustion chamber continues to send hot gases up the chimney. As this chamber loses air to the chimney, it replaces it with air from around the furnace or boiler. This in turn causes enough negative pressure in the home to result in outside air being drawn in through cracks and holes around windows, doors, and other openings (Straube, 2012).

The problems of an oversized heating system can be partially corrected by derating. This refers to adjustments that reduce the rate at which fuel is burned. In an oil-based heating system, a smaller nozzle is installed in the burner. A gas-based heating system is derated by reducing the burner orifice size or by decreasing the pressure in the manifold, the pipe that distributes gas to the burners. Derating a gas system also involves installing a fixed flue damper to modify the flue opening (U.S. Department of Energy, 2013b).

The amount of heat extracted from fuel depends on the efficiency of the combustion process. A combustion efficiency test provides a measure of the degree to which the burner converts fuel to useful heat. This test is performed by a heating system technician with special tools that analyze the composition of flue gas and measure its temperature, draft level, and smoke concentration. The efficiency of the combustion process is then calculated from these measurements. Standard tune-up procedures can usually result in a combustion efficiency rating between 75 and 85 percent for oil and gas systems.

In addition to combustion efficiency, there is seasonal efficiency, a gauge of how well the entire heating system extracts heat from fuel and warms the living space during the heating season. Seasonal efficiency takes off-cycle losses and the integrity of the distribution system into consideration. While seasonal efficiency is extremely complicated to determine for an existing system, it can nevertheless be estimated. The typical seasonal efficiency rating for an existing system is between 10 and 15 percent less than its combustion efficiency rating.

Manufacturers of new heating systems are required to present information on the efficiency of their furnaces and boilers and to compare this efficiency with other available units of the same size and type. The basis for comparison among units is a laboratory-tested seasonal efficiency known as the annualized fuel use efficiency (AFUE) rating, which is provided on the required energy guide fact sheet attached to each unit.

Improvements to space-heating efficiency can often be achieved by upgrading an existing system. Combustion efficiency can be increased through an annual tune-up that will insure that the maximum level of combustion efficiency is attained. Seasonal efficiency can be increased through a number of measures. A 5–15 percent increase, for example, can result from derating. Boiler pipes or furnace ducts that are leaky and uninsulated can waste over 10 percent of the heat produced by a system, especially if the ducts or pipes pass through unheated areas, such as a garage or crawl space. Furnace fan switches, automatic vent dampers, flue heat reclaimers, and setback thermostats also result in increased seasonal efficiency. However, improvements to seasonal efficiency might typically be limited once an existing system is over twenty years old. In this case, system replacement should be considered.

There are now a number of new gas and oil central heating systems with AFUE ratings of between 80 and 95 percent. Primarily, these high levels of efficiency are obtained through designs that minimize on-cycle losses. Some of the features that make these furnaces and boilers different from conventional units are forced draft systems, secondary heat exchangers, and heat-transfer modules. Probably the most striking difference between older and newer systems is that most newer furnaces do not require chimneys. In this case, many combustion products are vented through a wall with a plastic pipe, much like a dryer. As the water vapor resulting from combustion is condensed inside these furnaces, it must be drained away. This is achieved with a connection to a floor drain.

To select among several furnaces or boilers, a consumer should obtain gas prices from a utility or supplier or oil prices from a dealer and use these prices to estimate annual heating costs from the energy guide fact sheet for each unit. Heating contractor estimates should be used for installed prices of each unit. Purchase costs and operating costs of the different units should then be compared. A consumer can calculate a simple payback by dividing initial cost differences by annual savings but should be aware that the payback tells only part of the story. Savings continue to occur beyond the payback time, and a high-efficiency system is likely to increase the value of a home.

Cooling Efficiency

The purpose of an air conditioner is to cool and dehumidify the air. A central air conditioner is based on either a split-system unit or a packaged unit (U.S. Department of Energy, 2012a). A split-system is the most economical central air conditioner to install if a home already has a furnace but lacks an air conditioner (U.S. Department of Energy, 2012a). In a split-system central air conditioner, an outdoor metal cabinet contains the condenser and compressor and an indoor cabinet contains the evaporator (U.S. Department of Energy, 2012a). In many split-system air conditioners, this indoor cabinet also contains a furnace or the indoor part of a heat pump (U.S. Department of Energy, 2012a). The air conditioner's evaporator coil is installed in the cabinet or main supply duct of this furnace or heat pump (U.S. Department of Energy, 2012a).

In a packaged central air conditioner the evaporator, condenser, and compressor are all located in one cabinet, which is usually placed on a roof or on a concrete slab next to the house's foundation (U.S. Department of Energy, 2012a). This type of air conditioner is also used in small commercial buildings (U.S. Department of Energy, 2012a). Air supply and return ducts come from indoors through the home's exterior wall or roof to connect with the packaged air conditioner, which is usually located outdoors (U.S. Department of Energy, 2012a). Packaged air conditioners often include electric heating coils or a natural gas furnace (U.S. Department of Energy, 2012a). This combination of air conditioner and central heater eliminates the need for a separate furnace indoors (U.S. Department of Energy, 2012a).

Proper sizing and installation are key elements in determining air conditioner efficiency. A unit that is too large wastes energy and will not adequately remove humidity. While the unit will run long enough to satisfy the cooling temperature, it will not run long enough to remove the humidity. A unit that is too small will not be able to attain a comfortable temperature on the hottest days. Improper unit location, lack of insulation, and improper duct installation can greatly diminish efficiency (U.S. Department of Energy, 2012a).

Central air conditioners are rated according to their seasonal energy efficiency ratio (SEER) (U.S. Department of Energy, 2012a). SEER indicates the relative amount of energy needed to provide a specific cooling output (U.S. Department of Energy, 2012a). Many older systems have SEER ratings of 6 or less (U.S. Department of Energy, 2012a). Federal standards require air conditioners to have a SEER of 13 or higher (U.S. Department of Energy, 2012a). SEER 13 is 30 percent more efficient than the previous minimum SEER of 10 (U.S. Department of Energy, 2012a). The SEER 10 standard was implemented by Congress in 1987 (Environmental and Energy Study Institute, 2002). The Clinton administration mandated that the upgrade from SEER 10 to SEER 13 was to occur by 2006 (Environmental and Energy Study Institute, 2002). The SEER 13 standard applies only to appliances manufactured after January 23, 2006 (U.S. Department of Energy, 2012a). Equipment with a rating less than SEER 13 manufactured before this date may still be sold and installed (U.S. Department of Energy, 2012a; see chapter 18).

Other features to look for when buying an air conditioner include

- a thermal expansion valve and a high-temperature rating (SEER) greater than 11.6, for high-efficiency operation when temperatures are high;
- a variable-speed air handler for new ventilation systems;
- a unit that operates quietly;
- a fan-only switch, which can be used for nighttime ventilation to substantially reduce air-conditioning costs;
- a filter check light to remind a homeowner to check the filter after a predetermined number of operating hours; and
- an automatic-delay fan switch to turn off the fan a few minutes after the compressor turns off (U.S. Department of Energy, 2012a).

When installing a new central air conditioning system, a contractor should

- allow adequate indoor space for the installation, maintenance, and repair of the new system and install an access door in the furnace or duct to provide a way to clean the evaporator coil;
- use a duct-sizing methodology such as the Air Conditioning Contractors of America's (ACCA) *Manual D*;
- ensure that there are a sufficient number of supply registers to deliver cool air and a sufficient number of return air registers to carry warm house air back to the air conditioner;
- install duct work within the conditioned space, not in the attic, wherever possible;
- seal all ducts with duct mastic and heavily insulate attic ducts;
- locate the condensing unit where its noise will not keep the residents or their neighbors awake at night, if possible;
- locate the condensing unit where no nearby objects will block airflow to it;
- verify that the newly installed air conditioner has the exact refrigerant charge and airflow rate specified by the manufacturer; and
- locate the thermostat away from heat sources, such as windows or supply registers (U.S. Department of Energy, 2012a).

Water Efficiency

In the residential sector, total figures for water consumption are split between public withdrawals from fresh water and groundwater and water that is self-supplied from private wells and other systems (U.S. Geological Survey, 2009). Fifty-eight percent of public withdrawals in 2005, or 25,600 million gallons per day (Mgal/d), was for the residential sector; private withdrawals in the residential sector in that year consisted of 3,830 Mgal/d (U.S. Geological Survey, 2009).

An average family with 2.58 members (U.S. Bureau of the Census, 2010) in the United States uses three hundred gallons of water per day in a single-family home or in an apartment (U.S. Environmental Protection Agency, 2014d). Increasing the efficiency of water use can preserve more water for future generations and reduce current water supply, wastewater treatment, and related costs for communities. Table 19.2 shows a breakdown of water use in a typical U.S. home.

Toilets are responsible for the majority of a home's water consumption and account for 30 percent of the average home's water use (U.S. Environmental Protection Agency, 2014c). While some older toilets can use up to 3 gallons of water per flush, high-efficiency toilets (HETs) use 1.28 gallons, or 20 percent less than the federal standard of 1.6 gallons per flush, which was mandated for residential flush toilets in 1994 and for commercial flush toilets in 1997 based on the Energy Policy Act of 1992 (U.S. Environmental Protection Agency, 2014b). HETs can be identified through WaterSense®, a program sponsored by the EPA. A WaterSense® label issued by the EPA and affixed to a toilet indicates that it has been certified by an independent laboratory to meet criteria for performance and efficiency. While the first generation of high-efficiency toilets performed poorly by not emptying the toilet

TABLE 19.2
Typical Water Use in a U.S. Home

BATHROOM	
Toilet flush	3 gal. for older (pre–high efficiency toilet [HET]/1994) models; most new (post-HET/1994) toilets use 1.2 to 1.6 gal./flush
Bath	A full tub is about 36 gal.
Shower	2–2.5 gal./min; old shower heads use as much as 4 gal./min
Teeth brushing	<1 gal., especially if water is turned off while brushing; newer (low-flow) bath faucets use about 1 gal./min, whereas older (pre-low-flow) models use over 2 gal.
Hands/face washing	1 gal.
Face/leg shaving	1 gal.
KITCHEN	
Dishwasher	20 gal./load, depending on efficiency of dishwasher
Dishwashing by hand	4 gal./min for old faucets; newer kitchen faucets use about 1–2 gal./min
Drinking water	8 oz/glass
LAUNDRY	
Clothes washer	25 gal./load for newer washers; older models use about 40 gal./load
OUTDOORS	
Watering plants	2 gal./min

of waste products with one flush, this is not the case for WaterSense®-labeled toilets.

Another way to increase efficiency in residential water use is to use Energy Star® dishwashers and clothes washers. These appliances earn the Energy Star® label through third-party certification and testing. An Energy Star® clothes washer uses 70 percent less energy and 75 percent less water than a standard clothes washer used in the 1990s (U.S. Environmental Protection Agency, n.d.).

Sixty percent of the energy used by a dishwasher is for heating water (American Council for an Energy Efficient Economy, 2012). Energy Star® dishwashers use only 5.8 gallons of water per cycle, compared to 16 gallons used by standard dishwashers (U.S. Environmental Protection Agency, 2011). Thus less energy is used in an Energy Star® dishwasher to heat water. Dishwashing by hand is more energy intensive than using a dishwasher. Compared to dishwashing by hand, using an Energy Star® dishwasher reduces annual water consumption by five thousand gallons, annual utility costs by forty dollars per household, and a person's time by 230 hours (U.S. Environmental Protection Agency, 2011).

Water heating represents 17.7 percent of the energy consumed in the average U.S. home (U.S. Energy Information Administration, 2013). In most homes, water heated by natural gas, propane, electricity, fuel oil, a heat pump, or solar energy is stored in a fifty-gallon or larger tank. This heated water is distributed to kitchens, bathrooms, and laundry rooms by pipes. Another type of water heating system is a tankless, or instantaneous, water heater that is hung from a wall. Energy Star® storage tank (Energy Star, n.d.b) and tankless water heaters are also available (Energy Star, n.d.a; see chapter 3).

RENEWABLE ENERGY

Before the installation of any renewable energy system in a house, whether it is based on solar or wind energy or a geothermal or air-to-air heat pump, the home should be as energy efficient as possible (U.S. Department of Energy, 2014). Starting with a home's foundation, rigid board insulation, such as extruded polystyrene, should be underneath the concrete floor slab. If the home has a basement, the basement walls should be insulated, preferably from the exterior with rigid board insulation. A home's walls and attic should also be highly insulated. The U.S. Department of Energy provides climate-specific recommendations for home insulation levels through its Office of Energy Efficiency and Renewable Energy (U.S. Department of Energy, 2013a). Windows, doors, and skylights should all be Energy Star® labeled. The home itself could also be an Energy Star® certified home, which indicates that it uses 15 to 30 percent less energy than a conventional home.

The most important consideration about a home's level of energy efficiency is its ability to resist air leaks, which is referred to as its level of airtightness. A common misconception people have about a house is that it should not be airtight, as it needs to breathe. Indeed, a home needs to be built as airtight as possible. Ventilation that can be controlled by occupants should be provided.

Once a home is energy efficient, renewable energy systems should be considered. Photovoltaic systems convert sunlight to electricity. Other solar systems can heat a home and water. Wind systems can also generate electricity. Heat pumps recover heat from the ground, water, or air to heat a home (see chapter 18).

GREEN BUILDING AND SUSTAINABLE COMMUNITIES

Green Building

The term *green building* has been prominent in discussions about sustainability for about a decade (Laquatra et al., 2008). Homeowners, home buyers, builders, and remodeling contractors have become more aware of green building issues through information available from the U.S. Green Building Council, Green Builder College, *Green Builder* magazine, and many other resources. A green building, whether it is a residence, a commercial structure, or an institutional building, is energy and resource efficient and has healthy indoor air. However, other issues are critical as well, such as choices made regarding building materials and heating systems (Laquatra et al., 2008).

An important feature to consider when building green is siting, which reflects the use of sunlight for daytime lighting and energy. Damage to plants and vegetation is minimized at this stage. Another consideration is to build a small house that optimizes the use of building materials (Wilson, 2010).

Green building also focuses on materials, specifying reused or salvaged materials, those with the highest recycled content, and finally sustainably harvested or mined materials. Another issue to consider is the use of alternative construction techniques that use less building materials and provide higher levels of energy efficiency than conventional techniques. Examples of this are advanced framing, which is also referred to as optimum value engineering, and the use of structural insulated panels (SIPs). Embodied energy, the energy used in producing and transporting materials to the construction site, is another consideration, as is waste minimization during construction, as discussed earlier in this chapter.

Products are chosen for their durability and contributions to energy efficiency. Water use is also a factor. For example, a house without a lawn is considered to be greener than one that features native plants that are watered with recycled water (Vick & Tufts, 2006). Paints that do not emit volatile organic compounds (VOCs) are natural choices for green construction because they do not contribute to indoor air quality problems (Laquatra et al., 2008).

Green building may include green certification from one of various organizations that provide this service, including EarthCraft House, the U.S. Green Building Council's Leadership in Energy and Environmental Design (LEED) Program, and the National Green Building Standard of the International Code Council.

Green homes are not difficult to build, but before they are constructed as a matter of routine, training and education of general contractors and subcontractors, as well as home buyers, is necessary. Green homes contribute to energy independence and human health. As educational resources become increasingly available to help people understand issues related to green building, so do chances that building green homes will become routine (see chapter 18).

Sustainable Communities

When the concept of sustainability is applied to communities, the term refers broadly to various community attributes, including the built environment; transportation, including reduced or eliminated automobile dependency; water systems; local economies; health and safety; education; the arts; and more. Sustainable Tools for Assessing and Rating (STAR) Communities is a national certification system that recognizes sustainable communities (STAR Communities, 2014b). This system assigns scores to community features so that municipalities can assess their progress toward sustainability goals. For example, one hundred points can be earned in each of these areas: built environment, climate and energy, economy and jobs, energy and empowerment, health and safety, and natural systems. The category of education, arts, and community allows up to seventy points because it has fewer STAR objectives than the other categories.

Community sustainability rankings under STAR are 600 or more for a 5-STAR Community, 400–599 for a 4-STAR Community, 200–399 for a 3-STAR Community, and under 200 for a Reporting STAR Community. This rating system is used by many cities and counties throughout the United States and Canada, including Albany, New York; Northampton, Massachusetts; Cleveland, Ohio; Wichita, Kansas; and Vancouver, British Columbia; among others (STAR Communities, 2014a). As students in academic planning programs and practicing planning professionals, including city, village, town, and county planning board members and personnel of planning departments, become familiar with principles of sustainability, the implementation of these principles will eventually become routine (see chapter 18).

CONCLUSION

Housing is considered to be sustainable when efficiencies across various aspects are considered and deployed. These include efficiencies in the use of materials, energy, water, and other resources. Communities are considered sustainable when numerous attributes are planned and developed in ways that viably meet present and future needs. Much education of builders, subcontractors, planners, and other community officials is necessary before sustainability will be considered as a matter of routine when homes are built and communities are planned. For that to occur, policy makers need to understand the importance of this issue and advance the agenda through public discussions and, ultimately, legislation.

REFERENCES

American Council for an Energy Efficient Economy. (2012). *Dishwashing*. Retrieved May 29, 2014, from http://www.aceee.org/consumer/dishwashing.

Association of Science-Technology Centers Incorporated and Smithsonian Institution Traveling Exhibition Service. (1998). *Trash timeline—History of garbage*. Retrieved June 4, 2014, from http://www.alliedwastedalycity.com/kids_trash_timeline-printer.cfm.

Energy Star. (n.d.a). *Water heater, whole home gas tankless for consumers*. Retrieved September 14, 2014, from https://www.energystar.gov/products/certified-products/detail/water-heater-whole-home-gas-tankless?fuseaction=find_a_product.showProductGroup&pgw_code=WH.

Energy Star. (n.d.b). *Water heaters*. Retrieved September 14, 2014, from https://www.energystar.gov/index.cfm?c=water_heat.pr_water_heaters_landing.

Environmental and Energy Study Institute. (2002). *Air conditioner efficiency standards: SEER 13 vs. SEER 12* (Fact sheet). Retrieved March 10, 2015, from http://www.eesi.org/papers/view/fact-sheet-air-conditioner-efficiency-standards-seer-13-vs.-seer-12.

Laquatra, J., & Pierce, M. (2004). Waste management at the residential construction site. *Journal of Solid Waste Technology and Management, 30*, 67–74.

Laquatra, J. & Pierce, M. (2011a). *Toward more sustainable construction*. Retrieved September 17, 2014, from http://www.igreenbuild.com.

Laquatra, J., & Pierce, M. (2011b). Waste management at the construction site. In S. Kumar (Ed.), *Integrated waste management, volume 1* (pp. 281–300). www.intechopen.com: InTech, 281–300.

Laquatra, J., & Pierce, M. (2014). Waste management at the residential construction site. *Cityscape, 16*(1), 313–317.

Laquatra, J., Pillai, G., Singh, A., & Syal, M. (2008). Green and healthy housing. *Journal of Architectural Engineering, 14*(4), 94–97.

Memari, A., Huelman, P., Iulo, L., Laquatra, J., Martin, C., McCoy, A., Nahmens, I., & Williamson, T. (2014). Residential building construction: State-of-the-art review. *Journal of Architectural Engineering, 20*(4), 1–38.

National Solid Waste Management Association. (2008). *Modern landfill: A far cry from the past*. Retrieved June 3, 2014, from http://www.environmentalistseveryday.org/docs/research-bulletin/Research-Bulletin-Modern-Landfill.pdf.

Natural Resources Defense Council. (n.d.). *Your guide to more efficient and energy-saving lights bulbs*. Retrieved September 14, 2014, from http://www.nrdc.org/energy/lightbulbs/files/lightbulbguide.pdf.

Plymouth Rock Energy. (2015). *How do American home energy bills break down?* Retrieved March 10, 2015, from http://www.plymouthenergy.com/how-do-american-home-energy-bills-breakdown/.

Shaharir, B. M. Z., & Alinor, M. B. A. K. (2013). The need for a new definition of sustainability. *Journal of Indonesian Economy and Business, 28*(2), 257–274.

STAR Communities. (2014a). *Registered communities*. Retrieved September 14, 2014, from http://www.starcommunities.org/communities.

STAR Communities. (2014b). *STAR community rating system, version 1.1*. Retrieved March 26, 2015, from https://www.starcommunities.org/uploads/rating-system.pdf.

Straube, J. (2012). *Air leaks: How they waste energy and rot houses*. Retrieved January 11, 2017, from https://buildingscience.com/documents/published-articles/pa-air-leaks-how-they-waste-energy-and-rot-houses/view.

U.S. Bureau of the Census. (2010). *2010 census*. Washington, D.C.: U.S. Bureau of the Census.

U.S. Department of Energy. (2012a). *Central air conditioning*. Retrieved September 17, 2014, from http://energy.gov/energysaver/articles/central-air-conditioning.

U.S. Department of Energy. (2012b). *LED lighting*. Retrieved September 14, 2014, from http://energy.gov/energysaver/articles/led-lighting.

U.S. Department of Energy. (2012c). *Tips: Heating and cooling*. Retrieved June 15, 2014, from http://energy.gov/energysaver/articles/tips-heating-and-cooling.

U.S. Department of Energy. (2013a). *Building-science based climate maps*. Retrieved September 14, 2014, from http://apps1.eere.energy.gov/buildings/publications/pdfs/building_america/4_3a_ba_innov_buildingscienceclimatemaps_011713.pdf.

U.S. Department of Energy. (2013b). *Home heating systems*. Retrieved January 6, 2017, from https://www.energy.gov/energysaver/home-heating-systems.

U.S. Department of Energy. (2014). *Planning for home renewable energy systems*. Retrieved March 10, 2015, from http://energy.gov/energysaver/articles/planning-home-renewable-energy-systems.

U.S. Energy Information Administration. (2009). *Residential energy consumption survey*. Retrieved June 15, 2014, from http://www.eia.gov/consumption/residential/.

U.S. Energy Information Administration. (2013). *Heating and cooling no longer majority of U.S. home energy use*. Retrieved June 15, 2014, from http://www.eia.gov/todayinenergy/detail.cfm?id=10271.

U.S. Environmental Protection Agency. (n.d.). *About Energy Star*. Retrieved June 15, 2014, from http://www.energystar.gov/about/.

U.S. Environmental Protection Agency. (2011). *How much water do Energy Star dishwashers use?* Retrieved June 17, 2014, from http://energystar.supportportal.com/link/portal/23002/23018/Article/17719/How-much-water-do-ENERGY-STAR-dishwashers-use-Is-there-a-water-efficiency-metric-water-factor-for-ENERGY-STAR-dishwashers-like-there-is-for-ENERGY-STAR-qualified-clothes-washers.

U.S. Environmental Protection Agency. (2013). *ENERGY STAR certified homes, version 3 (Rev 07) national program requirements*. Retrieved September 12, 2014, from http://www.energystar.gov/ia/partners/bldrs_lenders_raters/downloads/National_Program_Requirements.pdf.

U.S. Environmental Protection Agency. (2014a). *Municipal solid waste*. Retrieved September 12, 2014, from http://www.epa.gov/epawaste/nonhaz/municipal/.

U.S. Environmental Protection Agency. (2014b). *Seven Georgia organizations receive 2013 Energy Star awards*. Retrieved September 12, 2014, from http://yosemite.epa.gov/opa/admpress.nsf/d0cf6618525a9efb85257359003fb69d/c84aadc8efd2f31685257b3a0069afaa!opendocument.

U.S. Environmental Protection Agency. (2014c). *WaterSense: Toilets*. Retrieved June 15, 2014, from http://www.epa.gov/WaterSense/products/toilets.html.

U.S. Environmental Protection Agency. (2014d). *WaterSense: Water use today*. Retrieved June 15, 2014, from http://www.epa.gov/WaterSense/our_water/water_use_today.html.

U.S. Environmental Protection Agency. (2016a). *Methodology to estimate the quantity, composition, and management of construction and demolition debris in the United States*. Retrieved January 11, 2017, from https://nepis.epa.gov/Adobe/PDF/P100NDZ0.pdf.

U.S. Environmental Protection Agency. (2016b). *Sustainable management of construction and demolition materials*. Retrieved January 11, 2017, from https://www.epa.gov/smm/sustainable-management-construction-and-demolition-materials.

U.S. Geological Survey. (2009). *Summary of estimated water use in the United States in*

2005 (Fact Sheet 2009–3098). Retrieved June 17, 2014, from http://pubs.usgs.gov/fs/2009/3098/pdf/2009-3098.pdf.

Vick, R. A., & Tufts, M. (2006). Low-impact land development: The practice of preserving natural processes. *Journal of Green Building, 1*(4), 28–38.

Wilson, A. (2010). Green building priority #5—build smaller. *Energy Solutions*. BuildingGreen.com. Retrieved September 14, 2014, from http://www2.buildinggreen.com/blogs/green-building-priority-5-build-smaller.

World Bank (2000). *Environmental strategies for cities: Solid waste*. Retrieved March 10, 2015, from http://web.mit.edu/urbanupgrading/urbanenvironment/sectors/solid-waste-landfills.html.

Chapter 20 Housing and Disasters

SARAH D. KIRBY AND
ANNIE HARDISON-MOODY

Disasters have been defined in a number of different ways. For example, Pearce (2000: 22) defines a disaster as "a non-routine event that exceeds the capacity of the affected area to respond to it in such a way as to save lives; to preserve property; and to maintain the social, ecological, economic, and political stability of the affected region." Saylor (1993) describes disasters as events that, first, involve damage to property, which may also include injury or death; second, have an exclusive start and end point; third, negatively impact a sizable group of people; fourth, are community and not individual experiences; fifth, are extraordinary circumstances; and sixth, cause significant stress in people's lives.

Many events occur during and after a disaster that relate directly to a community's ability to function: homes and businesses may be damaged and destroyed; the community infrastructure may be devastated; businesses and people may be forced to relocate; rebuilding, renovation, and mitigation actions may occur; and communities may be reconstructed and reestablished. However, as these communities rebuild, they are changed, and these changes are often felt deeply by those residents who experienced losses as a result of a catastrophic event (Elliot & Pais, 2006; see chapters 12 and 13). Disasters are not only felt through the destruction and loss of property or material things, they are also felt by residents in the loss of immaterial things, such as place and community. This chapter focuses on the effects of disasters on communities and their housing stock, paying close attention to the complicated reactions of individuals and families to the physical and emotional loss of home and community. This chapter then discusses disaster response, followed by discussion concerning housing and community disaster resilience, mitigation, and rebuilding.

EFFECTS OF DISASTERS ON COMMUNITIES AND HOUSING

Significance and Impacts of Disasters on Communities and Housing

Globally, disasters caused $1.7 trillion worth of damage, affected 2.9 billion people, and resulted in 1.2 million deaths between 2000 and 2012 (United Nations Office of Disaster Risk Reduction, 2015). In 2013 natural disasters forced the relocation of almost twenty-three million people, damaging or destroying 1.4 million homes (International Displacement Monitoring Centre, 2013a). In the United States, there were 359 natural disasters that affected over twenty-one million people between 2000 and mid-2015. These disasters resulted in over $544 million in damages, nearly 150,000 individuals becoming homeless, and over six thousand deaths (International Disaster Database, 2015).

Each year, a large number of homes are destroyed, damaged, or affected in some way by natural disasters. Table 20.1 illustrates the impacts of disasters on housing in the United States, as reported by the Federal Emergency Management Agency (FEMA), based on preliminary disaster reports from January 2014 to January 2015.

While table 20.1 shows the total number of homes that were affected in a twelve-month time period from 2014 to 2015, in any given year a single disaster may cause damage to a much larger number of homes. For example, in May 2013 a large tornado hit Moore, Oklahoma, with a population of almost sixty thousand, destroying over thirteen hundred homes in a single event (City of Moore, n.d.). Hurricane Sandy damaged more than 650,000 homes in the Northeast in the fall of 2012 (U.S. Department of Housing and Urban Development, 2015a).

Disasters impact the housing stock through damage or destruction. The most significant and most common damage from these events comes from earthquakes, tornadoes, hurricanes (tropical cyclones), and flooding. However, the frequency of each type of event and severity of the event vary. For example, in 1994 the Northridge earthquake left twenty thousand people homeless and damaged over five thousand homes (U.S. Department of Housing and Urban Development, 1994). In recent decades, earthquake damage to homes has been minimal, compared to tornadoes and hurricanes, resulting in slightly more than two hundred people becoming home-

TABLE 20.1
Disaster Effects on Housing in the United States, January 2014–January 2015

Type of damage	No. housing units affected
Homes destroyed—total loss of structure	594
Homes with major damage—substantial failure to structural elements	849
Homes with minor damage—uninhabitable but may be inhabitable with repairs	1,305
Homes affected—habitable, with damage to structure and contents	1,767
TOTAL HOMES AFFECTED	4,515

Source: Federal Emergency Management Agency, 2015d.

less (International Disaster Database, 2015). For example, in 2011 and 2012, there were 5,237 and 3,836 earthquakes in the United States, respectively, with the majority being between 2.0 and 4.9 on the 10-point Richter scale (U.S. Geological Survey, 2012).

There is also variation in terms of tornadoes. For example, in 2011 the United States recorded just fewer than 900 tornadoes. However, in 2012 that number was closer to 375 (National Oceanic and Atmospheric Administration, n.d.). While damage statistics for tornadoes are often difficult to gather, we can explore specific tornadic events to determine their impact on housing. For example, in 2011 thirty tornadoes in Alabama damaged or destroyed nearly fourteen thousand homes (State of Alabama, 2012). That same year, a tornado in Joplin, Missouri, damaged or destroyed seventy-five hundred homes (City of Joplin, 2012). In March 2012 tornadoes damaged more than twenty-two hundred homes in Kentucky (Federal Emergency Management Agency, 2012a).

In 2011 there were seven hurricanes in the United States; four of these were considered major hurricanes. In 2012 there were ten hurricanes, with two considered major (National Oceanic and Atmospheric Administration, 2014). Hurricanes caused significant housing damage in both years. For example, in 2011 Hurricane Irene moved up the East Coast of the United States, flooding homes and destroying structures from Florida to Maine. In 2012, in North Carolina alone, over twenty-eight thousand homes were damaged or destroyed (North Carolina Department of Public Safety, 2012).

Flooding may occur as a side effect of hurricanes, severe winter weather, or prolonged rainfall. In 2011 and 2012 the National Flood Insurance Program paid for almost 78,057 and 150,000 home losses, respectively (Federal Emergency Management Agency, n.d.d). In 2011 and 2012 there were over $2.4 million and over $9.0 million in claims, respectively (Federal Emergency Management Agency, 2015c). The National Flood Insurance Program, however, serves only those homeowners and renters who have private flood insurance. Those without flood insurance do not qualify for a reimbursement for a loss of their home. Thus the actual number of losses is much higher. According to the National Flood Insurance Program, in the five-year period between 2008 and 2012, the typical residential flood claim exceeded $38,000 (National Flood Insurance Program, 2015b). Flood risks change over time due to natural and human activity. Thus the Federal Emergency Management Agency revises flood maps regularly to reflect these changes (National Flood Insurance Program, 2015a).

Earthquakes, tornadoes, hurricanes, and flooding may have significant impacts on housing, ranging from nonstructural (i.e., minor damage, such as the loss of shingles or siding) to structural (i.e., major damage, such as moving a home off of its foundation, rending a home uninhabitable, or damage to columns, posts, trusses, beams, joists, foundations, and roofing and floor slabs) (Federal Emergency Management Agency, 2012c). The first, nonstructural type of damage might eventually lead to structural damage, including destruction of the architectural character; the mechanical, electrical, and plumbing systems; interior furnishings; and the building equipment. Additionally, nonstructural damage could lead to mold infestation, septic tank failure, and landscape destruction, to name a few potential problems. These components of a home, if damaged, compromise the home's structural integrity and the overall safety of its dwellers.

Community and Housing Vulnerabilities

Certain characteristics of some housing units make them more vulnerable to disasters than others. Older homes are more vulnerable to damage brought by a disaster because these homes were built before the establishment of disaster-resistant building codes and the development of improved design and construction standards for homes (U.S. Bureau of the Census, n.d., 2013). Older homes not built to the current seismic building code have the greatest risk of earthquake damage (Federal Emergency Management Agency, n.d.b). Homes constructed prior to the introduction of or without flood damage–resistant materials that are located in flood hazard areas have greater risk of excess damage in a flooding event (Federal Emergency Management Agency, n.d.c). Over time, however, building code improvements and advances in construction techniques and products have made housing more resilient to the destructive forces of wind, water, and movement (see chapters 5, 6, 18, and 19).

Manufactured housing is an affordable housing alternative for many low-income renters and owners (George & Barr, 2005; see chapter 10). However, manufactured homes, especially older ones, are susceptible to high wind damage and are generally less disaster resilient than other types of housing (Federal Emergency Management Agency, n.d.b). Residents of mobile homes have a greater risk of death during a tornado than residents of other types of housing (Brooks, 1997). In reviewing tornado fatalities from April 2011, the Centers for Disease Control and Prevention lists the lack of access to a basement or reinforced room, which typically occurs in mobile homes, as a housing-related risk factor for death and injury from tornadoes. The other two risk factors are related to the age of the home and the time of day the tornado struck (Centers for Disease Control and Prevention, 2012).

The location of a home also affects its vulnerability to disaster. While natural disasters can happen anytime and anywhere, some locations are more prone to certain types of events. Homes and communities built in hazard-prone areas are more likely to be affected by disasters. Hurricanes impact mostly coastal areas of the country; however, their effects can be felt far inland. "Tornado Alley," which includes Texas, Oklahoma, Kansas, Nebraska, and South Dakota, is particularly well-known for the occurrence of these major wind events, although all fifty states in the United States have experienced tornadoes (Federal Emergency Management Agency, 2011).

The earth's natural patterns of drainage and flooding have long been a part of its normal water cycle. Floodplains are those low-lying areas, usually near rivers or streams, that are prone to flooding. Human activity, such as road and building construction, changes the topography of the land, significantly impacting water drainage. These changes in topography can increase the amount and severity of flooding in some locations (Federal Emergency Management Agency, 1998). Additionally, with changes made to the landscape, individuals who once lived outside of a floodplain may find themselves in flood-prone areas (National Flood Insurance Program, 2015a). Currently, over ten million households live in floodplains in the United States (Federal Emergency Management Agency, 1998).

Disasters typically affect entire communities, although serious disasters can impact entire states or even regions. For example, in 2014 a mudslide devastated Oso, a rural neighborhood in Snohomish County, Washington.

Forty-three lives were lost and approximately forty-nine homes were destroyed as a wall of mud swallowed an area of about one square mile in this disaster (SR 530 Landslide Commission, 2014; Washington State Division of Emergency Management, 2014). This mudslide left the area not only dangerous but also uninhabitable for years to come. In a newspaper report about the event, one woman affected by the mudslide stated that she felt she lived in "a recurring dream [where] she still [saw] the wall of mud roaring toward her. She said she did not think any residents of Oso, which had a population of about 180 before the landslide, would ever go back and try to rebuild homes or their lives in the area" (Johnson, 2014: n.p.). Although many individuals and families want to return to homes and communities rebuilt after disasters, some disasters prevent that possibility by their sheer magnitude and scope (Dikmen, 2006).

Disasters and People

Disasters destroy homes and displace communities, and they have a tremendous impact on individuals and families. Loss of possessions as a result of home damage or destruction can be especially difficult after a disaster, particularly because homes and their contents are often reflections of the people who live there (Hayward, 1977). A home is a collection of reminiscences, both tangible in the form of artifacts and intangible in the form of treasured memories. Kleine and Baker (2004: 1) studied material attachment and found that it "is a multi-faceted property of the relationship between an individual or group of individuals and a specific material object that has been psychologically appropriated, decommodified, and singularized through person-object interaction." In other words, people give meaning to their personal possessions such that they are no longer just material objects but objects that have emotional significance. For example, the quilt a grandmother made for a grandchild is not only a covering to keep warm, it is also a symbol of love between generations, a piece of history of a life lived, and an item that not only reflects one's heritage but one that also elicits a feeling of comfort and affection. Because of this complex relationship between home, possessions, and people, the loss of any of these is stressful. DeLorme, Zinkhan, and Hagen (2004) studied the difference between voluntary and involuntary disposition of personal possessions. Voluntary discarding occurs when one chooses to let go of items by giving or throwing them away. Involuntary disposition is not a choice and may occur as a result of a disaster. Voluntary dispossession allows the individual to distribute possessions, whereas involuntary dispossession of items due to disaster causes an intense struggle in determining how to restore or replace items that might help an individual attempt to return to a predisaster life. As DeLorme, Zinkhan, and Hagen (2004: 195) found, "possessions can be meaningful to individual (and collective) memories and life story even, and perhaps especially, if that story is interrupted by a crisis such as a natural disaster and possessions are damaged or no longer physically present." In sum, a person's sense of self and life story are profoundly disrupted by the loss of possessions during and after a disaster.

The sense of loss is compounded when considering the multitude of losses often associated with disasters. This accumulated loss includes loss of possessions, home, neighborhood, community, job, schools, and other aspects of family life and lifestyle that can threaten one's "sense of self"

(Caruana, 2010: 84). These elements of the family, cultural, and social environment must be attended to for individuals and communities affected by disaster (see chapters 12 and 13).

Although disasters are a shared experience for a large group of people, they affect specific populations differently. Disasters are often "status levelers" (Fothergill & Peek, 2004) in that they affect everyone across economic classes, often leaving behind significant destruction in their wake. However, low-income communities often suffer greater losses and are affected for a longer period of time (Cutter, Boruff, & Shirley, 2003; Fothergill & Peek, 2004; Masozera, Bailey, & Kerchner, 2007). Some residents are more vulnerable to disasters than others (Rosenfeld, Caye, Lahad, & Gurwitch, 2010). Those with fewer resources are predisposed to the impacts of disasters because of the conditions in which they live. Low-income residents, older adults, and non-native-speaking individuals are often more vulnerable during disasters, especially during the preparedness and recovery phases (Rosenfeld et al., 2010; Torgusen & Kosberg, 2006). Many low-income people and people of color are more likely to experience job loss after a disaster (Elliott & Pais, 2006). For example, a post–Hurricane Katrina study found that black workers were four times more likely than their non-Hispanic white counterparts to lose their jobs after the storm (Elliott & Pais, 2006; see chapter 16).

Older adults often have chronic illnesses or diseases that may make disaster preparation and/or evacuation difficult or impossible. Mobility and sensory impairment may impede their ability to escape danger and to cope with the aftermath of disaster (Aldrich & Benson, 2007). Whether or not an older person is able to live independently may also play a role. Those who live in facilities such as retirement, assisted-living, or nursing homes typically rely on facility staff for safe evacuation. Those living independently in the community typically benefit from having an accessible living environment, a social network to allow for evacuation in the event of an emergency, and a plan for receiving assistance in evacuation, if necessary. Those who shelter in place must also deal with the potential vulnerabilities that occur when the infrastructure is not working. For example, lack of electrical power during winter storms or heat waves leaves older adults especially vulnerable to hypothermia or heat stroke (Dreyer, 2007; Oriol, 1999; see chapter 17).

Low-income families, who are disproportionately renters, tend to live in poorer quality, older, structurally flawed, and thus less durable housing. These housing characteristics make them more vulnerable to natural disasters (Cutter et al., 2003; Joint Center for Housing Studies of Harvard University, 2011; Peacock, Dash, & Zhang, 2007; U.S. Bureau of the Census, 2013; see chapter 9). Financial constraints may keep low-income homeowners from retrofitting their homes, which would help protect these homeowners from the impacts of future disasters (Vaughan, 1995). Government programs often do not include investor-owned housing units, so landlords have little incentive to rebuild damaged structures (Comerio, 1997). Also, low-income communities are typically left out of the rebuilding process after a tornado (Smart & Prohaska, 2014).

Low-income people are also less likely to have insurance coverage to help with recovery and rebuilding (Browne & Hoyt, 2000; Marshall & Mathews, 2010; Roth & Kunreuther, 1998). However, having insurance is a crucial part of recovering financially from the impact of disasters (Michel-Kerjan & Kousky, 2010). While private flood insurance, or insurance through the

National Flood Insurance Program, greatly benefits those who have experienced a flooding disaster, the cost is often prohibitive, especially for low-income people (Browne & Hoyt, 2000). Those who need this insurance often do not have it. For example, in New Orleans in 2005, in an area known to be vulnerable to flooding, only 40 percent of the residents had any type of flood insurance (Bayot, 2005). Low-income households often lack financial resources and may lack a social network that is financially strong to assist during recovery. Therefore, they often have a more difficult time navigating the recovery processes, including submitting insurance claims and qualifying for assistance programs (Been & Ellen, n.d.; Lindell & Perry, 2003; Peacock et al., 2007; see chapter 7).

In sum, some groups face greater risks before, during, and after disasters. In addition to supporting these groups as they move through processes of grief, loss of self and community, and rebuilding, it is essential that caregivers, government officials, and disaster responders take into account how these groups are treated, the resources available to them both financially and emotionally, and how best to respond to their needs. Disaster preparedness is essential to successful individual, family, and community handling of disasters. It is particularly important for those at-risk groups that are more vulnerable to disasters and their consequences.

DISASTER RESPONSE

Public Policies

How a community responds to a disaster event has a tremendous influence on how it will recover from that event. When disasters strike, it is the responsibility of the local municipality in which the disaster is located to serve as first responder. The community does so in conjunction with state and local emergency response teams made up of community, state, and volunteer organizations. If the event is extremely large or catastrophic in nature and overwhelms the community's and the state's ability to respond, the governor may request that the federal government declare a major disaster and assist by mobilizing resources through FEMA (Federal Emergency Management Agency, 2015b). However, the governor must commit matching state funds for recovery efforts. The type of disaster declaration is very important in terms of access to resources because it influences what long-term resources are available to help communities and individuals recover, including housing recovery.

After reviewing a governor's request, the "President may declare that a major disaster or emergency exists, thus activating an array of Federal programs to assist in the response and recovery effort. Not all programs, however, are activated for every disaster. The determination of which programs are activated is based on the needs found during damage assessment and any subsequent information that may be discovered" (Federal Emergency Management Agency, 2015a: n.p.). A major disaster declaration allows for longer-term national disaster recovery programs to provide assistance to victims. Some of these programs are matched by state programs and "are designed to help disaster victims, businesses, and public entities" (Federal Emergency Management Agency, 2015b: n.p.).

An emergency declaration provides a much smaller range of federal assistance and does not include the recovery programs that accompany a major disaster declaration. Any federal funds that are received are "provided to meet a specific emergency need or to prevent a major disaster from occurring" (Federal Emergency Management Agency, 2015b: n.p.).

At the housing level, there are five categories of government programs that benefit individuals affected by a disaster: disaster housing, disaster grants, low-interest disaster loans, other disaster aid programs, and the assistance process (Federal Emergency Management Agency, 2015b). Disaster housing assistance is the provision of housing for up to eighteen months for homeowners and renters who are displaced because their primary homes have been severely damaged or destroyed. This assistance also includes some funding for emergency housing repairs in order to make homes livable. Disaster grants, which do not have to be repaid, may also assist with housing-related loss, such as replacement of personal property in the home. These grants cover those needs that are not covered by individual insurance or other funding sources. In addition to grants, disaster victims may be eligible for low-interest Small Business Administration (SBA) loans. These loans, which have to be repaid, are to assist with long-term recovery and are designed to cover uninsured losses, such as home repairs or loss of personal property for homeowners or renters (Federal Emergency Management Agency, 2015b, n.d.a).

Private Resources

Historically, disaster victims have "relied on a combination of private insurance and limited government assistance to recover from the occasional destruction metered out by nature" (Comerio, 1997: 166). In addition to public policies discussed above, there are four general funding sources for rebuilding structures and communities after a disaster loss: personal resources, insurance coverage, government assistance, and other noninsurance sources. Each source has limited funding generally, as it takes a combination of these financial resources to rebuild homes and communities.

Personal resources are personal savings and social resources, such as friends and families who can assist monetarily, physically, or psychologically with repair and recovery. These funds and resources are often limited in nature, especially for low-income people, as discussed above (Rosenfeld et al., 2010; Torgusen & Kosberg, 2006).

Homeowner's and renter's insurance is designed, among other things, to cover housing and property loss in the event of damage. Most lenders require that a homeowner purchase homeowner's insurance. Renters are encouraged but generally not required to have renter's insurance that covers personal property losses (see chapter 9). Not all insurance policies provide needed coverage during a disaster (Michel-Kerjan & Kousky, 2010). For example, "standard multiperil homeowners insurance policies, which are normally required as a condition for a mortgage, cover damage from fire, wind, hail, lightning, and winter storms, among other perils. Coverage for flood damage resulting from rising water is explicitly excluded in homeowners insurance policies" (Michel-Kerjan & Kousky, 2010: 370; see chapter 7).

Government assistance may be available to individuals and communities after a disaster; however, these government programs assume that an individual's resources and insurance are the primary supports for recovery. Government assistance is meant to supplement individual private resources, not replace them (Federal Emergency Management Agency, 2015b).

Other noninsurance sources include a variety of groups, including private for-profit, nonprofit, and faith-based organizations. Nonprofit groups play a vital role in disaster preparedness, response, and recovery (Chikoto, Sadiq, & Fordyce, 2012). This sector may work alongside government entities to assist in providing food and shelter before, during, and after a disaster event. These organizations are also significant partners in rebuilding efforts, especially for those who may have depleted or are ineligible for other types of disaster assistance. Some well-known faith-based organizations that are actively involved in rebuilding homes after disasters include Brethren Disaster Ministries, Mennonite Disaster Services, Presbyterian Disaster Assistance, the Salvation Army, and Southern Baptist Disaster Relief. Many other non-faith-based groups provide disaster response and temporary housing, including the Red Cross (National Voluntary Organizations Active in Disaster, n.d.).

Community Participation

Another key practice in disaster recovery is respecting the losses faced by families by involving displaced residents in postdisaster situations. For example, in 2000 the Turkish government developed new housing for victims in nearby communities after the devastating Orta earthquake demolished their homes. Because of the scale of family and community displacement, rebuilding homes quickly after the disaster was a priority. The government built some of these homes in the same village where the devastation occurred, while other homes were built in nearby areas. Research exploring the success of the newly built communities found that many of the new developments failed because the earthquake victims refused to move to the new locations (Dikmen, 2006). Researchers determined that a lack of resident participation in site selection and a lack of understanding about family lifestyles in the region led to this outcome. Because families were not consulted in the design of the new communities, the government built housing that was outside of the existing villages where people had lived, which did not include structures that supported the agricultural lifestyle of the people, and which weakened kinship and neighbor relationships through physical separation. In other words, as disasters strike and it becomes necessary to rebuild communities in their wake, it is essential that those involved in the rebuilding process consult those who will live in the area about lifestyle needs, cultural nuances, and home design. Some key questions to examine with the community might include, first, where are people allowed to build or rebuild? Second, what are code requirements for communities and housing? Third, what resources exist or could be initiated to assist families who face disasters, regardless of the level of the ecological spectrum (i.e., family, social, and community)? Fourth, and finally, do people want to return to the community and where do they want to live?

DISASTER RESILIENCE, MITIGATION, AND REBUILDING

Resilience and Mitigation

Resilience is "the ability to recover from or adjust to misfortune or change" (Ligenza, Robinson, & Ogelsby, 2010: 18). To improve a community's resilience to disaster, researchers have explored the physical aspects of disaster, often focusing on technologies like strengthening levees or constructing disaster-resistant buildings. Resilience is an essential component of reducing risk and providing better protection from future disasters (U.S. Department of Housing and Urban Development, 2015b).

Mitigation is the effort to reduce loss of life and property by reducing the impact of disasters. Mitigation is taking current action (i.e., before a potential next disaster strikes) to reduce human and monetary consequences in the future by analyzing, reducing, and insuring against risk. Effective mitigation requires understanding local risks, addressing sometimes difficult and competing choices, and investing in long-term community well-being. A community's safety, security, and self-reliance are compromised without mitigation actions (Federal Emergency Management Agency, n.d.e; see chapter 12).

Addressing the disaster preparedness of communities and families requires more than mitigation to improve their resilience; it also requires exploring those individual, social, economic, political, and cultural influences that make people and communities vulnerable to disasters (Bankoff & Frerks, 2013; Birkmann, 2006; Caruana, 2010). Disaster outcomes can be improved for citizens and the communities and housing in which they live through proper preparedness and planning as well as rebuilding and mitigation practices. After a disaster, disaster-resistant construction and mitigation are key to reducing displacement and disruption for families in future disasters. Where, what, and how homes and communities are built and rebuilt are important components that help to ensure disaster-resistant housing and communities. Communities must carefully consider where homes and businesses are built. Those areas prone to disaster, such as coastal communities, must plan for and build in order to mitigate potential disasters. The goal of hazard-resistant construction is to build homes that protect residents from injury or death during a disaster and that sustain less damage as a result of the situations that often accompany disasters, such as high winds, electrical surges, flooding, and seismic movement (Center for Housing Policy, n.d.). Mitigation involves retrofitting existing homes and communities to prevent or reduce potential damage from disasters. Common mitigation techniques include elevating homes to protect against flooding, anchoring and bracing furnishings and walls to prevent damage during earthquakes, using fire-resistant building materials to prevent fire hazards, and reinforcing and bracing building components to protect from high winds (Federal Emergency Management Agency, 2012b, 2013b; see chapters 5, 6, and 9).

Rebuilding

Building codes provide minimum standards by which structures should be constructed in order to provide for the health, safety, and welfare of their occupants (Federal Emergency Management Agency, 2015f). Building codes have been in existence for thousands of years (Insurance Institute for Business and Home Safety, 2015; Lindamood & Hanna, 1979). They vary depending on the municipality, county, state, or country.

Building codes are particularly important when considering the potential for natural disasters. Poorly constructed housing and inferior building materials can compromise the integrity of a building and may lead to greater damage and destruction of property and even result in loss of life (Insurance Institute for Business and Home Safety, 2015). Disaster-resistant construction is designed to strengthen structures so that they can survive a disastrous event, as well as to provide for easier cleanup and rebuilding after a disaster. Disaster-resistant building codes, supported by FEMA, go beyond minimal building codes and include strengthened standards for earthquakes, tornadoes, hurricanes, and flooding that improve the overall performance of a home during an event. The most cost-effective and simplest way to make homes disaster resistant is to build them to code.

For many homeowners and landlords of existing homes, mitigation of potential disasters includes improving and retrofitting their homes. Earthquake-resistant housing uses seismic retrofits to make a structure safer and more resistant to the impact of earth movement (Federal Emergency Management Agency, n.d.b). These retrofits include bolting the home to its foundation, strengthening crawlspace walls, reinforcing masonry foundations, and strengthening chimneys (Federal Emergency Management Agency, 2005). Inside the home, water heaters should be braced to the wall studs and tall and heavy items should be secured to walls to keep them from falling during an earthquake event (Federal Emergency Management Agency, 2005).

Flooding retrofits may include moving the home to higher ground or raising the elevation of a home so that the first floor of the home is above the flood level. Dry and wet floodproofing are also mitigation actions that assist with limiting flooding effects on housing. Dry floodproofing involves sealing the exterior of the home so that water cannot infiltrate. This can be done using waterproof membranes along the outside of a wall or using watertight closure systems on windows to prevent water entry (Federal Emergency Management Agency, 2007). Wet floodproofing is making lower level, nonliving areas of the home water resistant so that floodwaters can enter and recede without damaging it. This may include additional anchoring of the structure and providing openings to protect against and allow for movement of floodwaters. Another example may include using flood-resistant materials, such as paperless drywall, below the flood elevation level (Federal Emergency Management Agency, 2007).

Wind events, such as hurricanes, tornadoes, and high winds from severe weather, can also be mitigated. Features of a home that make it vulnerable to winds include roofs, attics, walls, windows, doors, garage doors, porches, and carports. As wind gets under the surface of these structures, it can provide significant pressure and vertical uplift. Basic wind retrofits include securing the roof deck with fastenings, installing an underlayment that protects the roof from water intrusion (often associated with wind events), installing new roofing with very specific types of fasteners and spacing, and replacing vents and soffits. Standards for roof installation vary according to the type of roof installed (metal, tile, asphalt shingle). The protection of openings in the home is essential, as these openings can fail during high winds (Federal Emergency Management Agency, 2010; see chapters 5, 6, 18, and 19).

Homeowners and landlords can also designate safe rooms and storm shelters. These are special rooms or structures designed to protect a home's occupants from the effects of tornadoes and hurricanes. Safe rooms are separate buildings or rooms in a building that are designed and constructed according to International Code Council 500 standards and specific FEMA P-361 guidelines. They provide "near-absolute protection from the deadly winds and wind-borne debris associated with extreme-wind events" (Federal Emergency Management Agency, 2015e: i; International Code Council,

2013). To help incentivize the installation of safe rooms, some states and municipalities have instituted safe room programs, in which citizens receive a rebate for a portion of the cost of the safe room once installation is complete (Federal Emergency Management Agency, 2013a; State of Oklahoma, 2015). Storm shelters are separate structures or rooms in a building that comply with the International Code Council (ICC) 500 standards (Federal Emergency Management Agency, 2015e).

There are two categories of safe rooms: residential and community. FEMA (2015e) defines residential safe rooms as places for individuals living within a single housing unit. These rooms can be inside of the home or stand-alone units that are outside of the home. Residential safe rooms typically hold no more than sixteen people. Community safe rooms may be public or privately owned and generally serve businesses and organizations. As with residential safe rooms, they can be inside the building or be a separate structure outside of the building (Federal Emergency Management Agency, 2015e).

As discussed above, technology and building science has evolved such that it is possible to make housing more disaster resilient. One example of a disaster-resilient home is the LaHouse Home and Landscape Resource Center (LaHouse). Located on the Louisiana State University campus, LaHouse demonstrates a variety of construction technologies and building techniques that can improve the performance of a home in high winds and flooding events. The home includes multiple examples of roofing systems, window protection, storm shelters, and flood-resistant features that increase a home's ability to withstand various types of natural disasters and that allow individuals living in that home to restore their home to living condition after an event (Louisiana State University Agricultural Center, n.d.).

People's Attachment to Place

Relocation may be a necessary effect of a disaster, leading people to feel displaced from their homes and communities. Individuals often hold long-standing connections to the places they call home, and the disruption of that home and those places can lead to a sense of dispossession from the self. When a home or possessions are lost, family members might experience significant grief, given the ties they felt to their homes and their possessions (Prigerson et al., 1997). A lifetime of memories can be destroyed with a single disaster, leading individuals and families to feel as if they are no longer whole. Perhaps those who have suffered such significant loss say it best. Bridget Dugan, a resident of New Orleans during Hurricane Katrina, describes the loss of her home and community and subsequent relocation in this way: "It feels as though my skin has been ripped off and I am exposed, just dangling there, lost amidst a group of people. I do not know as I search for my place, my new skin. I fervently try to sew together ripped shards of the old me, hoping they will hold. To my dismay they never do and so I continue my search for my new skin" (Dugan, 2007: 41).

While much of the literature on disaster recovery focuses on the ways that families and communities can repair physical capacities, there are more abstract—and yet no less important—conceptions of place that affect how people are able to heal and thrive after a disaster event. Postmodern place theorists have emphasized the importance of bodies in their relation to places; in other words, a location or place is more than just a point on a map.

Rather, place is understood by and through our bodies and how they interact within that space and time. Place is one way that we come to know who we are and where we are from. This is particularly salient when people talk about the places they call home. As Fulkerson states,

> Hometown is constructed by the people of a particular geographically defined reality—from family and friends to the strangers who make up our environment and its past and present. Hometown is our surroundings in the fullest aesthetic and experiential sense. Particular buildings—our family home, school, church, the park—make up place, but so do their associations (as spacious or cramped, light or dark, safe or dangerous). Reducible neither to the geographic boundaries on a map, nor to our projections onto an ostensible physical "outside," then, the place hometown is better described as a matrix of feelings that a place "releases" to us (Fulkerson, 2010: 27).

Home is more than a location. It is an environment of relationships, memories, and embodied feelings that connect us to a place. When a hometown is lost, then, through a disaster, the effects of the loss on the sense of self, and of community, can be tragic (Fulkerson, 2010).

Attachment to place is often twofold: attachment to the location or the physical space itself and attachment to the relationships or the social aspects of place (Lewicka, 2010). Both aspects are important when attempting to understand loss associated with disasters. Hayward (1977) supports the idea that home is more than a physical structure that protects its occupants from the elements. He argues that home is the relationship one has to the physical environment. Home is a place of continuity and connection, with recognizable surroundings and a sense of constancy and permanence. The home's environment is a symbol of one's identity and character. This includes the "size and physical condition of the building, the appearance of the street block as well as the front door, and even the kind of people and community life that one finds in the neighborhood" (Hayward, 1977: 10). It is a place where one grows up, and, as such, it is a piece of history that is a meaningful part of an individual's life. Knowledge of the depth of the relationship that people have with their homes can therefore help professionals and volunteers who respond following a disaster to understand the magnitude of loss people feel when their home and/or community is destroyed. Attachment to place increases with length of time lived in an area (Lewicka, 2010) and has personal connotations characterized by personal memories, symbolic meaning, and even sacred significance (Scannell & Gifford, 2010).

This feeling of displacement is magnified when entire communities are relocated in the wake of a disaster, as Chamlee-Wright and Storr (2009) found in their study of the Ninth Ward in post–Hurricane Katrina New Orleans. This area of the city was among the poorest and most susceptible to the effects of disaster. In working with residents, the researchers identified several key themes that they heard postdisaster. First, residents felt a strong attachment to the area; second, residents had a sense of loss over cultural resources that were destroyed; and third, residents described place as an important factor in the desire to move back to the area (Chamlee-Wright & Storr, 2009). While some Katrina evacuees moved to other areas and chose to remain there because of greater opportunities in terms of jobs, schools, and homes, other evacuees wanted to move back to the Ninth Ward, despite the challenges they faced there, including barriers posed by the government, such as the inability to qualify for reconstruction financing and constraints on rebuilding in hazardous areas (Giegengack & Foster, 2006). These barriers were traumatic because "the evacuation experience separated people not only from their homes, but from their identity" (Chamlee-Wright & Storr, 2009: 628). For evacuees, the social and cultural characteristics of place were of paramount importance.

When dealing with the effects of displacement after a disaster, grief is a common outcome. As Prigerson et al. (1997) discovered, individuals who experience material losses after a disaster also experience complicated grief, although their levels of grieving might not be as high as those of individuals who lost loved ones. Their study of post-Katrina New Orleans was the first of its kind to measure the effects of nonbereavement losses on grief. As might be expected, their study found that as losses due to disaster increased (including tangible losses, like property and goods), participants reported higher instances of complicated grief (Prigerson et al., 1997). These findings echo the importance of place and property, including the home, in postdisaster recovery and healing (see chapters 12 and 13).

CONCLUSION

Disasters can affect any part of the United States at any time of the year, swiftly and without warning. In case they are multidimensional, they not only cause devastation to housing structures and community infrastructure but are traumatic for individuals as well. As communities face disaster, they encounter numerous stressors that test their resilience, reliance on community support, and connections to the physical environment where they live. Families react to these stressors, which include the loss of personal property, homes, social networks, and a sense of place or home. Those organizations and agencies that work with families in disaster situations must pay close attention to each of these levels of the families' environment in order to promote healing and physical and emotional survival in the aftermath of a disaster. This includes knowing about the resources available to families and communities in the aftermath of disaster—including government and nonprofit funding and supports as well as resilience and mitigation efforts—and being attentive to the ways different groups within communities (the elderly, low-income people, communities of color) experience disasters differently.

Additionally, given the importance of place in the life of many families and communities, it is imperative that organizations and volunteers who work with individuals and families affected by disaster understand the importance of home and community in the grieving and rebuilding processes. As research cited throughout this chapter confirms, when these experiences and feelings are not accounted for, families suffer from intense feelings of displacement, grief, and loss. To counter these effects, communities must be designed in such a way that disasters are planned for before they happen (mitigation), particularly focusing on the multiple environmental factors that impact how families are able to access services and support postdisaster.

Additionally, families and communities must be involved in rebuilding their communities. They understand the significance of not only the physical spaces or properties that were lost but also the more intangible aspects of community and familial life, such as connection to home, social supports, and community history (see chapters 12 and 13). As Caruana (2010: 86) states, "Loss is central to the experience of disaster—loss of home, loved ones, independence, identity and a sense of the world as a safe place—and it is the way in which this loss is accommodated that will determine how individuals, families and communities rebound." As individuals and communities work to rebuild and repair postdisaster, it is imperative that their social environments—home, family, community—are attended to in order to promote the flourishing and health of communities, individuals, and families.

REFERENCES

Aldrich, N., & Benson, W. F. (2007). Disaster preparedness and the chronic disease needs of vulnerable older adults. *Preventing Chronic Disease, 5*(1), n.p. Retrieved July 29, 2016, from http://www.cdc.gov/pcd/issues/2008/jan/07_0135.htm.

Bankoff, G., & Frerks, G. (2013). *Mapping vulnerability: Disasters, development and people*. New York: Routledge.

Bayot, J. (2005, August 31). Hurricane Katrina: Insurance; payouts hinge on the cause of damage. *New York Times*. Retrieved July 24, 2015, from http://www.nytimes.com/2005/08/31/business/31insure.html?_r=0.

Been, V., & Ellen, I. G. (n.d.). *Social vulnerability and disaster planning*. Rebuild by Design. Retrieved July 24, 2015, from http://www.rebuildbydesign.org/research/component/k2/54-research-advisory-group-reports/157/157.

Birkmann, J. (2006). *Measuring vulnerability to natural hazards: Towards disaster resilient societies*. Tokyo: United Nations University.

Brooks, H. (1997). *Mobile home tornado fatalities: Some observations*. NOAA/ERL/National Severe Storms Laboratory, Norman, Okla. Retrieved July 24, 2015, from http://www.nssl.noaa.gov/users/brooks/public_html/essays/mobilehome.html.

Browne, M. J., & Hoyt, R. E. (2000). The demand for flood insurance: Empirical evidence. *Journal of Risk and Uncertainty, 20*(3), 291–306.

Caruana, C. (2010). Picking up the pieces. *Family Matters, 84*, 79–88.

Center for Housing Policy. (n.d.). *Making homes more resistant to natural disasters*. Retrieved July 24, 2015, from http://www.nhc.org/media/documents/MkingHomes-DisasterResistant1.pdf.

Centers for Disease Control and Prevention. (2012). *Tornado-related fatalities: Five states, southeastern United States, April 25–28, 2011*. Retrieved July 24, 2015, from http://www.cdc.gov/mmwr/preview/mmwrhtml/mm6128a3.htm.

Chamlee-Wright, E., & Storr, V. H. (2009). "There's no place like New Orleans": Sense of place and community recovery in the Ninth Ward after Hurricane Katrina. *Journal of Urban Affairs, 31*(5), 615–634.

Chikoto, G. L., Sadiq, A. A., & Fordyce, E. (2013). Disaster mitigation and preparedness comparison of nonprofit, public, and private organizations. *Nonprofit and Voluntary Sector Quarterly, 42*(2), 391–410.

City of Joplin. (2012). *City of Joplin* (fact sheet). Retrieved July 24, 2015, from http://www.joplintornadoanniversary.com/resources/city-of-joplin-factsheet5-14-12.pdf.

City of Moore. (n.d.). *Comprehensive housing market analysis*. Retrieved July 24, 2015, from http://www.cityofmoore.com/housinganalysis.

Comerio, M. C. (1997). Housing issues after disasters. *Journal of Contingencies and Crisis Management, 5*(3), 166–178.

Cutter, S. L., Boruff, B. J., & Shirley, W. L. (2003). Social vulnerability to environmental hazards. *Social Science Quarterly, 84*(2), 242–261.

DeLorme, D. E., Zinkhan, G. M., & Hagen, S. C. (2004). The process of consumer reactions to possession threats and losses in a natural disaster. *Marketing Letters, 15*(4), 185–199.

Dikmen, N. (2006). Relocation or rebuilding in the same area: An important factor for decision making for post disaster housing projects. In *Proceedings of the International Conference and Student Competition on Post-disaster Reconstruction*, May 17–19, 2006, Florence, Italy.

Dreyer, K. (2007). Gerontology and emergency management: Discovering pertinent themes and functional elements within the two disciplines. In D. A. McEntire (Ed.), *Disciplines, disasters and emergency management: The convergence and divergence of concepts, issues and trends from the research literature* (pp. 206–212). Springfield, Ill.: Charles C. Thomas.

Dugan, B. (2007). Loss of identity in a disaster: How do you say goodbye to home? *Perspective in Psychiatric Care, 43*(1), 41–46.

Elliott, J. R., & Pais, J. (2006). Race, class, and Hurricane Katrina: Social differences in human responses to disaster. *Social Science Research, 35*(2), 295–321.

Federal Emergency Management Agency. (n.d.a). *Additional assistance with home repairs.* Retrieved July 24, 2015, from http://www.fema.gov/faq-details/Additional-Assistance-with-Home-Repairs-1370032124759/.

Federal Emergency Management Agency. (n.d.b). *Building codes.* Retrieved July 24, 2015, from https://www.fema.gov/building-codes#.

Federal Emergency Management Agency. (n.d.c). *Highlights of ASCE 24 flood resistant design and construction.* Retrieved July 24, 2015, from https://www.fema.gov/media-library/assets/documents/14983.

Federal Emergency Management Agency. (n.d.d). *Number of losses paid by calendar year.* Retrieved July 24, 2015, from http://www.fema.gov/number-losses-paid-calendar-year#.

Federal Emergency Management Agency. (n.d.e). *What is mitigation?* Retrieved July 29, 2015, from https://www.fema.gov/what-mitigation.

Federal Emergency Management Agency. (1998). *Managing floodplain development through the national flood insurance program.* Retrieved July 24, 2015, from http://www.fema.gov/media-library-data/20130726-1535-20490-7187/unit1.pdf.

Federal Emergency Management Agency. (2005). *Earthquake safety guide for homeowners.* Retrieved July 24, 2015, from http://www.fema.gov/media-library-data/20130726-1446-20490-6333/FEMA -530.pdf.

Federal Emergency Management Agency. (2007). *Selecting appropriate mitigation measures for floodprone structures.* Retrieved July 24, 2015, from http://www.fema.gov/media-library-data/20130726-1608-20490-9182/Federal Emergency Management Agency_551_ch_07.pdf.

Federal Emergency Management Agency. (2010). *Wind retrofit guide for residential buildings.* Retrieved July 24, 2015, from http://www.fema.gov/media-library-data/20130726-1753-25045-2304/508versioncombined_804.pdf.

Federal Emergency Management Agency (2011). *Tornado risks and hazards in the southeastern United States.* Retrieved July 24, 2015, from http://www.fema .gov/media-library-data/20130726-1801-25045-0298/ra1_2011_tornado_risks_tagged_011912.pdf.

Federal Emergency Management Agency. (2012a). *FEMA aid to Kentucky tornado recovery exceeds $7 million.* [Press release]. Retrieved July 24, 2015, from https://www.fema.gov/news-release/2012/03/23/fema-aid-kentucky-tornado-recovery-exceeds-7-million.

Federal Emergency Management Agency. (2012b). *Protect your property or business from disaster.* Retrieved January 26, 2017, from http://www.fema.gov/small-business-toolkit/protect-your-property-or-business-disaster.

Federal Emergency Management Agency. (2012c). *Reducing the risks of nonstructural earthquake damage: A practical guide.* Washington, D.C.: Federal Emergency Management Agency.

Federal Emergency Management Agency. (2013a). *Hazard mitigation grant program, pre-disaster mitigation grants and safe rooms.* Retrieved July 24, 2015, from http://www.fema.gov/media-library-data/20130726-1916-25045-9915/hmgp_and_safe_rooms_fact_sheet_2013_revised_05_25_2013.pdf.

Federal Emergency Management Agency. (2013b). *Mitigation ideas: A resource for reducing risk to natural hazards.* Retrieved July 24, 2015, from http://www.fema.gov/media-library-data/20130726-1904-25045-0186/fema_mitigation_ideas_final508.pdf.

Federal Emergency Management Agency. (2015a). *The declaration process.* Retrieved July 24, 2015, from https://www.fema.gov/declaration-process.

Federal Emergency Management Agency. (2015b). *The disaster process and disaster aid programs.* Retrieved July 24, 2015, from https://www.fema.gov/disaster-process-disaster-aid-programs.

Federal Emergency Management Agency. (2015c). *Loss dollars paid by calendar year.* Retrieved July 24, 2015, from http://www.fema.gov/loss-dollars-paid-calendar-year.

Federal Emergency Management Agency. (2015d). *Preliminary disaster reports.* Retrieved July 24, 2015, from http://www.fema.gov/preliminary-damage-assessment-reports.

Federal Emergency Management Agency. (2015e). *Safe rooms for tornadoes and hurricanes: Guidance for community and residential safe rooms.* Retrieved July 24, 2015, from http://www.fema.gov/media-library-data/1430758775177-353770961374f71c45383af7af4385d5/FEMA_P-361_2015r2.pdf.

Federal Emergency Management Agency. (2015f). What are building codes? Retrieved August 28, 2017, from https://www.fema.gov/building-codes.

Fothergill, A., & Peek, L. A. (2004). Poverty and disasters in the United States: A review of recent sociological findings. *Natural Hazards, 32*(1), 89–110.

Fulkerson, M. M. (2010). *Places of redemption: Theology for a worldly church.* Oxford: Oxford University Press.

George, L., & Barr, M. (2005). *Moving home: Manufactured housing in rural America.* Retrieved July 24, 2015, from http://www.ruralhome.org/storage/documents/movinghome.pdf.

Giegengack, R., & Foster, K. R. (2006). Physical constraints on reconstructing New Orleans. In E. Birch & S. Wachter (Eds.), *Rebuilding urban places after disaster: Lessons from Hurricane Katrina* (pp. 13–33). Philadelphia: University of Pennsylvania Press.

Hayward, D. G. (1977). Housing research and the concept of home. *Housing Educators Journal, 4*(3), 7–12.

Insurance Institute for Business and Home Safety. (2015). *Building code resources.* Retrieved July 29, 2015, from https://www.disastersafety.org/wp-content/uploads/Building_Codes_overview_2015.pdf.

International Code Council. (2013). *ICC/NSSA standard for the design and construction of storm shelters.* ICC 500–2013 edition. Retrieved July 24, 2015, from www.iccsafe.org/cs/standards/IS-STM/Documents/2013Dev/ICC500-2013_PC1.pdf.

International Disaster Database (2015). *United States disasters 2000–2015.* Retrieved July 24, 2015, from http://www.emdat.be/advanced_search/index.html.

International Displacement Monitoring Centre. (2013a). *Comprehensive response to wave of displacement crisis needed.* Retrieved July 24, 2015, from http://www.internal-displacement.org/south-and-south-east-asia/philippines/2013/comprehensive-response-to-wave-of-displacement-crises-needed.

Johnson, K. (2014, April 19). Leveled by landslide, towns mull how to rebuild. *New York Times.* Retrieved July 24, 2015, from http://www.nytimes.com/2014/04/20/us/leveled-by-landslide-towns-mull-how-to-rebuild.html.

Joint Center for Housing Studies of Harvard University. (2011). *Renter demographics.* Retrieved July 24, 2015, from http://www.jchs.harvard.edu/sites/jchs.harvard.edu/files/ahr2011-3-demographics.pdf.

Kleine, S. S., & Baker, S. M. (2004). An integrative review of material possession attachment. *Academy of Marketing Science Review, 1*, 1–29.

Lewicka, M. (2010). What makes neighborhood different from home and city? Effects of place scale on place attachment. *Journal of Environmental Psychology, 30*(1), 35–51.

Ligenza, L., Robinson, M., & Oglesby, H. (2010). *Resiliency in the face of disaster: Strategies for survivors and responders.* FEMA IA ESF-6 Conference, April 25–30, 2010, San Diego, Calif. Retrieved July 24, 2015, from http://www.fema.gov/pdf/conferences/iaconference/2010/tuesday_1045am_resiliency_in_face_of_disaster.pdf.

Lindamood, S., & Hanna, S. D. (1979). *Housing, society, and consumers.* St. Paul, Minn.: West Publishing.

Lindell, M. K., & Perry, R. W. (2003). *Communicating environmental risk in multiethnic communities* (Vol. 7). Thousand Oaks, Calif.: Sage.

Louisiana State University Agricultural Center. (n.d.). *La House.* Retrieved July 24, 2015, from http://www.lsuagcenter.com/en/family_home/home/la_house/.

Marshall, I., Jr., & Mathews, S. (2010). Disaster preparedness for the elderly: An analysis of international literature using symbolic interactionist perspective. *Journal of Aging in Emerging Economies, 2*(2), 79–92.

Masozera, M., Bailey, M., & Kerchner, C. (2007). Distribution of impacts of natural disasters across income groups: A case study of New Orleans. *Ecological Economics, 63*(2), 299–306.

Michel-Kerjan, E. O., & Kousky, C. (2010). Come rain or shine: Evidence on flood insurance purchases in Florida. *Journal of Risk and Insurance, 77*(2), 369–397.

National Flood Insurance Program. (2015a). *Flooding and flood risks: Undergoing a map change*. Retrieved July 24, 2015, from https://www.floodsmart.gov/floodsmart/pages/flooding_flood_risks/map_change.jsp.

National Flood Insurance Program. (2015b). *Residential coverage*. Retrieved July 24, 2015, from https://www.floodsmart.gov/floodsmart/pages/residential_coverage/rc_overview.jsp.

National Oceanic and Atmospheric Administration. (n.d.). *U.S. tornado climatology*. Retrieved July 24, 2015, from http://www.ncdc.noaa.gov/climate-information/extreme-events/us-tornado-climatology.

National Oceanic and Atmospheric Administration. (2014). *Frequently asked questions*. Retrieved July 24, 2015, from http://www.aoml.noaa.gov/hrd/tcfaq/E11.html.

National Voluntary Organizations Active in Disaster. (n.d.). *National organization members*. Retrieved July 24, 2015, from http://www.nvoad.org/voad-network/national-members/.

North Carolina Department of Public Safety. (2012). *Hurricane Irene*. Retrieved July 24, 2015, from https://www.ncdps.gov/Index2.cfm?a=000003,000010,002050,002063.

Oriol, W. E. (1999). *Psychosocial issues for older adults in disasters*. (DHHS Publication No. ESDRB SMA 99–3323). Washington, D.C.: Emergency Services and Disaster Relief Branch, Center for Mental Health Services, Substance Abuse and Mental Health Services Administration.

Peacock, W. G., Dash, N., & Zhang, Y. (2007). Sheltering and housing recovery following disaster. In H. Rodriquez, E. L. Quarantelli, & R. R. Dynes (Eds.), *Handbook of disaster research* (pp. 258–274). New York: Springer.

Pearce, L. D. R. (2000). *An integrated approach for community hazard, impact, risk and vulnerability analysis: HIRV* (Doctoral dissertation). University of British Columbia. Retrieved January 26, 2017, from http://blogs.ubc.ca/circlefacts/2010/08/10/ubc-theses-and-dissertations-collections/.

Prigerson, H. G., Shear, M. K., Frank, E., Beery, L. C., Silberman, R., Prigerson, J., & Reynolds, C. F. (1997). Traumatic grief: A case of loss-induced trauma. *American Journal of Psychiatry, 154*(7), 1003–1009.

Rosenfeld, L. B., Caye, J. S., Lahad, M., & Gurwitch, R. H. (2010). *When their world falls apart: Helping families and children manage the effects of disasters*. Washington, D.C.: NASW Press.

Roth, R. J., & Kunreuther, H. (Eds.). (1998). *Paying the price: The status and role of insurance against natural disasters in the United States*. Washington, D.C.: Joseph Henry Press.

Saylor, C. F. (1993). *Children and disasters*. New York: Plenum Press.

Scannell, L., & Gifford, R. (2010). Defining place attachment: A tripartite organizing framework. *Journal of Environmental Psychology, 30*(1), 1–10.

Smart, K., & Prohaska, A. (2014). *Hazard vulnerability and housing inequality after the Tuscaloosa, Alabama, tornado: A critical analysis of rebuilding efforts*. XVIII ISA World Congress of Sociology, July 13–19, 2014, Yokohama, Japan. Abstract retrieved July 24, 2015, from http://www.isa-sociology.org/en/conferences/world-congress/yokohama-2014/.

SR 530 Landslide Commission (2014). *The SR530 Landslide Commission final report*. Retrieved July 24, 2015, from http://www.governor.wa.gov/sites/default/files/documents/SR530LC_Final_Report.pdf.

State of Alabama. (2012). *Action plan for disaster recovery: Tornadoes of April 2011*. Montgomery: Alabama Department of Economic and Community Affairs.

State of Oklahoma. (2015). *SoonerSafe safe room rebate program*. Retrieved July 24, 2015, from https://www.ok.gov/OEM/saferoom/app/index.php.

Torgusen, B. L., & Kosberg, J. I. (2006). Assisting older victims of disasters. *Journal of Gerontological Social Work, 47*(1–2), 27–44.

United Nations Office of Disaster Risk Reduction. (2015). *Disaster impacts 2000–2012*. Retrieved July 24, 2015, from http://www.preventionweb.net/files/31737_20130312disaster20002012copy.pdf.

U.S. Bureau of the Census. (n.d.). *Physical housing characteristics for occupied housing units 2008–2012 American Community Survey 5-year estimates*. Retrieved July 24, 2015, from http://factfinder2.census.gov/faces/tableservices/jsf/pages/productview.xhtml?pid=ACS_12_5YR_S2504.

U.S. Bureau of the Census. (2013). *American Housing Survey for the United States: 2011*. Retrieved July 24, 2015, from https://www.census.gov/prod/2013pubs/h150-11.pdf.

U.S. Department of Housing and Urban Development. (1994). *Assessment of damage to residential buildings caused by the Northridge earthquake*. Retrieved July 24, 2015, from http://www.huduser.org/portal//Publications/PDF/earthqk.pdf.

U.S. Department of Housing and Urban Development. (2015a). *Management's discussion and analysis: Hurricane Sandy*. Retrieved July 24, 2015, from https://portal.hud.gov/hudportal/documents/huddoc?id=afrfy13_sandy.pdf.

U.S. Department of Housing and Urban Development. (2015b). *National disaster resilience competition*. Retrieved July 24, 2015, from http://portal.hud.gov/hudportal/documents/huddoc?id=NDRCFactSheetFINAL.pdf.

U. S. Geological Survey. (2012). *Earthquake facts and statistics*. Retrieved July 24, 2015, from http://earthquake.usgs.gov/earthquakes/eqarchives/year/eqstats.php.

Vaughan, E. (1995). The significance of socioeconomic and ethnic diversity for the risk communication process. *Risk Analysis, 15*(2), 169–180.

Washington State Division of Emergency Management. (2014). *Disaster resources*. Retrieved July 24, 2015, from https://www.liveandworkwell.com/images/member/spotlight/SA_WAmudslide14.pdf.

SECTION VI
HOUSING IN A GLOBAL CONTEXT

Chapter 21   Housing in Asia

SUK-KYUNG KIM

Among the continents in the world, Asia ranks first in land area (approximately seventeen million square miles or forty-four million square kilometers) and population (3.8 billion living in forty-eight countries) (World Atlas, 2014). Asia also has a diversity of national, regional, and local cultures, which translates into a diverse housing landscape (Kim, 2012b). Various factors affect housing design, planning, and market conditions in Asia. Many Asian countries' recorded history stretches back longer than that of the United States. This diversity and longer history make it difficult to characterize Asian countries' housing design and planning in a single chapter.

This chapter thus highlights major features of housing design and planning in select Asian countries, including Korea, Japan, China, India, and Singapore. Common housing features in these countries represent overall housing characteristics in Asia. Additional specific examples from different countries demonstrate how housing-related issues have been addressed in different or similar ways depending on the country. Common and nation-specific housing features are described within three historical periods—traditional, modern, and contemporary housing. Finally, this chapter briefly introduces homeownership rates in select Asian countries and national efforts to improve housing affordability.

Traditional housing is defined as that built before the 1910s (Kang, 1994; Martison, 2009).[1] This type of housing is a one- or two-story single-family home and is constructed with regionally produced natural materials such as wood or straw and locally produced bricks or roof tiles (Kang, 1994). In contrast, modern housing units, built from the 1920s to the 1960s, and contemporary housing, built from the 1960s to the present, have more mid- or high-rise multifamily housing structures. Modern housing began to have higher residential building structures using various construction technologies. Contemporary housing is characterized by sustainable housing, advanced architectural engineering technologies, a range of residential technologies such as Internet-based home automation systems (Kim, Lee, & Yim, 2009), and a diversity of housing types and designs to meet different lifestyles and residential needs, including aging in place (Kim, Ahn, & Tremblay, 2008).

1. Martison (2009) argues that modern architecture started in the 1920s in the United States.

Regardless of the historic period, housing in Asia shows significant influences of feng shui, a practice that was founded by the Chinese and provides practical guidance for planning, design, and architectural principles for many Asian homes and neighborhoods (Mak & Ng, 2005). It emphasizes harmonization between the built and the natural environment, such as mountains and watercourses surrounding a site (Mak & Ng, 2005). Feng shui also demonstrates environmentally conscious and harmonious relations between residents and their environment (Oh, Chang, Kim, & Lee, 2004). This principle is connected to sustainable housing principles in contemporary housing.

TRADITIONAL ASIAN HOUSING

In Asia evidence of human habitation dates back more than ten thousand years. Many early shelters have been preserved. For example, the Amsa-dong Prehistoric Sites, which date to 5,000 BCE, preserve the foundations of several round or rectangular human shelters from the Neolithic Era (Kang-dong-gu, 2014). Most of these shelters are located near rivers and mountains where people fished, hunted, or gathered fruits and vegetables. Although these shelters, constructed of straw, mud, and wood, may look temporary, the interiors were designated for basic residential functions such as dining, sleeping, and family gathering. Each shelter also has a designated area for cooking and heating,[2] which is adjacent to the dining area but separated from sleeping and family gathering areas.

Although traditional housing covers a broad range of historic periods, it usually dates back to AD 500 in Korea and China (Kang, 1994). During the planning and design process, designers considered the location, the layout, and the structure of the home and selected the building materials in response to the regional and local climate, wind direction, the amount of sunlight and shade, and the availability and accessibility of local and regional resources.

Many housing examples in these countries show that in colder climates homes are located closer to each other and have wooden roofs, facilitating heating and insulation; in warmer climates homes are located farther apart and have straw roofs, facilitating natural cooling and ventilation (Kang, 1994). These strategies take advantage of natural light and wind, improving indoor temperature control and ventilation (Kang, 1994; Kim, 2012b).

In Japanese traditional homes a type of local and natural flooring, a thick rectangular and environmentally friendly straw mat called tatami, has been used. The mats provide dryness in the humid summers and warmth in the cold winters. These mats measure approximately 0.995 by 1.91 meters (or 2.45 square feet) and are also used to measure space in Japanese homes (Paramore, Gong, & Murata, 2010).

In the past, certain roofing materials were permitted only for certain socioeconomic groups. For example, the *kiwa*, a building material for roofing, made of dried clay, was limited to middle- or upper-class households in Korea and China due to its cost and difficulty in manufacturing, while woven straw was used for the roof and mud and small rocks were used for the walls

2. Since there is little literature about the shelters, the author visited them in July 2013 and found these characteristics.

FIGURE 21.1
Traditional Single-Family House for an Upper-Class Family
Image credit: S.-K. Kim

in socioeconomically lower-class homes due to their affordability (Kang, 1994; Kim, 2012b). Figure 21.1 depicts an upper-class home located on a site with a brook right beside it and a low hill at the back, using *kiwa* for the roof and bricks for walls. This example shows the use of feng shui and natural materials for an upper-class household.

MODERN AND CONTEMPORARY ASIAN HOUSING

From the 1910s to the 1970s many Asian countries underwent various large-scale social upheavals. In the case of Korea these events were World War II, the Korean War, the Korean New Village Development Movement, and the crumbling of formerly fixed socioeconomic boundaries and layers, resulting in changed economic and social structures (Van Vliet & Hirayama, 1994). The evolution of housing mirrored these changes. First, the role of housing as a symbol of a household's socioeconomic status has diminished. Housing now utilizes various contemporary and convenient construction technologies. During this period in Korea, Japan, and China (Hirayama & Ronald, 2006), multifamily housing was developed to accommodate the needs of socioeconomically diverse populations, as opposed to traditional single-family housing units with one or two stories (Korea National Housing Corporation, 2002). The number of multistory housing structures has dramatically increased since the 1980s, particularly because of urban population growth (Kim, Ahn, & Tremblay, 2008; Van Vliet & Hirayama, 1994). As a result, high-rise multifamily housing buildings have become very common in Asia's metropolitan cities in the twenty-first century.

In contemporary Asian housing, sustainability (also called green, environmentally friendly, or energy-efficient design), high-rise residential buildings, high-tech amenities, and amenities for aging in place are common features (Kim, 2012b; Kim, Ahn, & Tremblay, 2008; Kim, Lee, & Yim, 2009), which may be similar to American housing. According to the U.S. General

Services Administration (2015), sustainable design takes a holistic approach to reduce the negative impact on the environment and to increase the health and comfort of building occupants. Sustainable design encompasses efficient, waste-reduced, and healthy and productive environments (Pile, 2007; Kim, Lee, Kwon, & Ahn, 2015; see chapter 19). In the 1990s, environmentally friendly design principles were of great interest among researchers in Korea and Japan (Oh, Chang, Kim, & Lee, 2004). *Green design* became a more popular term than *environmentally friendly design* in 2000, when the U.S. Green Building Council (USGBC) launched LEED rating systems for designing and assessing green building (U.S. Green Building Council, 2014). Many authors show that green, environmentally friendly, or energy-efficient design in Asia also considers the location of a building, the connectivity to public transportation, efficient water use, the quality of the indoor environment, recycling and reuse of architectural and interior elements, and space planning considerations in regard to the orientation of the building (Kim et al., 2015). These features are also emphasized in USGBC's LEED rating systems (U.S. Green Building Council, 2014).

Additionally in Asian housing, diverse technological systems for improving comfort and convenience are applied in many homes (Kim et al., 2009). Finally, Asian housing reflects the needs of aging populations in their societies (Kim & Kim, 2013; see chapter 17). The following sections highlight these characteristics of modern and contemporary Asian housing.

Housing Sustainability

Over the past few years, Asia, like many other continents across the globe, has increased its interest in sustainable housing, partly based on ideas presented at conferences hosted by the United Nations that declared the urgent need for sustainable human settlements for present and future generations (United Nations, 1996).

Measuring Housing Sustainability through Rating Systems

Many Western and Asian countries have established rating systems to assess the environmental friendliness and energy efficiency of single- and multi-family housing (Indian Green Building Council, 2015; Kim, Lee, Kwon, & Ahn, 2015). Examples of these rating systems are the USGBC's Leadership in Energy and Environmental Design (LEED), the Building Research Establishment Environmental Assessment Methodology (BREEAM) in the U.K., LEED-India, and Korea's Green Standard for Energy and Environmental Design (G-SEED) System (Building Research Establishment, 2015; Green Standard for Energy and Environmental Design Center, 2015; U.S. Green Building Council, 2014).

These systems aspire to reduce global warming, climate change, and greenhouse gas emissions and offer practical guidance for building sustainable communities in compliance with the Kyoto Protocol, an international agreement that emphasizes reducing greenhouse gas emissions (United Nations, 1996). These systems assess and rate the environmental performance of neighborhoods as well as residential and commercial buildings, regardless of whether they are newly constructed or existing buildings, attached or detached. Compared to the Western building rating systems, many Asian green building rating systems emphasize compact, high-density development because of Asia's larger population (Green Standard for Energy and Environmental Design Center, 2015; Japan Green Build Council and Japan Sustainable Building Consortium, 2015; U.S. Green Building Council, 2014). Their guidelines for development density are higher than those suggested by LEED.

In regard to Asian countries, India's Green Building Council adapted yet modified the USGBC's LEED rating system to reflect different national and regional situations (Indian Green Building Council, 2015). In addition to the modified LEED system, India developed another national green building standard that used both programs (Indian Green Building Council, 2015). In Korea developers and contractors widely adapted the USGBC's LEED rating system. Prior to adapting the LEED rating system, the Korea Ministry of Land, Infrastructure, and Transport (2013) launched a green building rating system, called the G-SEED System in 2002 (Kim et al., 2015). G-SEED certifies various types of neighborhoods, residential buildings that include multifamily housing units, and commercial and educational facilities, just as the USGBC's LEED rating system does.

The USGBC's LEED rating system and the G-SEED system show many similarities (Kim, Abrams, & Seidel, 2004). Both systems emphasize environmental friendliness and energy efficiency in systems ranging from land use to interior spaces and both take a holistic approach (Kim, Abrams, & Seidel, 2004). The LEED rating system consists of six main categories to assess green buildings: (1) land use and transportation, (2) sustainable sites, (3) water efficiency, (4) energy and atmosphere, (5) materials and resources, and (6) indoor environmental quality, including indoor air quality, temperature, ventilation, lighting, and acoustics (U.S. Green Building Council, 2014). The G-SEED system has four categories: (1) land use and transportation, (2) energy and natural resource management, (3) eco-environment, and (4) indoor environmental quality (Green Standard for Energy and Environmental Design Center, 2015).

The main differences between the two systems are the amount of points that can be earned. The USGBC's LEED rating system allows 110 points as the maximum, which consists of 100 points from categories 1, 2, 4, 5, and 6

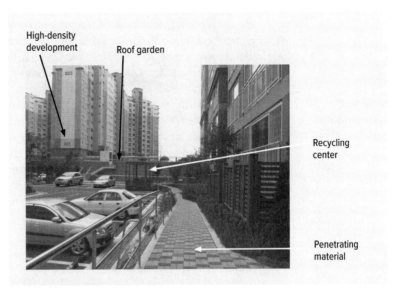

FIGURE 21.2
Multifamily Housing Complex Certified by the Korean G-SEED (Green Standard for Energy and Environmental Design) System for the Humansia Community, Andong City, Korea
Image credit: S.-K. Kim

and 10 points from two incentive categories: innovation in design and regional priority (U.S. Green Building Council, 2014). The G-SEED system consists of required elements to receive a rating and an additional section for incentives. The maximum score is 100 points, which includes incentives (Korea Ministry of Land, Infrastructure, and Transport, 2013). Figure 21.2 shows Asian high-rise multifamily housing complexes certified by the G-SEED system.

In Japan, the Comprehensive Assessment System for Built Environment Efficiency (CASBEE), established in 2001, assesses and rates the environmental performance of buildings (Japan Green Build Council and Japan Sustainable Building Consortium, 2015). Similar to the LEED and G-SEED systems, the CASBEE is a tool for assessing new construction, renovation of existing buildings, and detached homes. It pursues the goals of designing buildings and homes to be energy efficient and environmentally friendly.

Examples of Sustainable Housing in Asia

As of August 2014, about one hundred low-rise multifamily housing developments and several thousand housing units in Asia had been certified by the U.S. Green Building Council's LEED for Homes rating system (U.S. Green Building Council, 2014). In addition to LEED for Homes, many highrise or experimental residential projects are certified by LEED for New Construction and Major Renovation. Among them are Green Tomorrow, an experimental home built in Seongnam City in Korea by the Samsung Engineering and Construction Group, which achieved LEED's platinum certification in 2009, based on the USGBC's LEED for New Construction and Major Renovation system (Samsung C&T Corporation, 2013). This model home demonstrates various energy-saving technologies and management systems, as an example of green and smart home practices (Kim et al., 2009; Sakamura, 1989; see figure 21.3).[3]

Green Tomorrow utilizes solar, geothermal, and water-saving systems. The Green Tomorrow model home faces south to maximize sunlight and natural heating and cooling. The roof is covered by solar panels, which collect solar energy, then send it to a battery for water- and space-heating purposes. In addition to this active solar system, the home also uses a geothermal system that gains heat from the ground or exports the heat to the ground and uses it for heating and cooling spaces and a gray-water system that recycles water from the sink, washing machine, and dishwasher to use for flushing the toilet. The garage also offers an electrical outlet for charging a hybrid car.[4] (See figure 21.4.)

A monitoring panel that hangs on the living room wall tracks and reports energy consumption of the home. This panel can be applied in multifamily housing units, enabling the comparison of energy use among units in the same complex (Samsung C&T Corporation, 2013). Regional or reclaimed materials are used for the interior and exterior parts of the building. All home appliances carry the U.S. Energy Star® label. Light switches are linked to motion detectors, so the lights turn off whenever no movement is detected. For more detailed design and technology features, see Kim et al. (2015).

---

3. A smart home is defined as a dwelling incorporating a communications network that connects electrical appliances and services and allows them to be remotely controlled, monitored, or accessed (Poulson, Nicolle, & Galley, 2002).

4. The author visited this home in July 2014 and collected this information from the visit.

FIGURE 21.3
Green Tomorrow: Kitchen and Dining Room with Smart Technologies
Image credit: S.-K. Kim.

FIGURE 21.4
Green Tomorrow: Garage with Geothermal and Gray-Water Systems
Image credit: S.-K. Kim.

The parking lot uses the open-grid pavement method, which allows rainwater to penetrate the ground and to be returned to the natural environment. The roof garden collects rainwater. Many of the technologies demonstrated in this experimental home have been applied to actual homes since the early 2010s; however, some expensive technologies installed in this home are still in the testing phase (Samsung C&T Corporation, 2013).

Between January 2013 and January 2017, eight hundred housing projects that include over eighty thousand residential units were certified by G-SEED in Korea (Korea Environmental Industry and Technology Institute, 2017). The increase in CASBEE-certified homes is also evident (Institute for Building Environment and Energy Conservation, 2017). Since the number of certified homes consistently grows in Asia, sustainable design features in Asian housing will continue.

In Asia there are many environmentally friendly neighborhood or new town developments. For example, Japan shows many sustainable housing developments. The Japanese National Housing Corporation (JNHC) has designed and constructed many environmentally friendly and energy-efficient multifamily housing complexes and communities since the 1960s (Lee,

1997). Tama New Town, planned by JNHC from 1964 to 1966, had its first group of residents move into the community in the early 1970s. This development uses the natural topography of the site, preserving the landscape, planning low- and high-rise buildings, and providing open spaces, streams, and playgrounds (Park, 1995). Tama New Town offers residential units and commercial and retail areas. It also has a transit system that links the development to the Tokyo metropolitan area. Planning and design strategies used for the development process of Tama New Town have been applied in other new town developments in Asian countries, for example, Bundang and Ilsan New Towns (Park, 1995). Any of these new town projects try to preserve the natural landscape as much as possible, to provide walkable environments, and to encourage socioeconomic diversity among residents (Oh et al., 2004).

Bundang, located in the city of Seongnam in Korea and built in the 1990s, was planned to accommodate 160,000 to 170,000 residents, ninety thousand housing units, and commercial, retail, educational, health care, and entertainment facilities to reduce commute times and achieve work-life balance (Korea National Housing Corporation, 2002). This city-scale development offers various types of housing units that include high-rise, midrise, and low-rise multifamily housing complexes, single-family homes and townhouses, and mixed-use developments, facilitating socioeconomic diversity among residents. It also provides public transportation, walkability, and bikeability within the community (Lee, Oh, Kim, & Jang, 2000). Figure 21.5 shows the central park located in Bundang New Town.

Energy efficiency and environmental friendliness are also demonstrated in many single-family homes. Some of them were built to achieve the goals of zero-energy homes, which are defined as homes that produce as much energy as they consume (Johnston & Gibson, 2010). In South Korea several zero-energy homes have been constructed since 2010. One example is located in Dae-Jeon city, in an area called zeeHomes (or Jugdong Zero-Energy Home Neighborhood) (Kim, 2012b; Kim et al., 2015). This neighborhood development consists of six detached and seven attached single-family, owner-occupied homes that utilize energy-saving technologies such as solar

FIGURE 21.5
Bundang New Town, Developed during the 1990s
Image credit: S.-K. Kim.

systems with solar panels and batteries, geothermal heat pumps, and energy-efficient floor heating systems.

ZeeHomes use both active and passive solar design strategies to assist with heating and cooling. Active systems use mechanical means to collect, store, and distribute solar energy within the home. Passive systems use nonmechanical means to gain solar heat in the winter and prevent solar heating in the summer through design elements, including home orientation, walls, windows, and overhangs (Johnston & Gibson, 2010). Interior space planning also adapts passive design strategies. The floor plan offers natural air circulation and a comfortable indoor temperature without using mechanical ventilation or a furnace. In zeeHomes, for example, a home is divided into left and right sections. The left section has a living room and a kitchen with a dining space on the first floor and two bedrooms with a small living room on the second floor. The right section has a bedroom for the couple on the 1.5th floor. Family members can use the first floor as social space and the 1.5th floor and the second floor as private spaces. The high ceiling void that is continued from the first floor to the second floor in the living room space improves natural air circulation. The optimum void size avoids unnecessary heat loss, according to the architect. As a result of these energy-saving considerations, zeeHomes generate more energy than they consume, selling this energy back to energy providers. A postoccupancy evaluation survey conducted in 2013 shows that most residents are satisfied with the functions and efficiency of their zeeHomes (MA Architect, 2013).

High-Rise Multifamily Housing

In many Asian countries high-rise multifamily housing, defined as residential buildings higher than five or more stories, is common (Generalova & Generalova, 2014; Kim, 2012a; Pusca, 2010; Yeh & Yeun, 2010). Indeed, most high-rise residential buildings have more than fifteen stories (Park, 1995; Urban Redevelopment Authority, 2013; Yeh & Yeun, 2010).

Among the reasons for these high-rise residential complexes in many Asian urban areas are the high population density, the high job density, and the availability of good-quality schools in those areas (Zhang, Li, & Xue, 2015). These employment and educational opportunities have an important influence on housing choices and attract new residents to urban areas. To accommodate more people on limited lots, high-rise multifamily housing became an inevitable option in many Asian countries (Generalova & Generalova, 2014). Although there are no comprehensive data about the proportion of high-rise multifamily housing compared to single-family housing in Asia, the 2010 Korean census shows that 71 percent of all Korean housing units are found in multifamily housing buildings that are more than ten stories high (Statistics Korea, 2013). Singapore also includes famous urban housing projects led by the government (e.g., City View at Boon Keng, Park Central at Ang Mo Kio, and Natural Loft at Rishan) that are high-rise multifamily buildings (Generalova & Generalova, 2014; Yeh & Yeun, 2010).

The literature shows that many Asian governments support the construction of high-rise housing (Generalova & Generalova, 2014; Yeh & Yeun, 2010). The history of high-rise housing construction differs among Asian countries, but many began constructing this type of housing in the 1950s or 1960s (Korea National Housing Corporation, 2002). Many Asian countries lost their housing stock in wars. For instance, about 20 percent of the Korean housing stock was destroyed during World War II (Japanese colonial rule) and the Korean War (Korean Research Institute of Human Settlements, 2012). Japan and China also lost a number of housing units during World War II. These countries faced a shortage of housing and had to replace demolished or damaged units. Massive housing construction was undertaken during the modernization period so that the government could provide homes for many people quickly and efficiently (Hinokidani, 2006). The construction of high-rise multifamily housing after World War II was influenced by Western countries such as the United States and the UK (Korea National Housing Corporation, 2002; Korean Research Institute of Human Settlements, 2012). In the case of Singapore, where public housing is supplied for many citizens, the government has relied on high-rise housing as an efficient way of providing enough units of adequate residential quality for owners or renters (Generalova & Generalova, 2014).

High-rise residential buildings have reinforced concrete and solid building foundations (Korea National Housing Corporation, 2002). They are structurally durable, making it easy to stack up many units in one building. To avoid monotonous building designs, however, architects try to offer various floor plans in one building (French, 2006). In addition, exteriors of high-rise housing in new towns in Japan, Korea, and Singapore show interesting shapes and textures. Punggol Waterfront Housing in Singapore and Minami Osawa Housing Complex in Japan are good examples of varied exteriors (Park, 1995; Singapore Urban Redevelopment Authority, 2013). Instead of being simple cubic shapes, these buildings include sections of differing heights. Window frames, balconies, and exterior walls combine different shapes and colors and mixes of rough and smooth textures (Park, 1995; Singapore Urban Redevelopment Authority, 2013).

Another characteristic of high-rise multifamily housing in Asia is the incorporation of sustainable design principles. This movement is encouraged by policy through awarding tax incentives to construction companies and designers whose buildings are sustainable (Lee, 1999). The New Millennium Greenville development in Yongin, Korea, is a good example of a sustainable multifamily housing neighborhood where environmentally friendly design strategies and construction technologies are applied. The development was planned in 1998 and completed in 2002 by the Korea Land and Housing Corporation, a government-associated housing construction and planning company, and certified by the G-SEED system (Green Standard for Energy and Environmental Design Center, 2015). This housing community, consisting of about two thousand units, utilizes sustainable design principles for housing, community-oriented design for improving social interactions and sense of community, and smart home technologies for improving the quality of life.

Examples of sustainable design in this community include the development's proximity to public transportation and commercial areas, the south-facing orientation of housing units to capture daylight through walls and windows, and the use of energy-efficient heating boilers and environmentally friendly materials and finishes. Some of the housing units have large terraces connected to a patio of the building, providing rooftop gardens.

This housing site is also distinguished by community design strategies that promote social interactions among residents and a child-friendly neighborhood design. There are six open spaces within the site, offering child-friendly, safe play areas with water streams, sculptures, water wheels, and

FIGURE 21.6
Common Space with Water Streams in New Millennium Greenville
Image credit: S.-K. Kim.

fountains. Seating and gathering spaces around the play areas encourage social interaction among residents. Figure 21.6 shows one playground space in New Millennium Greenville.

This type of high-rise multifamily housing development is expected to spread in many Asian countries. Urban population densities are increasing and government-led housing supplies still exist in many Asian countries (Generalova & Generalova, 2014). Moreover, high-rise multifamily housing is regarded as an efficient way to increase homeownership rates by offering more housing units (Daelim, Inc., 2015; Hyundai, Inc., 2015). As seen in recent examples, the improvement in interior and neighborhood design quality and the affordability (i.e., lower purchasing prices, low interest rates for mortgage loans, and reasonable maintenance fees) of high-rise multifamily housing developments may positively affect the quality of residents' lives. Therefore, many countries still support this type of high-rise housing.

High-Tech Amenities in Housing

Amenities enhance the quality of built environments for occupants. High-tech amenities improve the convenience and comfort for residents through the use of the Internet or other communication services (Kim, Lee, & Yim, 2009; Schmitz, 2000). Examples of such amenities are small systems planned in the interior of a home, such as a home automation system installed on the living room wall, or large, community-scale systems, such as renewable energy collectors (Kim et al., 2009; Schmitz, 2000). High-tech amenities are found in single- and multifamily housing along with numerous inventions and applications of Internet-based devices (Kim et al., 2009).

One of the most progressive examples of high-tech homes is found in Japan. It is the Real-time Operating System Nucleus (TRON) model home in Japan, designed by Ken Sakamura in Nishi Azabu and built in 1988 (Sakamura, 1989). A total of 380 computers were used for communications among the interconnected appliances, remotely controlled by engineers. Dozens of speakers were placed throughout the home because many gadgets were voice

TABLE 21.1
High-Tech Systems Offered in Residential Environments

System	Characteristics
SAFETY AND SECURITY	
Invasion and robbery prevention	Automatically reports to police or maintenance office when homes or apartments are invaded
Apartment building gate control	Coded access control system for an apartment building
Fire and gas detection	Automatically trips alarm and reports to police or fire station when a fire or gas leak is detected
Elevator safety	Automatically trips alarm and reports to maintenance office or elevator service center
Emergency alarm	Automatically trips alarm and reports to maintenance office or hospital when residents become ill
Apartment unit gate control	Coded access control system for an apartment unit
Closed-circuit television (CCTV) monitoring	Monitors hallways and elevators for security purposes
Integration key	Allows people to open an apartment building entrance and a unit entrance with one key
INDOOR ENVIRONMENT CONTROL	
Automatic lighting	Automatic on/off system with a sensor that detects movement
Dimming control	Remote-control system for adjusting brightness of indoor lighting
One-button lighting on/off	With one button, every light in the home can be turned on or off
Automatic curtain and blind	Remote-controlled curtains and blinds
Heating control	Maintains the temperature set by residents
Air-conditioning control	Maintains the temperature set by residents
HOUSEKEEPING ASSISTANCE	
Indoor garbage collecting	A garbage drop installed on the wall inside of an apartment; residents can dump their garbage through the drop and it will be transferred to a collection spot
Automatic water	Water on/off system with a sensor detecting movement
Cleaning	Air intakes on the walls designed for removing the dust that is collected by a vacuum cleaner
HEALTH RELATED	
Intelligent bathtub	Whirlpool bathtub that controls the amount and temperature of water
Central water purification	Water filtration and purification system located in the center of an apartment complex; purified water is distributed to individual apartment units through pipes
INTERNET-BASED SERVICE	
Communication	Interphone and telephone system that operates through the Internet
Remote meter reading	Automatically monitors and records utility meter readings
AUTOMATIC CONTROL	
Indoor remote control	Remote control to turn electronic devices on or off
Speech recognition	Allows voice commands to perform functions or turn devices on or off
Remote control	Allows remote control of home electronic devices through the Internet

Source: Kim, Lee, & Yim, 2009. Reprinted by permission of Taylor and Francis Ltd., http://www.tandfonline.com.

activated. The kitchen is equipped with one-touch water faucets and a water temperature control system. The bathroom has an emergency call button that connects to the police station or the hospital (Sakamura & Koshizuka, 2005). The TRON model home concept has been developed further under the name U-Home (ubiquitous home) and applied in many residential building projects in Taiwan and Japan (Sakamura & Koshizuka, 2005).

Another example of an experimental home that provides high-tech amenities is the Toyota Dream Home PAPI, which was also designed by Ken

Sakamura but applied more advanced technologies and equipment. The technology-friendly features of this home reflect "ubiquitous computing technologies." That is, several computer technologies control various home automation systems (Sakamura, 1987). The Toyota Dream Home PAPI is also environmentally friendly, made of recyclable aluminum and glass. This home uses computer networking for controlling machines and equipment in the home, which is similar to TRON, but the networking technologies used for the PAPI are more advanced. A system named Ubiquitous Communicator (UC) is used to control the appliances and systems in the PAPI.

In Korea high-tech amenities for housing have been supported by policies since 1998, when vision Cyber Korea 21 was proposed. The Ministry of Information and Communication recommended the provision of free high-speed Internet service in residential buildings as a default at the beginning of policy implementation (Kim et al., 2009). This enabled more households of different socioeconomic levels to have Internet service in their homes. This policy also expedited the development of Internet-based home automation systems, which can be remotely controlled by the residents (Kim et al., 2009). This strong support through incentives from the government resulted in an increase in new multifamily housing buildings offering various systems as high-tech amenities for residents. These can be categorized into six types based on the function of the systems or devices, as presented in table 21.1.

Some of these technologies are more complicated and expensive than others to implement in homes. Several systems, such as the apartment building gate control system, the emergency alarm system, the one-button lighting on/off system, and the remote meter reading system, have been installed in low-income housing complexes in Korea (Yim, Kim, Lee, & Lee, 2000). These systems have also been installed recently in many homes in other Asian countries, such as Singapore, China, and Japan, in order to improve energy efficiency, provide security for residents, and enhance the convenience of residents' daily lives (Piller, 2016).

Housing for Aging in Place

Like many Western countries, Asian countries have seen a growth in their aging population. The Asian population age sixty-five or older was about 206,800,000 in 2000, and it is expected to increase to over 450,000,000 in 2020 (East-West Center, 2002). For example, in Korea more than 9 percent of the population was sixty-five years or older in 2007. This proportion is expected to increase to 24 percent by 2030 (Korea National Statistical Office, 2007). Japan is expected to go through a similar increase in terms of its aged and aging population (World Population Review, 2014; Yashiro, 2001).

Many seniors in Asia prefer aging in place, living close to their children, relatives, or support networks (Kim, 2006; Yoon, Kang, & Song, 2004; see chapter 17). Until the late 1980s, retirement communities, independent living communities, continuing care retirement communities (CCRC), and nursing homes were rare in Asian countries because it was a familial norm for elderly parents to live with their adult children (Park, Choi, Kwon, Yoo, & Paik, 2006; Yoon et al., 2004). Yet such facilities have become popular due to the increasing proportion of seniors and the decrease in family size (Kim & Kim, 2015).

For example, the first CCRC in Korea was built in 1988, although acceptance of this type of housing was slow (Yoodang-maeul, 2014). However, the socioeconomic and familial characteristics of older people have changed. Older people have become more financially and physically independent compared to the elderly in previous generations (Kim et al., 2009). Much literature indicates that seniors in Asia are better educated, more independent of their adult children, and more familiar with technology than previous generations (World Population Review, 2014; Yoon et al., 2004). Using the computer or the Internet, home appliances, or electrical devices became popular among the older population in the 1990s (Kim et al., 2009; Kim & Ahn, 2010). More senior residents were willing to move to retirement communities while staying connected with their family members (Kim & Oh, 2014). The senior housing supply has thus been active since the 1990s, which results in a number of quality senior housing options available for people at different socioeconomic levels in these countries (Kim & Oh, 2014; Park, 2007; Yashiro, 2001).

Many postretirement communities in Asia are neighborhood-type developments that include residential buildings and shared outdoor spaces (Kim & Oh, 2014). However, some postretirement homes are in mixed-use buildings with retail and commercial spaces on the first floor and residential units on the upper floors (Chun, 2010; Kim & Oh, 2014). This is because of higher land prices and development density restrictions in urban areas (Kim & Oh, 2014). Common features of postretirement communities are shared spaces such as swimming pools, fitness rooms, libraries, and big gathering spaces. Outdoor spaces in such communities provide walking, biking, and exercising areas (Kim, 2011). Housing units in these communities are typically wheelchair accessible and have universal design features (Kim et al., 2009; Yoodang-maeul, 2014). The features of Asian housing for seniors present a rapid growth in quantity and quality of housing, despite its short history compared to Western countries.

Homeownership

Among Asian countries homeownership rates differ depending on each country's housing market condition; housing policies and programs of the government; the level of engagement of governments, the private sector, and nonprofit organizations in housing supply and management; and housing finance (Zhu, 2006). Many Asian governments, similar to U.S. federal and local governments, offer diverse home mortgage programs, housing vouchers, and tax credits (Chan, Davies, & Gyntelberg, 2006) to improve housing affordability for purchasing, renting, and maintaining homes.

Overall homeownership rates and the residential property index in 2013 in select Asian countries are presented in table 21.2. The residential property index is calculated based on the price of land and detached homes and condominiums (Trading Economics, 2017a, 2017b). As table 21.2 shows, China and Singapore, where social housing is common, have higher homeownership rates than Korea and Japan.

Unsurprisingly, these homeownership rates are lower in urban areas, however. As mentioned earlier, the population, jobs, housing construction, and good-quality schools are concentrated in urban areas in many Asian countries (Zhang et al., 2015). These unequal housing opportunities increase housing prices in urban areas, which consequently restrains many urban

TABLE 21.2
Homeownership Rates (2013) and Residential Property Index (2016) in Select Asian Countries

Country	Homeownership rate, 2013	Residential property index, 2016
China	90.0%	11.80
Singapore	90.9%	137.20
Korea	53.6%	101.40
Japan	61.9%	106.28

Source: Author, based on Trading Economics, 2017a, 2017b.
Note: Index value for the United States is 0.00.

households from purchasing their own home. Therefore, diverse efforts have been made by various housing-related stakeholders to reduce housing inequality and unaffordability in urban areas in many Asian countries (Ronald & Jin, 2010).

CONCLUSION

Asian housing that predated the modernization period served as a symbolic entity that reflected occupants' socioeconomic status and followed a long tradition, exhibiting diverse cultural characteristics (Kim, 2012b). Simultaneously, homes designed and built during this period respected nature and complemented their natural surroundings. Construction techniques were vernacular and neutral looking, using various wood structures.

Asian housing in the twentieth and twenty-first centuries has merged with new social and global trends. Housing design and planning follow a variety of sustainability principles and practices. Fast-growing technologies facilitate the construction of high-rise housing structures. This residential type became most representative in many Asian countries, particularly in urban areas, because it provides a great quantity of housing units and homeownership opportunities within the limited amount of developable lands. In contemporary Asian housing sustainable design practices are frequently realized in high-rise housing projects that target low- to high-income families.

At the same time, advanced residential technologies are being invented and applied in the interior and the exterior of homes designed for various socioeconomic groups. Many countries in Asia have also experienced an increase in aging populations, so housing design and community planning consider how to accommodate their needs. Designers and planners in Asia are mindful of the aging-in-place concept and solutions. They are also willing to adapt residential technologies to accommodate housing arrangements for older residents (Kim et al., 2009).

These progressive and dynamic changes in housing have been improving the quality of residential environments in Asia. Considering the diversity in political, social, and demographic characteristics of Asian countries, each country's strategies and practical means for resolving housing issues can be different from others'. However, the ultimate goal of improving quality of life and well-being for individual residents seems to be agreed upon among Asian nations. Their ongoing efforts to reach this goal are expected to continue.

REFERENCES

Building Research Establishment. (2015). Building Research Establishment Environmental Assessment Methodology (BREEAM). Retrieved September 1, 2015, from https://www.bre.co.uk/page.jsp?id=829.

Chan, E., Davies, M., & Gyntelberg, J. (2006). The role of government-supported housing finance agencies in Asia. *BIS Quarterly Review*, December. Retrieved March 1, 2017, from https://ssrn.com/abstract=1632354.

Chun, S. (2010). Why are they paying attention to the urban silver town? Design House, Culture and People. Retrieved May 1, 2014, from http://happy.design.co.kr/in_magazine/sub.html?at=view&info_id=53434&c_id=00010005.

Daelim, Inc. (2015). *Annual development and construction plan*. Retrieved March 1, 2015, from http://www.daelim-apt.co.kr/Appl_list01.action.

East-West Center. (2002). The future of population in Asia: Asia's aging population. Retrieved December 1, 2015, from http://www.eastwestcenter.org/fileadmin/stored/misc/FuturePop08Aging.pdf.

French, H. (2006). *New urban housing*. New Haven, Conn.: Yale University Press.

Generalova, E., & Generalova, V. (2014). Designing high-rise housing: The Singapore experience. *International Journal of Tall Buildings and Urban Habitats, 4*, 40–45.

Green Standard for Energy and Environmental Design Center (2015). Overview of Green Standard for Energy and Environmental Design (G-SEED) System. Retrieved January 15, 2016, from https://ecohouse.lh.or.kr/index.do?menuno=132.

Hinokidani, M. (2006). Housing, family, and gender. In Y. Hirayama & R. Ronald, (Eds.), *Housing and social transition in Japan* (pp. 115–120). Oxford: Taylor and Francis.

Hyundai, Inc. (2015). *We build tomorrow: 2015 Hyundai E&C sustainability report*. Retrieved March 1, 2015, from http://www.hdec.kr/KR/PRRoom/FileSustainability.aspx#annual.

Indian Green Building Council. (2015). IGBC rating systems. Retrieved November 5, 2015, from https://igbc.in/igbc/redirectHtml.htm?redVal=showratingSysnosign.

Institute for Building Environment and Energy Conservation. (2017). Japan sustainable building database. Retrieved March 15, 2017, from http://www.ibec.or.jp/jsbd/index.htm.

Japan Green Build Council and Japan Sustainable Building Consortium. (2015). Comprehensive Assessment System for Built Environment Efficiency (CASBEE). Retrieved December 2, 2015, from http://www.ibec.or.jp/casbee/english/.

Johnston, D., & Gibson, S. (2010). *Toward a zero-energy home: A complete guide to energy self-sufficiency at home*. Newtown, Conn.: Taunton Press.

Kang, Y.-H. (1994). *History of Korean housing*. Seoul: Kimundang.

Kangdong-gu. (2014). Amsadong prehistoric stone age site. Retrieved May 2, 2014, from http://sunsa.gangdong.go.kr/main.jsp.

Kim, M. (2006). The preference of housing for the elderly among the middle-aged households for aging society. *Journal of the Korean Housing Association, 17*(1), 117–126.

Kim, M., & Kim, S.-K. (2013). Baby boomers' residential life images and supportive service needs at post-retirement homes: With a focus on Korean-American immigrants. *Journal of the Korean Institute of Interior Design, 22*(5), 3–10.

Kim, M., & Oh, J. (2014). The fundamental study for development and planning of Korean style university-based continuing care retirement communities: With focused on local university. *Journal of the Korean Institute of Interior Design, 16*(1), 108–113.

Kim, S.-K. (2012a). High-rise housing. In A. Carswell (Ed.), *The encyclopedia of housing* (pp. 262–265). Thousand Oaks, Calif.: Sage.

Kim, S.-K. (2012b). Housing abroad: Asia. In A. Carswell (Ed.), *The encyclopedia of housing* (pp. 312–315). Thousand Oaks, Calif.: Sage.

Kim, S.-K, Abrams, R., & Seidel, A. (2004). *Post-application of Korean sustainable indicators for multi-family housing with focus on the design of community centers*. Proceedings: The 2004 EAAE-ARCC (Architectural Research Centers Consortium) Conference (pp. 203–211), Dublin, Ireland, June 2–4, 2004.

Kim, S.-K., & Ahn, M. (2010). *Residential technology for elderly Americans and Koreans aging at home*. Proceedings of the Housing Education and Research Association (HERA) annual conference (pp. 135–148), Portland, Ore., November 3–6, 2010.

Kim, S.-K., Ahn, M., & Tremblay, K. (2008). Contemporary kitchen and dining space design in urban multifamily housing in Korea. *Housing and Society, 35*(2), 117–138.

Kim, M., & Kim, S. (2015). Future residents' opinions about architectural features and development strategies for the university-based retirement community. *Journal of the Korean Housing Association, 26*(6), 181–190. http://dx.doi.org/10.6107/JKHA.2015.26.6.181.

Kim, S.-K., Lee, S.-J., Kwon, H.-J., & Ahn, M. (2015). Zero-energy home development in Korea: Energy-efficient and environmentally friendly design features and future directions. *Housing and Society, 42*(3), 1–17.

Kim, S.-K., Lee, Y., & Yim, M. (2009). Hi-tech amenities for the elderly: The technological assistance needs of elderly Koreans aging at home. *Journal of Housing for the Elderly, 23*(3), 204–226.

Kim, S.-S. (2011). Living in a senior town Samsung Nobel County: Achieving ISO 9001. *Suwon* [newspaper]. Retrieved June 20, 2014, from http://www.urisuwon.com/sub_read.html?uid=14813.

Korea Environmental Industry and Technology Institute. (2017). G-SEED-certified home and building database. Retrieved March 15, 2017, from https://www.gbc.re.kr/app/data/authStatus/view.do.

Korea Ministry of Land, Infrastructure, and Transport. (2013). Green Standards of Energy and Environmental Design (G-SEED) Standards. Department of Green Architecture. Retrieved March 1, 2014, from http://www.law.go.kr/admRulLsInfoP.do?admRulSeq=2000000024359#AJAX.

Korea National Housing Corporation. (2002). *Housing and city 40 years*. Sungnam-city, Korea: Korea National Housing Corporation.

Korea National Statistical Office. (2015). *Current status and future prediction of world and Korea population*. Retrieved August 8, 2015, from http://kostat.go.kr/smart/news/file_dn.jsp?aSeq=347102&ord=1.

Korean Research Institute of Human Settlements. (2012). *2011 Modular business for economic development experiences: Strategies for the Korean affordable housing development*. Pyungchon: Korean Research Institute of Human Settlements.

Lee, K., Oh, S., Kim, S-K., & Jang, S. (2000). *Policies and systems for the development of sustainable human settlements III*. Seongnam, Kyonggido: Housing and Urban Research Institute, Korea Land and Housing Corporation.

Lee, K.-I. (1997). *World collective theme houses*. Seoul: Balen.

Lee, Y.-M. (1999). *Indicator development for assessing outdoor environmental quality in multifamily housing estates*. (Unpublished doctoral dissertation). Yonsei University, Seoul, Korea.

M.A. Architect. (2013). The zeeHome: Jokdong zero energy houses. Retrieved March 1, 2014, from http://www.amchamkorea.org/publications/GBF/4.%20Session%202_Mr.%20Jongil%20Kim(new).pdf.

Mak, M. Y., & Ng, S. T. (2005). The art and science of feng shui: A study on architects' perception. *Building and Environment, 40*, 427–434.

Martison, T. (2009). *The atlas of American architecture*. New York: Rizzoli International.

Oh, S., Chang, S., Kim, S.-K., & Lee, K. (2004). A study of the assessment of environment-friendly outdoor spaces in housing estates. *Journal of the Architectural Institute of Korea, 20*(6), 199–206.

Paramore, L., Gong, C. F., & Murata, N. (2010). *Japan home: Inspirational design ideas*. North Clarendon, Vt.: Tuttle.

Park, C.-S. (1995). Lesson of Tama New Town development and Belle-Colline Minami Osawa site. *Architecture, 39*(1), 52–61.

Park, J., Choi, E., Kwon, H., Yoo, B., & Paik, H. (2006). *Rental housing model development corresponding to the needs from the aging society*. Seongnam, Korea: Korea National Housing Corporation.

Park, S.-B. (2007). Fundamental study on housing for the elderly through an analysis of senior adults' needs. *Journal of the Architectural Institute of Korea: Planning and Design, 23*(5), 49–58.

Pile, J. F. (2007). *Interior design*. (4th ed.). London: Pearson.

Piller, F. (2016). The smart house: Japanese technology and standards. Retrieved March 1,

2017, from https://www.japanindustrynews.com/2016/05/smart-house-japanese-technology-standards/.

Poulson, D., Nicolle, C. A., & Galley, M. (2002). Review of the current status of research on smart homes and other domestic assistive technologies in support of the TAHI trials. Loughborough, UK: Loughborough University. Retrieved December 1, 2015, from http://citeseerx.ist.psu.edu/viewdoc/download?doi=10.1.1.463.8922&rep=rep1&type=pdf.

Pusca, A. (2010, August 23). High-rise housing. International Debate Education Association. Retrieved March 1, 2015, from http://www.idebate.org/debatabase/topic_details.php?topicID=572.

Ronald, R., & Jin, M. (2010). Homeownership in South Korea: Examining sector underdevelopment. *Urban Studies, 47*(11), 2367–2388.

Sakamura, K. (1987). The TRON project. *IEEE Micro, 7*(2), 8–16.

Sakamura, K. (1989). The TRON project. *Microprocessors and Microsystems, 13*(8), 493–502.

Sakamura, K., & Koshizuka, N. (2005). *Ubiquitous computing technologies for ubiquitous learning.* Proceedings of the 2005 IEEE International Workshop on Wireless and Mobile Technologies in Education, Tokushima, Japan, November 28–30, 2005.

Samsung C&T Corporation. (2013). *Green tomorrow: 2010 Raemian style special edition.* Gyeonggi, Korea: Samsung C&T Corporation.

Schmitz, A. (Ed.). (2000). *Multifamily housing development handbook.* Washington, D.C.: Urban Land Institute.

Singapore Urban Redevelopment Authority. (2013). *Designing our city: Planning for a sustainable Singapore.* Retrieved May 15, 2014, from https://www.ura.gov.sg/skyline/skyline12/skyline12-03/special/URA_Designing%20our%20City%20Supplement_July12.pdf.

Statistics Korea. (2013). Korea census. Retrieved October 1, 2015, from http://www.jkaptn.com/news/articleView.html?idxno=2176.

Steven Holl Architects. (2014). Linked hybrid. Retrieved September 30, 2014, from http://www.stevenholl.com/project-detail.php?id=58.

Trading Economics. (2017a). Japan home ownership rate, 1988–2017. Retrieved March 20, 2017, from http://www.tradingeconomics.com/japan/home-ownership-rate.

Trading Economics. (2017b). Japan residential property price index. Retrieved March 20, 2017, from http://www.tradingeconomics.com/japan/housing-index.

United Nations. (1996). Habitat II: Second UN Conference on Human Settlements, Istanbul, June 3–14. Retrieved March 1, 2014, from http://www.un.org/en/development/devagenda/habitat.shtml.

Urban Redevelopment Authority. (2013). *Designing our city: Planning for a sustainable Singapore.* Retrieved April 1, 2015, from https://www.ura.gov.sg/uol/publications/research-resources/books-videos/2012-07_designing_our_city.aspx.

U.S. General Services Administration. (2015). Sustainable design. Retrieved May 15, 2015, from www.gsa.gov/sustainabledesign.

U.S. Green Building Council. (2014). *LEED v4 AP BD+C candidate handbook: Building design and construction.* Retrieved April 25, 2014, from http://www.usgbc.org/resources/leed-v4-building-design-and-construction-redline-current-version.

Van Vliet, W., & Hirayama, Y. (1994). Housing conditions and affordability in Japan. *Housing Studies, 9*(3), 351–353.

World Population Review. (2014). Japan population. Retrieved June 20, 2014, from http://worldpopulationreview.com/countries/japan-population/.

Yashiro, N. (2001). *Social implications of demographic change in Japan.* Paper presented at "Seismic Shifts: The Economic Impact of Demographic Change," Federal Reserve Bank of Boston, June 2001. Retrieved June 20, 2014, from https://www.bostonfed.org/economic/conf/conf46/conf46k.pdf.

Yeh, A., & B. Yuen. (2010). Introduction: High-rise living in Asian cities. In B. Yuen & A. Yeh (Eds.), *High-rise living in Asian cities* (pp. 1–8). New York: Springer.

Yim, M., Kim, S.-K., Lee, Y., & Lee, C. (2000). *Development on the model of intelligent apartment housing corresponding to residents' demands I.* Kyeonggi: Housing and Urban Research Institute of Korea National Housing Corporation.

Yoodang-maeul. (2014). Introduction to Yoodang-maeul. Retrieved June 25, 2014, from http://yudang.co.kr/.

Yoon, J., Kang, M., & Song, H. (2004). *Aging population and senior housing: Current status of senior housing and policy directions in the aging society.* Anyang-City: Korea Research Institute for Human Settlements.

Zhang, D., Li, X., & Xue, J. (2015). Education inequality between rural and urban areas of the People's Republic of China, migrants' children education and some implications. *Asian Development Review, 32*(1), 196–224.

Zhu, H. (2006). The structure of housing finance markets and house prices in Asia. *BIS Quarterly Review.* Retrieved March 15, 2017, from https://ssrn.com/abstract=1632353.

Chapter 22 Housing in Europe

JEAN MEMKEN AND SHIRLEY NIEMEYER

This chapter explores households and housing in Europe. The European Union (EU) extends across many different cultures, climate zones, and landscape settings. More than five hundred million people are spread over the twenty-eight member countries, and they reside in a wide variety of building types. There are many differences among European countries in terms of housing policies, home design, and lifestyle (Economidou et al., 2011). However, the need for safe, accessible, quality housing is a common goal across the European Union (European Parliament, 2013). This chapter explores how the various countries in the European Union strive to meet that need. Below we discuss household structure, homeownership, renting, types of dwelling, and housing affordability in Europe.

HOUSEHOLD STRUCTURE IN EUROPE

Until recently, the nuclear family had been the predominant household type in Europe (European Union—Eurostat, 2013). However, over the past few decades there have been changes in the European household structure. Of all households in the EU in 2014, 32.7 percent were headed by a single person, followed by 24.7 percent with two adults without children and 20.2 percent with two adults with dependent children (European Union—Eurostat, 2015). These proportions impact the demand, supply, and design of housing.

The increase in the proportion of single-person households started in the twentieth century and has continued to emerge all over Europe. Reasons for this increase include postponing or foregoing marriage and childbearing, divorce, and increased life expectancy (Alders & Manting, 1999; Beier, Hofäcker, Marchese, & Rupp, 2010; Iacovou & Skew, 2011). As the proportion of single-person households has continued to grow, there has been greater demand for smaller living units with only one or two bedrooms, possibly on one level, particularly for single elderly people living independently (Organization for Economic Co-operation and Development, 2011). A comparison of the proportion of household types within the countries in the European Union can be found in table 22.1.

TABLE 22.1
Proportions of Household Types in the European Union, 2014

	Single adult with children	Single adult without children	Couple with children	Couple without children	Other type of household with children	Other type of household without children
EU (28 members)	4.5%	32.7%	20.2%	24.7%	5.6%	12.3%
Austria	3.0%	37.0%	17.2%	23.9%	5.7%	13.1%
Belgium	5.7%	28.3%	22.3%	27.3%	5.2%	11.2%
Bulgaria	2.8%	26.5%	17.4%	25.5%	8.5%	19.2%
Croatia	2.0%	24.5%	19.5%	18.0%	14.0%	22.0%
Cyprus	3.7%	20.0%	26.8%	23.2%	8.8%	17.4%
Czech Republic	4.7%	30.0%	22.8%	26.5%	4.6%	11.4%
Denmark	8.3%	42.5%	19.9%	23.9%	1.8%	3.7%
Estonia	6.8%	35.6%	21.5%	21.4%	5.1%	9.6%
Finland	1.6%	40.3%	19.0%	31.7%	2.0%	5.4%
France	6.1%	34.9%	21.9%	26.5%	3.6%	7.1%
Germany	3.8%	40.3%	15.2%	28.7%	3.1%	8.9%
Greece	1.8%	30.2%	21.1%	24.2%	4.7%	18.0%
Hungary	4.1%	32.7%	18.7%	21.3%	6.9%	16.3%
Ireland	6.3%	22.1%	28.9%	20.9%	6.3%	15.4%
Italy	2.8%	33.1%	21.5%	19.7%	6.0%	16.9%
Latvia	5.7%	32.2%	16.2%	17.7%	10.0%	18.3%
Lithuania	6.6%	36.2%	17.6%	18.0%	7.1%	14.5%
Luxembourg	4.5%	34.3%	27.4%	22.1%	4.8%	6.9%
Malta	3.2%	19.0%	23.8%	21.3%	9.9%	22.9%
Netherlands	4.3%	36.5%	21.8%	29.4%	2.9%	5.2%
Poland	3.7%	22.2%	23.3%	22.4%	11.8%	16.5%
Portugal	4.3%	20.9%	23.9%	23.8%	8.4%	18.7%
Romania	2.5%	27.4%	20.6%	19.3%	13.2%	17.0%
Slovakia	3.4%	21.8%	22.8%	20.9%	11.2%	19.8%
Slovenia	2.7%	32.8%	22.2%	20.4%	6.6%	15.2%
Spain	3.5%	25.0%	23.3%	21.8%	7.3%	19.1%
Sweden	6.3%	47.9%	19.5%	22.2%	1.7%	2.5%
United Kingdom	7.2%	31.4%	19.5%	26.3%	4.6%	10.9%

Source: European Union—Eurostat, 2015.

Another trend found in most European Union countries is that young adults are more likely to live in the parental household for a longer period of time than in previous decades (Alders & Manting, 1999). About 28.9 percent of young adults (ages twenty-five to thirty-four), or about fifty-one million, lived with at least one parent in 2016 (European Commission—Eurostat, 2016). Table 22.2 shows the proportion of young adults who lived in the parental home for each country in the European Union. Denmark, Sweden, and Finland have the lowest proportions of young adults living with their parents (3.0, 3.7, and 4.0 percent, respectively), whereas Slovakia, Greece, and Croatia have the highest proportions of young adults living with their parents (53.7, 51.5, and 57.1 percent, respectively) (European Commission—Eurostat, 2016).

TABLE 22.2

Percentage of Young Adults (Ages 25–34) Living with Their Parents in the European Union, by Country

	Total	Males	Females
EU (28 members)	**28.9%**	**35.6%**	**22.2%**
Austria	20.5%	25.1%	16.4%
Belgium	17.2%	22.0%	12.5%
Bulgaria	47.7%	62.2%	32.4%
Croatia	57.1%	68.1%	45.9%
Cyprus	27.3%	37.7%	17.6%
Czech Republic	34.1%	41.5%	26.0%
Denmark	3.0%	4.4%	1.7%
Estonia	22.7%	26.8%	18.5%
Finland	4.0%	6.2%	1.6%
France	11.1%	15.4%	7.1%
Germany	18.3%	25.2%	11.8%
Greece	51.5%	60.7%	42.3%
Hungary	47.5%	56.6%	38.2%
Ireland	21.4%	27.6%	16.2%
Italy	48.4%	56.8%	40.2%
Latvia	36.1%	42.6%	29.4%
Lithuania	29.4%	37.7%	20.8%
Luxembourg	24.6%	32.5%	17.0%
Malta	20.5%	55.1%	34.9%
Netherlands	9.5%	13.5%	5.5%
Poland	44.1%	49.9%	38.2%
Portugal	45.1%	50.8%	39.6%
Romania	47.9%	60.8%	34.0%
Slovakia	53.7%	60.6%	46.4%
Slovenia	43.6%	51.4%	34.8%
Spain	39.6%	45.9%	33.4%
Sweden	3.7%	4.9%	2.5%
United Kingdom	15.5%	20.9%	10.2%

Source: European Commission—Eurostat, 2016.

In every country in the European Union, a higher proportion of young men (35.6 percent) lived with their parents than young women (22.2 percent), as of 2015 (European Commission—Eurostat, 2016). The largest differences between genders living in the parental home are found in Bulgaria, Finland, Denmark, and the Netherlands, where the proportion of young men living with their parents exceeds that of young women by more than half (Choroszewicz & Wolff, 2010). Reasons for this phenomenon include the lack of affordable housing alternatives and/or being a student. Interestingly, around 20 percent of young adults in Europe regard living with parents as an alternative that offers fewer responsibilities and more comfort (European Commission—Eurostat, 2009; European Union—Eurostat, 2012). As leaving the parental home appears to be increasingly delayed for young adults in many European countries, demands for housing that better accommodates these households with adult children will increase (Forrest & Yip, 2013).

Other types of households are also emerging in Europe. One is the reconstituted family, which is composed of simple stepfamilies with children from just one side, complex stepfamilies with children from both sides or with shared children, and multifragmented families with more divergent family formations. Over time, these reconstituted or "patchwork" families, as they are also called, have been steadily increasing (Uhlendorff, Rupp, & Euteneuer, 2011). The other emerging family type is the rainbow family, which includes a same-sex couple with children or a single lesbian or gay adult raising children as a single parent. As more countries in the European Union give gay and lesbian couples the opportunity to legalize their unions, the predominance of these types of households will increase (Uhlendorff, Rupp, & Euteneuer, 2011).

Just as in the United States, European household types have important consequences for housing in terms of both structure and quantity. In the past, most urban planners, architects, and designers based their housing design ideas on the nuclear family. Today they must consider the needs and preferences of a variety of diverse households. As household types continue to evolve, a number of policy areas, including housing policy, will need to address this diversity in household forms (Organization for Economic Co-operation and Development, 2011).

HOMEOWNERSHIP IN EUROPE

In the European Union, 70 percent of households lived in owner-occupied housing in 2014, although there is a vast range among countries. For example, Romania, at 96.1 percent, has the highest homeownership rate, while Germany, at 52.5 percent, has the lowest homeownership rate (European Commission—Eurostat, 2016). Romania, Croatia, and Bulgaria, which were recently admitted to the European Union, have relatively high homeownership rates, with 96.1, 89.7, and 84.3 percent, respectively (European Commission—Eurostat, 2016). Table 22.3 shows a comparison of homeownership rates for all countries in the European Union.

More specifically, of all households in the European Union, approximately 70 percent were homeowners, with 27.1 percent living in an owner-occupied home with a mortgage and 42.8 percent living in an owner-occupied home without a mortgage in 2014 (European Commission—Eurostat, 2016). By comparison, in the United States 65.1 percent lived in owner-occupied housing in 2010. Of all homeowners in the United States, 30 percent of owner-occupied homeowners had no mortgage (U.S. Bureau of the Census, 2011a, 2011b).

Over the past decades, the homeownership rate in the European Union has increased, mostly due to policy changes. For example, in Great Britain and Wales, the British Right-to-Buy and Right-to-Acquire Programs have permitted a large number of tenants in social housing to become homeowners since 1980 and 1997, respectively (Mace, 2013). These programs have allowed tenants of public housing to purchase their units at a discounted price. Although tenants could take advantage of steep discounts, many units were still unaffordable to many low-income renters. Since 1980 (Right-to-Buy) and 1997 (Right-to-Acquire), about two million homes that were pre-

TABLE 22.3
Homeownership Rates in the European Union, by Country, 2014

	Rate		Rate
EU (28 members)	70.1%	Italy	73.1%
Austria	57.2%	Latvia	80.9%
Belgium	72.0%	Lithuania	89.9%
Bulgaria	84.3%	Luxembourg	72.5%
Croatia	89.7%	Malta	80.0%
Cyprus	72.9%	Netherlands	67.0%
Czech Republic	78.9%	Poland	83.5%
Denmark	63.3%	Portugal	74.9%
Estonia	81.5%	Romania	96.1%
Finland	73.2%	Slovakia	90.3%
France	65.0%	Slovenia	76.7%
Germany	52.5%	Spain	78.8%
Greece	74.0%	Sweden	69.3%
Hungary	89.1%	United Kingdom	64.8%
Ireland	68.6%		

Source: European Commission—Eurostat, 2016.

viously classified as social or public housing have been sold (Wilson, 2014). This homeownership option stands in sharp contrast to public housing in the United States, which includes only rental units that are owned by the Public Housing Authority. Rent in public housing in the United States is based on the tenant's income, and there is currently no option to buy.

While some European households have been able to purchase a former social housing unit with the help of a conventional lender, others have been able to purchase these units with the help of mortgages made by local housing authorities. In Ireland citizens can acquire loans that can cover up to 97 percent of the home's value, with a maximum loan of no more than €200,000 (about $180,000). Eligible applicants are households that consist of first-time home buyers between eighteen and seventy years of age, subject to income limitations, and depending on the number of household members (Department of Environment, Community and Local Government, 2016).

Another reason for the increase in the homeownership rate in Europe is the privatization of the housing stock in Eastern Europe after the breakup of the former Soviet Union in 1991. Thus, the three former Soviet republics of Estonia, Latvia, and Lithuania; the four former Soviet satellites of Poland, the Czech Republic, Hungary, and Slovakia; and the former Yugoslav republic Slovenia experienced the transfer of ownership of former state- and company-owned housing to existing tenants or renters (Pittini & Laino, 2012). Tenants had the option to buy the dwellings at deeply discounted prices. In these countries, except for Poland and Hungary, homes that "had been confiscated, nationalized, or in other ways taken from owners during or after World War II were privatized to benefit former owners or their heirs" if they could be found (Pittini & Laino, 2012: 12). The decrease in the number of public housing units has resulted in long waiting lists for social housing and in people being housed in an inadequate fashion (Amann, 2013).

In most Eastern European countries, the privatization of state housing stock led to individual ownership in the form of cooperative housing stock, although a very small share was left in public ownership and transferred to municipalities. However, the mass privatization of multifamily housing in Eastern Europe created a new group of poor owners who often do not have the funds to repair and maintain their units and the common areas, resulting in ineffective condominium management and higher housing cost overburden rates (Amann, 2013).

RENTING IN EUROPE

Rental Housing

Identifying market-rate, reduced-rate, and social housing is difficult in the EU due to the somewhat different classifications adopted by each of the twenty-eight member countries. The European Commission and Eurostat have attempted to identify each of the rental types to better compare data from each country. Despite data inconsistencies, 18 percent of the EU population lived as tenants with a market-rate rent and 11.2 percent as tenants in reduced-rent or free housing in 2013 (European Union—Eurostat, 2013). Market-rate rental housing refers to for-profit rental housing that may include rent totally or partially covered by housing allowances or other public, charitable, or private sources (European Commission—Eurostat, 2010). Reduced-rent housing is characterized by a rent that is lower than the market rate in social (European term) or public (U.S. term) housing, as well as housing owned by nonprofit organizations. Reduced-rate rental housing could also include situations in which tenants rent at a reduced rate from relatives or employers (European Commission—Eurostat, 2010).

Social/Public Housing

Social or public housing represents about 11 percent of the total housing in the European Union (Braga & Palvarini, 2013). People who are unable to afford market-rate housing utilize this type of housing. The economic crisis of the late 2000s caused all European countries to experience a significant increase in poverty rates and housing exclusion, which led to a greater demand for social housing throughout the European Union (Braga & Palvarini, 2013).

Social or public housing in the European Union includes a wide diversity of housing situations, policies, and approaches across countries (Czischke & Pittini, 2007). Diverse groups may be eligible for social or public housing. For example, until recently, there were no income restrictions for social housing in the Netherlands, making the entire population eligible to apply for social housing. Similarly, there were no income ceilings in Sweden in the allocation of dwellings from public housing companies (Pittini & Laino, 2012). Providers of social or public housing range from public companies and local authorities to nonprofit or limited-profit associations and companies. Some providers are cooperatives; others are private, for-profit developers and investors (Czischke & Pittini, 2007).

For Western European countries that invested heavily in social housing after World War II, social or public housing still plays a role, even with the increase in homeownership (Dol & Haffner, 2010). In many of these countries, such as Austria, Denmark, France, Finland, and Sweden, the market share of social housing has not declined much since 1990. Currently, the Netherlands has the largest social housing sector by market share (Dol & Haffner, 2010). In the new member states of the EU, social or public housing represents about 3–5 percent of the housing stock due to the privatization discussed above.

Housing Cooperatives

Overall, about 10 percent of households in the EU live in housing cooperatives, compared to 1 percent in the United States (Co-operative Housing International, 2010; Moreau & Pittini, 2012). However, there is a range. For example, 20 percent of the housing stock in Poland and 17 percent of the housing stock in Sweden and the Czech Republic are housing cooperatives. On the other hand, only 0.1 percent of the total housing stock in the United Kingdom is occupied as housing cooperatives (Confederation of Co-operative Housing, 2000; Moreau & Pittini, 2012). Shareholders, who may live in a unit or rent it out, democratically control housing cooperatives (one share, one vote). The first independent housing cooperatives were formed in the mid-1800s in Berlin, when several structures were constructed. Many of these century-old cooperatives are still operating (Moreau & Pittini, 2012).

Housing cooperatives vary within the EU in how they are structured and operated. They may be social housing cooperatives created by public authorities that own most of the capital and where tenants are not members of the cooperative. The tenants or public companies may also own cooperatives collectively. Credit cooperatives extend loans to purchase a social dwelling, which is constructed by others. Other arrangements may be not-for-profit associations that join together in a cooperative but whose members are not the persons who reside there. Tenants' cooperatives are typically managed and owned by the tenants (Moreau & Pittini, 2012).

TYPES OF DWELLINGS IN EUROPE

In some European countries, such as Croatia, Hungary, and Slovenia, more than 60 percent of the housing stock consists of single-family homes, many of which have been preserved for several centuries. In other countries with large urban populations, such as Greece, Spain, and Estonia, about 60 to 65 percent of contemporary units are located in multifamily structures (see figure 22.1 for an example in Italy). Most Eastern European countries have a greater proportion and number of multiunit structures than other countries in the European Union (European Union—Eurostat, 2014b).

Almost 42 percent of people in the European Union lived in flats (European term) or apartments (U.S. term), 34 percent lived in a detached house, and about 24 percent lived in a semidetached or terraced house in 2012 (European Union—Eurostat, 2014b) (see figure 22.2 for an example in the United Kingdom). In the United States, about 35 percent live in apartments, flats, or semidetached homes and about 60 percent live in detached homes (U.S. Bureau of the Census, 2011a, 2011b).

Table 22.4 shows the proportions of dwellings in the European Union

FIGURE 22.1
High-Rise Multifamily Housing in Italy
Image credit: S. Niemeyer.

FIGURE 22.2
Row Housing in the United Kingdom
Image credit: S. Niemeyer.

TABLE 22.4
Proportions of Dwelling Types in the European Union, by Country, 2012

	Apartment/flat	Detached house	Semidetached/ terraced house	Other
EU (28 members)	**41.6%**	**34.0%**	**23.7%**	**0.7%**
Austria	42.5%	49.2%	7.2%	1.2%
Belgium	20.8%	37.1%	41.8%	0.3%
Bulgaria	43.2%	46.0%	10.5%	0.3%
Croatia	20.7%	73.0%	6.1%	0.2%
Cyprus	24.1%	47.0%	27.7%	1.3%
Czech Republic	52.6%	37.2%	9.9%	0.3%
Denmark	29.9%	57.1%	12.5%	0.4%
Estonia	65.1%	29.8%	4.6%	0.5%
Finland	33.6%	47.2%	18.6%	0.5%
France	33.1%	44.2%	22.5%	0.1%
Germany	53.2%	28.6%	16.7%	1.5%
Greece	59.7%	32.1%	8.1%	0.0%
Hungary	30.1%	63.9%	5.4%	0.7%
Ireland (2009)	3.1%	39.1%	57.6%	0.2%
Italy	51.1%	22.0%	26.5%	0.4%
Latvia	64.4%	31.8%	3.6%	0.2%
Lithuania	57.6%	35.2%	6.8%	0.4%
Luxembourg	33.2%	36.4%	29.9%	0.5%
Malta	50.3%	4.5%	44.8%	0.3%
Netherlands	18.6%	16.2%	60.0%	5.2%
Poland	46.2%	48.9%	4.7%	0.2%
Portugal	41.3%	40.6%	17.8%	0.3%
Romania	37.8%	60.5%	1.7%	0.1%
Slovakia	48.1%	49.9%	1.8%	0.1%
Slovenia	28.9%	66.6%	4.1%	0.3%
Spain	65.0%	13.6%	21.2%	0.2%
Sweden	40.2%	50.6%	8.9%	0.4%
United Kingdom	14.5%	23.9%	60.9%	0.7%

Source: European Union—Eurostat, 2014c.
Note: "Other" includes accommodations that are situated in buildings used for other purposes than housing (schools, etc.) and fixed habitations, such as a hut.

by type by country. There are great differences in percentages of each type of dwelling among the EU countries, with no pattern of housing type by region, climate, degree of urbanization, economic conditions, or type of government. Several Eastern European countries (Czech Republic, Estonia, Latvia, and Lithuania) have some of the highest percentages of apartments or flats in the EU, but some countries along the southern coast of Europe (Spain and Greece) also have very high percentages of apartments or flats. In contrast, the majority of housing units in Ireland and the United Kingdom are semidetached and/or terraced housing units, but that is also the most common housing type in the Netherlands. Single detached units are the most common housing type in Denmark, Hungary, Romania, and Slovenia.

TABLE 22.5
Age Distribution of Housing Stock in the European Union, by Country, 2009

	Year of data	<1919	1919–45	1946–70	1971–80	1981–90	1991–2000	>2001
Austria	2009	15%	8%	28%	15%	12%	14%	8%
Belgium	2009	17%	24%	24%	14%	21%	N/A	N/A
Cyprus	2001	N/A	7%	17%	21%	27%	27%	N/A
Czech Republic	2005	11%	14%	25%	22%	16%	8%	3%
Denmark	2009	20%	16%	26%	17%	9%	5%	7%
Estonia	2009	9%	14%	30%	22%	20%	2%	3%
Finland	2009	2%	8%	28%	22%	19%	12%	10%
France	2006	17%	13%	17%	25%	10%	9%	8%
Germany	2006	14%	14%	46%	N/A	13%	9%	3%
Greece	2001	3%	7%	32%	25%	19%	14%	N/A
Hungary	2005	N/A	21%	27%	23%	18%	8%	3%
Ireland	2002	9%	8%	16%	14%	13%	20%	20%
Italy	2001	14%	10%	37%	19%	12%	8%	N/A
Latvia	2008	14%	13%	22%	19%	20%	7%	4%
Lithuania	2002	6%	23%	33%	18%	14%	6%	N/A
Luxembourg	2008	22%	26%	29%	12%	5%	5%	2%
Malta	2005	12%	10%	22%	16%	19%	17%	3%
Netherlands	2009	7%	14%	27%	17%	15%	12%	8%
Poland	2002	10%	13%	27%	18%	19%	13%	N/A
Portugal	2008	7%	10%	22%	16%	19%	18%	8%
Romania	2002	4%	12%	37%	24%	15%	7%	1%
Slovakia	2001	3%	7%	35%	26%	21%	6%	1%
Slovenia	2004	15%	8%	28%	23%	16%	7%	3%
Spain	2001	9%	4%	34%	24%	14%	16%	N/A
Sweden	2008	12%	15%	37%	17%	9%	6%	5%
United Kingdom	2004–5	17%	17%	21%	22%	20%	N/A	N/A

Source: Dol & Haffner, 2010; slightly modified by authors.
Note: Ages of countries' housing data vary somewhat due to how the data are collected and when. In addition, totals from Slovenia include vacation homes as well as permanent residences. Dwellings in multifamily housing were classified by the period in which the construction of the building containing them was completed.

Almost three-fourths of the housing units in Croatia are detached houses (European Union—Eurostat, 2014b).

The age of the housing stock varies greatly throughout Europe. In many countries, about 10 percent of the housing stock was built before 1919; only Greece, Finland, Romania, and Slovakia have smaller percentages (Dol & Haffner, 2010). For example, approximately 20 percent of the housing stock in Denmark and Luxembourg was built before 1919. In contrast, Ireland leads the European Union in new housing stock, with almost 20 percent of housing built after 2000, evidence of the Irish real estate bubble in the 2000s (Dol & Haffner, 2010). Almost all countries had an increase in building activity from 1946 to 1970, some of which was due to reconstruction efforts after World War II. Table 22.5 shows the age distribution of the housing stock in each of the European Union member countries.

HOUSING AFFORDABILITY IN EUROPE

As in the United States, affordable, quality housing is an issue in all countries of the European Union. Not surprisingly, housing-related expenditures make up the biggest component of spending of many households (Economidou et al., 2011). On average, European households spend 22.9 percent of their disposable income on housing. However, a majority of those living below the poverty line spend more than 40 percent of their disposable income on housing, which indicates an overburdened household (Pittini & Laino, 2012). In the United States, those who spend over 30 percent of their income on housing costs are considered housing cost burdened (Schwartz & Wilson, 2008).

The average proportion of households spending more than 40 percent of their income on housing in the European Union (12.2 percent) masks significant differences among member states. At one extreme, there are many countries where a relatively small proportion of the population lives in households where housing costs exceeded 40 percent of their disposable income, including Malta (2.6 percent), Cyprus (3.3 percent), and Finland (4.5 percent). However, 33.1 percent of households in Greece, 18.2 percent of households in Denmark, and 16.6 percent of households in Germany spent more than 40 percent of their equalized disposable income on housing (European Union—Eurostat, 2014a).

CONCLUSION

Housing in the European Union is as diverse as its various cultures, and yet there are some important similarities. Much of the housing stock was designed and built for the traditional nuclear family, but countries face the challenge of housing a population with a higher proportion of older people and an increasingly higher proportion of nontraditional households. While many European households are owner-occupiers, the homeownership rate varies greatly among countries. There is a great need for more affordable housing options across the European Union. As a higher proportion of households are paying an increasing percentage of their income for housing, European countries are striving to meet the demand for affordable housing through a variety of social housing programs. In addition, many European nations are encouraging innovative uses of technology to increase the energy efficiency and accessibility of housing, leading the way into the twenty-first century.

REFERENCES

Alders, M., & Manting, D. (1999). Household scenarios for the European Union, 1995–2025. *European Population Conference EPC99, Statistics Netherlands*. Retrieved January 18, 2016, from http://www.cbs.nl/nr/rdonlyres/ef9974d0-c3a5-4bef-a898-ff57b67c18ff/0/householdscenarios.pdf.

Amann, W. (2013). *Housing review on 23 countries in the Europe and Central Asia Region*. Atlanta: Habitat for Humanity. Retrieved January 18, 2016, from https://www.habitat.org/sites/default/files/housing_study_2013_final26112013_small.pdf.

Beier, L., Hofäcker, D., Marchese, E., & Rupp, M. (2010). *Family structures and family forms: An overview of major trends and developments*. FamilyPlatform. Retrieved

January 18, 2016, from http://www.ag-familie.de/media/agfdoc/EF1_Family_Structures_Family_Forms.pdf.

Braga, M., & Palvarini, P. (2013). *Social housing in the EU*. European Parliament, Committee on Employment and Social Affairs. Retrieved February 24, 2016, from http://www.europarl.europa.eu/RegData/etudes/note/join/2013/492469/IPOL-EMPL_NT(2013)492469_EN.pdf.

Choroszewicz, M., & Wolff, P. (2010). *51 million young EU adults lived with their parent(s) in 2008*. Eurostat: Statistics in Focus. Retrieved January 18, 2016, from http://ec.europa.eu/eurostat/documents/3433488/5565692/KS-SF-10-050-EN.PDF/877f8776-e7fe-4f2b-8bec-0a5cf54dcba4?version=1.0.

Confederation of Co-operative Housing. (2000) [website]. CCH: Confederation of Co-operative Housing. Retrieved January 18, 2016, from http://www.cch.coop.

Co-operative Housing International (2010). *About the United States*. Retrieved February 25, 2016, from http://www.housinginternational.coop/co-ops/usa.

Czischke, D., & Pittini, A. (2007). *Housing Europe 2007: Review of social, cooperative and public housing in the 27 EU member states*. Brussels: CECODHAS: European Social Housing Observatory. Retrieved January 18, 2016, from http://www.iut.nu/Literature/2007/CECODHAS_HousingEurope_2007_ENG.pdf.

Department of Environment, Community and Local Government. (2016). *Local authority mortgages*. Retrieved February 21, 2016, at http://www.environ.ie/housing/grantsfinancial-assistance/local-authority-loans/local-authority-loans.

Dol, K., & Haffner, M. (Eds.). (2010). *Housing statistics in the European Union 2010*. The Hague: Ministry of the Interior and Kingdom Relations.

Economidou, M., Laustsen, J., Ruyssevelt, P., Staniaszek, D., Strong, D., & Zinetti, S. (2011). *Europe's buildings under the microscope: A country-by-country review of the energy performance of buildings*. Brussels: Building Performance Institute Europe (BPIE). Retrieved February 15, 2015, from http://www.bpie.eu/uploads/lib/document/attachment/21/LR_EU_B_under_microscope_study.pdf.

European Commission—Eurostat. (2009). *Youth in Europe: A statistical portrait*. Retrieved February 16, 2016, from http://pjp-eu.coe.int/documents/1017981/1668203/YouthinEurope.pdf/40f42295-65e4-407b-8673-95e97026da4a.

European Commission—Eurostat. (2010). *The comparability of imputed rent: Methodologies and working papers*. Retrieved January 18, 2016, from http://ec.europa.eu/eurostat/documents/3888793/5847505/KS-RA-10-022-EN.PDF/45f3fd08-6f2a-4b58-942b-098570213790.

European Commission—Eurostat. (2016). *Share of young adults (aged 25–34) living with their parents by age and sex*. Retrieved February 22, 2016, from http://ec.europa.eu/eurostat/en/web/products-datasets/-/ILC_LVPS08.

European Parliament. (2013). *On social housing in the European Union*. Retrieved February 14, 2016, from http://www.europarl.europa.eu/sides/getDoc.do?type=REPORT&reference=A7-2013-0155&language=EN.

European Union—Eurostat. (2012). *Archive social statistics: Statistics explained*. Retrieved January 18, 2016, from http://ec.europa.eu/eurostat/documents/4031688/5930084/KS-FM-13-002-EN.PDF.

European Union—Eurostat. (2013). *European social statistics*. Retrieved January 18, 2016, from http://ec.europa.eu/eurostat/documents/3930297/5968986/KS-FP-13-001-EN.PDF.

European Union—Eurostat. (2014a). "Housing Affordability." *Housing statistics: Statistics explained*. Retrieved January 18, 2016, from http://ec.europa.eu/eurostat/statistics-explained/index.php/Housing_statistics#Housing_affordability.

European Union—Eurostat. (2014b). Source data for figures and tables. *Housing statistics: Statistics explained*. Retrieved January 18, 2016, from http://ec.europa.eu/eurostat/statistics-explained/index.php/Housing_statistics#Source_data_for_tables_and_figures_.28MS_Excel.29.

European Union—Eurostat (2015). *Statistics explained*. Retrieved February 15, 2016, from http://ec.europa.eu/eurostat/statistics-explained/.

Forrest, R., & Yip, N. (2013). *Young people and housing: Transitions, trajectories and generational fractures*. New York: Routledge.

Iacovou, M., & Skew, A. (2011). Demographic research: Household composition across the new Europe: Where do the new member states fit in? *Demographic Research* 25(14), 465–490. Retrieved January 18, 2016, from http://www.demographic-research.org/volumes/vol25/14/25-14.pdf.

Mace, A. (2013). *City suburbs: Placing suburbia in a post-suburban world.* New York: Routledge.

Moreau, S., & Pittini, A. (2012). *Profiles of a movement: Co-operative housing around the world.* Brussels: CECODHAS Housing Europe; Ottawa: ICA Housing. Retrieved January 18, 2016, from http://www.icahousing.coop/attachments/Profiles%20of%20a%20movement%20final%20web%20ISBN.pdf.

Organization for Economic Co-operation and Development (OECD), International Futures Program (2011). *The future of families to 2030. Projections, policy, challenges and policy options: A synthesis report.* Retrieved January 18, 2016, from http://www.oecd.org/futures/49093502.pdf.

Pittini, A., & Laino, E. (2012). *Housing Europe review: The nuts and bolts of European social housing systems.* Brussels: Housing Europe. Retrieved January 18, 2016, from http://www.housingeurope.eu/resource-105/the-housing-europe-review-2012.

Schwartz, M., & Wilson, E. (2008). *Who can afford to live in a home?: A look at data from the 2006 American Community Survey.* Washington, D.C.: U.S. Bureau of the Census.

Uhlendorff, U., Rupp, M., & Euteneuer, M. (Eds.). (2011). *Well-being of families in future Europe: Challenges for research and policy.* FamilyPlatform. Retrieved January 18, 2016, from http://europa.eu/epic/docs/family_platform_book1.pdf.

U.S. Bureau of the Census (2011a). *Historical census of housing tables.* Retrieved January 18, 2016, from https://www.census.gov/hhes/www/housing/census/historic/units.html.

U.S. Bureau of the Census (2011b). *Housing characteristics 2010.* Retrieved January 18, 2016, from https://www.census.gov/prod/cen2010/briefs/c2010br-07.pdf.

Wilson, W. (2014). *Incentivising the right to buy* (Briefing papers SN06251). UK House of Commons Library. Retrieved January 18, 2016, from http://researchbriefings.parliament.uk/ResearchBriefing/Summary/SN06251#fullreport.

Chapter 23

Housing in Latin America and the Caribbean

ROSA E. DONOSO AND
MARJA ELSINGA

This chapter is about adequate housing in Latin America and the Caribbean (LAC), providing an overview of housing programs in both the formal and informal housing markets. The formal housing market comprises housing that is generally mass-produced and that has building permits and property titles; the informal market occurs outside the borders of prescribed legal systems and formal urban development patterns. Informal housing includes dwellings that are self-built over time without the construction companies and investors that are typically present in the formal housing market. Both homeownership and renting are common forms of tenure that coexist within the formal and informal markets in LAC countries. About 60 to 70 percent of the housing stock in LAC countries is informal (Bouillon, 2012).

The Latin American countries in North and Central America are Mexico, Guatemala, Honduras, Nicaragua, El Salvador, Costa Rica, Panama, and Belize. The Latin American countries in South America are Venezuela, Brazil, Colombia, Ecuador, Peru, Bolivia, Paraguay, Uruguay, Chile, and Argentina. The Guianas (Suriname, Guyana, and French Guiana) and some of the Caribbean Islands (e.g., Haiti, Trinidad and Tobago, Cuba, and the Dominican Republic) are also included in discussions in this chapter.

This chapter is divided into six parts. The first part introduces the right to adequate housing, since many housing policies and programs are established under this right. The second part provides a historic overview of housing conditions. The third part focuses on informal housing strategies and housing policy answers to these informal strategies. The fourth part describes the development of formal housing policies. The fifth part discusses housing tenures and housing deficit statistics. The final section offers a synthesis of housing issues in LAC countries, highlighting the most important opportunities and challenges.

THE RIGHT TO ADEQUATE HOUSING IN LAC COUNTRIES

Article 25 of the United Nations' (UN) International Declaration of Human Rights states that every human being has "the right to a standard of living adequate for the health and well-being of himself and his family, including food, clothing, housing and medical care, and necessary social services" (United Nations, 1948: 1). Housing is therefore one internationally recognized factor in achieving an adequate standard of living (Rolnik, 2013). The UN-HABITAT division has identified seven main characteristics of an adequate standard of living regarding housing: (1) security of tenure; (2) availability of services, materials, and infrastructure; (3) affordability; (4) habitability; (5) accessibility; (6) location; and (7) cultural adequacy (UN-HABITAT, 2014: 4). The right to adequate housing implies more than a right to four walls and a well-constructed roof for a household. It is a comprehensive concept that connects housing issues to both urban development and institutional contexts.

In Latin America and the Caribbean, the right to housing is discussed not only with reference to the International Declaration of Human Rights but also with reference to constitutional social rights. The right to housing has been included in the national constitutions of many Latin American and Caribbean countries, including Brazil (1988), Colombia (1991), Paraguay (1992), Peru (1993), Venezuela (1999), Ecuador (2008), and Bolivia (2009) (Gargarella, 2013). Other countries have constitutional amendments that embrace the right to housing, including Argentina (1994), Mexico (1992), and Costa Rica (1989) (Uprimny, 2011).

Even though the International Declaration of Human Rights does not mention any preferred form of tenure involved in "adequate housing," homeownership in Latin America and the Caribbean has a central position in housing policies, as there are no housing programs for social or public rental housing even though a large share of households rent in cities (Blanco, Cibils, & Muñoz, 2014; Florian, 2012; Perez, 2007). The focus of policies on homeownership does not address the prevalence of such practices in formal and informal rental markets in many Latin American cities (Bouillon, 2012; Florian, 2012; Gilbert, 1993).

HISTORIC OVERVIEW

Latin America was once a primarily rural region, but today most of its population lives in cities. Population growth and industrialization triggered large-scale migration from rural to urban areas (Brea, 2003). In the 1950s about 40 percent of the population of Latin America lived in cities while about 60 percent lived in rural areas. The percentage of the urban population increased to almost 50 percent by the 1960s and to about 60 percent by the 1980s. Currently, almost 80 percent of the population in Latin America lives in urban settlements (United Nations, 2014).

In LAC countries, both rural and urban populations are racially and ethnically diverse (Telles & Paschel, 2014). This diversity has its origins in the migrations that began during the Spanish and Portuguese colonial era in the sixteenth century, when Europeans and enslaved Africans came into contact with indigenous Americans, continuing into the era of independent nation states in the 1820s. Today LAC countries are populated by Hispanic whites, indigenous people, Afro-Latinos, and mestizos (i.e., a mixture of the white race with other races and ethnicities) (Skidmore & Smith, 2005; Wade, 2010). This racial and ethnic diversity is reflected in socioeconomics and, particularly, in poverty (Hooker, 2005) and social and spatial segregation (Borsdorf & Hidalgo, 2010; Sabatini, 2006), as many Afro-Latinos and indigenous people tend to have lower incomes than mestizos and Hispanic whites (Hooker, 2005).

Housing problems in the early twentieth century were characterized by few urban housing options for migrants from rural areas. Thus they first found some accommodation in tenements located in the historic centers (Gilbert & Ward, 1982). These inner-city tenements are known by several names in Latin American and Caribbean countries. For example, in Mexico they are called *vecindades*, while in other countries (e.g., Argentina, Chile, Colombia, and Ecuador) they are called *conventillos* or *inquilinatos* (Moreno, 2001). Due to the rapid population growth in cities, overcrowding in tenements became one of the first evident housing problems that many national governments of LAC countries started to address with "hygienist" housing programs (Ormindo de Azevedo, 2001; Kingman, 2006).

The hygienist (*higienismo*) period, which ranged from 1890 to the 1930s, coincided with the City Beautiful Movement in the United States and the Haussmann period in France, bringing beautification and monumental grandeur to cities while demolishing tenements and other historic buildings in the United States and in Europe (Kingman, 2006). However, most tenements in LAC countries were located in the historic centers that contained buildings of recognized architectural value. Therefore, during the hygienist period many tenements did not experience demolition because LAC countries decided to preserve them, improving housing by regulating physical conditions. For example, in 1918 Colombia passed its first law requiring landlords to improve the precarious sanitary conditions in their housing units (Ceballos, 2008; see Magdaleno, 2001, and Moreno, 2001, for examples of other countries). Local housing policies for housing rehabilitation were implemented in the following decades to address the complexities of housing conditions in historic urban centers (Carrion, 2005; Contrucci, 1999; Delgadillo, 2011; Donoso, 2008; Rojas, 2004).

From the 1930s until the 1970s, the housing situation in many cities worsened because local policies and initiatives to improve conditions in urban centers were insufficient to cope with the housing needs of migrants moving from rural to urban areas. Therefore, it was necessary to increase the number of housing units to accommodate the new urban residents. At this point in history, housing markets and solutions started to split into the informal and formal housing markets.

On the one hand, informal settlements grew through incremental and self-built housing processes (Bromley, 2004). The poor started to find their own solutions since the market was not providing affordable options for them (Rojas, 2010); therefore, low-income households built their own dwellings on sometimes illegally acquired land. On the other hand, dwellings were produced in the formal housing sector for the upper and middle classes by the private residential construction sector. At the same time, many national governments created national housing agencies in charge of both building and financing housing for state workers.

The Inter-American Development Bank (IDB) is an international agency that has financed urban and housing development programs in LAC countries since the 1940s (Zanetta, 2001). The IDB recognizes the dual characteristics of the housing sector in LAC countries and has defined them as follows: "All countries [in LAC] have elements of both informal and formal sectors (and markets). Formal housing markets, in which officially valued housing properties are exchanged, function through highly developed systems of mortgage finance. Informal markets, which pertain to squatter settlements and housing built progressively, function through traditional approaches such as barter, sweat-equity, and squatter's rights" (Inter-American Development Bank, 2004: 15).

The IDB, like other financing agencies, such as the World Bank and USAID (U.S. Agency for International Development), currently recognizes these dual characteristics of urban and housing development conditions in LAC countries and supports both the physical and social upgrading of informal settlements and the provision of formal affordable housing with loans given to national governments (Imparato & Ruster, 2003; Inter-American Development Bank, 2004).

INFORMAL HOUSING STRATEGIES AND POLICIES

Given the varying levels of informality, there is no precise definition of the informal housing sector (Guha-Khasnobis, Kanbur, & Ostrom, 2006; Inter-American Development Bank, 2004). Informally built homes and neighborhoods have different names in different countries. Globally, they are known as slums (Davis, 2006) or as squatters' settlements (Inter-American Development Bank, 2004). In Latin America and the Caribbean, they are referred to as *barriadas* in Peru, *favelas* in Brazil, *barrios populares* or *invasiones* in Colombia and Ecuador, *villas* in Argentina, *arrabales* in Puerto Rico, and *cañadas* in the Dominican Republic (Gilbert, 2012; Sletto, Donoso, Strange, Muñoz, & Thomen, 2010; van Gelder, Cravino, & Ostuni, forthcoming). Along the U.S.-Mexico border, informal settlements can be found in informal subdivisions called *colonias* (Ward, 1999).

The informal housing sector typically features housing built by people who have a large degree of control over construction and design, called "self-building" or "self-help" housing (Turner, 1976; Ward, Jiménez, & Virgilio, 2014), and by people who may not have building permits. A household may start constructing and living in a small shack on a piece of land bought at a low price, reflecting the lack of services and access to roads. The household may progressively build the house according to their income constraints (Erazo, 2014; Moser, 2009; Ward et al., 2014). Eventually the household might seek to improve their housing conditions through extended consolidation (e.g., from a small shack to a three-story house) (Ferguson & Navarrete, 2003; UN-HABITAT, 2011). The goal is mainly owner occupancy, although sometimes a household may build an independent unit on the same lot to rent it out, generating additional income (Gilbert, 1993; Pradilla, 1983). Even though informal settlers may manage to formalize land tenure and to acquire a land title over time, there is typically no interest in moving out or selling the unit (Bromley, 2004; Ward, 2011).

As the IDB explains, "Informal settlements, regardless of their quality, provide affordable housing for the poor at minimal public investment" (Inter-

American Development Bank, 2004: 16). However, self-built housing units in the slums are often not classified as "adequate housing" in census statistics because many components of the UN definition discussed above are not met (e.g., lack of security of tenure, lack of services such as water and sewage systems, lack of permanent built structures, or poor connections with public transportation to areas providing employment and educational opportunities).

Even though slums were not the best housing option, migrants who lived in tenements in historic centers were the first ones to move into self-built areas "in search of a home" (Gilbert, 1993). This process did not occur individually or independently, though, as informality is a complex phenomenon characterized by rich social organization, social capital, and empowerment of vulnerable low-income communities whenever governments and markets do not provide sufficient affordable options for low-income people (Bellegooijen & Rocco, 2013; Moser, 2009; Rodriguez & Sugranyes, 2005; Rolnik, 2013).

Over the decades, informal settlements have been allowed to grow in most Latin American and Caribbean cities. In some cases, populist political parties, triggered by community pressure, have even promoted them in order to win votes, resulting in the provision of public services such as drinking water or paved streets (Bellegooijen & Rocco, 2013; Roy, 2005). Thus informal settlements have become a visible component of the Latin American urban physical and political landscape over time (Bellegooijen & Rocco, 2013; Gilbert, 2012).

Interestingly, over the decades informal settlements began to be seen less as a housing problem (Mangin, 1967; Turner, 1976) and more as a housing solution provided by and for the urban poor (Inter-American Development Bank, 2004; Rojas 2010). Also, international agencies have funded slum-upgrading programs (Imparato & Ruster, 2003) and land-titling programs since the 1990s in order to improve urban conditions for those who live in informal housing (Fernandez, 2011; Monkkonen, 2012; Ward et al., 2014). Slum-upgrading programs have been implemented with strong participa-

FIGURE 23.1
Formal Low-Cost Condominiums (Front) and Informal Settlements (Back) in Bogota, 2012
Image credit: R. E. Donoso.

tion of their respective communities with the goal of not only providing technical solutions but also comprehensively improving the quality of life by supporting community organization (Imparato & Ruster, 2003).

Although public services and security of tenure in informal settlements have improved greatly over the past few years (Economic Commission for Latin America and the Caribbean, 2013; Ward et al., 2014), the dichotomy between formal and informal housing has continued to exist, as can be seen in figure 23.1. Over time, informal settlements have kept growing informally, providing affordable housing for families in the lowest income brackets. However, there is much left to do, as about 70 percent of the housing stock in LAC cities either lacks public services or has issues in regard to the security of tenure.

FORMAL HOUSING STRATEGIES AND POLICIES

On the formal side of the housing sector, three eras of housing policies that favor owner occupancy can be distinguished: first, affordable housing construction by national housing institutions (from the 1940s to the 1970s); second, "sites and services" (from the 1970s to the 1980s); and third, a market-enabling approach (from the 1980s to the present) (Buckley & Kalarickal, 2006; Harris & Giles, 2003; Pugh, 2001; Roberts & Portes, 2006).

During the first era of housing policy (from the 1940s to the 1970s), national governments in LAC countries implemented mass-produced housing programs in order to provide housing for eligible low- and middle-income households. However, housing was mostly affordable only for state workers, who were often middle class and had a stable source of employment (Garcia, 2010). Consequently, households with jobs in the informal sector, like selling goods on the streets, or seasonal jobs, such as construction, were excluded from these programs. The only option for informal workers with housing needs was to live in informal rental or owner-occupied units in informal settlements (Rolnik, 2013; Ward et al., 2014).

Mass-produced housing was built in new neighborhoods as both single-family and multifamily units in midrise buildings following European and modernistic ideas for housing developments (Ballen, 2009; Hofer, 2003). In LAC countries, however, the formal provision of affordable housing was adapted to the specific institutional and cultural contexts. Unlike the United States' and Europe's experience with public or social housing developments, LAC governments decided to pursue affordable homeownership policies (Almandoz, 2006), calling these programs "social interest housing" (*vivienda de interés social*, VIS) (Jolly, 2004). In some countries, like Mexico and Colombia, national housing institutions first built affordable housing for renters, but these dwellings were eventually sold to their occupants at subsidized prices with low-interest mortgages (Ceballos, 2008; Garcia, 2010).

National housing institutions, together with private sector and worker organizations, directed mass-produced housing (Garcia, 2010). For example, Colombia founded the Institute of Territorial Credit in 1939, Ecuador created the Ecuadorian Housing Bank (BEV) in 1961 and the National Housing Board (Junta Nacional de la Vivienda, JNV) in 1974, Peru created the National Housing Board in 1963, Mexico created the INFONAVIT in 1972, and Argentina restructured its National Mortgage Bank into FONAVI, a national housing fund, in 1970. Some of these institutions also managed pension funds that built housing for workers (e.g., Institute of Territorial Credit in Colombia, FONAVI in Argentina, or INFONAVIT in Mexico) or managed loans from international agencies meant for improving housing conditions (e.g., BEV in Ecuador and JNV in Peru) (Abramo, Rodriguez, & Erazo, 2016; Ferguson & Navarrete, 2003).

The goal of the national housing institutions was to increase the number of housing units, since there had been a growing demand for affordable and adequate housing. In order to make housing units affordable, housing prices and mortgage interest rates were highly subsidized by governments (Ferguson, Rubinstein, & Vial, 1996). These supply-side programs operated until the end of the 1970s and 1980s in Chile and Colombia and until the 1990s in Ecuador, Argentina, and Mexico (Ceballos, 2008; Rojas, 2010).

International agencies have been important actors supporting the development of formal housing markets. In 1961 U.S. president John F. Kennedy initiated the Alliance for Progress program to cooperate with Latin American countries in partnerships that emphasized investing in economic and social development through lending with the goals of supporting political stability and democratic governments; building housing units and public infrastructure, such as schools, airports, hospitals, water and sewage systems, and water purification plants, among other facilities; and alleviating poverty in Latin America (Godwin & Harris, 2005). These investments included funds for infrastructure projects in informal settlements, resulting in improvements.

By the end of the 1950s all Latin American countries had legal property systems that allowed both public and private banks to provide mortgages to households to buy apartments, resulting in condominium ownership becoming a common form of ownership that was promoted by both private and public housing sectors (Donoso & Elsinga, forthcoming; Lujanen, 2010; Rosen & Walks, 2013). Condos promoted by the national housing institutions typically lack effective condominium property management by a homeowners' association, which would expect national housing agencies to provide management and make investments (Rojas 2010). Currently several authors have identified these dwellings as housing stock on a path toward deterioration (Donoso & Elsinga, forthcoming; Esquivel, 2008; Rodriguez & Sugranyes, 2005; Rojas, 2010).

During the second era of housing policy (from the 1970s to the 1980s), called "sites and services," new strategies were implemented based on the informal practices of the urban poor in previous decades. The programs based on this policy provided serviced plots of land on which households were responsible for constructing their own home. These approaches were developed by national housing institutions and promoted and funded by international finance agencies, such as the World Bank (Ferguson & Navarrete, 2003).

During the third era of housing policy, which can be characterized as a "market-enabling approach" (from the end of the 1980s to the present), national governments implemented a new housing program called System of Incentives for Housing (Sistema de Incentivos de Vivienda), which included a subsidy for a down payment for a so-called social interest house, constructed by the private sector, for eligible low-income households (Gilbert, 2012; Klaufus, 2010; Rojas, 2001).

Low-income households interested in participating in this program are required to open a savings account and to have a balance equaling 5 to 10 percent of the value of the house. The savings, together with the government subsidy, allow the household to cover 30 percent of the value of the house, thus requiring financing for the remaining 70 percent (Ferguson et al., 1996). This approach was first established in 1978 in Chile and then adopted throughout Latin America and the Caribbean (Ferguson et al., 1996; Gilbert, 2002; Rojas, 2001). The goal has been to incentivize the private sector to build affordable housing for eligible homeowners (Gonzales, 1999).

These policies constitute a liberal strategy that shifts the role of financiers and producers of affordable housing from the government to the private sector (Rojas, 2001). However, national governments have remained regulators in housing. For example, social interest housing regulations prescribe how the provision system should work, including, first, eligibility income thresholds; second, the maximum price of the affordable house; third, the roles of both private and public actors; and fourth, the minimum square meters (or feet), among other conditions such as construction quality and location.

For example, the Social Interest Housing Program in Ecuador is open to eligible households that earn from 1 ($366) to 3.5 times the minimum monthly salary (Salario Básico Unificado). The maximum value of an affordable house is set at $40,000, and the minimum size of the home is forty-six square meters (or 495 square feet). Within the system of incentives for social interest housing, there are also other subsidies for which eligible low-income households can apply, such as improving the physical condition of a housing unit, regardless of whether it is located in an urban or rural area, or building a new, affordable house on a plot in a rural area, subject to value and size limits (Ministerio de Desarrollo Urbano y Vivienda, 2015).

Many policy makers have regarded such subsidy-based programs as a successful strategy, since they have facilitated access to affordable homeownership (Rojas, 2001). However, the location of these units at the urban fringe, far from employment and educational opportunities, as well as the low construction quality of affordable homes, has remained a challenge (Rodriguez & Sugranyes, 2005). Due to the capped purchase price, quality is often compromised with inexpensive construction materials and basic interiors. Households purchase a somewhat basic house without finished

FIGURE 23.2
Affordable Condominium Housing in Bogota, 2012
Image credit: R. E. Donoso.

floors, built-in cabinets in kitchens, or closets in bedrooms. The low quality in location and in construction is evidenced in resident satisfaction surveys and high vacancy rates in affordable housing complexes in Mexico (Garcia, 2010; Paquette-Vasalli & Sanchez, 2009) and in dwellings built through the national My House My Life (Minha Casa Miha Vida) Program in Brazil (Santo, Zanin, & Rufino, 2015).

Since the 1990s mass-produced housing has been built where land is more inexpensive, gradually expanding the urban footprint of cities over time. LAC countries now realize that they should focus on providing affordable housing opportunities in more central locations. Decentralization and modernization of local planning systems in LAC countries have contributed to the development of municipal instruments aimed at the creation of urban plans that include land set aside for affordable housing provision and housing to be built by the private sector (Lentini & Palero, 2001; Smolka & Furtado, 2014). Since land policy is a local matter, some cities have inclusionary zoning policies similar to those in the United States (Calavita & Mallach, 2010). Thus cities such as Bogotá in Colombia, Sao Paulo in Brazil, and Quito in Ecuador have begun connecting local land policies to national affordable housing subsidies (Calavita & Mallach, 2010; Fernandez & Maldonado-Copello, 2009). While this approach has resulted in affordable housing for some eligible households, it has also resulted in increased land-price speculation that benefits landowners without addressing socioeconomic segregation (Roberts, 2011; Sabatini, 2006; Smolka & Furtado, 2014).

HOUSING TENURE AND HOUSING DEFICITS

Both the formal and informal housing markets in Latin America and the Caribbean are characterized by high rates of homeownership. There are three types of tenure: homeownership, renting, and sharing (i.e., shared with family or friends, known as *allegados* in Chile) as other types of occupancy. The average homeownership rate is about 65 percent in LAC countries, while about 20 percent of households rent and about 15 percent share housing or have other types of occupancy (Blanco et al., 2014). Among homeowners, about 65 percent own their homes without any debt, while about 35 percent have a mortgage (Pomeroy & Godbout, 2011).

As shown in figure 23.3, Nicaragua and Panama had the highest homeownership rates (82 percent), followed by Guatemala (75 percent), Honduras (74 percent), and Costa Rica (72 percent). Colombia has the lowest homeownership rate (44 percent) (Economic Commission for Latin America and the Caribbean, 2013). However, within these countries there are differences between urban and rural areas, the former having lower and the latter having higher homeownership rates.

Even though housing policy favors homeownership, renting is an important form of tenure in LAC countries (Gilbert, 2012). Interestingly, the rental market has a disproportionate share of middle- and high-income households, as illustrated in figure 23.4, especially in capital cities. For example, in Quito, Guatemala City, and Medellin, renters account for more than 30 percent of all households, and in Bogota and Santo Domingo they account for more than 40 percent, influenced by the age and familial status of householders and their type of employment (Blanco et al., 2014; Bouillon, 2012; Perez, 2007; Pomeroy & Godbout, 2011).

FIGURE 23.3
Housing Tenure in Latin American and Caribbean Countries, 2006–13.

Source: Authors, based on Economic Commission for Latin America and the Caribbean, CEPALSTAT, http://interwp.cepal.org/sisgen/ConsultaIntegrada.asp?idIndicador=166&idioma=i, data for 2006–13: Bolivia, 2011; Brazil, 2013; Chile, 2011; Colombia, 2013; Costa Rica, 2013; Ecuador, 2013; El Salvador, 2013; Guatemala, 2006; Honduras, 2010; Mexico, 2012; Nicaragua, 2009; Panama, 2013; Paraguay, 2013; Peru, 2013; Dominican Republic, 2013; Uruguay, 2013; Venezuela, 2012.

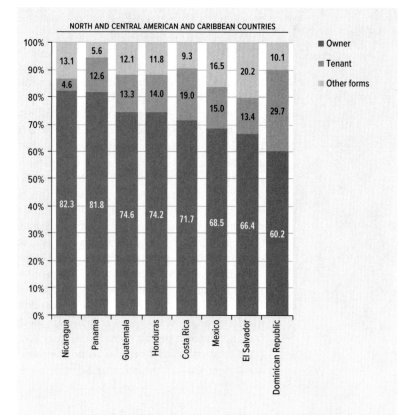

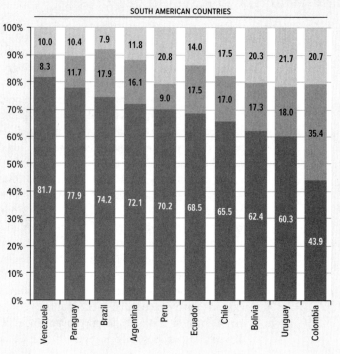

FIGURE 23.4
Proportion of Renters by Income Quintile in Latin American and Caribbean Countries, 2011.
Source: Authors, based on Pomeroy & Godbout, 2011.

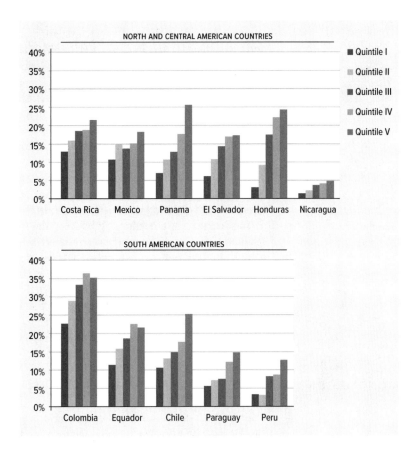

Most countries in Latin America and the Caribbean have both a quantitative and a qualitative housing deficit, as shown in their quintennial and decennial censuses gathered by the Economic Commission for Latin America and the Caribbean (ECLAC) (Economic Commission for Latin America and the Caribbean, 2015). The quantitative deficit occurs when there are more households than dwellings, resulting in overcrowding, as experienced by about 4 percent of households in LAC countries, and households living in units that cannot be rehabilitated due to poor construction quality (Blanco et al., 2014). The qualitative deficit occurs when numerous and diverse factors specified in the UN definition of an adequate home, discussed above, are not met (Rojas & Medellin, 2011).

The reasons for the quantitative deficit are manifold. For example, on the supply side, the production of a relatively low number of dwellings that do not satisfy the demand for housing could be a consequence of economic stagnation or the lack of a strong banking system. Other explanations include relatively high land and house prices and high poverty levels, which can create a mismatch between what the market offers and what home buyers can actually afford. Nevertheless, the quantitative housing deficit has been decreasing since the mid-1990s, possibly due to the impact of mass-produced, affordable housing (Blanco et al., 2014; Rojas, 2001). Indeed, as of 2007 a total of fifty-four million new dwellings were estimated to be needed in LAC countries (Scatigna & Tovar, 2007).

The qualitative deficit is measured by counting the presence or absence of at least one of the following dwelling features: piped water, sewage, a toilet connected to the municipal sewage system, fixed bath or shower facilities, and a designated space for cooking (UN-HABITAT, 2011). Nearly 37 percent of all households in Latin America and the Caribbean experience some kind of qualitative housing deficit (Blanco et al., 2014), with 52 percent of them from the lowest income quintile (Bouillon, 2012).

The qualitative deficit varies depending on whether the units are in rural or urban areas. In rural areas, 55 percent of the dwellings lack at least one feature, while in urban areas 26 percent do (Bouillon, 2012). Nevertheless, housing units in the countryside have vernacular forms of architecture and construction, such as a toilet located outside of the house, which is a typical part of culture and tradition. However, in the standard surveys these characteristics are marked as a deficit since the toilet is not inside.

In sum, there is a relationship between the informal housing sector and qualitative deficits. In 2009, 37 percent of households in LAC countries suffered some kind of housing problem, whether it was quantitative or qualitative. Informally built dwellings are often constructed with inadequate materials and located on sites that are not connected to the public infrastructure. While there is little agreement in LAC countries on how to measure qualitative and quantitative deficits (Rojas & Medellin, 2011), the UN definition of adequate housing helps establish a common ground.

CONCLUSION

Over the past decades, LAC countries have invested in and designed policies focusing on infrastructure and the social and economic needs of eligible low- and middle-income families. As a poverty reduction strategy, housing, regardless of whether it is formal or informal, is of high value, constituting a safety net in moments of uncertainty and job loss (Economic Commission for Latin America and the Caribbean, 2015; Moser, 2009).

Social movements, political representatives, and the research community have helped to visualize the great potential of and lessons learned from informality, such as the value of the self-built process that adapts to the socioeconomic reality of the urban poor. Informal settlements have been part of the unique character of the LAC city, demonstrating its positive effects on households that are fighting poverty and finding their own housing solutions with little assistance from either the government or the mortgage sector.

Despite considerable variation among LAC countries, three similar trends in their housing policies and housing sectors can be observed. The first is the coexistence of a formal and an informal housing sector, a situation that has lasted for many decades. The second is the focus on homeownership in formal housing policies. Finally, the third is the shift in affordable homeownership policy from strong government interference to a market-based approach.

The coexistence of and interaction between formal and informal markets have required governments to be creative and adaptive to the dynamics of these two types of markets. The quantitative and qualitative deficits, the level of maintenance of the housing stock within both the formal and informal sectors, and the absence of public infrastructure in some areas have been of concern across LAC countries. The challenge of housing in Latin America and the Caribbean in the twenty-first century will not only be to produce more dwellings but to produce adequate housing for all, including rural, urban, middle-, and low-income residents.

REFERENCES

Abramo, P., Rodriguez, M., & Erazo, J. (Coordinators) (2016). *Procesos urbanos en acción: ¿Desarrollo de ciudades para todos?* [Urban processes in action: City development for all?]. Quito: Abya-Yala.

Almandoz, A. (2006). Urban planning and historiography in Latin America. *Progress in Planning,* 65(2), 81–123.

Ballen, S. (2009). *Vivienda social en altura: Tipologias urbanas y directrices de producción en Bogotá* [Social housing in high-rises: Urban typologies and guidelines of provision in Bogota]. Bogota: Universidad Nacional de Colombia.

Bellegooijen, J. V., & Rocco, R. (2013). The ideologies of informality: Informal urbanization in the architectural and planning discourses. *Third World Quarterly,* 34(10), 1794–1810.

Blanco, A. G., Cibils, V. F., & Muñoz, A. F. (2014). *Rental housing wanted: Policy options for Latin America and the Caribbean.* Washington, D.C.: Inter-American Development Bank.

Borsdorf, A., & Hidalgo, R. (2010). From polarization to fragmentation: Recent changes in Latin American urbanization. In P. V. Lindert & O. Verkoren (Eds.), *Decentralized development in Latin America: Experiences in local governance and local development* (pp. 23–34). GeoJournal Library 97. Dordrecht: Springer.

Bouillon, C. P. (Ed.). (2012). *Room for development: Housing markets in Latin America and the Caribbean.* Washington, D.C.: Inter-American Development Bank.

Brea, J. A. (2003). Population dynamics in Latin America. *Population Bulletin,* 58. Retrieved December 20, 2015, from http://www.igwg.org/Source/58.1PopulDynamicsLatinAmer.pdf.

Bromley, R. (2004). Power, property and poverty: Why De Soto's *Mystery of Capital* cannot be solved. In A. Roy & N. AlSayyad (Eds.), *Urban informality: Transnational perspectives from the Middle East, Latin America and South Asia* (pp. 271–288). Lanham, Md.: Lexington Books.

Buckley, R. M., & Kalarickal, J. (Eds.). (2006). *Thirty years of World Bank shelter lending: What have we learned?* Washington, D.C.: World Bank.

Calavita, N., & Mallach, A. (Eds.). (2010). *Inclusionary housing in international perspective: Affordable housing, social inclusion and land value recapture.* Cambridge, Mass.: Lincoln Institute of Land Policy.

Carrion, F. (2005). *El centro histórico como proyecto y objeto de deseo* [The historic center as a project and as an object of desire]. *Eure-Revista Latinoamericana de Estudios Urbano Regionales,* 31(93), 89–100.

Ceballos, O. (2008). *Vivienda social en Colombia: Una mirada desde su legislación 1918–2005* [Social housing in Colombia: A view from its legislation, 1918–2005]. Bogota: Editorial Pontificia Universidad Javeriana.

Colombia, Republica de. (2009). *Generalidades del subsidio familiar de vivienda* [Family housing subsidy overview]. Bogota: Ministry of Interior and Justice of the Republic of Colombia. Retrieved June 12, 2009, from http://www.alcaldiabogota.gov.co/sisjur/normas/Norma1.jsp?i=36468.

Contrucci, P. (1999). *Repoblamiento del casco central de Santiago de Chile: Articulación del sector público y privado* [Bringing residents back to the central areas of Santiago, Chile: Working with public and private sectors]. Retrieved January 10, 2016, from http://www.flacso.org.ec/docs/sfdesculcontrucci.pdf.

Davis, M. (2006). *Planet of slums.* London: Verso.

Delgadillo, V. (2011). *Patrimonio histórico y tugurios: Las politicas habitacionales y de recuperación de los centros históricos de Buenos Aires, Ciudad de México y Quito* [Historic heritage and slums: Housing and rehabilitation policies in the historic centers of Buenos Aires, Mexico City and Quito]. Mexico City: UACM.

Donoso, R. E. (2008). *A case study of housing programs in the historic center of Quito: The need for planning direction (1990–2007).* (Unpublished thesis). University of Texas, Austin.

Donoso, R. E., & Elsinga, M. (forthcoming). Management of low-income condominiums in Bogotá and Quito: The balance between property law and self-organization. *International Journal of Housing Policy*.

Economic Commission for Latin America and the Caribbean. (2013). *Statistical yearbook for Latin America and the Caribbean*. Santiago: United Nations.

Economic Commission for Latin America and the Caribbean. (2015). *Poverty and indigence reduction stalls in most of Latin American countries*. [Press release]. UN Economic Commission for Latin America and the Caribbean. Retrieved June 25, 2015, from http://www.cepal.org/en/comunicados/se-estanca-la-reduccion-de-la-pobreza-y-la-indigencia-en-la-mayoria-de-paises-de-america.

Erazo, J. (2014). *Presentacion, ciudades populares* [Introduction: Popular cities]. *America Latina Hoy, 68*, 11–13.

Esquivel, M. T. (2008). *Conjuntos habitacionales, imaginarios de vida colectiva* [Housing complexes: Imaginaries of collective living]. *Iztapalapa, 64–65*(29), 117–143.

Ferguson, B., & Navarrete, J. (2003). New approaches to progressive housing in Latin America: A key to habitat programs and policy. *Habitat International, 27*(2), 309–323.

Ferguson, B., Rubinstein, J., & Vial, V. D. (1996). The design of direct demand subsidy programs for housing in Latin America. *Review of Urban and Regional Development Studies, 8*(2), 202–219.

Fernandez, E. (2011). *Regularization of informal settlements in Latin America*. Cambridge, Mass.: Lincoln Institute for Land Policy. Retrieved February 5, 2015 from https://www.lincolninst.edu/pubs/dl/1906_1225_Regularization%20PFR%20Rev%202012.pdf.

Fernandez, E., & Maldonado-Copello, M. M. (2009). Law and land policy in shifting paradigms and possibilities for action. *Land Lines*, July 14–19.

Florian, A. (2012). *El derecho a la vivienda* [The right to housing]. In J. F. Pinilla & M. Rengifo (Eds.), *La ciudad y el derecho* [The city and rights] (pp. 108–138). Bogota: Editorial TEMIS.

Garcia, B. (2010). *Vivienda social en Mexico (1940–1999)* [Affordable housing in Mexico (1940–1999)]. *Cuadernos de Vivienda y Urbanismo, 3*(5), 34–49.

Gargarella, R. (2013). *Latin American constitutionalism 1810–2010*. Oxford: Oxford University Press.

Gilbert, A. (1993). *In search of a home: Rental and shared housing in Latin America*. Tucson: University of Arizona Press.

Gilbert, A. (2002). Power, ideology and the Washington consensus: The development and spread of Chilean housing policy. *Housing Studies, 17*(2), 305–324.

Gilbert, A. (2012). Housing abroad: Latin America. In A. T. Carswell (Ed.), *The encyclopedia of housing* (pp. 323–25). Thousand Oaks, Calif.: Sage.

Gilbert, A. G., & Ward, P. M. (1982). Residential movement among the poor: The constraints on housing choice in Latin American cities. *Transactions of the Institute of British Geographers, 7*(2), 129–149.

Godwin, A., & Harris, R. (2005). Housing as a tool of economic development since 1929. *International Journal of Urban and Regional Research, 29*(4), 895–915.

Gonzales, G. (1999). Access to housing and direct housing subsidies: Some Latin American experiences. *CEPAL Review, 69*, 141–163.

Guha-Khasnobis, B., Kanbur, R., & Ostrom, E. (2006). *Linking the formal and informal economy: Concepts and policies*. Oxford: Oxford University Press.

Harris, R., & Giles, C. (2003). A mixed message: The agents and forms of international housing policy, 1945–1973. *Habitat International, 27*, 167–191.

Hofer, A. (2003) *Karl Brunner y el urbanismo europeo en América Latina* [Karl Brunner and European urbanism in Latin America]. Bogota: El Ancora Editores.

Hooker, J. (2005). Indigenous inclusion/black exclusion: Race, ethnicity and multicultural citizenship in Latin America. *Journal of Latin American Studies, 37*(2), 285–310.

Imparato, I., & Ruster, J. (2003). *Slum upgrading and participation: Lessons from Latin America*. Washington, D.C.: World Bank. Retrieved January 20, 2016, from http://www.schwimmer.ca/francesca/slum%20upgrading.pdf.

Inter-American Development Bank. (2004). *Reforming Latin American housing markets: A guide for policy analysis*. Washington, D.C.: Inter-American Development Bank.

Jolly, J.-F. (2004). *Algunos aportes para la conceptualizacion de la politica pública de vivi-*

enda de interes social—VIS [Some observations for the conceptualization of affordable housing public policy]. *Papel Politico, 16*, 77–102.

Kingman, E. (2006). *La ciudad y los otros: Quito 1860–1940. Higienismo, ornato y policía* [The city and the others: Quito 1860–1940. Hygienism, beautification and police]. Quito: FLACSO-Ecuador. Retrieved May 15, 2015, from http://www.flacsoandes.edu.ec/libros/100133-opac.

Klaufus, C. (2010). The two ABCs of aided self-help housing in Ecuador. *Habitat International, 34*, 351–358.

Lentini, M., & Palero, D. (2001). *Decentralizacion de la política habitacional y gestión territorial* [Decentralization of urbanization policy and territorial management]. *Bolentin INVI, 42*(16), 61–71.

Lujanen, M. (2010). Legal challenges in ensuring regular maintenance and repairs of common parts of owner-occupied apartment buildings. *Journal of Legal Affairs and Dispute Resolution in Engineering and Construction, 2*(1), 5–10.

Magdaleno, M. (2001). *Vivienda en centros historicos* [Housing in historic centers]. In F. Carrion (Ed.), *La ciudad construida: Urbanismo en America Latina* [The built city: Urbanism in Latin America] (pp. 367–375). Quito: FLACSO.

Mangin, W. (1967). Latin American squatter settlements: A problem and a solution. *Latin American Research Review, 2*(3), 65–98.

Ministerio de Desarrollo Urbano y Vivienda. (2015). *Acuerdo Ministerial No. 027* [Ministry of Urban Development and Housing, Ministerial Agreement No. 027]. Quito, Ecuador.

Monkkonen, P. (2012). The demand for land regularisation: Theory and evidence from Tijuana, Mexico. *Urban Studies, 49*(2), 271–288.

Moreno, J. R. (2001). *La vivienda en los centros historicos* [Housing in the historic centers]. In F. Carrion (Ed.), *La ciudad construida: Urbanismo en America Latina* [The built city: Urbanism in Latin America] (pp. 297–307). Quito: FLACSO.

Moser, C. (2009). *Ordinary families, extraordinary lives*. Washington, D.C.: Brookings Institution Press.

Ormindo de Azevedo, P. (2001). *Los centros históricos latinoamericanos y la globalización* [The Latin American historic centers and globalization]. In F. Carrión (Ed.), *La ciudad construida: Urbanismo en America Latina* [The built city: Urbanism in Latin America] (pp. 275–287). Quito: FLACSO.

Paquette-Vasalli, C., & Sanchez, M. Y. (2009). Massive housing production in Mexico City: Debating two policies. *Centro h, Revista de la Organización Latinoamericana y del Caribe de Centros Históricos, 3*, 15–26.

Perez, E. (2007). *Calidad habitacional del hogar arrendatario en Bogotá* [Residency quality of tenant households in Bogota]. Bogotá: Universidad Nacional de Colombia.

Pomeroy, S., & Godbout, M. (2011). *Development of the rental housing market in Latin America and the Caribbean*. Washington, D.C.: Inter-American Development Bank.

Pradilla, E. (1983) *El problema de la vivienda en America Latina* [The housing problem in Latin America]. Quito: CIUDAD.

Pugh, C. (2001). The theory and practice of housing sector development for developing countries, 1950–99. *Housing Studies, 16*(4), 399–423.

Roberts, B. (2011). The consolidation of the Latin American city and the undermining of social cohesion. *City & Community, 10*(4), 414–423.

Roberts, B., & Portes, A. (2006). Coping with the free market city: Collective action in six Latin American cities at the end of the twentieth century. *Latin American Research Review, 41*(2), 57–83.

Rodriguez, A., & Sugranyes, A. (Eds.). (2005). *Los con techo: Un desafío para la política de vivienda social* [Those with roofs: A challenge for social housing policy]. Santiago de Chile: Ediciones Sur.

Rojas, E. (2001). The long road to housing sector reform: Lessons from the Chilean housing experience. *Housing Studies, 16*(4), 461–483.

Rojas, E. (2004). *Volver al centro: La recuperación de areas urbanas centrales* [Return to the center: Central areas' urban renewal]. Washington, D.C.: Inter-American Development Bank.

Rojas, E. (Ed.). (2010). *Building cities: Neighbourhood upgrading and urban quality of life*. Washington, D.C.: Inter-American Development Bank.

Rojas, E., & Medellin, N. (2011). *Housing policy matters for the poor: Housing conditions in Latin America and the Caribbean, 1995–2006* (IDB Working Paper Series No. IDB-WP-289). Inter-American Development Bank. Retrieved February 26, 2016, from https://publications.iadb.org/handle/11319/3817?locale-attribute=en.

Rolnik, R. (2013). Late neoliberalism: The financialization of homeownership and housing rights. *International Journal of Urban and Regional Research, 37*(3), 1058–1066.

Rosen, G., & Walks, A. (2013). Rising cities: Condominium development and the private transformation of the metropolis. *Geoforum, 49,* 160–172.

Roy, A. (2005). Urban informality: Toward an epistemology of planning. *Journal of the American Planning Association, 71*(2), 147–158.

Sabatini, F. (2006). *The social spatial segregation in the cities of Latin America.* Washington, D.C.: Inter-American Development Bank.

Santo, C., Zanin, L., & Rufino, B. (Eds.). (2015). *Minha casa . . . E a cidade? Avaliacao do programa Minha Casa Minha Vida em seis estados Brasileiros* [My house . . . and my city? My House My Life Program evaluation in six Brazilian states]. Rio de Janeiro: Letra Capital.

Scatigna, M., & Tovar, C. E. (2007). Securitisation in Latin America. *BIS Quarterly Review,* 1–12.

Skidmore, T., & Smith, P. (2005). *Modern Latin America.* New York: Oxford University Press.

Sletto, B., Donoso, R. E., Strange, S., Muñoz, S., & Thomen, M. (2010). El Rincon de los Olvidados: Participatory GIS, experiential learning and critical pedagogy in Santo Domingo, Dominican Republic. *Journal of Latin American Geography, 9*(3), 111–135.

Smolka, M., & Furtado, F. (Eds.). (2014). *Instrumentos notables de políticas de suelo en América Latina* [Remarkable instruments in land policy in Latin America]. Ecuador: Lincoln Institute for Land Policy.

Telles, E., & Paschel, T. (2014). Who is black, white or mixed race? How skin color, status, and nation shape racial classification in Latin America. *American Journal of Sociology, 120*(3), 864–907.

Torres, C. A., & Vargas, J. E. (2009). Housing for displaced population in Colombia: Public policy and law enforcement recommendations. *Revista INVI, 24*(66), 17–86.

Turner, J. (1976). *Housing by people: Towards autonomy in building environments.* London: Marion Boyars.

UN-HABITAT. (2011). Affordable land and housing in Latin America and the Caribbean (Adequate Housing Series). Vol. 1. Nairobi: UN-HABITAT.

UN-HABITAT. (2014). *The right to adequate housing* (Fact Sheet No. 21 [Rev. 1]). Geneva: United Nations.

United Nations. (1948). *Universal declaration of human rights.* Retrieved June 1, 2015, from http://www.ohchr.org/EN/UDHR/Pages/Introduction.aspx.

United Nations. (2014). *World urbanization prospects.* Retrieved January 20, 2016, from http://esa.un.org/unpd/wup/highlights/wup2014-highlights.pdf.

Uprimny, R. (2011). The recent transformation of constitutional law in Latin America: Trends and challenges. *Texas Law Review, 89*(7), 1587–1610.

van Gelder, J.-L., Cravino, M. C., & Ostuni, F. (forthcoming). Housing informality in Buenos Aires: Past, present and future? *Urban Studies.*

Ward, P. M. (1999). *Colonias and public policy in Texas and Mexico: Urbanization by stealth.* Austin: University of Texas Press.

Ward, P. M. (2011). "A patrimony for the children": Low-income homeownership and housing (im)mobility in Latin American cities. *Annals of the Association of American Geographers, 102*(6), 1489–1510.

Ward, P. M., Jiménez, E., & Virgilio, M. D. (Eds.). (2014). *Housing policy in Latin American cities: A new generation of strategies and approaches for 2016 UN Habitat III.* New York: Routledge.

Zanetta, C. (2001). The evolution of the World Bank's urban lending in Latin America: From sites and services to municipal reform and beyond. *Habitat International, 25*(4), 513–533.

Chapter 24 Housing in Africa

AKIN S. AKINYEMI, PETRA L. DOAN,
AND LINDSAY SLAUTTERBACK

In order to understand the housing sector in Africa it is essential to understand several critical contextual elements. Although much greater attention has been paid to the long urban history of the Middle East, Asia, and Latin America, Africa also has a substantial urban history and the development of housing stock to match (Freund, 2007). Africa's experience with the ravages of the slave trade and later colonialism had profound influences on the urban sector and the types of housing that were deemed suitable (Myers & Owusu, 2008). Accordingly, the first section of this chapter briefly considers the influence of indigenous building traditions as well as the impact of colonialism on the housing sector. The second section explores the postcolonial period (from 1960 onward) and the failure of national urban policy measures and investment schemes by international donors such as the World Bank intended to provide adequate housing for large segments of the urban population, resulting in African cities having very large percentages of their populations living in slums and squatter settlements. The third and final section examines several more recent innovations in the housing sector that hold considerable promise for future developments in the sector.

To understand the diversity of housing in Africa it is helpful to consider briefly the history of this continent and its people. Africa is the second-largest continent both in terms of area (11.7 million square miles) and population (1.1 billion people). Its fifty-four sovereign nations represent diverse social and political characteristics with a rich history and an abundance of natural resources. Early European explorers incorrectly considered Africa south of the Sahara as backward and undeveloped, revealing more about the narrowness of the colonialist vision than the actual nature of sub-Saharan Africa.

Linguistic and cultural diversity abound across Africa, complicating flows of people and information. For the purposes of this chapter, we will subdivide Africa into five distinct regions: North, West, East, Central, and South, based on geography and predominant external influences. The northernmost region is bounded on the south by the Sahara Desert, which extends from the Atlantic Ocean on the west to the Red Sea on the east. The western region includes countries from the Sahel Region below the Sahara extending

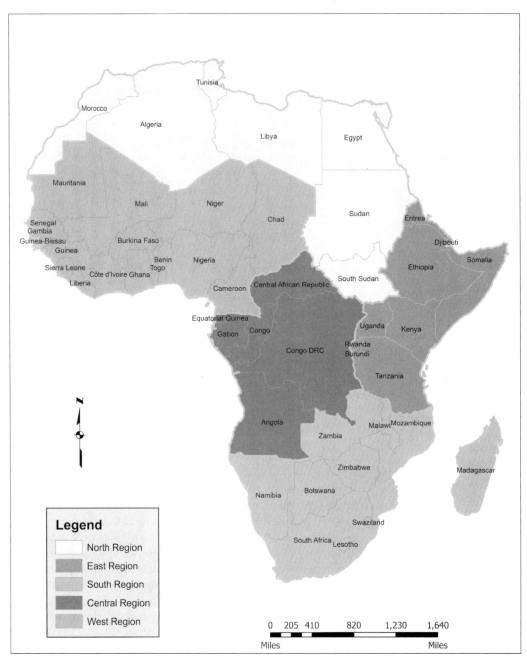

FIGURE 24.1
Africa's Five Regions
Source: Authors.

from the Atlantic coast of Senegal along the Gulf of Guinea as far as Cameroon. The central region is composed of tropical rain forests of a denser variety than the western region. The eastern region follows the coastline of the Indian Ocean from Ethiopia to Tanzania and includes several countries in the interior that are linked to the coast. The southern region has the greatest diversity of climate, from savannah to subarctic (in higher elevations). Figure 24.1 illustrates these regions.

TRADITIONAL FORMS OF RURAL HOUSING

The form, material, and other characteristics of indigenous (traditional) African housing is dependent on the climate, available raw materials, and local preferences. The oral tradition of storytelling, which is very prevalent in African culture, along with the hot climate and extended family cohabitation, makes the compound housing type the most predominant form in all regions. Generally speaking, traditional African housing is an organic form that harmonizes its geometry and materials with nature. Some homes are quite masterful, with ornate features mostly on gates, doors, windows, and perimeter walls. Housing construction in indigenous Africa is a communal activity that is a precursor to present-day concepts of self-help and aided self-help (as discussed below). During the dry, nonharvest seasons, families pool their resources by collecting earth (adobe) and vegetation to build their homes (Akinyemi, 1988).

Adobe, a mixture of moist clay and silt soil, is the primary material for constructing building walls in traditional housing. Depending on the wall height, region, or era, the adobe is often reinforced with fibrous materials such as straw, manure, or shredded sticks. Adobe is most commonly formed into brick-like shapes, dried in the sun, and then laid, but it is also used as rammed earth, a technique similar to today's poured concrete application.

FIGURE 24.2
Rammed Earth Construction Technique
Source: Authors.

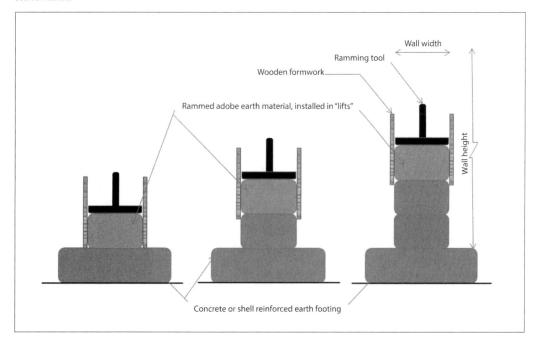

Rammed earth construction uses wooden forms in which semiliquid adobe is poured section by section. This gives the building façade a characteristically horizontal look with differently colored sections, due to different drying periods. This process is illustrated in figure 24.2.

The reinforcement and ramming of adobe also provides increased tensile strength, flexibility, and application to curvilinear walls and upper-floor decks. In the tropical rain forests, such as the Congo, wood studs with a bamboo covering and high-pitched, thatched-leaf roofs are most common. In the more mountainous areas, such as the Dogon of Mali and the Egba of western Nigeria, stone construction is common as well as post-and-beams systems of either stone or wood construction. In riverine areas, such as the rivers, cross-rivers, and delta states of south central Nigeria and along the Mono River in Benin, bamboo structures on pylons are prevalent in fishing communities (Akinyemi, 1988).

TRADITIONAL FORMS OF URBAN HOUSING

The urban history of Africa dates from the tenth to the fifteenth centuries AD and includes well-established urban settlements such as the Aksumite Empire in northern Ethiopia, the Yoruba Empire in western Nigeria, and Gao and Jenne in Mali (Anderson & Rathbone, 2000; Jenkins, Smith, & Wang, 2006). These cities formed the basis for intraregional trading networks within sub-Saharan Africa that resulted in the formation of urban areas with diverse building archetypes (Anderson & Rathbone, 2000; Coquery-Vidrovitch, 2005; El-Shakhs & Obudho, 1974; Freund, 2007; Goodwin, 2006; Jenkins et al., 2006). The physical layout of these cities mirrored the patterns of social stratification in indigenous African communities, with the king at the center and a family's distance from the center inversely proportional to its social status, except that very strong hunters and warriors were known to live on the outer rings for the community's protection. The threat of invasion also led to the construction of walled cities such as Zaria and Benin City in Nigeria. Although few communities can be described as being indigenous today, some cities have managed to preserve a distinctly African flavor in their town and building characteristics. For example, the city of Aksum in northern Ethiopia has maintained its indigenous building characteristics to the point that UNESCO designated it a World Heritage Site in 1993 (Anderson & Rathbone, 2000).

In the period just prior to colonization, some degree of social order, spatial organization, housing sophistication, and hierarchy had emerged in various centers of trade in Africa. While building materials of this era were largely limited to indigenous mud and vegetation, some evidence of increasing sophistication is evident in the form of buildings, number of stories, and complexity of wall-roof interconnectedness. An intra-African regional mix of housing types was beginning to emerge, especially along the trans-Saharan trade routes. The Mediterranean style, which comes from Arab influences to the north, can also be included in this era, primarily because the materials and most of the construction techniques are still indigenous to Africa, though the outward look is more sophisticated (Akinyemi, 1988; AlSayyad, 1991; Lejeune & Sabatino, 2010).

COLONIAL HOUSING

Colonial housing developments were established in the wake of the Berlin Conference of 1884, at which European countries divided up the continent into areas where individual countries could pursue colonization (Acemoglu & Robinson, 2012; Rakodi, 1997). After 1884 colonial authorities established administration centers and built houses for European officers, administrators, and business expeditions. Social stratification followed the patterns of a master-servant relationship, with a typical colonial house consisting of a single-family mansion and a detached servants' quarter. This period brought new building materials and construction techniques, including bricks, shingles, tin, metal forging, brick or block molds, scaffolding, and multilevel buildings. Although these materials have good plasticity and the potential for great variety of form, by and large they were used to produce rectilinear, box-like houses in new town layouts that followed the strict grid forms common in European cities.

Variations in this era of housing include British Victorian, American Richardsonian, and Brazilian brick mansions. Overlap between this and the modern/contemporary era includes the use of sand-cement blocks, corrugated asbestos cement, sheet-metal- and shale-tiled shingles, plastering, and steel-reinforced precast or cast-in-place concrete. The influence of this era went far beyond housing's brick and mortar, introducing a whole new social order and the beginning of land surveying, documented town planning, and residential subdivision and zoning, which probably codified segregation (Akinyemi, 1988).

HOUSING IN THE AFTERMATH OF COLONIALISM

Most African countries gained independence in the 1960s, stimulating high hopes and expectations for new directions as well as encouraging substantial rural-to-urban migration across the continent. Rural populations looking for more stable economic livelihoods with which to increase their standard of living and better provide for their families were powerfully attracted to the promise of life in the capital cities of these newly independent African countries. According to the World Bank's African Development Indicators, the proportion of the total population of Africa that was urban jumped from just 18.7 percent in 1960 to 32 percent in 1990. As of 2005, the urban population had continued to grow, with 37.4 percent of the total population in Africa residing in cities (World Databank, 2015). Governments were unprepared for this rapid influx of rural populations and were increasingly disenchanted by the proliferation of squatter settlements on the peri-urban fringes of their cities (Arimah, 2011).

Several authors (Njoh, 1999; Simon, 1992) have suggested that planning and construction methods continued in the tradition of past colonial masters, resulting in only two new forms of housing development: apartments (or flats) and squatter settlements. Apartments or flats were seen as a formal response to the problem of providing modern housing and were built in the international architecture style emerging in Europe, reminiscent of social or public housing developments in England and the United States. This type of housing was typically provided by the public sector and was therefore in limited supply. The remainder of the burgeoning urban population found housing in squatter settlements (UN-HABITAT, 2003).

STATE-PROVIDED HOUSING

The 1970s marked the era of state-provided housing, in which the state developed some large-scale housing projects intended to accommodate poor urban residents and discourage people from settling illegally on land in the cities. The following planned housing types had emerged: the compound house, a loose or closed loop of huts joined together by perimeter walls and inhabited by a multigenerational family; the courtyard house, containing a few one- or two-story buildings with rooms lining verandahs that face a central courtyard, which were more common in northern areas; the single-family house, which emerged in the colonial era and consists of a main one- or two-story house and a detached servants' quarter separated by a well-manicured garden; the single-room occupancy, commonly referred to as "face me, I face you," usually a two-story tenement building with shared kitchen and bathroom; and apartments or flats, usually a two- to four-story self-contained multifamily apartment unit (Akinyemi, 1988).

Unfortunately, in many places state-provided housing did not live up to the intentions of housing the poor because any new housing was frequently claimed by upper-income citizens and those employed by the state. Under colonialism, many employees of the state were provided with housing, and this prerogative continued to prevail following independence in many African countries. State-provided housing also proved to be hugely expensive, and many states found that there was no way to implement these housing projects with the meager budgets they had. Additionally, while these projects were described as "large-scale," they were unable to meet the continuing demand for new housing units as urban populations continued to grow (Stren, 1990). Adenuga (2013) suggests that in Nigeria the public sector does not produce a sufficient number of houses, and those it does produce are of low quality. Another author suggests that part of the problem in Nigerian public-housing programs can be linked to corruption, political interference, and the lack of trained technical staff overseeing construction (Ademiluyi, 2010).

The debacle faced by many countries in Africa regarding state-provided housing is illustrated by the case of public housing in Nairobi, Kenya. While city agencies, including the Nairobi City Council, claimed to maintain a commitment to low-cost affordable housing, the program was marked by lack of affordable, rentable, and available units. The lack of units continued to be a major issue, and every few years the significant increase in population further illustrated the disparity. Temple and Temple (1980) argue that public housing in Nairobi consistently failed to keep pace with population growth, resulting in severe shortages. In addition, biases persisted in favor of those associated with the government and higher-income groups, leaving those with the most need unable to find housing (Temple & Temple, 1980).

Coping with Squatter Settlements

Many low-income rural-to-urban migrants had few skills and little formal education, making work in the informal sector their only option. The jobs available in the informal economy include activities that are not formally recognized by the government (either through taxation or registration), but work within this informal sector can be lucrative and offer a viable means of making ends meet. However, informal-sector workers frequently earn irregular incomes that are difficult to quantify or document, making it difficult for them to qualify for formal-sector loans or mortgages needed to purchase more established housing in the city. Mitullah (1992) argues that in both sites and services and upgrading schemes designed for low-income urban households, the poor did not have access to these programs. Accordingly, the only means of obtaining housing in these cases is to rent or build outside planned and developed areas (Arimah, 2011).

In addition, since the option of owning land via formal land tenure procedures was not available for many residents, they either settled on unoccupied land or made irregular payments to intermediaries to gain access to buildable land. These areas are often called squatter settlements because the land may be illegally occupied or not formally registered with government authorities. In many cases, a majority of the urban population lives in these types of settlements (Obudho & Aduwo, 1989). This form of housing in many African cities, sometimes called shantytowns or bidonvilles, consists of sporadic shelter using makeshift, repurposed building materials, often in unplanned clusters of shacks. There has been much study and attempted definition of these sporadic shelters (Arku, 2009; Davis, 2006; Jenkins & Andersen, 2011; Lupala, 2002; Mbiba & Huchzermeyer, 2002) as well as recent efforts to reform housing in Africa (Arku, 2009; Danso-Wiredu & Loopmans, 2013; Hamid & Elhassan, 2014; Obeng-Odoom & Amedzro, 2011).

The initial response to the proliferation of squatter housing was to bulldoze these communities in an effort to discourage their proliferation. However, despite the violent destruction of property in such attempts, squatter settlements have continued to spring up, often linked to outright rebellion and political organization against the state (Abrams, 1966). African countries continue to struggle with housing shortages as rural-to-urban migration continues and new residents are forced into slums and squatter settlements either as squatters or as renters from other squatter settlements. The scale of the problem in Africa is massive; according to United Nations estimates, 71.9 percent of the urban population, or roughly 166 million people, lived in slums in 2001 (UN-HABITAT, 2003). A number of countries have explored alternatives to address housing issues in Africa with financing from international lending institutions. The two most common alternatives consist of projects within the squatter settlements themselves (in situ upgrading) that upgrade basic infrastructure such as roads and electrical and water services and providing new sites with basic services (sites and service projects) along with concrete foundation pads upon which residents can build their own homes. Both of these types of projects require land tenure solutions as well as housing solutions (De Soto, 1989). However, international donors are reluctant to intervene if squatters have not resolved issues related to land tenure, complicating the usefulness and wide applicability of these strategies (Arimah, 2011; Gulyani & Basset, 2007).

Aided Self-Help and Sites and Services Schemes

As governments continued to struggle with providing housing and ensuring that land tenure rights were secured, a different option was needed to accommodate the ever-increasing numbers of rural-to-urban migrants who were continuing to settle in "spontaneous housing" on the fringes of cities. Planned development was slow and unable to provide adequate amounts of land for residential development to meet the demand for housing from the increasing urban population. High rates of urban population growth in Africa surpassed the ability of the public sector to provide urban services, including housing and basic infrastructure, resulting in the vast growth of the informal sector (Stren, 1990). In response, many new urban residents simply began building on any land that was not otherwise developed, without waiting for planning permission or the acquisition of formal tenure.

The international lending community, stimulated by Turner and Fichter's work in Latin America (1972), recognized that providing more security of tenure (either by providing pathways to legal ownership of land or by reducing fears of imminent destruction of squatter housing) would encourage individuals to help themselves or undertake what came to be known as self-help projects. In Africa, self-help projects were partly a reaction to earlier state-provided housing efforts that had failed miserably and partly a recognition that any assistance for low-income housing would need to rely on individuals and families taking an active role in helping themselves in conjunction with international donors. One solution for achieving this blend was called sites and services. This scheme was intended to provide large numbers of serviced, buildable lots with very basic infrastructure and concrete foundations upon which houses could be built. The costs of these projects were covered by large loans from international institutions, such as the World Bank, to national housing entities, which in turn distributed these funds as loans to individuals and families, who would then, in principle, repay the loans over time.

According to a paper published by the World Bank (Mayo and Angel 1993), African housing projects had a significantly lower rate of return than projects in other regions. Over 25 percent did not generate a positive rate of return (Mayo and Angel, 1993). While countries such as Tanzania, Kenya, and Senegal continued to accept structural adjustment loans related to housing, most projects were affected by stagnating economies. Sanyal (1987) describes a squatter upgrading and sites and services project in Lusaka, Zambia, and notes that cost recovery was a virtual failure. Sanyal (1987) notes that since residents did not fully understand the extent of their financial obligations, they were not motivated to repay loans. In addition, the system developed to collect on these loans was not well planned or implemented, resulting in additional delays. The lack of political will to enforce existing sanctions further exacerbated the problem.

Self-help projects funded by the World Bank all across the continent were, and in a few cases still are, marked by a lack of understanding of the needs of changing and increasing populations in urbanized areas. Because of this lack of understanding, housing projects have struggled to meet the needs of impoverished people they aimed to help, and projects have often lacked a specific timeline and have been nowhere near ready when needed. The first major sites and services project funded by the World Bank in Africa was located in Dakar, Senegal (White, 1985). The planners anticipated that the project would help meet the housing needs of about fourteen thousand low-income families, but by 1984 only thirty-six hundred houses were built and occupied, while another three thousand were still under construction. In addition to slow progress in completing housing construction, less than 20 percent of those built were actually serving low-income families. This example illustrates the problems inherent in many self-help projects funded by international donors who do not understand the scale of the issues or the underlying causes of the scarcity of affordable housing (White, 1985). As a result, donor interest in large-scale self-help projects has waned, although self-help continues at a community level (see the discussion of Slum Dwellers International below).

Large-Scale Private or Public-Private Housing Initiatives

In recent years, a number of city and national governments have sought to create world-class cities by allowing private investors free reign to establish new settlements at the fringes of African cities (Cain, 2014; Grant, 2015; Jordhaus-Lier, 2015). Watson (2014) offers a strong critique of attempts by African urban planners and international consulting firms to impose modernist megaprojects on the superstructure of African urbanism. Many of these efforts attempt to leapfrog existing urban problems by building sleek, modern satellite cities at the urban periphery and beyond. Widespread efforts along these lines include Tatu City and Konza Technocity in Nairobi, parts of a planned world-class city with several urban developments; satellite cities outside of Luanda in Angola; New Kigamboni City, a planned eco-city in Tanzania; Cité le Fleuve, a grand vision to make Kinshasa a world-class city; Hope City, a planned technology hub outside Accra in Ghana; and the massive Eko Atlantic development in Lagos, built on reclaimed land (Grant, 2015; Watson, 2014). Each of these plans has involved attempts by local development actors and their international consultant partners to bypass planning processes, with only limited local input. Watson (2014) concludes that these projects exacerbate the abandonment of low-income people by municipal governments and that the sheer scale of this policy shift may lead to organized resistance to such programs by shack dwellers, unemployed youth, and local, informal, and formal businesses. Jordhaus-Lier (2015) studied the N2 Gateway megaproject in Cape Town, South Africa, and suggests that these kinds of projects are likely to be politically controversial and to stimulate more radical forms of dissent. Furthermore, the cost of housing in these modernist dream cities can be prohibitive. In the case of Luanda, Angola, large investments from China combined with large Angolan subsidies resulted in massive ghost cities that are too expensive for most local residents and have led to "a dramatic collapse in real estate values in that section of the market" (Cain, 2014: 567).

Other housing projects utilize public-private partnerships in which public-sector involvement is used to encourage private-sector investments from both domestic and international investors. For instance, in Nigeria these developments often involve the construction of new communities. Ikejiofor (2014) examined new communities outside Abuja and Lagos that were intended to promote private-sector investment to meet the social needs of the majority of the urban population, which is low income. Unfortunately, the implementation of these projects has been plagued by corruption and the purchase of units intended for low-income residents by wealthy Nigerian residents. Ikejiofor (2014) finds that the strategy of using public-private partnerships is effectively a scheme for building fancy homes for very high income consumers by using large-scale private-sector developers. Although the intent of public-private partnership efforts was to build affordable two-bedroom units, in the five case studies Ikejiofor (2014) analyzed, three projects provided three- or four-bedroom homes with expensive finishings and the other two projects had a combination of two- and three-bedroom units. The most inexpensive of the two-bedroom units was estimated to cost 10 million Naira ($62,500), far more than the yearly salary of an average civil servant, who earns 216,000 Naira ($1,360).

Recent Innovations in the Housing Sector in Africa

Several promising innovations in the housing sector in sub-Saharan Africa suggest a shift toward more recognition and respect for residents of slums and shantytowns. One of the unique features of the African context is the complex nature of land tenure in the region. Prior to colonialism, customary land tenure, a form of usufruct or use rights, was the predominant landownership pattern across most of the continent. Colonial powers, particularly Britain and France, imposed freehold land tenure on urban areas but for the most part were unsuccessful in making changes to traditional or customary land tenure in the countryside (Njoh & Akiwumi, 2012). Part of the push for urban land to be treated as freehold derives from the assumption that private landownership (freehold) is a prerequisite for urban investments in permanent housing and building materials. Turner (1976) argues that if squatters were given ownership of their parcels, they would begin to make substantial improvements in their housing structures. His work was based on his experience in Latin America but resonated throughout the developing world, including Africa, and policy makers have for many years sought to provide formal land tenure so that residents of former squatter areas would be incentivized to begin investing in more permanent materials. Other research has confirmed the importance of landownership in the Latin American context (De Soto, 1989).

More recently, scholars and practitioners have begun to rethink the necessity for outright ownership of land in favor of more emphasis on security (Payne, 2001; Payne, Durand-Lasserve, & Rakodi, 2009). The United Nations Human Settlements Programme (UN-HABITAT) has argued that a critical component to enhancing urban security is for cities to recognize that the informal city exists and that forced evictions must cease (UN-HABITAT, 2007). In Western countries, legal procedures are required to register a deed for a piece of property, which proves who owns the land in question, but in many developing countries determining who owns a piece of land is more complex. In many parts of the informal city, ownership in terms of a formal deed is not the same as security of tenure. Slum dwellers may not have a formal deed to the property on which they live for a number of reasons. They may consider the cost of registering ownership to be too high, they may have purchased the land from a prior occupant who had not registered that ownership, or they may be squatting on land owned by the state or by an absentee landlord. There are many gradations to tenure security, and steps should be taken to increase the security of tenure for those whose claim to a dwelling in a city is based on less formal, unregistered, and often unrecognized means of documentation.

Noting the limited amount of freehold land available for urban development, Rakodi and Leduka (2004) suggest that the majority of urban residents in Africa continue to utilize informal connections to find appropriate land or housing. The supply of land is frequently constrained by the contested nature of land tenure in the peri-urban areas that are transitioning from rural and agricultural land to urban uses. Customary tenure arrangements designate tribal authorities to allocate rural land according to need, but this system has difficulty coping with the sharp increase of demand from higher population density and, especially, the demand for housing and business locations that are semipermanent (Oduro, 2010). Kalabamu (2014) suggests that in Botswana the expansion of demand for urban land in the traditional village of Mogoditshane adjacent to Gaborone led to many illegal subdivisions of agricultural land and an increasing number of competing land claims, disagreements, and litigation that made the tenure of many plots unclear. Furthermore, because land registration systems in many countries are overly bureaucratic and require official surveys and documents, security of tenure is difficult to obtain for many residents of these peri-urban areas.

One important innovation in increasing the supply of buildable land for housing is enabling the use of alternative forms of documentation for claims to land. Research conducted at the International Institute for Environment and Development in the United Kingdom suggests that when governments recognize land claims based on informal contracts, witnessing, and testimony of nongovernmental organizations, greater security of tenure can be obtained, incentivizing residents to invest in the quality of their housing (International Institute for Environment and Development, 2006). Some governments have experimented with issuing less-formal certificates of occupancy in place of land titles, which have proven to be effective at providing security of tenure, if not necessarily formal tenure (Rakodi & Leduka, 2004).

Previous government efforts to provide housing for low-income and homeless populations were fraught with tension and difficulties. One means of coping with these challenges that provides a ray of hope is the growth of local federations of homeless people who are taking greater responsibility for their own housing. As noted above, outright public provision of housing has not worked in most developing contexts. For example, sites and service projects established by governments, often in cooperation with the World Bank, are often plagued by very low repayment rates or are taken over by middle-income residents (Sanyal, 1987). Mitlin and Satterthwaite (2007) suggest that an innovative mechanism for housing low-income people is linked to the increasing recognition of the vital role that can be played by community-based organizations affiliated with Slum/Shack Dwellers International (SDI). This international nongovernmental organization (NGO) was formed in 1996, when representatives of the Asian Coalition for Housing Rights, the South African Homeless People's Federation, and other African and Latin American NGOs met (Patel, Burra, & d'Cruz, 2001). Support from international actors such as UN-HABITAT and several NGOs from the Global North enabled a series of international meetings, which encouraged the launch of a number of national federations. The SDI website (http://www.sdinet.org/) currently lists nineteen African countries that have local affiliates, in addition to five other affiliates in Latin America and five in Asia.

In the SDI model, residents of squatter settlements take a lead role in setting up a local federation that will be managed by residents themselves. Mitlin (2013) suggests that SDI has helped about two hundred thousand households obtain more secure tenure arrangements and has enabled the construction of about fifty-five thousand homes overall. A key ingredient is the establishment of savings and credit societies to support slum dwellers in accumulating sufficient capital to improve their homes and their neighborhoods. These savings groups enable low-income people, and especially women, to more fully participate in upgrading efforts (Mitlin & Satterthwaite, 2007). Greater local autonomy also enables these civil society movements to create "spaces of governmentality" (Watson, 2009) that can result in significant policy shifts toward a pro-poor orientation.

The South African Homeless People's Federation is the oldest of these federations in Africa and has had some success with rotating loan funds, like those used by the Grameen Bank in Bangladesh (Yunus, 1998), that are administered by members of the federation themselves (Bolnick, 1996). The National Slum Dwellers Federation of Uganda in Jinja has had some success in fighting evictions and arguing for the importance of local interventions before city council (Nyamweru & Dobson, 2014). In Jinja the federation has enabled slum dwellers to exert some influence over planning and development decisions being made by the local government for the first time. SDI local affiliates in Malawi (Manda, 2007) and Zimbabwe (Chitekwe-Biti, 2009) have also begun to play influential roles in encouraging slum residents and local governments to find common ground.

Elsewhere in Kenya, two groups, Muungano wa Wanvijiji (the Kenyan urban poor federation) and the Pamoja Trust (a Kenyan NGO working to oppose demolitions and forced evictions), have cooperated to put pressure on government agencies in favor of low-income people and, at the same time, have created housing savings groups in the poorest slum areas outside Nairobi (Weru, 2004). These grassroots groups have worked closely with SDI to learn basic skills and basic community self-governance techniques. Weru (2004) indicates that developing community-based management skills is critical to creating strong communities and establishing the groundwork for future upgrading. One of the most difficult issues in conducting upgrading work is the need to understand the layout of the often congested and densely packed settlements. In Tanzania, grassroots community organizations have taken on the task of mapping their settlements in order to obtain water and sanitation upgrading (Glöckner, Mkanga, & Ndezi, 2004). By involving the community, these efforts have created trust in the process and stimulated greater involvement in decisions about the upgrading plans. Although community-led enumerations continue to be challenging to implement, they remain a very useful tool for building local capacity among slum dwellers to begin producing alternative solutions and influence local government decision making (Patel, Baptist, & d'Cruz, 2012).

CONCLUSION

This chapter has provided an overview of housing conditions across Africa. Many of the current problems in the housing sector are linked to an ongoing failure to recognize the value of indigeneity, especially vis-à-vis the capacity of people to create their own viable housing. Clearly a portion of this neglect can be attributed to colonialism, in which foreign administrators persisted in viewing native and traditional solutions as inherently inferior and unworthy of support in modern colonial cities. These same attitudes were adopted and perpetuated by the governments of newly independent countries during the latter half of the twentieth century as they adopted Western-style building codes and tried to replicate cities of the developed world. A shift in perspective from a top-down to more of a bottom-up perspective is slowly gaining strength along with the recognition that slums and squatter settlements are not a problem but rather are a solution that is in process (Peattie, 1994).

The formal housing sector modeled on Western standards has been unable to supply housing at an affordable rate for the vast majority of the rapidly growing urban population. Some observers have suggested that mismanagement, poor maintenance, and outright corruption by government housing programs have combined to exacerbate the supply problems in the modern sector. The shantytowns ringing most African cities are a result of this failure and, at the same time, are evidence that low-income people in these cities have found housing and have established a toehold in the urban economy. While some African governments (most recently Zimbabwe in its Operation Murambatsvina [Restore Order]) continue to attempt to eradicate illegal housing (Potts, 2007), many have begun to recognize the importance of working with residents of informal settlements to improve basic conditions. These more enlightened schemes, with the help of international NGOs such as SDI, have shown considerable promise in South Africa, Uganda, Kenya, and a number of other African settings.

International donors have for the most part been supportive of these changes. The World Bank has dramatically reduced its direct support of urban-sector projects, choosing to focus instead on revitalizing the financial markets that are a part of the problem for middle-income families seeking to purchase housing. Ongoing projects in Nigeria and Uganda have the explicit goals of helping build more robust financial institutions that can more efficiently and effectively provide loans for housing and other infrastructure projects. The U.S. Agency for International Development (USAID) has also moved away from direct housing provision and has begun to focus on sustainable infrastructure and service provision to existing settlements. In addition, the Department for International Development (DFID) of the United Kingdom has adopted the most explicit emphasis on pro-poor development, encouraging host country partners to recognize and work with grassroots organizations in urban areas. Finally UN-HABITAT has also established a new initiative, the Participatory Slum Upgrading Program, which recognizes that slum dwellers must play a central role in improving their settlements. These new programs and initiatives suggest that while a great deal of work remains to be done in this sector, there is mounting evidence that an important shift from top-down to bottom-up and pro-poor approaches is starting to take hold in a number of African countries.

REFERENCES

Abrams, C. (1966). *Squatter settlements: The problem and the opportunity* (Agency Report #63). Washington, D.C.: U.S. Agency for International Development.

Acemoglu, D., & Robinson, J. A. (2012). *Why nations fail*. New York: Crown.

Ademiluyi, I. A. (2010). Public housing delivery strategies in Nigeria: A historical perspective of policies and programs. *Journal of Sustainable Development in Africa, 12*, 153–161.

Adenuga, O. A. (2013). Factors affecting quality in the delivery of public housing projects in Lagos State, Nigeria. *International Journal of Engineering and Technology, 3*, 332–344.

Akinyemi, A. S. (1988). *Self-help housing technology: Designing an autonomous, self-sustaining community* (Unpublished master's thesis, Department of Architecture). Florida A&M University, Tallahassee.

AlSayyad, N. (1991). *Cities and caliphs: On the genesis of Arab Muslim urbanism.* New York: Greenwood Press.

Anderson, D. M., & Rathbone, R. (Eds.). (2000). *Africa's urban past.* Oxford: James Currey.

Arimah, B. (2011). *Slums as expressions of social exclusion: Explaining the prevalence of slums in African countries.* Nairobi: United Nations Human Settlements Programme (UN-HABITAT).

Arku, G. (2009). Housing policy changes in Ghana in the 1990s. *Housing Studies, 24,* 261–272.

Bolnick, J. (1996). uTshani buyakhuluma (The grass speaks): People's dialogue and the South African People's Homeless Federation (1994–96). *Environment and Urbanization, 8,* 153–170.

Cain, A. (2014). African urban fantasies: Past lessons and emerging realities. *Environment and Urbanization, 26,* 561–567.

Chitekwe-Biti, B. (2009). Struggles for urban land by the Zimbabwe Homeless People's Federation. *Environment and Urbanization, 21,* 347–366.

Coquery-Vidrovitch, C. (2005). *History of African cities south of the Sahara.* Princeton, N.J.: Markus Wiener.

Danso-Wiredu, E. Y., & Loopmans, M. (2013). The gap between visions and policies: Housing the poor and urban planning in Ghana. *Planum: The Journal of Urbanism, 26,* 2–11.

Davis, M. (2006). *Planet of slums.* London: Verso.

De Soto, H. (1989). *The other path: The invisible revolution in the Third World.* New York: HarperCollins.

El-Shakhs, S., & Obudho, R. (Eds.). (1974). *Urbanization, national development, and regional planning in Africa.* New York: Praeger.

Freund, B. (2007). *The African city: A history.* Cambridge: Cambridge University Press.

Glöckner, H., Mkanga, M., & Ndezi, T. (2004). Local empowerment through community mapping for water and sanitation in Dar es Salaam. *Environment and Urbanization, 16*(1), 185–197.

Goodwin, S. (2006). *Africa's legacies of urbanization: Unfolding saga of a continent.* Lanham, Md.: Lexington Books.

Grant, R. (2015). Sustainable African urban futures: Stocktaking and critical reflection on proposed urban projects. *American Behavioral Scientist, 59,* 294–310.

Gulyani, S., & Basset, E. (2007). Retrieving the baby from the bathwater: Slum upgrading in sub-Saharan Africa. *Environment and Planning C: Government and Policy, 25,* 486–515.

Hamid, G. M., & Elhassan, A. A. M. (2014). Incremental housing as an alternative housing policy: Evidence from Greater Khartoum, Sudan. *International Journal of Housing Policy, 14,* 181–195.

Ikejiofor, U. C. (2014). Dashed hopes: Public-private partnership and sustainable low-income housing delivery in Nigeria. In J. Bredenoord, P. van Lindert, & P. Smets (Eds.), *Affordable housing in the urban global south* (pp. 349–362). New York: Routledge.

International Institute for Environment and Development. (2006). *Innovation in securing land rights in Africa: Lessons from experience* (IIED Working Paper). London: International Institute for Environment and Development. Retrieved January 26, 2017, from http://pubs.iied.org/pdfs/12531IIED.pdf.

Jenkins, P., & Andersen, J. E. (2011). *Developing cities in between the formal and informal.* Paper presented at the ECAS Fourth European Conference on African Studies, Uppsala, Sweden.

Jenkins, P., Smith, H., & Wang, Y. (2006). *Planning and housing in the rapidly urbanizing world.* New York: Routledge.

Jordhaus-Lier, D. (2015). Community resistance to mega-projects: The case of the N2 Gateway project in Joe Slovo informal settlement, Cape Town. *Habitat International, 45,* 169–176.

Kalabamu, F. T. (2014). Divergent paths: Customary land tenure changes in Greater Gaborone, Botswana. *Habitat International, 44*, 474–481.

Lejeune, J., & Sabatino, M. (2010). *Modern architecture and the Mediterranean: Vernacular dialogues and contested identities*. New York: Routledge.

Lupala, J. M. (2002). *Urban types in rapidly urbanizing cities: Analysis of formal and informal settlements in Dar es Salaam, Tanzania* (Unpublished doctoral dissertation). Royal Institute of Technology, Stockholm.

Manda, M. A. Z. (2007). Mchenga—urban poor housing fund in Malawi. *Environment and Urbanization, 19*, 337–359.

Mayo, S. K., and Angel, S. (1993). *Housing: Enabling markets to work; with technical supplements*. Washington, D.C.: World Bank.

Mbiba, B., & Huchzermeyer, M. (2002). Contentious development: Peri-urban studies in sub-Saharan Africa. *Progress in Development Studies, 2*, 113–131.

Mitlin, D. (2013). A class act: Professional support to people's organizations in the towns and cities of the global south. *Environment and Urbanization, 25*, 483–499.

Mitlin, D., & Satterthwaite, D. (2007). Strategies for grassroots control of international aid. *Environment and Urbanization, 19*, 483–500.

Mitullah, W. V. (1992). *State policy and urban housing in Kenya: The case of low-income housing in Nairobi*. Nairobi: University of Nairobi.

Myers, G., & Owusu, F. (2008). Cities of sub-Saharan Africa. In S. Brunn, M. Hays-Mitchell, & D. Ziegler (Eds.), *Cities of the world: World regional urban development* (pp. 341–383). Lanham, Md.: Rowman and Littlefield.

Njoh, A. J. (1999). *Urban planning, housing and spatial structures in sub-Saharan Africa: Nature, impact and development implications of exogenous forces*. Aldershot, U.K.: Ashgate.

Njoh, A., & Akiwumi, F. (2012). Colonial legacies, land policies, and the millennium development goals: Lessons from Cameroon and Sierra Leone. *Habitat International, 36*, 210–218.

Nyamweru, Hellen, and Dobson, Skye. 2014. *Building partnerships between urban poor communities and local governments: The case of the National Slum Dwellers Federation of Uganda in Jinja* (IIED Working Paper). London: IIED. http://pubs.iied.org/10700IIED.

Obeng-Odoom, F., & Amedzro, L. (2011). Inadequate housing in Ghana. *Urbani izziv, 22*, 127–137.

Obudho, R. A., & Aduwo, G. O. (1989). Slum and squatter settlements in urban centres of Kenya: Towards a planning strategy. *Netherlands Journal of Housing and Environmental Research 4*, 17–30.

Oduro, C. Y. (2010). *Effects of rapid urbanization on livelihoods in the peri-urban areas of Accra, Ghana* (Unpublished Ph.D. dissertation, Department of Urban and Regional Planning). Florida State University, Tallahassee.

Patel, S., Baptist, C., & d'Cruz, C. (2012). Knowledge is power: Informal communities assert their right to the city through SDI and community-led enumerations. *Environment and Urbanization, 24*, 13–26.

Patel, S., Burra, S., & d'Cruz, C. (2001). Slum/Shack Dwellers International (SDI): From foundations to treetops. *Environment and Urbanization, 13*, 45–59.

Payne, G. (2001). Urban land tenure policy options: Titles or rights? *Habitat International, 25*, 415–429.

Payne, G., Durand-Lasserve, A., & Rakodi, C. (2009). The limits of land titling and home ownership. *Environment and Urbanization, 21*, 443–462.

Peattie, L. (1994). An argument for slums. *Journal of Planning Education and Research, 13*, 136–143.

Potts, D. (2007). "Restoring order"? Operation Murambatsvina and the urban crisis in Zimbabwe. *Journal of Southern African Studies, 32*, 273–291.

Rakodi, C. (Ed.). (1997). *The urban challenge in Africa*. New York: United Nations University Press.

Rakodi, C., and Leduka, C. (2004). *Informal land delivery processes and access to land for the poor: A comparative study of six African cities*. Birmingham: International Development Department, University of Birmingham. Retrieved January 26, 2017, from http://r4d.dfid.gov.uk/pdf/outputs/mis_spc/r8076-comparative_land_delivery.pdf.

Sanyal, B. (1987). Problems of cost-recovery in development projects: Experience of the Lusaka squatter upgrading and site/service project. *Urban Studies, 24*, 285–295.

Simon, D. (1992). *Cities, capital and development: African cities in the world economy.* London: Belhaven Press.

Stren, R. E. (1990). Urban housing in Africa: The changing role of government policy. In P. Amis & P. Lloyd (Eds.), *Housing Africa's urban poor* (pp. 35–54). Manchester: Manchester University Press.

Temple, N., & Temple, F. (1980). The politics of public housing in Nairobi. In M. Grindle (Ed.), *Politics and policy implementation in the Third World* (pp. 235–250). Princeton, N.J.: Princeton University Press.

Turner, J. F. C. (1976). *Housing by people: Towards autonomy in building environments.* London: Marion Boyars.

Turner, J. F. C., & Fichter, R. (1972) *Freedom to build: Dweller control of the housing process.* New York: Macmillan.

UN-HABITAT. (2003). *The challenge of slums: Global report on human settlements 2003.* Nairobi: United Nations Center for Human Settlements.

UN-HABITAT. (2007). *Enhancing urban safety and security: Global report on human settlements.* Nairobi: United Nations Center for Human Settlements.

Watson, V. (2009). The planned city sweeps the poor away: Urban planning and 21st century urbanization. *Progress in Planning, 72*, 151–193.

Watson, V. (2014). African urban fantasies: Dreams or nightmares? *Environment and Urbanization, 26*, 215–231.

Weru, J. (2004). Community federations and city upgrading: The work of the Pamoja trust and the Muungano in Kenya. *Environment and Urbanization, 16*, 47–62.

White, R. R. (1985). The impact of policy conflict on the implementation of a government-assisted housing project in Senegal. *Canadian Journal of African Studies, 19*, 502–528.

World Data Bank. (2015). *World development indicators.* Retrieved January 26, 2017, from http://databank.worldbank.org/data/.

Yunus, M. (1998). Poverty alleviation: Is economics any help? Lessons from the Grameen Bank experience. *Journal of International Affairs, 52*, 47–65.

Chapter 25

Global Housing Challenges in the Twenty-First Century

CORIANNE PAYTON SCALLY

People and places across the globe face a variety of housing challenges. This chapter—complementing and supplementing previous chapters in this volume—will highlight some of the most critical challenges that need to be addressed before housing can be a vehicle for a more equitable, just society. These challenges include securing the right to adequate housing, tenure security, ensuring the quality of housing and basic services, affordability, residential segregation and discrimination, and environmental sustainability (see chapters 9, 10, 11, 12, 14, 18, 19, and 20). The chapter concludes with a discussion of the growing need to view housing as intricately connected to a variety of quality-of-life issues.

THE RIGHT TO ADEQUATE HOUSING

One of the fundamental housing challenges of the twenty-first century is that of securing a right to housing and property. Some have argued on moral grounds that housing is a fundamental right and necessity for people to thrive. Developed by the economic theorist Amartya Sen (1999) and expanded by political philosopher Martha Nussbaum (2011), the capabilities approach emphasizes what people need in order to function with the freedom to choose, change, and achieve what is most valued in life. Adequate shelter—defined in detail below—is identified as one such need. Failure to meet such needs can have negative social and economic costs.

Internationally, housing has been recognized as a human right through a variety of statements and ratified agreements, the most notable of which is Article 25 of the Universal Declaration on Human Rights, passed by the United Nations (UN) in 1948. The right to adequate housing includes both *freedoms*—from forcible eviction, from interference in home and privacy, and to choose where to live and move—as well as *entitlements*—to secure tenure, restitution, equal access, and participation in housing-related decisions (OHCHR & UN-HABITAT, n.d.). In order to be considered "adequate," housing must be affordable, habitable, available, accessible, connected to services and infrastructure, and culturally appropriate (OHCHR

& UN-HABITAT, n.d.; see chapters 2, 3, 5, 6, 9, 10, 11, 12, 13, 17, 19, and 20). Some nations include a basic right to housing within their constitutions, although many advanced countries do not (OHCHR & UN-HABITAT, n.d.). The UN Special Rapporteur on the Right to Adequate Housing researches national conditions around the world and reports back to the UN Human Rights Commission on countries' progress and shortcomings in meeting international standards of a right to housing.

In general, those who are more likely to suffer from inadequate housing are women, children, people with disabilities, residents in informal settlements, refugees and migrants, and indigenous people (OHCHR & UN-HABITAT, n.d.). The most vulnerable people are those already homeless or at risk of homelessness due to forced eviction through either private market or government actions (OHCHR & UN-HABITAT, 2014; see chapter 11).

The failure to ensure a right to adequate housing has resulted in the proliferation of informal settlements—in developing countries also referred to as slums—throughout the world, which lack most entitlements and many freedoms required for adequate housing. Slum residents often lack secure tenure, live in substandard structures, have poor access to basic services, receive no restitution when they are forcibly moved from their homes, and have little say in housing decisions that affect them (UN-HABITAT, 2003a). Around 30 percent of the world's urban population lived in slums in 2014, including almost 880 million people throughout the cities of developing countries in Asia, Africa, and Latin America (United Nations, 2015). In contrast, less than 10 percent of the urban population in Europe and North America resides in informal settlements (UN-HABITAT, 2011). Informal settlements are much more uncommon in these developed countries, where property rights are stronger and more rigidly protected and enforced, housing quality is higher, and units are more readily available and supported by adequate public services. However, such housing may be unaffordable to households with low incomes and other vulnerabilities (Bratt, Stone & Hartman, 2006; UN-HABITAT, 2011).

TENURE SECURITY

One way of ensuring adequate housing is by granting some level of secure tenure through a formal system of property ownership and use rights (Durand-Lasserve & Royston, 2002). Tenure security is challenging for countries without a strong history of recognized or defended property rights, where large proportions of the population have been excluded from whatever system may exist and forced to settle in slums. One possibility for addressing these challenges is to implement a completely formalized ownership structure, such as regularizing informal (illegal) settlements by granting legal ownership and property titles (Durand-Lasserve & Royston, 2002). This has been the approach advocated by de Soto (2003), but it can be a costly and lengthy process in countries with large proportions of the population experiencing insecure tenure (M. Davis, 2006). Another possibility is to grant basic protections against forced evictions by providing use rights apart from ownership (Durand-Lasserve & Royston, 2002). This includes mechanisms such as ensuring occupancy rights through long-term leases or granting use rights based on unopposed, continuous occupation of public or private land, as is the case in Brazil (Handzic, 2010). This can be a temporary or permanent measure and can be an effective mechanism for dealing with rapid, unplanned urbanization.

Within countries with strong, formal property rights systems, the challenges to securing a right to housing are somewhat different. Since uncontested illegal occupancy of public or private property is rare, the challenge is expanding narrowly defined concepts of tenure and securing additional protections to make formal property rights more accessible to poor households. This approach may include innovations such as regulated rental systems and shared equity models for homeownership. Rents may be controlled or restricted to maintain an affordable supply of units within both privately owned and government-financed units (Keating, Teitz, & Skaburskis, 1998; Schwartz, 2015; see chapters 9, 10, and 14). However, these restrictions have been weakened in recent years within the United States, Europe, and even China, where state-controlled rents were the norm for decades (Man, 2011; Schwartz, 2015; UN-HABITAT, 2011). To increase access to affordable ownership, shared equity ownership models in the United States include Community Land Trusts and cooperative housing. In these models, property rights and equity are secure but shared between owners, and therefore more limited than sole ownership, in exchange for more affordable housing costs (J. Davis, 2006).

QUALITY OF HOUSING AND BASIC SERVICES

Housing habitability relies on the quality of the standards and materials used in construction, having a reasonable number of inhabitants per dwelling, and the adequacy of the service infrastructure available to support residential life (see chapters 5, 6, 12, 13, 18, and 19). These components are so critical to adequate housing that they were used as indicators for measuring progress toward the UN's Millennium Development Goal 7 of improving the lives of at least one hundred million slum dwellers by 2015. The indicators tracked were the proportion of residents without access to improved water or sanitation, living in overcrowded conditions (i.e., more than three people per room), or living within structures made of nondurable materials (United Nations, 2008; see chapter 19). Access to safe housing and adequate services remains a priority within the new post-2015 Sustainable Development Goals, specifically through Goal 11 on creating safe cities and communities that include adequate, safe, affordable housing and basic services along with slum improvement (Open Working Group of the General Assembly on Sustainable Development Goals, 2014; see chapter 10).

Many countries have adopted residential building standards meant to ensure a high degree of safety and appropriateness of home design and construction in keeping with local climate and materials, either by adopting standards promulgated by the International Organization for Standardization (ISO standards) or locally modified versions (Vierra, 2014; see chapters 5, 6, 18, and 19). A lack of building standards or enforcement of such standards can lead to poor-quality housing as well as unauthorized, illegal dwellings that are not appropriate for habitation (UN-HABITAT, 2003a). For example, due to rapid urban population growth in many major Chinese cities, coupled with a lack of legal, affordable housing options, migrants have been living in unauthorized basement units with substandard infrastructure

(Kim, 2014). Up to one million people in Beijing alone live in such dwellings (Kim, 2014). In a different context of depopulation and disinvestment, the U.S. city of Detroit recently found that 20 percent of the city's housing stock is unfit for habitation or rehabilitation due to prolonged vacancy and abandonment and needs to be demolished (Detroit Blight Removal Task Force, 2014).

Another challenge to providing adequate housing is ensuring that an appropriate infrastructure exists for safely and affordably accessing energy, water, and sanitation. This challenge is magnified within informal settlements with little to no formalized property or use rights, which are often required to access public and private utilities. As a result, millions of households lack access to clean water, adequate sanitation, and safe energy, particularly in Asian, African, and Latin American and Caribbean cities (UN-HABITAT, 2003b; see chapters 23 and 24). This lack of access leads to pollution of natural waterways and the spread of disease through exposed human waste, not to mention the added cost to residents of accessing water in terms of both money and time (UN-HABITAT, 2003b). Households without formal electricity may tap into existing lines illegally or utilize more dangerous sources, such as propane, coal, or wood, creating fire and health hazards (UN-ENERGY, 2005). Many alternatives have been deployed to enhance access and safety in these areas. These include community water standpipes, water delivery services, renewable fuels, and modern cookstoves (UN-HABITAT, 2003b; UN-ENERGY, 2005).

Two common models used to address the twin problems of rapid urbanization and poor-quality housing infrastructure are slum upgrading strategies to improve existing informal settlements and sites and services approaches that enable households to build incrementally or progressively on newly designated land. Slum upgrading projects try to improve the housing, infrastructure, and services in existing informal settlements by providing tenure security, offering home improvement loans, extending public road and infrastructure systems, and developing community-managed alternatives to water and waste management, among other interventions (Mehta & Dastur, 2008). This can be challenging given the complicated histories of informal settlements and the haphazard and sometimes hazardous placement and construction of buildings and infrastructure; some structures have to be torn down during the upgrading process (UN-HABITAT, 2003a).

The second model—sites and services—was most popularly utilized in the 1970s and 1980s for creating new "legalized" communities by subdividing unsettled land into plots suitable for housing development that are already tied into public infrastructure or alternative systems (Patton, 1988). Sometimes modules of the home are provided; other times the newly settled households construct the homes incrementally through their own or hired labor using more of a self-help model. Sites and services projects require large areas of undeveloped land and are therefore often developed on the periphery of urban areas, exacerbating transportation difficulties in accessing employment and disrupting local social networks (Patton, 1988).

While housing quality generally improves for residents who participate in either improvement approach, both models are criticized for increasing the cost of housing and services, failing to meet diverse household needs—socially, culturally, and economically—and lacking environmental sustainability, as discussed in more detail below (M. Davis, 2006; Golubchikov & Badyina, 2012). Such challenges have been generally replaced by more holistic models of urban governance and land use reform (Pugh, 2001), although some advocate for the inevitability and practicality of continuing to assist self-help efforts of housing development and improvement in rapidly urbanizing areas (Bredenoord & van Lindert, 2010).

AFFORDABILITY

Having a right to quality housing does not necessarily guarantee affordability. In many places, there is a shortage of low-cost housing units (see chapters 9 and 10). One source of low-cost housing units comes about through the process of filtering: as newer, more expensive units are constructed, older stock becomes available at more affordable prices (Galster & Rothenberg, 1991). However, this older stock may be poorer in quality and require higher maintenance costs. Additionally, in some housing markets where home values and rents are rapidly appreciating, lower-cost units may be absorbed by more moderate-income households, as opposed to poorer households, leaving a shortage in supply affordable at lower incomes (Skaburskis, 2006).

One solution to the lack of low-cost housing is to build more, often through the assistance of government subsidies or incentives. Government construction and management of housing units has varied globally. On one end, there are countries like China that have an extensive history of providing public housing to residents on a large scale (Man, 2011). At the other end, countries like the United States have provided such housing only on a small scale relative to their respective populations and national housing stock (Schwartz, 2015; see chapter 14). Currently, many public or social housing models are being challenged as failures, and in many countries there are movements to sell the existing units to tenants and permanently reduce the public housing stock. In China the private ownership rate rose from under 20 percent in 1981 to over 80 percent by 2003, primarily through the private sale of public housing (Man, 2011). Through its Right to Buy Program, the UK has sold off more than 1.3 million units of social housing since 1980 (Whitehead, 1993; see chapter 22). Such programs may significantly expand affordable homeownership opportunities for those tenants fortunate enough to benefit from privatization, but they simultaneously reduce the stock of permanently affordable rental housing.

Due to continued deficits in affordable housing units compared to resident needs, some countries are trying new methods of enticing the private sector to develop more affordable units. As one example, Brazil has launched its My House, My Life (Minha Casa Minha Vida) Program to stimulate the production of one million new affordable housing units with private investment (UN-HABITAT, 2013; see chapter 23). In the United States, the Low-Income Housing Tax Credit (LIHTC) Program has generated equity for over 2.4 million affordable units since 1986 through private investments in return for tax benefits (Schwartz, 2015; see chapter 14). It is unclear, however, if a one-time capital investment through private market mechanisms yields a permanent supply of quality, affordable housing.

Another solution to the affordability crisis is to reduce development barriers and encourage the development of low-cost units in tandem with market-rate housing through inclusionary housing programs (Calavita & Mallach, 2010). In some local contexts, exclusionary zoning and other regulatory barriers prevent the development of lower-cost, multifamily housing by requiring large amounts of land to build a single unit and not allowing any multiunit developments (Advisory Commission on Regulatory Barriers to Affordable Housing, 1991; see chapter 5). There are a number of initiatives trying to reduce such barriers and promote low-cost unit development. Many North American and Western European countries—including Canada, the United States, England, France, and Spain—are using inclusionary housing programs to provide incentives to private developers to include low-cost units in their projects. In exchange, the developers receive special development benefits, such as access to publicly owned land or increases in the number of units that can be built at a given location (Calavita & Mallach, 2010; see chapter 14). China has also been experimenting with inclusionary housing, using its state land ownership as a lever to sell land lease rights to private developers on condition of including a certain amount of subsidized housing on the site (Huang, 2015). These types of strategies have worked best within housing markets with high housing demand and for ownership units (Calavita & Mallach, 2010; Schwartz, Ecola, Leuschner, & Kofner, 2012).

Finally, if supply cannot keep up with the demand for more affordable units, a variety of mechanisms can be used to help households afford existing housing costs in the private market. This means lowering either the cost of borrowing money for home purchase or the cost of renting. Home mortgage costs can be lowered through government guarantees and insurance that reduce risk and interest rates, government bond financing, down payment assistance or reductions, or shared equity ownership models, as discussed above (Schwartz, 2015; see chapters 7, 8, and 10). Rental payment assistance is often provided directly to the landlord to supplement rental payments from the tenants. In the United States, this is done primarily through the Housing Choice Voucher (HCV) Program; in the UK this is known as the housing benefit (Kemp, 2007; see chapter 14). While these policies seem more cost-effective than large capital investments, they do not result in an increased supply of permanently affordable units and still require ongoing subsidies to households and landlords (Kemp, 2007).

RESIDENTIAL SEGREGATION AND DISCRIMINATION

There is a high level of residential segregation in the world due to both policy and preference. Some places have long histories of active discrimination in housing markets against people according to race, ethnicity, age, sex, economic status, family status, religion or creed, disability, nationality, refugee status, and other characteristics. To ensure better human and housing rights, and to promote residential choice, a variety of current laws and policies try to fend off discrimination. In many places, however, residential segregation is still increasing by many measures, in part through community opposition often referred to as the Not In My Backyard (NIMBY) syndrome (Scally & Tighe, 2015; see chapters 9, 10, 12, 13, 14, and 16).

In some countries, specific policies have excluded people with certain characteristics from certain neighborhoods or worked to contain them within others. Often there are historical patterns that reflect active policies of segregation, particularly of racial and ethnic minorities, usually linked to the denial of property and housing rights. Examples include black Africans during South African apartheid (Durand-Lasserve & Royston, 2002) and blacks/African Americans as a result of what some have labeled the

American apartheid (Massey & Denton, 1993; see chapter 16). China's *hukou* household registration system notably links property rights to place of birth, particularly disadvantaging those with rural registrations who later move to cities in search of employment opportunities (Man, 2011). In many countries, migrant workers can be clustered in housing in specific neighborhoods and either denied certain amenities and services or forced to pay for them at higher rates than the general resident population.

Attempts to fix or undo histories of residential segregation resulting from discrimination can range from reallocation of land and property rights, to laws making certain types of discrimination illegal, to programs promoting greater residential mobility and choice. South Africa has attempted to directly redistribute to black Africans land that was taken from them during apartheid, with both successes and failures (Ntsebeza & Hall, 2007). The United States has focused more on preventing future discrimination by passing the Fair Housing Act in 1968 and the Fair Housing Amendments Act in 1988. These acts made discrimination against people due to certain personal characteristics—race, color, national origin, religion, sex, family status, and disability—illegal in home sales, lending, and leasing transactions (Silverman & Patterson, 2011). A final way to combat legacies of discrimination is to create opportunities for households to move to communities of their choice, such as programs moving households out of concentrated public housing units and into the general housing market with the help of rental assistance. In the United States, examples include the HOPE VI, Moving to Opportunity (MTO), and Gautreaux Programs, which have yielded mixed results in moving households to more socially and economically integrated neighborhoods (Chetty, Hendren, & Katz, 2015; Kleit, Kang, & Scally, 2016).

Despite some advances in promoting more choices and residential integration, many people continue to prefer greater exclusivity in selecting their neighbors. Gated communities have become increasingly popular around the world, both as symbols of wealth and privilege and as secured spaces from which to exclude others (Bageen & Uduku, 2010; Blakely & Snyder, 1997). There can actually be social and economic benefits, particularly for new immigrants, in choosing to live within smaller ethnic enclaves within larger urban or suburban communities (Abrahamson, 2005). Some communities can also exercise their residential preferences by acting in concert to oppose the development of low-cost housing, which can be viewed as a threat to private property values, service quality, environmental sustainability, and social cohesion (Scally & Koenig, 2012). Such NIMBY opposition can apply pressure on decision makers to adopt exclusionary zoning or other regulatory barriers, discussed above, to limit or prohibit low-cost housing options (Pendall, 1999; see chapters 9, 10, 12, 13, 14, and 16).

ENVIRONMENTAL SUSTAINABILITY

While the challenges discussed so far have focused on issues of access to housing, the challenge of environmental sustainability relates to the effects that the construction and use of housing have on the natural environment. As a built structure that consumes natural resources, housing has significant impacts on the environment. Innovative measures are being taken to reduce these negative effects in key ways, including using more sustainable building materials and employing practices that reduce waste, energy usage, and water usage (Golubchikov & Badyina, 2012; International Energy Agency, 2013). To encourage the use of such materials and practices, a number of systems have been developed to guide and certify the construction of more environmentally friendly housing structures (Vierra, 2014). Using more sustainable building methods and materials can increase the cost of the construction of the home compared to conventional methods, but over the life cycle of the building's operations and maintenance, it can result in significant savings in addition to lessening the environmental burden (see chapters 6, 18, and 19).

To reduce the consumption of natural resources, construction practices in advanced countries are being modified to include the recycling and reuse of existing materials, with an emphasis on using locally appropriate and available building materials (Chini & Bruening, 2003; Vierra, 2014). Deconstruction is encouraged to reduce construction waste by taking a building apart carefully in order to reuse or recycle existing materials rather than demolishing and disposing of them (Chini & Bruening, 2003). New housing can then reuse these materials. When new materials are required, they can be made from recycled products (e.g., water bottles turned into carpeting), come from sustainably harvested sources (e.g., fast-growing woods like bamboo and cork), and be made locally to minimize transportation costs and energy (Vierra, 2014). A variety of certifications exist to validate that materials are sustainably sourced, including the Forest Stewardship Council, Green Seal, and Cradle to Cradle (Vierra, 2014; see chapter 19).

A significant proportion of the world's energy is consumed by the residential sector (International Energy Agency, 2013). Heating and cooling use the most energy, followed by home appliances and electronics (International Energy Agency, 2011). To reduce the negative environmental impacts of this energy consumption, there are many efforts to develop renewable energy sources, such as solar and wind, to replace the use of fossil fuels, such as coal and oil (International Energy Agency, 2011). Innovations in building design, as well as using alternative systems for heating and cooling, can also reduce energy consumption. In terms of building design, this includes reorienting homes to minimize heat intake during hot months, installing roofs that reflect rather than absorb sunlight, and mounting solar panels on roofs to turn sunlight into energy (International Energy Agency, 2013). Geothermal systems, which are installed in the ground next to the home, can draw on the stable temperature of the earth to naturally heat and cool homes through heat exchange. More energy efficient appliances and electronics are being manufactured today to use less energy to operate; some, like solar water heaters, are specifically engineered to use sustainable energy sources (International Energy Agency, 2011; see chapters 3, 5, 6, 18, and 19).

Water is a critical natural resource necessary for human nourishment and hygiene, and it therefore plays a central function within the home (see chapter 3). In areas where water is plentiful and infrastructure abounds, there is a tendency to waste water, often by overusing clean, potable water and failing to capture and reuse rainwater. In other areas of the world, there is a shortage of water safe for drinking, bathing, and cooking. In both cases, reducing residential use of potable water is a critical strategy (UN-HABITAT, 2003b). Gray water, or recycled water, and rainwater can be reused for tasks such as flushing toilets and watering gardens (Vickers, 2001; see chapter 3). In some places with an abundance of developed, impermeable surfaces or that experience heavy periods of rain, managing runoff is a critical strategy for ensuring safe, quality housing. Installing living roofs, rain gardens, bioswales, and other types of green infrastructure on and around housing can help capture excess storm-water runoff to prevent flooding and to filter and remove surface pollutants before returning the water to the groundwater supply (Lovell & Johnston, 2009; see chapter 19).

A growing number of home-rating systems exist that issue guidelines on design, materials, systems, and processes for home construction and operations (Vierra, 2014). When a residential building meets the guidelines, it is certified as reaching a certain level of sustainability. Ratings systems are typically based on (1) the construction materials and processes used in building a home, or (2) the home's postconstruction performance on energy usage. Residential rating systems based on building materials and processes include the U.S. Green Building Council's LEED (Leadership in Energy & Environmental Design) for Homes, the U.S. National Association of Homebuilders' and International Code Council's National Green Building Standard, BREEAM in the UK and European Union, and Japan's CASBEE (Vierra, 2014). Typical of these systems, LEED rates homes on their sustainability on a scale ranging from Certified (lowest) to Platinum (highest) based on the total number of points attained by meeting specific guidelines, which are independently verified through site inspections during construction. Systems that rate residential buildings based solely on their energy performance include the U.S. Energy Star® Program (Vierra, 2014) and the Home Energy Rating System (HERS) maintained by the U.S.-based Residential Energy Services Network (2015). These systems conduct audits on homes following construction to measure energy consumption and leakages, including the building envelope, windows and doors, and heating and cooling systems. Homes need to score well against performance benchmarks to receive a good rating (see chapter 19).

CONCLUSION

As a foundational, basic need, housing plays a vital role in human flourishing. However, there are a variety of challenges to ensuring that everyone has access to safe, quality, affordable, and environmentally sustainable housing in communities where they choose to live (see chapters 6, 10, 14, 18, and 19). At the root of many of these challenges are poverty and political disenfranchisement. People who lack the income to pay for housing accommodations often lack the political power to draw attention to the issue and demand better access to this most basic need. Living wage and fair trade movements take one particular approach to addressing this problem (Luce, 2004; Raynolds, Murray, & Wilkinson, 2007). They work to pass wage-labor laws or reach agreements on fair prices for consumer goods that link wages to actual local costs of living. The goal is to lift people out of poverty and enable them to cover the costs of their basic needs, including housing. Other approaches, such as research missions of the Advisory Group on Forced Evictions within UN-HABITAT (2007), seek to uncover unmet housing needs and abuses against marginalized populations, bring these issues to international attention, and suggest remedies to these situations on behalf of affected residents.

While these challenges seem daunting, there is significant impetus for solving them. Many recognize that housing is more than just shelter, or an individual asset, or a commodity in which to invest. Instead, they promote the right to housing as key to individual and community quality of life and success (Bratt et al., 2006; OHCHR & UN-HABITAT, n.d.). As a basic need, housing influences individual physical and mental health, educational achievement, and employment and determines access to basic needs, amenities, and opportunities, such as food, health care, transportation, schools, and jobs, among others (Hays, 2012). The next step, therefore, beyond solving the specific housing challenges of tenure security, housing quality, access to basic services, affordability, segregation and discrimination, and environmental sustainability discussed here, is exploring the linkages between housing, transportation, health, and education and increasing our understanding of housing as one important link within a system of global human development (see chapters 9, 10, 12, 13, 14, 18, and 19).

REFERENCES

Abrahamson, M. (2005). *Urban enclaves: Identity and place in the world*. New York: Worth.

Advisory Commission on Regulatory Barriers to Affordable Housing. (1991). *Not In My Backyard: Removing barriers to affordable housing*. Washington, D.C.: U.S. Department of Housing and Urban Development.

Bageen, S., & Uduku, O. (Eds.). (2010). *Gated communities: Social sustainability in contemporary and historical gated developments*. Washington, D.C.: Earthscan.

Blakely, E. J., & Snyder, M. G. (1997). *Fortress America: Gated communities in the United States*. Washington, D.C.: Brookings Institution Press.

Bratt, R. G., Stone, M. E., & Hartman, C. (Eds.). (2006). *A right to housing: Foundation for a new social agenda*. Philadelphia: Temple University Press.

Bredenoord, J., & van Lindert, P. (2010). Pro-poor housing policies: Rethinking the potential of assisted self-help housing. *Habitat International, 34*(3), 278–287.

Calavita, N., & Mallach, A. (Eds.). (2010). *Inclusionary housing in international perspective: Affordable housing, social inclusion, and land value recapture*. Cambridge, Mass.: Lincoln Institute of Land Policy.

Chetty, R., Hendren, N., & Katz, L. (2015). *The effects of exposure to better neighborhoods on children: New evidence from the Moving to Opportunity experiment*. Cambridge, Mass.: Harvard University and National Bureau of Economic Research.

Chini, A. R., & Bruening, S. F. (2003). *Deconstruction and materials reuse in the United States* (Report No. 10). Delft: International Council for Research and Innovation in Building and Construction.

Davis, J. E. (2006). *Shared equity homeownership: The changing landscape of resale-restricted, owner-occupied housing*. Montclair, N.J.: National Housing Institute.

Davis, M. (2006). *Planet of slums*. New York: Verso.

De Soto, H. (2003). *The mystery of capital: Why capitalism triumphs in the West and fails everywhere else*. New York: Basic Books.

Detroit Blight Removal Task Force. (2014). *Detroit Blight Removal Task Force plan*. Detroit, Mich.: Detroit Blight Removal Task Force.

Durand-Lasserve, A., & Royston, L. (Eds.). (2002). *Holding their ground: Secure land tenure for the urban poor in developing countries*. London: Earthscan.

Galster, G., & Rothenberg, J. (1991). Filtering in urban housing: A graphical analysis of a quality-segmented market. *Journal of Planning Education and Research, 11*(1), 37–50.

Golubchikov, O., & Badyina, A. (2012). *Sustainable housing for sustainable cities: A policy framework for developing countries*. Nairobi: UN-HABITAT.

Handzic, K. (2010). Is legalized land tenure necessary in slum upgrading? Learning from Rio's land tenure policies in the Favela Bairro program. *Habitat International, 34*(1), 11–17.

Hays, R. A. (2012). *The federal government and urban housing*. Albany, N.Y.: SUNY Press.

Huang, Y. (2015). *Bolstering inclusionary housing in Chinese cities*. Chicago: Paulson Institute.

International Energy Agency. (2011). *Technology roadmap: Energy-efficient buildings—Heating and cooling equipment*. Paris: International Energy Agency.

Glossary

Note: Some definitions in this glossary are based in part on the following sources:

>Arlington County, Virginia, https://building.arlingtonva.us/glossary-of-terms/.
>Canada Mortgage and Housing Corporation, https://www.cmhc-schl.gc.ca/.
>Consumer Financial Protection Bureau (CFPB), https://www.consumerfinance.gov/.
>Investopedia, http://www.investop=edia.com/terms/a/accessory-dwelling-unit-adu.asp.
>Office of Policy Development and Research (PD&R) of the U.S. Department of Housing and Urban Development (HUD), https://www.huduser.gov/portal/glossary/glossary.html; https://portal.hud.gov/hudportal/documents/huddoc?id=hhpgm_final_gloss.pdf.
>U.S. Bureau of the Census, https://www.census.gov/glossary/.
>U.S. Department of Labor, https://www.dol.gov/.
>U.S. Environmental Protection Agency, https://iaspub.epa.gov/sor_internet/registry/termreg/searchandretrieve/termsandacronyms/search.do.

accessibility: A situation in which public or common-use areas of a building can be approached, entered, and used by individuals with physical challenges.

Accessory Dwelling Unit (ADU): A legal and regulatory term for a secondary building or structure with its own kitchen, living area, and separate entrance that shares the building lot with a larger, primary house.

activities of daily living (ADLs): A defined set of activities necessary for normal self-care. The activities are movement in bed, transfers, locomotion, dressing, personal hygiene, and feeding.

adaptive reuse: The repurposing of a building from one form and function to another, such as converting a warehouse to an apartment building.

adjustable-rate mortgage (ARM): A mortgage with an interest rate that changes periodically, usually in relation to an index. Payments may go up or down accordingly.

affirmatively furthering fair housing (AFFH): The 1968 Fair Housing Act's obligation for state and local governments to improve and achieve more meaningful outcomes from fair housing policies, ensuring that every American has the right to fair housing, regardless of his or her race, ethnicity, national origin, religion, sex, disability, or familial status.

affordable housing: Housing for which the occupant(s) is/are paying no more than 30 percent of household income for gross housing costs, including utilities.

age-restricted housing: Housing for older persons; housing intended and operated for occupancy by at least one person fifty-five years of age or older per unit.

alternative-A (Alt-A) prime mortgage: A mortgage characterized by borrowers with less than full documentation, lower credit scores, and higher loan-to-value ratios.

Alternative Mortgage Transaction Parity Act (AMTPA) of 1982: An act that authorized state-chartered or state-licensed lenders to originate mortgages and loans with variable rates.

American Community Survey (ACS): A data set based on a nationwide sample designed to provide information on age, race, ethnicity, income, commute time to work, home value, veteran status, and other important data from U.S. households.

American Housing Survey (AHS): A data set, released every other year, based on a nationwide sample and on select metropolitan samples that provides information on apartments, single-family homes, mobile homes, vacant homes, family composition, income, housing and neighborhood quality, housing costs, equipment, fuels, size of housing units, and recent movers.

American Recovery and Reinvestment Act of 2009 (ARRA; "Recovery Act"): A response to the economic crisis (Great Recession) that included measures to modernize the national infrastructure, enhance energy independence, expand educational opportunities, preserve and improve affordable health care, provide tax relief, and support eligible households in need.

Americans with Disability Act of 1990 (ADA): A broad civil rights law guaranteeing equal opportunity for individuals with disabilities in employment, public accommodations, transportation, state and local government services, and telecommunications.

amortization: A regular, fixed payment to repay the mortgage principal over time.

annual percentage rate (APR): A mortgage or credit interest rate that reflects the interest rate and other charges, for example, fees or points (also known as discount points, which may lower the borrower's interest rate in exchange for an upfront fee).

apartment: One or several rooms forming a residence or a studio, which combines a living room, a bedroom, and a kitchenette into a single room, in a building.

appraisal: A written document that provides an opinion of how much a property is worth, describing what makes the property valuable and how it compares to other properties in the neighborhood. An appraisal helps assure the borrower and the lender that the value of the property is based on facts, not just the seller's opinion.

appreciation (house price appreciation): The increase in the value of an asset (such as a house) over time.

area median income (AMI): The household income for the median (or middle) household in a metropolitan statistical area (MSA), annually calculated by the U.S. Department of Housing and Urban Development (HUD).

asbestos: An incombustible, chemical-resistant, fibrous material of pure magnesium silicate occurring in rock and soil form and used for fireproofing, electrical insulation, and building materials. Exposure to asbestos fibers may be associated with lung cancer, mesothelioma, and asbestosis. The EPA has banned or severely restricted its use in manufacturing and construction.

Asian: A person having origins in any of the original peoples of the Far East, Southeast Asia, or the Indian subcontinent, including, for example, Cambodia, China, India, Japan, Korea, Malaysia, Pakistan, the Philippine Islands, Thailand, and Vietnam.

assisted living: Facilities that offer a housing alternative for adults who may need help with dressing, bathing, eating, and toileting but do not require the intensive medical and nursing care provided in nursing homes. They may be part of a retirement community, nursing home, or senior housing complex, or they may stand alone.

baby boomer: A person born between 1946 and 1964. The baby boom resulted from a large increase in birth rates following World War II, and the boomers are one of the largest generations in U.S. history.

balloon payment: A larger-than-usual payment at the end of a mortgage term (the length of time over which the mortgage is paid back).

black/African American: A person having origins in any of the black racial groups of Africa. It includes people who indicate their race as "black or African American," or report origins such as African American, Kenyan, or Nigerian. It excludes a person from the West Indies (who may identify as black only).

boom (house price boom): A rapid increase of house prices in a neighborhood, city, county, state, or nation, fueled by an increase in demand or speculation.

borrower: A person who incurs debt.

broken windows model: A model suggested by George Kelling and James Wilson, focusing on the importance of broken windows in generating and sustaining more serious crime.

broker (mortgage broker): A person who helps a borrower find a mortgage lender to facilitate a real estate transaction.

Brooke Amendment (1969): An amendment passed in 1969, capping public housing rent at 25 percent of a resident's income as a response to rent increases and complaints about services in public housing. Congress raised the cap to 30 percent in 1981.

building and loan society: A society or association with a cooperative character, established in the United States from the 1830s to the 1980s for homeownership purposes. Members pledge to contribute a certain amount of money at a constant rate over a specified period, first in the down payment phase, followed by the mortgage phase.

building code: A set of building construction requirements developed and administered by international, national, and local bodies to ensure that buildings meet certain minimum standards for structural integrity, safety, design, and durability.

building permit: The approval provided by a local jurisdiction to proceed on a construction project.

bust (house price bust): A rapid decrease of house prices in a neighborhood, city, county, state, or nation, fueled by a decrease in demand.

census tract: A small, relatively permanent statistical subdivision of a county or statistically equivalent entity, delineated for data analysis purposes. In many urban cases it is equivalent to a neighborhood.

certificate of occupancy (CO): A certificate issued by an inspector that is required for any occupancy, change of occupancy, use, or change of use of any land or building, regardless of whether it is new or existing, or change of ownership of any business or building, or condo/co-op conversion of a building. This document states that the building or proposed use of a building or land complies with all provisions of law and of county ordinances and regulations.

Chicago School of Urban Sociology (Chicago School of

Ecology): A major body of work that emerged in the 1920s and 1930s, focusing on urban sociology and ecology. Major contributors were Ernest Burgess, Everett Hughes, Roderick D. McKenzie, and Robert E. Park, among others.

Choice Neighborhood Program: A program that supports locally driven strategies to address struggling neighborhoods with distressed public or HUD-assisted housing through a comprehensive approach to neighborhood transformation. Local leaders, residents, and stakeholders, such as public housing authorities, cities, schools, police, business owners, nonprofits, and private developers, come together to create and implement a plan that transforms distressed housing and addresses the challenges in the surrounding neighborhood.

Civil Rights Act of 1964: An act, signed into law by President Lyndon B. Johnson on July 2, 1964, that prohibited discrimination in public places, provided for the integration of schools and other public facilities, and made employment discrimination illegal. This act was among the most sweeping civil rights legislation since Reconstruction.

closing (also called settlement): The last step in buying and financing a home, when the buyer, the seller, and other parties in a mortgage loan transaction sign the necessary documents.

cohousing: A group of private detached or attached homes clustered around shared indoor and outdoor space that may include a common house with a large kitchen and dining area, laundry facilities, parking, walkways, open space, gardens, and recreational spaces. Cohousing may allow residents to take an active role in their community's development and each other's lives.

collateral: A guarantee, for example, a property, pledged as security for payment of a debt.

community: A group of people living in the same neighborhood.

community-based organization (CBO): A public or private nonprofit organization of demonstrated effectiveness that is representative of a community or significant segments of a community and provides educational and related services to individuals in the community.

Community Development Block Grant (CDBG): A program, created under the Housing and Community Development Act of 1974, that provides grant funds to local and state governments to develop viable urban communities by providing decent housing with a suitable living environment and expanding economic opportunities to assist low- and moderate-income residents.

community development corporation (CDC): A nonprofit entity characterized by its community-based leadership and work primarily in housing production and/or job creation. CDCs are typically formed by residents, small business owners, faith-based congregations, and other local stakeholders to revitalize a low- and/or moderate-income community in order to produce affordable housing, create jobs for community residents, and provide a variety of social services within its target area.

Community Land Trust (CLT): An entity, typically a nonprofit organization, that preserves public investment and protects affordability. A CLT acquires and retains ownership of the real property and sells the improvements via a ninety-nine-year ground lease to a homeowner, another nonprofit, a cooperative housing corporation, or a for-profit entity. This arrangement between the owner and the CLT protects housing affordability in perpetuity by ensuring that the property will remain affordable to low- and moderate-income households upon the sale of the property.

Community Reinvestment Act (CRA) of 1977: An act intended to encourage depository institutions to help meet the credit needs of the communities in which they operate, consistent with safe and sound operations. The CRA requires that each depository institution's record in helping meet the credit needs of its entire community be evaluated by the appropriate federal financial supervisory agency periodically. A bank's CRA performance record is taken into account in considering its application for deposit facilities.

Complete Streets: A relatively new design and construction approach that enables safe access and travel to all users of the street network, including pedestrians, bicyclists, motorists, transit users, and travelers of all ages and abilities.

Comprehensive Housing Affordability Strategy (CHAS) plan: A local plan that shows the extent of housing challenges for low- and moderate-income, elderly, and disabled households, including households of color.

condominium: A form of ownership in which the separate owners of individual units jointly own the development's common areas and facilities.

construction: Building, altering, maintaining, or repairing building or engineering projects, for example, highways or utility systems.

Consumer Financial Protection Bureau (CFPB): A U.S. government agency that makes sure banks, lenders, and other financial companies treat households fairly.

covenant (restrictive covenant; racially restrictive covenant): A legally enforceable contractual agreement imposed upon a buyer, for example, restricting the purchase, lease, or occupation of a piece of property. Racially restrictive covenants were contractual agreements made between 1926 (*Corrigan v. Buckley*) and 1948 (*Shelley v. Kraemer*) that prohibited the purchase, lease, or occupation of a piece of property by blacks/African Americans.

credit score: A number that predicts how likely a borrower is to pay back a loan or a mortgage on time, based on a scoring model. Credit scores are based in part on an individual's bill-paying history, current unpaid debt, the number and type of loan accounts he or she has, how long he or she has had his or her loan accounts open, how much of the available credit he or she is using, the number of new applications for credit, and whether he or she has had a debt sent to collection, a foreclosure, or a bankruptcy.

Current Population Survey (CPS): The primary source of labor force statistics for the population of the United States, sponsored jointly by the U.S. Bureau of the Census and the U.S. Bureau of Labor Statistics (BLS). The CPS is the source of numerous high-profile economic statistics, including the national unemployment rate, and provides data on a wide range of issues relating to employment and earnings.

debt-to-income ratio (DTI): A ratio that consists of a borrower's monthly debt payments divided by his or her gross monthly income. This number is one way that lenders measure a borrower's ability to manage monthly payments.

deed (deed of trust; trust deed): A legal document that passes, affirms, or confirms an interest, right, or property, often associated with transferring title to a property.

default: A failure to make any payment or to perform any other obligation under a mortgage.

defensible space: A concept of structuring or restructuring the physical layout of a community to allow residents to control the areas around their homes, including the streets and grounds outside their buildings and the lobbies and corridors within them, based on the work of Oscar Newman.

demolition: The dismantling, razing, destroying, or wrecking of any building or structure or any part thereof.

density bonus: A rule that allows developers more density in exchange for community improvements, for example, open space, affordable housing, special building features, or public art.

deposit: Money placed in an account for safekeeping.

Depository Institutions Deregulation and Monetary Control Act of 1980: An act to facilitate the implementation of monetary policy, to provide for the gradual elimination of all limitations on the rates of interest that are payable on deposits and accounts, to authorize interest-bearing transaction accounts, and for other purposes.

discount points: Additional fees paid at the closing process of a real estate transaction by the buyer to lower the loan's interest rate. One discount point costs 1 percent of the mortgage amount.

discrimination/housing discrimination: An act that actually or predictably results in a disparate impact on a person or a group of persons and that may create, increase, reinforce, and perpetuate segregated housing patterns because of race, ethnicity, religion, sex, handicap, familial status, or national origin.

Dodd-Frank Wall Street Reform and Consumer Protection Act of 2010 ("Dodd-Frank"): An act passed as a response to the Great Recession that made changes in the U.S. financial regulatory environment, which affects all federal financial regulatory agencies and most parts of the financial services industry.

down payment: A proportion of the house price saved up before and paid upon purchase. Typically 20 percent for a conventional mortgage and 3.5 percent for a mortgage insured by the Federal Housing Administration (FHA).

duplex: A residential building with separate entrances for two households.

earnest money: Money paid by the buyer of a home at the beginning of a real estate transaction, applied toward the total cost of purchase.

eminent domain: The application of the power of the government or quasi-government agencies, such as airport authorities, highway commissions, community development agencies, or utility companies, to take private property for public use. In return, the landowner is provided just compensation for the value of the property taken.

empty nester: A parent who remains behind after the last adult child has left home to attend college or to live in his or her own home.

energy efficiency: Using technology that requires less energy to perform the same function, resulting in a lower energy bill.

Energy Star® Program: A joint program of the U.S. Environmental Protection Agency and the U.S. Department of Energy. The Energy Star® Program was introduced in 1992 as a voluntary labeling program designed to identify and promote energy-efficient products in order to reduce greenhouse gas emissions. Currently the Energy Star® label is affixed to major appliances, office equipment, lighting, home electronics, homes, and more.

equity/home equity: The amount left after the unpaid debt balance(s) on the property from the property's current market value as assessed by an assessor. It increases as the debts are paid off and as the property's value appreciates.

escrow (account): An account established by the mortgage servicer. The borrower makes a fixed monthly payment that covers the monthly mortgage payment (principal and interest), the quarterly or biannual property tax payments, and the annual homeowners' insurance premium.

ethnicity: Identification as a person of Hispanic or Latino origin, as defined by the U.S. Office of Management and Budget (OMB). There are two minimum categories for ethnicity: Hispanic or Latino and not Hispanic or Latino. OMB considers race and ethnicity to be two separate and distinct concepts. Hispanics and Latinos may be of any race.

eviction: The dispossession of a tenant from a leased unit as a result of the termination of tenancy, including a termination prior to the end of a lease term.

exclusionary zoning: Zoning that excludes a specific class of people, possibly based on income, or a specific type of business.

extremely low income (ELI) household: A household with an income below 30 percent of area median income.

Fair Housing Act of 1968: An act passed in 1968 and

amended in 1974 and 1988 that provides the U.S. Department of Housing and Urban Development (HUD) with fair housing enforcement and investigation responsibilities. This law prohibits discrimination in all facets of the home-buying process on the basis of race, ethnicity, national origin, religion, sex, familial status, or disability.

Fannie Mae (Federal National Mortgage Association): A housing-related, government-sponsored (i.e., authorized by Congress and established for public purposes) enterprise, chartered by Congress to create a secondary market for residential mortgages.

Federal Deposit Insurance Corporation (FDIC): An independent agency of the U.S. federal government that preserves and promotes public confidence in the U.S. financial system by insuring deposits in banks and thrift institutions up to at least $250,000 by identifying, monitoring, and addressing risks to the deposit insurance funds and by limiting the effect on the economy and the financial system when a bank or thrift institution fails.

Federal Home Loan Bank Act of 1932: An act designed to lower the cost of homeownership through the creation of Federal Home Loan Banks, which lend to building and loan associations, cooperative banks, homestead associations, insurance companies, savings banks, community development financial institutions, and insured depository institutions in order to finance mortgages.

Federal Housing Administration (FHA): A federal agency that provides mortgage insurance on loans made by FHA-approved lenders throughout the United States and its territories. The FHA insures mortgages on single-family, multifamily, and manufactured homes. It is the largest insurer of mortgages in the world, having insured over thirty-five million properties since its inception in 1934.

Federal Housing Enterprises Financial Safety and Soundness Act (FHEFSSA) of 1992: An act to improve supervision and regulation of Fannie Mae (Federal National Mortgage Association), Freddie Mac (Federal Home Loan Mortgage Corporation), and the Federal Home Loan Bank System, among other purposes.

Federal Housing Finance Agency (FHFA): An agency established by the Housing and Economic Recovery Act of 2008, responsible for the effective supervision, regulation, and housing mission oversight of Fannie Mae (Federal National Mortgage Association), Freddie Mac (Federal Home Loan Mortgage Corporation), and the Federal Home Loan Bank System. Since 2008, the FHFA has also served as conservator of Fannie Mae and Freddie Mac.

Federal Reserve System: The central banking system of the United States, established in 1913 in response to a series of financial panics that showed the need for central control of the monetary system.

FICO (Fair, Isaac and Company) credit score: A number that is used to predict how likely a borrower is to pay back a loan on time. Credit scores are typically used by companies to make decisions such as whether to offer an applicant a mortgage or a credit card. They are also used to determine the interest rate a borrower receives on a loan or credit card, as well as the credit limit. The FICO score is a particular brand of credit score.

filtering: The negative change in property value of the housing stock from higher- to lower-income households as the housing stock ages, among other factors.

fixed-rate mortgage: A mortgage with an interest rate that will not change over time. Thus the mortgage payments remain the same throughout the life of the loan.

flexible housing: An approach that allows homeowners to reconfigure their home as their lifestyle and economic situation change, making housing accessible for young children, persons with disabilities, and elderly people.

foreclosure: The legal process by which a property may be sold and the proceeds of the sale applied to the mortgage debt. A foreclosure occurs when the loan becomes delinquent because payments have not been made or when the borrower is in default for a reason other than failure to make timely mortgage payments.

Freddie Mac (Federal Home Loan Mortgage Corporation): A housing-related, government-sponsored (i.e., authorized by Congress and established for public purposes) enterprise, chartered by Congress to create a secondary market for residential mortgages.

gated community: A residential area with gates to control the movement of people into and out of the area, signifying status.

Gautreaux vs. Chicago Housing Authority: A lawsuit based on a charge by Dorothy Gautreaux, who claimed that the Chicago Housing Authority and the U.S. Department of Housing and Urban Development were contributing to racial segregation by the very rules established for selecting sites for public housing and assigning tenants to them. The charge was ultimately upheld in court. In 1976, after a Supreme Court ruling, the U.S. Department of Housing and Urban Development agreed to a series of efforts to increase the housing opportunities of public housing tenants in the greater Chicago area.

Generation X: a person born between 1965 and the early 1980s. Generation X is a smaller demographic cohort than baby boomers and millennials.

gentrification: A form of neighborhood change that occurs when higher-income groups move into low-income neighborhoods, increasing the demand for housing and thus driving up house prices.

GI Bill of Rights (formally Servicemen's Readjustment Act of 1944): An act that provides a range of benefits for veterans returning from wars. Benefits include dedicated payments of tuition and living expenses to attend high school, vocational school, or college; a mortgage with no down payment requirement and a low interest rate; a loan to start a business; and unemployment compensation.

Ginnie Mae (Government National Mortgage Association): A wholly government-owned corporation that guarantees mortgages by approved mortgage lenders and sells them to capital markets.

government-sponsored enterprise (GSE): Organizations authorized by Congress and established for public purposes, such as Fannie Mae and Freddie Mac, which were chartered by Congress to create a secondary market for residential mortgages.

Gramm-Leach-Bliley Act (Financial Services Modernization Act) of 1999: An act that repealed restrictions imposed by the Glass-Steagall Act of 1933 that prevented banks from affiliating with nonbank firms, such as insurance or security companies.

Great Depression: A period of business cycle contraction that lasted from August 1929 to March 1933 and from May 1937 to June 1938, triggered by a major fall in stock prices, which caused the gross domestic product and thus personal incomes, tax revenues, profits, prices, and trade to decrease while the unemployment rate increased.

Great Recession: A period of business cycle contraction that lasted from December 2007 to June 2009, triggered by a major fall in house prices, which caused the gross domestic product and thus personal incomes, tax revenues, profits, prices, and trade to decrease while the unemployment rate increased.

green building: The practice of creating structures and using processes that are environmentally responsible and resource efficient throughout a building's life cycle, from siting to design, construction, operation, maintenance, renovation, and deconstruction.

gross domestic product (GDP): The market value of goods and services produced by labor and property in the United States, regardless of nationality.

Habitat for Humanity (International): A global nonprofit housing organization working in nearly fourteen hundred communities across the United States and approximately seventy countries around the world. Habitat for Humanity envisions a world where everyone has a decent place to live, which it pursues by building strength, stability, and self-reliance in partnership with people and families in need of a decent and affordable home.

Healthy Home Rating System (HHRS): A visual assessment tool adapted from the British Housing Health and Safety Rating System (HHSRS) to examine twenty-nine hazards, or categories of hazards, to determine the risks to occupants' health and safety. An assessment using the HHRS is made based on the condition of the entire dwelling.

height restriction: The maximum height of a structure, based on local zoning laws and building codes.

hierarchy of human needs: A theory in psychology, suggested by Abraham Maslow in 1943, with needs ranging from physiological, safety, love/belonging, and esteem to self-actualization.

Hispanic/Latino: A person of Cuban, Mexican, Puerto Rican, South or Central American, or other Spanish culture or origin, regardless of race.

historic preservation: A way to transmit understanding of the past to future generations through the designation of historic sites, including federal, state, or private properties, through written, photographic, and technical documentation as well as oral histories and physical preservation, including stabilization, rehabilitation, restoration, and reconstruction.

Home Affordable Modification Program (HAMP): A program that provides eligible borrowers the opportunity to modify their mortgage to make it more affordable.

Home Affordable Refinance Program (HARP): A program through which government-sponsored enterprises (GSEs) will purchase any refinanced mortgages that they owned or guaranteed, if the property is owner occupied, the borrower has sufficient income to support the new mortgage debt, and the first mortgage does not exceed 125 percent of the current market value of the property.

Home Energy Rating System (HERS): An analysis of a home's energy performance and efficiency based on a nationally recognized scoring system that results in an index.

home equity: The amount left after subtracting the unpaid debt balance(s) on a property from the property's current market value as assessed by an assessor. It increases as debts are paid off and as the property's value appreciates.

Home Equity Conversion Mortgage (HECM): A mortgage that a senior homeowner (age sixty-two or older) can use to convert the equity in his or her home into a monthly stream of income and/or a line of credit to be repaid when he or she no longer occupies the home. A lender typically funds the mortgage, which is insured by the Federal Housing Administration (FHA). Also called a reverse mortgage.

home equity line of credit (HELOC): A form of revolving credit in which a home serves as collateral to finance large expenditures of a borrower, for example, home improvements, tuition, or medical bills. The HELOC is determined by the existing equity in the home.

home inspection: An examination of a property's condition, typically conducted in connection with a property's sale.

home Investment Partnerships Program (HOME): Provides formula grants to states and localities, which communities use—often in partnership with local nonprofit groups—to fund a wide range of activities that build, buy, and/or rehabilitate affordable housing for rent or homeownership or to provide direct rental assistance to low-income people.

homeless: An individual who lacks a fixed, regular, and adequate nighttime residence, including individuals who have a primary nighttime residence that is a shelter that is supervised either publicly or operated privately, designed to provide temporary living accommodations.

Home Mortgage Disclosure Act (HMDA) of 1975: An act that requires most mortgage lenders located in metropolitan areas to collect data about their housing-related lending activity, report the data annually to the government, and make the data publicly available.

homeowner: A person who owns a property.

homeowners' association (HOA; also called a common-interest community association): An association of homeowners responsible for the upkeep of a building or a development and its maintenance. Homeowners pay monthly, quarterly, or annual HOA fees to fund expenses.

homeownership rate: The proportion of owner-occupied homes divided by the total number of occupied housing units.

Home Owners' Loan Corporation (HOLC): A federal agency established to refinance home mortgages that were in default or at risk of foreclosure due to the stock market crash in 1929 and the ensuing collapse of the housing market; about 20 percent of mortgages were owned by HOLC in 1934. By the HOLC's final year in 1936, it had provided about one million new mortgages and had lent out approximately $350 billion ($750 billion in today's dollars).

HOPE VI: A program charged with proposing a national action plan to eradicate severely distressed public housing. HOPE VI operated from 1993 until 2009, awarding planning, revitalization, demolition, and Main Street grants, in addition to creating neighborhood networks, resulting in a total of $6.7 billion invested in communities.

household: One or more people who occupy a housing unit. A household may include related family members as well as unrelated people, if any, such as lodgers, foster children, wards, or employees who share the housing unit.

house price bubble: A rapid increase in house prices in a neighborhood, city, county, state, or nation, fueled by an increase in demand or speculation.

Housing Act of 1934: An act that created the Federal Housing Administration (FHA) and the Federal Savings and Loan Insurance Corporation, making housing and home mortgages more affordable.

Housing Act of 1937: An act that authorized federal loans and annual contributions to local public housing agencies for low-rent public housing.

Housing Act of 1949: An act that declared that the general welfare and security of the nation requires the establishment of a national housing policy to realize, as soon as feasible, the goal of a decent home and a suitable living environment for every American family. The act authorized federal advances, loans, and grants to localities to assist with slum clearance and urban redevelopment. It substantially expanded the public housing program by authorizing federal contributions and loans for up to 810,000 additional units of housing over a six-year period. The Housing Act of 1949 significantly increased the Federal Housing Administration (FHA) mortgage insurance program for nondefense housing.

housing affordability: A threshold indicating that a household pays more than 30 percent of its income (considered cost burdened) or more than 50 percent of its income (considered severely cost burdened) for housing, thus potentially having difficulty affording other necessities such as food, medical care, transportation, and clothing.

Housing and Economic Recovery Act (HERA) of 2008: An act designed to address the subprime mortgage and economic crisis through several additional acts: the Federal Housing Finance Regulatory Reform Act of 2008, the HOPE for Homeowners Act of 2008, and the Foreclosure Prevention Act of 2008.

Housing Choice Voucher (HCV) Program: The federal government's major program for assisting very low income households, the elderly, and the disabled, allowing them to afford decent, safe, and sanitary housing in the private rental market.

housing code: A set of laws or regulations that relate to property maintenance and housing business licenses.

housing cost burden/burdened: Households that pay more than 30 percent of their income for housing and thus may have difficulty affording other necessities such as food, clothing, transportation, and medical care. A severe housing cost burden is defined as paying more than 50 percent of one's income on housing.

housing counselor: An expert who can provide advice on buying a home, renting, defaults, foreclosures, and credit issues. The U.S. Department of Housing and Urban Development (HUD) maintains a nationwide list of HUD-approved counseling intermediaries.

Housing Finance Agency (HFA): A state or local agency responsible for financing and preserving low- and moderate-income housing within a state or a municipality.

Housing First: An approach to quickly and successfully connecting individuals and households experiencing homelessness to permanent housing without preconditions and barriers to entry, such as sobriety, treatment, or service participation requirements. Supportive services are offered to maximize housing stability and prevent returns to homelessness as opposed to addressing predetermined treatment goals prior to permanent housing entry. Housing First emerged as an alternative to the linear approach in which people experiencing homelessness were required to first participate in and graduate from short-term residential and treatment programs before obtaining permanent housing.

housing market: The supply of and demand for houses, typically at a local or regional level.

housing norms: A model that states that households judge their housing based on cultural and family norms. The latter are defined as standards for housing developed by the household itself that may or may not match cultural norms. The concept is based on the work of Earl W. Morris and Mary Winter.

housing starts: An economic indicator that is based on the number of new single or multifamily housing units.

housing stock: The number of existing housing units, based on data compiled by the U.S. Bureau of the Census.

housing trust fund: A fund created in connection with an affordable housing production program that will complement existing federal, state, and local efforts to increase and preserve the supply of decent, safe, and sanitary affordable housing for extremely low and very low income households, including homeless families. The (national) Housing Trust Fund was established under Title I of the Housing and Economic Recovery Act of 2008.

housing unit: A house, apartment, or single room occupied or intended for occupancy as separate living quarters.

inclusionary zoning: A mandatory or voluntary local policy that has requirements that benefit residents in return for incentives geared toward developers, for example, density bonuses, expedited approval, and fee waivers.

independent living: A way of living for people with a disability or for senior citizens that may include convenient services, user-friendly surroundings, and increased social opportunities. Most people will not require assistance with daily activities or around-the-clock skilled nursing.

Individual Development Account (IDA): An asset-building tool designed to enable eligible low-income households to save toward homeownership, postsecondary education, or small business ownership.

inequality (wealth inequality): The unequal distribution of resources, such as wealth.

informal settlement: An area where a housing unit has been constructed on land that the occupants have no legal claim to.

in-law suite: A unit that is part of a single-family home but may or may not be attached to the primary residence. *See also* Accessory Dwelling Unit; secondary dwelling unit.

interest: A fee paid for the use of another party's money. For a borrower, interest is the cost of renting money; for a lender, interest is the income from lending it.

interest-only loan: A loan with scheduled payments that require a borrower to pay only the interest for a specified amount of time. Once the interest-only period ends, the borrower may pay off the loan balance all at once, refinance the loan, or begin to pay off the balance in monthly payments, which are typically higher than the interest-only payments.

International Code Council (ICC): An association dedicated to developing model codes and standards used in the design, construction, and compliance processes to provide safe, sustainable, affordable, and resilient structures.

International Energy Conservation Code (IECC): A building code created by the International Code Council for the establishment of minimum design and construction requirements for energy efficiency.

International Residential Code (IRC): A comprehensive, stand-alone residential code that creates minimum regulations for one- and two-family dwellings of three stories or less and that combines all building, plumbing, mechanical, fuel gas, energy, and electrical provisions for one- and two-family residences.

land bank: A governmental or nongovernmental nonprofit entity established, at least in part, to assemble, temporarily manage, and dispose of vacant land for the purpose of stabilizing neighborhoods and encouraging reuse or redevelopment of urban property.

landlord: The owner of real estate that is leased or rented to another person, such as a tenant or renter, for a fee.

large-lot zoning: A requirement that specifies the minimum lot size with the goal of limiting development densities to preserve the rural character of agriculture, forestry, or environmentally sensitive areas, among others.

Latino/Hispanic: *See* Hispanic/Latino.

lead-based paint: Paint or other surface coatings that contain lead equal to or exceeding 1.0 milligrams per square centimeter or 0.5 percent by weight or 5,000 parts per million (ppm) by weight; banned in 1978 in the United States.

lease: A written agreement between an owner and a household for the temporary use of a decent, safe, and sanitary dwelling unit.

LEED (Leadership in Energy and Environmental Design): The green building rating system most widely used in the world. LEED provides a framework that project teams can apply to increase healthy, highly efficient, and cost-saving green building.

lender: A person who provides money, as in the case of a residential transaction, that is, the purchase of a home.

lien: A public notice attached to a property stating any claims the owner owes to someone, generally filed with a county records office in the case of real estate. Liens must be resolved before a property is refinanced or sold.

limited equity cooperatives: A type of shared homeownership in which individuals purchase a share in a cooperative. The share entitles the shareholder to occupy one unit and participate in decision making within the cooperative. Market-rate cooperatives allow shareholders to sell their shares at market value. Limited equity cooperatives limit the return that share owners are allowed to receive when they sell their share.

loan-to-value (LTV) ratio: A measure used by lenders to compare the amount of the mortgage to the appraised value of the property. The higher the borrower's down payment, the lower his or her loan-to-value ratio.

Low-Income Housing Tax Credit (LIHTC): A tax incentive intended to increase the availability of low-income housing. The program provides an income tax credit to owners of newly constructed or substantially rehabilitated low-income rental housing projects.

Making Home Affordable (MHA): A program launched by the U.S. Department of the Treasury in 2009 to help borrowers avoid foreclosure through voluntary modifications of mortgage contracts.

manufactured home: A structure, transportable in one or more sections, that is built on a permanent chassis and designed to be used as a dwelling with or without a permanent foundation when connected to the required utilities and includes the plumbing, heating, air conditioning, and electrical systems contained in the structure. Manufactured homes are built to the Manufactured Home Construction and Safety Standards (Code of the U.S. Department of Housing and Urban Development). *See also* mobile home; modular home.

metropolitan statistical area (MSA): An area that consists of one or more counties that contain a city of fifty thousand or more inhabitants or that contains an urbanized area defined by the U.S. Bureau of the Census that has a total population of at least one hundred thousand (seventy-five thousand in New England).

millennial(s): A person born during the early 1980s to the early 2000s. The millennials are the largest generation in U.S. history; the baby boomers are the second largest.

mixed-income housing: A development that comprises housing units with differing levels of affordability, typically with some market-rate housing and some housing that is available to low-income occupants below market rate.

mobile home; modular home: A structure, transportable in one or more sections, that is built on a permanent chassis and designed to be used as a dwelling with or without a permanent foundation when connected to the required utilities and includes the plumbing, heating, air conditioning, and electrical systems contained in the structure. *See also* manufactured home.

mortgage: All forms of debt for which a property is pledged as security for payment of the debt.

mortgage-backed security (MBS): A security that represents an undivided interest in a group of mortgages. Principal and interest payments from the individual mortgage loans are grouped and paid out to the MBS holders.

mortgage broker: A professional who matches a borrower with a lender in a real estate transaction.

Mortgage Credit Certificate (MCC): A certificate issued by certain state or local governments that allows a borrower to claim a tax credit for some portion of the mortgage interest paid during a given tax year.

Mortgage Interest Deduction (MID): A policy that allows a taxpayer in an owner-occupied unit to reduce his or her taxable income by the amount of interest and property taxes paid on a mortgage that is secured by his or her principal residence (and in some cases a second home).

mortgage revenue bond (MRBs): A tax-exempt bond that state or local governments issue through housing finance agencies (HFAs) to help fund below-market-interest-rate mortgages for first-time qualifying home buyers. Eligible borrowers are first-time home buyers with low to moderate incomes (below 115 percent of median family income).

Moving to Opportunity (MTO): A demonstration designed to ensure a rigorous evaluation of the impacts of assisting very low income households with children in moving from public or assisted housing in high-poverty neighborhoods to lower-poverty neighborhoods throughout a metropolitan area.

multifamily housing: A building with more than four residential rental units.

multigenerational household: A household that includes two or more adult generations, for example, baby boomer parents and their adult children.

Multiple Listing Service (MLS): A nonpublic database created, maintained, and paid for by real estate professionals to share with other real estate professionals in order to help clients buy and sell property.

Mutual Mortgage Insurance (MMI) Fund: A fund that insures mortgages originated by the Federal Housing Administration (FHA) on single-family homes. The MMI pays the lender if the mortgagor defaults.

National Affordable Housing Act of 1990 (Cranston-Gonzalez National Affordable Housing Act of 1990): An act to help households not owning a home to save for a down payment for the purchase of a home; to retain wherever feasible as housing affordable to low-income households those dwelling units produced for such purpose with federal assistance; to extend and strengthen partnerships among all levels of government and the private sector, including for-profit and nonprofit organizations, in the production and operation of housing affordable to low-income and moderate-income households; to expand and improve federal rental assistance for very low income households; and to increase the supply of supportive housing, which combines structural features and services needed to enable persons with special needs to live in dignity and independence.

National Foreclosure Mitigation Counseling (NFMC) Program: A program launched in December 2007 with funds appropriated by Congress to address the nationwide foreclosure crisis by dramatically increasing the availability of housing counseling for households at risk of foreclosure.

naturally occurring retirement community (NORC): A housing development or neighborhood that was not originally built for seniors but that now is home to a significant number of senior citizens.

Neighborhood Stabilization Program (NSP): A program that provides grants to every state and certain local communities to purchase foreclosed or abandoned homes and to rehabilitate, resell, or redevelop these homes to stabilize neighborhoods and stem the decline of property values of adjacent homes. The program was authorized under Title III of the Housing and Economic Recovery Act of 2008.

NeighborWorks: A congressionally chartered, nonpartisan nonprofit that has created places of opportunity in communities across the country for almost four decades. Its network of more than 245 independent nonprofit organizations helps households and communities through comprehensive approaches to affordable housing and community development.

net zero energy house: A building that produces a sufficient amount of renewable energy to meet its own annual energy consumption requirements, thereby reducing the use of nonrenewable energy in the building sector.

New Deal: A set of federal policies launched by President Franklin D. Roosevelt in response to the Great Depression and that lasted until 1942.

New Urbanism: A planning practice that incorporates interrelated patterns of land use, transportation, and urban form to create communities that foster neighborliness, environmental sustainability, economic efficiency and prosperity, historic preservation, participation in civic processes, and human health.

non-Hispanic white: A person who reports being white and not of Hispanic/Latino origin.

Not In My Back Yard (NIMBY): Community opposition to a housing development, for example, affordable housing, housing that benefits people with disabilities, or the homeless, based on fears of increased crime, decreased property values, and other negative impacts on the community.

nursing home: A place for individuals who cannot be cared for at home but who do not need to be in a hospital. Most nursing homes have nursing aides and skilled nurses twenty-four hours a day, providing medical care as well as physical, speech, and occupational therapy.

occupant: Any individual who is living, sleeping, cooking, or eating in or having possession of a dwelling unit or a rooming unit; except that in dwelling units a guest is not considered an occupant.

occupied housing unit: A housing unit classified as occupied, the usual place of residence of the person or group of people living in it at the time of enumeration.

Office of the Comptroller of the Currency (OCC): An independent bureau of the U.S. Department of the Treasury that charters, regulates, and supervises all national banks and federal savings associations as well as federal branches and agencies of foreign banks. OCC's mission is to ensure that national banks and federal savings associations operate in a safe and sound manner, provide fair access to financial services, treat customers fairly, and comply with applicable laws and regulations.

overcrowding: The condition of having more than one person per room in a residence.

owner: Any person who, alone, jointly, or separately with others, (a) has legal title to any premises, dwelling, or dwelling unit, with or without accompanying actual possession thereof, or (b) has charge, care, or control of any premises, dwelling, or dwelling unit, as owner or agent of the owner, or as executor, administrator, trustee, or guardian of the estate of the owner.

owner-occupied unit: A unit occupied by any private person or entity, including a cooperative, an agency of the federal government, or a public housing agency, having the legal right to lease or sublease dwelling units.

pay-option ARM: An adjustable-rate mortgage with several possible payment choices, for example, paying an amount that covers both the principal and interest, paying an amount that covers only interest, or paying a minimum (or limited) amount that does not cover the interest.

permanent supportive housing (PSH): Housing with indefinite leasing or rental assistance paired with supportive services to assist homeless persons with a disability or households with an adult or child member with a disability.

planner: A government official who is responsible for managing long-term change within a community, usually through the issuance of building permits and the implementation of zoning changes.

postoccupancy evaluation (POE): The process of obtaining feedback on a building's performance in use.

poverty: A situation in which the total income of a household falls below the poverty threshold established by the U.S. Office of Management and Budget (OMB), varying by household size and composition.

prepayment: A payment for a mortgage or loan before the due date.

prime mortgage: A mortgage that carries an interest rate offered to customers with the best credit histories. A prime mortgage can be either a fixed- or an adjustable-rate loan.

private mortgage insurance (PMI): A type of mortgage insurance a borrower might be required to pay for if he or she takes out a conventional loan (with a down payment of 20 percent or less). PMI protects the lender, not the borrower, in case the borrower stops making payments on his or her mortgage.

public housing agency (PHA): Any state, county, municipality, or other government entity or public body, or agency or instrumentality of these entities, that is authorized to engage or assist in the development or operation of low-income housing under the U.S. Housing Act of 1937.

race: A classification of a person based on self-identification, reflecting a social, not a biological, anthropological, or genetic definition of race. For data collection, the U.S. Office of Management and Budget (OMB) specifies the following five groups: white, black/African American, American Indian or Alaska Native, Asian, and Native Hawaiian or other Pacific Islander. Respondents may report more than one race.

radon: An odorless, colorless radioactive gas that is a form of uranium and that moves through fractures and porous substrates in the foundations of buildings. It can collect in high concentrations in certain areas.

Radon may also enter a building through water systems in communities where groundwater is the main water supply, most commonly in those dependent on small public systems and private wells.

rapid rehousing (RRH): Housing that emphasizes search and relocation services and short- and medium-term rental assistance to move homeless persons and households into permanent housing as rapidly as possible.

rating agency: A company that calculates a credit rating, which shows the ability of an institution to pay back debt by making timely payments and the likelihood of default. Examples of ratings agencies are Standard & Poor's, Moody's Investor Service, or Fitch Ratings.

real estate owned (REO) property: A foreclosed property now owned by the lender.

realtor: A licensed real estate sales person who is a member of the National Association of Realtors, the largest trade group in the United States.

recession: A period of business cycle contraction that may be triggered by a major fall in stock, oil, or house prices, among other factors, which cause the gross domestic product (GDP) and thus personal incomes, tax revenues, profits, prices, and trade to decrease while the unemployment rate increases.

redlining: Discrimination based on location. Historically, some lending and insurance institutions were found to have maps with red lines delineating neighborhoods within which they refused to conduct business.

rehabilitation; remodeling: The labor, materials, tools, and other costs of improving buildings, other than minor or routine repairs.

renewable energy: Energy sources that regenerate, unlike finite fossil fuels. Examples of renewable energy sources are biomass (e.g., wood and wood waste, municipal solid waste, landfill gas and biogas, ethanol, and biodiesel), hydropower, geothermal, wind, and solar.

renovation: Rehabilitation that involves costs of 75 percent or less of the value of the building before rehabilitation.

rent: A tenant's regular payment to a landlord for the use of property or land.

rent control: The regulation of rent within certain municipalities.

renter: A person who rents property or land from a landlord for a fee. *See also* tenant.

restrictive deed covenant: *See* covenant.

risk-based pricing: The offer of different interest rates or other mortgage terms to different customers, based on the estimated risk.

savings and loan society: A financial institution that specializes in accepting savings and deposits to originate a mortgage or other loans.

secondary dwelling unit (SDU): A unit that is part of a single-family home and that may or may not be attached to the primary residence. *See also* Accessory Dwelling Unit; in-law suite.

secondary mortgage market: A financial marketplace created in the 1930s by the U.S. Congress to provide lenders a much bigger, steadier, and more evenly distributed stream of money for lending purposes to stabilize the nation's residential mortgage markets and expand opportunities for homeownership and affordable rental housing. The secondary mortgage market connects lenders, home buyers, and investors in a single system that benefits home buyers in multiple ways.

segregation: Separation of different racial and ethnic groups in a community.

Servicemen's Readjustment Act of 1944 (GI Bill of Rights): An act that provides a range of benefits for veterans returning from wars. Benefits include dedicated payments of tuition and living expenses to attend high school, vocational school, or college; a mortgage with no down payment requirement and a low interest rate; a loan to start a business; and unemployment compensation.

setback: The distance between a building and the street.

settlement (also called closing): The last step in buying and financing a home, when the buyer, the seller, and other parties in a mortgage-loan transaction sign the necessary documents.

settlement house: An institution that provides educational, social, recreational, and other social services to a community.

Shelley vs. Kraemer, 334 U.S. 1 (1948): A landmark U.S. Supreme Court case that held that courts could not enforce racial covenants on real estate.

shelter: A place giving protection from the elements.

shelter poverty: A concept, suggested by Michael Stone, that determines how much a household can realistically afford for housing by taking the difference between their disposable income (income after taxes) and the cost of meeting nonhousing needs at a basic level of adequacy. This concept is different from housing affordability, which is based on a threshold, indicating that a household pays more than 30 percent of its income or more than 50 percent of its income for housing, thus potentially having difficulty affording necessities such as food, medical care, transportation, and clothing.

single-family housing unit: A residence that is either fully detached, semidetached (semiattached, side-by-side), or a row house or town house.

single-room occupancy (SRO) housing: A furnished efficiency apartment for a single householder, typically with a short renewal option.

smart home: A home that incorporates advanced automation systems to provide the inhabitants with sophisticated monitoring and control over the building's functions. A smart home may control lighting, temperature, multimedia, security, and window and door operations, as well as many other functions.

strategic default: A decision by a borrower to stop making payment on a mortgage despite the ability to do so.

subprime mortgage: A mortgage that carries an interest rate higher than the rates of prime mortgages. A subprime mortgage is sometimes offered to prospective borrowers with impaired credit records. The higher interest rate is intended to compensate the lender for accepting the greater risk in lending.

subsidy: Support given by the government to a natural or legal person, either in the form of cash or a tax reduction, often in the interest of a greater good. Examples of subsidies are Housing Choice Vouchers and the Mortgage Interest Deduction.

supportive housing: A combination of affordable housing and support services designed to help households to use housing as a platform for health and recovery, sometimes following a period of homelessness, hospitalization, or incarceration, or for youth aging out of foster care.

sustainability: A concept based on the principle that everything needed for survival and well-being depends on the natural environment.

sweat equity: Using one's own labor to build or improve a property as part of the down payment.

tax-increment financing (TIF): A public financing method to promote public and private investment.

teaser rate: A low introductory interest rate for a mortgage that resets to a much higher rate after two, three, or five years.

tenant: A person who is leasing or renting real estate from a landlord for a fee. *See also* renter.

tenement housing: Rental units occupied by low-income households, the primary form of working-class housing from the 1840s to the 1930s in many major cities.

tenure: The manner of holding a housing unit (including a cooperative or condominium unit), either owner occupied or renter occupied. Whereas an owner is someone whose name is on the deed, mortgage, or contract, a renter is someone whose name is on the lease.

tiny house: A house between one hundred and four hundred square feet. A newly constructed single-family detached home has about twenty-four hundred square feet.

tipping point: A threshold that is passed as a particular racial or ethnic group moves into a neighborhood with a different racial or ethnic group. The concept is based on the works of Morton Grodzins and Thomas Schelling.

title (property title): A legal document that passes, affirms, or confirms an interest, right, or a property, often associated with transferring title to a property.

toxic asset: An asset on a lender's balance sheet impacted by default or foreclosure.

transit-oriented development (TOD): Development of commercial space, housing services, and job opportunities close to public transportation, thereby reducing dependence on automobiles. TODs are typically designed to include a mix of land uses within a quarter mile (walking distance) of transit shops or core commercial areas.

underwater (negative home equity): A property with a market value less than the outstanding mortgage balance.

underwriting: A service provided by a financial institution, evaluating a borrower's creditworthiness and eligibility for a mortgage, consistent with standards provided by the lender.

universal design: A design concept that encourages the construction or rehabilitation of housing and elements of the living environment in a manner that makes them usable by all people, regardless of ability, without the need for adaptation or specialized design.

urban redevelopment; urban renewal: Clearance, redevelopment, rehabilitation, and/or conservation in a blighted, deteriorated, or deteriorating area.

U.S. Bureau of the Census: The leading public source of quality data about U.S. people and the economy.

U.S. Department of Energy: A department tasked to ensure the country's security and prosperity by addressing its energy, environmental, and nuclear challenges through transformative science and technology solutions.

U.S. Department of Housing and Urban Development (HUD): Established in 1965, HUD's mission is to increase homeownership, support community development, and increase access to affordable housing free from discrimination.

U.S. Department of the Treasury: The executive agency responsible for promoting economic prosperity and ensuring the financial security of the United States. Its mission is to maintain a strong economy and to create economic and job opportunities by promoting the conditions that enable domestic and international economic growth and stability, strengthen national security by combating threats and protecting the integrity of the financial system, and manage the U.S. government's finances and resources effectively.

U.S. Department of Veterans Affairs (VA): A department tasked to fulfill President Lincoln's promise "to care for him who shall have borne the battle, and for his widow, and his orphan" by serving and honoring the men and women who are veterans.

U.S. Environmental Protection Agency (EPA): An agency created for the purpose of protecting human health and the environment by writing and enforcing regulations based on laws passed by Congress.

U.S. Housing Act of 1937 (USHA): An act authorizing loans for local public housing agencies (PHAs) to achieve lower-rent public housing construction expenses.

usufruct: A property system characterized by limited property rights where the owner does not hold legal title.

vacancy; vacant unit: A dwelling unit that has been vacant for not less than nine consecutive months.

Veterans Affairs (VA) mortgage: A mortgage with a zero down payment requirement provided by a private lender but guaranteed by the Veterans Administration.

Veterans Affairs Supportive Housing (VASH) Program: A collaborative program between the U.S. Department of Housing and Urban Development and the Veterans Administration that combines housing vouchers and supportive services to assist homeless veterans and their families to find and sustain permanent housing.

visitability: A design approach for homes, the main principle of which is that an individual in a wheelchair should be able to visit the home. Accessibility features are a zero-step entrance, interior doors wide enough to allow a wheelchair to pass through, and a bathroom on the main floor.

voucher (formerly Section 8 voucher): A voucher that allows eligible very low income households, the elderly, and the disabled to move to a rental unit owned by a landlord who participates in the Housing Choice Voucher Program.

walkability: A measure of how friendly a neighborhood is to walking.

Walk Score: An index that measures the walkability of any home.

Wall Street: The location of a major part of the U.S. financial industry in New York City.

WaterSense®: A program by the U.S. Environmental Protection Agency (EPA) designed to encourage water efficiency through the use of a special label on consumer products.

zoning: The classification of land by types of uses permitted and prohibited in a given district and by densities and intensities permitted and prohibited, including regulations regarding the location of a building on a lot.

Contributors

Mira Ahn, Ph.D., is an associate professor of interior design in the School of Family and Consumer Sciences at Texas State University. Her research focuses on the behavioral and psychological aspects of residents in relation to the residential environment in aging societies, including aging in place, residential satisfaction, and sustainable living.

Akin S. Akinyemi is a doctoral student in the Department of Urban and Regional Planning at Florida State University. His background is in architecture, housing, and community development, and his dissertation is about developing a new paradigm of community redevelopment for marginalized communities in West Africa.

Katrin B. Anacker, Ph.D., is currently an associate professor at the Schar School of Policy and Government at George Mason University in Arlington, Virginia. She is the North American editor of the *International Journal of Housing Policy* and the former coeditor of *Housing Policy Debate*. She is also the editor of *The New American Suburb: Poverty, Race, and the Economic Crisis*, published with Ashgate. She earned her Ph.D. in city and regional planning from The Ohio State University.

Jorge H. Atiles, Ph.D., is associate dean and professor of housing, College of Human Sciences at Oklahoma State University. Dr. Atiles holds degrees in architecture, urban and regional planning, and housing. He has worked in the private and public sectors, managing housing finance and development projects in the United States and the Dominican Republic.

Julia O. Beamish, Ph.D., CKE, is professor of housing and head of the Department of Apparel, Housing, and Resource Management at Virginia Tech. She teaches and conducts research in the areas of universal design, kitchen and bath design, housing alternatives for older adults, housing satisfaction, and postoccupancy evaluation.

Marilyn J. Bruin, Ph.D., is a professor in housing studies at the University of Minnesota. She teaches courses on housing development, research ethics, methods, and grant writing. Dr. Bruin's research agenda focuses on the influence of housing and neighborhood environments and housing polity on housing stability, economic well-being, and housing policy and practice.

Andrew T. Carswell, Ph.D., is a tenured associate professor at the University of Georgia in the Department of Financial Planning, Housing, and Consumer Economics. He has been on faculty at the university since 2003. He has authored over 140 publications on a broad range of housing issues, such as mortgage fraud, housing counseling, homeowner and household finances, multifamily property management operations, and aging in place.

Christine C. Cook, Ph.D., is an emeritus professor at Iowa State University in the Department of Human Development and Family Studies. Her focus of research and teaching includes the provision of affordable housing and community resources for low-income families, children with disabilities, and aging adults.

Dennis Patrick Culhane, Ph.D., is a professor and Dana and Andrew Stone Chair of Social Policy at the University of Pennsylvania. His primary area of research is homelessness and assisted housing policy, and his work has contributed to efforts addressing the housing and support needs of people experiencing housing emergencies and long-term homelessness.

Petra L. Doan is a professor in the Department of Urban and Regional Planning at Florida State University. Her research explores planning for human settlements and marginalized people in both the developing world (emphasis on Africa and the Middle East) and the United States. She teaches courses on global urban development, housing in developing countries, and gender in the city.

Rosa E. Donoso, Ph.D., is a research affiliate at OTB Department of the Faculty of Architecture and the Built Environment at TUDelft, the Netherlands. She is an architect and has a master of science in community and regional planning from the University of Texas at Austin. She is a housing adviser at the Secretariat of Territory, Habitat, and Housing at the Municipality of the Metropolitan District of Quito, Ecuador.

Rachel Bogardus Drew, Ph.D., is a freelance policy analyst and expert in housing markets. She was formerly a research associate at the Joint Center for Housing Studies at Harvard University. She has a degree in economics from Dartmouth College and received her Ph.D. from the University of Massachusetts, Boston.

Marja Elsinga is a full professor of housing institutions and governance at the Faculty of Architecture and the Built Environment at Delft University of Technology, the leader of the research program "Housing in a Changing Society," and a visiting professor at the College of Architecture and Urban Planning at Tongji University Shanghai. Her focus is on affordable housing, homeownership, and comparative research.

Heidi H. Ewen, Ph.D., is an assistant professor at the University of Georgia with appointments in the College of Family and Consumer Sciences and the College of Public Health, representing the Department of Financial Planning, Housing, and Consumer Economics, the Department of Health Promotion and Behavior, and the Institute of Gerontology. She has an established research program focused on the housing and health of older adults, with emphasis on residential adjustment to changes in psychosocial well-being and life events.

Rosemary Carucci Goss, Ph.D., is the Residential Property Management Advisory Board Professor and associate director of the Program in Real Estate at Virginia Tech. She received her B.S. from Concord University in 1974, her master's degree from Virginia Tech, and her Ph.D. from Florida State University. Dr. Goss has been an Alpha Sigma Alpha volunteer since 1974, serving in a variety of positions, most notably as national president and as chairman of the Alpha Sigma Alpha Foundation, which was begun during her presidency. For fourteen years she was a member of the Alpha Sigma Alpha delegation to the National Panhellenic Conference (NPC) and chaired the NPC president's group in the mid-1980s.

Annie Hardison-Moody is an assistant professor in the Department of Agricultural and Human Sciences at North Carolina State University. She is co-PI of "Voices into Action: The Families, Food, and Health Project," a USDA-funded study of the home and food environment of low-income families, and author of *When Religion Matters: Practicing Healing in the Aftermath of the Liberian Civil War* (Wipf & Stock).

Sandra C. Hartje, Ph.D., is a professor of interior design and housing at Seattle Pacific University. Her teaching, research, and outreach interests focus on affordable housing, accessible and universal design, housing and health, and policy issues related to housing and to the broader mission of family and consumer sciences.

Kathryn Howell, Ph.D., is an assistant professor at the Wilder School of Government and Public Affairs at Virginia Commonwealth University. Howell's research focuses on affordable housing and neighborhood change. Her recent research has focused on the origins and effects of mixed-income housing on long-term residents in Washington, D.C.

Suk-Kyung Kim, Ph.D., LEED green associate, is an associate professor of interior design at the School of Planning, Design, & Construction at Michigan State University. She received a Ph.D. in architecture from Texas A&M University and MS and BS degrees in housing and interior design from Yonsei University in Seoul, Korea.

Sarah D. Kirby, Ph.D., is a professor, extension housing specialist, and department extension leader in the Department of Youth, Family, and Community Sciences at North Carolina State University. Her work is primarily focused in three areas: residential energy efficiency, healthy homes, and disaster management.

Joseph Laquatra, Ph.D., is professor emeritus in the Department of Design and Environmental Analysis at Cornell University. He is a past president of the Housing Education and Research Association and served two terms as chair of the National Consortium of Housing Research Centers.

Kirk McClure, Ph.D., is a professor in the Department of Urban Planning at the University of Kansas. McClure's research in housing policy has been published in many of the top academic journals in urban planning and has won multiple awards. He has won multiple competitive research grants and has served as scholar in residence with the U. S. Department of Housing and Urban Development.

Jean Memken, Ph.D., has been a housing educator for over thirty years, teaching and conducting housing research at the University of Nebraska, Illinois State University, and Northwest Missouri State University. In addition, Dr. Memken has served as the executive director for the Housing Education and Research Association.

Deborah Mitchell is pursuing a doctoral degree in housing studies from the University of Minnesota in the Department of Design, Housing, and Apparel. Her research focuses on homeless African Americans and low-income households. Her academic objective is to generate research findings to inform housing policy and practice.

Ann Elizabeth Montgomery, Ph.D., is an assistant professor in the Department of Health Behavior at the University of Alabama at Birmingham School of Public Health and an investigator with the U.S. Department of Veterans Affairs, National Center on Homelessness among Veterans and Birmingham VA Health Services Research.

Elizabeth Mueller, Ph.D., is an associate professor of community and regional planning and social work at the University of Texas at Austin. Her research centers on issues of equity in cities, particularly access to affordable housing. Her current work focuses on strategic preservation of affordable rental housing in gentrifying transit-rich neighborhoods.

Shirley Niemeyer, Ph.D., has held many leadership positions in state and national professional organizations, was president of the Housing Education and Research Association, and received the Distinguished Service Award for education and research. Niemeyer has provided housing educational programs to thousands of consumers and professionals and conducted research. She is professor emerita, extension specialist/research, housing & environment, University of Nebraska Lincoln.

Kathleen R. Parrott, Ph.D., is a professor in residential environments and design at Virginia Tech. She has comprehensive experience in the field of housing with primary expertise in environmentally sustainable housing and residential design. She also has experience in extensive research, classroom teaching, and outreach education, resulting in numerous publications. She has special expertise and certification in kitchen and bath design.

Deirdre Pfeiffer, Ph.D., is an associate professor in the School of Geographical Sciences at Arizona State University. Her research focuses on housing strategies in the United States relevant to an aging and diversifying society, the outcomes of the foreclosure crisis, and the relationship between suburban growth and racial equity.

Corianne Payton Scally, Ph.D., is a senior research associate in the Metropolitan Housing and Communities Policy Center at the Urban Institute. Her areas of expertise include U.S. and international affordable housing policies and programs. She was previously associate professor of urban planning at the University at Albany, SUNY.

Martin C. Seay, Ph.D., CFP®, is an associate professor of personal financial planning at Kansas State University. His research focuses on borrowing decisions, how psychological characteristics shape financial behavior, and methodology in financial planning research. He received his Ph.D. in housing and consumer economics from the University of Georgia.

Lindsay Slautterback is a student at Florida State University in the Master's International Program in the Department of Urban and Regional Planning. She served in Nicaragua for the Peace Corps until November 2017 and works as an environmental educator in her community.

Cherie Stueve, MBA, CPA (inactive), AFC®, is a Ph.D. candidate in personal financial planning at Kansas State University. She works with working and military households on debt reduction and savings goals. Her research interests include barriers that prevent households from seeking appropriate professional assistance with financial decisions and general financial behaviors.

Daniel Treglia, Ph.D., is a postdoctoral fellow at the University of Pennsylvania. Dr. Treglia's research focuses on the causes of, policy implications of, and solutions to poverty and homelessness, with a focus on veteran homelessness and program evaluation. He is also leading efforts to understand the impact of protective psychological factors on shelter use by homeless families.

Kenneth R. Tremblay, Ph.D., was a professor at Colorado State University. He served as an influential coeditor of the first edition of *Introduction to Housing* and wrote more than 270 publications for scholarly and lay audiences. He served as editor of *Housing and Society* for many years and as president of the Housing Education and Research Association in 2010. He earned the 2014 Distinguished Service Award of the Housing Education and Research Association.

Becky L. Yust, Ph.D., is a professor of housing studies, College of Design, University of Minnesota. She teaches courses on housing adequacy and affordability; multifamily housing development, finance, and management; and interior structures, systems, and life safety. Her current research includes investigating healthy housing initiatives and the design of affordable housing.

Index

Note: Page numbers followed by *n* indicate a footnote with relevant number; page numbers in italic refer to figures, and those followed by *t* indicate tables.

accessibility: and aging, 13–14; in Asian housing, 378; costs of, 16; and disabled persons, 69, 93, 100–101, 112; in European housing, 406; incentives for, 113; as part of adequate standard of living, 410; policies and programs on, 110–11. *See also* universal design; visitability
Accessory Dwelling Units (ADUs), x, 158, 301
activities of daily living (ADL), 100, 303, 310. *See also* universal design
adequate housing, 27, 183; definition of, 420, 441, 443; provision of, 413, 415, 421, 425, 444; right to, 409, 410, 442
adjustable-rate mortgages (ARMs). *See* subprime mortgages
affordable housing, xi, 167–79: Affordability Index (LAI), 169–71; assistance programs, 172, 240, 305; below market interest rate (BMIR) loans, 174–75; block grant programs, 240; Comprehensive Housing Affordability Strategy Plan, 247–48; definition of, 168–69; in European Union, 398, 406; and expanding concepts of tenure, 443; federal policy on, 221, 245, 250, 286–87; and filtering, 445; limited equity cooperatives, 174; and minimum wage, 156, 163, 172, 179; and opportunity maps, 225, 226; removal of, 172–73, 211, 245, 248, 411, 436; and residual income measure, 171; senior-oriented, 301–2, 304–5; and shelter poverty, 300–301, 302; siting of, 221; status of, 167, 249, 250, 443–44; subsidized public housing, 111–12; trust funds, 112; vacancy rates, 211, 417. *See also* housing cost burden; U.S. Department of Housing and Urban Development
Affordable Housing Act of 1990, 240, 247
Affordable Housing Design Advisor, 84
African Americans: and American apartheid, 446–47; and concentrated poverty, 223; foreclosure rate of, 160, 277–78; as Home Affordable Modification Program (HAMP) clients, 288–89; and homelessness rate, 187, 188; homeownership rate, 32, 146, 276, 277, 286, 287; household size, 25; and housing mobility programs, 210–11, 212, 224–25; median household income and net worth, 27, 281, 282, 300; migration from South by, 201; and neighborhood amenities, 219; obesity and asthma rates of, 229; and residential segregation, 202, 203–4, 213, 281; and suburbanization, 202, 221, 223; and urban renewal, 204–5; as urban underclass, 209
African housing: affordable, 430, 433; background, 425–26; colonial, 429–30; and formal land tenure, 431–32, 434–35; and ghost cities, 433; public, 430; and public-private partnerships, 433–34; rural, 427–28; and rural-to-urban migrants, 431; and self-help projects, 432–33; and squatter settlements, 431, 434–37; urban, 428–29, 433
age-restricted housing, 113, 307. *See also* universal design
aging: and affordable housing, 304; and age-restricted communities, 113, 294, 301, 307, 309–11; and assisted living, 31, 93, 296, 299, 300, 307–11, 361; and community amenities, 309; and continuing care retirement communities (CCRC), 310–11, 389–90; demographics, 294–95; and empty nesters, 295; and financial independence, 390; and housing needs, 301–2; and rural areas, 298–99; and social isolation, 297, 298, 302, 307, 309, 310; and supportive housing, 29, 294, 301, 304, 305, 307; and walkable environments, 307–8. *See also* activities of daily life (ADL); aging-in-place; baby boomers; mortgage loans: reverse; multifamily residential housing; universal design
aging-in-place, 299–300; in Asian housing, 378, 379, 389, 391; design and, 66, 77, 108, 310; focus on, x; in NORCs, 308; and sense of self, 104; and social interaction, 309. *See also* universal design
Alliance for Progress, 415
Alternative-A (Alt-A) prime mortgage, 149
American Association of Retired Persons (AARP): aging-in-place, 299; Home and Community Preferences, 99; walkable communities, 308
American Community Survey (ACS), 24; and affordable housing, 249
American Dream, 32, 121, 122, 150, 237, 256
American Housing Survey (AHS), 24, 34, 158
American Recovery and Reinvestment Act of 2009 (ARRA), 244t, 264; and homelessness, 189; and housing construction industry, 238
American Woman's Home, 45
Americans with Disability Act (ADA), 67
Annual Homelessness Assessment Report (AHAR), 185–86
apartment: and Asian housing, 389; and baby boomers, x, 29, 31; choice of, 21, 26, 36; and high-rise buildings; 82; and Housing First, 190; and

471

apartment (*continued*)
life cycle, 31; and limited equity cooperatives, 174; and low-income seniors, 305, 310; micro-unit, 163; and millennial generation, 30; and mixed-use development, 228; mother-in-law, 108; and prohibition of buildings, 203; and proportion of renters, 33, 402, 404; and rural areas, 159; as secondary dwelling units, 301; and single individuals, 81. *See also* condominium housing; Housing Choice Voucher Program; U.S. Department of Housing and Urban Development
Applecroft Home Experiment Station, 45
Asian Coalition for Housing Rights, 435
Asian housing: aging population of, 389; Bundang, 384; contemporary, 377–78; *feng shui*, 378, 379; modern, 377; sustainability, 391; Tama New Town, 384; traditional, 377, 378; and universal design, 390
Asians: foreclosure rate, 278; homeownership rate, 277, 279; household size, 25; median income and net worth, 27, 281; and suburbanization, 213

baby boomers, x, 12, 16, 24; aging of, 13, 295; borrowing practices of, 301; and homelessness, 192; housing preferences of, 29, 298; retirement of, 296, 299; values of, 30, 31
bathroom design: accessible, 48; by function centers, 58–61; green building of, 49–50; history of, 43–44; and materials, 52–53; modern, 46–47; process of, 53; space clearances, 59; and technology, 51; types of, 58; and ventilation, 327. *See also* universal design
Beecher, Catherine, 45
blacks. *See* African Americans
Brethren Disaster Ministries, 364
Brooke Amendment of 1969, 245
building and loan societies (B&Ls), 139, 140–43
building codes: and adoption of model codes, 328; and African housing, 437; disaster-resistant, 359, 365–66; federal policy on, 242; and height of structure, 68; international standards for, 319, 443; kitchen and bathroom, 46, 48; and secondary dwelling units, 302; and universal design, 106; and ventilation requirements, 50, 326
Building Research Establishment Environmental Assessment Methodology (BREEAM), 380, 449

Center for Housing and Environmental Studies, 47
Center for Universal Design (CUD), 48–49, 98, 101–3
Chicago Housing Authority, residential segregation by, 210, 224. *See also* Gautreaux programs
China: and *hukou* household registration system, 447; urban population growth in, 443–44. *See also* Asian housing
Choice Neighborhoods Program, 248, 251
Civil Rights Act of 1964, 205
Civil Rights Act of 1968, 162
civil rights movement, and urban renewal, 163, 205
Claritas Corporation, 28
cohousing, 307, 309, 311
communities: age-restricted, 31, 113, 294, 301, 307, 309; and aging, x, 35, 307; broken window theory, 210; and Complete Streets policy, 308; definition of, 200; destruction of, 204–8; diversity in, 91; and gentrification, 173, 200, 209; and mass transportation, 91; mixed income, x–xi, 168, 200, 209; mixed-use, 92; multifamily, 83, 174; perceptions of, 198–99, 200–202; revitalization of, 167, 219; and social capital, 210; sustainable, 12, 69, 88. *See also* affordable housing; immigrants; neighborhoods; New Urbanism; non-Hispanic whites; residential segregation; transit-oriented development
Community Development Act of 1974, creation of, 208, 240
Community Development Block Grant (CDBG), 177; and community-based organizations, 214; as consolidating program, 246; creation of, 208, 240; focus of, 240; and secondary dwellings, 302
community development corporations (CDCs), 205; and inequality, 206
Community for Creative Nonviolence, 184
Community Land Trust (CLT), 174, 177, 443
Community Reinvestment Act (CRA), 243, 244, 246
community-based organizations (CBOs), 206
Complete Streets, 308
Comprehensive Assessment System for Built Environment Efficiency (CASBEE), 382, 383, 449
Comprehensive Housing Affordability Strategy Plan, 247–48
condominium housing, x, 31; in Asia, 390; in Eastern Europe, 401; and homeowners' association, 89; in Latin America, 413, 416; multifamily, 83, 89, 92, 94; ownership of, 131, 415; upgrading of existing housing to, 159
construction of housing, x, 47, 64; and building permit, 113; and building practices, 325–31; common requirements, 68; costs, 4, 17, 69, 70, 105t, 160, 174; debris (C&D), 342–43; economic stimulation of industry, 238, 244–45, 256, 284; multifamily, 93; overall quality of, 11; process, 71–72, 72; secondary dwelling units, 302–3; sound mitigation, 90; standards, 55, 67, 68t, 145; starts, 7; "sweat equity," 175; and technology, 69–70; and universal design, 100–106, 112, 304. *See also* accessibility; manufactured homes; visitability
Consumer Financial Protection Bureau (CFPB), establishment of, 266, 288
Continuums of Care (CoCs), 185
Convention on the Rights of Persons with Disabilities, 98
cooperative housing, 241, 242; age-segregated, 93; in Europe, 401, 402; limited equity, 174; ownership of, 83, 131–32, 309, 443
Cost of Funds Index (COFI), 127
covenants, 131; Cradle to Cradle certification, 448; and needs assessment, 53; racial, 146, 203, 220; restrictive deed, 203–4, 220
credit scores, 123, 149, 306; effect of Great Recession on, 256; effect of short sale on, 134; effect on downpayment, 147, 265; and interest rate, 127; and qualifying for mortgage, 128, 143, 267, 285–86; race and ethnicity and, 279, 281. *See also* FICO
Current Population Survey (CPS), 24, 25

Defensible Space, 88
Depository Institutions Deregulation and Monetary Control Act, 260, 283
design, x, 6, 8; of multifamily residential, xi, 53, 64–78, 80–94; occupant needs, 72; open floor plan, 75, 75–76; process, 72, 73; setback, 71, 81, 302, 347; of single-family residential, 70–77; of spatial organization, 73–77; and technology, 51; trends in, 10–11. *See also* accessibility; bathroom design; kitchen design; universal design; visitability
disabled persons, 69, 70, 173, 304; and affordable housing, 173, 305. *See also* affordable housing
disasters and housing, 356; and bereavement, 368–69; community participation in recovery, 364; community response, 362; definitions, 356; demographics, 357–58; effect on people, 360–62; federal policy on, 362–63; and job loss, 361; and mitigation, 365; nongovernmental assistance, 364; and sense of self, 360, 367–68; vulnerabilities, 359–60
discrimination: and Community Reinvestment Act (CRA), 246; and Fair Housing Administration (FHA), 258; and Home Mortgage Disclosure Act (HMDA), 246; prohibition, and protected classes, 242
Dodd-Frank Wall Street Reform and Consumer Protection Act, 266

Earth Advantage Institute, 50
EarthCraft House, 50, 352
EasyLiving^{cm} Home, 113
Eleanor Smith Inclusive Home Design Act of 2015, 111
Emergency Economic Stabilization Act (EESA), 263
Energy Independence and Security Act of 2007, 343
Energy*Star Program, 50, 69, 343, 350, 351, 382, 449. *See also* sustainable housing
environment-health interaction: air quality, 331–32; asbestos, 34, 317, 343, 429;

building materials, 324–25; climate variables, 319; household chemicals, 332; household water source, 333–34, 335; industrial contamination, 322; lifestyle issues, 335–37; moisture control, 329–31; older home hazards, 325; overcrowding, 34, 67, 68, 161, 167, 276, 298, 411, 419; radon, 34, 317, 318, 325t, 328, 331; risk factors, 317–18; siting of building, 320–21; ventilation, 325–29; water control, 321–24

Equifax, 127

European Union: affordable housing in, 396, 398, 406; age of housing stock in, 405; and homeownership, 399–400; household types, 397; housing cooperatives, 402; and millennial generation, 397–98; nontraditional households in, 406; and older persons, 406; public housing in, 399–401; and Right to Acquire program, 399; and type of dwelling, 402–4

Experian, 127

Fair Housing Act of 1968: and residential discrimination, 207, 221, 258, 447; and restrictive covenants, 204

Fair Housing Amendments Act (FHAA) of 1988, 111, 112

Fannie Mae (Federal National Mortgage Association), 139, 144–45, 243–44, 245, 258–59; elimination of, 150; establishment and evolution of, 147–48; federal conservatorship of, 15, 244, 248, 265; and Federal Reserve discount window, 259; future of, 265; and HARP, 134; and mortgage banks, 143; and mortgage credit availability, 144; and National Housing Trust Fund, 178; and secondary mortgage market, 259; solvency of, 149–50

Federal Deposit Insurance Corporation (FDIC), 264

Federal Emergency Management Agency (FEMA), 357, 358, 362. *See also* disasters and housing

Federal Home Loan Bank (FHLB), creation of, 257

Federal Home Loan Bank Act of 1932, passage of, 257

Federal Home Loan Mortgage Corporation. *See* Freddie Mac

Federal Housing Administration (FHA), xi, 15, 121, 139, 144–47, 284; and borrowers of color, *286*; and capital reserve ratio, 264–65; countercyclical role of, 285; creation of, 244, 258; and discrimination, 146, 245; downpayment requirement, 124–25, 158, 258, 285; and easing of lending requirements, 147; FHA Secure Program, 288; focus on affordability by, 245, 246; and Great Recession, 264; Home Affordable Modification Program (HAMP), 288; Home Affordable Refinance Program (HARP), 288; and homeownership expansion, 15–16; and increase in market share, 146, 245; and loan insurance, 241; Making Home Affordable (MHA), 288; minimum property standards (MPS), 46; mortgage insurance, 121; and multifamily rental housing, 245; National Foreclosure Mitigation Counseling (NFMC) Program, 288; Neighborhood Stabilization Programs, 288; proportion of mortgage loans, 144, *145*, 285; space recommendations of, 46

Federal Housing Enterprise Financial Safety and Soundness Act (FHEFSSA), 148, 284, 286

Federal Housing Finance Agency (FHFA): and conservatorship of GSEs, 149; and reduction of benchmarks, 287–88

federal housing policy: and affordable-housing goals, 236–37, 286–87; capital gains, 242; and Federal Home Loan Bank (FHLB), 284; and government-sponsored enterprises (GSEs), 243–44; and Great Depression, 244–45, 257; homeownership as full-employment objective, 237; and homeownership versus rental housing, 257; and Housing Act of 1937, 245; loan insurance, 241; mortgage interest, 242; mortgage revenue bonds (MRBs), 242; and place-based subsidies, 240; and project-based subsidies, 238, 239, 240, 250; and property taxes, 242; and reduction of goals, 287–88; role of, 235–36; and secondary mortgage market, 243–44; special needs populations subsidies, 240–41; and support for homeownership, 284; tax breaks and, 241–42; and tenant-based subsidies, 239–40, 247, 250–51

Federal Mortgage Insurance Corporation (FMIC), 265

Federal National Mortgage Association. *See* Fannie Mae

FICO (Fair Issac & Company), 127, 267, 281, 285; scores, and downpayment requirements, 285

Field Guide to American Houses, A, 65

financial counseling, and affordable housing assistance, 178, 179

Financial Stability Act of 2009, 266

foreclosure crisis, xii, 149; and adjacent property values, 262; and adjustable rate mortgages (ARMs), 261; and Affordable Care Act (ACA), 261; and African Americans, 278; and FHA Secure Program, 265; and financial markets, 256–57; and Home Affordable Modification Program (HAMP), 265, 266, 288; and Home Affordable Refinance Program (HARP), 266; and house price bubble burst, 259–60, 261; and Housing and Economic Recovery Act (HERA), 264, 265, 288; and housing market boom, 4, 10, 14, 16, 260–62; impact on people of color, 288; and Making Home Affordable (MHA), 266; and mortgage securitization, 261; and National Foreclosure Mitigation Counseling (NFMC) Program, 265; and rating agencies, 261; and rental housing, 159, 160; roots of, 260; starts and completions, 260; and total loss of equity, 262; as trigger for Great Recession, 261; underwater status and strategic default, 261, 262; and unplanned personal emergencies, 261; and use of eminent domain, 263. *See also* Great Recession; subprime mortgages

Forest Stewardship Council, 448

Frankfurt Kitchen, *45*

Freddie Mac (Federal Home Loan Mortgage Corporation), xi, 139, 243–44, 259; elimination of, 150; establishment of, 147–48; federal conservatorship of, 15, 244, 248, 265; future of, 265; and mortgage banks, 143; and mortgage credit availability, 144; and National Housing Trust Fund (NHTF), 178; solvency of, 149–50

Fredrick, Christine, 45

gated communities, 447

Gator Tech Smart House, 69

Gautreaux programs, 210–11, 212, 224–25, 447

Gautreaux v. Chicago Housing Authority, 224

Generation X, 12–13, 16, 30; housing choice of, 31

gentrification: and affordable housing removal, 173; and neighborhood conflict, 200, 212, 213; and structural view of poverty, 209

GI Bill of Rights (Servicemen's Readjustment Act of 1944), 259, 284

GI generation, 30, 31

Ginnie Mae (Government National Mortgage Association), 284; creation of, 143, 147, 244t; and secondary mortgages, 243

Giuliani, Rudolph, 210

Government National Mortgage Association. *See* Ginnie Mae

government-sponsored enterprises (GSEs): and affordable housing goals, 287t; and Federal Housing Enterprises Financial Safety and Soundness Act (FHEFSSA), 286; and Federal Mortgage Insurance Corporation (FMIC), 265; HUD oversight of, 246; market share in underserved areas, 287; and mortgage-backed securities, 149, 261, 265; reform of, 250. *See also* Fannie Mae; Freddie Mac; Ginnie Mae

Gramm-Leach-Bliley Act (Financial Services Modernization Act), 261

Great Depression, 4; and federal housing policy, 244–45; and homeownership, 144; Home Owners' Loan Corporation (HOLC), 141

Great Recession: and Dodd-Frank Wall Street Reform and Consumer Protection Act, 266; effect on financial services industry, 263; effects on labor market, 281; and Federal Housing Administration (FHA), 146; and Financial Stability Act

Great Recession (*continued*) of 2009, 266; and government intervention, 263–64; and homeownership, xii; and homeownership rate, xi, 32; house price bubble burst, 248; and housing construction industry, 238; and immigrant reduction, 24; impact of, ix–x; and insufficiency of economic stimuli, 266; and median income, 27; and rental housing supply, 33; and retirement, 295; and secondary mortgage market, 244; and toxic assets, 263–64; and Troubled Assets Relief Program (TARP), 263–64; and unemployment rates, 255–56; and wealth creation, 300
Green Builder, 351
Green Building Council, 381
green housing, 386; construction materials, 351–52; importance of siting, 351; structural insulating panels (SIPs), 352; volatile organic compounds (VOCs), 352. *See also* Asian housing; sustainable housing
Green Seal, 448
Green Standard for Energy and Environmental Design (G-SEED), 380, 381, 382, 383, 386
Green Tomorrow, 382, *383*

Habitat for Humanity, 105, 112, 175, 304. *See also* universal design; visitability
health: and built environment, 227, *317*; determinants of, 222; and education, 224; and exposure to environmental hazards, 228; and homeownership, 256; and neighborhood amenities, 226; social determinants of, 229. *See also* environment-health interaction
health care: access to, 167, 309; advances in, 295; aging and, 299–301, 306, 307; costs of, 311; expansion of industry, 299; homelessness and, 192; housing cost burden and, 16, 276, 294, 298; and rural areas, 298–99; shelter poverty and, 172, 300
HEARTH Acts, 185
Hispanics/Latinos: credit scores of, 281; discrimination against, and real estate industry, 281; expansion of homeownership among, 146; and FHA-originated mortgages, 286; and fore-

closure, 160; as Home Affordable Modification Program (HAMP) clients, 288–89; homeownership rate among, 32, 276–79, 287; household size of, 25; median household income and net worth of, 281, 282; underemployment rates of, 281; and wealth creation, 300
Home Affordable Modification Program (HAMP), 265, 266, 288, 289t
Home Affordable Refinance Program (HARP), 134, 266
home buying, 128–30; appraisal, 129, 130, 134, 142; broker, 123, 128; closing, 130; closure meeting, 130; final approval contingency, 129; home inspection, 129; lead-based paint disclosure, 129; protected classes, 128; purchase agreement, 129–30. *See also* homeownership; mortgage loans
Home Energy Rating System (HERS), 449
Home Equity Conversion Mortgage (HECM), 133, 306–7
HOME Investment Partnership Program (HOME), 177, 240, 247, 305
Home Mortgage Disclosure Act (HMDA), 244t, 246
Home Owners' Loan Corporation (HOLC), 284; establishment of, 144–45; and foreclosures, 257–58; redlining practices of, 146, 204
homeless: characteristics of, 186; number of, 184, 185; vulnerability of, 442. *See also* homelessness
homelessness, 188; and baby boomers, x, xii, 13; definition of, 183; direct and peripheral costs of, 191; and enforcement of social norms, 212; of families, 186–87; health issues among, 187; prevention-driven approach to, 189; risk for, 187; and women, 186–87. *See also* McKinney-Vento Act of 1987
Homelessness Prevention and Rapid Re-housing Program (HPRP), 189, 191
homeownership, 121–35; in Asia, 390–91; boom, 9–10, 15, 259; costs of, 130–31, 132; demographics of, xii; and discrimination in real estate industry, 281; as economic stimulus, 256–57; effect of Great Recession on, xii, 121,

134–35, 266–67; equity, 122–23; in European Union, 399; exclusion from, 289; and federal policy, 237, 264; forms of, 131; and Great Depression, 245; and health outcomes, 256; and millennial generation, x, 285; positive characteristics of, 256–57; and racial and ethnic diversity, 276; and rapid rehousing (RRH), 189, 190, 191; rate of, xi, 14–16, *15*, 149, 150, 259, 445; and redlining, 204; risks of, 122–23; shared equity models of, 443; tax incentives for, 121, 122; as unaffordable, 284; and wealth building, 134, 144, 150; and World War II, 258. *See also* European Union; foreclosure crisis
Homestead Act of 1882, 121
HOPE VI, xii, 211–12, 248, 447; and mixed-income communities, 200, 251; and senior renter, 305
house price bubble burst, 30, 248, 262. *See also* foreclosure crisis; Great Recession; subprime mortgages
household: and amenities, 34; composition, 11–14; family type, 13; and housing choice, 447; life cycle, 25–26, 31; multigenerational, 297–98, 302; size, 25; socioeconomic characteristics, 26–27
Housing Act of 1934, 121, 144
Housing Act of 1937, 244t, 245
Housing Act of 1949, 244t, 245
Housing Affordability Index (HAI), 169, *170*
Housing and Community Development Act of 1974, 238; and housing affordability, 246; passage of, 240
Housing and Economic Recovery Act (HERA), 264, 265, 288
Housing Assistance Council, 175
housing choice: and cultural orientation, 29; and demographics, 22, 23, 23–24; generational differences, 29–30; and hierarchy of human needs, 21–22, 22; influences on, 21–36; life cycle, 33; lifestyle factors, 28–29; and neighborhood amenities, 219; and norms, 22, 31–32, 35; and value hierarchy, 28
Housing Choice Voucher Program (HCVP), xii, 446; and deconcentration of poverty, 251; and high-opportunity neighborhoods, 209

housing codes, 242; and health, 161; and height restrictions, 161; reform of, 202
housing cost burden, 16, 83, 88, *168*, 169, 173, 236, 276–77, 277t, 406
housing counselors, 123, 125
housing finance industry, xi, 139–50; attitude of, toward homeownership, 256; and Great Recession, 4; and homeownership opportunities, 16
Housing First, 190
Housing Homeless Act of 1986, 183
housing landscape, and demographics, ix–x xii
Housing Management Information System (HMIS), 185
housing market, 3–18; and affordability, 16–17, 445; in Asia, 390; boom, 4, 6, 159, 306; boom-and-bust cycle, 237; and certificates of occupancy, 435; collapse of prices, 241, 262; and decline in home value, 222; discrimination in, 162, 207, 446; and Federal Housing Administration (FHA), 144; formal and informal, 409, 411–12, 415, 417; government intervention in, 211, 238, 241–42, 244, 263; and Great Recession, 4; and homeless, 188; and household growth, 17–18; median price increase, 169; multifamily, 83; and production bubble, 237; and racial homogeneity, 222; rental sector of, 156, 159, 160, 163; separate, 220; single-family, 33, 159; smart home, 66, 382n3, 386; stabilization of, 257–58; starts, 6–7; supply-and-demand conditions in, 247; and tenant-based assistance, 240, 250, 447; trends, 3–18; and unemployment rate, 255; and universal design, 114; urban, 211; vacancy rate, 9. *See also* foreclosure crisis; Great Recession, subprime mortgages
housing norms, 21, 22, 31–32, 67, 77; changing of, 24, 32; conceptual framework of, 23, 35; and cultural orientation, 28; generational differences in, 28; and life cycle, 25t, 26; and lifestyle, 23, 28; neighborhood, 35; and socioeconomic characteristics, 26, 32; and spending habits, 35. *See* life cycle; tenure

Housing Opportunities for People with AIDS (HOPWA), 177t
Housing Opportunity Index (HOI), 169, *170*

ICC 700 National Green Building Standards, 50
ICE Inc., 184
immigrants, 44; and discrimination, 200; and gated communities, 447; and millennial generation, 24; reduction in, 24; and tenement housing, 82, 201, 411, 413; and urban housing, 202
Inclusive Home Design Act of 2002, 110–11
income: annual median family, 239; and area median, 83, 148–49, 173, 179, 287; low and moderate, 83, 124, 148, 156, 158–59, 160, 167, 172–74, 179, 205, 239, 286; median household, 281; and unemployment rate, 24, 146, 188, 255–56, 267, 279, 280
Individual Development Accounts (IDAs), 178
informal settlements, 411; efforts to improve conditions in, 437; inadequate housing in, 442; infrastructure projects in, 415, 444; and security of tenure, 414; social upgrading of, 412; upgrading strategies, 444; and urbanization, 140, 201–2. *See* tenure
Institute for Human Centered Design (IHCD), 101
instrumental activities of daily living (IADL), 100. *See* universal design
insurance, 105; disaster, 361; exclusion for food damage, 363; Federal Housing Administration (FHA), 121, 133, 145–47, 220, 241, 244, 258, 264–65, 285; Flood Insurance Program, 358, 362; as government subsidy, 241; and home-buying process, 128; homeowners', 122, 124, 129, 131, 306, 363; and housing cooperatives, 131; mortgage, xii, 124, 131, 134; mortgage insurance premium, 285; private, 241, 244, 261; private mortgage insurance (PMI), 124; proof of, 130; renter's, 363; title search, 130; for veterans, 121
Inter-American Development Bank (IDB), 412
International Code Council (ICC), 67, 352, 366, 367, 449
International Declaration of Human Rights, 410

International Energy Conservation Code (IECC), 50, 67, 319, 328
International Organization for Standardization (IOS), 443
International Residential Code (IRC), 47, 59, 67, 68t, 319, 328

Japanese National Housing Corporation (JNHC), 383
John Burns Real Estate Consulting, 31

Kerner Commission, on segregation in the United States, 207
King, Martin Luther, Jr., 207
kitchen design: closed arrangement, 55; configurations, 53–55; "fitted," 45; by function centers, 55–58; green building, 49; history of, 43–44; *Kitchen Industry Technical Manuals*, 46, 47; materials in, 52–53; modern, 44–45; open arrangement, *54*; process of, 53; and quality of life, 44–45; recommendations for shelf and drawer frontage, 58t; and technology, 51; ventilation in, 326–27. *See also* universal design

Ladies Home Journal, 45
LaHouse, 69
land use, xii; and affordable housing, 172; and "chain of exclusion," 220; and density bonus, 174; and green construction, 381; and history of site, 322; nontraditional, 174; reform of, 445; restrictions on, 220; and state land ownership, 446; strategies on, 174, 228; and walkable environments, 229, 307–8. *See also* Not in My Back Yard; zoning
Latin American and Caribbean housing, 409; affordable rental housing, 414–15; condominium ownership, 415; deficits, 419–20; formal and informal markets, 411–12, 413–15; homeownership rates, 417; preferred forms of tenure, 410; and property title, 409, 442; racial and ethnic diversity, 410–11; and right to adequate housing, 409, 410; social-interest housing, 416–17; and System of Incentives for Housing, 415–16; tenement demolition, 411; and urbanization of population, 410–11

LEED (Leadership for Energy and Environmental Design), 50, 69, 352, 382, 449
LEED-India, 380, 381
life cycle: 23; changes during, 35; concept of, 25–26; of house, 129, 448; and housing space, 33; of mortgage, 147, 258, 284; and older persons, 295; and renters, 160; and socioeconomic characteristics, 26; stages of, 31, 36; and trajectory of housing, 160
Life Wise Home, 68
limited equity cooperatives, 174. *See also* cooperative housing
Link, 185
London Interbank Offered Rate (LIBOR), 127
Low-Income Housing Tax Credit (LIHTC), 177; and affordable housing, 445; expansion of, 249; and low-income developments, 239; and low-income seniors, 305; and mixed-income developments, 251; as tax credit, 247

Mace, Ron, 101, 103, 303
Making Home Affordable (MHA), 266
manufactured homes: as affordable housing, 174; definition of, 5; and disaster vulnerability, 359; and HUD Code, 174; insurance for, 241, 258, 284; in rural areas, 299
McKinney-Vento Act of 1987, 177t, 183, 185, 189
Mennonite Disaster Services, 364
millennial generation: definition of, 30, 31; diversity of, 30; homeownership rate among, 32, 285; and housing in Europe, 396–97; postponement of homeownership by, 121; and rental housing, 163; size of, 13, 24; and suburbs, 298; and wealth-building opportunities, 144
minimum property standards (MPS), 46
mixed-income communities: benefits of, 200; and poor households, 209; and public housing, 209; and social capital, 210, and social interaction, 213. *See also* mixed-income housing
mixed-income housing, *92*, 168, 238, 248. *See also* income: low and moderate

mobile homes. *See* manufactured homes
Mortgage Bankers Association (MBA), 143
Mortgage Credit Availability Index (MCAI), 143–44
Mortgage Credit Certificate (MCC) Program, 242
Mortgage Electronic Registration Systems (MERS), 139
Mortgage Interest Deduction (MID), 241–42, 250, 257
mortgage lenders: abandonment of lending, 146; and adjustable rate mortgages (ARMs), 283–84; and Alternative Mortgage Transaction Parity Act, 260, 283–84; bankruptcy of, 263; and credit availability, *143*, 143–44; credit certificate (MCC) program, 242; and decline in thirty-year interest rates, 283; and Depository Institutions Deregulation and Monetary Control Act, 260, 283; and downpayment requirements, 258, 267, 284, 285; and Federal Mortgage Insurance Corporation (FMIC), 265; and financial markets, 256; and Financial Services Modernization Act, 261; and home equity line of credit (HELOC), 306–7; and insurance premium (MIP), 285; and North Carolina Predatory Lending Law, 260–61; preemption of state laws regulating national banks, 260–61; proportion of loans, 263, 285; and qualifications for mortgage, 260, 283; and securitization, 143; and subprime mortgages, 259, 260; "too big to fail," 261
mortgage loans, 127; Alternative-A (Alt-A) prime, 149; and amortization, 258, 284; and annual percentage rate, 124, 127; availability of, 139; and balloon payments, 145, 258, 284; borrower of, 122, 124–29, 134, 143, 145, 258, 262, 285, 306; collateral for, 133; and design norm, 145; fixed-rate, 122, 127, 128, 132, 134, 145; and Great Depression, 244–45; interest-only, 284; and loss mitigation tools, 134; low-income, 148–49; pay-option ARM, 284; preapproval for, 123–24; prepayment penalties for, 125; refinancing of, 132–33; reverse, 133, 301, 304, 306; and secondary mortgage

mortgage loans (continued) market, 243–44; securitization of, 143, 148, 149, 261, 263; and short sale, 134; and tax breaks, 241–42. *See also* credit scores; foreclosure crisis; insurance; subprime mortgages
—downpayment requirements: 5, 123, 128, 169, 267, 415; assistance with, 125, 446; and baby boomers, 301; and conventional loans, 158; definition of, 124; and earnest money, 130; and equity, 122; escrow account, 124, 130; FHA-insured, 124, 147, 258, 265, 285; and GI Bill, 259; low, 14, 15, 124; special savings programs for, 178; tighter standards on, 285; wealth and, 281
—interest rates, 4; below-market, 175, 239; and credit score, 127; and Federal Reserve discount window, 259; and government guarantees, 446; influences on, 125; and lifetime cap, 127; monthly housing costs, 125t; and refinancing, 132–33; simulated payments, *126*; thirty-year fixed, *283*. *See also* subprime mortgages
Moving to Opportunity (MTO), 447; and economic inclusion, 225; and mixed-income communities, 200; mixed results of, 212; and relocation, 211
multifamily residential housing: and Americans with Disability Act (ADA), 67; appeal of, 33–34; concerns about, 87–90; definition of, 5; density of, 94; design of, 80–94; duplexes, 80, 113; in European Union, 402; and exclusionary zoning, 445–46; expansion of, 245–46; high-rise, 379, 382, 385–86; history of, 82; and insurance, 241, 258, 284; mass-produced, 414–15, 417; opposition to, 93; and owner-occupied housing unit, 90; and socioeconomic diversity, 379; sustainability of, 383; types of, 82–83; and *Village of Euclid v. Ambler Realty Co.*, 203; and visitability, 112–13, 304
Mutual Mortgage Insurance (MMI) Fund, 264
Muungano wa Wanvijiji, 436
My House, My Life Program, 445

National Affordable Housing Act of 1990, 247, 258
National Association of Home Builders, 449; certification by, 69; housing affordability indices, 169
National Association of Realtors (NAR), housing affordability indices, 169
National Bureau of Economic Research (NBER), 184
National Commission on Severely Distressed Public Housing, 211
National Fenestration Rating Council, 50
National Flood Insurance Program, 358, 362. *See also* disasters and housing
National Foreclosure Mitigation Counseling (NFMC) Program, 265
National Green Building Standard, 50, 352, 381, 449
National Housing Act of 1949, 34
National Housing Trust Fund (NHTF), 176, 177t
National Kitchen and Bath Association (NKBA), 46; and bathroom planning, 59; and home ventilation, 325–26
National Low Income Housing Coalition (NLIHC), 172
National Multifamily Housing Council, 32
National Slum Dwellers Federation, 436
natural disasters. *See* disasters and housing
naturally occurring retirement communities (NORC), 31, 294, 301; retrofitting of, 307–9
negative home equity, "underwater" status. *See* subprime mortgages
neighborhood amenities: defining of, 219; and housing prices, 218, 219; and lack of choice, 221; and physical and social characteristics, 229; and school quality, 224, and settlement house movement, 199, 202, 226. *See also* New Urbanism
Neighborhood Stabilization Programs, 288
neighborhoods, xii; and access to opportunity, 225; and appraisals, 204; decline of, 207; diversity of, 167; and effects of isolation, 223; enhancement of, 81, 84; and foreclosure crisis, 263; and ghettos, 202–3; and inequality, 201; physical and social characteristics of, 226; and

PRIZM, 28; and protection of residential areas, 227; and racial homogeneity, 222; and strong and weak ties, 212. *See also* communities
NeighborWorks, 265, 288
New Housekeeping, The, 45
New Millennium Greenville, 386–87
New Urbanism, 30, 227, 228; and Cohousing communities, 309
New York City: causes of homelessness in, 187; gentrification in, 212; homelessness in, 185, 191; homelessness prevention programs in, 189–90; mixed-income housing in, 83; tenements of, 161
Nixon, Richard, and federal housing policy, 208, 240
non-Hispanic whites, xii; debt-to-income ratio of, 279, 281; and denial of housing, 281; and Federal Housing Administration mortgages, 146; and foreclosure rates, 277, 288; historic privilege of, 277; and homeownership rates, 16, 276, 277, 281, 288; households headed by, 12; and loan-to-value (LTV) ratio, 279; and median income, 27, 281; as minority population, 275; mortality rate of, 275; neighborhood abandonment by, 209; and neighborhood associations, 203; neighborhood mobility of, 223; and postdisaster job loss, 361; relocation of, 204; return to cities by, 212, 214; and shelter poverty, 300; social norms of, 212–13; suburbanization of, 202, 204; unemployment rate of, 279, 281; use of covenants by, 204; wealth of, 220–21, 300; and white flight, 213
Not In My Back Yard (NIMBY): and land-use controls, 178, 220; and manufactured homes, 175; and mixed-income housing, 168; and political pressure on local governments, 208, 447; and rental housing, 161; and residential segregation, 207, 446

older persons: and affordable housing, 173; and disaster vulnerability, 361; and federal housing subsidies, 241; and homelessness, 192; and homeownership, 256; and Section 202 program, 245.

See also aging; aging-in-place; baby boomers opportunity maps, 225–26
Out of Reach, 172
owner-occupied housing: in European Union, 399; frequency of, 83; preference for, 414; prevalence of, 121; transition to rental, 159. *See also* single-family residential housing; tenure

Pamoja Trust, 436
people of color: and credit scores, 281; demographics of, 275–76; discrimination and real estate industry, 281; and FHA originations of mortgages, 286; homelessness of, 186; and homeownership rates, *278*; households headed by, *12*; and income levels, 281; as majority in United States, 275–76, *276*, 289; and subprime mortgages, 284; and underserved communities, 202; unemployment rate, *282*; and urban underclass, 209; and use of homeless shelters, 188; and wealth creation, 277. *See also* African Americans; Hispanics/Latinos
permanent supportive housing (PSH), 190–91
post-occupancy evaluation (POE), 71
poverty: and bridging capital, 223; concentration of, 239; and home values, 222; and inner-city concentration, 209; and lack of access to resources, 222; and relocation, 214; structural concentration of, 209, 222; tipping point, 222; and white flight, 213. *See also* income: low and moderate; public housing
Presbyterian Disaster Assistance, 364
Principles of Universal Design, The, 101–2
Pruitt-Igoe housing complex (St. Louis), as symbol, 211
public housing: Brooke Amendment of 1969, 245; and change in federal policy, 248; creation of, 245; curtailment of, 250; demolition of, 248; in European Union, 400–401; and *Gautreaux*, 210–11; and homeownership option, 400; legal challenges to, 224; in New Deal era, 208; redevelopment of, 209, 248; scale of, 445; and stock con-

traction, 249. *See also* HOPE VI
Public Housing Authority (PHA), and federal funding, 238, 239

race and ethnicity. *See* people of color
real estate industry: and attitude toward homeownership, 256; and discrimination, 221; and multiple listing service (MLS), 128
Real-time Operating System Nucleus (TRON), 387–88
Red Cross, 364
redlining: continuation as policy, 213; and Federal Housing Administration, 146, 204; institutionalization of, 204; reaction to, 243
rehabilitation, 8, 101, 131, 173, 174, 175, 239, 240, 245, 246, 305, 411, 444
remodeling, 7–8, 43, 51, 104, 361
renovation, 104, 105, 131, 240, 356, 382
rental housing, xi, 5, 6; advantages and disadvantages, 157–58; affordability of, 156, 159–60; characteristics of, 158–59; deposit for, 6; discrimination in, 162; and duplexes, 33, 158; in European Union, 400; and fair-market rent (FMR), 172; federally assisted units, 177t, 249t; and house price bubble burst, 248; housing vouchers, 177; and landlords, 5, 8, 159, 172, 175, 176, 239; and project-based rental assistance, 177; and regulated rental systems, 443; and rent control, 157, 162; rural, 177; senior-oriented, 301; shortage of, 445; single-room occupancy (SRO), 184
renters, 32, 33, 156–63; assistance programs, 156; and disaster vulnerability, 361; extremely low-income (ELI), 173, 175, 238, 239; and foreclosure crisis, 262; and housing cost burden, 169, 173, 276–77, 277t; and landlord-tenant relations, 157, 161, 162–63; in Latin American and Caribbean housing, 417–18; and leases, 5–6, 33, 88, 92, 157, 162–63; low- and moderate-income, 156; low-income senior, 305; and national housing wage, 172; as proportion of households, 158; and public housing, 238–39, 245; and public

transit, 228; and Section 8 program, 238–39; and senior-targeted housing, 304, 305; social status of, 157; tenants' rights, 157, 162, 163
residential segregation, xiii, 441; private property deed restrictions, 220; worldwide, 446–47. *See also* African Americans; Latinos/Hispanics; redlining
Resource Conservation and Recovery Act of 1976 (RCRA), 342
restrictive covenants, 203–4, 220
Right to Acquire Program, and European Housing, 399
Right to the City, 206
Roosevelt, Franklin D., 144, 148; and economic stimulus programs, 257, 258, 259, 284; and federal housing policy, 244–45
rural areas, 28; and aging population, 298–99; and Latin America, 410–11, 417, 420; and manufactured housing, 159, 299; migration of seniors to, 298; and multifamily residential housing, 93

Salvation Army, 364
savings and loan associations (S&Ls): and building and loan societies (B&Ls), 141; and Freddie Mac, 143, 147–48
Schütte-Lihotzky, Margarete, 45
Sears, Roebuck & Company, 70
secondary dwelling units, 301–2, 303; and Community Development Block Grant (CDBG), 302; and in-law suites, 301
Section 8 Existing Housing Certificate Program, 239–40
Section 8 New Construction/Substantial Rehabilitation Program, 246, 247, 259, 284
Section 8 programs, 238–39; contraction of, 249; Housing Choice Vouchers program (HCV), 246, 249; initiation of, 246
Section 811 Supportive Housing for People with Disabilities, 305
segregation. *See* African Americans; Hispanics/Latinos; redlining; residential segregation
Servicemen's Readjustment Act of 1944 (GI Bill of Rights), 259, 284

Shelley v. Kraemer (1948), 146; and property values, 220
silent generation, 31
single-family residential housing: definition of, 5; desirability of, 202; as dominant housing type, 64–65; in European Union, 402; and fixed rate mortgages, 145; forms of ownership of, 131; and homogenous neighborhoods, 220, 221; and insurance, 258, 284; interior space of, 73–77; mass-produced, 414–15; as preference, 33, 67; visitability guidelines for, 112–13; and zoning, 203
single-room occupancies (SROs), 158, 241
Slum/Shack Dwellers International (SDI), 435, 436
slums: upgrading strategies for, 444; urban population in, 442. *See* informal settlements
Small Homes Council, 46, 47
Snyder, Mitch, 184
social capital: loss of, 223; and mixed-income communities, 210
socioeconomic status: and Asia, 378–79; and assisted housing, 178; and diversity, 167, 384, 389; and Latin American and Caribbean housing, 411; and neighborhood amenities, 219; and segregation, 213; strong and weak ties, 223
Southern Baptist Disaster Relief, 364
Stowe, Harriet Beecher, 45
subprime mortgages, 4, 123, 248, 262, 306; and balloon payments, 260, 283; and defaults, 4, 10; and Fannie Mae and Freddie Mac, 149; and foreclosures, 259; and house price bubble burst, 30, 248, 262; and inability to refinance, 262; and mortgage credit availability, 143; national crisis in, 139; and people of color, 284; and risk-based pricing, 260, 283–84; triggering of Great Recession, 261. *See also* foreclosure crisis; Great Recession
suburbanization, 202; and African Americans, 202, 221, 223; and non-Hispanic whites, 222, 225; and residential segregation, 221
suburbs: and automobile dependency, 298; and housing market, 211; job growth in, 223; and low-income rent-

ers, 225; and migration from city, 202, 204; and older persons, 294, 298; and racial covenants, 146; rural outmigration to, 298; share of housing in, 11; white flight to, 213; and World War II housing boom, 144
Supportive Housing for the Elderly Program, 304, 305
sustainable communities, 341, 351; definition of, 352; rating systems for, 380. *See also* green housing; LEED; sustainable housing
sustainable housing: and annualized fuel use efficiency (AFUE), 347; and construction waste management, 342–43; definition of, 341, 353; and energy efficiency, 343, 344–49, 350; and environmental impact, 447–48; and high-efficiency toilets (HET), 349; and light-emitting diodes (LEDs), 344; and proximity to transportation, 386; rating systems for, 380–83, 449; and seasonal energy efficiency ratio (SEER), 348; and Tama New Town, 384; and waste management, 342; and water-use efficiency, 348–49; and zero-energy homes, 384–85. *See also* Asian housing; Energy*Star Program; LEED; sustainable communities; WaterSense*
Sustainable Tools for Assessing and Rating Communities (STAR), 352. *See also* sustainable communities

tatami, as measuring unit, 378. *See also* Asian housing
tax breaks: and Mortgage Interest Deduction (MID), 241, 250, 257, 284; and property tax deduction, 242. *See also* Low-Income Housing Tax Credit
Taylor, Frederick, 45
tenure: definition of, 6, 417; and foreclosure, 262; importance of, 134; and income as determinant, 158; informal, 409–15, 417, 420, 431–32, 434–35, 437, 442, 444; preferences on, 17, 23, 32, 67, 410, 412; security of, xiii, 410, 413, 414, 433, 434–35, 441–43, 450; and shelter poverty, 300; and usufruct, 434; and vacancy rates, 8. *See also* homeownership; multifamily residential housing; rental housing;

tenure (*continued*)
single-family residential housing
Toxic Wastes and Race in the United States, 228
Toyota Dream Home PAPI, 388–89
traditionalist generation, definition of, 31
transit-oriented development (TOD), x, 91, 308
transportation: and affordable housing, 167, 169, 172, 276, 305; and aging population, 299, 307; and "complete communities," 228; connectivity to, 380, 386; and housing location, 69, 100–101, 267; and millennial generation, 30, 35; and mixed-use development, 92; and neighborhood retrofitting, 307–8; public, 94, 225, 384, 413, 444; and sustainable communities, 50, 352, 381; viability of mass, 91
TransUnion, 127
Troubled Assets Relief Program (TARP), 263–64

U.K. Department for International Development (DFID), 437
"underwater" (negative home equity). *See* subprime mortgages
unemployment. *See* income
United Church of Christ Commission for Racial Justice, 227–28
United Nations Human Settlements Program, 434
Universal Declaration on Human Rights, and right to adequate housing, 441
universal design (UD): and aging, 300, 303; and aging-in-place, 301; Asian housing use of, 390; Baldwin house (Seattle), 99, *108, 109, 110*; benefits of, 99, 103; and cohousing communities, 309; and cost considerations, 104–5; design principles of, 106–10; evolution of, 100–101; federal funding of, 304; and financial incentives, 113; and independent living, 93; integration of, 103–4; policies and programs of, 110–13; principles of, 101–3, *107*. *See also* visitability
urban planning: and accessibility, 228; and civil rights movement, 205; and development of focus, 227–29; neighborhood context in, 218. *See also* New Urbanism
urban renewal: and community destruction, 204–8; and Housing Act of 1949, 244t, 245; and slum clearance, 245; termination of, 246
urbanization, 140; as employment based, 201–2. *See also* African housing; Asian housing; Latin American and Caribbean housing
U.S. Agency for International Development (USAID), 412, 437
U.S. Bureau of Labor Statistics, 27
U.S. Bureau of the Census, 23, 24; census tract, 225; homeless count by, 184; and household type, 25; and housing construction, 6, 7; and housing quality, 34
U.S. Department of Agriculture: and housing affordability standard, 168; mortgage guarantees by, 144; and rural market, 124; and universal design modification funding, 304
U.S. Department of Energy, and climate zones, 319
U.S. Department of Housing and Urban Development (HUD), 24; affordable housing goals of, 148, 286; assessment of fair housing (AFH), 242–43; Assisted Living Conversion Program, 310; and below market interest rate (BMIR) loans, 175; budget authority of, 249; conflicts with state governments, 208; creation of, 246, 258; definition of homelessness, 183, 184; enforcement powers of, 207; and fair-market rent (FMR), 172; and *Gautreaux*, 210–11; HOPE VI programs, 305; and housing affordability standard, 168–69; Housing Choice Voucher Program (HCV), 239, 241, 305; housing counselors, 123
U.S. Department of Labor, and monthly statistics, 24
U.S. Department of Veterans Affairs: Home Improvements and Structural Alterations grant, 304; homelessness prevention programs, 190; mortgage downpayment, 124–25; mortgage guarantees, 121, 144; Supportive Services for Veteran Families program, 190; Veterans Affairs Supportive Housing Program (VASH), 241. *See also* disabled persons
U.S. Federal Reserve, and low interest rates, 261, 283
U.S. Green Building Council, 351. *See also* green housing; LEED
U.S. League of Local Building and Loans, 142
U.S. Savings and Loan League, 142
U.S. Supreme Court, on multifamily housing, 203
U.S. Treasury Department, conservatorship of GSEs, 149

Veterans' Administration (now U.S. Department of Veterans Affairs; VA), and post–World War II homeownership, 259, 283. *See also* U.S. Department of Veterans Affairs
Village of Euclid v. Ambler Realty Co., 203
visitability: concept of, 111–12; and federal policy, 110; financial incentives for, 113; and senior overlay district, 309; and universal design, 303–4. *See also* accessibility; aging-in-place
Voting Rights Act of 1965, 205

wages. *See* income
WaterSense®, 50, 51, 349–50
wealth creation: exclusion from, 160, 221, 277, 289; factors influencing, 218, 283; federal housing policy supporting, 236, 264; and Great Recession, 264, 266; homeownership as foundation for, 14, 134, 144, 150, 266, 267; and liquidity of home equity, 123; and racial and ethnic diversity, 277; restoration of potential for, 256. *See also* African Americans; foreclosure crisis
World Bank, 412, 415; and adequate housing, 425; African Development Indicators of, 429; project funding in Africa, 432–33; reduction of support by, 437; sites and services projects of, 435
Wright, Frank Lloyd, 65

zeeHomes, 384–85. *See also* Asian housing
zoning: and affordable housing, 172; and discrimination, 203; exclusionary, 445, 447; inclusionary, 174; large-lot, 220; local and state control of, 208; and neighborhoods, 201; and parking places, 87; and property values, 220; and secondary dwelling units, 302; and senior overlay districts, 308–9; Standard State Zoning Enabling legislation, 203. *See also* land use; Not in My Back Yard